A DICTIONARY OF ENGLISH PHRASES

A DICTIONARY
OF ENGLISH PHRASES

PHRASEOLOGICAL ALLUSIONS, CATCHWORDS, STEREOTYPED MODES OF SPEECH
AND METAPHORS, NICKNAMES, *sobriquets*, DERIVATIONS FROM PERSONAL
NAMES, ETC. WITH EXPLANATIONS AND THOUSANDS OF EXACT REFERENCES
TO THEIR SOURCES OR EARLY USAGE

BY

ALBERT M. HYAMSON, F.R. HIST. S.

Author of *A Dictionary of Universal Biography*, *A Dictionary of the Bible*,
A Dictionary of Artists and Art Terms, etc.

LONDON:
GEORGE ROUTLEDGE & SONS, LTD.
NEW YORK: E. P. DUTTON & CO.
1922

To Marie

PREFACE

It is somewhat difficult, perhaps impossible, to define exactly the scope of the present volume. The title, " A Dictionary of Phrases," gives the key to its intention, but does not unlock the whole of its contents. It may be described as a book about terms and phrases that have been incorporated in the English language. An endeavour has been made to cover the whole field of phrases, but so far as the terms, for the most part single words, are concerned, as far as possible only those have been included which owe their existence not so much to a process of natural development, a course to which all words and phrases owe their present form, but in response to some sudden demand to meet some sudden emergency. For instance, crises in British history, such as wars, have brought many words directly into the language—*maffick, camouflage, poilu,* and others. Inventions and discoveries have brought yet others, *e.g., Lyddite, Bessemer steel, Cæsarean operation.* Historical personages, and heroes and villains of romance, have formed yet another means of enriching the language. From this source come such words as to *hector,* a *Solomon,* a *Stiggins.* Words of this character have come direct into the language and are still practically unchanged. The process of their development has hardly yet commenced. As part of a living language they will undergo changes so as ultimately perhaps, in certain cases, to be barely recognizable. And centuries hence, when some successor in the same field takes up his pen to prepare another " Dictionary of Phrases," he may find in the present work a guide to the first stages of many words that might other-wise prove to be insoluble puzzles. The words of this class that are to be found in the following pages are in every case derived from proper names. In dealing with material of this description there is a natural tendency to include too many words, to take, for instance, a classical name, to place an indefinite article before it and then introduce it as the description of a class. This temptation has, however, been evident to the writer throughout, and he has steadfastly endeavoured to avoid it, rejecting all such words for the use of which he has been unable to find good authority.

A kindred class of phrases is that formed by the appropriation of the name of a classical hero, of a city, etc., to some modern successor. Such are the *Briareus of Languages,* the *Carthage of the North,* the *Russian Byron.* Here again the temptation to insert attributions has been great, but it has been resisted. An independent authority has always been found before any such descriptive title has been admitted to the volume. Descriptions of this character form but a part of a larger class which may be entitled nicknames, although they are not altogether nicknames in the narrow sense, and in almost every instance there is a good historical reason for attaching the appellation to the person or place concerned. In many instances the reason is self-evident, *e.g.*, *The Brighton of Scotland*, and explanation is unnecessary. Where, however, it is thought that an explanation is called for it is given.

A third class of words that have been included in this work are those which are usually to be found in slang dictionaries. They consist of slang words and colloquialisms that have degenerated, and references are generally given to the former position of the words in question in literary English. Side by side with these are to be found other words, which have ascended in the scale, and although of low, vulgar origin, are now received in the best social circles. In treating of words belonging to this third class there may sometimes have been some anticipation, words having been included which have not yet obtained admission to the highest circles, but which one is justified in expecting will shortly secure that privilege. An endeavour has, in fact, been made to exclude ordinary slang words and phrases, but so rapid has been the development of the English language, especially during the recent war, in the course of which it was enriched but not always embellished by new phrases and words, that it has at times proved very difficult to decide. However, those words and phrases of which there is a promise of permanency have been included, but in deciding the author has had to rely on instinct rather than on judgment.

Many foreign words and phrases that have become incorporated in the English language without change also find their places in the following pages.

A large proportion of the following items consists not of words but of phrases. Many of them belong to one or another of the classes that have already been mentioned. But phrases give one a wider opportunity than do words. The number of phrases in current use in the English language that are in fact metaphors, although the user seldom stops to notice the fact, is legion. Nearly all words and phrases are, of course, in their ultimate origin metaphors, but in most cases the metaphor has been concealed by the deposits of ages. However, there are still a very large number of phrases in which the metaphor is patent to anyone who stops for a moment to look for it. One of the purposes of the present volume is to collect for the curious these metaphorical phrases and to throw a little light on their origins and on their growth. Here one comes closely into contact with proverbs. But proverbs have not been included *qua* proverbs. A dictionary of proverbs deserves a volume to itself. Only when a proverb has given rise to a word or phrase which is in fact a crystal of the proverb has attention been given to it.

In many instances the earliest known—or an early—use of the phrase is mentioned—in a few instances a parallel phrase in a foreign language. References are also given to the origin of foreign phrases that are now part of the English language.

The present volume, although it contains some fourteen thousand entries, is necessarily imperfect, for no work of this description can well be complete. Even if an author with superhuman self-confidence is satisfied with his work, there are sure to be hosts of critics to point out deficiencies, and it is seldom that they are not justified. There is, there-

fore, no desire to put forward a claim to exhaustiveness, and the author
will welcome suggestions for additional entries for incorporation in a second
edition of the work, if the demand for the present one justifies it. In
preparing the list of words and phrases with which he has dealt, he has
had to rely mainly on the notes he has made in the course of his reading,
but the nucleus of the list, and a very large nucleus, he owes to Mr.
William Swan Stallybrass, who very generously placed unreservedly at
his disposal his own vast collection of words and phrases made in the
course of catholic reading during a long period of years, together with
scores of thousands of extracts from writers from the Homeric age to
the present time. In fact, if it had not been for Mr. Stallybrass, from
whom the suggestion for the book first came and whose wide knowledge
and critical advice were always at the disposal of the author, it is very
doubtful whether the book would ever have been brought into being.

Finally, it is desired to point out that this book, although of the nature
of a dictionary, is not intended to be used merely as a dictionary. If it is
so used it will fail of its full purpose. It is hoped that it will be consulted
whenever enlightenment is desired on any word or phrase that is proper
to its scope. It is hoped also that when the reader turns to it for reference
he will find it sufficiently interesting to induce him to turn from entry
to entry and browse on it before he closes the book and returns to that
which first sent him to it. Only in such a case will the book have justified
the work that has been put into it.

A. M. H.

A FEW OF THE
PRINCIPAL REFERENCE WORKS CONSULTED

BARTLETT (J.). Familiar Quotations. 9th edition. 1898.

BENT (S. A.). Familiar Short Sayings of Great Men. New edition. 1887.

BORCHARDT (W.). Die Sprichwörtlichen Redensarten im deutschen Volksmunde. 5th edition. By G. Wustmann. Leipzig. 1895.

BREWER (E. C.). Dictionary of Phrase and Fable. New edition, n.d. (1894).

—— The Reader's Handbook. New edition. 1898.

BÜCHMANN (G.). Geflügelte Worte. 16th edition. By W. Robert-tornow. Berlin. 1889.

Century Cyclopaedia of Names, edited by B. E. Smith. 1894.

DAWSON (L. H.). Historical Allusions. 1907.

DIXON (J. M.). Dictionary of Idiomatic English Phrases. 1912.

EDWARDS (E.). Words, Facts and Phrases. 1882.

Encyclopaedia Britannica. 9th and 10th editions. 1875–1903.

Encyclopaedic Dictionary.

FARMER (J. S.). Americanisms—Old and New. 1889.

—— and HENLEY (W. E.). Slang and its Analogues, Past and Present. 7 vols. 1890–1904.

—— Dictionary of Slang and Colloquial English. (The above abridged). 1905.

FENNELL (C. A. M.) Stanford Dictionary of Anglicized Words and Phrases. Cambridge. 1892.

FOSTER (J). A Shakespeare Word-book, n.d. (1908).

FOURNIER (E.). L'Esprit des Autres Recueilli. Paris. 1879.

Gentleman's Magazine (The). 1731–1873.

HALLIWELL (J. O.). Dictionary of Archaic and Provincial Words. 6th edition. 1904.

HARBOTTLE (T. B.). Dictionary of Historical Allusions. 1904.

HEYWOOD (John). Proverbs and Epigrams (1562). Spenser Society. 1884.

HOTTEN. (Pub.) Slang Dictionary (1873). New edition, n.d. (1891).

JAMIESON (J.). Etymological Dictionary of Scottish. 2 vols.; Supplement, 2 vols. Edinburgh. 1808–25.

JOHNSON (T. H.). Phrases and Names.

JONES (H. P.). New Dictionary of Foreign Phrases. New edition. 1902.

LATHAM (E.). Dictionary of Names, Nicknames and Surnames. 1904.

—— Famous Sayings and Their Authors. 1904.

LEAN (V. S.). Collectanea. 4 vols. in 5. 1902–4.

LEMPRIERE (J.). A Classical Dictionary. New edition. 1919.

MACKAY (C.).   Glossary of Obscure Words and Phrases.   1887.

MURRAY (Sir J. H.), etc.   New English Dictionary on Historical Principles.
   Oxford.   1888 *sqq.*

NARES (R.).   Glossary of Words, Phrases, Names and Allusions.   New
   edition.   By J. O. Halliwell and Thomas Wright.   1905.

PALMER (A. SMYTH).   Folk-Etymology : A Dictionary.   1882.

ROZAN (C.).   Petites Ignorances de la Conversation.   11th edition.
   Paris.   1887.

—— Petites Ignorances Historiques et Littéraires.   Paris.   1888.

SKEAT (W. W.).   Etymological Dictionary of the English Language,
   Oxford.   1882.

SMITH (H. P.).   Glossary of Terms and Phrases.   1883.

SPENCE (Lewis).   Encyclopaedia of Occultism.   1920.

SVARTENGREN (J. H.).   Intensifying Similes in English.

TRENCH (R. C.).   A Select Glossary of English Words used formerly in
   senses different from their present.   New edition.

WALSH (W. S.).   Handy Book of Literary Curiosities.   1894.

WARE (J. R.).   Passing English of the Victorian Era.   1909.

WEATHERBY (C.).   Routledge's New Dictionary of the English Language.
   1914.

WHEELER (W. A.).   Familiar Allusions.   1882.

ABBREVIATIONS

A.-S.	= Anglo-Saxon	Consp.	= Conspirator
A.V.	= Authorized Version	Contemp.	= Contemptuously
Abbrev.	= Abbreviation	Contr.	= Contraction
Acc.	= According	Cor.	= Corinthians
Adm.	= Admiral	Corrup.	= Corruption
Admin.	= Administrative	Ct.	= Count
Adv.	= Adverb	Cttee.	= Committee
Afr.	= African	D.	= Died
Agric.	= Agricultural	Dem.	= Democratic
Alex.	= Alexander	Dept.	= Department
Amb.	= Ambassador	Der.	= Derivation; derived
Amer.	= American	Dial.	= Dialect
Anc.	= Ancient; anciently	Dimin.	= Diminutive
Antiq.	= Antiquities	Dist.	= District; distinguished
Arab.	= Arabian; Arabic	Div.	= Divine
Arch.	= Architecture	e.g. (*exempli*	
Assoc.	= Association	*gratia*)	= For example
Astrol.	= Astrological	Eccles.	= Ecclesiastical
Astron.	= Astronomical	Econ.	= Economic; Economist
Aug.	= August; Augustus	Edw.	= Edward
Aust.	= Austrian	Eliz.	= Elizabeth; Elizabethan
Austral.	= Australian	Emp.	= Emperor
B.C.	= Before Christ	Eng.	= England; English
Batt.	= Battalion	Equiv.	= Equivalent
Bec.	= Because	Esp.	= Especially
Belg.	= Belgian	Est.	= Established
Bibl.	= Biblical	Et seq. (*Et*	
Bot.	= Botanist	*sequentes*)	= And following
Brit.	= British	Europ.	= European
C. (*circa*)	= About	Exam.	= Examination
Camb.	= Cambridge	Exch.	= Exchange
Canad.	= Canadian	Fav.	= Favourite
Cap.	= Capital	Fig.	= Figuratively
Card.	= Cardinal	Fl.	= Flourished
Cath.	= Catholic	Flem.	= Flemish
Cent.	= Century; Central	Fndr.	= Founder
Cf. (*confer*)	= Compare	For.	= Foreign
Ch.	= Church	Form.	= Formerly
Chas.	= Charles	Fr.	= French
Chem.	= Chemist; chemistry	Fred.	= Frederick
Chin.	= Chinese	Gen.	= General
Christ.	= Christian	Geo.	= George
Class.	= Classical	Germ.	= German
Coll.	= College	Gov.	= Governor
Colloq.	= Colloquialism; colloquial;	Govt.	= Government
	colloquially	Grk.	= Greek
Comb.	= Combination	Heb.	= Hebrew
Cong.	= Congress	Hind.	= Hindustani
Conseq.	= Consequently	Hist.	= Historian
Conserv.	= Conservative	Hse.	= House

Hy.	= Henry	Polit.	= Political; Politician
i.e. (*id est*)	= That is	Pop.	= Popular
Imp.	= Imperial	Port.	= Portuguese
Indiv.	= Individual	Poss.	= Possibly
Ind.	= Indian	Pres.	= President
Inhab.	= Inhabitant	Presbyt.	= Presbyterian
Inv.	= Inventor	Prev.	= Previous; previously
It.	= Italian	Prob.	= Probably
Jap.	= Japanese	Prot.	= Protestant
Jas.	= James	Prov.	= Province; proverb
Jos.	= Joseph	q.v. (*quod*	
Journ.	= Journalist	*vide*)	= which see
Kg.	= King	R.C.	= Roman Catholic
Lang.	= Language	R.C. Ch.	= Roman Catholic Church
Lat.	= Latin	Rad.	= Radical
Lib.	= Liberal	Regt.	= Regiment
Lieut.	= Lieutenant	Rel.	= Religious
Lit.	= Literally	Rep.	= Republic; Republican
M.E.	= Middle English	Rev.	= Revolution
Marq.	= Marquis	Revol.	= Revolutionary
Marsh.	= Marshal	Rich.	= Richard
Mathem.	= Mathematician	Rob.	= Robert
Matt.	= Matthew	Rom.	= Roman
Med.	= Medieval	Russ.	= Russian
Metaph.	= Metaphorically	Sam.	= Samuel
Metro.	= Metropolitan	Scand.	= Scandinavian
Mil.	= Military	Scot.	= Scottish
Min.	= Minister	Sec.	= Secretary
Moham.	= Mohammedan	Soc.	= Society
Myth.	= Mythology	Span.	= Spanish
N.T.	= New Testament	Sqq. (*se-*	
Naut.	= Nautical	*quentes*)	= And following
Nonconf.	= Nonconformist	Subseq.	= Subsequently
O.-E.	= Old-English	Swed.	= Swedish
Orig.	= Originally; origin	T.C.D.	= Trinity College, Dublin
O.T.	= Old Testament	Tech.	= Technical
Oxf.	= Oxford	Theol.	= Theologian; theology
Parl.	= Parliament	Thos.	= Thomas
Part.	= Particular; particularly	Trans.	= Translation; translator
Pert.	= Pertaining	U.S.	= United States
Pers.	= Persian	Univ.	= University
Philos.	= Philosopher; philosophy	Wm.	= William

DICTIONARY OF PHRASES.

A1 : first class. From the symbol denoting ships in the best condition in *Lloyds' Registry of Shipping*. **A** denotes the quality of the vessel, **1** that of its stores. Introduced into literature by Capt. Marryat in *Peter Simple* (1834).

a fortiori (*Lat.*) : with a stronger reason. [Whitaker, *Disput.* (1588)]

à la (*Fr.*) : in the manner of. Employed by Thomas Gray 1716-71 in his letters, lxiii.

à la bonne heure (*Fr.*, at the good hour): luckily. [Horace Walpole, *Letters*, p. 19 (1762)]

à la mode (*Fr.*, in the manner) : fashionably. [Nashe, *The Unfortunate Traveller* (1594)]

à la mort (*Fr.*) : to the death. [Shakespeare, 1 *Henry VI*, III, ii ; Wyrley, *Armorie* (1592)]

à la volée (*Fr.*, at the flight) : at random, inconsiderately. [Sir Thomas Browne, *Religio Medici*, Pt. II (1643)]

à outrance (*Fr.*, to a finish) : to the bitter end. Originally applied to a contest between two antagonists, both determined to conquer or die. [Holland, *Translation of Suetonius* (1606)]

a posteriori (*Lat.*, from the latter) : from effect to cause. [Adams, *Diary* (1758)]

a priori (*Lat.*, from the former) : of an argument from that which went before; from the antecedent. [P. Bayne, *Commentary on Ephesians* (1618)]

à propos (*Fr.*, to the purpose) : [Dryden, *Mock Astrologer*, V (1669)]

a vinculo matrimonii (*Lat.*, from the bond of matrimony) : a complete divorce. [Coke, *Littleton* (1628)]

Aaron's beard : popular name of several plants, especially Great St. John's Wort.

Aaron's rod : popular name of the Golden Rod ; also of Great Mullein.

Aaron's serpent, An : that which is powerful enough to overcome and neutralise all rivals. [*Exodus*, vii, 10-12]

A.B., An : an able-bodied seaman, the lowest rank but one in the Royal Navy.

Ab extra (*Lat.*) : from without. [Thomas Goodwin, *Works* (1650)]

Ab ovo (*Lat.*, from the egg) : from the beginning. Eggs formed the first dish at a Roman repast. [Sidney, *Apologie for Poesie* (1595)]

Abaddon (*Heb.*) : the destroying angel ; hell. [*Rev.* ix, 11 ; Bunyan, *Pilgrim's Progress* (1678)]

Abaton, As inaccessible as : the Abaton was the fortification erected by the Rhodians around the statue of Rhodes erected by Artemisia.

Abbas Letitiæ : see Abbé de Liesse.

Abbé de Liesse (*Fr.*) : the Abbot of Jollity, Abbot of Misrule (*q.v.*).

Abbethdin : a Lord Chancellor. Properly a principal judge in a Jewish court of law. [Dryden, *Absalom and Achitophel*, Pt. I, ii, 188-91 (1681)]

Abbey Laird : an insolvent debtor. After the Abbey of Holyrood, the precincts of which were a sanctuary for insolvent debtors.

Abbey Lubber: a lazy monk, or other idler. In general use after the Reformation.

Abbot of Misrule, Lord of Misrule : the Master of the Ceremonies at the Christmas celebrations. *See also* Abbot of Unreason ; Abbé de Liesse.

Abbot of Unreason : in Scotland, Master of the mediæval Christmas revels.

A B C book : see Absey book.

A B C-darian : see Abecedarian.

A B C nations : originally Argentina, Brazil, and Chile. Subsequently extended to the Latin States of South America.

A B C of . . The : the elementary principle or rudiments of . . [Dekker, *The Gull's Horn Book*, ch. 6 (1609)]

A B C Process, The : the manufacture of manure from alum, blood and clay, its principal ingredients.

Abdael : George Monk, 3rd Duke of Albemarle. So called by Dryden in *Absalom and Achitophel*, after Abdiel in Milton's *Paradise Lost*, Bk. V (1665).

Abderitan : foolish. From Abdera in Thrace, proverbial for the stupidity of its inhabitants.

Abderitan laughter : ceaseless, scoffing laughter. From Democritos of Abdera, 'the Laughing Philosopher.' An *Abderite*, a scoffer.

Abdul the Damned : Abdul Hamid II (1842-1918), Sultan of Turkey. So-called by Dr. Joseph Parker, on account of the Armenian atrocities perpetrated during his reign.

Abecedarian : (1) a member of an Anabaptist sect of the 16th cent., which taught that believers could learn the Bible without knowing how to read ; (2) one engaged in learning or teaching the alphabet.

Abhorrers : the predecessors of the Tories and Conservatives in English politics, who in 1680 signed addresses abhorring proposals to limit the power of the king.

Abigail, An : a lady's maid. After the wife of Nabal (I *Sam.* xxv). Abigail is ' the waiting gentlewoman ' in Beaumont and Fletcher, *The Scornful Lady* (1616).

Abingdon Law : ' Hang a man first and try him afterwards '—the policy of Major Brown of Abingdon, an officer in the Parliamentary Army in the English Civil War. Or, perhaps, from the execution without trial of the Irish prisoners taken by the Earl of Essex and Waller during the defence of Abingdon (1644-5).

Aboard of .. To fall : to meet and abuse. A nautical metaphor.

Abolitionist, An : an advocate of the abolition of slavery in the U.S. Still earlier the term was applied in Great Britain to the advocates of the abolition of slavery.

Abomination of Desolation, An : any thing very hateful or damaging ; properly, the Roman standard (*Mat.* xxiv, 15), which, being set up in the Holy of Holies, was an abomination and brought destruction or desolation.

Abonde, Dame : the French Santa Claus (*q.v.*).

Aborigines : the earliest known inhabitants of a land, originally applied to a Central Italian tribe settled in Italy before the Roman period. From the Lat. *ab origine* (from the beginning).

Above-board : straightforward, without concealment. Originally a gaming term, meaning above the table, affording no opportunity for the changing of cards or other form of cheating.

Above par : a commercial term, used to indicate value in excess of the nominal value. Also used figuratively.

Abracadabra : meaningless gibberish ; a magical charm used by the Gnostic sect of Basilides. The charm took the form of a triangle composed of the word repeated eleven times but on every occasion with the loss of one letter, so that on the last occasion it appeared as A only. Origin unknown ; first used in 2nd cent. by Q. Severus Sammonicus. A suggested derivation is from the Heb. *ab* (father) *ben* (son) and *ruach akodesh* (holy spirit).

Abraham man ; Abram man, An : a wandering beggar, one of a class that came into existence after the dissolution of the Monasteries ; esp. a lunatic beggar from Bethlehem (Bedlam) Hospital, whose wards were formerly named after different Saints. The inmates of the Abraham ward were allowed to go out to beg in the streets on certain days.

Abraham Newland, An : a Bank of England note. After the cashier whose signature was appended to ehe notes at the beginning of 19th c)nt.

Abraham (Abram), To sham : (1 to pretend, for begging purposes, to be insane (*see* Abraham man) ; (2) to forge a bank-note (*see* Abraham Newland).

Abrahamic Covenant, The: (1) the covenant entered into by God with Abraham, whereby the latter was to become the ancestor of a great nation and ultimately of the Messiah ; (2) the rite of circumcision, whereby Abraham's descendants dedicated themselves to the service of God.

Abraham's Bosom : the repose of the blessed after death (*Luke* xvi, 22). From the ancient practice of resting on the bosom of a friend.

Abraham's Eye, An : a charm used to render a thief who refuses to confess his crime blind.

Abram-coloured : a corruption of auburn-coloured. [Shakespeare, *Coriolanus*, II, iii (? 1607)]

Abram man : *see* Abraham man.

Abraxas Stones : gems used as amulets by the Basilides and engraved with the Abraxas, a magical word, probably a Gnostic title of God. Perhaps derived from the Greek letter-numerals which make up the symbolic number 365.

Abroad, To be all : to have one's mind wandering from the subject.

Absalom, An : an undutiful son. After Absalom the son of David (II *Sam.*). The Absalom in Dryden's satire *Absalom and Achitophel* (1681-2) represents James, Duke of Monmouth.

Absentee Tax : a tax on absentee Irish landlords, imposed in the reign of Richard II and attempted to be reimposed in 1773.

Absenteeism : the practice, esp. on the part of a landlord, of living away from the source of one's income. Irish in origin.

Absent-minded Beggar, An : an English common soldier. From a poem of that title by Rudyard Kipling (1900).

Absey book, An : an A B C book or elementary spelling-book. [Shakespeare, *King John*, I, i (?1595)]

Absolute, A Captain : a persistent and high-spirited lover. After the character in Sheridan, *The Rivals* (1775).

Absolute Monarchy : government by the absolute will of the monarch. [Francis, Lord Bacon, *Essays : Of Superstition* (1624)]

Absolute, A Sir Anthony : an obstinate, passionate yet generous old man. After a character in Sheridan, *The Rivals* (1775).

Absquatulate, To : for a squatter suddenly to leave his holding.

Abstainer, A Total : one who abstains entirely from alcoholic liquor. Formerly a Nazarite.

Acacetus : one who does nothing badly ; a name borne by the god Mercury. From the Grk. *a* (not) and *kakos* (bad).

Academic Legion, An : an armed corps of students which participated in European insurrections, esp. at Vienna in 1848.

Academy : an educational institution ; a learned society. From the School of Philosophy founded by Plato in the Garden of Academus, near Athens.

Academy, French, The : a French association of the 40 members (the 'Forty Immortals') supposed to be the most illustrious living French men-of-letters. Formally established in 1635 by Card. Richelieu for controlling the French language and directing literary taste.

Academy headache, An : a headache due to attention to picture and other similar exhibitions. Phrase coined, 1885, with reference to the Royal Academy Exhibition.

Acadia : an early French name for Nova Scotia. After the river Shubenacadie.

Accessory after the Fact, An : one who shields or assists a criminal, knowing him to be guilty of the crime. [*A Warning for Faire Women*, II, l. 1289 (1599)]

Accessory before the Fact, An : one who is aware of the intention on the part of another to commit a crime, but does not disclose that intention. [*A Warning for Faire Women*, II, l. 1289 (1599)]

Accident of an Accident, An : high birth. First used by Lord Thurlow (1731-1806), Lord Chancellor, in a debate in the House of Lords.

Account of, To give a good : to punish severely.

Account, Of small : of little consequence. [Lyly, *Euphues* (1579)]

Account, To call to : to demand an explanation of. [Francis Bacon, *Essays : Of Friendship* (1625)]

Account, To go to one's : to die.

Account, To turn to : to make use of.

Accusative, The : John Calvin (1509-64), the founder of Protestantism. So-called by his college companions from his habit of accusing error.

Ace, To bate an : to hesitate ; to show reluctance. Properly, to give a competitor a slight advantage. An ace is the lowest numeral. The phrase is said to have originated at the court of Henry VIII, from the mouth of Bolton, one of his courtiers. [Wm. Haughton, *Englishmen for My Money*, II, ii (1597)]

Ace of, Within an : On the point of. ' Ace ' in the sense of a jot or tittle, a playing-card with a solitary pip.

Aceldama : a field of slaughter. After the ' field of blood ' bought by Judas with the money derived from the betrayal of Jesus.

Acephalites : religious sects that acknowledged no worldly superiors. Grk., *a* (not, without) and *kephale* (a head).

Acestes, The arrow of : Acestes, a Sicilian competitor in a contest, discharged his arrow with such rapidity that it caught fire. [Virgil, *Æneid*, V, 525 ; Burton, *Anatomy of Melancholy* (1621)]

Achaian prophet, The blind : Tiresias, the legendary blind prophet of Thebes.

Achan, An : a looter. After the biblical personage who was stoned to death for looting (*Joshua*, vii).

Achates, A Fidus : a trusty friend. After Achates, Æneas' faithful friend.

[Virgil, *Æneid*, I, 188 ; Turner, *Letter to Fox* (c. 1587)]

Acheron : the lower world. After a fabulous river in that region.

Acheron, Food for : *see* Pabulum Acherontis.

Acheron, The Pit of : *see* Acheron.

Acherusia Palus (*Lat.*, the Acherusian bog) : the lower world. After the name of several small lakes in Pontus which were supposed to be connected with Hades.

Achilles, An : a splendid military hero. After the King of the Myrmidons in Thessaly, the central character of Homer's *Iliad*, and the Greek hero of the Trojan War.

Achilles of England, The : (1) the Duke of Wellington (1769-1852) ; (2) John Talbot, 1st Earl of Shrewsbury (1373-1453).

Achilles of Germany, The : Albert III, Elector of Brandenburg (1414-86).

Achilles of Rome, The : Lucius Licinius Dentatus (d. 450 B.C.), Roman Tribune. Also called The Second Achilles.

Achilles of the West, The : Roland, the Paladin (8th cent.).

Achilles, The heel of : a vulnerable spot. From the story of Achilles, who was held by the heel when dipped in the Styx to make him invulnerable, the heel being thus the one vulnerable spot in his body.

Achilles, The Second : *see* Achilles of Rome.

Achilles tendon, The : the tendon which connects the heel with the calf ; *see* Achilles, The heel of.

Aching Almanac An : rheumatism.

" Some men ('gainst raine) doe carry in their backs
　Prognosticating Aking Almanacks :
　Some by a painefull elbow, hip, or knee,
　Will shrewdly guesse what wether's like to be."

[John Taylor, *Drinke and Welcome* (1637)]

Aching void, An : sorrow caused by the recollection of a loss. [Cowper, *Walking with God*]

Achitophel, An : a treacherous friend and adviser. After the man who seceded from David to Absalom. [II *Sam.*] Achitophel is also a character in Dryden's satire *Absalom and Achitophel* (1681-2).

Ack pirate, An : a pirate who follows his calling on inland waters.

Acknowledge the corn, To : to admit oneself beaten. From the story of an American countryman who, finding himself for the first time in New Orleans, was cheated at cards, losing, in addition to his money, two barges, one of corn the other of potatoes, which he had brought to sell in the town. While he was gambling the barge of corn was accidentally sunk. When in the morning the creditor came to receive his property, the debtor replied, ' I acknowledge the corn ; but the potatoes you can't have, by thunder ! ' Another suggested derivation is from a debate in the U.S. Congress in 1828 between Andrew Stewart and Charles A. Wickliffe, which the latter concluded, ' I acknowledge the corn.'

Acmonian Wood, The : a trysting-place for the practice of immorality. From the spot where Mars met Harmonia to become the father of the Amazons.

Acquaintance, A nodding : *see* Nodding Acquaintance.

Acre Fight : a duel between English and Scots on the Border, erroneously derived from the mistranslation of a mediæval Lat. phrase in *The Annals of Burton* (1237).

Acre, God's : a churchyard. ' Acre ' in the sense of enclosed land.

Acre shot, An : a charge rated per acre.

Acres and a cow, Three : a small agricultural holding ; facilities for the acquisition of which by agricultural labourers were made by Jesse Collings a part of the Radical Party's campaign previous to the General Election of 1885.

Acropolis, An : the fortified buildings in the centre of a Greek city, esp. the Acropolis of Athens.

Across lots : by a short cut. ' Lots ' means allotted or private property. The phrase was rendered famous by Brigham Young, the Mormon leader's threat, ' We'll send them (the Gentiles) to hell across lots.'

Act of Faith : *see* Auto da Fé.

Act of God, An : an accident due to causes over which no man has control.

Actæon, An : (1) a hunter ; (2) the husband of an unfaithful wife.

Actæon-like : Actæon, a hunter, who witnessed Diana bathing and as a punishment was turned by her into a stag, which was torn to pieces by his own hounds.

Actæon's hounds : *see* Actæon-like. [James Puckle, *The Club: ' Dear Kinsman '* (1711)]

Actian years : years in which the Actian Games instituted at Actium, in honour of Apollo, were celebrated.

Action-sermon, An : a sacramental or Communion discourse (Scottish).

Adam, A Son (Child) of : a human being. After Adam, the first man.

Adam, An : (1) a humorous epithet for a sergeant or bailiff who wore buff. After Adam who ' wore his native buff.' [Shakespeare, *Comedy of Errors*, IV, iii] (2) a faithful, devoted old servant. After a character in Shakespeare, *As You Like It* (1600).

Adam Bell, An : an accomplished archer. After a northern outlaw, celebrated for his archery. [Percy, *Reliques*, I (1868)]

Adam Cupid : Cupid as an archer : *see* Adam Bell. [Shakespeare, *Romeo and Juliet*, II (1592)]

Adam, Father : *see* Father Adam.

Adam furniture (etc.) : in the style of the Brothers Adam (John, Robert, James, William), English architects who flourished in the latter half of the 18th cent.

Adam, Not to know from : to have no knowledge of at all.

Adam, The offending : the original inclination to evil in man. [Shakespeare, *Henry . V*, I, i (1599)]

Adam, The old : man's natural tendency towards evil. After Adam, the first man, who succumbed to temptation. [*Romans*, vi, 6, etc.]

Adam, As old as : in allusion to Adam, the first man. Used as a rule in connection with stale news.

Adam, The Second (New) : Jesus Christ.

Adam's ale : water. The phrase was introduced by the Puritans. [Prynne, *Sovereign Power of Parliament* (1643)]

Adam's apple : the thyroid cartilage visible in the human throat ; the ' huggle-guggle.' After the superstition that it arose from a piece of the forbidden fruit that stuck in Adam's throat.

Adam's arms : a spade, in allusion to the first man.

Adam's profession : gardening. On account of the occupation of Adam in the Garden of Eden. An ' Adamist,' a gardener.

Adam's sin : disobedience.

Adam's wine : Adam's ale (*q.v.*) (a Scotticism).

Adams, Parson : a simple, kind-hearted, honest old country clergyman. After a character in Fielding, *Joseph Andrews* (1742).

Adamant, A heart of : a cold, unemotionable disposition, impervious to influence. The adamant is the diamond. [*Ezekiel*, iii, 9 ; and Greene, *Selimus*, II, 47-8 (1594)]

Adamant, As hard as : as hard as the diamond. [Ovid, *Heroides*, X, 109 ; and Lyly, *Euphues* (1579)]

Adamantine chain, An : an unbreakable bond. [Æschylus, *Prometheus Vinctus*; Ovid, *Tristia*, Bk. IV, viii, 11, 45-6 ; and Milton, *Paradise Lost*, I, 48 (1667)]

Adamite, An : (1) a descendant of Adam ; (2) a member of a religious sect that practised nudity in imitation of Adam. The sect flourished at intervals from 2nd to 19th cent. ; (3) an adherent of John Quincy Adams, 10th president of the U.S.

ad captandum (*Lat.*, for catching) : addressed to ignorance, prejudice, etc., rather than to reason.

ad crumenam: An argument (*Lat.*, to the purse, pocket) : an argument that appeals to one's material interests. [Scott, *Rob Roy*, ch. 27 (1818)]

ad hominem (*Lat.*, at the man) : of an argument directed to the special interest or feelings of the individual, instead of to abstract or general principles.

ad valorem (*Lat.*) : applied to customs and excise duties calculated on the value of the goods on which they are levied. Also used generally for ' up to the value of the goods.'

Addison of the North, The : Henry Mackenzie (1745-1831), Scottish essayist and novelist.

Addition, division and silence : corrupt practices supposed to be necessary to an unscrupulous politician. Believed to have been first used in a letter alleged to have been written by W. H. Kemble, State Treasurer of Pennsylvania, and published in the *New York Sun*, March 15, 1872.

Addled Parliament, The : summoned in 1614 and dissolved without having passed any legislation.

Addle-headed (-pated) : muddle-headed. A metaphor derived from an addled egg.

Address, The : the reply to the King's Speech moved on the opening of a session of Parliament,

Adelantado, An (*Span.*, 'His Excellency') : an important personage ; esp. the head of a small community. It is the title of a Spanish governor of a province.

Adjutators : nominees of the Army appointed to represent their grievances before Parliament in 1647.

Admirable, The : Abraham Aben-Ezra (1093-1167), Spanish-Jewish scholar and biblical commentator.

Admirable Crichton : *see* Crichton.

Admirable Doctor, The : Roger Bacon (c. 1214-94), English scholar and scientist.

Admiral of the Blue, An : (1) formerly an admiral hoisting a flag on a blue ground and commanding the rear ; (2) a tapster, from the colour of his apron ; (3) a butcher, for the same reason.

Admiral of the Red, An : (1) formerly an admiral hoisting a flag on a red ground and commanding in the centre ; (2) a tippler, from the colour of his face or nose.

Admiral of the Red, White and Blue, An : a beadle ; hall-porter ; etc. From their gorgeous uniforms.

Admiral of the White, An : (1) formerly an admiral hoisting a flag on a white ground, who commanded in the van ; (2) a coward ; (3) a fainting person.

Admiral, To tap the : to drink secretly. Originally a nautical phrase.

Admiral's Regiment, The : the Royal Marines.

Admonitioners, Admonitionists : the Puritans who made representations to Parliament in 1571 against ceremonies in the Church of England. From the 'admonition' which they presented.

Ado, To keep : to be always astir. [Earle, *Microcosmographie : A Medley Man* (1628)]

Ado, To make an : to make a fuss. [Thos. Preston, *King Cambyses*, I, 832 (c. 1561)]

Adonai (*Heb.*) : (1) a name of God ; (2) My lords ; (3) the god of light among the Rosicrucians.

Adonis, An : an extremely handsome youth or man ; a dandy. After Adonis, the beloved of Venus, famous for his beauty.

Adonis garden, An : an ephemeral toy or pleasure. From the Adonis gardens or lettuce jars of the ancient Greeks in which herbs were grown for the annual festival of Adonis, and then discarded.

Adonis of fifty : George IV of England. So-called by Leigh Hunt, who suffered imprisonment on account of the epigram which contained the phrase.

Adoptive Emperors, The : Nerva, Trajan, Hadrian, Antoninus Pius and Marcus Aurelius, Roman emperors who were adopted and nominated by their immediate predecessors.

Adriatic, Marriage of the : the ceremony formerly performed annually by the Doge of Venice of throwing a consecrated ring into the water. Instituted c. 1177 to commemorate the victory over Emperor Frederick Barbarossa.

Adullam, Cave of : *see* Adullamites.

Adullamites : seceders from the Liberal Party in 1866 on the subject of Parliamentary Reform. The secession was termed the Cave of Adullam by John Bright (*see* I *Sam.*, xxii). Hence any body of political seceders.

Adventurer ; Merchant Adventurer : one engaged in a trading expedition in the 16th or 17th cent., or a member of a society engaged in such an enterprise. In the Elizabethan period a volunteer who participated in a naval enterprise was sometimes called an ' Adventurer.'

Adventurer upon return, An : a traveller who gambled on his return from a voyage. He lent money on his departure and was repaid with heavy interest in the event of his return.

Adventurers of 1642, The : those who advanced money to the Government in 1641 and were repaid by grants of land in Ireland 12 years later.

Adversary, The : Satan. [I *Peter*, v, 8]

Advocatus Diaboli (*Lat.*, the devil's advocate) : an adverse critic. Properly, the official appointed by the Pope to argue against the proposed canonization of a saint.

Ægean civilization : prehistoric civilization centering in Crete and spreading around the shores of the Eastern Mediterranean, or Ægean, Sea.

Æger, An (*Lat.*, ill) : (1) a certificate of illness held by a student at a university or school ; (2) the excuse for absence on account of illness.

Ægis of .. Under the : under the protection of .. The ægis was the shield given by Jupiter to Athena. It was the former's protection in his war with the Titans.

Ægrotat, An (*Lat.*, he is ill) : an excuse from examination at a university on account of illness.

A.E.I.O.U. : *Austriae Est Imperare Orbi Universo ; Austria Erit In Orbe Ultima ; Alles Erdreich Ist Oesterreich Unterthan ;* Austria's Empire Is Over all Universal. Adopted by the Emperor Frederick III, Archduke of Austria (1415-93).

Ælia Lælia : an insoluble riddle. From the title of a Latin inscription discovered at Bologna.

Æmonian arts, The : magic. After Æmonia in Thessaly, famous for its magic.

Æolian : (1) borne by the wind, after Æolus, the god of the winds ; (2) lyric, after Æolis, the N.W. Coast of Asia Minor, where the early lyric poetry of the Greeks flourished.

Æolian harp, An : a musical instrument played by the wind. After Æolus, the god of the winds.

Æolus, A cave (temple) of : a very windy place. After Æolus (Greek mythology), the keeper of the winds.

Æolus, The breath of : scandal.

Æschylus of France, The : Prosper Jolyot de Crébillon (1674-1762), French dramatist and poet. After Æschylus (525-456 B.C.), the founder of the Greek drama.

Æsculapius, An : a physician. After Æsculapius, the Greek god of medicine. ' Æsculapian,' medicinal.

Æson's bath : a hair-dye [according to Sir T. Browne, *Religio Medici* (1643)] The reference is to the rejuvenation of Æson by Medea.

Æsop of Arabia, The : Lokman (fl. 5th cent.). After Æsop (c. 620-560 B.C.), the famous Greek fabulist.

Æsop of England, The : John Gay (1688-1732), author of *Fables* (1726).

Æsop of France, The : Jean de la Fontaine (1621-95), author of *Fables* (1668-95).

Æsop of Germany, The : Gotthold Ephraim Lessing (1729-81).

Æsop of India, The : Pilpay or Bidpai, author of *Fables* (c. 300 B.C.).

Affaire de coeur, An (*Fr.*, affair of the heart) : a love-affair.

Affaire d'honneur, An (*Fr.*, affair of honour) : a duel.

Affliction, Bread of : a living earned in painful or unpleasant circumstances. [*Deuteronomy*, xvi, 3]

Afrancesados : Napoleon's supporters in Spain and Spanish America.

African dust : gold.

African Slave, The : Terence (B.C. 194-159), Latin comedian, who was brought to Rome from Carthage as a slave.

Africander, An : a white South-African, generally of Dutch extraction.

Africander Bund, The : a political association formed in 1882 to secure the independence of South Africa.

After us the Deluge : *see* Deluge.

After-cast : (1) a second throw at dice ; (2) anything done too late.

After-clap, An : a sudden attack occurring after the contest is supposed to have concluded ; an unexpected demand suddenly put forward. [Occleve, *De Regimine Principum*, 855 (1411-2)]

After-dinner mood, An : a comfortable and good-tempered condition.

After-meal, An : an entertainment following a banquet.

Afternoon of one's days, The : the second half of a life of normal length. [Shakespeare, *Richard III*, III, vii, (1594)]

Afternoon's man, An : a tippler. [Sir T. Overbury, *Characters, A Water-man*, (1616)]

Aga Khan, An : (1) a descendant of Ali, the husband of Fatima, Mahomet's daughter ; (2) an Indian prince of this descent possessing spiritual authority.

Agamemnon, An : a great military ruler. After the legendary king of Mycenæ, who led the Greek expedition against Troy and who, on his return home, was murdered either by his wife or by her paramour.

Aganice, As the moon obeys : from an ancient Greek proverb, used in allusion to boasters ; more remotely from the legend of Aganice of Thessaly, who, learning to calculate eclipses, pretended, until her secret was discovered, that she could control the moon.

Agape (*Grk.*, love) : a love-feast in the ritual of the Early Christians.

Agapemone : (1) an institution of the religious sect of Agapemonites ; (2) an ' abode of (sexual) love.'

Agate, An : an undersized person. From the small figures cut in agate, which stone was named after Achates, the Greek name of a Sicilian river in whose bed agates were found in profusion.

Agathocles' pot : a poor relation. From Agathocles (B.C. 361-289), Tyrant of Syracuse, who was the son of a potter, himself at first followed that trade, and in his period of greatness always kept an earthen pot near him to remind him of his origin.

Age, Of a certain : generally of a woman, no longer young. [R. Cumberland, *The Mysterious Husband*, I, i (1783)]

Age of the Bishops, The : The ninth century (according to Hallam).

Age of the Popes, The : the twelfth century (according to Hallam).

Age, The Wire : the present. On account of the universal use of the telegraph.

Ages, The Five : (1) according to Hesiod : the Golden or Patriarchal ; the Silver or Voluptuous ; the Brazen or Warlike ; the Heroic or Renaissant ; the Iron or Present ; (2) according to Fichte : the Antediluvian ; the Postdiluvian ; the Christian ; the Satanic ; the Millenian.

Ages, The Three : (1) according to Varro : the Beginning of Mankind to the Deluge ; the Deluge to the First Olympiad (the mythical) ; the First Olympiad to the Present Time (the Historic) ; (2) according to Lucretius : the Age of Stone (when implements of stone were used) ; the Age of Bronze (when implements of copper or brass were used) ; the Age of Iron (the present, when implements of iron are used).

Ages of Man, The Seven : *see* Seven Ages.

Ages of Man, The Three : (1) " At 20 years of age the will ripens ; at 30 the wit ; at 40 the judgment." [Benj. Franklin, *Poor Richard's Almanac* for 1741, June] (2) an infant in a cradle, a shepherd playing a flute, an old man meditating on two skulls ; as symbolized by Titian.

Ages of a State, The Three : *see* State, The Three Ages of a.

Agent Provocateur, An (*Fr.*) : a secret agent employed by governments to encourage suspected revolutionists or other political offenders so far to commit themselves as to justify their arrest.

Agitator, An : one who stirs up feelings of discontent. Originally one of the delegates of the private soldiers in the English Parliamentary Army (1647).

Agnes, An : a simple girl who innocently makes remarks into which an improper interpretation can be read. After a character in Molière, *L'Ecole des Femmes* (1662).

Agnus Bell, An : the bell rung while the Agnus Dei is being recited or chanted.

Agnus Dei (*Lat.*, the Lamb of God) : (1) the symbol of Christ : in the Catholic Church a cake of candle-wax impressed with the symbol of a lamb and blessed by the Pope ; (2) a prayer commencing with the words *Agnus Dei*, O Lamb of God.

Agog, To set (*Fr.*, *à gogo*, in clover) : to excite to eager expectation, like a horse in clover.

Agony Column, An : the advertisement column of a newspaper which contains inquiries for missing friends, communications between lovers, etc. In allusion to the obvious distress of some of the advertisers.

Agony, To pile on (up) the : to exaggerate esp. in sensational narratives. [Mrs. Gaskell, *Life of Charlotte Brontë*, ch. xxv (1857)]

Agrarian League, The : a German league formed in 1893 to secure the adoption of bimetallism and protection.

Agraviados (*Span.*, men with a grievance) : Spanish insurgents of 1826-8.

Agree to differ, To : to refrain from dispute although not in agreement. [Sidney, *Arcadia*, Bk. I (1590)]

Agur's wish : ' Give me neither riches nor poverty.' [*Proverbs* xxx, 8]

Ahitophel : *see* Achitophel.

Aholibah : the personification of prostitution. [*Ezekiel*, xxiii]

Ahriman : the principle of evil, according to the old Persian mythology.

Aid, An : a feudal tax levied in England on vassals ; also sometimes a voluntary grant.

Aide de Camp, An (*Fr.*, camp-assistant) : an officer in attendance on a general. [Cotton, *Espernon*, III, xi (1670)]

Aim-crier, An : an abettor. A metaphor drawn from archery.

Aim at, To take an : to estimate. [Francis Bacon, *Essays : Of Superstition* (1625)]

Aim, To cry : to consent ; approve of ; applaud. Originally derived from archery where it was used to encourage a competitor to accept a challenge. [Rob. Garnier, *Cornelia* (Thos. Kyd's Translation), IV, i, 172 (1594)]

Aim, To give : to stand aloof ; to guide one who aims, by informing him of the result of his previous shot. Originally an archery term. [Dekker and Webster, *Westward Ho*, II, ii (1607)]

Air one's opinions, To : to state one's views publicly ; to propound one's opinion.

Air, To live on : to have no visible means of existence.

Air, To plough the : *see* Plough.

Air, To take : to be spread abroad. [Bunyan, *The Holy War* (1682)]

Air, To take the : to enjoy a walk or promenade.

Air, To vanish into thin : to disappear. [Homer, *Odyssey*, Bk. VIII, 409 ; Shakespeare, *The Tempest*, IV, i, 11. 148-56 (?1609)]

Air, To walk on : to be light-hearted.

Air weeps, The : it rains. [Nich. Grimald, *Epitaph on the Death of Sir James Willford* (1557)]

Airs, To give oneself : to make pretensions to superiority.

Airy nothings : matters of no consequence. Attributed to Dr. Johnson by Mrs. Piozzi.

Ajax, An : (1) a hero, distinguished by stature, strength, and physical beauty. After the Greek hero in the Trojan War ; (2) a water-closet ; properly, a jakes.

Alabama Claim, The : a privateer, fitted out in England, which preyed on the commerce of the Northern States during the American Civil War, in consequence of which more than £3,000,000 compensation had to be paid by England.

Aladdin's cave of wealth, An : vast stores of wealth. From the tale of *Aladdin and the Wonderful Lamp* in *The Arabian Nights.*

Aladdin's Lamp : a talisman that brings good fortune and success. From the tale of *Aladdin and the Wonderful Lamp* in *The Arabian Nights.*

Aladdin's Window, To finish : to attempt to complete a task beyond one's powers. From the tale of *Aladdin* in *The Arabian Nights.*

Alamode : *see* à la mode.

Alaric Cottin (Cotin) : a nickname given to Frederick the Great of Prussia by Voltaire. After Alaric, the Visigothic King, a famous warrior (c. 376-410), and Charles Cotin, a mediocre French poet (1604-82).

Alarm, A false : an unnecessary warning of approaching danger. From *all' arme*, to arms. [Langland, *Piers Plowman*, XX, 91 (14th cent.)]

Alascons : Protestant refugees in England in the 16th cent. After Jan à Lasci, a Polish refugee in England (1499-1560).

Alasnam's Mirror : the test of virtue ; a mirror given by one of the genii to Prince Zeyn Alasnam, whereby he could tell immediately whether a maiden would remain faithful to him or not. [*The Arabian Nights*]

Albany ; Albion : a poetical name for Scotland. Properly, Northern Scotland.

Albany Regency, The : an American political Party, with headquarters at Albany, New York State. It acquired considerable influence (c. 1820-54).

Albertine, An : a very careful domestic manageress. After a character in Alexandre Dumas (fils), *Le Père Prodigue* (1859).

Albigenses, The : Pre-Reformation heretics ; esp. Reformers in the South of France in the 12th and 13th centuries who were severely persecuted by Innocent III and Simon de Montfort, and who were the progenitors of the Reformation in England and on the Continent. From Albi, a town in Languedoc, one of their centres.

Albin : Albion (*q.v.*) ; Albany (*q.v.*)

Albino-poets : minor poets, noteworthy for sweetness rather than for strength. A term invented by Oliver Wendell Holmes in *The Autocrat of the Breakfast Table* (1857-8) in reference to Kirke White, on whose name the term is a play.

Albion : the ancient and poetical name of Britain. From a Celtic word, meaning White Land, in allusion to the chalk cliffs on the southern coast.

Alcantara, Knights of : a Spanish order of knighthood, established in 1177 for service against the Mohammedans.

Alcinous, An : a protector and host. After the king of the Phæacians, with whom Odysseus, Jason and Medea took refuge.

Alcinous, A feast of : an extravagant entertainment.

Alcinous, Apples to : *see* Apples.

Alcmena's night, An : a night apparently as long as three ordinary ones.

Alcyon : *see* Halcyon.

Alderman, An : (1) a crowbar as a burglar's tool, on account of its important position in the outfit ; (2) two-shillings-and-sixpence ; because just as an alderman is half a king in his ward, a two-and-sixpenny coin is half-a-crown ; (3) a turkey ; from its usual appearance at municipal banquets, and also from the red and purples of its head and neck.

Alderman in chains, An : a turkey with sausages hung around it. On account of its resemblance to a portly City alderman wearing the chain of office.

Alderman's pace : a slow, stately pace.

Aldgate Pump, A draught on : a dishonoured cheque. A play on draught (draft).

Aldine Editions : books printed by Aldus Manutius of Venice (1450-1515), who invented the italic (formerly Aldine) type. Esp. editions of the classics printed by the Aldine press.

Ale, March : *see* March Ale.

Ale mends in summer, To mend as sour : not at all. [Heywood, *Proverbes* (1546)]

Ales : rustic festivals. On account of the ale consumed on such occasions.

Ale-bush, An : a tavern-sign. [Henry Porter, *Two Angry Women of Abington* (1599)]

Ale-clout, To wash one's face in an : to get drunk. [Heywood, *Proverbes* (1546)]

Ale-conner, An : a mediæval English official appointed to prevent depreciation in the quality of ale sold.

Ale-dagger, An : a dagger worn for use in taverns.

Ale-draper, An : a tavern-keeper. By analogy with linen-draper. [Chettle, *Kinde-Hart's Dreame* (1593)]

Ale-Knight, An : a tippler. [*Eccl. Proc. Chester* (1575)]

Ale-silver : a tax formerly paid to the Lord Mayor of London by those who sold ale within the City.

Ale-stake : (1) the sign before an inn, or its support ; [Chaucer, *Canterbury Tales*, Prologue 667 (1386)] (2) a tippler (16th cent.).

Ale-wife, An : (1) a kind of herring ; (2) the wife of an innkeeper.

Alexander Newski, Order of : a Russian Order of Knighthood, founded by Peter the Great.

Alexander of the North : Charles XII of Sweden. In allusion to Alexander the Great, King of Macedon (356-323 B.C.).

Alexander, The Albanian : Iskander Beg or Scanderbeg (George Castriot) (1403-67), Prince of Albania.

Alexander the Corrector : Alexander Cruden (1701-70), author of the *Concordance to the Bible*, who petitioned Parliament to appoint him ' Corrector of the People.'

Alexander, The English : Henry V. After Alexander the Great, Conqueror of the World.

Alexander, The Persian : Sandjar (1117-58).

Alexanders at five sous a day : soldiers, so-called by Voltaire.

Alexander's beard : no beard.

Alexandra limp, The : an artificial limp fashionable in English society (1872 *et seq.*) when Queen Alexandra was suffering from an injury to the knee.

Alexandrian : (in mediæval times) Eastern, because all oriental produce was imported from Alexandria.

Alexandrine (Verse) : The French heroic verse ; in English a kind of verse. After the French poet Alexandre Paris or from a poem on the subject of Alexander the Great.

Alexandrine Age, The : A.D. 323-640 when Alexandria was at the culmination of its career.

Alfred's Scholars : Werfrith, Bp. of Worcester ; Ethelstan and Werwulf, Mercian priests ; Plegmund of Mercia, Abp. of Canterbury ; Asser, a Welshman ; Grimbald, a Frenchman.

Algerism : administrative incapacity. After Russell Alger, American Secretary for War (1897-99), who was driven from office on account of his inefficient management of the Spanish-American War.

Alibi clock, An (*Lat.*, elsewhere) : a clock that strikes one hour and shows another.

Aliboron, An : a fool ; an ass. The name of a jackass in one of La Fontaine's *Fables*.

Alive and kicking : very much alive. In allusion to the child in the mother's womb after quickening. [Peter Pindar, *Hair Powder* (1795)]

All and some : everyone. [*The Pardoner and the Friar* (1533)]

All and sundry : all without exception.

All Fools' Day : the 1st of April : *see* April Fool.

All fours, To go on : to crawl on hands and knees.

All fours with .. On : quite conforming with .. ; entirely agreeing and harmonious with .. ; ' squaring ' with .. Of Masonic origin, denoting the completeness and harmony of the four sides of a square.

All Halloween summer, An : a late summer. After the Festival of All Hallows (All Saints) on the 1st of November.

All my eye (and Betty Martin) : all nonsense. Supposed to be a corruption of *ah mihi, beate Martine,* ' Woe to me, Blessed Martin,' the invocation of Italian beggars to their saint. It is said that an English sailor wandered into an Italian Church, and, when asked by his companions what was transpiring therein, replied : ' All my eye and Betty Martin.' In all probability the phrase has some kinship with ' to have in one's eye,' to have in mind, the suggestion being that not only is it in the mind, but it will remain there and never materialize.

All one : of no difference. [Lilly, *Campaspe* III, ii (1584)]

All, One's (little) : all one's property. [Peter Pindar, *Mr. Pitt's Flight to Wimbledon* (1795)]

All Red Cable : the cable-route, completed in 1902, from England to Australia, not touching foreign soil.

All Saints' Day : November 1st.

All serene : all right. Span., *serena,* a pass-word used in Cuba.

All Soul's Day : November 2nd. A Catholic festival in memory of the dead.

All talk and no cider : much cry and little wool ; a great deal of fuss but very little result. An Americanism. Said to have arisen out of a cider party met in Bucks County, Pennsylvania, which quickly developed into a political meeting, to the resentment of many of the guests who considered that they had been brought to the gathering on false pretences.

All the go : popular at the moment. Originally a draper's term, that which is going (by sale) and will soon be sold out.

All the Hacks : the British ministry which succeeded that of ' All the Talents ' in 1807.

All the Talents : Lord Grenville's Coalition Ministry of 1806-7, which included representatives of both political parties.

All there : quick-witted and in full possession of his senses.

All things to all men : of one who endeavours by agreeing with everybody to displease nobody. [I *Corinthians,* ix, 22 ; Edgeworth, *Belinda,* ch. 1 (1801)]

All the world and his wife : the whole of society. [Swift, (Simon Wagstaff), *Polite Conversation,* Dial. III (1738)]

All, To throw (push) at : to risk everything. [Dekker, *Whore of Babylon* (1607)]

All waters, To be for : to be able to turn to any occupation, like a fish that can live in either fresh or salt water. [Shakespeare, *Twelfth Night,* IV, ii (1601)]

All-fathering river, The : the Nile, so-called by G. W. Steevens.

Alley, To be good only in one's own : metaphor drawn from the bowling-alley. [Bacon, *Essays : Of Cunning* (1625)]

Alliance Society, The : a Belgian political Society formed in 1897 to secure the union of the different branches of the Liberal Party.

Allodial lands : lands held absolutely among the Franks, subject to no burdens and passing on death to next of kin.

Alma Mater (*Lat.,* benign Mother) : the university or college at which one has been educated. [Trapp, *Commentary on Old Test.,* III (1657)]

Almanac, As uncertain as an : metaphor derived from Marston, *Jacke Drum's Entertainement* (1601).

Almighty dollar, The : money regarded as a god. Term coined by Washington Irving in *The Creole Village* (1837). *See also* Ben Jonson, *Epistle to Countess of Rutland,* ' almighty gold.'

Almond for a parrot, An : a trifle to amuse a silly person. [Ray, *Proverbs* (1670)]

Almond tree, The : the grey hair of old age. [*Ecclesiastes,* xii]

Alms basket : charity.

Alms penny, An : a lucky penny. [Peele, *Old Wives' Tale* (1595)]

Alnaschar dream, An : a day-dream. From the story of Alnaschar in *The Arabian Nights.* He invests all his possessions in glass-ware, begins to imagine his success step by step until he becomes a millionaire, when with a careless kick he upsets his merchandise and thereby destroys the whole basis of his dreams.

Alnaschar of Modern Literature, The : Samuel Taylor Coleridge (1772-1834), who said that he derived his *Kubla Khan* from a dream.

Alpha and omega (*Grk.*) : the first and the last ; the beginning and the end. They are the first and the last letters of the Greek alphabet. [*Revelations,* i, 8]

Alruna-wife, An : a household god, after the Alrunes or household gods of the ancient Germans.

Alsatia : a sanctuary ; a resort for bad characters. From Alsace, for many centuries a debatable province between Germany and France. In 16th cent. the region between the River Thames and Fleet Street in London was termed Alsatia, and was a sanctuary for rogues.

Alsatian, An : a street bully, from Alsatia (*q.v.*).

Alter ego, An (*Lat.*, other I) : one's other self. [Mobbe's transl. of Aleman, *Guzman de Alfarache* (1623) ; *Suppression of Monasteries*, p. 156 (1537)]

Alter Fritz (*Germ.*, old Fritz) : Frederick the Great of Prussia (1712-86).

Althæa's brand : a fatal event. From the legend of Althæa's son Meleager, who was to live so long as a log then on the fire remained unconsumed. [Ovid, *Metam.*, VIII, 4]

Altrincham (Cheshire) : a proverbially small and poor corporation.

Alumbrados : a Spanish mystical sect, the forerunners of the Illuminati (*q.v.*) which flourished in the first quarter of the 16th cent.

Alumnus, An (*Lat.*, foster-child) : a pupil of an educational establishment : see Alma Mater. [Evelyn, *Diary*, I (1644)]

Alvina weeps : the wind blows loudly. From a Flemish legend of Alvina, a princess cursed by her parents, who took to the air where she continued to wander and weep.

Amaimon ; Amaymon ; Amoymon : (in mediæval demonology) one of the four kings of hell.

Amalekites, To smite the : to root out .. utterly destroy .. [*Exodus*, xvii, 8-16 ; I *Sam.*, xxx ; I *Chron.*, iv, 43]

Amalfitan Code, The : the earliest-known code of maritime law (11th cent.). After Amalfi, in Italy.

Amalthea's horn : the horn of plenty. After the horn of the goat Amalthea, the foster-mother of Jupiter.

Amaranthine flower of faith : everlasting flower of faith. The amaranth was reputed to be unfading. [Wordsworth, *Weak is the Will of Man*]

Amaryllis, An : a country girl. After a country girl in Theocritus, *Idyls*, Ovid, and Virgil, *Eclogues*.

Amati, An : a violin of excellent quality. After the maker, Andrea Amati, of Cremona (fl. 1550).

Amazon, An : a female warrior ; a physically powerful woman ; a virago. According to Herodotus the Amazons, a race of female warriors, inhabited Scythia.

Amazone : A riding habit.

Amazonian chin, An : a beardless chin.

Amber, A fly in the : see Fly.

Ambesas, Ambes-ace, Ames-ace (*Lat.*, *ambo asses*: two aces, *i.e.*, the lowest cast of the dice) ; bad luck.

Ambree, A Mary : a woman of strength and spirit. After an English heroine at the siege of Gaunt (1584), the subject of a ballad. [Ben Jonson, *Tale of a Tub*, I, 4 (1633)]

Ambrosia : food or drink of a most delicious character. In Greek mythology, the food of the gods.

Amen to, To say : to approve of. [Bunyan, *Pilgrim's Progress* (1678)]

Amende honorable, An (*Fr.*) : a public and generous admission of wrong done ; honourable compensation. Formerly (in France), a disgraceful form of punishment for traitors, parricides and sacriligious persons.

Amends, To make : to apologize and compensate for a slight offence, probably unintentional. [*Paston Letters*, No. 408 (1461)]

American Party, The : A United States political party which flourished in the middle of the 19th cent. It advocated differentiation against Americans of foreign birth. It was also known as the Know Nothing Party, because, being at first a secret organisation, its members refused to furnish any information concerning it or its objects.

American Volunteers, The : An American Salvation Army, formed as a secession from the Salvation Army by Mr. and Mrs. Ballington Booth in 1896.

Ames-ace : see Ambesas.

Ami des Hommes, L' (*Fr.*, friend of man) : Victor Riquetti, Marquis de Mirabeau (1715-89), French politician, father of the great Mirabeau. After his book *L'Ami des Hommes* (1756).

Ami du Peuple, L' (*Fr.*, friend of the people) : Jean Paul Marat (1743-93), French Revolutionary leader. After the title of the paper which he edited.

Amicus curiae (*Lat.*, friend of the Court): one in court, not a party to the suit, who assists or corrects the judge.

Aminadab, An : a Quaker. A term used by the earlier English dramatists.

Ammonian horn, The : the cornucopia or horn of plenty. Orig., a tract of very fertile land, in the shape of a ram's horn, given by Ammon, king of Libya, to Amalthea, the mother of Bacchus.

Amnesty oath, The : the oath required of those to whom an amnesty was granted after the conclusion of the American Civil War.

Amok (amuck), To run : to attack frenziedly and indiscriminately all within reach. From *amuco*, the Malay name for those who act in this manner.

Amort, All (*Fr.*, *à la mort*, to the death): lifeless ; in a state of death.

Amour propre (*Fr.*, self-love) : self-esteem ; self-respect.

Ampersand : the sign ' &.' Literally, ' and per se—and,' and by itself, and.

Amphidromical feast, An : a sacramental feast. After the Amphidromia, a family festival in ancient Athens at which a newly-born infant was conse-crated.

Amphigouri : nonsense verses.

Amphisbæna : a mythical Libæan serpent with a head at both ends.

Amphitryon, An : a host who gives good dinners. After a play of that name by Molière. This was based on a play by Plautus, who on his part used a Greek legend for his basis.

Ampoule, La Sainte (*Fr.*) : the vase that contained the oil with which the kings of France used to be anointed at their coronations. Destroyed in the first French Revolution.

Amsterdam religion : extreme Puritan-ism or Nonconformity, after the Puritans who fled from England to Amsterdam and other cities of Holland at the beginning of the 17th cent.

Amuck : *see* Amok.

Amurath succeeds an Amurath, An : one tyrant or oppressor follows another. In allusion to Amurath III, Turkish sultan, who reigned from 1574-95, and whose first act after his accession was to invite all his brothers to a banquet and strangle them. [Shakespeare, 2 *Henry IV*, V, ii (1598)]

Amyclæan Brothers, The : Castor and Pollux. They were born at Amyclae.

Amyclæan silence : the inhabitants of Amyclae, in consequence of repeated false reports, were forbidden to an-nounce the approach of the Spartan enemy, who in consequence ultimately took the city by surprise.

Amysis plays the fool : said of someone assuming stupidity or some other false attribute. Amysis, sent to Delphi to consult the oracle, learnt that his city was about to be destroyed, and, to escape its fate, fled to Peloponnesus.

Anabaptists : (1) an extreme religious and revolutionary communistic sect, which seized the City of Munster in 1535, but was afterwards suppressed ; (2) a sect of Baptist dissenters, who advocated a second baptism.

Anacharsis among the Scythians : a wise man among fools. The Scythians were proverbially foolish. Anacharsis, one of them, was an exception.

Anack, Sons of : *see* Anakim.

Anacreon, An : a poet singing of love and wine, after the Greek lyric poet (c. 563-478 B.C.).

Anacreon Moore : Thomas Moore (1779-1852), Irish poet, the translator of Anacreon, who also wrote poems in the same style.

Anacreon of painters, The : Francesco Albano (1578-1660), Italian painter of lovely women.

Anacreon of Persia, The : Mohammed Hafiz (d. 1389).

Anacreon of the French, The : (1) Pontus. de Tyard (1521-1605) ; (2) P. Laujon (1727-1811).

Anacreon of the Guillotine, The : Bertrand Barère de Vieuzac (1755-1841), President of the National Con-vention ; from his addresses to his victims condemned to the guillo-tine.

Anacreon of the Temple, The : Guillaume Amfrye (1639-1720).

Anacreon of the Twelfth Century, The : Walter Mapes (1150-1208).

Anacreon, The Scottish : Alexander Scot (c. 1530-70).

Anacreon, The Sicilian : Giovanni Meli (1740-1815).

Anagram of a man, An : a person physically deformed. [*The Spectator*, No. 60 (1711)]

Anakim ; Sons of Anak : giants. [*Joshua*, xv, etc.]

Ananias, An : a liar. [*Acts*, v]

Anathema Maran-atha : an intensified form of anathema, a curse, something accursed. In Hebrew antiquity an-athema was an offering dedicated to Jehovah, esp. one set apart for destruction ; in classical antiquity a thank-offering. [I *Corinthians*, xvi, 22]

Anatomy, An : a thin, half-starved person, old or young ; a skeleton. [Shakespeare, *Comedy of Errors*, V, i (1591)]

Ancestor, To be one's own : to have performed services (usually military) of such outstanding value to one's country that one's status demands no pedigree. [Voltaire, *Nérope*, I, 3 (1743) : ' Qui sert bien son pays n'a pas besoin d'aïeux,' He needs no ancestors who serves his country well.]

Anchor of salvation, The : hope. [Nich. Breton, *The Good and the Bad : A Holy Man* (1616)]

Anchor, To have cast : to have made up one's mind, fixed one's course. [Dekker and Webster, *Sir Thomas Wyat*, sc. 6 (1607)]

Anchor, To ride at : to be in a position of security. [Congreve, *Old Bachelor*, V, 1 (1693)]

Anchor, To weigh : to start on one's course.

Anchors, It is safe riding at two : it is safe to ' have two strings to one's bow.'

Ancien Régime ; Ancient Régime, The (*Fr.*) : the social and political system in France previous to the Revolution that commenced in 1789.

Ancienne Noblesse, The (*Fr.*, ancient nobility) : the nobility of the ancient Régime.

Ancient, An : a banner ; banner-bearer. A corruption of ' ensign.' [Wright, *Certain Errors in Navigation* (1599)]

Ancient history, That's mere : said when disparaging another's forecast as something stale or known to everybody. The Romans had a saying, ' de Remo et Romulo praedicari,' to prophesy about Remus and Romulus (Cicero, *De Legibus*, I, 3, 8)

Ancient lights : light through a window which has been enjoyed at least twenty years. The enjoyment of it then becomes a legal right.

Ancient Mariners : graduates who row in college races, Cambridge University.

Ancient of Days, The : a biblical term for God.

Ancient Pistol, An : see Ancient (An). After Pistol, Falstaff's ' ancient' or ensign in Shakespeare's plays.

Ancient than chaos, To speak of things more : see Speak.

Ancient Way, The : ' and ask for the old paths, where there is the good way, and walk therein, and ye shall find rest for your souls.' (*Jeremiah*, vi, 16).

[Bacon, *Essays : Of Innovations* (3rd edn. 1625) ; *Advancement of Learning*, I, 5, 2 (1605)]

Ancients, The Council of : the Upper House of the French Directory (1794-99).

.. and his wife : added for emphasis and exaggeration. Cf. All the world and his wife (*q.v.*) ; Coach and horse and his wife (*q.v.*) ; *also* Devil and his dam (*q.v.*).

Andalusian eye (etc.), An : a dark eye. [Barham, *Ingoldsby Legends : Mrs Botherby's Story* (1840)]. An ' Andalusian dame ' [Ainsworth, *Rookwood*, III. 18 (1834)]

Andrea Fer(r)ara, An : a sword of fine quality. After Andrea of Ferrara, a famous Italian swordsmith of the 16th cent. [Scott, *Waverley*, (1814) ; *Fortunes of Nigel*, ch. 3 (1822)]

Andrew, An : (1) a merchant-vessel. After Andrea Doria (1466-1560), Genoese admiral. [Shakespeare, *Merchant of Venice*, I, i, 27 (?1596)]. (2) a man-servant.

Andrew, A merry : a buffoon. After Andrew Borde or Boorde (c. 1490-1549), a learned English physician possessed of great wit, who used to address the people in the market-place.

Andromache, An : a heroic and devoted wife. After the wife of Hector. [*The Spectator*, No. 57 (1711)]

Anecdote, An : a short account of an incident. Originally a secret history, a narrative of unpublished events ; so used by Procopius of his private life of Justinian and Theodora.

Anes, Journée des (*Fr.*) : see Journée.

Angel : a gold coin of the value of 6s. 8d. (Edw. IV to Chas. I) with a figure of St. Michael on the reverse. Orig., Angel-noble, being a new minting of the noble.

Angel altogether, An : a habitual drunkard. A West-Indian slang phrase.

Angel goes a-hunting, When the : *i.e.*, in foul weather. A Jewish saying. [Zangwill, *Children of the Ghetto*, I, 2 (1892)]

Angel of the Schools, The : St. Thomas Aquinas, the angelic doctor (*q.v.*).

Angel, One's good (better), or bad : one's better, or worse, self. It was previously held by some that ' every man hath a good and a bad angel attending on him in particular all his life long.' [Burton, *Anatomy of*

Melancholy, Pt. I, Sect. ii, Mem. i, Sub-sect. 2 (1621)]

Angel, There spoke an : used in approval of a proposal made by another. [Old play of *Sir Thomas More*, p. 6]

Angel, To write like an : in allusion to Angelo Vergecio (Vergetius) (fl. 1535-65), copier of Greek MSS., after whose design a font of Greek type was cast by order of Francis I of France. The phrase was later applied to authors as well as to calligraphists, *e.g.*,

'Here lies Nolly Goldsmith, for short-
ness called Noll,
Who wrote like an angel, and talked
like Poor Poll.
Garrick, *Epitaph on Goldsmith.*

Angel unawares, To entertain an : to entertain a stranger for charity's sake and find him a highly worthy person. [After *Hebrews*, xiii, 2]

Angels and ministers of grace ! : an exclamation of surprise. [Shakespeare, *Hamlet*, I, iv, 39 (1602)]

Angel's music : the ringing of the Church bells. [Geo. Herbert, *Temple : The Church Porch*, st. 65 (1631)]

Angels, To be on the side of the : to agree with the orthodox and more pleasant view of a moot question. In 1864, when Darwinism was somewhat of a novelty, Benjamin Disraeli (after-wards Lord Beaconsfield) said in a speech before the Oxford Diocesan Society, 'That question is this : Is man an ape or an angel ? I am on the side of the angels.'

Angels' visits, few and far between, Like : said of rare joys or periods of happiness. Forms 1. 376 of Campbell's *Pleasures of Hope* (1799). [Norris, *The Parting* (1699) ; Blair, *The Grave*, l. 589 : 'Like those (visits) of angels, short and far between.']

Angels weep, Enough to make the : said of something particularly evil, sad or foolish. [Shakespeare, *Measure for Measure*, II, ii, 122 (1603)]

Angelic Doctor (Angel of the Schools), The : St. Thomas Aquinas (c. 1227-70), Italian scholastic theologian. From his discussions on the nature of angels.

Angelica's draught : a draught which changes one's affection. From a potion drunk by Angelica in Ariosto, *Orlando Furioso* (1516).

Angelical Stone, The : a superstition of the alchemists. From the speculum claimed by the alchemist, Dr. John Dee (1527-1608), to have been given to him by the angels Raphael and Gabriel.

Angelus, The : a Roman Catholic prayer in memory of the Annunciation, said at 6 a.m. and 6 p.m. *Also* the bell which summons worshippers to the prayer. From *Angelus Domini nun-tiavit Mariae*, the Angel of the Lord announced unto Mary, the first words of the prayer. It is also the name of a famous painting by J. F. Millet, of the Barbizon School.

Angle, A Brother of the : *see* Brother.

Angle with a silver hook, To : to buy fish instead of catching it; to bribe.

Anglo-Catholic : one who, while remain-ing in communion with Rome, desired to secure the independence of the Church in England ; a member of the Church of England who claims for it a Catholic character.

Anglo-Celtic : a term suggested by Sir Arthur Conan Doyle (*Review of Reviews*, June, 1898), as a substitute for Anglo-Saxon.

Anglo-mania : a passion for imitating English fashions, customs, etc.

Anglophobia ; Anglophobe, An : Un-reasonable hatred for and fear of England ; one who suffers from Anglophobia. [*Ibis*, p. 83 (1862)]

Angora : a fabric made of goat's hair ; from Angora in Anatolia, where a special brood of goats, famous for their silky hair, flourishes.

Angostura ; angustura : a tonic bitters. From the name of a town in Venezuela, now known as Ciudad Bolivar.

Angry as a wasp, As : viciously angry. [Geo. Gascoigne, *The Steel Glass* (1576)]

Anguilles de Melun, Les : crying out before one is hurt. In allusion to one Languille who took part in a mystery play at Melun. When in the course of the play the executioner came to flay him alive, he became so nervous as to shriek out in his mental agony.

Animal, To go the entire : to go the whole hog (*q.v.*).

Animal Spirits : a vivacity due to youth and good health. Animal is used in the sense physical, as opposed to vital and natural.

Ann, Like Sister : who in the fairy-tale of *Bluebeard* kept watch from a tower to see whether or when the expected assistance for her sister Fatima would come in sight.

Anna Matilda, An : an extremely sentimental girl. From the *nom de plume* used by Mrs. Hannah Cowley (1743-1809), English dramatist and poetess.

Annates : the first year's income from a benefice, claimed by the Pope. Transferred to Queen Anne's Bounty in 1704. From Lat., *annus*, a year.

Annual compliment, An : a salary. [Dickens, *Hard Times* (1854)]

Annunciator, An (*Amer.*) *:* a bell or gong.

Annunziata, Order of the : the highest Italian Order, founded by Amadeus V of Savoy in 1362.

Annus mirabilis (*Lat.*, the wonderful year) : the year 1666, famous for two English victories over the Dutch fleet and the great Fire of London.

Annus mirabilis, An : a wonderful year.

Anodyne Necklace, An : a hangman's rope. An anodyne is a reliever of pain. *Nodus*, on which the phrase is a pun, is the Latin for ' knot.'

Anointed, The : Christ, the Messiah.

Anon : the reply of waiters in the 16th cent. when called.

Anonyma (*Lat.*, a nameless female) : a woman of loose morals. A term invented by *The Times* (1862).

Another gates : another sort. [Lyly *Mother Bombie*, I (1594)]

Anserine (*Lat.*, *anser*, a goose) : stupid, silly.

Answer like a Norman, To : to reply evasively.

Answer for the consequences, To : to be held responsible for the consequences of one's action.

Ant, As busy as an : *see Proverbs*, vi, 6-8.

Antaeus, An : a powerful giant. From the Libyan giant and wrestler in Grk. mythology.

Antediluvian : antiquated. Lit., before the Flood (Scriptural).

Antelope State, The : Nebraska ; on account of the number of the antelopes to be found there.

Anthology : a collection of literary passages, esp. poems. From Grk., *anthos* (flower) and *legein* (to choose). First used by Philippus of Thessalonica, epigrammatist (fl. c. 100). The first anthology was compiled by Meleager of Gadara about a cent. and a half earlier.

Anthony, St. : *see* St. Anthony.

Anthony pig, To whine like an : from the starved pigs which the proctors of St. Anthony's Hospital, London, used to protect and feed. These pigs used to follow their benefactors whining for food.

Anthony's fire : a pop. name for erysipelas. From the tradition that those who sought the intercession of St. Anthony recovered from the disorder.

Anthropophagi (*Grk.*, man-eaters) : cannibals.

Anti-Birmingham : a Tory, *i.e.*, opposed to counterfeit, given to the opponents of the Exclusion Bill in 1680, by its supporters, who had themselves been dubbed ' Birmingham ' by the Tories. The connection between Birmingham and counterfeit was due to the coining of counterfeit groats in that town.

Antiburgher : the section of the Secession Church of Scotland which seceded on their part in 1747 on the ground that it was unlawful to take the Burgess Oath.

Anti-Christ : Satan, the man of sin ; (with the Early Christians) the Roman Empire, the persecuting emperors ; (with the Protestants) the Pope. [I *John*, ii, 18]

Anti-Corn Law League : an English political society formed in 1838 to secure the repeal of the import duties on corn.

Anti-Federalists : the precursors of the Democrats in American politics ; supporters of the rights of the States of the Federation.

Anti-Jacobin : opposed to the Jacobins (*q.v.*). *The Anti-Jacobin* was the name of a weekly periodical founded by George Canning and Wm. Giffard in 1797.

Anti-Masonry : opposition to freemasonry, the policy of a political party in the United States, during the second quarter of the 19th cent.

Anti-Masque : a ridiculous interlude introduced into the Masque in the 16th and 17th cents.

Anti-Parnellites : the members of the Irish National Party who seceded and formed a new party in 1890 in consequence of the connection of their former leader Chas. Stewart Parnell, with the O'Shea divorce suit.

Anti-Remonstrants : Irishmen who refused in 1666 to sign the remonstrance protesting against the theory that toleration of Catholicism was inconsistent with the security of the English State.

Anti-Renter : one of the party of rebels in Albany, U.S.A. (1839-47), who took up arms in opposition to an attempt to collect overdue rents.

Antic, An : Orig. a fantastic form found in class. sculpture. Subseq. (1) an archit. term to denote the grotesque ; (2) anything or anybody in any way grotesque ; (3) a ludicrous gesture or behaviour ; (4) a ludicrous performance.

Antic, To dance (To play the) : to behave like one of the comic characters that took part in the Anti-Masque (*q.v.*).

Anticyra, Go to : Go to Bedlam (*q.v.*). From the city in Phocis, Greece, or that of the same name in Thessaly, both of which were noted for hellebore, the ancient remedy for madness.

Antigone, The modern : Marie Thérèse, Duchess of Angoulème, daughter of Louis XVI of France, a name given to her by Louis XVIII. The original Antigone was the unhappy daughter of Oedipus, king of Thebes, and the subject of a tragedy of Sophocles.

Antilegomena : the doubtful books included in the Canon of the New Testament.

Antimacassar, An : a covering of a chair, etc., used as a protection. From Greek *anti* (against) and Macassar, the name of an oil.

Antinous, An : a beautiful youth. From the name of a youth of Bithynia who was a favourite of Emperor Hadrian.

Antipodes : the land exactly opposite on the other side of the world ; its inhabitants. From Grk. *anti* (opposite), *podos* (a foot).

Anti-Pope : a pope improperly elected and not generally recognized.

Antonines, Age of the : the reigns of the Emperors Antoninus Pius and Marcus Aurelius ; the period of domestic tranquility in Roman history.

Antrustion : one of the military household or bodyguard of the Merovingian Frankish kings.

Anxious bench, On the : in a state of great difficulty or depression. At Methodist and other religious revivals in the U.S. the anxious benches used to be set aside for those members of the congregation who had repented of their previous life and desired to be admitted to the Church.

Anzac, An : an Australian or New Zealand soldier. From the initial letters of Australian and New Zealand Army Corps. Another derivation is from the Arab. *anzak*, to cause to jump, a suggested equiv. for kangaroo, a term applied to the first Australian soldiers in Egypt.

Anziani : a council of the fourteen principal citizens (the Ancients) of Florence, appointed in the 13th cent. for the government of the State.

Aonian : poetical. From Aonia, where the muses dwelt.

Aonian Maids, The : the Muses.

Ap- (*Welsh*, son) : found in compound names, *e.g.*, Pryce-Ap-Ryce.

Apache, An : a Parisian street-ruffian. From the name of a tribe of N. Amer. Indians.

Apache State, The : Arizona. From the many encounters with the Apache Indians within its borders.

Ape, An : a fool. From the early phrase ' to put an ape into a person's hood,' *i.e.*, to make a fool of a person. [Chaucer, *Prioresses Prologue* (14th cent.)]

Ape, To : to imitate ; as an ape imitates. [Massinger, *City Madam*, IV, iv (1632)]

Ape-Carrier, An : a wandering buffoon. There used to be formerly a calling of professional buffoon, whose assistant was an ape.

Apes in Hell, To lead (of old maids) : from the monkish story that women married neither to God nor to man will be given to apes in the next world. *See also* Lead. [George Gascoigne, *Workes* (1577) ; Lyly, *Euphues and His England* (1580) ; Shakespeare, *Taming of the Shrew*, II, i (?1596)]

Ape's paternoster : chattering of the teeth, with fright or cold.

Appelles, An : a great painter. From the name of the greatest painter of antiquity. [fl. c. B.C. 332].

Aphrodisiac : exciting sexual desire. From Aphrodite, one of the names of the Greek Goddess of Love.

Apician : luxurious in food. From Apicius, a famous Roman epicure (1st cent.).

Apicius, An : a gourmand. *See* Apician.

Apocalypse : revelation. A name given to certain Jewish and Christian religious writings (B.C. 200-A.D. 300) which relate to the ' last things.'

Apocalyptic Number, The : 666. [*Revelations*, xii, 18]

Apocrypha : books whose inclusion in the canon of the Bible is questioned.

Originally Heb. writings whose meaning is hidden.

Apocryphal : of doubtful authenticity ;
not to be taken literally.

Apollo : the sun. From the name of the
Sun-god in Grk. mythology.

Apollo, An : an extremely handsome
youth. From the Olympian god
famous for his manly beauty. *Also*
a banqueting-chamber. [Herbert,
Travels]

Apollo Belvidere, An : a handsome
youth. The Apollo Belvidere is the
famous statue of Apollo in the Vatican
at Rome. (3rd cent. B.C.).

Apollo of Portugal, The : Luis Camoens
(1524-80), Portug. poet.

Apollonize, To : to set oneself up as an
authority on music, poetry, etc. From
Apollo, the patron of music and
poetry.

Apollyon (*Grk.*, destroying) : the Angel
of the Bottomless Pit. [*Revelations*,
ix, 11]

Apostle : one of the original missionaries
or messengers of the Gospel ; one of
the twelve principal officers of the
Mormon Church.

Apostle Gems : jasper (St. Peter),
sapphire (St. Andrew), chalcedony (St.
James), emerald (St. John), sardonyx
(St. Philip), carnelian (St. Bartholomew), chrysolite (St. Matthew), beryl
(St. Thomas), chrysoprase (St. Thad-
deus), topaz (St. James the Less),
hyacinth (St. Simeon), amethyst (St.
Matthias).

Apostle of Andalusia, The : Juan de
Avila (1500-69).

Apostle of the Ardennes, The : St.
Hubert (d. 727).

Apostle of Brazil, The : José de Anchieta
(1533-97).

Apostle of Culture : one who claims to be
a judge of good taste. Prob. invented
by Sir Francis Burnand in *Punch*
(c. 1880).

Apostle of the English, The : St. Augustine
(d.c. 613).

Apostle of Free Trade, The : Richard
Cobden (1804-65).

Apostle of the French, The : St. Denis
(3rd cent.).

Apostle of the Frisians, The : St.
Willibrod (c. 657-738).

Apostle of the Gauls, The : St. Irenæus
(c. 130-200).

Apostle of the Gentiles, The : St. Paul.

Apostle of Germany, The : St. Boniface
(680-754).

Apostle of the Highlanders, The : St
Columba (521-97).

Apostle of the Indians, The : John Eliot
(1604-90).

Apostle of the Indies, The : St. Francis
Xavier (1506-52).

Apostle of Infidelity, The : Voltaire (1694-
1778), Fr. philosopher.

Apostle of Ireland, The : St. Patrick
(373-468).

Apostle of the Iroquois, The : François
Piquet (1708-81).

Apostle of Liberty : *see* Liberty.

Apostle of the New World, The : José de
Anchieta (1533-97).

Apostle of the North, The : Ansgar (9th
cent.) ; Bernard Gilpin (1517-83).

Apostle of the Peak, The : William
Bagshaw (1628-1702), Eng. ejected
Nonconformist.

Apostle of Peru, The : Alonso de
Barcena (1528-98).

Apostle of the Picts, The : St. Ninian
(d. 432).

Apostle of the Scots, The : John Knox
(1505-72).

Apostle of the Slavs, The : St. Cyril
(c. 315-86).

Apostle spoon : a spoon with a figure of
one of the Apostles on the handle,
given at baptisms in the 16th and
17th cents.

Apostle of the Sword, The : Mahomet,
because he used his sword as an aid
in his mission.

Apostle of Temperance, The : Theobald
Mathew (1790-1856), Irish Preacher.

Apostles of Murder : Anarchists,
Nihilists, or similar physical-force
politicians.

Apostles, Prince of the : St. Peter.
[*Matthew*, xvi, 18, 19]

Apostles, The Twelve (*Camb. Univ.*) :
the last twelve candidates who obtained the ordinary B.A. degree when
the candidates were still ranged in
order of merit. *Lat.*, *post alios*, after
the others.

Apostolic Fathers : the Early Christian
Fathers, contemporaries of the
Apostles. Clement of Rome, Barna-
bas, Hermas, Ignatius and Polycarp.

Apostolic Majesty : one of the titles of
the King of Hungary, conferred by
Pope Sylvester II in 1000 A.D.

Apostolical succession : spiritual succession by ordination from the Apostles.

Appanages : in France, the lands held
by the Crown for the benefit of the
younger sons of the French kings ; in

Russia, the imperial and grand ducal estates.

Apple with an Ave Maria : an unknown superstitious or magical practice. [Lyly, *Euphues and His England* (1580)]

Apple because of the core, To throw away the : to reject the good on account of a slight blemish. [Bunyan, *The Pilgrim's Progress* (1678)]

Apple-cart, To upset a person's : to disarrange his plans and frustrate his intention.

Apple, Dead Sea : a beautiful fruit that turns to ashes when bitten. From a fruit that grows on the shores of the Dead Sea. [Curzon, *Monasteries of the Levant*] Used metaphorically for hollow and unsatisfactory pleasures.

Apple of Discord : a cause of dispute. The prize of Beauty, assigned by Paris to Venus, which was one of the ultimate causes of the Trojan War.

Apple of one's eye, The : the pupil of the eye ; hence that which is specially prized. Perhaps from Coptic *al-bal*, the ball (of the eye). [*Deuteronomy*, xxxii, 10] [King Alfred, *Gregory's Past*, XI, 68 (885)]

Apple John : a species of long-keeping apple which ripens about St. John's Day (May 6). It keeps for a very long time and consequently generally withers.

Apple-monger : a bawd. From the activity in the 16th cent. of fruiterers as go-betweens in the service of lovers.

Apple of perpetual youth, The : the apple of Idun, wife of Bragi, in Scand. mythology.

Apple, Prince Ahmed's : a universal cure. [*Arabian Nights : Prince Ahmed*]

Apple of Sodom : *see* Apple, Dead Sea.

Apple squire, An : a bawd ; an apple-monger (*q.v.*).

Apples to Alcinous, To give : ' to carry coals to Newcastle,' *i.e.*, to perform a work of supererogation. The reference is to the fertility of the apple-orchards of Alcinous, King of Coreyra in Corfu.

Apples swim ! How we : An exclamation of self-congratulation by a pompous individual ; in allusion to the fable of the apples floating down the river supported by horse-dung.

Apple-pie bed, An (*Fr., nappe pliée*, a folded sheet) : a bed deliberately disordered by folding up and over the lower sheet, as a practical joke.

Another derivation is from ' apple turn-over,' a piece of pastry folded up and over from the sides.

Apple-pie order : perfect and trim order. Several derivations have been given : (1) *cap-a-pie* order (*Fr., de pied en cap*) with reference to a fully caparisoned knight ; (2) *à plis* (in plaits), in neat and regular plaits ; (3) (*Fr., nappes pliées*, folded linen) neat as folded linen ; (4) ' Order is an old word for a row, and a properly made apple-pie had, of old, always an order or row of regularly cut turrets, or an exactly divided border ' (Barrère and Leland) ; (5) *alpha beta* order, as orderly as the alphabet.

Apple-pie, To give a child : when correcting a child for sitting with one or both elbows on the table, the parent raises the arm and knocks it on the table.

April and May, To smell of : to be young and of a courting age.

April Fish, An : An April fool (*q.v.*), who is caught as easily as a fish.

April Fool (Gowk) : the victim of a hoax on the 1st of April, a day on the forenoon of which hoaxers have full licence. The custom originated in France, where in 1564 the beginning of the year was changed from the 25th of March to the 1st of January. In the earlier period New Year presents were exchanged on the 1st of April. After the change people were made April fools by the pretence of giving them presents on the 1st of April. Other derivations are : (1) from a mystery play performed at Easter, which frequently fell in April, in which Christ was depicted running fruitless errands ; (2) the alleged anniversary of the first return of the dove to Noah and the Ark ; (3) an echo of the Roman Cerealia which fell at the beginning of April. The story runs that Proserpina, playing in the Elysian meadows, was carried away to the lower regions by Pluto. Her mother, Ceres, hearing her voice, went on a fool's errand in search of it.

April Fool's Day : the 1st of April ; *see* April Fool.

April gentleman, An : a newly-married husband, who has made himself by his marriage an April fool.

April poetry : that in which the reader is kept in expectation of two good lines to come after twenty bad ones. [Dryden, *Discourse on Satire*]

April squire, An : a newly-made squire ; a parvenu.

Apron, Blue : *see* Blue.

Apron, Green : a lay preacher. [Warren, *Unbelievers* (1654)]

Apron-man, An : a mechanic.

Apron-strings, Tied to the : under the influence of a wife, mother, or other female relative.

Apron-strings Tenure : tenure in virtue of a wife.

Apropos de Bottes (*Fr.*, apropos of boots) : something unconnected with the preceding remarks. The suggested origin is as follows :—A French noble having lost a lawsuit, told the king, Francis I, that the court had unbooted him (*l'avait débotté*) instead of having decided against him (*il avait été débouté*). The error was due to the employment of Latin in the courts. The King reformed the practice, but the members of the bar, who were annoyed at the change, said that it was made *apropos de bottes*. [Lord Chesterfield, *Letters*, II, No. 96 (1757)]

Aqua Regia (*Lat.*, royal water) : an acid capable of dissolving gold and platinum, the ' noble ' metals.

Aqua Tofana : a colourless poison invented by a woman named Tofana of Palermo (d. 1730).

Aqua Vitae (*Lat.*, water of life) : strong spirits ; orig. used by the alchemists.

Aqua Vitae Man, An : a dram-seller.

Aquinian Sage, The : Juvenal (c. 55-135), the Roman satirist, who was born at Aquinium.

Arab, An ; Arab, A street : a boy-frequenter of the streets. Orig. Arab (*i.e.*, wanderer) of the City.

Arabesque : fantastic ; of a style of decoration.

Arabian bird, The : the phoenix ; a marvellous man ; something unique. [*Histrio-mastix*, III, 1, ll. 2-4 (1610)]

Arabian Night, An : a fabulous story ; from *The Thousand and One Nights*, usually called *The Arabian Nights*.

Arachne, An : a spider ; a weaver. From the name of a Lydian maiden who competed with Minerva in needlework and was changed by her into a spider.

Arachne's Art : weaving.

Arachne's Labours : spinning or weaving.

Arachnean : gossamer ; web-like.

Arbor Day : a day set apart in the United States, Canada, Australia, and New Zealand for the planting of trees.

Arcades ambo (*Lat.*, both Arcadians) : (of two people) both simpletons, innocents. *See* Arcadia. [Virgil, *Eclogues*, VII, 4 ; Burton, *Anatomy of Melancholy* (1621), to the Reader ; Byron, *Don Juan* (1821) canto iv, st. 93]

Arcadia ; Arcady : a Utopia of poetical simplicity and innocence. After a pastoral and mountainous district of the Peloponnesus ('the Greek Switzerland ').

Arcadian ; Arcadic : rustic, simple, innocent. After the Arcadians, the least intellectual of the Greeks. ' Arcadian poetry,' pastoral poetry ; An ' Arcadian,' a shepherd.

Arcadian nightingales : asses. [Rabelais, *Pantagruel*, V, 7, note]

Arcadian youth, An : a simpleton [Juvenal, *Satires*, VII, 159-60].

Arch Fiend, The : Satan.

Arch Monarch of the World, The : Napoleon III(1808-73) reigned 1852-70.

Arches, Court of : an English ecclesiastical court. From the original place of meeting, the Church of St. Mary-le-Bow, or S. Maria de Arcubus.

Arches, Dean of the : Judge of the Court of Arches.

Arched eyebrow, With an : with an expression either of (*a*) derision, or (*b*) horror. [(*a*) Pope, *Epistle to Arbuthnot* (1735) ; (*b*) Gray, *Agrippina* Act I, sc. 1 (1742)]

Archie ; Archy, An : a Court-fool. After Archibald Armstrong (d. 1672), Court-jester. [Ben Jonson, *Staple of News* (1625), III, 2]

Archilochian bitterness, etc. : keen, stinging. After Archilochus, a Greek satirist (fl. 650 B.C.), ' The Swift of Greek Literature.'

Architect, The Universal : God. [Cowley (1618-67), *Essays, The Garden*, III]

Ardennes, The Boar of the : William de la Marck (d. 1485), Renaissance noble and soldier. On account of his resemblance, both in appearance and manner, to a boar.

Areopagus : a tribunal of the highest rank. After the locale, the Hill of Ares, of the highest judicial Court in Athens.

Argie-bargie, To : a portmanteau-word made up of to argue and bargain. A Scotticism. [Crockett, *The Raiders* (1896), ch. 15]

Argo, An (*Grk.*) : a ship sailing on an adventure. After the name of the vessel on which Jason sailed to Colchis in his search for the Golden Fleece.

Argonaut, An : one who sails on a voyage of adventure. *See* Argo.

Argonauts of Forty-Nine, The : the adventurers who settled in California on the discovery of gold there in 1849.

Argosy, An : a large warship or richly laden merchant-ship. Formerly ' Ragusy.' Either from (1) Ragusa, an Adriatic port ; or (2) the ' Argo ' (*q.v.*).

Argumentum ad baculinum (*Lat.*, argument at the stick) : club-law.

Argumentum ad hominem (*Lat.*, argument at the man) : an argument at the individual himself. [Locke, *Essay on the Human Understanding*, IV, xvii (1690)]

Argumentum ad pocketum : an argument addressed to the pocket. *Pocketum* is, of course, artificial Latin.

Argus, An : a watchful guardian. After Argos, the hundred-eyed guardian who was set by Juno to watch Io. His eyes were transferred by Juno to the tail of the peacock.

Argy-bargy, To : *see* Argie-bargie.

Argus-eyed : vigilant.

Ariadne, An : a devoted female lover. After Ariadne, daughter of Minos, King of Crete, who assisted her lover Theseus to escape from the labyrinth in which he had been confined.

Ariadne, The thread of : the thread by which Ariadne enabled Theseus to escape.

Ariosto of the North, The : Sir Walter Scott. So-called by Byron in *Childe Harold*, canto IV, st. 40 (1818). After Ariosto (1474-1533), author of *Orlando Furioso.*

Aristides, An : a man of inflexible impartiality. After Aristides the Just (c. 530-468 B.C.), Athenian statesman and general.

Aristides, The British : Andrew Marvell (1621-78), English poet and satirist.

Aristides, The French : Albert Grévy (1813-91), President of the French Republic.

Aristippus, An : an advocate of luxury and self-indulgence. After the founder of the Cyrenaic sect of Greek philosophy (c. 435-356 B.C.).

Aristocracy of Accident (of Nature) : the high-born, as distinguished from the high-principled low-born. [Harriet Martineau, *Autobiography* (1877)]

Aristocracy of Labour, The : ' those (labourers) whose lives are industrious,

temperate, and moral, and want only to be enriched by the culture which has hitherto been supposed to be the special possession of the better educated.' Sir W. Besant, *The Alabaster Box* (1900).

Aristocracy, The cold shade of : the unsympathetic patronage of the highly-placed. Term originated by Sir Wm. Napier in his *History of the Peninsular War* (1851).

Aristophanes, The English : Samuel Foote (1720-77), comedian and dramatist. After Aristophanes (c. 448-385 B.C.), the greatest of the Greek comedians.

Aristophanes, The French : Molière (1622-73), dramatist.

Aristotle, An : a philosopher. After Aristotle (384-322 B.C.), known as the ' Father of Greek Philosophy.' Sometimes semi-ironically, *e.g.*, ' The Aristotle of the village.' [Mrs. Oliphant, *The Cuckoo in the Nest*, ch. 2 (1892)] Reverence for Aristotle is enshrined in Jewish and Yiddish literature and idiom, *e.g.*, ' If I had Aristotle's head, I might be able to find out why my legs are inferior.' [I. Zangwill, *Children of the Ghetto*, Bk. I, ch. 2 (1892) possibly on account of the popular Jewish belief that he was a Jew]

Aristotle of China, The : Tehuke (d. 1200).

Aristotle of Christianity, The : Thomas Aquinas (1224-74), Scholastic philosopher and theologian.

Aristotle of the Nineteenth Century, The : George Leopold, Baron de Cuvier (1769-1832), French naturalist.

Ark, To have come out of the (To have been born in the) : to be very old-fashioned. In allusion to Noah's ark. [Sydney Smith (1768-1845), *Memoir* 157]

Arkansas Civil War : a dispute which developed into fighting between the supporters of rival candidates for the governorship of Arkansas in 1874.

Arkansas tooth-pick, An : bowie-knife, as used in the State of Arkansas.

Arm out further than one can draw it back again, To put one's : to over-reach oneself. [Sir W. Scott, *Rob Roy*, ch. 22 (1818)]

Arm, The Secular : the authority of a secular or temporal tribunal, as distinguished from ecclesiastical authority.

Arm's length, At : at a short distance from . . ; on formal terms with.

Arms, Passage of : a controversy, esp. between men of letters.

Arms and the Man : a military hero. [Virgil, *Æneid*, I, l. 1 ; title of a play by Bernard Shaw (1898)]

Arms of courtesy : with lances at the extremities of which a piece of round flat board was fixed to avoid all danger except that from the shock of horses and riders. [Sir W. Scott, *Ivanhoe*, ch. 8 (1830)]

Arms reversed, To have one's : to be dishonoured. [Sir W. Scott, *Ivanhoe*, ch. 24 (1830)]

Arms, Up in : in a state of active indignation. [Burton, *Anatomy of Melancholy*, To the Reader (1621)]

Arms, With open : whole-heartedly ; cordially. [Sydney Smith, *Peter Plymley's Letters*, V (1808)]

Armada, An : any great fleet of warships. After the Spanish Armada sent by Spain against England in 1588.

Armageddon, An : any wide-spread and bloody battle ; the site of such a battle. After the name of the place of the great battle which is to precede the Resurrection (*Rev.*, xvi, 16) ; possibly connected with Megiddo, a battle-field in Palestine.

Armagnac War, The : the war between the Emperor Frederick III and the Swiss in 1444. On account of the number of Armagnac mercenaries in the Imperial armies.

Armagnacs, The : the party of the Orleans princes in the French Civil War of 1410. After Bernard, Count Armagnac (d. 1418), one of the leaders.

Armed Man, The : Death. [Dekker, *The Seuen Deadly Sinnes : Crueltie* (1606)]

Armed Neutrality : action just short of war by a neutral power in time of war, jealous of its rights and anxious to safeguard them. The first Armed Neutrality was formed under the lead of Russia in 1780 and directed against England, at war with France, Spain, and the United States.

Armed Soldier of Democracy, The : Napoleon I.

Armed to the teeth : heavily armed.

Armida, The Garden of : gorgeous luxury. After Armida, a beautiful sorceress in Tasso, *Jerusalem Delivered*, who enticed, by means of her charms and her luxuries, Crusaders from their duty. [R. L. Stevenson, *Familiar Studies : S. Pepys* (1888)]

Arminians : (1) the followers of Jacob Harmensen Arminius (1560-1609), who led a secession from the Calvinist Church in Holland ; (2) the English High Church Party in the reign of Charles I.

Arnauts : the Albanians. So-called by the Turks. Lit., brave men.

Arras : tapestry-hangings. After Arras, in N. France.

Arrière Ban : *see* Ban.

Arrière pensée, An: (*Fr.*, back thought) : an unstated motive ; a mental reservation.

'Arry (and 'Arriet) : 'Arry as the type of the good-natured, easy-going, but vulgar, flashy, and loud-mouthed costermonger, who drops his *h*'s and is usually seen with his 'Arriet on Sunday afternoons and Bank Holidays, was the creation of Edwin J. Milliken, the *Punch* artist. *'Arry on 'orseback* in *Punch's Almanac* for 1874 was 'Arry's début.

Arsie-versie : upside-down. [N. Udall, *Erasmus' Apophthegmes* (1542)]

Art and part of .. (in ..) : an essential part of .. [Huxley, *Life and Letters*, Vol. I, p. 237 (1862)]

Arts, The Seven : arithmetic, geometry, astronomy, music, logic, rhetoric, grammar. [*Histrio-mastix*, I, 1, 6 (1610)]

Artful Dodger, An : one who combines considerable skill with disingenuousness. After the nickname of John Dawkins, a boy pickpocket in Dickens, *Oliver Twist* (1838).

Arthur's : a London club-house, founded in 1765. After the keeper of White's Chocolate House, who had died four years previously. [A. Murphy, *Three Weeks After Marriage*, Act II (1776)]

Articles, Lords of the : the Committee which prepared measures for submission to the Scottish Parliament.

Articulo mortis, In (*Lat.*, at the point of death) : in the last throes of death. [*Estate of English Fugitives*, p. 75 (1596)]

Artillery of Heaven, The : thunder and lightning. [Shakespeare, *Taming of the Shrew*, I, ii, 205 (1596-7)]

Artists, The Prince of : Albrecht Dürer (1471-1528), Germ. painter.

Arviragus, An : a husband whose sense of honour leads him even to sacrifice his wife. After a character in Chaucer, *Franklin's Tale*, derived from Boccaccio, *Diavora and Gilberto*.

As in praesenti ' (Propria quae maribus), To learn one's : to be starting on the rudiments of some study. These portions of sentences are, respectively, the first words of the parts of the old *Eton Latin Grammar* which treat of the conjugation of verbs and the genders of nouns, the sentences being *As in praesenti perfectum format in avi* (*As* in the present forms its perfect in *avi*), and *Propria quae maribus*.

Ascapart, An : a giant. After a giant ' ful thyrty fote long ' in the ballad of *Sir Bevis of Southampton*. [Shakespeare, 2 *Henry*, II, iii (4to) (?1592-4)]

Ascii (*Grk.*, shadowless) : the inhabitants of the Tropical Zone.

Ascræan Poet (Sage), The : Hesiod (fl. 859-824 B.C.), who was born at Ascra in Boeotia.

Asculum, An : a Cadmean victory (*q.v.*), a victory that brings no advantage. After the victory of Pyrrhus over the Romans at Asculum (Ascoli) B.C. 278.

Asgard : the abode of the gods, in Scand. mythology. ' As ' was one of the major gods.

Ash Pole, The : selected in 1828 as the symbol of the American Whig party. After Ashland, Henry Clay's plantation nr. Lexington, Kentucky. The Democratic symbol was Hickory (*q.v.*).

Ash Wednesday : the first day in Lent. From the Roman Catholic practice of sprinkling ashes on the heads of penitents, the priest saying : ' Remember, man, that thou art ashes, and unto ashes thou shalt return.' The practice was abolished early in the reign of Edward VI.

Ashes, As pale (white) as : very pale.

Ashes in the mouth, To turn to : to prove a great disappointment on realization.

Ashes, To recover the : to win in a return contest, after a previous defeat. A cricketing metaphor, derived from a mock epitaph published in the *Sporting Times* in August 1882 on the final defeat of the English team by the Australians. ' English cricket .. which died at the Oval, August 29, 1882 .. the body will be cremated and the ashes taken to Australia.'

Ashlanders : a political club identified with Ashland Square, in Baltimore.

Ashkenazim : Jews who follow the Germ. or N. European ritual, as distinguished from the Sephardim, who follow the Span. ritual. From *Ashkenaz* (Med. Heb.), Germany, after Ashkenaz the son of Gomer (identified or confused with Germany). [*Genesis*, x, 3]

Asian Mystery, The : Lord Beaconsfield. So described by Beresford Hope in 1867 in the debate on the Reform Bill, in allusion to his Hebrew extraction.

Aside, To go : to absent oneself. [*Terence in English* (1614)]

Asiento (*Span.*, agreement) : permission granted by Spain to England, Portugal, and France to trade in slaves with America.

Asinego (Asinigo) : *see* Assinego.

Asked in Church, To be : to have the banns of marriage put up in church. [*Wily Beguiled*, l. 1515 (1606)]

Asking, To be had for the : to be had very cheaply. [Susan Ferrier, *Inheritance*, ch. 18 (1824)]

Asmodeus : the destroyer of domestic happiness. From the Heb. demon who, according to the *Book of Tobit*, destroyed Sara's seven husbands in succession.

Asmodeus flight, An : from the flight of the demon Asmodeus in Le Sage, *Le Diable Boiteux* (1726), in which the interiors of the houses were laid bare as he passed over them.

Aspasia, An : a fascinating courtesan. After the mistress of Pericles.

Aspen leaf, An : one who is always chattering. After the aspen-leaf, which, from the nature of its formation, is almost invariably quivering. To ' tremble like an aspen-leaf ' is to tremble violently. [Chaucer, *Troilus and Creseide*, Bk. III, ll. 1200-1 (c. 1380)]

Ass ascends the ladder, Until the : *i.e.*, never. A rabbinical saying.

Ass, Burial of an : no burial at all. [*Jeremiah*, xxii, 19]

Ass, To come from a horse to an : to descend in the social or financial scale.

Ass to a horse, To go from an : to ascend in the social or financial scale.

Ass in a lion's skin, An : a coward who attempts to bully ; a fool who pretends to be wise. From the fable of the ass concealed in the lion's skin that was betrayed by his bray.

Ass of oneself, To make an : to behave foolishly. ' Ass ' was a generic term for a stupid person even in the early Greek period.

Ass, To give straw to one's dog and bones to one's : *see* Straw.

Ass, To mount the : to become bankrupt. From the French custom in the 16th cent. of mounting a bankrupt on an ass with his face to its tail.

Ass, To seek wool on an : *see* Wool.

Ass, To shave an : *see* Shave.

Ass with two panniers, An : a man walking between two women. *Faire le panier à deux ânes*, to put one's arms akimbo ; lit., to make with one's arms a basket with two handles.

Ass' Bridge ; Pons Asinorum : the 5th proposition of 1st Book of Euclid ; owing to the difficulty found by beginners in mastering it.

Ass' shadow, To wrangle for an : to quarrel or argue about a trifle. From a story told by Demosthenes.

Assassin, An : a secret murderer, esp. of a public personage. The Assassins were a fanatical Moslem sect, which fl. in Persia and Syria from 11th to 14th cent. One of their doctrines was the assassination of all opponents. Their chief was Sheikh-al-Jabal, the chief (Old Man) of the Mountain.

Assassins commencent ! Que Messieurs les (*Fr.*, Let the assassins begin !): the remark made by Alphonse Karr (1808-90) on the proposal to abolish capital punishment.

Assault and battery : attack on the person with injury. When the hurt is inflicted the battery is committed. [*Bartholomew Faire* (1641)]

Assault-at-arms, An : an exhibition of military skill.

Assaye Regiment, The : the 74th Regt. of Foot, now the 2nd Highland Light Infantry. From its gallantry in the Battle of Assaye (1803).

Assays, At all : at all hazards ; prepared for anything that may happen. [Stubbes, *Two Wonderful and Rare Examples* (1581)]

Assiento : *see* Asiento.

Assignat, An : paper-currency issued by the 1st Revolutionary Government in France.

Assinego (Asinego), An (*Port.*, a little ass) : a fool, a silly fellow. [Shakespeare, *Troilus and Cressida*, II, i, 49 (?1606-7)]

Assize of Arms, An : a universal military levy for national defence. Instituted by Henry II in 1181.

Assize of Bread, The : regulation of the price of bread. Instituted by Henry III in 1266.

Assize, The Last : the Last Judgment ; the Day of Doom.

Assizes of Jerusalem, The : the code of legislation adopted by the Crusaders for Palestine in 1099.

Assizes, The Bloody : *see* Bloody.

Associated Counties, The : Norfolk, Suffolk, Essex, Hertford, Cambridge, Huntingdon, and Lincoln, which combined in 1642-6 to keep the Civil War outside their boundaries.

Assume the mantle of, To : to adopt the manners or responsibilities of .. In allusion to the mantle of Elijah to which Elisha succeeded.

Astolpho's book, Like : purveying universal knowledge. In Ariosto, *Orlando Furioso*, Astolpho is one of Charlemagne's paladins.

Astolpho's horn, Like a blast from : causing terror. From the horn given to Astolpho by Logistilla in *Orlando Furioso*, which, when blown, created a panic.

Astræa : equity ; innocence. The name of the Greek goddess of Justice.

Astræa, The Divine : Mrs. Aphra Behn (1640-89), Eng. dramatist, poetess and novelist. So called by herself.

Astronomer of Dublin, The : the head of the most prominent rebel or traitor mounted on a stake, in the City of Dublin.

At stake, To be : to be in jeopardy.

Atalanta, An : a girl swift of foot. After a maiden in Grk. legend, who used to race with suitors for her hand.

Atalantis, An : a scandalous narrative. After the title of a *chronique scandaleuse* by Mrs. Manley (1709).

Atchison, An : a coin. Thomas Atchison was assay-master at the mint at Edinburgh during the reigns of Mary and James VI. His name was given to the base-metal coins that were then in circulation and which were in the year 1587 'cryed down by Proclamation, because counterfeit in England and other foreign parts.'

Ateliers Nationaux : national workshops established for the unemployed by the French government in 1848.

Atellan Fables : farces in ancient Rome performed by amateurs. After Atella in the Romagna.

Athanasius contra mundum (*Lat.*, A. against the world) : one against an enormous majority. In allusion to Athanasius (293-373), one of the most illustrious defenders of the Christian Faith, and author of the Athanasian Creed.

thenæum : a literary or scientific institution. After the Athenaion, the Temple of Athene, at Athens. A school or university called the Athenæum was founded at Rome by Emperor Hadrian.

Athenian Bee ; Bee of Athens, The : *see* Bee.

Athens of America, The : Boston, Massachusetts, the literary capital of the U.S.

Athens of England, The : Melton Mowbray.

Athens of Ireland, The : (1) Cork ; (2) Belfast.

Athens of Scotland : Edinburgh.

Athens of Switzerland, The : Zurich.

Athens of the New World : Boston, Mass., literary capital of the U.S.

Athens of the North, The : (1) Edinburgh ; (2) Copenhagen.

Athens of the South, The : Nashville, Tennessee, U.S. On account of the number of its educational institutions.

Athens, The Thief's : the Grisons.

Athens of the West, The : Cordova, the intellectual centre of Spain from 8th to 13th cent.

Athens, The German : Saxe-Weimar.

Athens, The Modern : (1) Edinburgh ; (2) Boston, Mass, U.S. ; (3) Weimar.

Athens, The Mohammedan : Bagdad, in the period of Haroun al Raschid.

Atlantean shoulders : powerful shoulders. After Atlas (*q.v.*). [Milton, *Paradise Lost*, II, 300 (1667)]

Atlantes : figures of men used as supports in architecture ; *see* Atlas.

Atlantic Greyhounds : fast liners plying between Europe and America.

Atlantis : the legendary ' lost continent ' in the Atlantic Ocean ; mentioned by Plato and other early writers ; the site of the Elysian Fields.

Atlantis, The New : an island, the home of a philosophical commonwealth devoted to the cultivation of the natural sciences, the product of Lord Bacon's imagination.

Atlas, An : a book of maps. After the mythical King of Mauretania, Atlas, who was said to support the world on his shoulders, an illustration of whom appeared on the title-page of old atlases.

Atlas shoulders : *see* Atlantean shoulders.

Atomy, An : a dwarf or deformed person. A contraction of anatomy (*q.v.*). [Shakespeare, 2 *Henry IV*, V, iv (1597-8)]

Atonement : complete agreement and harmony ; the condition of being at one with others : at-one-ment.

Atra cura (*Lat.*, black care) : intense anxiety. [Horace, *Odes*, III, i]

Atropos : that one of the Fates who used to sever the thread of human life. Atropine, the alkaloid poison, is named after her.

Attalus, The wealth of : unbounded riches. After Attalus I, King of Pergamum (241-197 B.C.). [Horace, *Odes*, Bk. I, i, 11-3]

Attendance on, To dance : to be at all times at the service of another. [Heywood, *Proverbes* (1546)]

Attic : (1) classical ; of elegant literary style ; from the Grk. State Attica, whose capital was Athens ; (2) the top storey of a building with sloping roof. Originally, the room enclosed by the Attic architectural decoration.

Attic Bee, The : (1) Sophocles (495-406 B.C.), the Grk. tragic poet ; (2) Plato (427-347 B.C.), the Grk. philosopher.

Attic Bird, The : the nightingale ; because Philomel was the daughter of the King of Athens. [Milton, *Paradise Lost*, Bk. IV, l. 244 (1667)]

Attic Boy, The : Cephalos, beloved by the Morn.

Attic Faith : inviolable faith.

Attic Muse, The : Xenophon (c. 435-354 B.C.), the Grk. historian. On account of the elegance of his style.

Attic Salt : delicate wit. In both Greek and Latin, salt was a synonym for wit. The Athenians were noteworthy for their wit.

Attic storey, In the : in the head. A metaphor drawn from architecture.

Attic Warbler, The : the Attic Bird (*q.v.*).

Attic Wit : *see* Attic Salt.

Atticus, The Christian : Reginald Heber (1783-1826), Bp. of Calcutta, poet and hymn-writer. The original Atticus (109-32 B.C.) was reputed to be the most elegant and finished scholar of the Romans.

Atticus, The English : Joseph Addison (1672-1719), Eng. essayist. So called by Pope.

Atticus, The Irish : George Faulkner (1699-1775). So-called by Lord Chesterfield.

Attila, An : one who commits brutal atrocities. After Attila, ' The Scourge of God,' King of the Huns, who ravaged the Roman Empire in 5th cent. *See also* Hun.

Attorney-General of the Lantern, The : Camille Desmoulins (1762-94), French Revolutionist. In allusion to his practice of indiscriminately condemning political opponents to be hanged from street-lamps.

Attorney-General's Devil, The : the Junior Counsel to the Treasury. *See* Devil for . . (To).

Au courant (*Fr.*, in the current) : conversant with.

Au fait (*Fr.*, in the fact) : expert, well-acquainted with . .   [Horace Walpole, *Letters*, II (1748)]

Au grand sérieux : *see* Sérieux.

Au pied de la lettre (*Fr.*, at the foot of the letter) : strictly, literally.   [Horace Walpole, *Letters*, VIII, (1782)].

Au revoir! (*Fr.*, until seeing you again) : farewell for the present !   [17th cent.]

Aubade, An (*Fr.*) : a morning serenade or concert.   In early Fr. poetry, a love-song sung at dawn.

Audience to . . To give : to listen to . . ; to grant an interview to another for the purpose of hearing his views.

Audit-ale : ale brewed for Audit days at Trinity College, Cambridge and other colleges.

Audley (a matter), To John (Lord) : to bring it to a close.   In the 18th cent. Shuter, manager of a travelling theatrical company, was accustomed to spin out the performance until an audience sufficient to fill the theatre again had collected ; whereupon a boy in front called out ' John Audley,' and the performance inside was brought to a rapid close.

Audley over, To come Lord : to gull, deceive.   Possibly from Mervin, Lord Audley, who was hanged for stealing in 1631.   *See also* the previous entry.

Auf Wiedersehen ! (*Germ.*, Until seeing you again !) :   Farewell for the present !

Auge of . . In the : in the highest pitch.   From ' auge,' the highest point in the course of the sun, the moon, or a planet.

Augean task, An : an extremely difficult task.   *See* Augean Stables.

Augean Stables, To cleanse : to perform a dirty or unpleasant task which has long called for attention.   After the stables of Augeas, King of the Epeians, in Elis.   The cleansing of them, after 30 years' of neglect, was one of the Labours of Hercules.

Augmentation Office, The : the office in which the records of the Augmentation Court (estab. by Henry VIII) were kept after its dissolution by Queen Mary.   The Court's function was to decide claims against monasteries and abbeys.   The name was derived from its augmentation of the royal revenues.

Augur, To ; Augur, An ; Augury, An : (*a*) to foretell, esp. by omens ; (*b*) a prophet from the Roman College of Augurs who foretold events from the flight of birds and other signs ; (*c*) an omen.

August : (1, pronounced Aug'ust), the 8th month, named in honour of Emperor Augustus, whose lucky month it was ; (2, *pron.* aug-ust'), inspiring respect, majestic ; also after Augustus.

Augusta : the Roman name for London.

Augustan Age, The : the greatest literary period in the history of a people.   After the reign of Emperor Augustus, the greatest period in Latin literature.

Augustan Age of England, The : (1) the reigns of Elizabeth and James I ; (2) the reigns of William III and Anne.

Augustan Age of France, The : that of Louis XIV.

Augustan Age of Germany, The : the nineteenth century.

Augustan Age of Portugal, The : that of Don Alphonso Henrique.

Augustine, The Second : Thomas Aquinas (1224-75). St. Augustine, the greatest of the Latin Fathers, lived from 353 to 430.

Augustus, An : a great king whose reign confers peace and prosperity on his people.   After the title of the first of the Roman emperors.

Auld Farrant-like ;   Auld Farrand : (*Scottish*) : old-fashioned ; possessing the attributes of age.

Auld Hornie (*Scottish*) : Satan ; in allusion to his horns.   From representations of the heathen god Pan.

Auld Lang Syne : lit., old long since ; past times.   [Title of a song by Robert Burns (1788)]

Auld Reekie : ' Old Smoky,' a name for Edinburgh.   On account of the clouds of smoke that so often appear above it.   Originally the name of the old town only.

Aulic Council, The : the supreme Council of the Holy Roman and subsequently of the Austrian Empires.   Estab. in 1501.

nt, An : a prostitute or procuress. [Shakespeare and his contemporaries.]

nt Sally, An : an object put up to be aimed at. From the popular name of a cockshy at a fair, race-course, etc. Earlier, a black-faced doll used as a sign of a rag-shop. From Black Sal, a character in Pierce Egan, *Life in London* (1821).

uri sacra fames (*Lat.*, accursed (sacred) hunger for gold) : overpowering desire for wealth. [Virgil, *Æneid*, III, 57]

urora : the dawn. After the Roman goddess of the Dawn.

urora's Tears : the morning dew.

usgleich, An (*Germ.*) : an agreement between Austria and Hungary, that was renewable every ten years, for the settlement of economic, financial, and other differences between the two governments.

usterlitz, The Sun of : a symbol of good-fortune. In allusion to the sun that dispersed the clouds on the morning of the Battle of Austerlitz (Dec. 2, 1805).

ustrian Leeds, The : see Leeds.

ustrian lips : the thick under-lip characteristic of the Hapsburg family, that of the Austrian emperors, said to have first appeared in the family in the person of Emperor Maximilian I.

ut Cæsar aut nullus (*Lat.*, either Cæsar or nobody) : everything or nothing. It was Cæsar who said, 'Sooner first in a village than second in Rome.'

Author of Evil, The : Satan.

Authentic Doctor, The : Gregory of Rimini (d. 1358), Scholastic philosopher.

Authorized Version, The : the English translation of the Bible of 1611 : ' King James' Version.'

Autocrat, The ; Autocrat of all the Russias, The : the Tsar of Russia.

Autocrat of the Breakfast Table, The : Oliver Wendell Holmes (1809-94), American man-of-letters. It forms the title of his most popular book.

Auto-da-fé ; Auto-de-fé (*Port.*, act of faith) : the public sentence and execution of one condemned to death by the Spanish or Portuguese Inquisition.

Autolycus, An : a witty, not too honest, pedlar. After a character in Shakespeare, *Winter's Tale* (1611). In Grk. legend, a famous thief.

Automedon, An : a coachman. After Achilles' charioteer.

Avatar : the appearance on earth of a deity. Hindu mythology.

Ave Bell : see Ave Maria Bell.

Ave Maria, An : a prayer to the Virgin in the Roman Catholic Church : its two first words are ' Ave Maria,' ' Hail, Mary.'

Ave Maria Bell : the bell that summons to prayer when the Ave Maria is said.

Avernus : hell. After a lake in the Roman Campagna, said to be the entrance to the Infernal Regions.

Avignon Captivity, The : the period of the residence of the Popes at Avignon under the control of the French kings, A.D. 1305-77.

Avoirdupois : the general English standard of weight. Old-Fr., *aveir de peis*, goods of weight.

Awful Unnamable, The : God, so-called by Thomas Carlyle (*Heroes and Hero Worship*, lect. VI).

Awkward Squad, An : an untrained party ; a squadron or party of un-trained or insufficiently-trained recruits.

Awls and be gone, To pack up one's : to make a complete and permanent departure. Either from ' all,' everything ; or from ' awl,' the shoemaker's tool.

Axe after helve, To send : to throw good money after bad. [John Heywood, *Proverbes* (1546)]

Axe on the helve, To put the : to have solved a difficulty.

Axe to grind, To have an : to have a personal end to serve. From the American backwoodsmen's practice of calling at houses ostensibly to grind an axe but in reality to obtain a drink. Based on a story told by Charles Miner (1780-1865), ' Who'll turn the grindstone ? ' in the *Wilkesbarre Gleaner* of 1811, of a man who, by flattery, induced a boy to turn the grindstone while he sharpened his axe.

Axe, To hang up one's : to retire from business ; an allusion to the battle-axe of the *passé* warrior.

Axe, To open a door with an : see Open.

Ayankeeados : Mexican sympathizers with the U.S. during the war between the two countries in 1846.

Ay-ma ; Ay-mee, An : a lamentation. A corruption of ' Ah me.' [Beaumont and Fletcher, *Tamer Tam'd*, III, 1 (1604)]

Ayrshire Poet, The : Robert Burns (1759-96), born near Ayr.

Azazel : the scapegoat ; on which the sins of the Jewish people were laid by the High Priest. Properly, a name of Satan.

Azrael, The Angel of : the angel that separates the soul from the body at the moment of death.

Azrael, The Wings of : the coming of death.

B. and S. : brandy and soda, as a drink. The initial letters.

B from a battledore, Not to know a : to be quite illiterate or stupid. A battle-dore was a horn-book from which children were taught the alphabet. [John Halle, *Historiall Expostulation* (1565)]

B from a bull's foot, Not to know a : to be quite illiterate. In allusion to the supposed resemblance of a bull's parted hoof to the letter B. [*Pol. Poems*, II, 57 (A.D. 1401)]

B-flat, A ; a bug. On account of the flatness of these insects.

B's, The Four : blood, brains, brass (impudence), brads (money). An Americanism.

B, Marked with a : of little value. Owing to the coincidence that in French many physical defects are expressed by words beginning with the letter B, *e.g.*, *bigle*, squint-eyed ; *borgne*, one-eyed ; *bossu*, humpty.

Baal, A : a false god. The name of the principal god of Canaan.

Babel, A : a confusion of tongues, an uproar. After Babel, the tower of which the building was interrupted by the miraculous confusion of tongues. (*Genesis*, ix). [*Bartholomew Faire* (1641)]

Babel, A Tower of : a lofty structure ; a visionary scheme.

Babes in the Wood : (1) a pair of harm-less but ill-used orphans, a boy and a girl ; (2) rebels who infested the woods of Wicklow and Enniscorthy in the 18th cent. ; (3) men confined in the stocks. From characters in an old pathetic ballad so-entitled.

Babies in the Eyes : the reflection of oneself in a lover's eyes. [Drayton ; Herrick ; possibly alluded to by Shakespeare, *Timon of Athens*, I, ii. (?1607)]

Babu ; Baboo : a semi-educated Hindu ; an Indian clerk. Now the Hindu equivalent of Mr. or Esquire.

Babylon, A : any luxurious and magnifi-cent capital city ; esp. Rome and the Vatican. After the capital of the ancient Empire of Chaldæa.

Babylon, The Modern : (1) London (2) the Church of Rome.

Babylonian Numbers : astrology attempts to foresee the future. The Chaldæans of Babylon were devoted to magic.

Babylonish Captivity, The : the period o residence of the Popes at Avignon (*see* Avignon Captivity). Properly the exile of the Jews in Babylon, from the time of Nebuchadnezzar to tha of Cyrus.

Baca, A Valley of : a place or period o depression. [*Psalm* lxxxiv, 6]

Bacchus : wine. After the Grk. go of wine.

Bacchus, A Son (Priest) of : a drunkard

Bachelor girl, A : an unmarried girl who lives away from home, either in apartments or at a club.

Bachelor, To be a lady's : to act a knight to a lady.

Bachelor President, The : James Buchanan (1791-1868), 15th President of the U.S.

Bachelor's buttons, To wear : to be un-married. From the superstition attached to the campion-flower (' bachelor's button '), which was supposed to have a magical effect on the fortunes of lovers. [Thos. Heywood, *Fair Maid of the West* (1631)]

Bachelor's fare : bread, cheese and kisses.

Bachelor's wife, A : the ideal wife. [John Heywood, *Proverbes* (1546)]

Back, To : to bet or wager on. From the commercial practice of backing, or endorsing, a bill or cheque on behalf of another.

Back and edge : completely. The back and the edge comprise the whole of the knife, etc. [*Lady Alimony*, III, vii (1659)]

Back, Behind a person's : surreptitious-ly ; in his absence ; without his privity. [Lilly, *Campaspe*, IV, i (1584)]

Back, To cast behind one's : to reject. [*Nehemiah*, ix, 26]

Back down, To : to yield, submit. Perhaps a metaphor drawn from the game of leap-frog.

Back, To give a person the : to turn away from.

ack into .. To put one's : to put the whole of one's energy into ..

ack (neck) of .. To break the : to perform the essential, usually the hardest, part of ..

ack Number, A : a person whose ideas or methods are out of date. A journalistic metaphor.

ack of .. To ride on the : to deceive. [*The Wizard* (1640)]

ack of .. To see the : to complete (a task) ; to see the last of (a person). As if it (or he) had gone away from you.

ack on .. To turn one's : to throw over .. ; to give up, withdraw from ..

ack out of .. To : to withdraw from ..

ack, Thrown on one's : completely defeated. A wrestling metaphor.

ack to the wall, To have one's : to stand at bay, facing odds. The natural desire in such circumstances is to have the back protected.

Back up .. To : to support .. as if standing behind.

Back up, To get a person's : to arouse his active opposition. From the cat's habit of raising its back when faced by an opponent. [*Dame Huddle's Letters* (1710)]

Back-bite, To : to slander or speak ill of a person in his absence. Lit., to bite a person in the back. [*Proverbs*, xxv, 23 ; *Cott. Hom.* 205 (1175)]

Back-door : clandestine. Since beginning of 17th cent., when it was possible to gain one's way at Court by underhand intrigue. [Shakespeare, *Cymbeline*, V, iii, 45 (1611)]

Back-friend, A : a false friend, or secret enemy. [Falkland, *The Marriage Night*, III, i (1664)]

Back-hand, To hold a person's : to support.

Back-hander, A : a blow with the back of the hand ; an unexpected rebuff.

Back-lane Parliament, The : an assembly of Irish representatives in 1792, which requested the grant of the franchise.

Back-rag (rack) : a German wine. From Bacharach, where it was grown.

Back-seat, To take a : to withdraw into a less prominent position. The phrase was popularized by Andrew Johnson (President of the U.S.) in 1868.

Back-sheesh : *see* Bakshish.

Back-slide, To : to deteriorate or fall away morally.

Back-stairs influence : secret, underhand influence. From the private stairs of some palaces which could be secretly mounted.

Backward blessing, A : a curse. According to superstition to recite the Lord's Prayer backwards was to incite evil.

Backbone : (1) firmness of character ; steadfastness ; (2) the main support. Metaphorical use of backbone as spine.

Backfish, A (Germ., *Backfisch*, fish for frying) : a girl of about 16 or 17.

Backwoodsmen : reactionary members of the House of Lords who very seldom attended its sittings but were always available when needed to outvote the advocates of reform.

Bacon, To baste a person's : to thrash him. From the Norman habit of calling the Saxons ' hogs.'

Bacon, To save one's : to rescue oneself from an awkward situation. [Peter Pindar, *The Lousiad*, II (1786)]

Bacon of Theology, The : Bishop Joseph Butler (1692-1752), author of *Analogy of Religion*. After Francis Bacon (1561-1626), the intellectual giant.

Baconian, A : one who holds that Francis Bacon, Lord Verulam, wrote the works attributed to Shakespeare by almost universal consent. This contention is called ' The Baconian Theory.'

Baconists : the Liberal Party in Virginia and in Maryland at the end of the 17th cent. After Nathaniel Bacon (1642-76), The Virginia Rebel.

Bactrian Sage, The : Zoroaster (9th cent., B.C.), the founder of the Magian religion. He was born in Bactria.

Bad blood : ill-feeling. [*Brother Jonathan*, I, 74 (1825)].

Bad books, In a person's : *see* Books.

Bad cess to you ! : ill-luck attend you ! Irish ' cess,' board and lodging.

Bad debt, A : an unrecoverable debt.

Bad egg, A : *see* Egg.

Bad form : behaviour not in accordance with etiquette. A metaphor derived from the racing-stable.

Bad hat, To be a (shocking) : *see* Hat.

Bad Lands : a desolate region in the North-West of U.S.

Bad, To go to the : to degenerate, deteriorate ; to fall away in the direction of ruin.

Badge of poverty, The : in reference to the badge at one time borne by those who received parish relief.

Badge-men : licensed beggars. In allusion to the badge formerly worn by inmates of almshouses.

Badger, To : to annoy, to worry ; as a badger-hunter treats a badger.

Badger State, The : Wisconsin. From the badger on its coat of arms. It is said that this emblem is derived from the habit of the early miners in the State, who in the winter lived in the earth like badgers.

Badger, As uneven as a : very uneven. From the vulgar error that the two right legs of a badger are shorter than the left.

Badinguet : Napoleon III. After the name of the workman in whose clothes he escaped from prison at Ham in 1846.

Badminton : (1) a drink made of claret ; (2) a game played with battle-dores and racquets, after Badminton, the seat of the Dukes of Beaufort, where it was introduced ; (3) blood (a pugilistic term), after Henry Somerset, 7th Duke of Beaufort (1792-1853), a patron of the prize-ring.

Bag and baggage : originally all the property of an army. [Rymer, *Foedera*, X (1422)]. ' Bag ' was an allusion to the soldier's receptacle for his portable property ; ' baggage ' was the term used for the female followers of an army, either from the baggage wagons in which they rode or from Ital. *bagascia*, harlot.

Bag and baggage, To march out with : (of an army) to withdraw honourably with all its impedimenta ; (of an individual) to be turned out with all his belongings.

Bag and baggage policy, The : the policy advocated by W. E. Gladstone in 1876-78 of the expulsion of Turkish rule from Europe. [Speech of 7th May, 1877]

Bag and bottle provisions : cf. *Ballad of Robin Hood and the Shepherd*. [Fulwell, *Like Will to Like*, l. 559 (1568)]

Bag of tricks, The whole : everything. From the fable of *The Fox and the Cat*.

Bag, The bottom of the : the last resource.

Bag, To empty the : to tell the whole truth. Fr., *vider le sac*, to expose everything to view.

Bag-man, A : a commercial traveller of an inferior class. From the practice of carrying samples in a bag.

Bag-of-bones, A : an emaciated person.

Bagatelle, A (mere) (*Ital, bagatella*, a little property) : a trifle.

Baggage, A : a disreputable woman. [Shakespeare, *Taming of the Shrew*

(?1596)] ; a young woman, in familiar sense. [Davenant, *The Wi* (1636)] *See* Bag and baggage.

Baily's Beads : the appearance of th sun (like a string of beads) when a eclipse reduces it to a thin disc. Aft Francis Baily (1774-1844), by who the resemblance was first pointed ou

Baiting-stock, A : a laughing-stock ; a object to be baited.

Bajulus, A : a pedagogue. After a officer of the Greek Imperial Court.

Baker, The ; Baker's Wife, The : (a Louis XVI ; (b) Marie Antoinett From the trade in corn conducted i the environs of their palace a Versailles.

Baker, To meet a splay-footed : to receiv a warning of ill-luck.

Baker, To spell : to undertake a difficul task. In the old spelling-book ' baker ' was the first word of tw syllables.

Baker's dozen, A : thirteen. Pedlar in bread were formerly supplied wit thirteen loaves for the price of twelve the additional loaf representing thei profit. Another derivation gives a ' Devil's Dozen ' as an equivalent thirteen being the quorum at a Witches' Sabbath. (Bakers were formerly very unpopular and as a sign of their unpopularity ' Baker was substituted for ' Devil.') It i also said that to avoid the risk o giving short weight (an offence former ly visited with heavy punishment) bakers were accustomed to give thirteen loaves for twelve.

Baker's dozen, To give a : to give a sound thrashing (more than was expected).

Bakshish ; Baksheesh ; Bucksheesh (*Persian, bakhshidan*, to give alms) : a tip or bribe, in Moslem countries.

Balaam (Balaamite), A : one who approves when he is expected to dis- approve ; one who makes a profit out of his religion. After the prophet whose story is told in *Numbers*, xxii- xxiv.

Balaam : (journalistic) odds and ends of ' copy ' used to complete columns in a newspaper. Possibly from the prophet on the asumption that, like Balaam's ass, these odds and ends are of little value.

Balaam Box (Basket), A : a receptacle for odds and ends of ' copy ' for which a use may be found. *See* previous entry.

Balaam's Ass, A : a servant who is more far-seeing than his master. From the story of Balaam and his ass. [*Numbers*, xxii-xxv]

Balaam's Blessing, A : an intended curse that becomes a blessing. [*Ibid.*]

Balance and to be found wanting, To be weighed in the : to fail when tested. From the writing on the wall at Belshazzar's Feast. [*Daniel*, v, 27]

Balance, Not to go above the : to reverence justice ; for neither fear nor flattery to lean to anyone partially. [Lyly, *Euphues : The Anatomy of Wit* (1579)]

Balance of Power, The : military and naval equilibrium between the ' Great Powers ' of Europe. [*London Gazette*, No. 3758 (1701)]

Balance of Trade, The : the difference between the value of the imports into and the exports from a country. [Child, *Discourse on Trade* (1668)]

Balance, To be thrown off one's : to be taken at a disadvantage through surprise.

Bald as a coot, As : very bald. In allusion to the absence of feathers from the front portion of the head of a coot. [Tyndale, *Works*, II, 224 (1530)]

Baldachin ; Baldaquin : a canopy-like structure ; a canopy over the altar or over the Holy Sacrament when carried in procession. From Bagdad, the source of the silk of which the canopies were made, through Ital., *baldacco* and *baldacchino*.

Bale out the sea, To : to undertake a useless task.

Balkanize, To : to split up into small and mutually hostile states, such as those of the Balkan Peninsula. Term introduced during the discussion of the treaties that concluded the European War of 1914-18.

Ball, A : a dancing-party. From the early practice of combining a game of ball with the dancing, derived from the game of ball played in church by the Dean and choir-boys of Naples during the Feast of Fools.

Ball at one's feet, To have the : to have a desired opportunity at hand. A football metaphor. [Bunyan, *The Holy War*, (1682)]

Ball before the bound, To catch (take) the : to anticipate an opportunity. A ball-game metaphor. [Howell, *Familiar Letters*, Bk. I, §4, Letter ix (1647)]

Ball of Fortune, To be the : to be subject to the fluctuations of fortune, tossed about as is a ball.

Ball on the bound, To catch the : to seize an opportunity that offers itself. A ball-game metaphor.

Ball rolling, To keep the : to prevent an enterprise, conversation, etc., from coming to a standstill. From the game of Bandy, or of Lacrosse.

Ball, To be a tennis- : to be bandied about by other people, as if one were a tennis-ball. [Warner, *Albion's England*, VI, xxx, 151 (1589)]

Ball one's own way, To have the : to do oneself a good turn.

Ball, To open the : to start an enterprise. A dancing metaphor.

Ball under the line, To strike the : to fail. A tennis metaphor. [John Heywood, *Proverbes* (1546)]

Ball up, To keep the : to prevent a conversation from flagging or a movement from coming to a standstill. A ball-game metaphor.

Balls, Three Golden : the sign of a pawnbroker. From (1) three purses of gold, the emblem of St. Nicholas ; or (2) the arms of the Medici family (three golden pills, referring to the origin of the family name from *medicus*, physician) ; or (3) the balls of the mace of the giant Mugello, killed by Averardo de Medici, one of the Knights of Charlemagne.

Ballambangjan, Straits of : a sailor's term for a region of incredible adventures.

Ballast, A man of no : a man of no stability. From the unsteadiness of a ship deficient in ballast. [Bacon, *Essays : Vainglory* (1612)]

Ballon d'Essai, A (*Fr.*, a trial balloon): a proposal or scheme put forward to test public opinion or interest.

Ballot-box, To stuff the : to obtain false returns at an election by means of a fraudulent ballot-box.

Ballplatz, The : the Foreign Office of the late Austro-Hungarian Government. From the name of the street in Vienna in which it was situated.

Ballyrag, To : *see* Bullyrag.

Balm in Gilead : a soothing agency or influence. [*Jeremiah*, viii, 22]

Balmoral, A : a Scotch cap. After the royal residence in Scotland.

Balmy : sleepy. Frequently misused for Barmy (*q.v.*).

Balmy stick, To put on the : to feign madness. Prison slang. *See* Barmy.

Baltimore, A ; Baltimore bird, A : a North American bird with plumage of the same colours as the arms of Lord Baltimore, founder of Maryland.

Balts : inhabitants of the Baltic provinces of Russia, *i.e.*, Esthonia, Livonia, Courland.

Bambocciades : pictures of low-life. From Pieter van Laer (1613-73) (*bamboccio*, Ital. for ' cripple '), who first painted such pictures.

Bamboozle, To : to deceive by a trick. A slang word, possibly of gipsy origin, introduced into the English language about 1700. [*The Tatler*, No. 230 ; Colley Cibber, *She Would and She Would Not*, II, i (1703)]

Ban, Arrière : a proclamation of the French kings, summoning to military service.

Banal : commonplace. From Ban, the service imposed on subjects in mediæval France.

Bananaland : Queensland. On account of the number of bananas grown there.

Banbury, As wise as the Mayor of : very foolish. The Mayor is reputed to have held that Henry III preceded Henry II.

Banbury cheese, As thin as a : Banbury cheese was reputed to be the thinnest of poor cheese. [Shakespeare, *Merry Wives of Windsor*, I, i (1598)]

Banbury, As drunk as a tinker at : the allusion is unknown. [*The London Chanticleers*, V (1659)]

Banbury Man (Saint), A : a Puritan. Banbury was a centre of Puritanism in the 16th and 17th cents.

Banda Oriental : the former name of the Republic of Uruguay.

Bandbox, As neat as a : as neat as clothes packed in a bandbox.

Bandbox, To look as though one had stepped out of a : to be very trim and dapper. *See* previous entry.

Bande Noire (*Fr.*, black band) : (1) certain regiments in the French service in the 16th cent. ; (2) speculators who bought Church property and confiscated estates in the course of the French Revolution and acted as vandals in their treatment of buildings of archæological value.

Bandy, To : to exchange (words, blows, etc.). A metaphor drawn from the game of tennis, formerly called Bandy.

" Bang went saxpence ! " : a reference to the proverbial meanness (?frugality) of the Scots. Immortalized by Charl Keene in *Punch*. Originally overhear by Sir John Gilbert as passing th lips of a recently arrived visitor fro Glasgow who complained of the e travagance of London.

Banian : *see* Banyan.

Banjo A : a stringed musical instrumen From Pandoura, a Greek stringe instrument named after the god Pa

Bank Holiday, A : a general holiday o which banks are compelled by Act o Parliament to close.

Bank, In : in hand. Lit., readil available at one's bank. [Vanburg and Cibber, *The Provoked Husban* III, i (1728)]

Bank, Sisters of the : loose women wh frequented the Bankside (*q.v.*).

Bank, To break the : to be so successfu in gambling as to exhaust, temporaril the resources of the director of th game.

Banks's Horse : a performing hors belonging to a man named Bank between 1590 and 1601. Both th horse and its owner are said to hav been burnt ultimately by the Inqu sition at Rome.

Banker Poet, The : (1) Samuel Roger (1763-1855), English poet ; (2) Ed mund Clarence Stedman (1833-1908) American poet.

Bankside : the Southern bank of th Thames between Waterloo and Black friars Bridges, the resort of women c loose character.

Banshee, A (*Gaelic, bean sidhe*, woman fairy) : an Irish spectre believed t warn certain Irish families of ap proaching death.

Bant, To : to practise the bantin system (*q.v.*).

Bantam-weight, A : a boxer not ex ceeding 8 st. 4 lb. in weight. Afte the bantam, a small variety of fowl hence anything below the average i height or weight.

Banting System, The : a system fo reduction of corpulence by dieting After Wm. Banting (1797-1878), fo whom it was prescribed by Willian Harvey and by whom it was recom mended to the public in *A Letter on Corpulence*.

Banyan (Banian) Days : days on which meat is not eaten. After Banian, a native class in India, whose member abstain from eating meat, holding animal-life sacred.

Banyan Hospital : a hospital for animals. See previous entry.

Baptism of fire : the first occasion on which a soldier goes under fire ; an introduction to any situation of danger. Used by Napoleon at St. Helena (Aug. 2, 1817). [O'Meara, *Voice from St. Helena*]

Bar, To pitch the : to exaggerate. [*Spectator*, Nov. 17, 1712]

Bar, To pitch over the : to discard as no longer of use. [Sir Thos. Overbury, *Characters: A Meere Pettyfogger* (1616)].

Bar, A trial at : a trial before a full bench of judges.

Bar sinister, A : a device in heraldry ; erroneously considered an indication of illegitimate birth. Properly the bar drawn the reverse way, *i.e.*, from right to left.

Barabas, A : a thief. After the criminal who was pardoned on the occasion of the Crucifixion.

Barathron ; Barathrum : hell ; a deep pit. After a pit at Athens into which criminals were thrown.

Barbadoes Leg : a form of elephantiasis. After the island in the West Indies, where it is prevalent.

Barbarossa (*Lat.*, red-beard) : the Emperor Frederick I (1121-90). On account of his red beard.

Barbary : North Africa generally. Grk., *Barbaria*, land of *barbaroi* (foreigners).

Barbary Latin : uncultured Latin as distinguished from literary Latin. The Latin of the Roman colonies in N. Africa.

Barbecue, A : (*Haytian, barbacoa*, ' a framework of sticks set upon posts.' E. B. Tylor). (1) a frame for roasting or drying large joints of meat ; (2) an animal roasted whole ; (3) an open-air entertainment at which animals are roasted whole ; (4) the wooden framework of a bed.

Barber Poet, The : Jacques Jaomin (1798-1864), Provençal poet who was also a barber.

Barber-shop, Forfeits in a : barber-shops were formerly places of popular resort ; and, in order to preserve order among the company, forfeits were inflicted. [Shakespeare, *Measure for Measure*, II, ii (?1603)]

Barber's chair, As common as a : which was proverbial for giving accommodation to anybody.

Barber's news, As true as : untrustworthy. Barbers' shops have, since Roman times, been the centres of gossip and rumour. [Middleton, *The Roaring Girle*, III, iii (1611)]

Bard of all times, The : William Shakespeare (1564-1616).

Bard of Avon, The : William Shakespeare (1564-1616), born at Stratford-on-Avon.

Bard of Ayrshire, The : Robert Burns (1759-96), born at Alloway in Ayrshire.

Bard of Hope, The : Thomas Campbell (1777-1844), author of *The Pleasures of Hope*.

Bard of the Imagination, The : Mark Akenside (1721-70), author of *Pleasures of the Imagination*.

Bard of Memory, The : Samuel Rogers (1763-1855), author of *The Pleasures of Memory*.

Bard of Olney, The : William Cowper (1731-1800), who lived at Olney, Bucks.

Bard of Prose, The : Giovanni Boccaccio (1313-75), author of *The Decameron*.

Bard of Rydal Mount, The : William Wordsworth (1770-1850), who lived at Rydal Mount, near Grasmere.

Bard of Twickenham, The : Alexander Pope (1688-1744), who lived at Twickenham, on the Thames.

Bare as one's nail, As : penniless. [Fulwell, *Like Will to Like* (1568)]

Bare Poles : a man at the end of his resources. From a sailing-vessel in a gale sailing under bare masts.

Barebones Parliament : Cromwell's ' Little Parliament ' of 1653. After one of its prominent members, Praisegod Barebones (Barbon).

Bargain, A wet : a bargain sealed by the parties to it drinking together.

Bargain, Into the : in addition. [Dryden, *Sir Martin Marr-all*, II, i (1668)]

Bargain, To make the best of a bad : to reconcile oneself to ill-luck or misfortune and take whatever little advantage it may offer.

Bargain, To sell a : to return a coarse answer.

Bargain, To strike a : to come to an agreement. [Bp. Hall, *Cases of Conscience* (1650)]. From the practice of striking or shaking hands on the conclusion of a bargain.

Bargains for, More than one : more than one has expected.

Bargain-penny : money in part payment when a bargain is made.

Bargain-Saturday, A : a day appointed for the hiring of servants at fairs.

Bark and flee, To : to hasten to ruin.

Bark and the tree, To put the hand between the : to interfere in matters which do not concern one, esp. between husband and wife. [Lyly, *Euphues and his England* (1580) ; John Heywood, *Proverbes* (1546)]

Bark at the moon, To : (1) to labour in vain ; (2) to speak ill of one's superiors. [*Paston Letters*, No. 296 (1456)]

Bark to be worse than the bite, The : said of a person prone to ill-speaking but not ill-doing.

Bark up the wrong tree, To : to strive towards a mistaken object ; to adopt means unlikely to attain to the desired end. Based on an American racoon-hunting anecdote.

Barker, A : a pistol ; which ' barks ' when it is fired.

Barker's knee, As stiff as : after one Barker, who rashly declared that he did not believe in the existence of knockers (sprites that haunt the tin-mines of Cornwall). He was waylaid by knockers as a punishment and permanently injured.

Barkis is willin' : a phrase used to denote willingness to agree if asked to do so. It was the repeated message of Barkis, a character in Dickens, *David Copperfield* (1849), in offering marriage to Peggotty.

Barkshire : Ireland. From Bark, an Irishman.

Barley-bree : strong ale.

Barley in a brulzie, To cry : to ask for a truce. The phrase is derived from children's games in Scotland.

Barley-cap, A : a tippler ; one into whose head barley-bree has risen.

Barleycorn, John : (1) the personification of malt liquor ; hence (2) an inn-keeper. From the song *Sir John Barleycorn* (1651).

Barmecide, A : one who arouses one's expectations without satisfying them.

Barmecide's Feast : an empty meal or illusory benefit. One of the Barmecides (rulers of Bagdad) is said to have invited a beggar to a banquet, the dishes at which were without exception empty when the covers were removed. [*The Barber's Sixth Brother* in *The Arabian Nights*]

Barmy : slightly insane. A corruption of St. Bartholomew, the Patron Saint of the insane. *See also* Balmy ; Balmy-stick.

Barnaby thistle, A : a thistle which flowers about the 11th of June, St. Barnabas' Day.

Barnaby-bright : St. Barnabas' Day, June 11th, according to the Old Style, the longest day.

Barnacle, A : (1) a species of Arctic goose ; (2) a shell-fish which attaches itself to the bottom of a ship or other object floating on the sea ; hence (3) a person who attaches himself to another against his wish, or a man who clings to office although no longer serving a useful purpose. The barnacle-goose was popularly supposed, on account of the similarity of the name, to be produced out of the shell fish. [Dekker and Webster, *Northward Ho*, III, i (1607)]

Barnacle Tite, A : an official steeped in forms and precedents and bound round with red tape. After a character in Dickens, *Little Dorrit* (1855).

Barnburners, The : the Radical wing of the Democratic Party in New York in the middle of the 19th cent. Originally the participants in the " Dorr Rebellion " of 1842 who were accused of burning barns and other offences.

Barnstormer, A : a second-rate travelling actor. Dates back to the time when travelling companies often gave their performances in barns.

Barnumese : an exaggerated journalistic style. After Phineas Taylor Barnum (1810-91), American showman.

Baron of Beef, A : the two sirloins joined by the end of the backbone.

Barragouin : gibberish. Breton, *bara*, bread and *gwenn*, white. On account of the surprise expressed by Breton soldiers at seeing white bread. [Sir Thos. Overbury, *Characters : A Meere Common Lawyer* (1616)]

Barratron (um) : *see* Barathron.

Barrell's Blues : the King's Own (Royal Lancaster) Regiment form. the 4th Foot. After William Barrell, their colonel (1734-9), and the colour of their facings.

Barrier Treaty, A : a treaty fixing national boundaries ; esp. the treaty of 1715 between Austria, Gt. Britain and the Netherlands, fixing the boundary between the first and third of these Powers.

Barriers, To fight at : to fight within lists. [Lyly, *Euphues and His England* (1580)]

Bartholomew Baby (doll), A : (1) a doll (2) an overdressed woman. From Bartholomew Fair at West Smithfield at which these dolls were sold.

Bartholomew Pig, A : a fat person. After the roast pigs that were sold at Bartholomew Fair.

Bartholomew, A Saint : a massacre of heretics or nonconformists to the prevalent faith. After the massacre of the French Huguenots which commenced on St. Bartholomew's Day in 1572.

Bartholomew's Day : 24th August, the festival in honour of the Apostle Bartholomew. In England celebrated by a great fair at West Smithfield, from 1133 to 1855.

Bartholomew-tide : Bartholomew's Day.

Bartolist, A : a learned French lawyer. After Bartole (1313-56), an Italian jurist with a great reputation among French lawyers.

Bas Bleu, A (*Fr.*) : a Bluestocking (*q.v.*).

Base, To bid a : to run away while encouraging pursuit. From the rustic game ' base ' or ' prisoners'-base.'

Bashaw, A Three-tailed (*Arabic, pasha*, a high official) : a Turkish Pasha of high rank, bearing three horse-tails on his standard.

Bashi-Bazouk (*Turk.*, one whose head is turned) : (1) a Turkish irregular soldier ; (2) a ruffian ; from the atrocities committed by Bashi-Bazouks.

Basilisco, A : a braggart. After a character in *Solyman and Perseda* (1599).

Basilisco-proof : shameless, unabashed. From the basilisco (basilisk), a fabulous reptile, whose mere look was fatal to the beholder.

Baskerville, A : an edition of a book printed by John Baskerville (1706-75), a Birmingham printer.

Basket, To be left in the : not to be selected ; like the worst of the apples.

Basket to .. To give a : to refuse to marry. From the German practice of fixing a basket on the house of a rejected lover.

Bason, To beat the : to attract attention to another's disgrace. From the practice of the mob in preceding a cart containing criminals and other bad characters and beating basins, etc., in order to attract a still larger crowd.

Baste a person's jacket, To : to thrash him.

Bastille, A : a State prison in which political prisoners are incarcerated. After the French State-prison, which

was attacked by the mob at the outbreak of the French Revolution. In English use in 14th cent.

Bastinado (*Span., bastonada*) : punishment of beating on the soles of the feet, practised by the Chinese, Turks, Persians, etc.

Bat, Off one's own : by one's own sole exertions ; without assistance. A cricket metaphor.

Bat, To carry one's : to be still ' in,' *i.e*, undismissed, when the innings is brought to a conclusion ; to succeed in an undertaking by tiring out all opposition. A cricket metaphor.

Bat, As warm as a : bat in South Staffordshire is that slaty coal which will not burn.

Bat-fowling : swindling. [Dekker and Webster, *Westward Ho*, V, iii (1607)]

Bate, Clean at the : at loggerheads. [R. Wever, *Lusty Juventus*, I, 480 (c. 1560)]

Bath ! Go to : an exclamation of dismissal addressed to people who behave foolishly. From the former practice of sending insane people to Bath for the benefit of their health.

Bath, Order of the : a British Order of knighthood, derived from the ceremonial bath formerly taken before the conferment of the honour. Instituted 1399.

Bath of Blood, The : (1) the massacre of the Huguenots at Vassy in France, in 1562, by order of the Duke of Guise ; (2) the massacre of seventy Swedish nobles, in 1520, by order of Christian II of Denmark.

Bath, The King of : Richard Nash (Beau Nash) (1674-1761), for many years Master of Ceremonies at Bath and a typical ' buck.'

Bath, The Maid of : Miss Linley, who afterwards married Sheridan (1751-1816).

Bathing to steal clothes, To catch : see Whigs.

Batrachomyomachia (*Grk.*, battle of the frogs and mice) : much excitement over a trivial matter. From the title of an early Greek mock-heroic poem.

Battels : college-accounts, esp. for food. University of Oxford.

Batter-fanged : beaten ; torn with the nails. [Taylor, *Works* (1630)]

Battersea to be cut for the simples, To go to : addressed to a stupid person. The London apprentices used formerly to make an excursion to Battersea to see the medicinal herbs (simples) cut by the market-gardeners of the neighbourhood.

Battle of the Books, A : a controversy between literary men. After the title of a satire by Swift (1697).

Battle of Flowers, A : an incident in many Carnivals, in which the participants pelt one another with flowers.

Battle of the Frogs and Mice : see Batrachomyomachia.

Battle of the Giants, The : the Battle of Marignano (1515), between Francis I of France and the Swiss under the Duke of Milan. Because on both sides there were mighty men of valour, who fought like giants.

Battle, Half the : the greater or more difficult part of an undertaking.

Battle of the Nations, The : the Battle of Leipzig (Oct. 16-19, 1813), in which French, Prussians, Austrians, Russians, Swedes, Saxons, etc., took part.

Battle of the Three Emperors, The : Austerlitz (Dec. 2, 1805), in which Napoleon, the Emperor of Russia, and the Emperor of Austria took part.

Battles over again, To fight one's : to narrate one's exploits to an admiring circle. [Sophocles, *Antigone*, ll. 1286-8]

Battle royal, A : a free fight, in which more than two combatants are engaged. Originally a cock-fighting term.

Battle, The British Soldiers' : the Battle of Inkerman (Nov. 5, 1854), in which, in consequence of the disorder, the soldiers had to fight for the most part deprived of the leadership of their officers.

Battle-born State, The : Nevada, which was admitted into the Union in the midst of the American Civil War.

Battledore, To say Bee to a : see Bee.

Baubee : see Bawbee.

Bauble, To deserve the : to act very foolishly. After the bauble, the emblem of office of the professional fool.

Bavius, A : an incompetent poet. From *The Baviad*, a satire on the poetry of the Della Cruscan School (*q.v.*) by William Gifford (1756-1826). Also the name of two Roman poets who were immortalized on account of their bad verses by Virgil and Horace, respectively.

Bawbee, A : a halfpenny. Originally a Scotch coin of the value of a halfpenny. Probably derived from an early mint-master, the Laird of Sillebawby.

Bawcock, A : a good fellow. Possibl from Fr., *beau coq*, fine cock, or fror boy and cock. [Shakespeare, *Henry V* III, ii (1599)]

Bawtry who was hanged for leaving hi liquor, Like the saddler of : criminals o the way to execution were accustome to stop at a tavern in York to partak of a parting draught. According to Yorkshire proverb a saddler of Bawtr declined to do so and in consequenc failed to escape hanging. A shor delay would have enabled his repriev to arrive in time.

Bay : fame and glory. From the wreat of bay-leaves placed on the head of victor.

Bay State, The : Massachusetts. Afte the original name of the colony Massachusetts Bay.

Bay, To wear the : to be the recipient o honour. see Bay.

Bays, The Queen's : the 2nd Dragoo Guards. From the colour of thei horses.

Bayard, A : (1) a man of courage an honour, after the Chevalier d Bayard, ' sans peur et sans reproche (1473-1524) ; (2) a valuable horse after Baiardo, Rinaldo's horse, i Ariosto, *Orlando Furioso* (1516).

Bayard, As bold as blind : of a perso who acts hastily and without du consideration. [Langland, *Pier Plowman* (1362) ; Chaucer, *Canon' Yeoman's Tale*, Pt. II (14th cent.)]

Bayard of the Confederate Army, The Robert Lee (1807-70).

Bayard in the stable, To keep : to kee close guard over one's valuables [John Heywood, *Proverbes* (1546)]

Bayard of the East, The : Sir Jame Outram (1803-63).

Bayard of India, The : Sir James Out ram (1803-63), so-called by Sir Charle Napier.

Bayard of ten toes, To ride : to go on foot

Bayard of the Indian Army, The : Si James Outram (1803-63).

Bayard of Nations, The : Poland.

Bayard, The British : Sir Philip Sidne (1554-84).

Bayard, The Polish : Prince Josep Poniatowski (1763-1814).

Bayard's bun : bread given to horses After Bayard, the horse. Se Bayard (2).

Bay-leaf eater, A : a poet. See Bay To wear the. [Dekker and Webster *Northward Ho*, V, i (1607)]

Bayonet, A : a blade attached to a rifle. From (1) Bayonne, in France, where bayonets were first made ; (2) Bayonnetta, in the Basque province, whose troops improvised them in the course of a battle in 1647.

Bayou State, The : Mississippi. From the number of bayous or marshy creeks along its coast.

Bayreuth Festival : the musical festival held annually at Bayreuth for the representation of Wagner's operas.

Bayreuth Hush : intense silence. From the silence that precedes the opening of a Wagner Festival at the Bayreuth Opera House.

B.C., Marked with : dismissed from the Army with a ' bad character.' From the mark formerly set against a soldier's record in such circumstances.

Beachcomber, A : in Australasia, a vagrant who lives on the sea-shore ; earlier, a European settler on one of the Pacific Islands ; still earlier, a pirate.

Bead on .., To draw a : to attack. Orig., to fire at, the foresight of many rifles being of the ' bead ' pattern.

Bead, To raise a : to bring to the point ; to assure success. Metaphor drawn from strong spirits which will not ' raise a bead ' unless of sufficient strength.

Beads, St. Martin's : *see* St. Martin's Beads.

Beads, To bid : to count the beads on a rosary. Originally, to say prayers. *See* Bead roll.

Beads, To count one's : to say one's prayers. From the Roman Catholic practice of telling beads while at prayer.

Beads, To pray without one's : to lose one's bearings.

Bead-folks : pensioners who offer prayers on behalf of their benefactors. *See* Bead-roll. [*Interlude of Calisto and Meliboea* (1530)]

Bead-roll, A : a list of persons ; originally of persons to be prayed for. Saxon *bead* or *bede*, a prayer.

Beadsman, A : one who prays for another ; a pensioner ; an inmate of an almshouse. *See* Bead-roll.

Beak, A : a magistrate. From the *beag* (gold collar) worn by that officer, Formerly the same word was used for a constable.

Beam in one's eye, To have a : to have a fault in one's own character ignored in one's desire to discover a much smaller fault (a *mote*, speck) in another's. [Cf. *Matthew*, vii, 3]

Beam, To kick the : to be wholly outweighed. Properly, of one scale of a balance being so lightly loaded that it flies up and strikes the beam of the balance.

Beam-ends, To be thrown on one's : to be reduced to one's last resource. A nautical metaphor.

Bean for .., Not to care a : to hold as of next to no account. Owing to the small value of a bean. [1297]

Bean in the cake, A : a means of choosing the king in Twelfth Day festivities.

Bean in the cake, To find the : to gain an unexpected prize.

Beans are in flower, The : a suggested explanation of a person's stupidity. It was formerly believed that the scent of the flowering bean induced stupidity in the recipient of it.

Beans, Full of : in good condition, like a horse fed on beans.

Beans go to make five, To know how many : to be mentally very alert, ' wide-awake,' ' up to snuff.' From the former practice of using beans when counting.

Beans in a blue bladder, Three blue : one who talks much but displays little sense. Possibly from a jester's bladder ornamented with peas or beans. It has also been suggested that blue beans (small bullets) in a bladder make a great rattling noise without serving any useful purpose.

Beans in the wind, To sow : to labour to no purpose. [*The Marriage of Witt and Science* (1569-70)]

Beans, To abstain from: not to meddle in politics, ' for in the old times the election of magistrates was made by the pulling of beans.' [*See* Lyly, *Euphues* (1579)]

Beans, To give a person : to punish a person. From the French proverb, ' If he gives me peas I will give him beans,' *i.e.*, more punishment than he gives me.

Beanfeast, A : an annual excursion provided for workers by their employer, usually a festival of a somewhat vulgar character. A bean-goose used invariably to form one of the dishes at a beanfeast. Another origin is derived from Daniel Day, a Wapping pumpmaker of the 18th cent., who on one day in the year used to offer all-comers a hearty meal of beans and bacon beneath the great oak at Fairlop, then a part of Epping Forest.

Bear, A : a gruff, ill-tempered person, resembling in manners the quadruped.

Bear and Bull (Stock Exchange terms) : the bear is one who speculates for a fall in prices ; the bull, for a rise. From the proverb of selling the skin of a bear before he is caught. [Jas. Puckle, *The Club : Knave* (1711)]

Bear by the Tooth, To take a : to take foolhardy risks. [Martial, *Epigrams*, Bk. VII, 11, 27-8]

Bear State, The : Arkansas ; formerly noted for the number of its bears.

Bear the bell, To : to be successful. From the now obsolete practice of awarding the bell to the victor in a race. [Heywood, *Proverbs* (1546)]

Bear the market, To : to depress the value of shares for the purpose of buying them cheap. *See* Bear and Bull.

Bear, The (Northern) : Russia. From its cognizance.

Bear-garden, A : a place of disorder and strife. Orig., a place set apart for bear-baiting and other rough sports.

Bear-garden, To speak : to use bad language ; in allusion to the language used at bear-baiting.

Bear-leader, A : a tutor and companion of a boy whose education and manners need polishing.

Beard a person, To : to face and oppose a person openly. From the idea of seizing him by the beard. [Shakespeare, *1 Henry IV*, IV, i (1596)]

Beard ablaze, To put a person's : to arouse a person's wrath.

Beard on shoulder, To have a : to be listening with a view to overhearing.

Beard the lion, To : *see* Beard, To ; to attack an esp. powerful opponent.

Beard, To laugh at one's : to endeavour to make a person ridiculous.

Beard, To laugh in one's : to laugh to oneself at having fooled a person.

Beard, To make a person's : to have a person at one's mercy.

Beard, To put in a person's : to charge a person with. [*Paston Letters*, No. 483 (1464)]

Beard, To run in a person's : to oppose a person to his face.

Beards, To wag : to feast. [*Life of Alexander* (1312)]

Bearded Master, The : Socrates (468-399 B.C.) ; so-called by Persius, the Roman poet.

Beardsleyism, A : a pictorial illustration in black-and-white in the style of Aubrey Vincent Beardsley (1872-98)

Bearings, To bring to : to bring a person to reason. A nautical metaphor.

Bearings, To lose one's : to become bewildered. A nautical metaphor.

Bearings, To take one's : to consider the position in which one finds oneself. A nautical metaphor.

Béarnais, The : Henri IV of France. From Béarn, the province in which he was born.

Beast, The : the Roman Catholic Church ; the Anti-Christ in the *Apocalypse* of St. John.

Beast, The mark of the : *see* Mark.

Beast, The number of the : *see* Apocalyptic Number.

Beat a retreat, To : to withdraw from a situation. A military metaphor.

Beat about the bush, To : to approach a subject with hesitation, and apparent desire to avoid the main issue. A sporting metaphor. [Robert Whittington, *Vulgaria*, I (1520)]

Beat the air, To : to strive or work uselessly. A pugilistic metaphor [*I Corinthians*, ix, 26 ; Bacon, *Essayes : Of Despatch* (1625)]

Beat the bounds, To : to trace the bounds of a parish by beating the landmark with willow wands on Ascension Day ; an old custom.

Beat the dog before the lion, To : to punish a person of lesser degree in the presence of and in order to intimidate one of greater. From the French proverb, ' Battre le chien devant le lion.' [Chaucer, *Squire's Tale*, Pt. II (?1393)]

Beat the Dutch, To : *see* Dutch, To beat the.

Beat a person with his own staff (rod), To : to refute a person out of his own mouth. [Heywood, *Proverbs* (1546)]

Beat the record, To : to exceed all forerunners. [Prynne, *Histrio-Mastix* (1599)]

Beat the same ivy bush, To : to make the same boasts ; to play the same game as another. [Dekker, *The Gull's Hornbook*, ch. 7 (1609)]

Beaten gold and ivory, To be all : to be super-excellent.

Beaten track, The : the conventional course.

Beati possidentes (*Lat.*, Happy are those in possession) : a contraction of the legal phrase *Beati in jure consentiuntur* *possidentes*. It is generally agreed that those in possession are happy in law. The phrase was applied by Bismarck to the Christian provinces of Turkey, esp. Bosnia and Herzegovina, after the Russo-Turkish War.

Beau, A (*Fr.*, handsome) : a dandy ; a man who devotes special attention to his attire ; a male lover. [In English use in 14th cent.]

Beau Brummel, A : a dandy. After George Bryan (1778-1840), (Beau Brummel), the greatest of the dandies and the leader of fashion in his day.

Beau ideal, The (*Fr.*, the ideally beautiful) : the highest type of excellence.

Beau monde (*Fr.*, beautiful world) : the fashionable world. [Wycherley, *Gentleman Dancing-master* (1659)]

Beau Nash : Richard Nash (1674-1761), ' The King of Bath,' an English leader of fashion in his day.

Beau Sabreur, Le (*Fr.*, the Handsome Swordsman) : Joachim Murat, one of Napoleon's marshals and afterwards King of Naples (1767-1815), famous as a cavalry leader.

Beauchamp, As bold as : from the proverbial bravery of the Beauchamps, Earls of Warwick ; or from that of Thomas, the first earl in particular, who in 1346 with the assistance of a squire and six archers defeated a hundred Normans. A play, *The Three Bold Beauchamps*, was published about 1610 and *Bold Beauchamp* was the title of one of the lost plays of Thos. Heywood (d. 1650).

Beauclerc : Henry I of England. In acknowledgment of his scholarship.

Beaumontague : literary padding ; hack-work. From Emile Beaumont (1798-1851), geologist, and Germ., *Teig*, dough.

Beauté du Diable (*Fr.*, beauty of the Devil) : a type of beauty that indicates ill-health or disease.

Beautiful Parricide, The : Beatrice Cenci (d. 1599), who is said to have justifiably murdered her father.

Beauty and the Beast : a couple of whom the woman is beautiful and the man ugly. After the title of Mme. Villeneuve's fairy tale (1740).

Beauty-sleep : sleep obtained before midnight, the most healthy period.

Beauty-spot, A : a patch placed on the face of a lady to act as a foil to her complexion.

Beaux esprits : plural of Bel esprit (*q.v.*).

Beaux yeux (*Fr.*, beautiful eyes) : attractive ' looks,' appearance.

Béchamel : a white sauce used in cookery. After the French inventor, the Marquis de Béchamel (d. 1703), steward to Louis XIV.

Beck and call, To be at a person's : to be within his absolute control, to have to dance attendance on him.

Becky Sharp, A : an unscrupulous, worldly young woman. After a character in Thackeray, *Vanity Fair* (1847).

Bed and board : full connubial relations. [*York Manual* (1403)]

Bed of down, A : an easy, pleasant situation. [Shakespeare, *Othello*, I, iii (?1604) ; Sir Thos. Wyatt, *How to Use the Court* (1557)]

Bed of Justice : a meeting of the French Parliament under the presidency of the king. From the pile of cushions which originally formed the royal seat.

Bed of roses, A : a pleasant situation.

Bed of thorns, A : an unpleasant situation. [Thos. Watson, *Aurora Now Began to Rise Again* (1593)]

Bed the wrong side (with the left foot or leg foremost), To get out of : to be in a bad temper. From the superstition that it is unlucky to put the left foot first to the ground on getting out of bed. [John Still, *Gammer Gurton's Needle*, II, i (1566)]

Bed-post, Between you and me and the : between ourselves, to the exclusion of others ; strictly, privately.

Bed-post, In the twinkling of a : instantaneously. Previously, ' in the twinkling of a bedstaff.' The bedstaff was used to keep the clothes on the bed, and also served as a substitute for a rapier in fencing. [Colman, *Heir at Law* (1808)]

Bed-rock : the ultimate basis ; the end of one's resources. A mining metaphor.

Bedfordshire, To go to : to go to bed. A pun.

Bedlam, A : a lunatic-asylum ; an uproar. After the Hospital of St. Mary of Bethlehem (Bedlam) in London, a lunatic-asylum.

Bedlam beggars : discharged incompletely-cured inmates of Bethlehem (Bedlam) Hospital, licensed to beg in the streets from passers-by.

Bedlam, Bess o' : *see* Tom o' Bedlam.

Bedlamite, A : one who is, or ought to be, an inmate of a lunatic-asylum.

Bee, A Spelling : a party engaged in a spelling-game. Bee in the (Amer.) sense of a gathering of people, a ' swarm ' of bees. *See* Swarm.

Bee in one's bonnet, To have a : to have a craze on some definite subject ; to be slightly unhinged in mind ; to be of a choleric disposition. *See* Bees in the head.

Bee of Athens (Attica), The ; The Athenian (Attic) Bee : (1) Plato (c. 427-347 B.C.), a native of Athens, in allusion to the sweetness of his style ; (2) Sophocles (496-405 B.C.), a native of Athens ; (3) Xenophon (444-350 B.C.)

Bee of Hymettus, The : *see* Bee of Athens.

Bee to a battledore, To say : to have at least an elementary knowledge. A battledore was a cardboard book used for teaching young children in the earlier half of the 19th cent.

Bee-line, In a : direct ; following the straight line which a bee is reputed to take when returning home. Of Amer. origin.

Bees, In the : confused.

Bees in the head, To have : to be of a choleric disposition, *i.e.*, to have that in the head which is easily provoked. [Gawin Douglas, *Æneis*, VIII (1512)]

Bees of Hybla : *see* Hybla.

Beef nor brose of mine, Neither : no concern of mine. Brose is, in Scotland, a porridge made by pouring boiling water over oatmeal.

Beefeater, A : a yeoman of the guard. From buffeter, in the sense of a menial servant, or the beefeater, a bird whose strong thick bill bore some resemblance to their arms.

Beelzebub : the Devil. From the name of the God of Flies, one of the heathen gods mentioned in II *Kings*. In Milton, *Paradise Lost*, it is the name of one of the fallen angels.

Beelzebub to cast out Satan, To call in : to employ one evil to neutralize another.

Beer and Bible : the Conservative Party (according to their opponents) from 1873 onwards. In that year the party which had always included a number of religious leaders, received an accession of strength from the brewing interest, which took serious objection to legislation proposed by the Liberal Government.

Beer and skittles : all that one could desire ; the height of pleasure. A public-house metaphor.

Beer, To chronicle small : to write (talk about trivialities. [Peter Pinda: *The Remonstrance : Ode to My As* (1791) ; Shakespeare, *Othello*, II, : (?1604)]

Beer of . . To think small : to have (poor opinion of . . Small beer is wea: beer. [Shakespeare, *Othello*, II, (?1604)]

Beer-money : money paid to a servan: in lieu of an allowance of beer ; a tip

Beerage, The : the brewer-peers. A: artificial word modelled on ' peerage.

Beerocracy : the class of wealth: brewers. An artificial word modelle(on ' aristocracy.'

Beersheba, Dan to : *see* Dan.

Beetle, As quick as a : very slow.

Beetle-browed : having heavy, darl eyebrows. An allusion to the insect [14th cent.]

Beetle-crusher, A : a large, flat foot [First used in *Punch* by John Leech.]

Befana, The : in Ital. folklore, a sort o: combination of the Wandering Jew and Santa Claus. An old woman who was too busily employed in domestic work to go to the window to see the Three Wise Men of the East pass on their way to greet the Infant Jesus, and has been awaiting their return ever since. On Twelfth Night she acts as a sort of Santa Claus. A corruption of Epiphany (Twelfth Night).

Before the lights : on the stage. A theatrical phrase.

Before the mast, To serve : to be a member of the ordinary crew of a vessel whose quarters are in the forecastle, before the mast.

Beg : a Turkish governor ; a bey.

Beg the question, To : to assume the conclusion without proving it. The phrase in its Grk. equivalent was first used by Aristotle.

Begbie murder, A : an unsolved mystery or problem. After the mysterious murder and robbery of William Begbie, a bank manager, in Edinburgh, on the 13th Nov., 1806.

Beggar description, To : to exhaust the powers of description. [Shakespeare, *Anthony and Cleopatra*, II, ii (?1606)]

Beggar on horseback, A : an upstart ; a person suddenly raised in social status and rendered giddy by his promotion. From the Germ. proverb, ' Set a beggar on horseback and he'll outride the Devil.' [Burton, *Anatomy of*

Melancholy, Pt. II, Sect. II, Memb. 2 : ' Set a beggar on horseback and he will ride a gallop ' (1621)]

Beggar to his dish, As true to one as the : From the clap-dish, the beggar's receptacle for alms.

Beggar's brown : Scotch snuff.

Beggars' Bush, To go by : to proceed to ruin. The Beggars' Bush was a tree on the road between Huntingdon and Caxton, which formed a rendezvous for beggars. [Robert Greene, *Quip for an Upstart Courtier* (1592)]

Beggars of the Sea : Dutch privateers who preyed on Span. commerce in the latter part of the 16th cent.

Beggars, The Wild : Dutch revolutionary brigands active in the latter half of the 16th cent.

Beghard, A : a member of a lay religious Order ; from Lambert de Bègue (d. 1187), the founder, a priest of Liége. *See* Beguine.

Begonia : a species of ornamental plant ; from Michel Begon (1638-1710).

Beguine, A : a female member of a continental lay Order ; *see* Beghard.

Bejan : a freshman. From *Fr.*, *bec jaune*, a yellow-beak, a young bird. Scot. and Fr. Universities.

Bel Anglais, Le (*Fr.*, the handsome Englishman) : the Duke of Marlborough (1650-1722).

Bel esprit, A (*Fr.*, a fine spirit) : a man of brilliant intellect ; a wit.

Bel's two fires, Between : between alternate difficulties. In allusion to the two fires kindled in Irish villages on the eve of the 1st of May between which all devoted to sacrifice had to pass.

Belcher, A : a neckerchief with white or coloured spots. After James Belcher (1781-1811), Eng. pugilist, by whom a neckerchief consisting of white spots on a dark-blue ground was introduced.

Belial, A son (man) of : an evil man. A Biblical phrase denoting a son of evil. The name Belial was given by Milton in *Paradise Lost* to one of the fallen angels. [II *Samuel*, xvi, 7]

Belisarius, A : a great general, hero of his army. After the Roman General of that name (c. 505-65).

Belisarius, To play : to act the beggar. From the Latin proverb,' *Date obolum Belisario* ' (Give an obolus or small coin to Belisarius). Belisarius (c. 505-65), Commander-in-Chief of the army in the East under Justinian, being

accused of conspiracy, forfeited his rank and fortune. According to a doubtful tradition he lost also his sight and was reduced to beggary, so that he had to beg for pennies at the gate of Rome.

Bell, Book and Candle, To curse by : a form of excommunication in the Roman Catholic Church. The Bell called the attention of the public to the forthcoming announcement ; the Book contained the sentence that was pronounced ; the Candle was extinguished to symbolize the spiritual darkness of the object of the curse. The concluding lines of the formula were : ' Cursed be they from the crown of the head to the sole of the foot. Out be they taken from the Book of Life (at this point the priest closed the book), and as this candle is cast from the sight of men, so be their souls cast from the sight of God into the deepest pit of hell (at this point a lighted candle is cast to the ground). Amen.' Then the bells were rung in discord to signify the passing of the souls of the excommunicated persons out of grace.

Bell the cat, To : to undertake a dangerous task. From La Fontaine's fable of the mice appointing one of themselves to put a bell on the cat. The phrase was coined by the 5th Earl of Angus (c. 1449-1514) when in a company of Scot. nobles he offered to face their common enemy, the Earl of Mar. [Heywood, *Proverbes* (1546)]

Bell, The Passing : a church-bell tolled to announce a death. Orig. the bell that was rung when a person was dying in order to scare away the evil spirits that were supposed to be waiting for his soul. It also served the purpose of summoning all good Christians to pray for the admission of his soul into paradise.

Bell, To bear the : *see* Bear.

Bell, To lose the : to be defeated. From the medieval practice of presenting a bell as a prize to the victor in a race.

Bells and let her fly, To give the : to make the best of a misfortune and not to attempt hopelessly to reverse it. A hawking metaphor. When a hawk was worthless the bells were taken off and it was allowed to escape.

Bells backwards, To ring the : to ring a muffled peal as a sign of mourning. In earlier times the bells were rung backwards to sound the alarm.

Bells on one horse, To have all one's : to leave all of one's property to one child.

Bell-wavering : inconstancy (Scottish).

Bellarmine, A : a jug with the face of a man on it made at Cologne. After Card. Robert Bellarmino, the opponent of the Protestants (1542-1621).

Belle, A (*Fr.*, beautiful) : a good-looking young woman, esp. one who dresses to enhance her charms.

Belle of the ball, The : the centre of attraction at a dance.

Belle Passion, La (*Fr.*, the beautiful passion) : passionate love.

Bellerophon, Letters of : documents which are a source of danger to those who hold them. From the letter sent with Bellerophon to the King of Lycia ordering the latter to have the bearer put to death.

Belles Lettres (*Fr.*, fine literature) : literature in which regard to style is given prominent consideration.

Bellibone, A : a good-looking girl. A corruption of *belle et bonne*. [Spenser, *Shepherd's Calendar* (1579)]

Bellona's handmaids : blood, fire and famine. Bellona was the Roman Goddess of War.

Belly god, A : a glutton ; one who worships his belly.

Belly-cheer : provisions. [Eliote's *Dictionarie* (1559)]

Belly-piece, A : an apron ; hence, a woman. [Shadwell, *Bury Fair* (1689); Randolph, *Jealous Lovers* (1646)]

Belly-timber : provisions. [*Terence in English* (1614)]

Beloved Disciple, The : St. John. [*John*, xiii, 23 *et seq.*]

Beloved Physician, The : St. Luke.

Below par : not in the best of health or condition. A metaphor drawn from the money-market with reference to securities below their nominal value (par).

Below stairs : among the servants.

Belt, To hit below the : to act unfairly ; from the language of the prize-ring.

Belt, To hold the : to champion ; to support. A pugilistic metaphor.

Beltane : May-day (in Scotland) ; June 2 (in Ireland). A festival celebrated by the extinguishing of all domestic fires and the lighting of bonfires, from which the domestic fires are re-kindled. Apparently a heathen survival from the period of fire-worship.

Ben, Big : *see* Big Ben.

Ben trovato (*Ital.*, well found) : well invented. The phrase is derived from the remark *Se non è vero, è ben trovato* (If it is not true, it is certainly well invented), attrib. to Hippolito, Card. d'Este (1479-1520), patron of learning, on the occasion of the dedication to him by Ariosto of his *Orlando Furioso* (1516).

Bench and bar : the body of judges and barristers. From the bench on which the former sit, and the bar that used to separate the latter from the public in Court.

Bench-whistler, A : an idler ; a loafer one who sits whistling on a bench.

Bend, Above one's : beyond one's power or capacity. In allusion to the bending power of a bow which, if exceeded leads to a break.

Bend, The Grecian : *see* Grecian.

Bend Sinister, To have a : to be of illegitimate birth. An allusion to the device in a coat of arms supposed to indicate bastardy.

Bendigo, A : a fur cap, similar to that worn by William Thompson (1811-80), Eng. pugilist, born at Bendigo Australia.

Benedicite (*Lat.*, bless ye) : a very brief grace before a meal ; invocation of a blessing.

Benedick, A : a newly-married man. After a character in Shakespeare, *Much Ado About Nothing* (1599).

Benedict, A : a bachelor. After St. Benedict, patron of celibates.

Benedictine : a liqueur, formerly made by the Benedictine monks at Fécamp France.

Benefit of Clergy : exemption of the clergy, and at one time of all who could read, from criminal proceedings before a secular Court.

Benevolence, A : a tax arbitrarily inflicted by the king. Introduced by Edward IV in 1473, as a suggested proof of loyalty to the king.

Bengal stripes : striped gingham. From Bengal, India, whence the material was exported in the 17th and 18th cents.

Bengal Tigers : the Leicester Regt. or 17th Foot, who, after approved service in India (1802-23) were given a tiger as a badge.

Benjamin : aromatic resin. A corruption of benzoin.

Benjamin, A : (1) a dark-blue or black long jacket, fitting close to the figure after one Benjamin, a sailors' tailor at Portsmouth, its inventor; (2) a favourite son; the youngest son. After the youngest son of Jacob.

enjamin's mess : the largest share. [*Genesis*, xliii, 34 : ' Benjamin's mess was five times so much as any of theirs']

ennett, To receive : to be tonsured as a priest. [*Paston Letters*, No. 286 (1479)]

ent, Out of one's : beyond one's powers.

ent, To the top of one's : as far as it is possible for one to go, as far as the bow can be bent without breaking. [Shakespeare, *Hamlet*, III, ii (1602)]

ent, To take the : to take the flight.

ent with Robin Bruce, To take the : to take to the open country ; to provide for one's safety.

enton's mint drops : gold coins of the U.S., esp. the smaller ones. After Thomas Hart Benton (1782-1858), mainly through whose influence in Congress gold became relatively common as currency.

ergæan, A : a great liar. From Antiphanes of Berga, Grk. fabulist.

ergaize, To : to tell incredible stories.

ergamot, A : a species of orange ; the perfume obtained therefrom ; a coarse tapestry. From Bergamo, a town in Italy ; or from Turk., *beg-armudi*, prince's pear.

ergen-op-zoom, A : a dunce, a person impermeable to impressions derived from reading. From the successful defence of the Dutch town of that name against all attacks in 1588, 1605, 1622 and 1814. [De Quincey (1785-1859), *Collected Writings*, iii, 93]

erlin, A : a closed carriage with a seat and a hood behind. After the capital of Germany.

erlin wool : a wool used for fancywork. After the capital of Germany.

ermudas : a tobacco. After the Bermuda Isles in the North Atlantic, whence the tobacco was orig. obtained.

ermudas, To live in : to live in hiding. After Bermudas, a term applied to the alleys and courts in the neighbourhood of Covent Garden, London, in the early 17th cent., where debtors and others who wished to conceal themselves hid. The name was derived from the Bermuda Isles, in which those who wished to defraud their creditors settled.

ernesque poetry : serio-comic poetry. From Francesco Berni (1490-1536), Ital. poet.

Berserk rage : the martial frenzy of a soldier on the battlefield.

Berserker, A : a reckless hero ; a Viking hero. From the Scand. mythological hero, Berserk, who fought without armour. Icelandic, *berserkr*, bear-skin.

Berth, A good (bad) : a comfortable (uncomfortable) office or employment. A nautical metaphor.

Berth to .. To give a wide : to avoid. A nautical metaphor.

Bertillonism : anthropometry. From Alphonse Bertillon (1853-1914), French inventor of identification by measurement.

Bertolde, Imperturbable as : very imperturbable. After a character in a piece by J. Cesare Croce.

Berwick to Land's End, From : from one extreme limit to the other. Berwick-on-Tweed and Land's End mark the extremes of the kingdom of England.

Besant : *see* Bezant.

Besom, To hang out the : to enjoy oneself in the absence of one's wife. A besom, originally a birch, now means a broom.

Besom, To jump the : to live together as man and wife, without being married.

Besonio ; Besognio : *see* Bezonian.

Bespeak, A : a benefit-night at the theatre, when the play is chosen or bespoken by the person to benefit or by his friends.

Bessemer steel : steel made by the Bessemer process. After Sir Henry Bessemer (1813-98), the inventor.

Bess of Bedlam, A : a female vagrant lunatic. *See* Bedlam. There is an old chap-book entitled ' Bess of Bedlam's Garland.'

Best leg foremost, To put one's : *see* Leg.

Best of the matter, To make the : to face disappointment or misfortune courageously and take whatever slight benefit it may still offer. [Wm. Combe, *Tour of Dr. Syntax in Search of the Picturesque*, Canto xxvi (1812)]

Bête noire (*Fr.*, black beast) : a cause of annoyance. Apparently from a black sheep in a flock, always of less value than a white one and at times an object of superstitious aversion.

Bethel, A : a dissenting chapel ; in the U.S. a chapel for seamen. After Bethel, the House of God, a place-name and sanctuary in Biblical Palestine.

Bethel, A calf of : a Roman Catholic priest.

Bethel, A Little : a nonconformist place of worship.

Betonica ; Betony : a dye and a medicine, and the plant from which they are obtained. From the Vetones, a people of Spain, who are supposed to have discovered the plant.

Better days, To have seen : to be reduced in fortune. [Shakespeare, *As You Like It*, II, vii, l. 113 (1601) ; *Timon of Athens*, IV, ii, l. 27 (1607)]

Better, for worse, For : in all circumstances and conditions. A phrase employed in the Anglican marriage-service. [*Appius and Virginia*, l. 308 (1563)]

Better than one's word, To be : to exceed one's promise.

Better-half, The : a wife, man and wife being theoretically one. Originally applied to a close friend. [Sidney, *Arcadia*, Bk. III, l. 280 (1580)]. The idea is anticipated in an oriental story of a Bedouin whose wife pleaded for him in the following words : ' O great Prince . . . the blasphemy is horrible, I confess . . . but it is not my whole husband who has thus rendered himself guilty towards thee.' ' Not thy whole husband ? ' ' Nay,' she continued,' it is but the half of him that has committed the insult ; for am I not the other half—I who have never offended thee ? Now the guilty half places itself under the protection of the innocent half and the latter cannot suffer the former to be punished.' (*Percy Anecdotes*).

Better of a matter, To think : to revise one's opinion of a matter.

Better of . . To get the : to get the advantage of . .

Better off : in more comfortable circumstances.

Better oneself, To : to improve one's circumstances. [*The Return from Parnassus*, V, iii (1606)]

Better self, One's : one's husband or wife. [John Cooke, *Greene's Tu Quoque*, I, 1430 (1614)]

Better than one should be, To be no : (said of a woman) ; to be of doubtful virtue or reputation. [Beaumont and Fletcher, *The Coxcomb*, IV, iii (c. 1610)]

Betters, One's : one's social superiors. [Layamon, 3749 (1205)]

Betterment : increase in value of land and house-property as a consequence of public improvements. [First used in this sense in the U.S.]

Betty, A : a man who engages in fema pursuits.

Between ourselves (you and me) : spea ing confidentially. [Foote, *T Author*, I, i (1757) ; Goldsmith, *T Goodnatured Man*, IV, i (1768)]

Between you and me and the bed (gat post : speaking confidentially. [Pet Pindar, *Peter's Pension* (178-)]

Beulah, The Land of : *see* Land.

Bever : drink ; drinking time ; a ligl meal between breakfast and dinne Old Fr., *beivre*, to drink.

Bezant ; Byzant, A : a gold coin, (varying value, of the Eastern Empir and also of Europe until the 14t cent. From Byzantium, the capit: of the Eastern Empire.

Bezoar stone, A : a supposed antidot for poison. Bezoar stones are th round, hard concretions formed in th intestines of wild goats of masses (hair swallowed by them.

Bezonian, A : a young untrained soldier a needy person. From Ital. *bisogno* want. Applied first to badly clad an(accoutred Span. soldiers who lande(in Italy. [Middleton, *Blunt Maste Constable* (1602)]

Bezonian ? Under which king, : mak your choice of sides. [Shakespeare *2 Henry IV*, V, iii (1597-8)]

Bianchi and Neri (*Ital.*, whites an(blacks) : supporters of the House o Savoy and the Papal Tempora claims, respectively. The names o two factions in the Guelph Party.

Bible oath, A : an oath sworn upon th(Bible.

Bible of . . The : that which one hold: sacred and swears by.

Bible-backed : round-shouldered, like one much given to reading.

Bible-clerk, A : a scholar at Oxford whc reads lessons in chapel.

Bibliolatry : a superstitious worship of the Bible ; worship of books. Invented by S. T .Coleridge (1772-1834).

Biblion abiblion (*Grk.*, a book that is not a book) : ' Literature ' of the character of directories, railway-guides, etc., which possess no quality of books except in their appearance. The word was invented by Charles Lamb (1775-1834).

Bibulus, A : a cipher in office. After the colleague of Julius Cæsar.

Bickerstaff, Isaac : a name assumed by Jonathan Swift in his controversy with Partridge, the almanac-maker ;

adopted by Sir Richard Steele as his nom-de-plume in *The Tatler* (1709) ; and later by Benjamin West in his *Boston Almanac*.

Bid beads, To : to say prayers. *See* Beadsman, and Bidding Prayer.

Bid-ale, A : a benefit-entertainment for which a general invitation is issued, From bid, to invite, and ale, a festival.

Bidding-prayer, A : a prayer, esp. one for the repose of souls. Lit., a praying prayer, or perhaps one that the congregation is bidden to utter. *See* Beadsman.

Biddy (Bridget), A : a maid-servant, esp. in the U.S. where at one time most of the domestic servants were Irish.

Bideford Postman, The : Edward Capern (1819-94), postman and poet.

Bidet, A (*Fr.*, *bidet*, pony) : a post-horse, or small horse.

Bidri ; Bidree ; Biddry : a kind of damascening in metals. After Bidri, a city in the Deccan, India.

Bien-Aimé, Le (*Fr.*, the well-beloved) : Louis XV of France (1710-74).

Bien venu (*Fr.*) : welcome. Now almost obsolete in England.

Bienseance (*Fr.*) : proper behaviour. Now almost obsolete in England.

Bierbalk, A : the road by which a corpse has been carried to the churchyard, which was at one time popularly supposed to grant thereby a permanent right of way to the public.

Bierway, A : (in East Anglia), a bier-balk (*q.v.*).

Big as a bee's knee, As : of infinitesmally small size.

Big Beggarman, The : Daniel O'Connell (1775-1847). A nickname given to him by the Irish landlords.

Big Ben : the great bell in the clock-tower at Westminster. From Sir Benjamin Hall (1802-67), who was First Commissioner of Works when the bell was hung.

Big Bend State : Tennessee, which in one of the Indian languages is 'River of the Big Bend.'

Big bird, To get the : to be hissed off the stage. Theatrical slang.

Big Bo : a hobgoblin.

Big Gooseberry Season : the period after Parliament has risen when, in consequence of lack of news, the newspapers devote undue attention to topics such as the growth of giant gooseberries, the appearance of the sea-serpent, etc.

Big as a pin's head, As : very small. [J. Still, *Gammer Gurton's Needle*, I, v (1566)]

Big for one's shoes, To get too : to have become very conceited ; to ' have a swollen head.'

Big gun, A : a person of consequence.

Big Pot, A : a person of consequence.

Big, To speak (talk) : to boast.

Big-wig, A : an important official. A wig of large size was formerly worn by men of high rank or importance. [Ned Ward, *The English Spy* (1703)]

Biggin, A : a pot for making and serving coffee. After the name of the inventor who lived in the 18th-19th cents.

Biggin ; Biggen, A : a child's cap ; a night-cap. From Beguine (*q.v.*).

Bighes, To be in the : to be in an excellent humour. From bighes, women's ornaments.

Bike, A : a corrupt contraction of bicycle.

Bilbo, A : a sword of a fine temper. From Bilbao in Spain, where such swords were first made.

Bilboes : the irons used as manacles for sailors. From (1) Bilbao in Spain, where they were made ; or (2) the Bilboes, the windings of a river in Spain.

Bile, To rouse (stir) the : to enrage. The ancient view was that an excited bile caused anger.

Bilk, To : to cheat (esp. cabmen). A corruption of ' balk.' [Ben Jonson, *The Tale of a Tub*, I, i (1633)]

Bill and coo, To : to make love ; to show signs of mutual affection, like turtle-doves. [Dryden, *Amphitryon*, I, ii (1690)]

Bill, A true : a *prima facie* case against a person. Legal term.

Billet à La Châtre, A : a broken promise ; a promise to be broken. From the remark made by Ninon L'Enclos (1615-1705), Fr. wit and beauty, when, in the absence of the Marquis de la Châtre, she took to herself another lover : ' *Ah, le bon billet qu'a La Châtre !* ' (' Ah, the fine promise I made to La Châtre !).

Billet-doux, A (*Fr.*, sweet little letter) : a love-letter. [Vanbrugh, *The Provoked Wife*, IV, iv (1697)]

Billingsgate : foul language. From the fish-market at Billingsgate, notorious for the bad language in common use there. [Wycherley, *The Plain Dealer*, III (1677)]

Billingsgate pheasant, A : a red herring. From the fish-market at Billingsgate.

Billy Barlow, A : half-witted street fool. After a character in the East End of London (d. 1851).

Billycock (hat), A : a hard round felt hat. Formerly ' bully-cocked,' *i.e.*, cocked like a street bully. Another derivation is from William Coke of Holkham (1752-1842) who is said to have introduced them at his great shooting parties.

Bingham's Dandies : the 17th Lancers. After one of their colonels, Lord Bingham.

Birchin(g) Lane, To send to : to order to be punished. From Birchin Lane in the City of London, a pun on ' birch.' [Ascham, *The Schoolmaster* (1570)]

Bird in one's bosom, The : one's loyalty. From an expression used by Sir Ralph Percy, a Lancastrian, killed at the Battle of Hedgly Moor (1464).

Bird is flown, The : the person sought has escaped. [John Heywood, *Proverbes* (1546)]

Bird in the hand, A : a certainty, as compared with a possibility. From the proverb ' A bird in the hand is worth two in the bush.'

Bird of ill-omen, A : one supposed to bring ill-luck. In allusion to the ancient practice of augury by birds.

Bird of Juno, The : the peacock.

Bird of the night, The : the owl. [Shakespeare, *Julius Caesar*, I, ii (1601)]

Bird of passage, A : a sojourner ; one who, like the migratory birds, does not stay long anywhere.

Bird of Washington, The : the American eagle.

Bird, The Arabian : the phœnix.

Bird, To get the big : *see* Big Bird.

Bird told me, A little : a fictitious explanation of the source of knowledge. [*Ecclesiastes*, x, 20 : ' Curse not the king, no not in thy thought . . for a bird of the air shall carry the voice, and that which hath wings shall tell the matter.' Heywood, *Proverbes*, ' I hear by one bird that in mine ear was late chanting.']

Bird-spit, A : a sword. Lit., a spit for cooking birds on.

Bird-witted, To be : to be apparently incapable of mental concentration ; to flit from one subject to another, like a bird. [Bacon, *Advancement of Learning*, I, 7, §7 (1605)]

Bird's-eye view, A : a general view take from above, as seen by a bird (or from an aeroplane).

Bird's tail, As bare as a : stripped naked [*Terence in English* (1614)]

Birds of Diomedes : swans. From th legend that after the death of th legendary Grk. hero, Diomedes, h companions were changed by the god into swans.

Birds of a feather : people of simila character. Generally deprecatingly From the proverb, ' Birds of a feathe flock together.' [*Life and Death o Captain Thomas Stukeley*, I. 362 (1605)

Birds with one stone, To kill two : t attain two objects by one effort [Plautus, *Casina*, 476]

Birds' milk : *see* Pigeons' milk.

Birgham ! Go to : go away (emphatic ally). From Birgham in Scotlan where the nobles who betrayed thei country to Edward I were assembled.

Birkenhead, The : an Eng. troop-shi that sank with a loss of 400 lives i 1852. The discipline and unselfishnes of the men has become proverbial.

Birmingham : *see* Brummagem.

Birmingham Doctor, The : Samuel Par (1747-1825), so-called by De Quince on account of ' his spurious and wind imitation of Dr. Johnson.' *Se* Birmingham.

Birmingham Milton, The : Gottlieb Friedrich Klopstock (1724-1803) Germ. poet ; so-called by De Quincey *See* Birmingham.

Birmingham of Belgium, The : Liége.

Birmingham of Russia, The : Tula.

Birmingham Poet, The : John Freeth (1730-1808).

Birmingham School, The : orig. (previou to 1886) extreme Radicalism a preached by Joseph Chamberlain afterwards Liberal Unionism ; and still later Tariff Reform. In both the latter cases as advocated and promoted by the same political leader.

Birrell, To : to write in ' a style, light, easy, playful, pretty, rather discursive, perhaps a little superficial. Its characteristic note is grace.' [G. W. E. Russell, *Collections and Recollections* (1898)] After Augustine Birrell (b. 1850), English essayist and politician.

Birthday honours : honours and titles conferred on the occasion of a royal birthday.

Birthday suit, In : nude.

irthright for a mess of pottage, To sell one's : to exchange a permanent advantage for a temporary benefit. From the action of Esau, as narrated in *Genesis*, xxv. [G. Wilkins, *Miseries of Enforced Marriage*, III, ll. 307-8 (1607)]

ishop of Chester, As poor as the : a sarcasm. The wealth of Bishopric of Chester in the 15th cent., when this simile originated, was immense.

ishops, Age of the : see Age.

ishop's cope, To quarrel over a : see Quarrel.

ismarck of Asia, The : the Chinese statesman, Li Hung Chang (1823-1901). Otto, Prince Bismarck (1815-98), was the greatest statesman of the German Empire.

it and sup, A : a little food and drink. [Verney, *Memoirs*, II (1665)]

it in (between) the teeth, To take the : to be obstinately determined, like a horse that catches the bit between his teeth when about to bolt. [Heywood, *Proverbs* (1546)]

it of one's mind, To give a person a : to reprove a person sharply.

ite a person's nose off, To : to answer a person snappishly. [Nashe, *Lenten Stuffe*, 47 (1599)]

ite, Bark to be worse than the : see Bark.

ite the hand that feeds one, To : to show base ingratitude.

ite off more than one can chew, To : to undertake more than one can carry out ; in allusion to tobacco-chewing.

ite one's thumb at, To : to insult. The thumb represented a fig and the action amounted to an intimation that the other party to the controversy was not considered of the value of a fig. [Shakespeare, *Romeo and Juliet*, I, i (1591)]

ite the dust, To : see Dust.

ite, To teach a fish to : see Teach.

iter bit, The : an aggressor unexpectedly caught in his own trap.

ites of a cherry, To make two : to perform a work in unnecessary instalments ; linger unnecessarily over a task. [Rabelais, *Works*, Bk. V, ch. xxviii]

itten to the brain : drunk. [Heywood, *Proverbes* (1546)]

itter end, The : the last extremity ; the dregs. [*Proverbs*, v, 4 : ' Her end is bitter as wormwood.'] Another derivation is a nautical one ; from the very end of the cable 'abaft the bitts.'

Bitter as gall, As : very bitter. [Burton, *Anatomy*, II, 120 (1621)]

Bitter as wormwood, As : very bitter, sour tempered. [*Proverbs*, v, 14 ; Shakespeare, *Love's Labour Lost*, V, ii (1588) ; Burton, *Anatomy of Melancholy*, I, 338 (1621)]

B.K.S. : barracks. A military term.

Blab (abroad), To : to talk or utter indiscreetly. ' Blab ' as a noun (one who talks much and unnecessarily) was in common use until the 18th cent., from the time of Chaucer, who used it. The verb ' blabber ' was in use even earlier.

Black Act, The : the Eng. statute of 1722, directed against certain lawless persons who designated themselves ' The Blacks,' and blackened their faces as a means of disguise.

Black Acts, The : acts of the Scottish Parliament passed between the accession of James I and 1587. So-called because they were printed in black characters.

Black and blue, To beat a person : to beat a person until he is badly bruised. [Dryden, *Sir Martin Marr-all*, IV, i (1688)] ' Blak and bla ' and ' blak and blo ' were in use in the 13th cent.

Black and white : right and wrong. [Ascham, *The Schoolmaster*, Bk. I (1570)]

Black and white, In : in writing or print. Black for the ink, white for the paper. [Ben Jonson, *Every Man in His Humour*, IV, ii (1596)]

Black Art, The : witchcraft.

Black as a Newgate knocker : the Newgate knocker is the curl worn by costermongers and criminals.

Black as night, As : [Spenser, *Fairie Queen*, VI, vii, 43 (1590-6)]

Black as pitch, As : absolutely black. [Ovid, *Ars Amatoria*, II, 657-8 ; R. de Brunne, *Handlyng Synne* (1303) ; Earl of Sackville, *A Mirrour for Magistrates* (1563)]

Black as soot, As : pitch black. [Jos. Hall, *Satires*, Bk. I, vii, ll. 21-2 (1597)]

Black as thunder, As : pitch black ; gloomy.

Black Assizes, The : assizes held at Oxford in 1577, when several hundred persons died of an epidemic.

Black Bands : German mercenaries employed by Louis XII of France in his Italian wars.

Black Bartholomew : St. Bartholomew's Day, 1661, on which, in consequence of the Act of Uniformity, 2,000 Presbyterian pastors were ejected.

Black book, A : a record of offenders and offences.

Black books, To be in a person's : to be in disgrace with him. In the 16th cent. and later a Black Book was used for recording offenders.

Black Brunswickers : troops raised by the Duke of Brunswick in 1809 to avenge the death of his father at the Battle of Auerstadt. Their uniforms were black, in mourning for the late Duke, and their badge a skull-and-crossbones.

Black Cap, The : a cap worn by Eng. judges when pronouncing sentence of death ; properly, the cap that forms part of the full official dress of a judge.

Black Cattle : Negro slaves.

Black Clergy, The : the Russian regular monastic Orders. The parish priests are called 'The White Clergy.'

Black Coat, A : a parson ; in allusion to his dress. [Earle, *Microcosmography : A Profane Man* (1628)]

Black Code, The : legislation regulating the treatment of negroes in the Southern of the U.S. before the emancipation of the slaves. Properly, the *Code Noir* or Black Code, introduced by Bienville, the French governor of Louisiana, about 1723.

Black Country, The : the coal and iron districts of Staffordshire and Warwickshire, on account of their grimy state.

Black as a crow, As : [Apuleius, *Metamorphoseon*, Bk. II, ix ; Chaucer, *Knight's Tale* (14th cent.)]

Black Death, The : an epidemic of putrid typhus which ravaged Europe in the middle of the 14th cent. and is said to have carried off a quarter of the population of the world.

Black Diamonds : coals. Coal and diamonds are closely allied chemically.

Black Dog : (1) base coin, current in the early 18th cent. ; (2) depression ; ill-humour.

Black dog, To blush like a : not to blush at all. [Withal, *Dictionarie* (1634)]

Black Douglas : William Douglas, Lord of Nithsdale (d. 1392).

Black Eagle, Order of the : the highest Prussian order, founded by Frederick I in 1701.

Black Fast, The : the Jewish Day Atonement, a day of strict abstentie from food and drink.

Black flag, A : the standard of a pirate also used as the announcement of th infliction of capital punishment.

Black Flags : (1) Chinese pirates in th service of Annam in the war wit France ; orig. Chinese rebels ; (Moslem soldiers, from the colour of th banner of the Abbasides.

Black Friday : (1) May 11, 1866, th date of the failure of Overend an Gurney, the Glasgow bankers, whic led to a financial panic ; (2) Dec. 1745, the day on which the new reached London that the Youn Pretender had reached Derby ; (3) i the U.S. Sept. 24, 1869 and Sept. 1 1873, days of financial panic in Ne York ; (4) Good Friday, on account c the black vestments worn in th Roman Catholic Church.

Black Gown, A : a parson, collegiar or other learned man. In allusio to the uniform of the two forme classes.

Black as Hell, As : (1) pitch-black (2) infernally wicked. [Earl of Dorset *A Mirrour for Magistrates* (1563)]

Black Hole, A : a prison or place o internment of insufficient size. Afte the Black Hole of Calcutta (*q.v.*) Until 1868 it was the official designa tion of a military place of punish ment.

Black Hole of Calcutta : the smal dungeon in which Surajah Dowla placed his British prisoners in 1756 123 of the 146 prisoners died o suffocation or heat during th night.

Black Horse, The : the 7th Dragoon Guards, whose facings are black.

Black as ink, As : pitch black. [Spenser *The Faerie Queen*, I, i, 22 (1590-6)]

Black is white, To swear : to swear wha is visibly or obviously untrue.

Black Ivory : Negro slaves.

Black Jack : (1) John Alexander Logan (1826-86), American general ; so-called by his soldiers on account of his complexion and the colour of his hair ; (2) J. P. Kemble (1757-1823), Eng. actor, for a similar reason.

Black Jack, A : a large leather bottle with a tarred exterior.

Black Letter : the heavy Gothic type used generally by the early printers in England.

Black Letter Day, A : a day of misfortune ; from the practice of the Romans of marking such days in the calendar with charcoal.

Black Letter Dogs : Antiquaries searching for Black-Letter books.

Black List, A : (1) a list of persons under suspicion or noted as bad characters ; (2) in the Navy, a list of defaulters.

Black Man, The : the Devil.

Black Maria, A : a popular name for the black vehicle in which criminals are conveyed to prison. Said to derive from a negress named Maria Lee (or Black Maria) of Boston, U.S., who used frequently to assist the police in controlling refractory prisoners. Other derivations are from ' black ' the colour of the vehicle, and ' marinated ' (transported to a convict-settlement abroad) or ' married ' (chained to another prisoner).

Black Monday : (1) Easter Monday, on account of a great death-dealing storm which arose on that day in 1360 ; (2) in Melbourne, Feb. 27, 1865, the date of a wind-storm that caused great destruction ; (3) in use among schoolboys for the first Monday after the return to school.

Black Money : false money introduced into England in the time of the Plantagenets.

Black monkey : *see* Black dog.

Black Museum, The : the collection of criminal relics at Scotland Yard, the headquarters of the London police.

Black ox has trodden on his foot, A : misfortune has overtaken him. Black oxen were sacrificed to the gods of the Lower Regions. [Heywood, *Proverbes* (1546)] The phrase has special reference to marriage. The proverb, 'The black ox never trod upon his foot,' means 'He is not married.' ' The black ox hath trampled on him ' is an equivalent of ' He is hen-pecked.'

Black Pope, The : the General of the Order of Jesuits.

Black Prince, The : the eldest son of Edward III. On account of (1) the colour of his armour, or (2) the terror of his arms. [Froissart].

Black Republic, The : Hayti ; a West Indian State formed for the most part of negroes.

Black Republicans : Republican opponents of slavery, during the period which preceded the American Civil War.

Black Rod (properly, Gentleman Usher of the Black Rod) : an Eng. Court and Parliamentary official ; from his wand of office.

Black Sanctus : a burlesque hymn ; a parody of the Sanctus, the hymn which concludes the Eucharistic preface.

Black Saturday : in Scotland, Aug. 4, 1641, when the Scottish Parliament committed the country to episcopacy.

Black Saunt : *see* Black Sanctus.

Black sheep, A : a person of bad character. In a flock a black sheep is of less value than its white fellows.

Black swan, A : a great rarity.

Black Thursday : Feb. 6, 1851, in Victoria, Australia ; a day on which many alarming bushfires following a long period of drought did much damage.

Black to be white, To swear : to commit perjury.

Black, To look : to look displeased. From the black clouds that indicate stormy weather.

Black Watch, The : a regiment of Highlanders, formerly the 43rd and afterwards the 42nd Regt. of the line. On account of their dark tartan uniform. They were orig. appointed to watch the Highlands.

Black Wednesday : Jan. 8, 1878, on which a large number of civil servants in Victoria were dismissed in consequence of the refusal of the Legislative Council to pass the Appropriation Bill.

Blacks, The : mourning ; mutes at funerals. *See* Bianchi and Neri.

Blacks, The : the 7th Dragoon Guards. From the colour of their facings.

Black-and-Tan, A : a member of the militarized police, temporary members of the Royal Irish Constabulary, recruited for service in Ireland in 1920. In allusion to their uniforms—black caps and khaki (tan) clothing.

Black-and-tan Country, The : the Southern States of the N. Amer. Union. From the colour of the negro inhabitants and to ' tan,' to ' thrash '—the country where the negroes were thrashed.

Black-and-White artist, A : an artist who draws in ink or black crayon on a white surface.

Black-birder, A : a vessel engaged in conveying Kanaka labour to the place of its employment.

Black-fisher, A : one who engages in blackfishing.

Black-fishing : the catching of salmon, which have just spawned, by torch-light at night.

Blackamoor, A : a dark-skinned person ; properly a W. African.

Blackamoor white, To wash a : to undertake an impossible task. From the fable of Æsop, *Washing the Blackamoor White*.

Blackamoors' teeth : cowry-shells, widely used as money by natives of Africa.

Blackball, To : to ostracize, or refuse membership to a club or society. From the black ball formerly used to signify the negative in the ballot for admission.

Blackfoot, A : a messenger between the two parties to a love-affair.

Blackfriar, A : a Dominican ; on account of the colour of his garb.

Blackguards : men of bad character, esp. criminal loafers of the lower classes, or in a higher rank of society swindlers and men prone to dishonourable conduct. Orig. the servants of the lowest rank in a palace or in the army, who were called ' blackguards ' on account of their grimy appearance as contrasted with the guards of honour and other guards. While on journeys their duty was to guard the kitchen utensils.

Blackguard, To : to abuse in insulting language.

Blackleg, A : one who, not a member of a trade union, replaces a workman out on strike (1889). Formerly one who swindled on the turf or in other gambling occupations. These latter generally wore black gaiters or high boots.

Blackmail : payment to avoid exposure or annoyance. Originally, tribute levied on residents on the Scot.-Eng. border by freebooters in order to secure freedom from molestation.

Blacksmith's Daughter, The : a key, esp. that of a sponging-house.

Blacksmith, The Learned : Elihu Burritt (1811-79), Amer. author.

Blackthorn Winter, A : cold weather, when the blackthorn is in blossom.

Blade, A : a young man about town, of good spirits, somewhat self-indulgent, but inspired by no deliberately evil intent. Possibly connected with ' blade,' a sword, on account of the

swords such men formerly wore. The sense of the word has degenerated since the 18th cent. [*The Merry Devil of Edmonton*, l. 262 (1608)]

Blague (*Fr.*) : humbug. [Introduced by Carlyle, *French Revolution*, V, vi (1837)]

Blanes d'Espagne : the extreme French royalists who support the claim of the Spanish Bourbons to the French throne.

Blank cheque to .. To give a : to give unlimited or undefined authority. A blank cheque is a cheque which has been signed without the amount to be paid having been inserted.

Blanket Fair : (1) the fair held on the Thames during the great frost of 1683-4 ; (2) a bed.

Blanket, On the wrong side of the : of illegitimate birth.

Blanket term, A : an omnibus term ; a term describing an important member of a group extended to cover the whole of the group. An Americanism.

Blanket, A wet : one who seeks to discourage others in an enterprize, who looks on the gloomy side, who 'throws cold water' on an undertaking, etc. [R. Cumberland, *The Fashionable Lover*, I, i (1772)]

Blanketeers : (1) Lancashire working-men who, furnished with provisions and a blanket, marched to London in 1817 to demand assistance from Parliament ; (2) a party of unemployed who marched on the American Congress with blankets on their backs in 1894.

Blarney : flattery. From the Blarney Stone at Blarney Castle, Ireland, which is said to endow him who kisses it with the power of cajolery. The reputation of the stone may have been derived from the endless plausible excuses invented by Lord Clancarty in 1602 to relieve him of the necessity of fulfilling his promise to surrender Blarney Castle to the Queen's forces.

Blarney-stone, To kiss the : to be given to the practice of wheedling flattery, such as that which is supposed to be characteristic of the Irish. *See* Blarney.

Blatant Beast, The : (1) calumny ; a term invented by Spenser in his *Faerie Queen* (1590-6) to describe the child of Cerberus and Chimæra, in whom calumny was symbolized ; (2) the multitude. [Spenser, *The Returne from Parnassus* (1606)]

Blayney's Bloodhounds : the 2nd Battalion of Princess Victoria's Irish Fusiliers (form. the 89th Foot). After their colonel, Lord Blaney, and their tireless pursuit of the Irish rebels in 1798.

Blazer, A : a sporting jacket of light, bright colour or colours. From 'to blaze.' First applied to that worn (a bright red) by the members of the Lady Margaret Boat Club of St. John's College, Cambridge.

Blazes ! Go to : a euphuism for 'Go to hell !' In allusion to the fires that are supposed to blaze there.

Bleed a person, To : to extort money from a person. [Dryden, *An Evening's Love*, IV, i (1668)]

Bleed a person white, To : to extort the last penny from him.

Bleeding Kansas : the State of Kansas, U.S.; so-called on account of its many fights over the slavery question. Orig. coined as a newspaper headline.

Blenheim Spaniels : the electors of Oxford who for a long period could be trusted to vote in accordance with the wishes of the Duke of Marlborough, whose residence was at Blenheim.

Blenheim Steps, To go to : said of a corpse surreptitiously removed from its grave and sold for dissection. There was formerly a famous anatomical school at Blenheim Steps, where corpses found a ready market.

Blighty : English and Anglo-Indian soldiers' term for England. Possibly from Urdu *walayate*, foreign, akin to Turkish *vilayet*.

Blind, A : a pretence, in the sense of that which deceives or mentally blinds a person. [South, *Sermons* II, 208 (1664)]

Blind alley, A : a street, or road, closed at one end ; a *cul-de-sac*. ' Blind ' in the sense of secret, dark.

Blind as a bat : bats are not blind but are unable to distinguish objects in a good light.

Blind as a beetle : beetles are not blind, but flying ones sometimes knock against people and objects as if they were so.

Blind as a harper, As : blind. In allusion to the many blind minstrels who used to wander about the country. [Lilly, *Sapho and Phao*, IV, iii (1591)]

Blind as a mole : moles are not blind, but have very small eyes. In one species the eyes are covered by membranes and it was probably to these that Aristotle referred when he said ' The mole is blind.'

Blind as an owl, As : owls are not blind, but see better in the dusk than by day.

Blind Bard, The : Homer.

Blind Boy, The : Cupid, the Roman god of love ; depicted as a blind boy.

Blind Department, The : the department of the Post Office which deals with insufficiently or obscurely addressed letters.

Blind ditch, A : a hidden ditch: *see* Blind alley.

Blind eye, To have (apply) the : deliberately to ignore or pretend not to see that which is inconvenient. After the story of Lord Nelson who at the Battle of Copenhagen applied his telescope to his blind eye so as to avoid seeing an inconvenient signal.

Blind Harry : a Scottish minstrel (d. c. 1492).

Blind hedge, A : a hawthorn hedge, not easily detected : *see* Blind alley.

Blind Hookey : a leap in the dark. After a card game so-called.

Blind in the purse : poor. [*Rare Triumphs of Love and Fortune*, III, l. 93 (1589)]

Blind journey, To have a : to have a fruitless journey. [Hy. Porter, *Two Angry Women of Abington*, l. 2569 (1599)]

Blind leaders of the blind : *see* the allusion to the Pharisees in *Matthew* xv, 14 ; also Plato, *Republic*, viii.

Blind man's holiday : the period of dusk, when it is too dark to work, but not yet dark enough to justify the use of artificial light. [Nashe, *Lenten Stuffe* (1599)]

Blind man's lantern : a blind man's walking-stick.

Blind manuscripts : anonymous manuscripts. [Fenton, *Treatise of Usurie* (1612)]

Blind side of a man, The : the tender or yielding part of a man's nature. [Chapman, *The Gentleman Usher*, I, i (1606)]

Blind Master, The : Cupid. *See* Blind Boy.

Blind men's dinner, The : a meal for which no payment was made. From the story of the twelve blind men who obtained a good dinner at an inn, each believing that one of the others had received a gift wherewith to pay for it.

Blind writing : writing in ink intended to fade.

Blizzard, A : a violent gale of snow and sleet. A word of Amer. origin, not in general use before 1880, but known as early as 1834. Perhaps onomatopoeic in origin.

Bloc, A : a close co-operation between Parties in a Parliament, in support of a common policy.

Block, Ben : a sailor.

Block a bill, To : to prevent progress of a bill in Parliament by means of making full use of the forms of the House.

Blockade, A pacific : a blockade exercised without a declaration of war and without the use of arms.

Blockade, A paper : a blockade that is merely nominal or ineffective.

Blockhead, A : a stupid person. Lit., a wooden-head. [Coverdale, *Erasmus' Paraphrase*, I xl, 14 (1549)]

Bloke, A : a somewhat contemptuous term for a man.

Blood, A : a rake, a man of pleasure. ' Blood' as the seat of the emotions, or as denoting good or noble family. [Thos. Kyd, *Jeronimo*, Pt. I, l. 76 (1591)]

Blood and Iron, The Man of : Prince Otto von Bismarck, Germ. statesman (1815-98). From a phrase in a speech made by him before the Budget Commission of the Prussian House of Delegates in 1862. The phrase had previously been used by him in a letter to Baron von Schleinitz, the Foreign Minister, in May, 1859. Bismarck did not, however, coin the phrase. It had been employed by (1) Quintilian, the Rom. rhetorician (c. 35 to 95) ; (2) Ernst Moritz Arndt, the Germ. patriot, political writer and poet (1769-1860) ; (3) by others.

Blood and thunder novel, A : cheap, sensational fiction.

Blood, Bad : ill-feeling. [Bacon, *Henry VII* (1622)]

Blood, Blue : *see* Blue.

Blood boil, To make one's : to arouse to anger. [Benj. Franklin, *Poor Richard's Almanac for* 1742]

Blood from a stone, To attempt to get (draw) : to endeavour to obtain something from a person who does not possess it.

Blood into . . To infuse new : to introduce new and vital elements into . .

Blood of the Grograms : pseudo-aristocracy. From ' grogram ' a material composed of silk and mohair, from Fr. *gros*, coarse, and Engl. *grain*.

Blood, The Man of : Charles I ; so-called by the Puritans on account of his armed opposition to them.

Blood, A Prince of the : *i.e.*, of the Blood Royal.

Blood Tax, The : (1) the section of the Crimes Act of 1882 which authorize the levy of a fine on a district in whic a political murder had been committed (2) military conscription, so-describe by Gen. Maximilian Sebastian Foy i the French Chamber, May 28, 1824

Blood, To run in the : to be inherited o heritable. [Evelyn, *Diary*, (Apl. 1646)

Blood, To taste : to enjoy a pleasure fo the first time.

Blood upon the head of . . : responsi bility for murder or other offence [*Joshua*, ii, 19]

Blood, A young : a young energeti member of a political party or othe movement.

Blood money : (1) money paid to a ma as an inducement to him to betray o give evidence against another ; (2 money paid to a man as an inducemen to forego the right to revenge.

Blood-sucker, A : one who extorts mone from another. [Jasper Fisher, *Fuimu Troes*, III, i (1633) ; for To suck a per son's blood used in this sense, se *Description of an Ungodly World*, l. 4 (1557)]

Bloody Assizes, The : the trials by Judg Jeffreys in the West of England afte the suppression of Monmouth Rebellion (1685), when very man people were condemned to death an executed.

Bloody Bill, The : the Statute of the Si Articles (1539), which made denial o the doctrine of Transubstantiation capital offence.

Bloody Butcher, The : *see* Butcher o Culloden.

Bloody Chasm, To bridge the : to softe the memory of the Amer. Civil Wa and its effects.

Bloody Eleventh, The : the 11th Reg of Foot, now the Devonshire Reg From their heavy losses in the Batt of Salamanca, and elsewhere.

Bloody Mary : Mary I, Queen of Englan On account of her persecution of t Protestants.

Bloody Tower, The : that part of t Tower of London in which the bodi of the two princes, murdered in 148 were buried.

Bloody Wedding, The : the Massacre St. Bartholomew, which took pla during the marriage-festivities Henry of Navarre (Henri IV) a Marguerite de Valois (1572).

Bloody Week, The : May 21-28, 1871, when Paris was set on fire by the Communists.

Bloomers : knickerbockers for women. After Amelia Jenks Bloomer, the Amer. inventor of the costume (1818-94).

Blot on the ' Scutcheon,' A : a stain on the character. Metaphor drawn from heraldry.

Blow great guns, To : (of the wind) to blow so fiercely as to resemble the discharge of artillery. [Charles Dibdin (1745-1814), *The Sailor's Consolation*] Also used metaphorically.

Blow hot and cold, To : to affirm and to contradict at the same time. From the fable of a traveller who was entertained by a satyr who blew his fingers to warm them and his broth to cool it. [W. Bullinger, *Decades* (1577)]

Blow the coals, To : to inflame passion ; to excite discord. [Lyly, *Euphues : Anatomy of Wit* (1579)]

Blow off steam, To : to disperse one's superfluous energy.

Blow one's own trumpet, To : *see* Trumpet.

Blows, To come to : to fight.

Bluchers : military half-boots, as worn by Field-Marshal Gebhard von Blücher (1742-1819).

Blue, A : (1) at Oxford or Cambridge, Eton or Harrow, a representative of the Univ. or school in sport ; (2) a blue stocking (*q.v.*).

Blue, To : to squander ; to spend recklessly. From either (1) to pass into the blue, *i.e.*, into the sky or the blue sea, or (2) to blow away.

Blue, Out of the : quite unexpectedly.

Blue Apron, A : (1) a tradesman, from the apron formerly worn by all shopkeepers ; (2) an amateur statesman. *See* next entry.

Blue Apron Statesman, A : an amateur politician ; a tradesman who poses as a statesman. From the blue apron formerly worn by all tradesmen.

Blue beans : bullets. From the colour of lead.

Blue Bird, The : happiness. After Maeterlinck's play of that name.

Blue Blazes : Hell, in allusion to the colour of burning sulphur.

Blue Blood : royal or noble birth ; orig. used in Spain to denote freedom from Jewish or Moorish taint. In the fair Gothic type the veins show blue through the skin.

Blue, A bolt from the : *see* Bolt.

Blue Bonnets : *see* Blue Caps.

Blue Book, A : an Eng. Parliamentary or Privy Council publication. From the colour of the paper cover in which they are bound. Hence any government publication.

Blue Bottle, A : a policeman ; a servant ; a beadle ; a harlot. From the colour of their clothing, the last-mentioned in the House of Correction.

Blue Caps ; Blue Bonnets : (1) Scotsmen; from the colour of the caps worn by them ; (2) the Dublin Fusiliers ; from the reference to them during the Indian Mutiny by Nana Sahib as ' blue-capped.'

Blue, Dark (A) : a student of Oxford or scholar of Harrow. From the University and school colours.

Blue Devils, To get the : to become unreasonably and morbidly depressed. [Steine, *Letters*, No. 33 (1762)]

Blue dog, To blush like a : not to blush at all. [Swift (Simon Wagstaff), *Polite Conversation* (1738)]

Blue Fish, The : the shark. From the colour of its upper parts.

Blue flag, To hoist the : to turn publican or fishmonger, in allusion to the blue aprons worn in those trades.

Blue glasses, To look through : to regard objects wrongly.

Blue God, The : Neptune, the god of the sea.

Blue Gown, A : (1) in Scotland, a licensed beggar, from the colour of his attire ; the Bluegowns were orig. patronized and authorized to beg by the kings of Scotland ; (2) a harlot ; from the colour of their former uniform in the House of Correction.

Blue Grass State, The : Kentucky, which includes the blue grass region.

Blue Guards, The : the Royal Horse Guards, formerly the Oxford Blues.

Blue Hen, The : Delaware. The name was derived from the ' Game Cock Regt.' raised in Delaware, which distinguished itself in the War of Independence. One of its officers, Capt. Caldwell, a game-cock fancier, held the view that a true game-cock must be the offspring of a blue hen. Hence the appellation.

Blue Horse, The : the Fourth Dragoons. From the colour of their facings.

Blue Law State, The : Connecticut : *see* next entry.

Blue Laws : supposed draconic laws enacted in Connecticut in 1640, by which several offences, even disobedience to parents, were made capital. Hence a general name for Puritanical legislation.

Blue Light, A : a person of excessive and unconcealed piety. Nautical term.

Blue, A Light : a student at Cambridge University and scholar of Eton. From the University and school colours.

Blue, A Man in : a policeman. From the colour of his uniform.

Blue Monday : (1) the Monday before Lent ; a day of dissipation ; (2) a workingman's Monday spent in idleness and dissipation.

Blue Moon, Once in a : exceedingly rarely. [Roy and Barlow, *Rede Me and be not wrothe* (1528)]

Blue Noses : Nova Scotians. After the name of a potato grown widely in that Province, or possibly in allusion to the coldness of the winter there.

Blue Peter : (1) a flag hoisted by a vessel as a signal of immediate sailing ; (2) the playing of an unnecessarily high card at whist as a signal to one's partner. 'Peter' is a corruption of *partir*, to set out.

Blue Ribbon, The : (1) a distinction of the highest character ; probably from the blue ribbon of the Order of the Garter, the highest Eng. Order of knighthood ; (2) a badge of total abstention from alcoholic liquor ; after the Blue Ribbon Army (*q.v.*).

Blue Ribbon Army : a band of total abstainers from alcoholic liquor, who wear a small piece of blue ribbon as a badge. Instituted in 1882.

Blue Ribbon of the Turf, The : the Derby, the principal Eng. horse-race. So designated by Lord Beaconsfield in the *Life of Lord George Bentinck* (1852).

Blue Roses : unattainable objects of desire. Blue roses were unknown until a few years ago, when the Germans introduced a climbing-rose called *Veilchonblau* (violet blue).

Blue Stocking, A : a learned, somewhat pedantic woman. After The Blue Stocking Club, a literary society, founded by Mrs. Elizabeth Montagu (1720-1800), about 1750, to which one of the members (Benjamin Stillingfleet) came in blue worsted, instead of the usual silk stockings. It is said, however, that the blue stockings were first worn not at Mrs. Montagu's but at Mrs. Vesey's, and by a Frenchman who took his invitation literally, 'You may come in your blue stockings if you like.'

Blue, To look : to appear annoyed [Lilly, *Sapho and Phao*, II, ii (1591)]

Blue, To talk : to be indecent in conversation, possibly from the colour of the uniform worn by harlots in the House of Correction.

Blue True : thoroughly reliable and steadfast ; loyal ; conservative. *See* Coventry Blue, True as. Blue was considered the colour of truth and loyalty as far back as Ancient Rome.

Blues, The : *see* Blue Devils.

Blue-eyed Maid, The : Minerva ; so-called by Homer.

Bluejacket, A : a sailor. In allusion to the colour of his costume.

Blue-mantle : the Eng. pursuivant-at-arms. From the colour of his official robe.

Blue-pencil, To : (of an editor) to delete portions of a M.S. From the blue pencil usually employed in the process.

Bluebeard, A : a brutal husband ; one who marries and murders wife after wife successively. From the name of a character in a popular tale told by Charles Perrault (1628-1703), based perhaps on the career of Gilles de Laval, Baron de Retz (1396-1440), Marshal of France.

Bluecoat Boy, A : a pupil at Christ's Hospital. From the colour of the school uniform.

Bluecoat School : Christ's Hospital. From the colour of the school uniform.

Bluejackets : sailors as distinct from marines. From the colour of their jackets.

Bluewater School, The : the school that holds the view that the function of a navy in war is to seek out and attack the enemy and not to concentrate its efforts on defence.

Bluff, To : to deceive or hoodwink. A card-term adopted from the game of poker, possibly related to 'bluff' in the sense of a blinker for a horse.

Bluff Hal (Harry) : Henry VIII of England. On account of his bluff and burly manners.

Blush, At a ; Blush, At first : at first sight, speaking without consideration. In allusion to the habit of blushing when taken by surprise. [For 'At a blush,' Lilly, *Gallathea*, II, iii (1592) ; for 'At first blush,' Gosson, *Schoole of Abuse*, Ep. Dedic. (1579)]

Bo, Big : *see* Big Bo.

Bo-peep with, To play : to hide from while keeping the other person in view. [Hy. Porter, *Two Angry Women of Abington*, I, 2037 (1599)]

Bo to a goose, To say : to be not altogether lacking in courage. A proverbial phrase of considerable antiquity. [Arnim, *Italian Taylor and His Boy* (1609)]

Boanerges : a loud, over-bearing speaker. From Boanerges, 'the sons of thunder,' the name given to James and John, the sons of Zebedee. [*Mark*, iii, 17]

Board, To go by the : to be finally lost. A nautical term, meaning to fall overboard or by the ship's side. [Defoe, *Captain Singleton* (1720)]

Board School, A : a Public Elementary School in England, managed by a School Board. School Boards were abolished by Parliament in 1904.

Board, To sweep the : to secure everything. Orig. a card-term, meaning to secure all the stakes on the board or table.

Board wages : an allowance to domestic servants in lieu of board or food.

Boards, The : the stage. From the wooden planks of which it is formed.

Boat as (with) another, To be (row) in the same : to be involved in the same circumstances as another. First used by Pope Clement I (c. 30-100) in a letter to the Church at Corinth on the occasion of a dissension. Probably a reference to a boat launched from a wrecked ship.

Boat sails in smooth waters, One's : the opportunity is favourable. [Tibullus, I, v, 75-6]

Boats (behind one), To burn one's : by destroying one's means of retreat to strengthen one's courage for the assault. Armies were encouraged for victory in this manner by Agathocles of Syracuse in his expedition against Carthage (310-307 B.C.) ; the Emperor Julian in his expedition against Persia (363 B.C.) ; Robert Guiscard, Duke of Apulia and Calabria, in his expedition against Emperor Alexius (1084) ; and Hernando Cortes on the invasion of Mexico (1519).

Bob Acres, A : a coward ; a ludicrous boaster. After a character in Sheridan, *The Rivals* (1775).

Bob Sawyer, A : a medical student of not very high moral character. After a character in Dickens, *Pickwick Papers* (1836).

Bobadil, A : a boasting blusterer. After a character in Ben Jonson, *Every Man in his Humour* (1596).

Bobbing Joan : the Earl of Mar of 1715, who displayed opportunism in support of the two rival dynasties of Stuart and Hanover. After the name of an old dance.

Bobby, A : a slang nickname for a policeman. From Sir Robert Peel, the Home Secretary, who passed the Metropolitan Police Act of 1828, 'Bobby' being a pet-name for Robert.

Bob-wig, A : a wig with bobs or short curls ; hence, an important personage.

Bocardo, A : a prison ; a dungeon. After the name of a prison in Oxford, demolished in 1771.

Boche ; Bosche, A : a term of insult and contempt applied since 1914 to Germans, esp. by the French. From Germ., *bursch*, a lad, or from *bürschen*, to shoot (with a rifle). Another derivation is from *Les Alboches*, an invented nickname connoting ' The Blockheads,' given by French printers to their German colleagues a few years before the outbreak of the War of 1870-1. *Alboche* itself was derived from *boche*, a French colloquial term coined about the year 1860 to designate a person of bad character.

Bock-beer : a kind of Lager-beer. From Germ., *Bock-bier*, a corruption of *Einbecker*, from Einbeck, Hanover, famous for its beers.

Bodkin, To walk : of a man walking between two women. Because, like a bodkin, he is sheathed and harmless.

Body and soul together, To keep : to sustain life. [Maria Edgeworth, *Castle Rackrent* (1799)]

Body Politic, The : the State. [Bacon, *Essays : Of Seditions and Troubles* (1625)]

Body-snatcher, A : one who opened a grave in order to steal the body from it and sell it for dissection. The earliest known instance of this offence occurred in 1777.

Boeotian : stupid, foolish. After Boeotia, in ancient Greece ; the inhabitants were proverbially rude and stupid.

Boeotian ears : ears that have no sense of music or of eloquence.

Boer, A : a Dutch inhabitant of S. Africa ; akin to boor. From Germ., *bauer,* a peasant.

Bog-trotters : robbers infesting the bogs of Ireland.

Bogus : counterfeit. Of Amer. origin, said to have appeared first in 1827 to represent an implement for coining false money and to have been derived from ' tantrabogus,' a word applied in Vermont to any ugly object. Another derivation is from Borghese, a swindler who about the year 1837 specialized in Boston in the manufacture and passing of false and worthless securities.

Bohea : a class of tea. After a range of hills in China.

Bohemian, A : one who leads a free, unconventional life apart from the society to which he naturally belongs. Used esp. of men of artistic or literary tastes and occupations. The word used in this sense was introduced by W. M. Thackeray in *Vanity Fair* (1847). In French it had been previously used to denote a vagabond, adventurer, person of irregular life or habits—a transference of the sense of gypsy. The word was first used to denote ' gypsy ' in the 15th cent. when, on their appearance in Western Europe, the gypsies were thought to have come from Bohemia.

Bohemian Tartar, A : a gypsy. By the French, gypsies are called ' Bohemiens '; by the Germans, ' Tartars.' Shakespeare combined both terms in *Merry Wives of Windsor,* IV, v (1598-9).

Boil a bone, To : to act foolishly and to no purpose. From an ancient Grk. proverb.

Bold Beauchamp : *see* Beauchamp, As bold as.

Bold as brass, As : daring ; audaciously forward.

Bologna, A : a sausage of the kind orig. made at Bologna, Italy.

Bolshevik, A : an extreme revolutionary. The Anglicized form of the name of a socialist-political Party in Russia. Russ., *Bolshinstivs,* majority ; from the majority who voted with Lenin at the Russian Socialist Congress held in London in 1903.

Bolt, To : to break away from a political party.

Bolt from the blue, A : a sudden an surprising event, like a thunde bolt from the sky. [Horace, *Ode,* xxxiv, 5-8 ; Virgil, *Æneid,* IX 630]

Bolt-upright : as straight as a bolt c an arrow. ' Upright ' orig. mean straight, not necessarily vertical.

Bolus, A : a dispensing chemist. Afte the bolus which he dispenses.

Bomba : Ferdinand II of Naples an Sicily (1810-59) On account of h having bombarded his people. Se *also* Bombalino.

Bombalino or **Bomba II :** Francis II, th last king of the two Sicilies (1836-94 *See* Bomba.

Bombast : empty boasting. From Lo Lat., *bombax,* cotton, which wa formerly used for stuffing clothing, t give a deceptive appearance of a fin figure.

Bombastes Furioso, A : a boaster an employer of long words. After th hero of a play so-entitled by W. P Rhodes (1772-1826).

Bon mot, A (*Fr.,* good saying): an epigram witty saying, or repartee. [First usec in English by Jonathan Swift.]

Bon ton (*Fr.*) : good style ; fashionabl society. [Chesterfield, *Letters,* Bk. II No. 20 (1747)]

Bon vivant, A (*Fr.,* living well): gourmet ; one devoted to comforts esp. of the table.

Bon voyage ! (*Fr.,* a good journey t you !) [15th cent.]

Bona fide (*Lat.*) : in good faith ; genuine Orig. a legal term. [Rob. Wilson *Three Ladies of London,* II, l. 931 (1584)]

Bona Roba, A : a loose woman. Ital. *buona roba,* good dress ; attractive clothing being customary with Italian courtesans. [Shakespeare, 2 *Henry IV,* III, ii, 267 (1597-8)]

Bona Socia, A : a boon companion.

Bonanza, A : a stroke of luck. After the Bonanza silver-mine in Nevada which was at first considered a failure but which suddenly produced immense wealth.

Bonanza State : Nevada. After its rich Bonanza mines.

Bond, To have one's : to have one's legal rights no matter how the other party to the transaction may be affected. In allusion to one of the main incidents of the plot of Shakespeare, *Merchant of Venice* (1596).

Bone, To : to filch; to seize as a dog seizes a bone. [Shakespeare, 2 *Henry VI*, I, iii, (1593), where 'bone' is used in the sense of finger]

Bone, To bite near the : to be grasping. [Geo. Cavendish, *Life and Death of Wolsey* (1557)]

Bone, To boil a : *see* Boil.

Bone of one's bone and flesh of one's flesh : closely related, of the same family. [*Genesis*, ii, 23]

Bone of contention, A : a cause of difference or dispute, as a bone between two dogs. [Lambarde, *Perambulation of Kent* (1576)]

Bone in one's leg, To have a : an excuse, frequently given to children for refraining from exertion.

Bone to pick with .. To have a : to have cause for recriminatory discussion with .. [Calfhill, *Answere to the Treatise of the Crosse*, 277 (1565)]

Bone in one's throat, To have a : an excuse for not answering a question.

Bones to one's ass, To give straw to one's dog and : *see* Give.

Bones, To break no : to do no harm. [Goldsmith, *The Good-natured Man*, III, i, (1768)]

Bones of .. To make no : to have no hesitation. Orig., to find no bones (*i.e.*, obstruction) in. [*The Paston Letters*, 331, I (1422-1509)]

Bones, To make old : to live to a good old age.

Bone-lace : a kind of lace made by means of bobbins of bone.

Bone-setter, A : a surgeon. [Brome, *Queen and Concubine* (1659)]

Bone-shaker, A : (1) a bicycle without rubber tyres; in allusion to the rough course it pursues when ridden; (2) a four-wheeled cab.

Boney : Napoleon I. A term used by the English, contracted from the surname Buonaparte.

Bonhomme, A : a member of a branch of the Order of Franciscans. The term 'Bon Homme' (good man) was applied to their founder, St. Francis de Paule, by Louis XI of France.

Bonhomme, Jacques : *see* Jacques Bonhomme.

Boniface, A : the host of an inn, esp. a good-tempered, cheery one. After (1) a character in Farquhar's *Beaux' Stratagem* (1707); or possibly (2) Pope Boniface, who granted indulgences to all who drank the Pope's health.

Boniface's Cup, St. : a glass of wine at the conclusion of a meal; in allusion to the indulgence granted by Pope Boniface to all who drank the Pope's health on the conclusion of a meal after grace.

Bonne Bouche (*Fr.*, a good mouth) : a dainty morsel; an unexpected stroke of luck.

Bonnet, A Blue : *see* Blue Caps.

Bonnet Rouge (*Fr.*) **A :** (1) the red Cap of Liberty, emblem of Republicanism, introduced at the first French Revolution; (2) a Republican.

Bonnet-piece, A : a Scotch gold coin on which King James V was depicted wearing a bonnet.

Bonnet, To have a green : to have failed in business. After the French custom until as late as the 17th cent. of obliging bankrupts to wear green headgear.

Bonnet, To play the : to act as a decoy for rogues. Because he blinds his dupes just as if he knocks their hats over their eyes.

Bonnet, To vale the : to take off one's hat to .. [Lilly, *Endimion*, III, iii (1591)]

Bono Johnny : John Bull. Current in the East Indies.

Bontemps, A Roger : (*Fr.*, *rouge bon temps*, reddish and fair weather) : a cheery optimist; a free boon companion. [Jas. Howell, *Familiar Letters*, Bk. IV, Letter xix (c. 1647)]

Booby-trap, A : a practical joke, played by schoolboys.

Boodle : (1) a number of people; used contemptuously; (2) money used for bribery (American).

Book, A : an arrangement of bets by a bookmaker whereby he is almost certain to win on the whole.

Book and Candle, Bell : *see* Bell.

Book, Blue : *see* Blue Book.

Book in Breeches : Lord Macaulay (1800-59). So-called by Sydney Smith, on account of his wide knowledge.

Book of Books, The : the Bible.

Book of Hours, A : *see* Hours.

Book of Idiots, A : a picture. [Bp. Joseph Hall, *Characters: Premonition* (1608)]

Book of Life, The : the record of those who are to be for ever blessed. [*Revelations*, xx, 12]

Book of the Four Kings, The : a pack of cards. [Rabelais, *Gargantua and Pantagruel*, I, 22 (1532)]

Book, The : the Bible. [12th cent.]

Book, The People of the : the Jews. So-called by Mahomet.

Book, To bring to : to bring to account.

Book, To speak by the : to speak with punctilious care for the accuracy of one's statements.

Book, To speak like a : to be well provided with and free of information.

Book, To speak without : to speak without authority ; to speak extemporaneously. [Hy. Porter, *Two Angry Women of Abington*, l. 1576 (1599)]

Book, To suit one's : to fall in with one's arrangements. A betting metaphor. *See* Book, A.

Book, To write without one's : to speak or write without knowledge.

Books, Out of one's : no longer in favour. From the early practice of entering the names of one's retainers in a book. It was also customary to enter one's friends' names in a book.

Books, To be in a person's bad : to be out of favour with a person.

Books, To be in a person's good : to be in favour with a person. From the early practice of entering the names of one's retainers and servants in a book. It was also customary to enter one's friends' names in a book.

Book-maker, A : a betting agent who selects the bets he accepts and arranges them in a book so that in no circumstances is he likely to suffer loss. *See* Book, A.

Bookworm, A : a person devoted to reading. Lit., a maggot which makes its home in books and eats into them. According to *Revelations*, x, 9, the angel, in giving St. John the book with the seven seals, said, ' Take it, and eat it up ; and it shall make thy belly bitter, but it shall be in thy mouth sweet as honey.'

Boom, To ; Boom, A : (a commercial term) (*a*) to burst into favour with the public ; (*b*) a sudden great demand for a commodity, a sudden great success. A nautical metaphor, popularized in this country and in U.S. in 1879.

Boom, To top one's : to depart. A nautical metaphor.

Boon companion, A : a cheerful, jovial companion. Lit., good (*Fr.*, *bon*) companion. [Thomas Drant, *A Medicinable Morall* (1566)]

Boost, To : to assist upwards. An Americanism.

Boot forth, To : to go out ; sally forth.

Boot to be on the other leg, The : th responsibility to be transferred to th other party.

Boot, To get the : to be dismissed kicked out.

Boots, To go to bed in one's : to be ver drunk.

Boot-jack : *see* Jack.

Booty, To play : to give a person in th first instance a slight advantage so a ultimately to derive a far greate advantage from him. [Cartwright *Royall Slave* (1631)]

Borachio, A : a drunkard. Used by Shakespeare [*Much Ado* (1599)], and a little earlier by Stonyhurst in *Æneid* for a wine-bottle, the Span. for which is *borracho*.

Borak at, To poke : to deceive ; to supply with false news. A Colonial phrase.

Border, The : the frontier between England and Scotland.

Border Eagle State, The : Mississippi. After the Border Eagle in its coat of arms.

Border Minstrel, The : Sir Walter Scott, many of whose poems relate to the Border.

Border States : Delaware, Maryland, Virginia, Kentucky, Missouri, the States bordering on the Free States prior to the Amer. Civil War. North Carolina, Tennessee and Arkansas are also included sometimes.

Borderer, A : one who lives near the boundary between two States, esp. England and Scotland.

Boreal : northern. From Boreas, the god of the north wind.

Born in the purple : of royal or imperial birth. From (1) the official colour of the Roman emperors ; or (2) the decorations of the room prepared by one of the Roman empresses for her accouchement. *See* Purple.

Born with a silver spoon in the mouth : *see* Silver Spoon.

Borough English : a custom in the South of England by which manorial estates are inherited by younger sons. From Old-French, *Tenure en Burgh Engloys* (tenure in an English borough), the custom having been prevalent in certain English towns, but not in France.

Borough, A pocket : a borough carrying representation in Parliament owned, together with its representation, for practical purposes by an individual.

orough, A rotten : a Parliamentary borough, which had so degenerated through loss of population as to be practically in the hands of one person.

orrel folk : unlearned people. Middle-English, *borrel*, belonging to the laity, coarse cloth.

orrowed plumes, In : disguised; assuming a position superior to that which one really holds. [Lucian, *Prendolog*, 5 ; Webster and Dekker, *Westward Hoe*, II, ii (1607)]

osch (Boch) butter : margarine. From s'Hertogenbosch (or Bois-le-Duc), in Holland, where the manufacture was carried on.

osh : nonsense. From the Turkish for empty, vain. Introduced from J. J. Morier's Turkish novel, *Ayesha* (1834), and his *The Adventures of Hajji Baba of Ispahan* (1824).

osom, A bird in one's : *see* Bird.

osom, In one's : secretly.

osom, To be in a person's : to be in his secrets. [Terence, *Adelphi*, II. 707-9 ; Shakespeare, *Julius Cæsar*, V, i (1601)]

osom, To creep into a person's : to get into his confidence. [Rich. Edwards, *Damon and Pithias*, l. 474 (1567)]

osom sermons : written sermons, as opposed to sermons delivered extempore or from notes.

osom-friend, A : an especially close friend. [Greene, *Never Too Late* (1590)]

oss, A : (1) a workingman's term for his employer, master ; (2) in Amer. politics, the head of a caucus. Dutch, *baas*, master (earlier, uncle).

oss rule : control by a boss. Phrase invented by Wayne MacVeagh (b.1833).

oss the show, To : to occupy a controlling position in an undertaking. The slang word ' to boss ' *i.e.*, ' to miss,' is of different origin.

oston Tea Party, The : the destruction in Boston Harbour (Dec. 16, 1773) of a number of chests of tea by disguised citizens as a protest against the British proposal to tax the Amer. colonists.

oswell to . . To play : to write a biography rich in personal details, and in order to fit oneself for the task to be in constant close attendance on the subject of the biography ; as was James Boswell (1740-95), the biographer of Dr. Samuel Johnson.

oswellian : of biography, extremely intimate and detailed.

Botany Bay : a place of exile for convicts. From the name of an inlet on the coast of New South Wales, to which convicts were orig. sent in 1787.

Botany Bay dozen, A : twenty lashes of the ' cat.'

Botley Assizes : a reference to the tradition that the men of Botley once hanged a man because he could not drink as deeply as his neighbours.

Bottle-holder, A : (1) a second, or supporter, in a prize-fight ; one who holds the bottle out of which to give the pugilist refreshment ; (2) a second or moral supporter, generally. In 1851 *Punch* depicted Lord Palmerston as the bottle-holder of oppressed States.

Bottle-washer, A : one who makes himself generally useful in menial duties ; a general factotum.

Bottom dollar, One's (*Amer.*) : one's last coin.

Bottom drawer, The : an imaginary drawer in which is preserved the provision made from time to time by a prudent mother for the future trousseau of her daughter.

Bottom of one's heart, From the : unreservedly. [John Bale, *God's Promises*, V (1522)]

Bottom out of . . To knock the : to demolish the last resistance of . .

Bottom, To play : to be overweeningly conceited. After Nick Bottom, the weaver, a character in Shakespeare, *Midsummer Night's Dream* (1590).

Bottom, To touch : to fall to the lowest point of one's fortunes. A nautical phrase.

Bottomless pit, The : Hell. [James I, *A Counterblaste to Tobacco* (1604)]

Bough on which one is sitting, To saw off the : to deprive a person of support. [Cicero, *P. Scauro*]

Bougie, A (*Fr.*, *bougie*, candle) : a surgical instrument. From Bugia, a town of N. Africa which exported wax.

Bouguereau quality : extreme refinement, almost to effeminacy, in art and literature. After A. W. Bouguereau (1825-1905), French painter.

Boulangist, A : a follower of Gen. Boulanger (1837-91), Fr. reactionary politician.

Boule (*Grk.*, dissyllable) : the Grk. Parliament. The name of the Senate, or Council, of ancient Athens.

Boule : *see* Buhl.

Bounce : swagger ; impudence. [Steele, *The Lying Lover* (1704)]

Boundary, To go beyond the : to die.

Bounder, A : a pretentious vulgar man assuming a social position he does not possess by nature ; a 'cad.'

Bountiful, Lady : a kind-hearted generous lady. After a character in Farquhar, *The Beaux' Stratagem* (1707).

Bourbon, A : (1) a person who fails to profit by experience ; (2) a member of an Amer. political party ; ' a Democrat behind the age and unteachable.' After the French Royal Family, which was said to learn nothing and to forget nothing.

Bourgeois : (1) middle-class ; uninspired ; conventional ; [Horace Walpole, *Letters*, VI (1775)] (2) a size of printing type. After a French printer or type founder.

Bourgeoisie, The : the middle classes, especially the trading classes. From Fr. *bourgeois*, a citizen or freeman of a borough.

Bourne whence no traveller returns, The: death. [Shakespeare, *Hamlet*, III, i, (1602)]

Bourse, A : a stock exchange ; a centre for financial business. From the name of the family of Van der Burse of Bruges, whose coat of arms included a purse (*bourse*). The earliest exchange building was erected at Bruges.

Boustrapa: a nickname for Napoleon III. Coined from Boulogne, Strasbourg and Paris, the scenes of his three *coups d'état*, the last only of which was successful.

Bouts-rimés (*Fr.*, rhymed ends) : rhymed endings of lines, from which verse was constructed.

Bow and scrape, To : to salute with much obeisance. The scraping refers to the drawing back of the foot in making the obeisance. [Earle, *Microcosmography : A Plaine Country Fellow* (1628)]

Bow at a venture, To draw a : to make an intentionally random remark or effort on the chance that it may go home. [I *Kings*, xxii, 34]

Bow Bells, To be born within sound of : to be a cockney, *i.e.*, born within the City of London. From the Church of St. Mary-le-Bow in Cheapside, in the centre of the City.

Bow Street Runners : police-officers in charge of warrants of arrest, attached to Bow Street Police Court, London, in the late 18th and 19th cents.

Bow, To draw the long : to exaggerat From the marvellous stories former told of the skill of archers with th long-bow, and the feats of Robin Hoo and his foresters. [*The Spectato No. 538 (1712)]

Bow, To have two strings to one's : have two alternative courses open one. [Heywood, *Proverbes*, 30 (1546

Bow to . . To make one's : to introdu oneself to . . [Peter Pindar, *Subjec for Painters* (17—)]

Bow up at the castle, To have a famous to be a great braggart.

Bow-hand, To be too much of the : t fail in a design. Metaphor draw from archery. The bow-hand, th which held the bow, was the le hand.

Bow-wow way, A : a haughty, ove bearing manner. Term invented b the tenth Earl of Pembroke (1734-94 in allusion to Dr. Samuel Johnson.

Bowdlerize, To : to expurgate a book s as to render it unobjectionable fo family use. After Thos. Bowdle (1754-1825). Editor of *The Fami Shakespeare*.

Bowels, To have no : to be withou mercy. From the former belief tha the bowels were the seat of th quality of mercy. [Wm. Penn, *Som Fruits of Solitude*, Pt. I, §534 (1718)

Bowie-knife, A : a hunting-knife, usefu also as a weapon. After Jas. Bowie the Amer. inventor (1796-1836).

Bowl, The flowing : the bowl (of wine

Bowled out, To be : to be defeated ; t be put out of action. A cricke metaphor.

Bowler, A : a round hard-felt hat From its resemblance to a bowl.

Box and Cox arrangement, A : a arrangement whereby a room i occupied by one person during the da and another at night. After the titl of a comedy by J. Morton (1811-91).

Box, Christmas, A : *see* Christmas.

Box the compass, To : to turn roun completely. A nautical metaphor Properly, to repeat the names of th several points of the compass in thei correct order.

Box, To be in the wrong : (of people) t be out of place ; in a wrong position [Heywood, *Proverbes* (1546)]

Boxer, A : a member of a Chinese secre society formed for the expulsion o Europeans. Properly, a member o the League of United Patriots, which by a play upon words (Chinese) became known as a Boxer. [In common use in 1900]

Boy Bishop, A : a boy elected by his companions to act as bishop from St. Nicholas' Day (Dec. 6) to Innocents Day (Dec. 28). St. Nicholas was the Patron Saint of scholars.

Boy in buttons, A : *see* Buttons.

Boy with the bird-bolt, The : Cupid. The bird-bolt was a short, thick arrow without point.

Boys, Roaring : younger members of the aristocracy who used to frequent the streets seeking quarrels and annoying inoffensive citizens. [Originated in the reign of James I]

Boyar, A : a Russian noble. Orig. a member of a non-hereditary class attached to the Court. The Order was abolished by Peter the Great, but still survives in Roumania.

Boycott, To : to decline, for political reasons, to supply goods to, or have any intercourse with. After Chas. Cunningham Boycott (1832-97), first to be 'boycotted' under the Irish Nationalist 'Plan of Campaign' of 1880.

B.P., The : the British Public ; esp. in theatrical and journalistic slang.

Brabanconne, La : the Belgian national hymn, composed on the occasion of the Revolution of 1830 ; named from the Province of Brabant.

Brace of shakes, In a : in a moment.

Bradbury, A : a British Treasury Note ; after Sir John Bradbury, the Secretary to the Treasury, a replica of whose autograph was printed upon each note.

Brag, To : to boast ; lit., to make a loud noise like a trumpet.

Brag, Jack : a braggart. From the hero of a novel of that name by Theodore Hook (1837).

Braggadocio, A : a boaster ; also as an adjective, boasting. A pseudo-Italian word, formed from 'brag.' In Spenser, *Faerie Queen*, Braggadocchio is the personification of bragging and cowardice.

Bragi's Apples : fruit that refreshes but is not diminished ; an immediate cure for weariness. After Bragi, in Scand. mythology, the inventor of poetry.

Bragi's Story : a long story, but full of interest.

Brahminism : a social system in which priests are given great authority and power. After Brahmin, a member of

the highest or priestly caste among the Hindus.

Braidism : hypnotism as practised by Dr. James Braid (1795-1860).

Braille : a form of type consisting of raised dots to enable the blind to read by touch. After Louis Braille, the French inventor, (1809-52).

Brain, To bear a : to exert one's mental faculties. [Shakespeare, *Romeo and Juliet*, I, iii (1591)]

Brain, Bitten to the : *see* Bitten.

Brain, To have .. on the : to be over-devoted to .., obsessed by .. (some interest or hobby).

Brain, To turn a person's : to render a person insane, to arouse an all-absorbing enthusiasm in a person. [Sir S. Tuke, *Adventures of Five Hours*, III (1663)]

Brains, To pick a person's : to extract from another the fruit of his thought.

Brain-box ; Brain-pan, A : the cranium. [Latter form used in 14th cent.]

Brake, To take a person in a : to take a person at a disadvantage. [Geo. Cavendish, *Life and Death of Wolsey* (1557)]

Bramah lock (press, etc.), A : after the inventor Joseph Bramah (1748-1814).

Brambles grow, To seek figs where only : *see* Seek.

Bran it is Bran's brother, If not : a complimentary remark ; 'as good as the best.' Bran was the dog of Fingal, the Gaelic hero.

Bran-(Brand-)new : perfectly new ; showing clearly the brand of the maker. A.-S., *brand*, a torch.

Brand snatched from the burning, A : a rescued soul.

Brandy Nan : Queen Anne. A name given to her by Londoners on account of her alleged addiction to brandy.

Branghton, A : a vulgar, malicious, jealous person. After a family of that name in Fanny Burney, *Evelina* (1778).

Brantôme, A : a writer of scandalous biographical anecdotes. From the title (Seigneur de Brantôme) of Pierre de Bourdeilles (d. 1614), a Gascon biographer and writer of anecdotes.

Brass : (1) effrontery ; assurance ; [Shakespeare, *Love's Labour Lost*, V, ii, 395 (1588)] (2) money ; formerly copper or bronze coin. [Tyndale's *Matthew*, x, 9 ; Shakespeare, *Henry V*, IV, iv (1599)]

Brass Band, The Pope's : the Irish opponents of the Ecclesiastical Titles Bill of 1851.

Brass, As bold as : see Bold.

Brass farthing, Not to care a : to care nothing. [J. S., *Andromana*, I, i (1660)]

Bravado (*Span.*) : boastful behaviour, either as a sign of extreme courage or as a pretence to cover timidity. [Hakluyt, *Voyages*, II (1582)]

Brave des braves, Le plus ; The bravest of the brave : (1) Marshal Ney (1769-1815), a title given to him by Napoleon during the Russian campaign ; (2) the same title was given by Henri IV of France to Gen. Louis de Balbe de Crillon (1541-1615).

Bravo, A (*Ital.*, a brave man) : a bully ; a hired assassin. [Daniel, *Civil Wars*, III, lxxii (1597)]

Bray, Vicar of : see Vicar.

Brazil : a kind of hard wood ; a dye made from the Brazil wood.

Brazil, As hard as : supposed to be an allusion to copper, formerly known as brass, or iron pyrites once used for striking lights and therefore considered a symbol for hardness.

Bread and butter, To quarrel with one's : to be dissatisfied with one's earnings and act in a manner that will jeopardize even them. [Swift (Simon Wagstaff), *Polite Conversation*, Dial. I (1738)]

Bread and butter Miss, A : A girl of about 16 or 17 ; a High-school girl.

Bread and cheese : the minimum necessities of life.

Bread and salt, To take : to swear. Bread and salt, the two chief necessaries of life, were in ancient days regarded as giving solemnity to an oath.

Bread is buttered, To know on which side one's : to know where one's interests lie. [Heywood, *Proverbes* (1546)]

Bread of affliction : see Affliction.

Bread of idleness, To eat the : to neglect to support oneself.

Bread out of a person's mouth, To take the : to deprive a person of his livelihood.

Bread upon the waters, To cast (scatter) : to perform a small act in the hope or expectation of a disproportionate result. [*Ecclesiastes*, xi 1]. When the Nile overflows its banks rice-seed is thrown into its overflow, and when the waters subside the seed is found to have taken root.

Break a butterfly on the wheel, To : to use an instrument far more powerful than necessary for one's purpose. A reference to the former method of execution by breaking a person's body on a wheel. [Pope, *Epistle to Dr Arbuthnot*, l. 308 (1735)]

Break a person's heart, To : to cause a person irremovable grief. [*Acts*, xxi 13 ; Shakespeare, *The Rape of Lucrece* 1238-9 (1593-4)]

Break the ice, To : to open a conversation or other undertaking.

Break the neck of. . To : to overcome the first difficulties in an enterprise.

Breakers ahead : difficulties in front of one. A nautical metaphor.

Breakfast-table, Autocrat of the : see Autocrat.

Breast of . . To make a clean : to make a complete confession of . .

Breath, To slip one's : to die. [Peter Pindar, *Odes of Importance : Old Simon* (1792)]

Breeches Bible, The : the Eng. or Genevan Bible of 1560, in which *Genesis*, iii, 7, reads ' and they sewed figge-tree leaves together, and made themselves breeches.'

Breeches, To wear the : said of a wife who masterfully controls her husband even in details. [*Les Quinze Joyes de Mariage : La Dixieme Joye* (1450) ; Heywood, *Proverbes* (1546)]

Brentano, A : an extremely foolish person. From a Germ. proverb.

Brentford, The Old Woman of : a witch. After a famous witch of Brentford around whom several ballads were composed.

Brentford, Two Kings of : two persons who act exactly alike. After characters in the Duke of Buckingham, *The Rehearsal* (1672).

Brevier : a style of type orig. used for printing the Roman Catholic Breviary.

Briareus of Languages, The : Guiseppe Gaspar, Cardinal Mezzofanti (1774-1849), who knew 58 languages. In Homer *Iliad*, Briareos was a giant with 50 heads and 100 hands.

Briars, To be in the : to be in a difficulty. [*Terence in English* (1614)]

Bric-a-brac : portable objects of antiquarian and artistic interest. From *de bric et de broc*, by hook or by crook ; possibly referring to the means by which bric-a-brac is usually collected.

Brick, A : a good fellow ; one to be depended upon. From the description of the men of his army by Agesilaus, King of Sparta, when asked where his walled fortifications were.

rick, To drop a : to make a foolish mistake.

rick wall, To run one's head against a : to follow a course obstinately which must obviously lead to failure.

ricks without straw, To make : to attempt a task which is impossible in consequence of the absence of an indispensable tool or material. From the task of the Israelites as described in *Exodus*, v.

rickdusts, The : the 1st King's Shropshire Light Infantry, formerly 53rd Foot. On account of the colour of their facings.

ride of the Seas, The : Venice. In allusion to the Marriage of the Adriatic (*q.v.*).

ride-ale, A : a wedding-feast. 'Ale,' in the sense of a rural festival.

ride-bush, A : a bush hung out at a village ale-house in honour of a wedding.

ride-stake, A : a pole set up in a village to dance round at a wedding.

ridewell, A : a prison. After the palace near St. Bride's Well in London, used as a prison by Edward VI.

ridewell-man, A : a gaoler.

ridge of gold for .. To make a : to give a man an opportunity of withdrawing from a position without loss of dignity.

ridge over the sea, To build a : to attempt a futile task. From an ancient Grk. proverb.

ridge of Sighs : a covered bridge connecting the Doge's palace and the prison at Venice. Across it were taken prisoners for trial or judgment.

ridget, A : *see* Biddy, A.

ridgeting : obtaining money by false or other underhand pretences from the ignorant, esp. those of the servant-girl class (*see* Bridget). Irish servant-girls in the U.S. have subscribed largely, with more or less understanding, to the funds of Irish political movements.

ridgewater Treatises, The : a series of eight treatises written in accordance with the will of Francis Henry, Earl of Bridgewater (1756-1829), for the foundation of which he bequeathed £8,000. The writers selected by the President of the Royal Society, the Archbishop of Canterbury and the Bishop of London were Dr. Thomas Chalmers, Dr. John Kidd, Dr. Wm. Whewell, Sir Charles Bell, Peter Mark Roget, Dr. Wm. Buckland, Wm. Kirby, Dr. Wm. Prout, and the subject of the treatises, ' The Power, Wisdom and Goodness of God as manifested in the Creation.'

Bridle, To bite on the : to suffer great hardship. The bridle was the instrument formerly employed in the punishment of a scold.

Bridport dagger, A : a hangman's rope. Hempen goods were formerly mainly manufactured at Bridport.

Brieve of Furiosity, A : an inquiry into a person's sanity. In Scottish law, *brieve*, a writ issued in Chancery.

Brigand, A : a bandit ; an armed robber. Ital., *brigante*, an irregular foot-soldier. From Briga, a border-town near Nice.

Bright as the day, As : [Chaucer, *Canterbury Tales* (14th cent.)]

Bright's Disease : a disease of the kidneys. After Dr. Richard Bright (1789-1858), who investigated it.

Brighton of Scotland, The : St. Andrews.

Brillat-Savarin, A : an expert in gastronomy ; a bon-vivant. After A. Brillat-Savarin (1755-1826), author of *La Physiologie du Gout*.

Brilliant Madman, The : Charles XII of Sweden.

Bring Down the House, To : to induce very great applause (in a theatre).

Bring one's machines after the war is over, To : to act in a futile manner ; ' to lock the stable-door after the steed is stolen.' From an ancient Grk. proberb.

Briny, On the : on the ocean.

Brioche, A : a small fancy loaf ; a blunder. From the remark attributed to the daughter of Louis XVI, when she learnt that the people were starving for lack of bread : ' Si le peuple n'a pas de pain, qu'il mange des brioches.' ' If the people have no bread, let them eat brioches.'

Brisle dice : false dice. From the bristles inserted in them to influence their fall.

Bristol, A : a visiting-card ; formerly made of Bristol board (*q.v.*).

Bristol board, A : drawing-paper mounted on a thin board ; formerly made at Bristol.

Bristol Boy, The : Thomas Chatterton of Bristol (1752-70), poet.

Bristol fashion, In : in good order. Referring to the days when Bristol was almost the principal Eng. port.

Bristol man's gift, A : a gift of something that has no value to the giver.

Bristol Milk : sherry, a wine formerly imported via Bristol.

Bristol Stones (Diamonds) : brilliant stones, found near Bristol and used for cheap jewellery.

British Aristides, The : Andrew Marvell (1621-78). After Aristides the Just (c. 530-468 B.C.), the Athenian statesman and general.

British Common, The : the sea.

British Cuvier, The : Sir Richard Owen (1804-92). After G. L. C. Cuvier (1769-1832), a distinguished French naturalist.

British Jeremiah, The : Gildas (516-570), British historian. So-called by Gibbon.

British lion's tail, To twist : *see* Lion's tail.

British Solomon, The : James I, king of Great Britain.

Britisher, A : a citizen of the United Kingdom. Introduced and orig. used in the U.S. as a term of derision or contempt.

Brittle as glass, As : very fragile, easily broken. [*Mirror for Magistrates*, 179 (1559)]

Broad Arrow, A : a sign of British Government ownership. After the broad arrow-head marked on British Government stores, convicts, etc. Orig. the sign of Henry, Earl of Romney (1641-1704), Master-General of the Ordnance.

Broad as long, As : of two means, both leading to the same end.

Broad Bottom(ed) Ministry, The : the ministry formed by Henry Pelham in 1744. So-called because it included representatives of all Parties.

Broad Church, The : the Liberal school in the Church of England, which holds that the Church should be tolerant, and embrace wide differences of opinion. [First used at Oxford about 1850]

Broad Piece, A : a sovereign (20s.) Used after 1663 to distinguish the coin from the guinea then introduced, which was a more compact coin.

Broadbrim, A : a quaker. From the style of hat formerly worn by members of the Society of Friends.

Brobdi(n)gnag(ian) : huge ; immense. After the monstrous race of giants inhabiting Brobdingnag, in Swift, *Gulliver's Travels* (1726).

Brocard, A : a maxim. After Brocar Bp. of Worms (11th cent.), who ma a collection of ecclesiastical canons.

Broken beer : the unconsumed resid of beer left in the glass.

Broken English (etc.), To speak : speak English or other language u grammatically and with a forei accent. [Lyly, *Euphues and h England* (1580)]

Broken meat : remnants of food left aft a meal. [Chapman, *May Day* (1611

Broken posts, To erect : *see* Erect.

Broken reed, A : *see* Reed.

Broker, The Honest : *see* Honest.

Brooks of Sheffield : an assumed nam used when it is not desired to menti the real one. After an imaginar character in Dickens, *David Coppe field* (1849).

Broom, Dame (Mrs.) Partington's : s Partington.

Broom sweeps clean, A new : a pers newly appointed to an office starts h career with exceptional assiduity whic does not endure. [Heywoo *Proverbes* (1546)]

Broth of a boy, A : an Irish colloquialis for a high-spirited, good-nature young fellow. Irish, *brotha*, passionat

Brother Bung : a publican. In allusic to the bung of a beer-barrel.

Brother Chip : one of the same trad Properly, a fellow-carpenter.

Brother Jonathan : the popular nam for a citizen of the U.S. Said to hav arisen from Washington callir Jonathan Trumbull, Governor Connecticut, ' Brother.'

Brother of the Angle, A : a member the commonwealth of anglers. [Isa Walton, *The Compleat Angler*, Pt. ch. 1 (1653)]

Brother of the Blade, A : a soldie anyone of the same calling as tl speaker.

Brother of the Brush, A : a fellow-artis

Brother of the Buskin, A : an acto From the buskins worn by traged actors in ancient times.

Brother of the Coif, A : a sergeant-a law. From the coif or close-fittir cap worn by him.

Brother of the Quill, A : a member the commonwealth of letters. [*T Spectator*, No. 552 (1712)]

Brother of the String, A : a fiddler.

Brother of the Sword, A : a soldie [Dryden, *Epistle to Mr. Lee*, ll. 7 and (1677)]

Brother of the Whip, A : a coachman. [*The Spectator*, No. 498 (1712)]

Brougham, A : a closed, four-wheeled carriage. After Hy., Lord Brougham (1778-1868), by whom it was introduced.

Broughtonian, A : a pugilist. After John Broughton (1705-89), English pugilist.

Brown Bess : the flint-lock musket, formerly in use in the British Army. From the brown walnut stock.

Brown Bess, Married to : having joined the army.

Brown Bill, A : a brown halberd, formerly used by foot-soldiers. [Lyly, *Sapho and Phao*, II, iii (1591)]

Brown George, A : (1) a hard, coarse biscuit or bread ; (2) a brown earthenware vessel.

Brown, Jones and Robinson : the British public in a mass. These surnames are the most frequently met with in England. *Brown, Jones and Robinson* is the title of Richard Doyle's series of humorous *Punch* drawings depicting the adventures of three typical Englishmen on the Rhine and in Italy ; afterwards republished in book-form.

Brown study, A : a reverie. Connected with ' brown ' in the sense of ' gloomy,' or ' brow,' brain. [*The Marriage of Wit and Science* (1569-70)]

Browns, To astonish the : to say something that shocks the unsophisticated.

Brown-paper warrants : warrants that can be cancelled at the will of him who drew them. A nautical phrase.

Brownists, The : the original Congregationalists, followers of Rob. Browne (1550-1630), who seceded from the Church of England.

Bruin : a popular name for the bear. From the fable of *Reynard the Fox*. Dutch, *broun*.

Bruised reed, A : *see* Reed.

Bruiser, A : a prize-fighter. Lit., one who bruises. [Horace Walpole, *Letters to Horace Mann*, I, 57 (1744)]

Brummagem : cheap and showy ; counterfeit ; shoddy. A corruption of Birmingham, where cheap and spurious jewellery, etc., is made.

Brummagem Protestants : (1) counterfeit groats made at Birmingham ; (2) supporters of the Exclusion Bill of 1680. From Birmingham in its capacity of a Radical stronghold.

Brummell, Beau : *see* Beau.

Brunch : breakfast and lunch combined. A portmanteau word.

Brunswick, A : a lady's out-of-door costume. After Brunswick, Germany, whence they were introduced c. 1750.

Brunt, To bear the : to support the stress of a contest or undertaking. Icelandic, *bruni*, burning heat. [*The Louer Wounded of Cupide*, ll. 37-40 (1557)]

Brutum fulmen (*Lat.*, senseless thunderbolt) : an empty threat. [Pliny, *Historia Naturalis*]

Brutus, A : a kind of wig worn in the early 19th cent.

Bubble and Squeak : a dish of meat and cabbage cooked together. From the sounds made by the food in the process of cooking.

Bubble Company (Scheme), A : an unsound Company, of a fraudulent or semi-fraudulent character, as unsubstantial as a bubble. Perhaps connected with Middle English, to ' bubble,' to cheat.

Buccaneer, A : a pirate, a freebooter. Orig. the pirates of the West Indies, who preyed upon the Spanish trade in the 17th cent. From *Boucan* (Caribbean), a place where meat was dried. Many of the original buccaneers engaged in the occupation of drying meat.

Bucentaur, The : a large ship ; a gaily decorated barge. After the ' Bucentaur,' the state barge of Venice. The name was probably derived from a figure-head, half-man, half-ox.

Bucephalus, A : a spirited horse. After the favourite steed of Alexander the Great.

Buck, A : a dandy. From buckram, which was used in stiffening the dress of 18th-cent. men-of-fashion, or from to ' buck,' *i.e*, to wash clothes in lye, bucks' clothes being very carefully worked and prepared for wear.

Buck, To pass the : a phrase used in the game of poker, meaning to hand on a difficult decision to the next player.

Buck up, To : to make an effort. Orig. a Westminster School term.

Buck's horn, To blow the : to profit oneself nothing. [Chaucer, *Miller's Tale* (1393)]

Buck-eye, A : an inhabitant of the State of Ohio.

Buck-eye State, The : Ohio. On account of the number of its buck-eye or horse-chestnut trees.

Buck-horse, A : a blow on the face. After the name of a pugilist, Buck (fl. 1732-46).

F

Buck-tail, A : orig. a member of the Tammany Society of New York ; later a member of the Democratic-Republican Party.

Buck-tooth, A : a large projecting tooth, supposed to be evidence of the male sex.

Bucket, To kick the : *see* Kick.

Bucket Shop, A : the office or business of a dealer in stocks and shares who is not a member of an authorized Stock Exchange. From a gambling-office in Chicago to which clients were brought in a lift or 'bucket.'

Buckle and bare thong, To come to : to have exhausted one's means. [Heywood, *Proverbes* (1546)]

Buckle of one's belt behind one, To turn the : to prepare to fight to a finish. [Breton, *Poste with a Packet of Mad Letters* (1637)]

Buckle, To talk : to talk about marriage.

Buckle to, To : to enter seriously and resolutely into (a work). From the process of buckling on a knight's armour for the tournament or for battle. [Bacon, *Essayes : Of Deluges* (1625)]

Buckle-beggar, A (*Scot.*) : a person who performs irregular marriage ceremonies.

Bucklers, To give (yield) the : to admit defeat. [Shakespeare, *Much Ado About Nothing*, V, ii (1599) ; Greene, *Second Part of Coney Catching* (1592)]

Bucklers, To take up the : to issue a challenge to combat. [Wm. Rowley, *A Woman Never Vexed*, IV, i (1632)]

Buckra : superior ; white. The negro's term for a white man. Original meaning in Calabar language, a demon ; whence, powerful, superior.

Buckram Bag, A : an attorney of a low class. On account of the bags carried by them.

Buckram, Man in : *see* Man in Buckram.

Bud, To nip in the : *see* Nip.

Buddha to play with water, As dangerous as for a clay : from a Japanese proverb. Japanese children often amuse themselves by making little images of Buddha in mud which melt into shapelessness if placed in water.

Budget, The : the annual statement, together with estimates, of a Finance Minister. Orig. a bag, a despatch-box. In the Parliamentary sense probably derived from the Minister's despatch-box. First used about 1760.

Buff or sty, To say : to have a voice in a matter.

Buff, To stand : to stand firm. A nautical term. [Butler, *Hudibras' Epitaph* (1678)]

Buffs, The : the East Kent Regt. (3rd Foot). On account of the former colour of their facings.

Buffs, The Ross-shire : the 2nd Battn. Seaforth Highlanders (78th Foot). On account of the colour of their facings.

Buffer, An old : a good-natured, not over intelligent old gentleman. Middle-English, *buffen*, to stammer.

Buffer-State, A : a small State, whose independence is preserved in order that it may separate two larger rival states. From the contrivance inserted between them and thus neutralizing the shock when two powerful forces come into collision.

Buffle-head, A : a blockhead. From 'buffle,' a stupid person. [*Lady Alimony*, I, ii (1659)]

Bugaboo, A : a bogey.

Bug-bear, A : an object of needless terror. From a threat of something terrible (apparently a bear) used by nurses to frighten their charges. Welsh, *bwg*, a goblin.

Buhl : an inlay of metal, etc., in fine wood, etc., in cabinet-making. After André Boulle (1642-1732), Fr. cabinet-maker.

Build a bridge over the sea, To : *see* Bridge.

Bulbul, A (*Persian*) : a singer ; a nightingale.

Bull, A : an absurd verbal blunder, most commonly perpetrated by Irishmen : hence 'An Irish Bull.' Said to have been derived from Obadiah Bull, an Irish lawyer in London in the time of Henry VII.

Bull : (Stock Exchange) *see* Bear and Bull.

Bull by the horns, To take the : *see* Take.

Bull in a china shop : a person who causes damage or harm by his clumsiness.

Bull of Phalaris, A : an instrument of torture in the form of a hollow bull of brass in which the victims were burnt to death. Introduced by Phalaris, tyrant of Acragas in Sicily (c. 570-554 B.C.)

Bull to roar, To teach a : *see* Teach.

Bull-dog, A : an attendant on a proctor. A University term.

Bull-dog courage : unsubduable courage, like that of a bull-dog, which breed was formerly employed in bull-baiting.

Bull-doze, To : to threaten or bully. First used with reference to negro voters after the close of the Civil War. Lit., to flog with a strip of hide, used by drovers to control refractory animals.

Bull's-eye : the centre of a military target.

Bull's-eye, To hit the : *see* Hit.

Bulletin, To lie like a : *see* Lie.

Bulley-beef : tinned beef. Probably from (Fr.) *bouilli*, boiled.

Bullion State, The : Missouri. After its representative in Congress, Thos. Hart Benton, Old Bullion (*q.v.*).

Bullyrag, To : to threaten and abuse. Possibly derived from ' bully ' or ' bull ' and (red) ' rag.'

Bulwark of the North, The : Stirling, Scotland ; so-called by Sir Walter Scott in *The Lady of the Lake* (1810).

Bum-bailiff, A : a sheriff's officer ; one who comes up from behind to serve a summons.

Bum-boat, A : a clumsy-looking boat employed in taking provisions to a ship. Orig. a scavenger's boat on the Thames. Name derived either from the shape, or from Dutch *bon*, a box for holding fish.

Bumble, A : a parish beadle or other officer ; any pompous, minor official. After Mr. Bumble, the beadle, in Dickens, *Oliver Twist* (1838).

Bumbledom : (1) petty, fussy officialism ; (2) local officials as a class.

Bummer, A : (*Germ. Bummler*), a loafer. American slang.

Bumper, A : a glass of wine (etc.) filled to the brim ; anything filled to over-flowing.

Bumpkin, A country : (*Dutch boomken*), a fool. An awkward, uncouth rustic. [Peter Pindar, *Complimentary Epistle to James Bruce* (1790)]

Bumptious : aggressively conceited. Apparently a corruption of ' presump-tuous.' [Mme. D'Arblay, *Diary and Letters*, VI, 324 (1803)]

Bunch-clot, A : a farmer. N.-E. Eng. dialect, ' bunch,' to strike.

Buncombe : *see* Bunkum.

Bunco-steerer, A : a swindler ; a sharp. An Americanism. After Bunco (Ital. *Banco*), an American swindling card-game.

Bundesrath : the German Imperial Parliament.

Bung, A : (1) a pickpocket ; a sharper ; thieve's slang, possibly from Anglo-Saxon, *pung*, a purse ; (2) a publican ; from the bung of a beer-barrel.

Bung, Brother : *see* Brother.

Bungalow, A : a one-storied house. Persian, *bangalah*, a Bengalese (house).

Bungay with you ! Go to : orig. ' Go to Bungay and get your breeches mended ! ' Bungay was formerly famous for its manufacture of leather-breeches.

Bunk, To : to decamp ; to run away.

Bunkum ; Buncombe : humbug ; speech-making intended merely to deceive. From Buncombe County, N. Carolina, whose representative in the 16th Congress, Felix Walker, was addicted to such speech-making.

Bunny : pet name for a rabbit. From *bun*, a tail.

Burbolt, As much brain as a : as much sense as a bird-bolt or short, thick arrow, formerly used for shooting rooks. [Udall, *Ralph Roister Doister*, III, ii, ll. 100-1 (1550)]

Burchardize, To : to speak with authority. After Burchard (d. 1026), Bp. of Worms, compiler of a collection of canons.

Burgomaster : the Mayor of a German, Dutch, or Flemish town.

Buridan's Ass : the donkey, invented by the Fr. Schoolman, Jean Buridan (1297-1358). The ass, pressed by both hunger and thirst yet utterly unable to decide between a measure of oats and a bucket of water, both of which were within his reach, died of starvation and thirst.

Burke, To : to dispose of secretly ; later, to prevent another from securing ; to prevent ; suppress. After Wm. Burke (1792-1829), body-snatcher.

Burlaw : lynch-law (*q.v.*) ; a local law in Scotland. *Byr*, borough.

Burleigh nod, A Lord : a nod supposed to convey deep meaning, to have much wisdom behind it. From the nod of Lord Burleigh in Mr.Puff's *The Spanish Armada*, a part of Sheridan's *The Critic* (1779).

Burn one's boats behind one, To : *see* Boats.

Burn one's fingers, To : to get into trouble or suffer loss.

Burn the candle at both ends, To : *see* Candle.

Burn daylight, To : to waste time. [*Appius and Virginia*, l. 230 (1563)].

Burning question, A : a matter of intense and widespread interest and discussion. First used in English by Edward Miall, M.P. and Nonconformist minister (1809-81) ; prev. used in German (*brennende Fragen*) by Hagenbach in *Grundlinien der Liturgie und Homiletik* (1803). A 'red-hot' question is used with the same meaning.

Burning shame, A : a conspicuous disgrace. [Shakespeare, *King Lear*, IV, iii, 48 (1605–6)]

Burse, The (Fr., *bourse*, purse): one of the official insignia of the Lord Chancellor. A receptacle used in connection with the Eucharist.

Bury the hatchet, To : *see* Hatchet.

Bus, A : a contracted form of omnibus, a public vehicle for the conveyance of passengers on fixed routes. (Lat., *omnibus*, for everybody.)

Busby, A : a uniform hat worn by certain Eng. regiments ; formerly a species of wig. Either from the name of an Eng. village or an Eng. family name.

Busby's School : Westminster School. After Richard Busby (1606-95), a famous headmaster.

Bush, To beat about the : *see* Beat.

Bush-Whacker, A : (1) an irregular soldier in the Amer. Civil War ; lit., a backwoodsman, one who beats down bushes in order to make his way ; (2) (political) a free-lance.

Bushel, To hide one's light under a : to live modestly, not to obtrude one's excellences. [*Matthew*, v, 15 ; *Totus Mundus in maligno positus*, ll. 49-50 (1557)]

Bushel, To measure corn by one's own : to judge others by one's own standard. [Joseph Henshaw, *Horae Succesivae* 279 (1631)]

Bushido : the Japanese code of chivalry. Lit., the way of a military knight.

Buskin : tragedy. After the half-boot worn by Greek and Roman actors in tragedy.

Busman's (Busdriver's) Holiday, A : a holiday devoted to following one's ordinary occupation. From the apocryphal practice of a busman when on holiday riding by the side of one of his colleagues on duty.

Busy (fussy) as a hen that has one chick, As : fussy and over-anxious about trifles. [Clarke, *Paroemiologia* (1639)]

Busybody, A : one who concerns himself unnecessarily with other people's business. [Tindal, I *Peter*, iv, 15 (1526)]

But me no buts ! : speak clearly and to the point, without any qualifications.

[Fielding, *Rape upon Rape*, II, (1730)]

Butcher of Culloden, The : the Duke Cumberland (1721-65). On accou of his cruelties perpetrated after th defeat of the rebels at Culloden.

Butler's box, A : a box into which car players put a portion of their winnin (?) for the butler.

Butler's grace, A : a drink.

Butter would not melt in one's mouth, T look as if : to have the appearance perfect innocence and harmlessnes [Heywood, *Proverbes* (1546) ; Clarke, *Paroemiologia Anglo-Latin* (1639)]

Butter-box, A ; Butter-bag, A : Dutchman (contemptuously). Prob ably in reference to the production butter in Holland. [Lyly, *Sapho an Phao*, III, ii (1591)]

Butter-fingers, A : one who misses catch at cricket, or is otherwise clums with the fingers ; a duffer. [Markham *The English Housewife*, II, ii, 5 (1615)]

Buttered ale : a drink composed of bee butter, etc.

Butterfly on the wheel, To break a : t employ an unnecessarily great effo to overcome a slight obstacle.

Butterfly Journal, A : a financial new paper, not intended for *bona fide* sa but given away as an advertisemer to induce the purchase of shares, et

Butterfly('s) kiss, A : a kiss with th eyelashes.

Butternuts : (1) soldiers of the Con federate States ; on account of th colour of their uniforms, *i.e.*, brownish-grey ; (2) sympathizer with the Confederate cause, in th Northern States.

Button for . . Not to care a (brass) : t hold as of next to no account. O account of the small value of a butto [Taylor, *Workes* (1630)]

Buttons, A (Boy in) : a page ; the button on whose uniform are numerous an conspicuous.

Buttons, Not to have all one's : to b half-witted.

Buttons, To have a soul above : to b superior to one's employment. [Ge Colman, *Sylvester Daggerwood* (1795)

Buttonhole a person, To : to detain person in conversation, as if b inserting your finger in his butto hole ; to bore a person with one conversation.

utton-hole, To seize a person by the : to detain a person in conversation. [Goldsmith, *The Good-natured Man*, II, i (1768)]

uy cheap and sell dear, To : [Petronius, *Satyricon*, cap. 75]

uzfuz, A Sergeant : a bullying lawyer. After a character in Dickens, *Pickwick Papers* (1836).

uzzards : inhabitants of Georgia, U.S.A. Owing to the number of wild turkeys in that state.

uzzard, As blind as a : a buzzard was the name of a flying beetle; as in the evening it often struck people in its flight it was popularly supposed to be blind.

uzzard, Between hawk and : *see* Hawk.

yegones be byegones, To let : to ignore past wrongs or causes of offence and to start relations again with a clean slate.

yron, The Polish : Adam Mickiewicz (1798-1855).

yron, The Russian : Alexander Sergeivitch Puschkin (1799-1837).

ywoners : landless Boers in the Transvaal and Orange Free State.

yzant : *see* Bezant.

yzantism : a system of absolute monarchical government. From Byzantium, the name of the Eastern Empire.

aaba ; Kaaba : the building at Mecca in which the sacred stone, the centre of Mohammedan pilgrimage, is kept.

abal, A : a faction; an intrigue; a party of intriguers. Probably from Cabbala (*q.v.*). By a coincidence the initial letters of the names of the five members of the governing committee of the Privy Council in 1670, Clifford, Arlington, Buckingham, Ashley, Lauderdale, form the word Cabal.

abal, To : to intrigue, to plot.

abal, The American (Conway's) : an intrigue on the part of certain representatives of the Northern States against Geo. Washington and in the interests of Charles Lee. Its leader was Thos. Conway (1733-1805).

abbage, To : to crib; to steal. Orig. of a tailor (slang designation 'cabbage') who retains a portion of the cloth entrusted to him. Old Fr., *cabasser*, to steal.

abbage Garden Patriot, A : a coward. Smith O'Brien was discovered hiding among cabbages after his abortive rebellion.

Cabbala : the esoteric learning of the Jews; the mystical literature of Judaism.

Cabinet, A : the committee of ministers which forms the government of a country; a meeting of such a committee. From 'cabinet,' the private room of the sovereign in which the committee orig. met.

Cabinet Noir, A (*Fr.*, black cabinet) : an office in France created by Louis XIV for the supervision of the correspondence of suspected persons ; abolished in 1886.

Ca' canny : (of working men) intentional reduction of speed in working and of output ; from 'call,' to drive, and 'canny,' cautiously, deliberately.

Cachet, Lettres de : *see* Lettre de Cachet.

Cacique, A : a native chief of the Central or S. Amer. Indians.

Cackler, A : a chatterer; a tell-tale; resembling a cackling hen.

Cacoethes scribendi (*Lat.*, itch for writing) : an irrepressible desire to write. [Juvenal, *Satires*, VII, 52 ; Burton, *Anatomy of Melancholy* (1621)]

Cacus, As great a thief as : Cacus was a mythological robber, the son of Vulcan and Medusa.

Cad, A : (1) a vulgar, dishonourable fellow; (2) less often, an unskilled labourer; (3) an omnibus conductor; (4) a passenger carried for the profit of the driver and not of the owner of the coach. An abbreviation either of 'caddie' (*q.v.*), in which connection the term came into use at Oxford University, or of 'cadger.'

Caddie, A : a boy in attendance on a golf-player; a man who waits about for odd jobs. French, *cadet*, junior, younger. *See* Cad.

Cadets, The : a Russian political party, the Constitutional Democrats. From the initial letters C(= K)D.

Cadi, A (*Arab.*) : an inferior judge among the Moslems.

Cadmean Letters : the letters of the Grk. alphabet. From a Grk. legend that they were introduced by Cadmus, son of Agenor, king of Phoenicia, the legendary founder of Thebes.

Cadmean Victory, A : a victory purchased at great cost. From the legend of the armed men who sprang from the dragon's teeth sown by Cadmus, and fought with one another until only five survived. The term was first used by Herodotus in his description of the Battle of Alalia (535 B.C.). [*Hist.*, I, 166]

Cadmus Crop, A : in allusion to the legend of Cadmus. *See* Cadmean Victory. [Jasper Fisher, *Fuimus Troes*, Prologue (1633)]

Cadogan, A : a knot of ribbon worn at the back of the hair. After the 1st Earl Cadogan (1675-1726).

Cæsar, To appeal unto : to appeal to the highest authority. [*Acts*, xxv, 11]

Cæsar, To render unto : in allusion to *Matthew*, xxii, 21, ' Render to Cæsar the things that are Cæsar's, and to God the things that are God's.' Do not allow your religious duties to interfere with your duties as a citizen ! [Sir Thos. Overbury, *Characters : A Jesuite* (1616)]

Cæsar's Wife, A : one on whom even the breath of suspicion must not be allowed to alight. ' Because I would have the chastity of my wife clear even from suspicion,' was the reply of Julius Cæsar when asked why he had divorced his wife Pompeia through no fault of hers, but because Publius Clodius had fallen in love with her.

Cæsars, The City of the : a mythical city in South America, said to have been founded by a member of Cabot's party named Cæsar, who deserted or disappeared, in 1530.

Cæsarian operation, A : a surgical operation for the purpose of assisting child-birth. Julius Cæsar is said to have been born by this means.

Cæsarism : autocratic rule. After the Cæsars, Roman emperors.

Café in Europe, The most aristocratic : Spa, Belgium. In allusion to the resort to it of the royalty and nobility of Europe.

Caftan, A (*Turkish*) : a long outer garment worn in Asiatic countries.

Cain, The brand of : the mark of outlawry. [*Genesis*, iv, 15]

Cain, The curse of : condemnation to perpetual wandering. The punishment of Cain for the murder of Abel.

Cain-coloured beard (hair) : red beard (hair). From the traditional colour of Cain's hair.

Ça ira (*Fr.*, it will succeed) : a French Revolutionary song, composed in 1791. The refrain, *Ça ira, ça ira*, was taken from a mot of Benjamin Franklin, the

Amer. revolutionist, uttered during the dark period of the Amer. Revolution.

Cake and have it too, To eat the : to have the advantage of both sides of a bargain. [Plautus, *Trinummus*, II, iv ; Jno. Heywood, *Proverbes* (1546)]

Cake is dough, My : I have abandoned hope. A cake leaving the oven as dough is hopelessly spoilt. [Shakespeare, *The Taming of the Shrew*, V, i (?1596)]

Cakes, The Land of : *see* Land.

Cake, To take the : to gain the prize ; to be the best of several. In allusion to a cake as a prize in the cake-walking competition among the negroes of the U.S.A. A cake was awarded as a prize even in antiquity. [Aristophanes, *Thesmophoriazusae,*

Cakes and ale : the good things of the world ; luxuries. [Shakespeare, *Twelfth Night*, II, iii (1601)]

Cake-walk, A : a dance ; orig. a negro dance. *See* Cake, To take the.

Calabar bean, A : a poisonous plant ; the ' ordeal bean ' of the natives of Old Calabar.

Calais Cormorant, A : a man who had served in the French wars. [*Histriomastix*, III, i, ll. 100-1 (1610)]

Calais Sands : after duelling had become illegal in England, it was the custom to cross the Channel to Calais to settle disputes there.

Caledonia : a poetical name for Scotland. Celtic.

Calendar, A Newgate : a record of crime. *The Newgate Calendar*, first published in 1700, is a record of the lives, crimes, confessions, etc., of criminals.

Calends, The Greek : *See* Greek Kalends.

Calepin, A : a dictionary. After Ambrosio Calepino (1435-1511), Ital. lexicographer.

Calf, The Golden : the symbol of wealth as the object of worship. [*Exodus*, xxxii]

Calf's skin, A : a fool. From the coats of calf-skin worn by professional fools.

Calf-love : the first love of young lads, usually for their seniors.

Caliban, A : a degraded, semi-brutal being. After a character in Shakespeare, *Tempest* (1600)

Calico : a cotton cloth. Orig. Calicut cloth, after Calicut, in India.

California widow, A : a woman living apart from her husband. At the time of the California gold-fever many men left their homes to go in search of fortunes, leaving their wives behind them.

Caliph, A (*Arab.*, a successor) : (1) the spiritual head of all Moslems until 1517, when the dignity was transferred to the Turkish sultans ; (2) a descendant of Mahomet.

Call ; Call-bird, A : a decoy bird. [Shakespeare, *King John*, III, iv, 174 (?1595)]

Call Boy, A : a boy employed to warn actors that their appearance on the stage is about to come due.

Call in question, To : to challenge the truth of. [Sir Philip Sidney (1554-86), *Wooing-Stuff*, ll. 21-2]

Call out, To : to challenge to a duel.

Call over the coals, To : to haul over the coals (*q.v.*).

Called to one's last account : dead.

Caller Herrin' : fresh, newly-caught herrings. Scot. and Northern dialect.

Callipolis, A : a sweetheart. After a character in Peele, *The Battle of Alcazar* (1594).

Callot ; Calot ; Callet : a woman of bad character. After Kit Callot, said to have been the first Englishwoman to adopt the life of a gypsy.

Calumet of Peace, The : the pipe of peace. Among Amer. Indians the symbol of peace. Fr., *calumet*, the French-Canadian term for the plant out of which Indian pipes are made.

Calvary, A : a place of martyrdom. After the name of the place of the Crucifixion of Christ.

Calvert's Entire : the 14th Regt. of Foot, now the Prince of Wales' Own. After the name of their colonel, Sir Harry Calvert (1806-26) and in allusion to the three entire battalions that were kept up for his benefit.

Camacho's wedding : great, but useless, expenditure. From the story of the frustrated wedding of Camacho in Cervantes, *Don Quixote*.

Camarilla, A : a body of intriguers or plotters, esp. the secret advisers of a sovereign. Span., *camara*, a chamber. *See* Cabinet.

Cambays : a cotton-cloth made in India. After Cambay, a port of India.

Cambria : Wales.

Cambrian Shakespeare, The : Edward Williams (1746-1826).

Cambric : a linen fabric. From Cambrai, France.

Cambridgeshire nightingales : frogs. On account of the number to be found in that county.

Cambyses' vein, In King : pompously. After a character in Thos. Preston, *Cambyses* (1569). [Shakespeare, 1 *Henry IV*, ii, 4 (1596)]

Camel Driver of Mecca, The : Mohammed.

Camellia : a shrub. From G. J. Camellus, a Jesuit, who discovered it in the Philippines.

Camera obscura, A (*Lat.*) : a darkened room ; an optical instrument.

Cameronians, The : a Scottish regiment, formed orig. in 1689, to serve against the Jacobites, from some of the extreme Covenanting followers of Richard Cameron (1648-80).

Camisards : French Protestants who took up arms in defence of their liberties (1702-5). Lat. *camisa*, a shirt ; after the white blouses of the peasants who formed the majority of the rebels. *Camisard* is also a military term, meaning a night attack.

Cam(m)ock, As crooked as a : a camock is a crooked beam used in shipbuilding. Welsh, *kam*, crooked.

Camorra : a Neapolitan secret revolutionary Society, afterwards merged in the followers of Garibaldi ; later used for any secret revolutionary society.

Camouflage : disguise. The term was introduced during the European War of 1914-18, orig. to denote a disguise employed for military purposes. Probably from *camouflet*, smoke intentionally blown into another's face, though many other derivations have been suggested.

Campeachy : log-wood. After Campeachy, in Central America, whence it was imported.

Campo Santo (*Ital.*, holy field) : a cemetery, esp. in Italy.

Campus Martius (*Lat.*, field of Mars) : a place of military action. From Mars, the Roman god of war.

Canaan, A : a land of promise. After the land promised to the Israelites by God.

Canaille (*Fr.*, pack of dogs) : the rabble ; the lowest class in the population.

Canal Boy, The : James Abram Garfield (1831-81), President of the U.S., who served for a portion of his youth as a hand on a canal-boat.

Canapé, A (*Fr.*, sofa) : a slice of bread fried in butter and used as a support for caviare, anchovies, etc.

Canard, A (*Fr.*, duck) : a silly story that serves as a hoax. The word in this sense has been derived from the phrase *vendre un canard à moitié*, to half-sell a duck, *i.e.*, not to sell it at all. Another derivation is from a story told by the Dutch painter, Cornelissen, that he fed a flock of twenty ducks (Fr., *canard*) on one of their number which he killed every day. Ultimately the flock was reduced to one duck which had presumably eaten up all its fellows.

Canaries, To dance the : to take part in a lively Span. dance, called the Canary or Canaries, believed to have originated in the Canary Islands.

Canary, A : (1) a guinea, from the colour of that coin ; (2) a singing-bird, after the Canary Islands.

Canary Bird, A : a gaol-bird, a convict. Either on account of the colour of the uniform formerly worn by them, or, more probably, from the cage (prison) in which a convict is confined.

Cancan, The : a noisy, indecent dance. Suggested etymologies are : (1) Old-French, *caquehan*, a tumultuous assembly ; (2) Fr., *cancaner*, to quack as a duck ; (3) Lat., *quanquam*, about the pronunciation of which there was a noisy disputation in the Fr. schools.

Candle, As fine (gay) as the King's : generally applied to an overdressed woman. An allusion to the ancient practice of presenting gaily-coloured candles to the Three Kings of Cologne on the 6th January.

Candle, As upright as a : [Heywood, *Proverbes* (1546)]

Candle at both ends, To burn the : to use one's resources extravagantly, either by spending more than one earns, or by encroaching in work on one's time of rest and recreation. [Le Sage, *Gil Blas*, VII, 15]

Candle : Bell, Book, and : *see* Bell.

Candle, Sale by the : a kind of sale by auction, the bids being open until the candle has burnt down to a certain mark.

Candle, The game is not worth the : *i.e.*, not worth undertaking. Apparently in allusion to a game played by candle-light, the stakes in which were of small amount, barely sufficient to pay for the value of the candle. [Geo. Herbert, *Jacula Prudentum* (1640); Corneille, *Le Menteur*, I, i (1642)]

Candle to .. Not fit to hold a : altogether inferior to .. In allusion to the link-boys who used to hold the torches at places of entertainment.

Candle to seek another, To burn one : to throw good money after bad. [Gosson, *Schoole of Abuse* (1579)]

Candle to the Devil, To hold a : orig. to propitiate Satan, just as Saints are propitiated by candles ; later, to assist in evil courses. Lit., to attend on the Devil by holding a candle as a light for him. [*Paston Letters*, No. 428 (1461)]

Candle to the Sun, To hold a : to seek to compare one's little exploits with far greater ones. [Diogenianus, *Proverbia*, VI, 27 ; Earl of Surrey, *A Praise of his Love*, ll. 27-30 (1557)]

Candle to .. To hold a : to direct attention to. [Shakespeare, *The Merchant of Venice*, II, v (1596)]

Candles of the night, The : the stars. [Shakespeare, *Merchant of Venice*, V, i (?1596)]

Candle-ends, To drink off : a romantic manner of drinking a lady's health. [Shakespeare, 2 *Henry IV*, II, iv, 267 (1597)]

Candle-holder, A : an abettor. From the practice in the Roman Catholic Church of holding a candle to the reader.

Candle-rent : rent derived from property which is continually deteriorating in value.

Candle-waster, A : one who reads or studies or otherwise sits up at night, thereby wasting candles. [Ben Jonson, *Cynthia's Revels* (1599) ; Shakespeare, *Much Ado About Nothing*, V, i (1599)]

Candlemas Day : Feb. 2, the Festival of the Purification of the Virgin, when candles are burnt.

Candour, Mrs. : a slanderous hypocritical woman ; after a character in Sheridan, *The School for Scandal* (1777).

Canicular Days : the Dog Days ; period about Aug. 11, the time of the rising of the Dog-star. Lat., *canicularis*, relating to the Dog-star.

Canidia, A : a witch. [Horace, *Epodes*, V]

Cannae, A (To be one's) : to engage in a fatal battle, bringing one's period of success to a close. After the battle at which Hannibal defeated L. Aemilius Paulus (216 B.C.).

Cannibal, A : a human man-eater. A corruption of Span. *Caribal*, a Caribbean.

Cannon-fodder : infantry soldiers, esp. of an inferior quality. The term is derived from Shakespeare, 1 *Henry IV*, IV, ii, 60 : ' food for powder.'

anoe, To paddle one's own :   *see* Paddle.

anonical Hours : *see* Hours.

anossa, To go to : to submit ; to eat humble-pie. After the castle in Tuscany where the Emp. Henry IV made his submission to Pope Hildebrand in 1077. The phrase was coined by Bismarck in the Reichstag debates of 1872 in the *Kulturkampf*.

anossa Bill, The : the bill incorporating terms of settlement with the Catholic Party introduced into the Prussian Landtag in 1882.

ant : hypocrisy. Either (1) after Andrew Cant (1590-1663), Scot. Covenanter, who, while relentlessly persecuting those whom he considered heretics, prayed on their behalf ; or (2) more probably, from Lat., *cantus*, a chant, on account of the drawling, whining tones with which cant is associated.

antab, A : a member of the University of Cambridge. Abbrev. of Cantabrigian, from Cantabrigia, the Latin for Cambridge.

anter, A : an easy gallop. Contraction of ' Canterbury gallop,' the pace of the pilgrims to Becket's shrine at Canterbury.

anterbury Tale, A : a long or tedious story, or one not worthy of credence. After the title of Chaucer's poem. In latter sense term in frequent use in 16th cent. [Turbery, *Book of Falconrie*, 260 (1575)]

anting Coat : the Geneva gown ; the vestment of a Puritan divine. From ' cant ' in the sense of hypocrisy, applied in 17th cent. to Puritans and Presbyterians as a term of abuse.

anuck, A : an American term for a Canadian. Said to be a corruption of ' Connaught,' a term applied to English Canadians by their French fellow-nationals.

anvas, A : an oil-painting. After the material basis of the picture.

anvas, A man of : an artist.

anvas-back, A : the reverse of a thing far inferior to the front. Properly, the canvas back of a garment.

anvas City, A : a military camp. Orig. the Volunteer encampment at Wimbledon.

ap, A feather in one's : an achievement that justifies pride.

Cap a person, To : to confer a University degree (in Scotland).

Cap (an anecdote, etc.), To : to follow it by relating one still better. [Shakespeare, *Henry V*, II, vii, 124 (1584)]

Cap and bells, To wear the : to be an object of ridicule. From the symbol worn by a professional jester.

Cap at a person, To set one's : (of a woman) to endeavour to attract the favourable attention of a man ; possibly by wearing her most attractive cap for his benefit.

Cap at, To throw one's : to be envious of. [*Three-fold Discourse Betweene Three Neighbours* (1642)]

Cap and Feather Days : childhood.

Cap fits, The : the remark applies. Part of the Italian saying ' If the cap fits, wear it.' [Fiacchi, *Favole*, LXXVIII]

Cap of fools, The : the most foolish of the fools.

Cap of Liberty, The : the symbol of Republicanism. From the cap given to Roman slaves on their emancipation.

Cap of Maintenance, The : a cap carried before a dignitary on ceremonial occasions.

Cap, To put on one's considering : *see* Considering Cap.

Cap the globe, To : to surpass everything. *See* Cap an anecdote.

Cap to . . To : to assent to .. In allusion to the custom among French judges of signifying their assent to a conclusion by raising their caps.

Caps, Blue : *see* Blue.

Caps, To pull : to quarrel, like two women who pull at one another's cap.

Cap-à-pie (*Old Fr.*) : from head to foot. A feudal phrase referring orig. to armour.

Cap-in-hand : submissive. From the practice of uncovering the head in the presence of a superior.

Cape Merchant, A : a supercargo ; a head merchant in a factory. Probably the correct form is ' Cap merchant,' head merchant, from ' cap.'

Cape Sheep, A : a sailor's term for the albatross which frequents the vicinity of the Cape of Good Hope.

Capers, To cut : to frolic. Lat., *caper*, a wild-goat, *via* Fr., *capriole*, a frolicsome leap. [*A Match at Midnight*, IV, i (1633)]

Caperclaw, To : to scratch with the open hand. Properly, clapperclaw (*q.v.*).

Caperdochy, A : a prison. After Cappadocia, the king of which was, according to Horace, rich in slaves but poor in money.

Capernaite, A : a believer in transubstantiation. From Capernaum, in Galilee. [*John*, vi, 52]

Capital out of . . To make : to take advantage of an event or circumstance.

Capitals, To speak in : to lay great emphasis on certain words. [Sir Thos. Browne, *Religio Medici*, Pt. I (1643)]

Capitol, A : a legislative building, esp. in the U.S. After the legislative building in ancient Rome.

Capitularies : edicts of the early French kings.

Capitulations : arrangements whereby Europeans in most non-Christian States are not subject to the tribunals of the State but to that of the Consul of their own nation.

Capon, A Crail's : a dried haddock.

Capon, A Glasgow : a salt herring. *See* Glasgow Magistrate.

Capon, A Severn : a sole.

Capon, A Yarmouth : a red herring.

Caporal King, The : Frederick William I of Prussia. On account of his devotion and services to his army.

Caporal, Le Petit (*Fr.*, the Little Corporal) : Napoleon I. So-called by his soldiers.

Caporal Violet : Napoleon I. A name by which he was called by his friends in France during his exile in Elba, in the hope that he would return in the spring.

Cappadochio, A : a prison; *see* Caperdochy.

Captain of the Age, The : the Duke of Wellington, so-called by Sir Francis Burdett.

Captain Armstrong, To come : (of a jockey) to pull his horse so as to prevent it from winning. A play on ' strong arm.'

Captain Copperthorne's Crew : all leaders and no followers.

Captain of Kœpenick, A : a picturesque and amusing thief. From one Voigt, a shoemaker, who in Oct., 1906, masquerading as an army captain, induced the Burgomaster of Köpenick in Prussia to transfer to him the funds of the municipality.

Captain Podd : a showman. After one famous in the 16th and 17th cents.

Captain Stiff over, To come : to treat with extreme formality.

Captain of the suburbs, A : a pickpocket or other street criminal.

Capua, A : a scene of degeneration due to self-indulgence. After the Ital. city whose luxury demoralized Hannibal's army.

Capua, The wealth of : the luxury of Capua was proverbial in 2nd and 3rd cents. B.C.

Capuchins : a Roman Catholic religious Order, the mendicant friars of the Franciscan Order, founded in 1529. Fr., *capuche*, a pointed cowl, worn by them.

Caput mortuum : worthless residue. It is the technical term used in chemistry to denote the useless remnant after distillation or sublimation.

Carabas, A Marquis of : a pretentious, conservative old aristocrat. After a character in *Le Chat Botté* (Puss in Boots), one of Perrault's *Contes* (17th cent.).

Carabineers, The : the 6th Dragoon Guards. On account of the carbines with which they were formerly armed.

Caracole, To : to caper about. Properly (of a horse) to perform a series of half-wheeling motions.

Carat : a weight for precious metals and gems. From Grk., *keration*, the seed of the locust-tree, which was at one time used as the weight.

Caraway : an edible seed. From Caria, in Asia Minor, whence it was at one time obtained.

Carbonari : secret revolutionary societies in Italy and Portugal in the early 19th cent. Ital., *carbonari*, charcoal-burners, in whose huts the conspirators met. *Also* the extreme royalists who conspired against Louis XVIII in 1822.

Carcel-lamp, A : a clockwork lamp; a unit of illuminating power. After Carcel, the inventor.

Card, A : a slang-term, used generally in conjunction with an adjective, to describe a person with some peculiar trait, *e.g.*, ' queer,' ' knowing.' Perhaps descended from the phrase ' a sure card ' (*q.v. inf.*).

Card, A leading : a precedent.

Card, A sure : a safe card to play, one which is certain to win; later, a person who can be relied on.

Card, To play one's best : to make one's principal point in a contest.

Card, To play one's last : to make one's last remaining effort. A card-playing metaphor. [Bunyan, *The Holy War* (1682)]

Card, To speak by the : to speak with absolute accuracy ; in allusion to the card of the mariner's compass. [Shakespeare, *Hamlet*, V, i, 149 (1603)]

Cards, A house of : an unsubstantial, insecure scheme, which, like a ' house ' built by children of playing-cards, is liable to tumble to pieces at a mere touch.

Cards in one's hands, To have the : to have the opportunity with one. A card-playing metaphor. [*Life and Death of Jack Straw*, I, l. 208 (1593)]

Cards, To be on the : to be likely or possible to happen ; referring either to card-playing, from the possibility of any card to be turned up in the game ; or to the practice of forecasting the future from cards. Popularized by Dickens, but in literary use as early as Smollett.

Cards, To go in with good : to have excellent reasons for expecting success.

Cards well (badly), To play one's : to act with discretion (without discretion). A card-playing metaphor. [Arth. Murphy, *Three Weeks after Marriage*, I (1776)]

Cards, To show one's : to exhibit one's resources and intentions. A card-playing metaphor.

Cards, To throw up the : to abandon the contest. A card-playing metaphor.

Cardigan ; Cardigan-jacket, A : a knitted woollen waistcoat. After the 7th Earl of Cardigan (1797-1868).

Cardinal, The Gray : *see* Gray.

Cardinal of the Huguenots, The : Cardinal Richelieu (1585-1642), who granted tolerance to the Calvinists of France in 1629, supported the Protestants of Germany against the Emperor, and those of the Grisons and the Low Countries against Catholic Spain.

Cardinal virtues, The : justice, prudence, temperance and fortitude—the chief ' natural ' virtues, to which are sometimes added faith, hope and charity—the theological virtues.

Care (Careaway) Sunday : the fifth Sunday in Lent ; formerly the Sunday before Good Friday. *See* next entry. Perhaps (by folk-etymology) derived from ' care ' in the sense of ' grief.'

Carlin (Carling ; Carl) Sunday : the fifth Sunday in Lent. When there was great scarcity in Northumbria in 13th cent., a ship unexpectedly arrived with a cargo of carlin peas, and removed the danger of starvation. *See also* Care Sunday.

Carlists : supporters of Don Carlos, claimant to the throne of Spain, or of his descendants. Their claim is based on the illegality of the succession of a woman to the throne of Spain.

Carmagnole, The : a French revolutionary song and dance. After a dress of that name worn by the Jacobins in the French Revolution. From Carmagnola, in Italy.

Carmelites, The : the White Friars, a mendicant religious order, formed in Palestine in 12th cent. From Mount Carmel, whose hermits were the originators of the Order.

Carnival, A : a riotous festival ; the festival immediately preceding Lent. Medieval Lat., *carnelevarium*, Shrove Tuesday, from *caro*, flesh, and *levare*, to put aside.

Carpet, On the : under consideration. Lit., on the Council table. *Sur le tapis* is used in the same sense.

Carpet-bagger, A : a candidate for a constituency brought from outside and unknown to the electors. Orig. a U.S. political term applied to adventurers in the Southern States after the Civil War. In both cases the whole of their visible property could be enclosed in a carpet-bag.

Carpet knight (captain ; coward), A : a soldier who frequents carpeted rooms in preference to the field of battle. *See* Carpet-monger.

Carpet squire, A : a carpet-monger (*q.v.*).

Carpet-dance, A : a dance in a carpeted room, not in a ball-room with polished floors ; an informal dance.

Carpet-monger ; carpet-captain ; carpet-coward, A : a man who frequents drawing-rooms, boudoirs, and other carpeted chambers. A term suggesting effeminacy.

Carrageen ; Carragheen : Irish moss, a substitute for isinglass. After Carragheen, in Ireland.

Carriage-folk (company) : people who keep their own carriages.

Carrier's journeys, By : slowly. [Killigrew, *The Parson's Wedding*, II, v (1663)]

Carrière ouverte aux talents (*Fr.*, a career open to the talents): the principle expressed by Napoleon I.

Carronade, A : a short cannon with a large bore. From the Carron Iron-works in Scotland.

Carrots : a jocular term of address to red-haired people. Probably because the carrot is red, but derived by some from Judas Iscariot, who, according to tradition was red-haired. 'Ginger' is similarly an address to yellow-haired people.

Cart before the horse, To put the : to reverse the natural or correct order, either in an undertaking or a descriptive account. [Robert Whittington, *Vulgaria* (1520)]

Carta blanca (*Ital.*) ; **Carte blanche** (*Fr.*) : a free hand to act as one's discretion dictates. Lit., 'white paper,' *i.e.*, without instructions.

Carte de visite, A : a small-sized photo-graph. From the practice of the Duke of Parma (1857) of having his photo-graph on the back of his visiting-card.

Cartel, A : a combination of manu-facturers (esp. of sugar, in Austria) who, by means of heavy import-duties, are enabled to make large profits by sales at home and thus to sell abroad below cost-price.

Carthage of the North : Lübeck, the head of the Hanseatic League (*see* Hansa Towns).

Carthaginian Faith : *see* Punic Faith.

Carthaginian Peace, A : a treaty of peace, so harsh in its conditions as to involve almost the destruction of the defeated party. Applied in particular to the Treaty of Versailles of 1919. *See* Delenda est Carthago.

Carthago, Delenda est : *see* Delenda.

Carthusians : a monastic Order, founded in 1084 at Chartreuse, in France.

Carthusian Silence : almost complete silence. From the severe regimen of the Carthusian Order of monks, which includes frequent and long periods of silence.

Caryatid, A : a female figure in sculpture. From a woman of Caryae, Laconia, Greece, a priestess of Diana.

Casabianca, A : a heroic boy. After Giacomo Jocante Casabianca, son of a Fr. naval officer. He perished nobly at the Battle of the Nile. His deed was sung in a famous poem by Felicia Hemans, which has popularized his name.

Case-hardened : impervious to im-pressions. Lit., hardened on the surface. An engineering metaphor.

Cashmere : a fine woollen material made from the hair of the Cashmere goat.

Casket Letters, The : the letters sent by Mary, Queen of Scots, to Bothwell, which, if genuine, would prove her complicity in the murder of Darnley.

Cassandra, A : a prophetess of evil whose warnings are disregarded. After Cassandra, daughter of Priam, King of Troy, whose prophecies of woe were unheeded.

Cassius, Purple of : a purple pigment. After Andreas Cassius (d. 1680), Germ. physician and chemist, the inventor.

Cast beyond the moon, To : to calculate fancifully concerning something very remote. [Heywood, *Proverbes* (1562)]

Castalian : poetic. After the name of the fountain of the Muses on Mount Parnassus.

Caste, To lose : to suffer reduction in status. In allusion to the Indian caste-system.

Casting-counters : counters used for the process of calculation.

Castle, The : Dublin Castle, the seat of the Irish administration.

Castle of Maidens, The : Edinburgh.

Castle, Old Lad of the, An : a hail-fellow well met. Probably an equivalent of Castilian, once considered a perfect gentleman. [16th cent.]

Castles in Spain : daydreams ; castles in the air (*q.v.*). Orig. a Fr. phrase (11th cent.), Spain being the nearest Mo-hammedan country and therefore outside the pale of medieval civili-zation. The phrase may have arisen out of the wonderful rewards that fell to Henry of Burgundy and his followers on their invasion of Spain and Portugal to assist the Christians against the Moslems. One result was the creation of the kingdom of Portugal, of which Henry's son was the first monarch. It may be mentioned that at that period the castles of Spain were very few in number and every French baron who settled in the country had to build one for his occupation. [*Romaunt of the Rose* (1400)]

Castles in the air : daydreams ; projects never expected or even intended to be realized. [North, *Plutarch* (1580)]

Castles, To build : to give reins to one's imagination ; to be unduly optimistic *See* Castles in the air.

Casus belli (*Lat.*, a cause of war) : an international offence justifying a declaration of war.

Casus foederis (*Lat.*, a cause of a treaty) : an event that involves action by a State in accordance with the terms of an international treaty.

Cat, The : *see* Cat-o'-nine-tails.

Cat, As sick as a : in allusion to the proneness of cats to vomit. The original form was ' As sick as cats eating rats.'

Cat can lick her ear, Before a : *i.e.*, never, because a cat cannot lick her ear.

Cat, Cheshire, A : *see* Cheshire Cat.

Cat in, Not room to swing a : in allusion to the ' sport ' of hanging a cat to a tree as a target.

Cat in pan . . To turn : to prove perfidious ; to change one's side. A cookery metaphor ; from *cate*, cake. Another derivation is from the Catipani, a South-Ital. race, notorious for its perfidy. Yet another derivation is from the French, *tourner cote en peine*, to turn sides in trouble. [Heywood, *Proverbes* (1546)]

Cat i' the adage, The : in the adage the cat covets fish but does not like to wet its paws. [Shakespeare, *Macbeth*, I, vii (1605)]

Cat jumps, To see which way the : to watch which direction events are taking before one acts ; to ' wait and see.' Derived from the game of tip-cat.

Cat, Nine lives of a : *see* Nine lives.

Cat-o'-nine-tails, A : a whip, for use on human beings, with nine knotted lashes. Orig. used on board ship, where ropes are called ' cats.'

Cat out of the bag, To let the : to disclose a secret. From the swindle at country fairs of selling cats (in place of sucking-pigs) enclosed in bags.

Cat, To whip the : to play a practical joke. After a standing joke played on stupid country men in parts of England.

Cats and dogs, To rain : to rain very heavily. [Swift, *Polite Conversation* (1731)] Possibly a corruption of ' catalupe,' a waterfall.

Cat's foot, To live under the : to live under female control. In allusion to a mouse living on sufferance under the control of the cat.

Cats in a gutter, To agree like two : [Jno. Heywood, *Proverbes* (1546)]

Cats, Kilkenny : *see* Kilkenny cats.

Cat-a-mount ; Cat-o'-mountain : a popular name for the Amer. lynx.

Cat-call, A : unpleasant noises, made to disconcert speakers at a public meeting or to express disapproval of a theatrical performance.

Cat-and-dog life, A : a life filled with strife and quarrels, in allusion to the proverbial enmity between the two animals. [*How a Man May Choose a Good Wife from a Bad*, I, i (1602)]

Cat-and-dog money : a charitable fund administered at Christchurch, Spitalfields ; traditionally believed in the first instance to have been used for the benefit of cats and dogs.

Cataloon : a fabric. After Catalonia, in Spain.

Cat's-eye, A : a precious stone, which, when held to the light, resembles the contracted pupil of a cat's eye.

Catspaw, A : a person used as a tool by another to serve his purposes. From the fable of the monkey that used the paw or foot of a cat to take the roasting chestnuts from the fire. The monkey is said to have belonged to Pope Julius II. [Grose, *Dictionary of the Vulgar Tongue* (1785)]

Cat's-sleep, A : sham sleep, like that of a cat watching a mouse. [Dekker and Webster, *Northward Ho*, III, ii (1607)]

Cataian, A : a Chinaman ; a cheat. After Cataia (Cathay), an early name for China. Early travellers to China gave the people a reputation for stealing.

Catch a crab, To : in rowing, to raise the oar out of the water before pulling it. From the crab-like appearance of the rower as he falls backward.

Catch a hare, To sell an ox to : *see* Sell.

Catch a Tartar, To : to be held up by a prisoner one has oneself taken ; to get more than one bargained for. From the story of the Irish soldier who took a Turk prisoner, and, on being ordered to bring him along, replied : ' He won't let me ! ' and was then ordered to come on alone.

Catch a weasel asleep, To : to attempt the impossible. The weasel is reputed to be always awake.

Catch the Whigs bathing, To : *see* Whigs.

Catch the wind with a net, To : to attempt the impossible.

Catchpenny, A : something of little or no value made up to attract cheap purchasers. Corruption of Catnach Penny, after James Catnach (1792-1841), a publisher of cheap and trashy literature which was hawked in the streets.

Catchpoll (Catchpole), A : a minor official of a Court of Justice. In use in England as early as 12th cent.

Cathay : the name given to Northern China by Marco Polo. From Ki-tah, the race that ruled in that region in 10th cent.

Cathay, A cycle of : a period of 60 years.

Catherine's tresses, To braid : to live and die a virgin.

Catherine wheel, A : a revolving firework ; a circular window ; a somersault. After St. Catherine of Alexandria, who was martyred by being broken on the wheel.

Catherine wheel politicians : time-serving politicians.

Catherine wheel republics : ' always in revolution while the powder lasts.' Jas. Russell Lowell (1819-91) in *My Study Windows* (1870).

Catherine wheel, To turn a : to turn a somersault sideways, as distinct from backwards and forwards.

Catherine wheel window, A : a window, or compartment of a window, of a circular form with radiating divisions or spokes.

Catholic, A : a member of the Church which is under the allegiance of the Pope. Grk., *Katholikos*, universal.

Catholic Apostolic Church : a secessionist community founded by Edward Irving (1792-1834), the members of which are known as Irvingites.

Catholic Association, The : an association formed in 1823 by Daniel O'Connell to secure the emancipation of the Roman Catholics in the United Kingdom.

Catholic Majesty : a title of the kings of Spain ; conferred at the Council of Toledo in 590.

Catholic Rent : an unofficial tax levied in Ireland by Daniel O'Connell for the support of his Catholic Association (*q.v.*).

Catholics, Old : secessionists from the Catholic Church after the Vatican Council of 1870-1.

Catiline, A : a profligate conspirator. After Lucius Sergius Catilina (109-62 B.C.).

Catilinarian Existence, A : an existence supported by conspiracy. A phrase used by Bismarck in a debate in the Prussian House of Deputies in 1863 ; also the title of a novel, published by Theodor König in 1854.

Cat-lap : a non-intoxicating drink, such as tea ; that which a cat might lap.

Cato, A : a self-denying, quiet-living man, blunt of speech and renowned for his devotion to justice and patriotism. After Marcus Portius Cato (95-46 B.C.).

Cato's meal : a model meal.

Caucus, A : a private meeting of a political party, for the adoption of a programme or the selection of a candidate ; the political machine which chooses candidates and lays down policies. Coined in the U.S. early in 18th cent. A suggested derivation is from the Caulkers' Club, in Boston, U.S., one of the elements in the Amer. Revolution ; another is from Amer.-Ind. *caw-cawwassoughes*, elders.

Caudine Forks : a crushing defeat. After the defile near Caudium in Samnium where the Romans suffered an overwhelming defeat in the Second Samnite War (321 B.C.). The defeated army was forced to pass under the yoke (forks).

Caudle, A Mrs. : *see* Curtain-Lecture.

Caudle-cup, A : a warm drink given to invalids and also to their visitors. Lat., *caldus*, warm.

Caul on one's head, To be born with a : to be born lucky. From the superstition attaching to infants born with a caul or membrane on their heads.

Causa causans (*Lat.*, the cause causing) : the remote cause.

Causa causata (*Lat.*, a cause caused) : a secondary cause.

Cause of causes, The : love.

Cause célèbre, A (*Fr.*, celebrated lawsuit) : a lawsuit which attracts much attention.

Cause, The First : God, the Creator of the Universe. [Manasseh ben Israel, *Vindiciae Judaeorum* (1657)]

Cause with . . To make common : to co-operate with . .

Caution-money : money deposited as security for good conduct.

Cavaliers : supporters of Charles I, before and during the Civil War, the Party out of which grew the Tories. Fr., *chevalier*, knight.

Ça va sans dire (*Fr.*, that goes without saying) : that is a matter of course.

Cave, A : *see* Adullamites.

Cave of Adullam : *see* Adullam.

Cave in, To : to submit ; to withdraw from. Lit., of walls, etc., falling in from want of support.

Cave canem (*Lat.*, beware of the dog !) : an inscription frequently found on the thresholds of Roman houses.

Cave, To cry : to give warning. Lat., *Cave !* beware !

Caveat against . . To enter a : to issue a warning against ; to lay down conditions. A legal process. Lat., *caveat,* let him beware.

Caveat emptor (*Lat.*, let the buyer beware) : a legal maxim : it is for the purchaser to assure himself (*e.g.*, of the quality of the goods) he is about to buy.

Cavendish's wealth, Captain : in allusion to the wealth acquired by Thomas Cavendish in the course of his plundering expedition to South America in 1586-8.

Caviare to the general : said of something that is an acquired taste, not palatable to the majority. From *caviare*, the roe of the sturgeon, which is not pleasing to all tastes. [Shakespeare, *Hamlet*, II, ii (1602)]

Cayenne : hot red-pepper. After an island off the coast of Guiana.

Ceca to Mecca, From : aimlessly ; from one end of the world to another. Both Ceca and Mecca are places of Mohammedan pilgrimage. Ceca (Arabic, the mint) was the name given by Christians to the mosque at Cordova. [Cervantes, *Don Quixote*, I, iii, 4]

Cecil's fast : a meal of fish. From the legislation introduced by William Cecil, Lord Burleigh, making compulsory the eating of fish on certain days.

Cecrops, As noble as : according to tradition Cecrops was the first King of Athens and the introducer of civilization into Greece.

Celestial, A : a European designation for a Chinaman. *See* Celestial Empire.

Celestial City, The : Heaven. So-called by Bunyan in *The Pilgrim's Progress* (1678).

Celestial Empire, The : one of the native names for the Chinese Empire. The first Emperors were believed to be of divine origin.

Centaur, To be a very : to ride fast.

Centaur, A : a wild untamable creature ; an expert rider. After a fabulous race, half-man, half-horse, that is reputed to have lived in Thessaly.

Centennial State, The : Colorado, admitted into the Union in 1876, a century after the Declaration of Independence.

Centipedes, The : the 100th Regt. of Foot. After the insect popularly supposed to have 100 feet.

Centre, The : a political party holding opinions half-way between the two extremes. In France, the Moderate Republicans ; in Germany, the Catholic Party.

Century Plant, The : the agave, supposed to flower only once in a hundred years. Not to be confused with ' centaury.'

Cepola, Devices of : legal technicalities. After the devices of Bartholomew Cepola (d. 1474) for the prolongation of lawsuits.

Cerberus, A : a fierce, watchful guardian. Cerberus was the three-headed dog, the guardian of the entrance to Hades.

Cerberus, A sop to : *see* Sop.

Cerberus of the Muses, The : Lucian (120-80), Grk. writer and satirist, so-called by Scaliger.

Cereal : a grain. After Ceres (*q.v.*).

Ceremony, To stand on : to insist on the punctilious observance of formalities. [Shakespeare, *Julius Cæsar*, II, ii, 13 (1601)]

Ceres : Corn. After the name of the Roman goddess of the harvest.

Cervantic : in the style of *Don Quixote*, by Cervantes (1547-1616).

Cesarevich, The : (1) the eldest son of the Tsar (Czar) ; (2) an Engl. horse-race, founded in 1839 in honour of Alexander II, then Cesarevich.

Cess : *see* Bad Cess.

Cess, Out of all : out of all measure. [Shakespeare, 1 *Henry IV*, II, i (1596-7)]

Ceteris paribus (*Lat.*, other things being equal) : assuming that other things are equal.

Chadband, A : a canting hypocrite. After a character in Dickens, *Bleak House* (1852).

Chaff : banter. In use as early as 17th cent. Either from (1) the proverb, ' A bird is not caught with chaff ' ; or (2) to ' chafe,' to worry. Another suggested derivation is from a custom in the North Midlands of emptying a sack of chaff at the door of a man who ill-treats his wife, to indicate that thrashing is done there.

Chair, The : the office of President of a meeting, Speaker of the House of Commons, etc. Either a contraction of ' chairman,' or the transference of the word denoting the principal seat to the person who occupies it.

Chair, To pass the : to have been elected mayor.

Chair, To take up the : to assume the lead. [Rob. Johnson, *Essayes : Of Speech* (1607)]

Chair of St. Peter, The : the office of the Papacy, whose first incumbent was St. Peter.

Chair-days : old age, spent to a considerable extent resting in a chair. [Shakespeare, 2 *Henry VI*, V, ii (1593)]

Chalcedony : a precious stone. From Chalcedon, in Asia Minor, where it was first discovered.

Chaldean, A : an astrologer ; soothsayer. From Chaldea, whose inhabitants were reputed to be learned in magic.

Chalk from cheese, To know : to be wide-awake ; to be conscious where one's advantage lies. [*John Bow and Mast Person* (1548)] *See also* Gower, *Confessio Amantis* (1393), ' Lo ! how they feignen chalk for cheese ' ; Shacklock, *Hatchet of Heresies* (1565), ' Do not these thynges differ as muche as chalcke and chese ' ; and Jno. Heywood, *Proverbes* (1546), ' as well agreeth the comparison in these, as a lyke to compare in tast, chalke and cheese.'

Chalk it up, To : to make a public note of ; to advertise. From the practice of chalking a customer's indebtedness on a slate that was hung up in the ale-house.

Chalk of one and cheese of another, To make : to show favouritism, to treat two people differently.

Chalk, To glue : *see* Glue.

Chalks, By long : to a large extent ; greatly. In allusion to the use of chalk in scoring at games.

Chalybean-tempered steel : in allusion to the Chalybes, an ancient race of Asia Minor, famous for its skill in working iron. [Milton, *Samson Agonistes*, ll. 128-34 (1671)]

Cham : a title applied to the Emperor of China and other Tartar and Mongol rulers. A corruption of *Khan*, a title adopted by Chingiz (1162-1227) when he became ruler of the Mongols and Tartars.

Cham of Literature, The Great : Samuel Johnson (1709-84), so-called by Smollett.

Chambres Ardentes (*Fr.*, lighted chambers) : extraordinary tribunals under the French monarchy, held in rooms from which daylight was excluded.

Chameleon, To act as a ; To chameleonize : to change one's opinions frequently ; to be inconstant. From the chameleon, a lizard which adapts its appearance to its environment.

Chance, To have an eye to the main : to have one's own interest always in view. Metaphor drawn from the game of hazard. [Ben Jonson, *The Case is Altered*, IV, iv (1601)]

Chancelleries of Europe, The : the diplomatists of Europe. From chancellery, the official residence of the Chancellor of a legation.

Chancery, To get a person's head in : a term in pugilism, when the head is so held by the opponent as to be at his mercy. The helplessness of the litigant who gets into the Court of Chancery is well known.

Chandra (*Sanskrit*) : the moon ; hence any illustrious person.

Chaneph : a centre of hypocrisy. After the island of religious hypocrites in Rabelais, *Pantagruel* (1533).

Change a fly into an elephant, To : to undertake an impossible task. An ancient Grk. proverb.

Change (swop) horses while crossing a stream, To : to change one's instruments or weapons in a time of extreme difficulty. Phrase attributed by Abraham Lincoln to a Dutch farmer.

Change one's copy, To : to alter one's tactics. [Rich. Edwards, *Damon and Pithias*, ll. 268-70 (1567)]

Change out of . . To take the : to get an equivalent out of .. ; to get more than an equivalent out of ..

Change with every wind, To : to be very fickle. [Lyly, *Euphues : Anatomy of Wit* (1579)]

Changes, To ring the : to repeat the same words, actions, etc., with many slight variations. Metaphor from bell-ringing. [T. Adams, *The Devil's Banquet* (1614)] In slang, to cheat by means of coins.

Chanson de geste, A (*Fr.*) : a Fr. heroic song of the 11th to 15th cents.

Chantage : blackmail. A euphuism for singing to another man's tune, or paying blackmail under his pressure.

Chanticleer, A : a name of the farm-yard cock. After the name of the cock in *Reynard the Fox*. Fr., *chanter*, to sing ; *cler*, clear.

Chaonian Bird, The : the dove ; because it delivered the oracles of Chaonia.

Chaonian food : acorns. In allusion to the oak-trees of Chaonia.

Chaos, To speak of things more ancient than : see Speak.

Chap, A : a man, or boy. Contraction of ' chapman,' one who sold in a ' chepe ' (market).

Chap-book, A : a popular book sold in the streets and in villages by chapmen.

Chap-fallen : see Chop-fallen.

Chapel, A : an organization of printers' journeymen. From the disused chapel of Caxton set up his printing-press. Their representative is called the ' Father.'

Chapter of Accidents, A : a series of unexpected events. From the form in a book divided into chapters in which the Roman laws were kept.

Chapter, To the end of the : to the end. In allusion to the former practice of reading a complete chapter as the Lesson of the Church Service. [R. L'Estrange, in 1704]

Chapter of Possibilities, A : a series of possible happenings ; parallel with Chapter of Accidents.

Chapter and verse, To give : to give precise references to an authority for a statement. [Earle, *Microcosmography*, XLIII (1628)]

Chare Thursday : the Thursday in Passion Week. Properly, Shere Thursday, the Thursday before Easter, from the former practice of shearing the sheep on that day.

Charge, To return to the : to bring the conversation constantly back to the original topic.

Charivari, A : a travesty of a serenade ; an orchestra of discordant noises intended to express the unpopularity of the victim of it ; a babel.

Charlemagne of the East, The : Aurungzebe (1618-1707), Mogul Emperor.

Charlemagne, The Second : see Second.

Charles' head, King : see King Charles.

Charles' Wain : a constellation also known as The Great Bear. After Charlemagne (Charles the Great). The constellation Arcturus was supposed to be connected with King Arthur ; and the name of Charlemagne was therefore applied to a fellow-constellation. Another der. is from Ang.-Sax. *churles*, a farmer's

waggon, the constellation resembling a wagon in outline.

Charley, A : a night watchman. Possibly because King Charles I reformed the watch-system of London in 1640.

Charlie over the Water : the Young Pretender, Charles Edward Stuart, in exile on the Continent.

Charmed life, To bear a : to be impervious to harm, as if by magical protection. [Shakespeare, *Macbeth*, V, viii, 12-3 (1606)]

Charon, A : a ferryman. After the ferryman who ferried the souls of the dead to the Lower World.

Chartered Libertine, A : the Eng. press. So-called by William Pitt, Earl of Chatham. Shakespeare [*Henry V*, I, i (1599)] refers to the air as a ' chartered libertine.'

Chartist, A : an Eng. Radical reformer of the period, 1837-48. From ' The People's Charter,' a statement of the Chartists' programme.

Chartist Parson, The : Charles Kingsley (1819-75), clergyman and novelist, on account of his Chartist novel *Alton Locke* (1850).

Chartreuse : a liqueur made by the Carthusian monks, formerly at La Grande Chartreuse, their principal house near Grenoble, France. From Cartusio, a neighbouring village.

Charybdis : see Scylla and Charybdis.

Chase, A stern : a pursuit in which one vessel follows directly in the wake of the other, *i.e.*, keeps in a direct line with the other's stern.

Chassepot, A : a French breech-loading rifle. After the name of its inventor, Antoine Alphonse Chassepot (b. 1833).

Chaste as Ice, As : [Shakespeare, *Hamlet*, III, i, 136 (1602-3)]

Chaste as an icicle, As : chaste with a suggestion of lack of feeling. [Shakespeare, *Coriolanus*, V, iii, l. 64 (1609)]

Chastise the dead, To : to act in a futile manner. From an ancient Greek proverb.

Chastise with scorpions, To : to punish with special severity. From the rule of Rehoboam, King of Judah, as described in I *Kings*, xii, 11.

Chatterbox, A : one who talks incessantly.

Chaucer of France, The : Clément Marot (1496-1544).

Chaucer of Painting, The : Albert Dürer (1471-1528), Germ. painter.

Chaucer's Jest, A : an obscene or indelicate act or remark. In allusion to

G

some narratives in Chaucer, *Canterbury Tales* (14th cent.).

Chaunticleer, A : *see* Chanticleer.

Chautauqua : a society for the promotion of home-reading and study. After Chautauqua, a summer-resort in New York State, where the Chautauqua Literary and Scientific Circle has met since 1874.

Chauvinism : exaggerated patriotism ; extreme Imperialism. After Chauvin, a character in Scribe, *Soldat Laboureur*, fanatically devoted to Napoleon ; or from a character in *La Cocarde Trocolare* (1831) by Théodore and Hippolyte Cogniard.

Chaw-bacon, A : a country bumpkin. Bacon was at one time the only meat-food eaten by rustics.

Chawed up : demolished ; chewed up.

Cheap, To make oneself : to belittle one's own importance ; to be too accessible to others. [Wm. Penn, *Some Fruits of Solitude*, Pt. II, §203 (1718)]

Cheap as the Sardinians, As : in allusion to the number of Sardinian prisoners brought to Rome by Tiberius Gracchus (177 B.C.).

Cheap-Jack, A : a travelling hawker, who sells by Dutch auction, *i.e.*, reduces the price of his wares until he finds a purchaser. Anglo-Sax. *chepe*, a market. Sometimes **Cheap-John.**

Chebeek ; Chebacco, A : a boat used in the Newfoundland fisheries. After the name of a North Amer. coast-town.

Check-mate, A : a final defeat. A term used in the game of chess. (Pers. *Shah mat*, the king is dead.) [*Totus Mundus in Maligno Pontus*, ll. 37-40 (1557)]

Cheddar : a kind of cheese. Originally made at Cheddar, in Somerset.

Chedreux, A : a kind of wig. After a French wig-maker.

Cheek by jowl : side by side. [Du Bartas, *First Week, First Day* (1578)]

Cheek to the smiter, To offer the : to be meek and forgiving under a wrong. In allusion to *Matthew*, v, 39.

Cheeks, the Marine : a non-existent person. Invented by Captain Frederick Marryat. [*Peter Simple*, ch. vii (1834)]

Cheeryble, A ; Cheeryble Brothers : kind-hearted philanthropists, who do good as a pleasure. After characters in Dickens, *Nicholas Nickleby* (1838).

Cheeseparer, A : a mean, parsimonious person who might pare the last shred of cheese from the rind.

Cheeseparing (economy) : niggardliness.

Cheese-toaster, A : a sword. In allusion to an implement for toasting cheese.

Chef d'œuvre, A (*Fr.*, chief piece of work) : a masterpiece. [J. Chamberlain, *Court and Times of James I* (1619)]

Chelsea, As dead as : *see* Dead.

Cheque, To give a blank : *see* Blank.

Cherchez la femme (*Fr.*, find the woman) : a suggestion that a woman is at the bottom of every trouble. Phrase attributed to Gabriel de Sartine (1729-1801), Fr. Lieut.-Gen. of Police. [Dumas, *Les Mohicans de Paris*, III, 7 (1854) ; Richardson, *Sir Charles Grandison*, Letter 24 (1754)]

Cherethi and Pelethi : the Parties in Israel that remained faithful to David when he fled before the revolt of his son, Absalom.

Cherry Breeches : the 11th Hussars. On account of the colour of their trousers.

Cherry Fair, A : a symbol of the brevity of life and the ephemeral character of its pleasures. After the fairs, the occasion of boisterous enjoyment, held in cherry-orchards in Worcestershire and elsewhere.

Cherry Pickers, The : the 11th Hussars, captured by the French in the Peninsular War while robbing an orchard.

Cherry, To make two bites of a : to divide into two instalments a task which could easily be performed in one operation. [Bracciolini, *Lo Scherno degli Dei*, IV, 30]

Cherub, A : a beautiful child. The biblical name of a class of angels.

Cherubims, The : the 11th Hussars. A pun on their cherry-coloured trousers. (*Cherubim* is the plural of *cherub* ; the final *s* is redundant.)

Cheshire Cat, To grin like a : a simile popularized by 'Lewis Carroll' in *Alice in Wonderland* (1865). From the Cheshire cheese which was orig. moulded in the form of a cat. Other derivations are from (1) the unhappy results of a sign-painter's attempt to paint lions on some sign-boards ; (2) the result of a similar attempt to depict the arms of the Grosvenor family (of Cheshire), a wolf. [First used by Peter Pindar in 18th cent.]

Cheshire Round : a rough dance.

Chesterfield, A : a well-stuffed sofa with two upright ends ; an overcoat with long skirts. After an Earl of Chester-field.

Chestnut, A : (1) a kind of nut, from Kastana in Pontus ; (2) a hackneyed anecdote or joke, from a story of a chestnut-farm in America frequently told by the Amer. painter, E. A. Abbey (1852-1911). An alternative derivation is given in the following quotation from the Philadelphia *Press :*
' There is a melodrama, but little known to the present generation, written by William Dillon and called *The Broken Sword.* There were two characters in it—one a Captain Xavier and the other, the comedy-part of Pablo. The captain is a sort of Baron Münchausen, who, in telling of his exploits, says : " I entered the woods of Collaway when suddenly from the thick boughs of a cork-tree——" Pablo interrupts him with the words : " A chestnut, captain, a chestnut." " Bah ! " replies the captain ; "Booby, I say a cork-tree." " A chestnut," reiterates Pablo. " I should know as well as you, having heard you tell the tale these twenty-seven times." William Warren (1812-88) who had frequently played the part of Pablo, hearing a stale anecdote narrated at a dinner-party, interrupted with a quo-tation from the play, and the phrase " A chestnut " immediately became popular.'

Chestnut Sunday : a Sunday in May, when the chestnut trees in Bushey Park, nr. Hampton Court, are in full bloom, and ' all London ' goes to see them.

Chestnuts out of the fire, To pull the : to act as the tool of another. From the fable of the cat who used the monkey's hands for the purpose.

Cheval de Bataille, A (*Fr.*, battle-horse) : a strong argument.

Chevalier, A : a member of an Order of Knighthood. Orig. a horseman, or knight.

Chevalier, The : *see* Chevalier de St. George.

Chevalier of Fortune, A : a Chevalier d'Industrie (*q.v.*).

Chevalier d'Industrie, A (*Fr.*, knight of industry) : an adventurer ; one who lives by his wits.

Chevalier de St. George, The : James Stuart, the Old Pretender (1688-1766).

Chevalier sans Peur et sans Reproche, Le : Pierre du Terrail, Seigneur de Bayard

(1473-1524), a Fr. hero ; so-called by his anonymous biographer, ' Loyal Serviteur.'

Chevalier, The Young : Charles Edward Stuart, the Young Pretender (1720-88).

Chevaux de Frize (*Fr.*, Friesland horses) : a row of spikes at right angles to the ground. An epithet contemptuously applied, in 17th cent., by the French to the Dutch, who had no cavalry.

Cheveril conscience, A : an elastic conscience. From *cheveril,* a soft kid leather. [Burton, *Anatomy of Melancholy,* Pt. III, Sect. iv, Memb. ii, Sub-sect. 3 (1621) ; Shakespeare, *Henry VIII,* II, iii (1612-3)]

Cheviot : a cloth made from the wool of the sheep bred on the Cheviot Hills.

Chevy (Chivy), To : to chase. From Chevy Chace, an incident in the Battle of Otterburn (1388). Fr. *chevauchée,* a raid.

Chew the cud, To : to cogitate over. From the action of chewing the cud by certain quadrupeds. [Shakespeare, *As You Like It,* IV, iii, ll. 101-2 (1600)]

Chiabreresco : poetry which follows the Grk. model. After Gabriel Chiabrera (1552-1637), ' The Pindar of Italy.'

Chic (*Fr.*) : stylish, attractive. Possibly from ' chicane,' tact, skill.

Chichevache : a fabulous beast that devoured submissive wives. Old Fr., *chicheface,* ugly-face.

Chicken, No : (of a person) not young. [Swift, *Stella's Birthday* (1720)]

Chicken of St. Nicholas, The : the lady-bird, so-called by the Piedmontese.

Chickens before they are hatched, To count one's : *see* Count one's chickens.

Chicken-hearted : as timorous as a chicken. [Bunyan, *Pilgrim's Progress,* Pt. II (1684)]

Chiffney-bit, A : a kind of horse's-bit invented by Samuel Chiffney (1753-1807), a jockey.

Child away along with the bath, To throw the : to throw away the good with the bad, from a German saying.

Child's-play, Mere : a very simple task, comparable to the play of children.

Childermas Day : December 28th, the festival of the Holy Innocents in commemoration of the slaughter of the children by Herod.

Childhood, Second : dotage ; the period of failing faculties in extreme old age.

Children of the Mist : Scottish high-landers. In allusion to the mists prevalent in the north of Scotland.

Children of the West, The : the Americans.

Chiltern Hundreds, The : Burnham, Desborough, and Stoke, the stewardship of which is a sinecure office, used as a means of withdrawal from membership of the House of Commons. The constitution of Parliament does not permit of resignation, but a member on accepting an office of profit under the Crown vacates his seat. Orig. the stewardship of the Chiltern Hundreds carried with it the responsibility of suppressing the robbers who infested the Chiltern Hills.

Chimera, A : an imaginary goal; an empty fancy. After a mythical monster, a combination of lion, goat, and dragon, described by Homer.

Chimney Money : a tax on chimneys imposed during the reigns of Charles II and James II.

Chimney-corner Legend, A : an idle tale, suitable to be narrated by the fireside in winter in order to while away the time.

Chimney-pot hat, A : a tall black-silk hat. From its supposed resemblance to a chimney-pot.

Chin-music : chatter. An Americanism.

China : earthenware. Porcelain manufacture was introduced into Europe from China.

China to Peru, From : from one end of the earth to the other. [Johnson, *Vanity of Human Wishes*, ll. 1-2 (1749); Voltaire, *Lettres en Vers et en Prose* (1755)]

China-town : any urban district inhabited mainly by Chinese.

Chinee, The Heathen : *see* Heathen.

Chinese Gordon : Gen. Chas. Geo. Gordon (1833-85), also known as Gordon of Khartoum. On account of his services to China in the suppression of the Taeping Rebellion in 1863.

Chinese wall, A : an obstacle, very difficult to overcome. After the great medieval wall which bounds the north of China proper.

Chip of the old block, A : one who closely resembles his father generally, or in some special characteristic. Perhaps in allusion to the 'family tree.' [*Dick of Devonshire* (1626)]

Chippendale : furniture made by or in the style of Thos. Chippendale (d.1779).

Chitty-faced (Fr. *chicheface*, thin face) : with thin, pinched face; with a face like a baby's.

Chivan, To play the : to run away headlong.

Chivy, To : to worry and pursue. From Cheviot, in which Border region there used to be frequent cattle-driving and consequent chases. *See also* Chevy.

Chloe, A : a country-girl; a shepherdess. After a character in the Grk. romance, *Daphnis and Chloe*, by Longus. [Horace, *Odes*, I, 23; III, 26; Sidney, *Arcadia* (1590)]

Chocolate soldier, A : a soldier whose uniform and status are of more consequence than the demands of warfare. After one of the characters in Bernard Shaw, *Arms and the Man* (1894).

Choice Spirit, A : a young man of fashion, esp. one who carries the prevalent fashions to extremes. [Goldsmith, *The Good-natured Man*, III, ii (1768)]

Choke off, To : to check abruptly; to prevent; as if gripping a dog by the throat to compel him to relax his hold.

Choke-pear : an obstruction, difficult or impossible to overcome. Lit., the name of an unpalatable pear. [G. Harvey, *Letter Book*, 8 (1573)]

Choker, A : a neckerchief, esp. a large one.

Choker, A White : a clergyman. In allusion to the white tie which forms part of his uniform.

Chop and change, To : to change. 'Chop' has been introduced for alliterative and strengthening purposes. [Ascham, *Toxophilus*, Bk. I (1545)]

Chop logic, To : to argue. [Heywood, *Proverbes* (1546)]

Chops of the Channel, The : the entrance into the Eng. Channel from the Atlantic Ocean where the sea is esp. restless or 'choppy.'

Chop-church, A : one who dealt in ecclesiastical patronage.

Chop-fallen : chap-fallen; dejected; defeated in a contest. Lit., with the lower jaw hanging down. [Killigrew, *The Parson's Wedding*, V, iv (1663)]

Chopine, A : (*Span. chapin*), a shoe raised above the ground by exaggerated heels and soles, in fashion in Spain and Italy at the beginning of 17th cent.

Chopped Hay : unsubstantial learning.

Chortle, To : to express pleasure loudly; to chuckle and laugh. A word invented by Lewis Carroll in *Through the Looking Glass* (1872).

Chorus, A : a body of singers singing in unison ; a portion of a song to be sung by the company generally ; in drama, the character that speaks the prologue and the epilogue of the play. Grk. *choros.*

Chose jugée, A (*Fr.,* judged cause) : a matter that has been decided and should therefore not be re-opened. Introduced into England at the time of the Dreyfus Affair (1894).

Chosen People, The : the Jews. On account of the divine promises made to them.

Chouans, The : the Royalist insurgents in Brittany during the period of the French Revolution. From *chouan* (*chat huant,* screech owl), the nickname of one of the leaders, Jean Cottereau.

Chouse, To : to cheat ; to trick. From a Turkish *chiaous* or interpreter, who perpetrated a notorious swindle in London in 1609.

Chrisom child, A : a child of not more than a month. From the chrisom cloth it wears at baptism.

Chriss-cross : *see* Criss-cross.

Chriss-cross Row : *see* Criss-cross Row.

Christ Church Bells : an old dance.

Christian Cicero, The : Lactantius Firmianus (c. 260-340). After Cicero (106-43 B.C.) who was one of the greatest of the Roman orators.

Christian, To forgive as a : not to forgive at all. [Scott, *Ivanhoe,* ch. 32 (1830)]

Christian King, The most : a title of the kings of France, conferred by Pope Stephen III (714-68).

Christian name, A : the personal name given at christening.

Christian Seneca, The : Joseph Hall (1574-1656), Eng. satirist and Bishop of Norwich. After Lucius Annæus Seneca (B.C. 3-65 A.D.), who was the most eminent of the Latin writers of the Silver Age.

Christian Virgil, The : Marco Girolamo Vida (1490-1566). After Virgil (70-19 B.C.), who was one of the greatest of the Latin poets.

Christian Volume, The : *see* Volume.

Christians, New : *see* New.

Christmas box, A : a money present given at Christmastime ; orig. the earthenware box in which contributions were collected by apprentices at Christmas time.

Christmas King (Prince), A : a Christmas Lord (*q.v.*).

Christmas Lord, A : the Lord of Misrule (*q.v.*), at one time elected at Christmas time.

Christy Minstrels : negro or imitation-negro minstrels. The troupe organized by Edwin P. (1815-1862) and George N. Christy (1827-1868) in America.

Chronicle Small Beer, To : to busy one-self with matters of little importance. Small beer is beer of inferior quality. [Shakespeare, *Othello,* II, i (?1604)]

Chronique scandaleuse, A (*Fr.*) : a narrative of scandals.

Chrononhotonthologos, A : a bombastic talker. After a character in Henry Carey's burlesque of that name (1734).

Chronos, As old as : Chronos, in Grk. mythology, was the personification of time.

Chuck, To teach a hen to : *see* Teach.

Chuckle-headed : stupid. From chuckle, big and clumsy.

Chuff-headed : with a big, fat head ; stupid. [Nash, *Pierce Penilesse* (1592)]

Chum, A : a close associate. Possibly an abbrev. of ' chamber-fellow.' [1684]

Chump, To be off one's : to be out of one's mind. ' Chump,' a synonym for the head, is a block of wood.

Chunèe, A la : of great size. After Chunèe, the largest elephant ever brought to England (1810.)

Church ale, A : a joyful village gathering on a holiday. From the ale formerly brewed by churchwardens for such occasions.

Church Invisible, The : those who are known only to God as his children.

Church Parade, A : a fashionable promenade on Sunday mornings after church-time.

Church Triumphant, The : Christians who have died and, having fought the fight, are now triumphant in heaven.

Church Visible, The : the general body of Christians.

Church's wet nurse, The : Queen Anne. On account of her endowment of ' Queen Anne's Bounty,' so-called by Horace Walpole. [*Letters,* Vol. VII]

Churchwarden, A : a long clay pipe. Formerly smoked by churchwardens at their business-meetings.

Churchyard cough, A : a cough that suggests early death and consequent possible burial in a churchyard.

Churpatties : small cakes circulated in

India immediately before the outbreak of the Indian Mutiny and believed to have given the signal for the revolt.

Cicero, A : an eminent statesman, philosopher and orator. After Marcus Tullius Cicero (106-43 B.C.).

Cicero of France, The : Jean Baptiste Massillon (1663-1742), Fr. preacher and bishop.

Cicero of the British Senate, The : George Canning (1770-1827), Prime Minister of England.

Cicero, The British : William Pitt, Earl of Chatham (1708-78), Prime Minister of England.

Cicero, The Christian : Lucius Coelius Lactantius (260-340).

Cicero, The German : Johann Sturm (1507-89), Germ. divine.

Cicero of Germany, The : John III, Elector of Brandenburg (1455-99).

Cicero's Mouth : Philippe Pot (1428-94), Prime Minister to Louis XI of France.

Cicerone, A : a learned guide to objects of interest. From Cicero, the Roman orator (106-43 B.C.), in allusion to his learning and eloquence.

Cid, The : the Spanish Champion of Christendom, Don Roderigo Dias de Bivar, El Campeador (1040-99). The title Cid is the Arab. *Seid*, lord and conqueror, as which he was acknowledged by five Moorish chieftains after one battle.

Cid, The Portuguese : Nunez Alvarez Pereira (1360-1431), general and diplomatist.

Cider Country (Land), The : Herefordshire and Worcestershire. On account of the number of their apple-orchards.

Ci-devants (*Fr.*, formerly) : the members of the titled classes after they had been deprived by the French Revolutionists of their titles.

Cimmerian darkness : extreme darkness. In allusion to the Cimmerii, a fabulous people who dwelt in perpetual darkness.

Cinchona : quinine. After the Countess of Chincon, wife of a Viceroy of Peru, who was cured of a fever by the bark of the cinchona tree (c. 1640).

Cincinnatus, The American : George Washington. After Lucius Quinctius Cincinnatus (519-438, B.C.), saviour of Rome, who was fetched from his labours in the fields to assume the supreme power.

Cincinnatus of the West, The : William Henry Harrison, 9th President of the U.S. (1797-1801).

Cinderella, A : (1) (of a girl) a despised and ignored, yet virtuous member of a company of equals ; after the heroine of the fairy-tale, who, although repressed and ill-treated by her two sisters, ultimately married the Prince ; (2) a dancing-party which terminates at midnight ; from the fairy tale of *Cinderella*, who had to return home from the Prince's ball by midnight.

Cinderella of the Arts, The : architecture.

Cinque Port, A : one of the five (Fr., *cinque*) ports : Hastings, Romney, Hythe, Dover and Sandwich, to which were afterwards added Winchelsea and Rye. Sussex and Kent ports endowed as early as the reign of Edward the Confessor with special privileges, in return for which they were called upon to take a leading part in naval defence.

Cinquecento, The : the 16th century in its art and literature. Italian 500 = the century commencing in the year 1500. This was the period of Ariosto, Tasso, Raphael, Titian, Michael Angelo, Machiavelli, and other famous men.

Circe, A : a dangerously fascinating woman. After the mythological Grk. sorceress.

Circe of the Revolution, The : Madame Roland (1754-93).

Circean : *see* Circe.

Circumbendibus, A : a circumlocution. A word invented by Dryden (1681), from *circum*, around and ' bend,' with the ablative plural termination. [Dryden, *The Spanish Friar*, V, ii (1681)]

Circumlocution, A : a clumsy, involved manner of expressing oneself. [Barclay, *Mirror of Good Manners* (1510)]

Circumlocution Office, A : a Government Department or Office. Because its ' red tape '—*i.e.*, the observance of innumerable formalities—causes excessive and quite unnecessary delay. After the name of a Government Department in Dickens, *Little Dorrit* (1855).

Circumquaque : a circumlocution (*q.v.*).

Cisalpine Republic, The : a State formed by Napoleon in 1796 out of the conquered northern provinces of Italy.

Cisley, A : a dairymaid [Tusser, *A Hundreth Good Pointes of Husbandrie* (1557)]

Cistern, A : a reservoir for water, etc. From cista, the basket in which were carried the sacred vessels at the Eleusinian Mysteries.

Cit, A : a citizen or townsman (contemptuously). [Cleveland, *Rupeitismus* (1644)]

Cities, The Seven : Cairo, Jerusalem, Babylon, Athens, Rome, Constantinople, London (or Paris).

Citizen King, The : Louis Philippe, King of the French, the first elected King of France.

Citizen of Nature, A : one who feels himself at home in all countries.

Citizen of the World, A : a cosmopolitan ; one who regards—politically and morally—the whole civilized world as a unit. The phrase was apparently coined by Socrates (468-399 B.C.). It was also used as a *nom-de-plume* by Oliver Goldsmith (1728-74).

City, In the : in business. ' The City ' indicates the City of London.

City College, The : Newgate prison. Formerly situated in the City of London.

City Company, A : one of the Corporation guilds of the City of London.

City Editor, A : the financial editor of a newspaper.

City Father, A : one of the governing body of a city ; an alderman of the City of London.

City Golgotha, The : old Temple Bar, on which the heads of traitors used to be exhibited. Hebr. *Golgotha* is ' the place of skulls.'

City of Bells, The : Strassburg, in Alsace.

City of Brotherly Love, The : Philadelphia, which in Grk. means ' brotherly love.'

City of Churches, The : Brooklyn, New York. On account of the number of churches it contains.

City of David, The : Jerusalem. [II *Sam.*, v, 7, 9]

City of Elms, The : New Haven, Connecticut. On account of the number of elm-trees in its streets.

City of God, The : (1) Paradise ; (2) the Church, or the whole body of believers.

City of Magnificent Distances, The : Washington. On account of its wide and long avenues.

City of Masts, The : London. Owing to its great shipping industry.

City of the Midnight Sun, The : London, in allusion to its night-pleasures.

City of Monuments, The : Baltimore, U.S. On account of the number of monuments in it.

City of Oaks, The : Raleigh, N. Carolina ; which has many oak-trees in it.

City of Palaces, The : (1) Calcutta ; (2) Imperial Rome ; (3) Petrograd.

City of Refuge, A : an ' alsatia ' or place-of-refuge for criminals as well as the innocent. From the cities set apart when the Holy Land was occupied by the Hebrews as places of refuge for fugitives.

City of Refuge, The : Medina in Arabia, in which Mahomet took refuge in the year 622.

City of St. Michael, The : Dumfries, whose Patron Saint is St. Michael.

City of Saints, The : Montreal, whose streets are named after saints.

City of the Great King, The : Jerusalem. [*Psalms*, xlviii, 2 ; *Matthew*, v, 35]

City of the Prophet, The : Medina, the burial-place of Mahomet.

City of the Seven Hills, The : Rome, in allusion to the seven hills, the Aventine, Cælian, Capitoline, Esquiline, Palatine, Quirinal and Viminal, on which the city was originally built.

City of the Sun, The : (1) Baalbec, the centre of the worship of the Sun-God ; (2) Rhodes, whose tutelar deity was the Sun ; (3) Heliopolis in Egypt, on account of its Temple of the Sun.

City of the Tribes, The : Galway, ' the residence of the thirteen tribes.'

City of the Violated Treaty, The : Limerick. On account of the frequent breaches of the treaty of 1691.

City of the Violet Crown, The : Athens ; the violet being the symbol of the city. [Aristophanes, etc.]

City of Victory, The : Cairo.

City, The : the City of London, esp. the business-districts of London.

City, The Celestial : see Celestial.

City, The Eternal : see Eternal.

City, The Heavenly : Paradise.

City, The Holy : see Holy City.

Civis Romanus sum (*Lat.*, I am a Roman citizen) : phrase used by Cicero (106-43 B.C.) in his sixth oration against Verres, an expression of the pride, courage and steadfastness of a citizen of Rome. The phrase was quoted by Lord Palmerston in the House of Commons on 25th June,

1850, in defending his action in the Pacifico case.

Civvies, To be dressed in : to wear civilian costume. The phrase arose during the European War of 1914-18.

Clack-dish, A : a wooden receptacle with a cover carried by beggars and used as a means of attracting the attention of the alms-giver.

Claimant, The : Arthur Orton, an Australian butcher, who claimed to be the lost Sir Roger Tichbourne ; convicted of perjury in 1874.

Clanjamfray, The whole : the mob ; the rabble. Scottish.

Clan-na-Gael, The : an Irish secret political Society founded in 1881 to secure the separation of Ireland from Britain. Known also as ' The United Brotherhood.'

Clap-bread : a thin oatmeal cake. Lit., bread clapped (patted thin).

Clapham Sect, The : a sect of Evangelical Christians. From the district in London in which it centred in the late 18th cent.

Clapperclaw, To : to scratch with the open hand ; to abuse ; to beat. Lit., to claw with the clapper. Also ' caper-claw ' (*q.v.*). [Shakespeare, *Troilus and Cressida*, V, iv (1606)]

Clapper dudgeon, A : a beggar. From the clap-dish which beggars formerly carried. [Heywood, 1 *King Edward IV* (1600)]

Clap-shoulder, A : an officer of justice, who, when making an arrest. places his hand on the prospective prisoner's shoulder.

Clap-trap : cheap, insincere action or words intended to attract support.

Clarence, A : a four-wheeled carriage. After the Duke of Clarence, afterwards William IV.

Clarendon : a kind of printing-type. After the Clarendon Press, at Oxford, where it was introduced.

Class, No : *see* No Class.

Class, The Lower Middle : the lower division of the middle class of the population, consisting mainly of trades-people, clerks, etc.

Class, The Upper Middle : the second class in society, consisting of the richer professional and mercantile classes.

Classes, The : the upper or highest class in society.

Classes and Masses, The : the people as a whole, *viz.*, the Upper and Middle Classes and the mass of the people.

Phrase used by W. E. Gladstone (1809–98), and previously by Thos. Moore (1779–1852) in *The Fudges in England* (1835).

Claw-back, A : a flatterer. Lit., one who claws (strokes down) another's back. [Latimer, *Sermons* (1549)]

Claw-hammer coat, A : an evening-dress tail-coat. It resembles a claw-hammer, *i.e.*, a hammer with a claw for extracting nails.

Clay in the hands of the potter, As : easily influenced or moulded. [*Jeremiah*, xviii, 6]

Clay, Human : human beings. In allusion to *Genesis*, ii, 7.

Clay, A yard of : a churchwarden (pipe), *q.v.*

Clean breast of, To make a : *see* Breast.

Clean hands, To have : to be quite innocent in a certain matter.

Clean life, To live a : to live a blameless, virtuous life.

Clean pair of heels, To show a : to run away suddenly.

Clean sheet, A : a clear record.

Clean slate, With a : *see* Slate.

Clear as crystal, As : [1300]

Clear as the day, As : [Wager, *Rep. of Mary Magd.* (1566)]

Clear as daylight, As : perfectly plain. [Starkey, *England in the Reign of King Henry VIII*, 130]

Clear as noonday, As : absolutely plain. [Peter Pindar, *An Academie Ode* (1797)]

Clear out for Guam, To : not to be bound for anywhere in particular. In the rush to the Australian gold-fields ships were chartered to convey passengers outwards without having any definite cargo for the return journey. To seek this they used to sail from port to port. On leaving Melbourne, however, the captain had to state a destination, and for this purpose the name of Guam, a small island in the Ladrones, was usually given.

Cleargrits, The : the Canadian advocates of annexation to the U.S. in the middle of 19th cent.

Cleave the clouds, To : to act foolishly and to no purpose. From an ancient Grk. proverb.

Clemency Canning : Charles John, Earl Canning (1812–62), Governor-General of India. On account of his alleged extreme clemency to the Indian rebels.

Clenchpoop, A : a term of contempt ; orig. the designation of an artizan.

[Rob. Wilson, *Three Ladies of London*, II, l. 62 (1584)]

Clerk of the Weather, The : an imaginary official supposed to control weather-conditions.

Cliché, A : a hackneyed phrase or word. Fr., *clicher*, to stereotype.

Clicquot, King : Frederick William IV of Prussia. A name given to him in England.

Climacteric, The Grand : the 63rd year, supposed to be a critical one in human life. Seven and nine were the Climacteric Numbers, which had a fatal influence, and over which Saturn, the malevolent planet, was said to preside. Hence the 63rd (7 x 9) was considered especially fatal.

Climb the waves, To : to put out to sea. [Virgil, *Æneid*, Bk. I, l. 381]

Climb down, To : to abandon an attitude or view that one has adopted.

Clincher (Clencher), A : a conclusive argument. From ' clinch ' or ' clench,' to fasten securely.

Clink, A : a small prison. The name of a once famous prison in Southwark.

Clip the King's English, To : to speak corruptly. [Rich. Edwards, *Damon and Pithias* (1567)]

Clip the wings of .. To : to reduce the power or efficiency of .. [Peter Pindar, *Ode Upon Ode* (1785)]

Cloaca, A : a sewer. After the name of a sewer in ancient Rome.

Cloak, A : a cover; concealment; disguise. [Lyly, *Endimion*, II, i (1591)]

Cloak for the rain, A : an excuse. [Rich. Taverner, *Proverbes of Erasmus* (1552)]

Cloak and Sword plays : plays of modern life. The cloak and sword were part of the ordinary Spanish costume, when the phrase was invented.

Cloak and Sword romances : romances of adventure.

Cloak for every rain, To have a : to have an expedient for every requirement. [W. R., *A Match at Midnight*, III, i (1633)]

Clod-hopper, A : an agriculturist; an awkward man. One who walks over ploughed fields, or hops among the clods of earth.

Clootie, Auld : the Devil. Scot., *cloot*, a cloven hoof.

Close, To be : to be reserved. [*Destruction of Troy*, 3939 (1400)] Later, to be stingy.

Close trade, A : one that is confined to a few business firms that act in agreement.

Close-fisted : mean. Lit., with the hand tightly closed. [Lewis Machin, *The Dumb Knight*, V, i (1608)]

Close-time : a period during which it is illegal to kill certain game.

Closh, Mynheer : see Mynheer Closh.

Cloth, The : the clergy. [Swift, *Mrs. Harris's Petition* (1710)]

Cloth Breeches : members of the Lower or of the Middle Class. Formerly their distinctive dress.

Cloth, To cut the coat according to one's : see Coat.

Clothes for fishes, To make : see Make.

Clothes while bathing, To steal : see Whigs.

Cloud, Under a : in trouble; under suspicion. (1500 A.D.]

Clouds, In the : vague; obscure; imaginary. Lat., *in nubibus*. [Selden, *Laws of England* (1649)]

Clouds, To cleave the : see Cleave.

Clouds, To drop from the : to appear suddenly and from an entirely unexpected quarter.

Cloud-cuckoo-land : an idealistic scheme of reform. After Nephelokokuggia in Aristophanes, *The Clouds*.

Cloven hoof (foot), To show the : to display an evil intention. In Christian art Satan is depicted with a cloven hoof.

Clover, To be in : to be in a very comfortable situation; like a cow in a clover-field.

Club Land : that part of West London in which most of the principal clubs are located, *i.e.*, Pall Mall and St. James' Street.

Club Law : government by force; the law of the club, used to enforce obedience.

Clumber, A : a species of spaniel. After the seat of the Duke of Newcastle in Nottinghamshire.

Cluster-fist, A : a mean, grasping person. [Cotgrave, *Dictionary* (1611)]

Clutch-fist, A : a niggard. [Cartwright, *Ordinary* (1651)]

Cly-fake, To : to pick pockets. Thieves' slang. From ' cly,' a pocket, ' fake,' to steal.

Coach, A ; Coach, To : (*a*) a private tutor; (*b*) to prepare for an examination; to train for a boat-race, etc. Orig. a pun on a means of progressing quickly.

Coach, A slow : a dilatory person.

Coach, Fifth wheel of the : see Fifth.

Coach-and-four through .. To drive a : see Drive a coach.

Coal to blow at, A cold : an impossible task.

Coals of fire on the head of .. To heap : to put to shame by repaying evil with good. [*Proverbs*, xxv, 21-22]

Coals, To blow hot : to rage fiercely.

Coals, To blow the : see Blow.

Coals, To carry (bear) : to perform an unpleasant task ; to submit to humiliation. From the duties of the lowest menials in the household. [Ben Jonson, *Every Man Out of His Humour*, V, iii (1600) ; Chapman, *May Day* (1611)]

Coals, To haul (call) over the : to reprimand ; to blame. In allusion to the treatment of heretics.

Coals to Newcastle, To carry (send) : to perform a work of supererogation. Newcastle-on-Tyne is one of the principal English coal-mining centres. [Fuller, *Worthies : Northumberland* (1661)]. The phrase may have originated in ' as common as coales at Newcastle. [Heywood, *If You Know Not Me* (1606)]

Coals, To stir : to stir up strife and trouble. [Geo. Cavendish, *Life and Death of Wolsey* (1557)]

Coal-carrierly clown, A : a low, servile fellow.

Coast to be clear, The : the road to be open and unimpeded. Orig. a military phrase, signifying that the coast of a country was clear of defending forces ; also a smugglers' phrase, denoting the absence of coastguards. [Thos. Lodge, *Rosalind* (1590)]

Coat according to one's cloth, To cut one's : to adapt oneself to one's resources. A relic of the Sumptuary Laws. [Heywood, *Proverbes*, Pt. I, ch. viii (1546)]

Coat, To baste (pay) a person's : to beat him. [Bunyan, *Pilgrim's Progress*, Pt. I (1678)]

Coat, To be in a person's : to be in his place, esp. in time of trouble.

Coat off a person's back, To take the : to press a debtor or other person in one's power unduly.

Coat, To turn one's : to change one's principles and party. One who does this is called ' a turn-coat.'

Coat, To wear the king's : to be a soldier.

Cobalt : one of the metallic chemical elements. From Kobold, an imp of the Hartz Mountains. So-called by Paracelsus (1493-1541), on account of its elusive and impish quality.

Cobbler : an Amer. drink. First concocted by a shoemaker.

Cobbler Poet, The : Hans Sachs, of Nuremberg (1494-1574).

Cobbler should stick to his last, A : see Stick to one's last.

Cobbler's punch : a mixture of beer, spirit, sugar, and spice. See Cobbler.

Cobdenite School, The : After Richard Cobden. See Manchester School.

Coburg : an imitation merino fabric ; introduced shortly after the marriage of Queen Victoria with Prince Albert of Saxe-Coburg. There was no connection between the fabric and the Duchy of Coburg.

Cobweb-learning : learning of little substance. [Howell, *Familiar Letters* (1650)]

Cock, A. : (1) one who arouses ; a watchman ; a minister of religion ; in allusion to the crowing of the domestic cock that arouses the sleeper ; (2) one who shows spirit ; in allusion to a game-cock.

Cock and Bull story, A : a fictitious, far-fetched narrative, usually without any foundation in fact. Probably from some old absurd story or a fable of a cock and a bull. Cf. Coq à l'âne. [John Day, *Law Trickes*, IV (1608)]

Cock, To cry : to claim the victory ; to claim superiority.

Cock and Hen Club, A : a club for men and women.

Cock Lane Ghost, The : an imposture perpetrated in Cock Lane, Smithfield, London, in 1762, by a man named Parsons and his daughter.

Cock of the game, The : the leader in a game, esp. at school. Orig. a fighting-cock. [Munday and Chettle, *Death of Robert, Earl of Huntingdon*, II, ii (1601)]

Cock of the school, The : the leader of the school in sports, etc.

Cock of the walk, The : the leader of a circle or coterie ; the ' top dog.' From the farmyard, where one cock assumes the headship of the hen-run.

Cock to crow, To teach a : see Teach.

Cock, To live like a fighting- : see Fighting Cock.

Cock-a-hoop : defiant, boastful. Like a game-cock with his houpe or crest erect, or in allusion to the attitude of the triumphant cock perched on the hoop within which the fight is supposed to have taken place. [Heywood, *Proverbes* (1546) ; Shakespeare, *Romeo and Juliet*, I, v (1595)]

Cock-a-leekie : soup made of a cock boiled with leeks.

Cock-boat, A : a very small boat ; the small boat which is towed behind a ship.

Cock-brained : silly ; foolish ; with no more brain than a cock. [*Lomatius on Painting* (1598)]

Cock-fighting, To beat : to be most improbable. In allusion to far-fetched stories told of cock-fighting.

Cock-pit of Europe, The : Belgium. On account of the number of times it has been ravaged by the wars of other nations.

Cock-shy, A : an object at which sticks, etc., are thrown for prizes (*e.g.*, cocoanuts on sticks) at country fairs, etc. From the old sport of throwing sticks at cocks.

Cock-sparrow humour : amorous humour. [G. Wilkins, *Miseries of Enforced Marriage*, I, ll. 126–30 (1607)]

Cock-sure : absolutely certain : *see* Cocky. Or perhaps derived from cock-fighting. [Nat. Woodes, *Conflict of Conscience*, III, iii (1581)]

Cock-tail, A : (1) one who pretends to be a gentleman but is not one ; from cock-tailed horses (horses with their tails shortened), which as a rule are not thoroughbred ; (2) a drink, consisting of spirit, bitters, sugar, etc. ; from a Mexican favourite drink, Octel, after Xochitl, who first concocted it.

Cock's canny hinnies, As rich as : these were the daughters and heiresses of Alderman Ralph Cock, of Newcastle.

Cockade State, The : Maryland. On account of the cockades worn by the local regiment in the War of Independence.

Cockaigne ; Cockayne : London. Cockaigne is the fabulous land of luxury and idleness. Not connected with ' cockney.'

Cock-crow, At : at dawn. In allusion to the practice of cocks crowing as soon as light appears.

Cocked hat, To knock into a : to thrash thoroughly. A ' cocked hat ' (slang) is anything that has been damaged out of recognition. Another derivation is from the game of bowls. One of the figures in this game is designated

' a cocked hat.' To secure this figure is sufficiently exceptional to form the basis for a proverb.

Cocker, According to : accurate. After Edward Cocker, author of *The Compleat Arithmetician* (c. 1669). The phrase became common from the reference to Cocker and his arithmetic in Murphy's farce, *The Apprentice* (1756).

Cockle-brained : eccentric ; whimsical.

Cockles of the heart, To warm the : to give very great pleasure and satisfaction. Said to be an allusion to the resemblance in shape between a cockle-shell and the heart. An amusing derivation has been suggested, *viz.*, the resemblance between *kardia*, the Grk. word for ' heart,' and *cardium*, the technical Lat. name for ' cockle.' Another suggested origin is from the Lat. word *cochlea*, ventricle, used by Rich. Lower, an Eng. anatomist, in his *Tractatus de Corde* (1669). For the term ' Cockles of his heart ' *see* Eachard, *Observations* (1671).

Cockney, A : (1) a Londoner, one born within sound of Bow Bells. Orig. a cock's egg, *i.e.*, a small badly-shaped egg ; later, a countryman's nickname for a town-dandy ; in 17th cent. applied esp. to Londoners. Sir James Murray derives the modern use of cockney from the earlier sense of a pampered child, a milksop. At first applied to townsmen by countrymen, it later became attached to Londoners only. Yet another derivation connects the word with ' cock ' and relates it to the French phrase, *Le pais de cocagne*, the land of good cheer ; (2) a pet ; [Greene, *Liberality and Prodigality*, IV, i (1602)] (3) a member of the Cockney School (*q.v.*).

Cockney Accent : intonation or twang peculiar to the lower classes of East London.

Cockney School, The : a set of 19th-cent. London writers consisting of Leigh Hunt, Shelley, Hazlitt, Keats, etc. So-called by Lockhart.

Cockneys, The King of the : a Master of the Revels, chosen by the students of Lincoln's Inn on Childermas Day (Dec. 28th).

Cockoloach, A : a mean fellow ; a coxcomb.

Cocky : conceited ; formerly lecherous. Also (as a noun) a colloquial term of endearment.

Cocqcigrues, The : the future good time when all mysteries will be revealed. [Rabelais, *Gargantua*, I, 49]

Code Frédéric, The : a codification of the law made by Frederick the Great (1712–86).

Code Napoleon, The : the code of law introduced by Napoleon in 1803.

Codlin's your friend, not Short : an attempt to secure confidence at the expense of a rival. After Codlin and Short in Dickens, *Old Curiosity Shop*, ch. xix (1840).

Cod's head, A : a fool. The head of a codfish looks particularly silly.

Coelebs' Wife, A : a model wife in the opinion of a bachelor. After a character in Hannah More, *Coelebs in Search of a Wife* (1809).

Coeur de Lion (*Fr.*, heart of a lion) : (1) Richard I of England ; (2) also Louis VIII of France. On account of their exceptional bravery.

Coffee House Statesman (Politician), A : an amateur statesman. In allusion to the coffee-houses in which they used to gather for political discussion.

Coggeshall job, A : a stupidity. From the proverbial foolishness of the inhabitants of Coggeshall in Essex.

Cognac : brandy distilled from grapes grown at Cognac, France.

Cognoscente, A (*Ital.*) : one well versed in a subject, esp. one of the five arts.

Coin money, To : to make money rapidly, as if one were actually coining it.

Coin, To pay a person in his own : to treat a person in accordance with the treatment he himself meted out. [Plautus, *Pseudolus*, l. 743 ; Tomkis, *Alburnazar*, IV, ix (1615)]

Colberteen ; Colbertine : a kind of lace. After Jean Baptiste Colbert (1619–83), Fr. statesman and superintendent of the royal lace-factories.

Colchester, Weaver's beef of : *see* Weaver's.

Cold as a Key, As : cold. [Gawin Douglas, *Palace of Honour*, 674 (1501)]

Cold as a paddock, As : a paddock is a toad or frog, a cold-blooded rana.

Cold as a stone, As : (1290).

Cold blood, In : deliberately ; without excitement. [Wm. Brown, *Elegie to the Memory of Sir Thomas Overbury* (1613)]

Cold shoulder to . . To show (give) the ; To cold-shoulder: to be distant with . . ; to show a disinclination to friendship with . . [Scott, *The Antiquary*, ch. xxx (1816)]

Cold feet, To have : to be lacking, generally temporarily, in courage.

Cold steel : a bayonet ; a sword.

Cold, To leave out in the : to neglect ; to ignore.

Cold water upon . . To throw : to discourage.

Cold-blooded : unemotional ; heartless ; deliberate.

Cole (cold) prophet, To play : to pretend to tell fortunes. From ' cole,' a swindler. [Heywood, *Proverbes* (1546)]

Colin Tampon : a Swiss.

Coliseum : *see* Colosseum.

Collar, To : to seize. Lit., to lay hold of by the collar.

Collar of SS (Esses) : orig. the badge of the Lancastrians ; now worn by the Lord Chief Justice and other judges and officials.

Collectanea (*Lat.*) : a collection of an author's writings. First applied to those of Caius Julius Solinus (fl. 230), Roman grammarian, historian, and geographer.

Collective bargaining : negotiations on the part of workingmen in a body, *e.g.*, as a trade union, for improvements in pay or conditions of labour.

Colleen, A (*Irish*) : a young girl.

College, New : Newgate prison.

Collop Monday : the day before Shrove Tuesday on which collops (eggs fried on bacon) are eaten.

Cologne, The Three Kings of : Gaspar, Melchior, and Balthazar, the three Wise Men of the East, who visited the Infant Jesus, and according to tradition were buried at Cologne.

Colonial System, The Old : the system adopted by Britain towards her colonies in the 18th cent. and earlier, whereby she obtained considerable economic advantages at their expense. This system led to the secession of the North American colonies.

Colophon : the conclusion of a book, showing the date and place of publication, printer's name, etc. After Colophon, in Asia Minor, a troop of whose cavalry was famous for giving the finishing stroke.

Coloquintida, As bitter as : coloquintida, or colocynth, the bitter-apple. [Shakespeare, *Othello*, I, iii (1604)]

Colossal : immense, like a Colossus (*q.v.*).

Colosseum ; Coliseum : a place of amusement of the ' variety ' description; a music-hall. The Colosseum at Rome was the theatre for the public games. It derived its name from the colossal statue of Nero in its neighbourhood.

Colossus, A : an over-shadowing personality. After the Colossus, a gigantic statue of Apollo, which bestrode the harbour at Rhodes, one of the Wonders of the World.

Colossus of Independence, The : John Adams (1735–1826), second President of the U.S. On account of his efforts for the independence of the colonies.

Colour, A man of : a negro, or other dark-skinned person.

Colour of .. Under : under pretence of .. [Sir Thos. Wyatt, *The Louer Lamenteth His Estate* (1557)]

Colour to .. To give : to provide some sort of justification for .. [*Paston Letters*, No. 268 (1456)]

Colour, To turn : (of a person) to turn pale.

Colours, To desert one's : to withdraw one's support. A military metaphor.

Colours, False : a cover for dishonesty. A military metaphor referring to the flag or colours carried by a regiment.

Colours, Flying : *see* Flying.

Colours, To fear no : to fear no enemy. A military metaphor. [Shakespeare, *Twelfth Night*, I, v (1601)]

Colours, To join the : to join the army, *i.e.*, to range oneself under a military flag.

Colours, To paint in bright : to emphasize the pleasant aspects of ..

Colours to the mast, To nail one's : to remain steadfast in one's determination. A naval metaphor, referring to the flag or colours carried by a man-of-war.

Colours, To see a thing in its true : to see clearly, despite attempts at deception.

Colours, To stick to one's : to adhere to one's principles. A military metaphor.

Colours, To strike one's : to surrender, withdraw from a contest. A military metaphor.

Colours, True : honesty.

Colours, To wear a person's : to attach oneself to a person. [Shakespeare, *Love's Labour Lost* (1588)].

Coloured Frontispiece by 'Phiz,' A : a blush. A pun on 'phiz,' 'physiognomy,' and 'Phiz,' the *sobriquet* of Hablot K. Browne (1815–82), humorous artist.

Colporteur, A : one who travels from village to village hawking books, esp. Bibles and small devotional books, etc. From *col*, neck, and *porter*, to carry.

Colt Revolver, A : a fire-arm invented by Samuel Colt (1814–62).

Columbia : America. After Columbus, the discoverer.

Columbiad : a kind of heavy cannon, formerly used in the U.S. Army. After Columbia (*q.v.*).

Columbus' egg, As simple as : in allusion to the anecdote related of Christopher Columbus and the egg. The task set was to cause an egg to balance on one of its ends. Several scientists applied their knowledge to solving the difficulty but without success. Columbus, as soon as he learnt of the difficulty, indented one end slightly by cracking the shell, and immediately stood the egg upright.

Comb, A crab-tree : a cudgel, intended for use on the head. 'Crab' from crab-apple.

Comb of Germany, The : the four fingers and the thumb. [Rabelais, *Gargantua*, I, 21]

Comb the hair the wrong way, To : to annoy a person by opposing his prejudices, opinions, etc.

Come down, A : a humiliation; a reverse.

Come the old soldier over .. To : to deceive and cajole, esp. with a view to obtaining assistance. The phrase arose after the conclusion of the Napoleonic Wars from the public begging practised by disbanded soldiers and pretended soldiers.

Come to the end of one's tether, To : *see* Tether.

Comedy of character, A : ' not an exact drama, in which the actors deliver what is set down to them by the author; but one in which, the plot having been previously fixed upon and a few striking scenes adjusted, the actors are expected to supply the dialogue extempore.' [Scott, *St. Ronan's Well*, ch. 20 (1824)].

Comedy of Errors, A : a series of amusing mistakes. After the play of that title by Shakespeare (1589).

Comely as a cow in a cage, As : [Heywood, *Proverbes* (1546)]

Comfort(s), Creature : *see* Creature-comfort.

Comitadji, A (*Serbian*) : a member of a band of irregular soldiers or brigands in Macedonia, who, previous to the Balkan Wars, carried on a ceaseless warfare of extermination against the races other than his own living in that region.

Commandeer, To : to seize for military or other governmental use. From the South-African Dutch. Introduced at the time of the South African War of 1899.

Commander of the Faithful : the Caliph. The title was first assumed by Omar (581–644).

Commander of the Swiss Fleet, A : an ironical title for a paid holder of a sinecure. Switzerland, of course, possesses no fleet.

Commandment, The Eleventh : ' Thou shalt not be found out.'

Commando, A : a body of South African burghers summoned to take up arms for the defence of their lands. This system of compulsory service was introduced by the English in 1806.

Comme il faut (*Fr.*, as it should be) : in accordance with custom, convention or etiquette.

Commendation Ninepence, A : a bent ninepenny piece used as a love-token. Commendation, the act of commending.

Commercial drama, A : a play written for no other purpose than to make money.

Commodity of brownpaper, A : (1) goods purchased on credit by prodigals and swindlers to be turned immediately into ready money at a loss ; [Shakespeare, *Measure for Measure*, IV, iii (1603)] (2) worthless goods sold either as a make-weight or a deception.

Common cause with .. To make : to join one's fortunes with .. [Bacon, *Essays : Of Seditions and Troubles* (1625)]

Commoner, The Great : *see* Great.

Common or garden : quite ordinary and plentiful, not rare, as the context would have led one to expect. Like ordinary garden flowers. The phrase passed about 1875 from the technical use in the field clubs and naturalists' other popular societies into general use.

Common People, The : the people apart from those who enjoy titles or dignities.

Commons, Good : good feeding. ' Commons ' in the sense of provisions, orig. supplied to a number of people in common, as in a monastery or a college.

Commons, Short : insufficient rations. *see* Commons, Good.

Commonplace book, A : a book into which striking passages in literature, etc., are copied. ' Commonplace was a term used in old rhetoric to represent testimonies or pithy sentences of good authors which might be used for strengthening or adorning a discourse.' [Henry Morley, in a note to Sidney, *Defence of Poesie*]

Commonwealth of Letters : *see* Republic of Letters.

Commune, The : a socialist party in France during the period in 1871 in which the revolutionary socialists had control of Paris. From *commune*, a French municipal district, the independent unit for self-government, according to the theory of the Revolutionary Socialists.

Company, To keep : to associate with, esp. in the case of lower-class lovers. [*Wily Beguiled*, ll. 1053–4 (1606)]

Compass, To live : to return to one's starting-point ; to describe a circle. [Lyly, *Euphues and His England* (1580)]

Competition Wallah, A : a member of the Indian Civil Service appointed as a result of open competition. Urdu, *wala* is equivalent to the suffix - er in competitioner.

Complete Seaman, The : Admiral Sir Richard Hawkins (1562–1622). So-called by himself.

Compound householder, A : a householder whose rates are covered by his rent and are paid by his landlord. Act 14 and 15 Vict. (1851).

Comtism : Positivism. After Auguste Comte (1798–1857), the French founder of this school of philosophy.

Comus, A priest of : a cook. Comus was the god of revelry and feasting.

Con amore (*Ital.*, with love) : enthusiastically. [Warburton's edn. of *Pope*, IV (1757)]

Concert of Europe, The : agreement of the Great Powers of Europe in matters of common interest.

Conclave, A : an assembly of Cardinals for the election of a Pope. Properly, a set of rooms opened by a common key (*con clavis*), the range of rooms to which the Cardinals repair when a Pope is to be elected.

Conclusions with .. To try : to contest with .. Its former meaning was to experiment.

Concordat: the agreement of 1801 between Napoleon and the Pope for the restoration of the Roman Catholic Church in France.

Condog, To: to concur. Suggested derivation: dog = cur. [Lyly, *Galathea*, III, 3 (1592)]

Condominium, A (*Lat.*, joint dominion): a protectorate exercised jointly by two or more powers. [Burnet, *History of His Own Times*, III (1705)]

Condottiere, A: an Italian brigand. Orig. a soldier-of-fortune who fought in Italy in the wars of the 15th and 16th cents.

Confab, A: an intimate conversation. Contraction of confabulation. Lat., *confabulatio.* [*Dialogue: Marphorio and Pasquin*, 8 (1701)]

Confederate States, The: South Carolina, Alabama, Florida, Mississippi, Georgia, Louisiana, Texas, Virginia, Arkansas, Tennessee, North Carolina. The eleven southern States that seceded from the N. American Union in 1860. The secession led to the Amer. Civil War. The States were reincorporated in the Union on the conclusion of the war in 1865.

Confidence man, A: one who practices the Confidence Trick (*q.v.*); a respectably-dressed swindler.

Confidence Trick, The: a swindling trick which requires the confidence of the victim as a preliminary. Usually the deposit, as a token of good-faith, of money with which the holder runs away.

Congé d'élire (*Fr.*, permission to elect): the royal licence to elect a bishop.

Congleton Bears: the inhabitants of Congleton, Cheshire. From the tradition that when the town-bear died, the money subscribed for a new church Bible was appropriated to purchase another bear.

Congress: Parliament of the U.S., consisting of the Senate and House of Representatives.

Conqueror, To have come in (over) with the: phrase applied to those who claim long English lineage.

Conqueror's nose, A: a long straight nose with an elevated bridge; such as those of Charlemagne, the Duke of Wellington, Bismarck.

Conquistadores, The (*Span.*, the conquerors): the Spanish conquerors of Mexico and Peru in the 16th cent.

Conscience clause, A: a clause in an Act of Parliament that makes a concession to religious opinions.

Conscience, Court of: see Court.

Conscience money: money sent annoymously in payment of taxes of which the revenue had previously been defrauded by the sender.

Conscript Fathers, The: the Senators of ancient Rome: *Patres conscripti.*

Conservative Party, The: an English political party, formerly known as Tory. The name, which denotes the policy of conserving the institutions of the Country, came into use about 1832 on the initiative, it is said, of J. W. Croker (1780–1857). The term had, however, been used by George Canning in a speech at Liverpool in March, 1820.

Considering- (Thinking-) cap, To put on one's: to enter into deep consideration. [Rob. Arnim, *A Nest of Ninnies* (1608)]

Consistory, A: (1) a business-meeting of Cardinals under the chairmanship of the Pope; (2) an ecclesiastical Court.

Consolation prize, A: a prize awarded as the result of a contest in which only those who have failed in the regular contests are qualified to take part.

Consols: an English State debt, the interest on and principal of which are secured on the Consolidated Fund.

Conspicuous by its absence: phrase popularized in England by Lord John Russell in his *Address to the Electors of the City of London* (April 6, 1859). The phrase was derived by him from Tacitus, *Annales*, Bk. III, ch. 76. The equivalent phrase had already become familiar in French, by its use by the Jansenists in allusion to the omission of all reference to Pascal and Arnauld from Perrault's *History of Illustrious Men* (1696–1700).

Conspiracy of silence, A: a tacit agreement between several people to ignore a subject. Introduced in 1885 in connection with the general avoidance by the press of the disclosures of the *Pall Mall Gazette*, known as 'The Maiden Tribute.'

Constable, To outrun the: to run into debt; to succeed the bounds of moderation. [T. Powell, *Tom All Trades* (1631)]

Constitutional, A: a walk taken for the benefit of one's health, *i.e.*, physical constitution.

Consul Bibulus, A : one who holds office without power or influence. After Bibulus, who was joint-consul with Julius Cæsar (59 B.C.).

Contango, A : a Stock Exchange term : the rate of payment for permission to postpone the acceptance of stocks or shares purchased for one. An artificial word, possibly a corruption of ' continuation.'

Contention, Bone of : *see* Bone.

Conthoporian Spring, As cold as the : the Conthoporian Spring, near Corinth, was said to freeze the gastric juices of those who drank of it.

Contra bonos mores (*Lat.*, contrary to good conduct). [R. North, *Examen* (c. 1733)]

Contra bonum publicum (*Lat.*, against the public welfare). [Fielding, *Voyage to Lisbon* (1755)]

Contre vent et marée (*Fr.*, against wind and tide) : impetuously. [W. Roberts, *Memoirs of Hannah More*, I (1787)]

Convention Parliament, A : a parliament assembled without the summons of the sovereign.

Conway's Cabal : *see* Cabal (American).

Coo, To bill and : *see* Bill.

Cook accounts, To : to concoct or manipulate accounts, usually fraudulently. [17th cent.]

Cook and bottlewasher, Head : *see* Head Cook.

Cook the goose of .. To : to punish severely ; to over-reach. When Eric, King of Norway, arrived at a certain town, the inhabitants in derision hung a goose outside of the wall, inviting the king to shoot at it. Eric took the town within a few hours and burnt it, ' to cook your goose for you.' To ' cook one's own goose ' is to over-reach oneself.

Cool (Cold) as a cucumber, As : perfectly calm. Cool is here used in the sense of calm. [Beaumont and Fletcher, *Cupid's Revenge*, I, i (1615)]

Coolie, A : an Indian or East Asiatic indentured labourer, employed away from his native country. Hindu, *kuli*, labourer.

Cooling card, A : that which damps one's hopes. Phrase borrowed from a card game. [Lyly, *Euphues : Anatomy of Wit* (1579)]

Coon, A : a fellow. Formerly a member of the American Whig Party, which used to have a racoon for an emblem.

Coon, A gone : one whose case is hopeless. *See* Coon.

Coon's age, A : a long period of time. In allusion to the popular belief that the racoon lives to a great age.

Coot, As bald as a : in allusion to the bald coot or fulica. [Heywood, *Proverbes* (1546)]

Coot, As stupid as a : the bird is proverbial for stupidity.

Cophetua, A King : one who marries very much below his real station in life. After the legendary African potentate, famous for his wealth, who married a beggar-maid, according to a ballad in Percy, *Reliques* (1765).

Copper, A : (1) a policeman, from either (*a*) to ' cop,' to catch, or (*b*) the copper badge appointed for New York policemen by Fernando Wood ; (2) any bronze coin, usually a penny.

Copper : a metal. A corruption of Cyprus, an island in which in ancient times it was found in abundance.

Copper Captain, A : one who masquerades as a captain. [Beaumont and Fletcher, *Rule a Wife and Have a Wife* (1624)]

Copper-head, A : a pacifist of the North during the American Civil War. After the copperhead, an exceedingly venomous snake.

Copper-nosed Harry ; Coppernose : Henry VIII. In allusion to the silver coinage of his reign, which was an alloy of silver and copper, the copper showing first through the nose of his profile.

Copybook morality : formal, ' cheap,' morality. In allusion to the maxims given to school-children to copy as practice in caligraphy.

Coq à l'âne (*Fr.*, cock on the ass) : an impossible story ; a cock and bull story (*q.v.*).

Coqueligrues, At the coming of the : never. [Rabelais, *Pantagruel*]

Coral master, A : a juggler. From the scarlet costumes of the ancient Spanish jugglers.

Corbie messenger, A : one who returns too late, or not at all. In allusion to the raven in *Genesis*, viii, 7. (Scot., *corbie*, a raven.)

Cordelia's gift : a ' voice ever soft, gentle and low ; an excellent thing in woman.' [Shakespeare, *King Lear*, V, iii (1605–6)]

Cordeliers, The : a French revolutionary club (1790–94). It orig. met in the church of the Cordelier monks in Paris. The Cordelier or Franciscan Observantist monks derived the name from the knotted rope girdle they wore. Fr., *cordeler*, to twist.

Cordon Bleu, A : (1) the sash of the highest order of monarchical France, the St. Esprit; (2) humorously applied to a chief cook or *chef*.

Cordon Noir, Un : a knight of the French Order of St. Michael, distinguished by a black ribbon.

Cordon Rouge, Un : a chevalier of the French monarchical Order of St. Louis. In allusion to the red ribbon by which the decoration was suspended.

Cordon, Un Grand (*Fr.*, a broad ribbon) : a member of the Légion d'Honneur. the decoration of which is suspended by a broad ribbon.

Cordovan : leather. Orig. made at Cordova, in Spain.

Corduroy : a ribbed clothing-material. Fr., *cords du roi*, king's cord. From its use for the clothing of the Kings of France.

Corduroy, Mere : the working classes. After the material out of which their clothing used to be made.

Corduroy road, A : a road in marshy parts of N. America made with logs lying across it. From its resemblance to corduroy.

Cordwainer, A : a bootmaker. From Cordovan leather, used for making boots.

Coriander seed : money. Because the shape of the seed roughly resembles coins.

Corinth, A : a brothel. After the City of Corinth, which in classical days was proverbial for its luxury and immorality.

Corinthian, A : (1) roué; a rake; (2) (in America) a wealthy amateur who rides his own horses and navigates his own yacht. *See* Corinth.

Corinthian brass : (1) shamelessness; *see* Corinthian ; (2) a mixture of gold, silver and brass ; from the combination of these metals when Corinth was burnt by Mummius (146 B.C.).

Corinthian, To act the : to live the life of a prostitute.

Corinthianism : prostitution. *See* Corinthian.

Cormorant, To be a : to be greedy. A reference to the voracity of the cormorant. [*Joe Miller's Jests*, No. 179 (1739)]

Corn in the blade, To eat one's : to practise extravagance, especially by spending one's income in advance. [Rabelais, *Pantagruel*, III, 2]

Corn by one's own bushel, To measure other people's : to judge other people by one's own standard. [Simon Wagstaff (Jon. Swift), *Polite Conversation*, Dial. 1 (1738)]

Corn Crackers : poor whites in the Southern States of N. America. In allusion to their consumption of corn as a means of subsistence.

Corn in Egypt : plentifulness. In allusion to *Genesis*, xlii, 2.

Corn Law Poet (Rhymer), The : Ebenezer Elliott (1781–1849), author of *Corn Law Rhymes* (1831).

Corn Laws : legislation imposing an import duty on corn.

Corns, To tread on a person's : to offend against his susceptibilities.

Corn-cracker State, The : Kentucky. On account of its corn-cracker birds.

Cornelius and his tub : in allusion to one Cornelius and his cure for venereal disease.

Corner, A : a commercial operation whereby the price of a commodity is artificially raised by its concentration in the hands of one individual or corporation. To ' corner,' in the sense of to drive into a corner.

Corner Boy, A : (in Ireland) an idler who spends his time at street-corners.

Corner, To drive into a : to force into a position from which there is no escape.

Corner, To turn the : to pass successfully through the crisis of an illness, a trouble, a danger, etc.

Cornet of Horse, The Terrible : William Pitt, Earl of Chatham (1708–78). So-called by Sir Robert Walpole, who deprived him of his cornetcy in the Blues on account of his tireless criticism in Parliament.

Cornish hug, The : an allusion to the fame of Cornishmen as wrestlers.

Cornish Wonder, The : John Opie (1761–1807), the painter.

Cornstalks : Australians of European descent. In allusion to their tall, lithe figures, like cornstalks. Orig. limited to the inhabitants of New South Wales.

Cornuto, Dan : a cuckold; Lat., *cornutus*, horned. [Chapman, *All Fools*, II, i (1605)]

Corporal John : John Churchill, the great Duke of Marlborough (1650–1722). A name given to him by his men.

H

Corporal oath, A : an oath strengthened by touching some sacred object, in particular the corporale or cloth which covered the consecrated elements, [Cervantes, *Don Quixote*, Pt. I, Bk. IV, ch. x]

Corporal, The Little : *see* Caporal, Le Petit.

Corporal Violet : *see* Caporal Violet.

Corpse Candle, A : a luminous appearance in damp places, *e.g.*, cemeteries.

Corpus Christi Day (*Lat.*, body of Christ) : the Thursday after Trinity Sunday, a Roman Catholic festival in honour of the body of Christ in the Eucharist.

Corpus delicti (*Lat.*, body of the offence) : the aggregate of the various ingredients which make a given fact a breach of a given law.

Corpus vile (*Lat.*, a worthless body) : on which experiments may be made.

Correggesque : in the style of Antonio da Correggio (1494–1534), Italian painter.

Correggio of Sculptors, The : Jean Goujon (1510–72). Correggio (1494–1534) was one of the most distinguished of the Italian painters of the Cinquecento.

Corroboree, A : a dance of Australian natives. After the original native name for Port Jackson, N.S.W.

Corruptio optimi pessima (*Lat.*, the spoiling of the best is the worst) : the better a thing, the worse its abuse. [Purchas, *Microcosmus*, LXX (1619)] The phrase is traced back to Aristotle, *Nicomachean Ethics*, Bk. VIII, ch. x.

Corsican Ogre, The : Napoleon I. After Corsica, his birthplace.

Cortes, The : the Spanish or Portuguese Parliament.

Corvée : forced and unpaid labour—in France until 1776, in Egypt until 1888.

Corybantic Religion, The : the Salvation Army. So-called by Thomas Huxley (1825–1895), from a suggested resemblance between its extravagances and the ravings of the Corybantes or devotees of Bacchus.

Corycian Nymphs, The : the Muses. After the cave of Corycia, on Mount Parnassus.

Corydon, A : a shepherd. After a character in the *Idylls* of Theocritos, the *Eclogues* of Virgil, etc.

Coryphæus, A : the most active member of a committee, company, etc. After the title of the leader of the Greek chorus.

Coryphæus of German Literature, The : Goethe (1749–1832).

Coryphæus of Grammarians, The : Aristarchos of Samothrace (220–143 B.C.).

Costermonger, A : a street-hawker of fruit, vegetables, etc. From coster, a kind of apple, and monger, a dealer.

Cot-quean, A : (1) a low, vulgar woman ; lit., the housewife of a labourer's hut ; (2) a man who interferes in women's affairs. [Shakespeare, *Romeo and Juliet*, IV, iv (1591–3)]

Cotswold barley, To be as long a-coming as : Cotswold, in Gloucestershire, is backward in its vegetation on account of its cold, bleak situation, but it produces an excellent late supply of barley.

Cotswold lion, A : a sheep. In allusion to the flocks of sheep which graze on the Cotswold Hills. [*Thersites*, ll. 122–5 (1537)]

Cotton Lord, A : a prominent or wealthy cotton-manufacturer.

Cotton Plantation State, The : Alabama. Cotton is its staple industry.

Cotton (up) to .. To : to become closely attached to .. ; to cling to (like cotton). [*Life and Death of Capt. Thomas Stukeley*, l. 290 (1605)]

Cottonocracy, The : wealthy cotton-spinners, as a class.

Cottonopolis : Manchester, the centre of the cotton-spinning industry.

Couch-quail, To play : to cower ; to couch as a quail. [*Thersites*, ll. 19–20 (1537)]

Couleur-de-rose (*Fr.*, rose-colour) : promising success ; favourable ; ' rosy.' [J. Russell, *Babees Book* (c. 1447)]

Coulisse, The : the ' unofficial ' Stock Exchange in Paris ; the part of a theatre ' behind the scenes.' Properly, the groove in which the side-scenes of a theatre slide.

Coulomb : the unit in measuring current electricity. After Charles Augustin de Coulomb (1736–1806), French experimental philosopher.

Counsel of perfection, A : (1) one of the advisory declarations of Christ and the Apostles, the adoption of which assists towards the attainment of greater moral perfection ; (2) a recommendation of a course desirable but beyond attainment. [*Matthew*, xix, 21]

Count one's chickens before they are hatched, To : to assume success before it has been attained. [Butler, *Hudibras*, Pt. II, canto iii, 923 (1663)]

Counter-caster, A : an arithmetician (contemptuously). [Shakespeare, *Othello*, I, i (?1604)]

Counter-jumper, A : a shop-assistant.

Counties Palatine, The : orig. Chester, Lancaster, Durham, Kent, Shropshire, Pembroke, Hexham ; now the first three only. The privileges they enjoyed were granted in return for their defence of the frontiers of the kingdom.

Count-out, To : (Parliamentary) to lead to an adjournment of the House of Commons by calling attention to the absence of a quorum.

Counterfeit crank, A : a pretended epileptic.

Country Cousin, A : an ingenuous person from the country without experience of the complexities, luxuries, etc., of town life. [Foote, *The Lame Lover* (1770)]

Country Joan, A : an awkward country-girl.

Country Party, The : the political party which advocated the claims of the country, *i.e.*, agriculture, against those of the town—forerunner of the Tory and Conservative Parties.

Country, To appeal (go) to the : to dissolve Parliament and thus necessitate a General Election.

County Princess, A : a parvenu who apes the manners of the old county families.

Coup d'essai, A (*Fr.*, trial-blow) : a first attempt. [*Spectator*, 123 (1712)]

Coup d'état, A (*Fr.*, State-blow) : a sudden change of the system of government, esp. with the assistance of the Army, *e.g.*, Napoleon III's proclamation of himself as Emperor in 1851. [Howell, *Lewis* XIII (1646)]

Coup de grace, A (*Fr.*, stroke of grace) : a knock-out blow that ends a contest. From the fatal blow of the executioner that puts a victim who had been tortured out of his misery. [Peter Pindar, *Bozzy and Piozzi*, Pt. II (1796)]

Coup de main, A (*Fr.*, blow of the hand) : a sudden attack. Orig. a military phrase. [*Annual Register* (1758)]

Coup de maitre, A (*Fr.*, a masterstroke) : [Peter Pindar, *Lyric Odes to the Royal Academicians for* 1785, Ode VIII]

Coup manqué, A (*Fr.*, false stroke) : a miss.

Coup d'œil, A (*Fr.*, stroke of the eye) : a glance ; the scene as taken in at a glance.

Coup de pied de l'âne, A (*Fr.*, a kick by an ass) : a cowardly blow or insult.

Coup de théatre, A (*Fr.*, theatre-stroke) : an immediate theatrical success ; any sensational success. [Horace Walpole, *Letters*, II (1747)]

Couples, To hunt in : of two persons, to be inseparable. [Thackeray, *The Fatal Boots*, ch. 6 (1839)]

Courland weather : very rough weather. After Courland, a province of Russia.

Court card, A : a corruption of coat card. The figures on the court cards are coated.

Court Holy Water : flattery and empty promises. Translation of a French proverbial expression, *eau bénite de la Cour*. [Shakespeare, *King Lear*, III, ii (1605)]

Court of Arches, The : the Court of Appeal of the Archbishop of Canterbury, formerly held in the church of St. Mary-le-Bow, or St. Mary-of-the-Arches.

Court of Conscience, A : a Court of decision in cases of small debts ; figuratively, conscience as a moral tribunal.

Court of the Gentiles, To be in the : not to be included in the select, but to be only approaching to them. The Court of the Gentiles was the outermost court of the Temple at Jerusalem, but the furthermost point to which non-Jews were admitted.

Court, Out of : with no further say in the matter. Orig. referred to a plaintiff who has forfeited his claim to be heard in court.

Court plaster : sticking-plaster for the protection of slight wounds. From the plaster with which ladies at Court used to decorate their faces.

Court of Requests : a Court of decision in cases of small debts.

Courtesy title, A : a title enjoyed by courtesy, to which one has no legal right. Generally the subordinate title of a peer borne by his eldest son during the father's lifetime.

Cousin Betty : a semi-idiot.

Cousin Jacky (Jan) : a Cornishman. On account of the common practice in Cornwall of addressing people as 'Cousin.'

Cousin Michael (Michel): a German. From Michael, the typical German peasant.

Coûte que coûte (*Fr.*, cost what it may cost): at all costs. [Lord Bolingbroke, *Letters* (1715)]

Cove, A: a fellow; a chap. [16th cent.; Dekker, *Lanthorne and Candlelight*, ch. 1 (1609)]

Covenanter, A: one who had taken the Scotch National Covenant (1638), the Solemn League and Covenant (1643) or the Ulster Covenant (1912). *See* Solemn League and Covenant.

Coventry Act, The: the Act of Parliament (22–3, Chas. II, c. 1) directed against maiming, passed as a consequence of the mutilation of Sir John Coventry by the King's friends.

Coventry blue: a species of embroidery. After a thread formerly manufactured at Coventry.

Coventry blue, As true as: in allusion to the cloth and thread formerly made at Coventry and famous for the permanence of its colour.

Coventry Mysteries, The: a series of mystery-plays performed at Coventry in 16th cent. and earlier.

Coventry, To send a person to: to decline to speak to him. Possibly from an incident narrated in Clarendon's *History*, as having occurred at Birmingham, where certain supporters of King Charles were seized and sent to Coventry then strongly held for the Parliament. Another suggestion is that 'Coventry' is a corruption of quarantine. [Grose, *Dictionary of the Vulgar Tongue* (1785)]

Coverley, Sir Roger de, A: a typical Eng. country gentleman. After the *nom-de-plume* of the principal writer or writers in Addison and Steele's *Spectator* (1711–2).

Cow of Forfar did, To do as the: to take a long drink. The story runs as follows: A cow, passing a door in Forfar, drank the whole of a tub of ale that had been placed outside to cool. The owner of the ale sued the owner of the cow, but the decision was that as the ale was drunk at the door of the house it must be considered as a stirrup cup and no one could be so mean as to charge for that. [Scott, *Waverley* (1814)]

Cow and give the horns for charity, To steal the: [Bruno, *Candelaio*, I, ii]

Cow and the haystack, As much love as there is between the: (Simon Wagstaff (Jon. Swift), *Polite Conversation*, Dial. III (1738)]

Cow, Three acres and a: *see* Acres.

Cow of the wedding, To be the: to suffer for another's advantage or amusement. [Cervantes, *Don Quixote*, II, 69]

Cow with an iron tail, A: a pump.

Cow's tail, Like a: always behind.

Cowboy, A: a Western-American cattleman. Orig. a British marauder or irregular soldier active during the War of Independence.

Cowper Justice: *see* Cupar.

Coxcomb, A: a conceited person. On account of the cap, resembling the comb of a cock, formerly worn by a fool by profession.

Coxeyites: workingmen intent on forcing concessions from their employers. After Coxey, who led a large body of workingmen to the Congress at Washington.

Coze, To have a: to have a familiar conversation. Fr., *causer*, to talk.

Crab, To catch a: *see* Catch.

Crab-tree comb, A: *see* Comb.

Crack: first-rate; stylish. From 'crack up' (*q.v.*). So used by Arthur Young in *Annals of Agriculture*, XIX, 95 (1793).

Crack a bottle, To: open a bottle and drink the contents. [Shakespeare, 2 *Henry IV*, V, iii, 66 (1597–8)]

Crack a crib, To: to commit a burglary. Thieves' slang.

Crack of Doom, The: the Day of Doom or of Judgment at the end of the world, when all souls will be judged. [Shakespeare, *Macbeth*, IV, i (1606)]

Crack society: *see* Crack.

Crack up, To: to praise highly.

Crack-brained; Cracked: silly; semi-insane.

Crack-halter, A: a crack-rope (*q.v.*). [Josson, *Schoole of Abuse* (1579)]

Crack-jawed: difficult to pronounce; liable to crack the jaw.

Crack-rope, A: one fit to be hanged, who ought to have the chance of cracking a rope. [Hennyson, in *Tod's Confession* (c. 1450)]

Cracked in the ring: worn out. In Elizabethan coins, the sovereign's head was enclosed in a ring. If a crack extended from the edge beyond this ring the coin ceased to be current. [Shakespeare, *Hamlet*, II, ii (1602–3)]

Cracker State, The: Georgia.

Cracksman, A : a burglar. *See* Crack a crib.

Cracowe, A : a shoe with a long-pointed toe. After Cracow, in Poland, where the style of shoe originated.

Craddock (Cradock), As cunning as : after John Cradock, vicar of Gainford (1594), High Commissioner for Durham, Justice of the Peace, etc., notorious for his corruption and other misdemeanours.

Cradle of Liberty, The : Faneuil Hall, Boston, U.S., the meeting-place of the rebels during the Amer. Revolution.

Crail's capon, A : *see* Capon.

Crambo : rhyme ; rhyming. From the name of a game in which rhymes have to be found for a given line.

Cramp-ring, A : a ring which is supposed to be a charm against cramp, epilepsy, etc.

Crampart's horse, Swifter than : King Crampart made a wooden horse which could travel a hundred miles an hour, according to the story of *Reynard the Fox.*

Crank, A : one who holds views, or pursues a course almost peculiar to himself ; an eccentric person ; a faddist. In allusion to the crank of a barrel-organ which is continually grinding out the same tunes. The term is said to have been invented by Donn Piatt and applied by him to Horace Greeley (1811–72), the Amer. journalist and politician.

Crapeau, Jean (Johnny Crapaud), A : a popular name for a Frenchman. Lit., John Toad, probably, from the resemblance of a portion of the design of the former French standard to a toad. Term introduced by British sailors during the Napoleonic Wars.

Crape-man, A : a clergyman. From the material of which the dress of the clergy was made in 18th cent.

Crassus, As rich as : After Marcus Licinius Crassus (105–53 B.C.), surnamed Dives (the Rich), Roman general and statesman.

Cratur, A drop o' the : a drink of whiskey. An Irishism. Cratur, creature-comfort.

Cravat, A : a neckcloth. From Fr., *Cravates,* the Croatians, from whose dress the cravat was introduced into France in 1636.

Cravat, To wear a hempen : to be hanged. In allusion to the hempen rope.

Craw-thumper, A : a derisive term applied to a Roman Catholic, one who beats his breast (at Confession).

Crawley (Brook), As crooked as : alluding to the Crawley stream in Bedfordshire.

Crazy bone, The : the funnybone. An Americanism.

Crazy quilt, A : a patchwork quilt made on no definite design. An Americanism.

Cream City, The : Milwaukee ; from the colour of the bricks of which its houses are built.

Creature-comfort(s) : material comforts, *e.g.,* good food, clothing, housing, etc. [Scott, *St. Ronan's Well,* ch. 28 (1824)]

Credat Judæus (Apella) (*Lat.,* The Jew Apella may believe it) : of an incredible statement. The Jew Apella cannot be identified. [Horace, *Satires,* I, v, 100]

Credo, A : a creed or expression of belief. ' Credo ' is the first word in the Lat. version of the Apostles' (or Nicene) Creed.

Creep up the sleeve of .. To : to wheedle ; to attempt to get into the good graces of ..

Creke, To cry : to repent ; to capitulate. [Thos. Preston, *King Cambyses* (1561)]

Crême de la crême (*Fr.,* cream of creams): the choicest ; the very pick.

Cremona, A : a violin made at Cremona, in Italy.

Creole, A : a person of pure European descent born in Spanish America, or of pure French descent born in Louisiana.

Creole State, The : Louisiana. On account of its large Creole population.

Crescent, The : the Turkish Power. From the figure of the new moon in the Turkish flag.

Crescent City, The : New Orleans. In allusion to its situation on the Mississippi River.

Cresset ; Cresset-light, A : a beacon-light. From croisset, the cage or basket in which the fire in a raised light is held. [Rob. Wilson, *Three Lords and Three Ladies of London,* ll. 1364–5 (1590)]

Cressid ; Cressida, A : a faithless girl. After the mythical daughter of a Trojan priest of the period of the Trojan War. According to Homer her name was Briseis. The name Cressid was given to her in 12th cent. by Benoit de Ste. More, a French trouvère.

Cretan, To lie like a : Cretan lying has been proverbial from ancient days. Callimachos (fl. 260–240 B.C.), already referred to it.

Crete, The hound of : a bloodhound.

Cretonne : a kind of cotton fabric. After Creton, in Normandy.

Crib, A : a translation of a foreign (usually a Classical) book, used to avoid the trouble of study. Probably from 'to crib,' to steal (thieves' slang) ; Saxon, *crybb.*

Crib, To crack a : *see* Crack.

Crichton, The Admirable : James Crichton (1560–83), Scottish scholar and adventurer, famous for his learning and his many accomplishments.

Cricket, Not : not fair-play ; not the right thing to do.

Crime, Worse than a : a blunder. The phrase, 'It is worse than a crime, it is a blunder,' has been attributed to Talleyrand (1754–1838) in allusion to the execution of the Duc d'Enghien ; to Joseph Fouché (1763–1820), and to Boulay de la Meurthe (1761–1840).

Crispin, A : a shoemaker. After St. Crispin, the patron Saint of shoemakers.

Crispin's holiday, St. : Monday, a day on which shoemakers do no work.

Criss-cross : (properly Christ-Cross), (1) the sign of a cross made as a substitute for a signature ; (2) the alphabet, from the formula formerly recited before the alphabet was repeated : 'Christ's Cross me speed.'

Criss-Cross row : the alphabet. From the cross formerly placed at the beginning of a horn-book containing the alphabet, or from the form of a cross in which the alphabet was sometimes written. [Greene, *Selimus*, Pt. I, ll. 1900–3 (1594)]

Criticism, The Higher : *see* Higher.

Croakumshire : Northumberland. In allusion to the croaking manner in which the natives speak.

Crodocile('s) tears : hypocritical tears. From the belief formerly held that crocodiles wept in order to attract their victims. [Sir John Maundeville, *Voiage* (1356)]

Crœsus, A : an extremely wealthy man. After Crœsus, King of Lydia (d. 546 B.C.), who was famous for his riches.

Crœsus, A City : a wealthy merchant.

Crœsus, As rich as : *see* Crœsus.

Croggen, A : a Welshman.

Crokers : potatoes. After Croker's Field, Youghal, Ireland, in which they were cultivated.

Croker's mare, As coy as : as cautious as a mare that carries crockery. [Jno. Heywood, *Proverbes* (1546)]

Crop-ear, A : a person or animal whose ears have been cut down.

Cropper, To come a : to suffer a fall or a reverse. Possibly from ' to be turned out neck and crop'; more probably a metaphor drawn from the hunting-field.

Croppies : (1) a nickname given to the Roundheads (*q.v.*) ; (2) an Irish Republican Party in 1798 whose members cut their hair short in imitation of the French Republicans.

Crosbite, A : a swindler. From ' crossbite,' to bite the biter, to cheat in return.

Cross as a bear, As : in allusion to the sport of bear-baiting. [*The Actors' Remonstrance* (1643)]

Cross as the Devil, As : very bad-tempered. [Vanbrugh and Cibber, *The Provoked Husband*, III, i (1728)]

Cross, A Greek : a cross with four equal limbs.

Cross, A Latin : a cross with the lower limb longer than the top.

Cross, A Maltese : a cross with equal limbs indented so as to make eight points.

Cross, On the : crookedly ; not honestly.

Cross, A St. Andrew's : a cross with equal limbs like an " X."

Cross and pile : (1) the obverse and reverse side of a coin ; (2) money ; (3) pitch and toss. Some of the old French coins are said to have had a cross on one side and a column or pile on the other.

Cross as the tongs, As : a play on the word ' tongs.'

Cross as two sticks, As : a pun on ' cross ' (ill-tempered) and ' cross ' (placed across).

Cross, To bear one's : to suffer trouble patiently. Cf. *Matthew*, x, 38 ; xvi, 24. [Dekker and Webster, *Sir Thomas Wyat*, sc. 14 (1607)]

Cross, To take the : to enter on a crusade or other unselfish course of action.

Cross-bench mind, A : a mental constitution naturally independent and impartial, that sees and weighs both sides of a question. From the cross-benches in several Parliamentary buildings on which the independent members definitely committed to no Party sit.

Cross-bones : bones of the arm and leg crossed. Together with a skull, the device of pirates.

Cross-grained : ill-tempered and argumentative. Lit., of wood with an irregular grain and consequently a cause of difficulty in working.

Cross-patch ; Cross-piece, A : an ill-tempered person, esp. a woman.

Cross-purposes, To be (play) at : to misunderstand one another mutually. [Vanbrugh, *The Provoked Wife*, IV, vi (1697)]

Cross-sticks, Miss (Mrs.) : a cross or bad-tempered woman. [Fielding, *The Miser*, I, i (1733)]

Crossed in love, To be : to have a successful rival in an affair of the heart.

Crotchets in the head, To have : to hold curious but not very important views opposed to those of the majority ; to give expression to eccentric opinions. [Shakespeare, *Merry Wives of Windsor*, I, i (1600)]

Crouchmas Day : May 3rd, the festival of the finding of the Cross.

Crow, To eat : to recant ; to humiliate oneself. Two derivations have been offered for the phrase. According to the one, an American crossed the Canadian boundary and shot a crow. The man on whose land he was trespassing caught him and forced him to eat his quarry. According to the second story a Federal soldier, in the course of the Civil War, shot a tame crow belonging to a planter and was forced by the latter to eat a portion of it. The soldier, when he obtained the opportunity, in retaliation compelled the planter to eat the remainder of the dish. Crow is, of course, a most unpalatable food.

Crow, A white : see White crow.

Crow flies, As the : in a straight line ; the shortest distance between two points. [Bunyan, *Pilgrim's Progress*, Pt. II (1684)]

Crow over .. To : to exult in success over .. From the crowing of a cock after a victory in a fight. Orig., ' to overcrow.'

Crow, To pluck (pull) (pick), A : to have a quarrel. Orig. the phrase meant to concern oneself in a matter of little importance, a crow being considered of no value. [Towneley, *Plays*, II : *The Killing of Abel*, ll. 308–11 (1450)]

Crow, To teach a cock to : see Teach.

Crow, To wash the : see Wash.

Crow with .. To pluck (pull) A : to settle an unpleasant matter with .. Possibly in allusion to the longevity of crows and their corresponding toughness.

Crows'-feet : small wrinkles at the corners of the eyes. On account of their supposed resemblance to the feet of crows. [Chaucer, *Troylus*, II, 354] (14th cent.)

Crowbar Brigade, The : the Royal Irish Constabulary. In allusion to the crow-bars used by them in effecting evictions at times of agrarian unrest.

Crowder, As cunning as : see Cunning.

Crown of the East, The : Antioch in Syria.

Crown Office, To have been in the : to be drunk. A pun on ' crown ' as the equivalent of head.

Crown of Thorns, A : grief or pain patiently borne. After the crown of thorns worn by Christ at the Crucifixion.

Crowner's Quest : a vulgar corruption of Coroner's Inquest. [Shakespeare, *Hamlet*, V, i (1602)]

Crowning mercy, A : the description given by Oliver Cromwell to his victory over the Royalists at Worcester (Sept. 3, 1651).

Crumbs, To gather up the : to improve in health and appearance. [Lyly, *Euphues and His England* (1580)]

Crusoe, A : a solitary person. After the hero of Defoe, *Robinson Crusoe* (1719).

Crusty : short-tempered ; peevish. From cross, ill-tempered. [Thos. Preston, *King Cambyses*, l. 389 (1561)]

Cry off, To : to withdraw from an undertaking or projected undertaking.

Cry, A far : a long distance. ' Cry ' in the sense of the distance which a cry carries.

Cry and little wool, Much : more excitement than result ; ' much ado about nothing.' From the mystery-play of *David and Abigail*, in which the Devil is depicted shearing a pig in imitation of Nabal shearing a sheep. The remark is attributed to the Devil.

Cry out before one is hurt, To : to protest prematurely. [Rabelais, *Gargantua*, I, 47 ; Montluc, *La Comédie de Proverbes*, I, ii]

Cry, Out of : beyond measure. [*Wily Beguiled*, ll. 1641–2 (1606)]

Cry over spilt milk, To : to grieve uselessly, *i.e.*, when it is impossible to remedy the harm.

Cry stinking fish, To : to depreciate one's own goods or interests. [Jeremy Taylor, *Ductor Dubitantium*, 805 (1660)]

Cry-baby, A : a term of contempt for a big child who is moved to tears over a trivial matter.

Crying evil (shame) (sin), A : an evil (cause of shame) (sin) so obvious that it may be said to cry out. [Burton, *Anatomy of Melancholy*, Pt. I, Sect. 1 (1621)]

Cub, A half-licked (unlicked) : an ill-mannered lout, like a bear-cub insufficiently licked by its dam. [Congreve, *Old Bachelor*, IV, 8 (1693)]

Cube, A faultless : an almost perfect man. [Aristotle, *Nicomachean Ethics*, I, ii, Sect. 11.]

Cucking-stool, A : a chair in which offenders, esp. women, were formerly fastened and dipped as a punishment.

Cuckoo storm, A : a spring wind that brings the cuckoo earlier than usual.

Cucumber-time : the dull season of the year. From the Germ. phrase, *die saure Gurken-Zeit*, the pickled cucumber-time.

Cuddy, A : (1) a bribe or gift ; formerly rent paid to a landlord ; still earlier, entertainment due by a tenant to his lord ; Irish, *cuid oidhche*, evening portion ; (2) a fool, a gipsy term ; Hindu, *ghudda*, an ass.

Cudgel one's brains, To : to make mental exertions. [Shakespeare, *Hamlet*, V, i, 63 (1602)]

Cudgels, To take up the : to take the part of in a contest or dispute. [Jas. Puckle, *The Club* (1711)]

Cuerpo, In (*Span.*, in the body) : naked ; without a cloak, so as to display the form of the body. [R. Cock, *Diary*, I (1622)]

Cui bono ? (*Lat.*, to whose advantage ?) : quoted by Cicero in the Second Philippic, 14, 35, and elsewhere as a saying by Lucius Cassius in trying a man for murder.

Culturkampf : *see* Kulturkampf.

Cum grano salis (*Lat.*, with a grain of salt) : making allowance for overstatement ; with reserve.

Cunctator, A (*Lat.*, one who delays) : after the title given to Quintus Fabius Maximus (275–203 B.C.), who defeated

Hannibal by avoiding a general engagement.

Cunning as Crowder, As : after Samuel Crowder, a carrier in North-West England, who displayed great ingenuity. An alternative derivation is from 'cunning,' skilful, and 'crowder,' fiddler.

Cup that cheers but not inebriates, The : tea. [Cowper, *The Task : The Winter Evening*, IV, 34 (1784)]

Cup, To drink the : to bear whatever sorrows befall one. [*Matthew*, xx, 22]

Cup of life to the bottom, To drink the : to participate in all the experiences of life.

Cup and lip, Between : on the point of achievement. From the proverb, 'There is many a slip 'twixt the cup and the lip.' [Aulus Gellius, XIII, 18]

Cup to run over : blessings to overflow. [*Psalm* xxiii, 5–6]

Cups, In one's : intoxicated. [Thos. Preston, *King Cambyses*, ll. 916–8 (1561)]

Cupar Justice ; Jedburgh Justice : lynch Law. From a practice formerly in force in Coupar-Angus.

Cupboard love : love dependent on the prospect of advantage. [Herrick, *Poor Robin* (1661)]

Cupid, A : a beautiful boy. From the pictorial representations of the God of Love.

Cupid's golden arrow : virtuous love.

Cupid's leaden arrow : sensual love.

Cupids in the eyes, To look for : to look closely into one's lover's eyes so as to see oneself reflected there. Cf. Babies in the eyes. [Drayton, *Polyolbion*, II (1613)]

Curaçoa : a liqueur. Orig. made in the island of Curaçoa.

Curfew (-bell), A : an evening bell. Orig. a public signal to extinguish lights. From *couvrir*, to cover, and *feu*, fire.

Curled darlings : (1) well-dressed idle young men in general ; [Shakespeare, *Othello*, I, ii (1604)] (2) military officers, a term applied to them during their period of popularity after the close of the Crimean War.

Curmudgeon, A : a miser ; a surly bad-tempered man. Possibly from *coeur mechant*, evil heart.

Currant, A : (1) a small dried grape. From *raisins de Courauntz*, grapes of Corinth, Greece, whence they are exported.

Currant (2) ; **curranto, A :** a liar. After the currants or newspapers (' currant newes') of 17th cent. They were notorious for their general unreliability.

Currant, As true as a : false. [Donald Lupton, *London and the Country Carbonadoed* (1632)] *See* Currant (2).

Currente calamo (*Lat.*, with a running pen) : on the spur of the moment ; without premeditation. [Horace Walpole, *Letters*, VI (1776)]

Curse, Not worth a : either from the name of the wild cherry, or perhaps derived from Anglo-Sax. *cerse*, watercress. [Langland, *Piers Plowman* (1362)]

Curse of Scotland, The : the Nine of Diamonds. Possibly from the armorial bearings of Dalrymple, Earl of Stair—nine lozenges on a saltire—who was much hated and was termed ' The Judas of the Country.' Other derivations are : (1) a similar resemblance to the armorial bearings of Col. Packer who commanded the forces in Scotland during the time of the Commonwealth ; (2) the playing-card on which the Duke of Cumberland gave instructions on the night before the Battle of Culloden (1746) to his generals to give no quarter ; (3) the importance of the card in the game of Comet, introduced into Scotland by James II of England shortly before his accession it proved the ruin of many Scottish families ; (4) the designation of the card in the game of Pope Joan as ' The Pope ' ; (5) nine tyrannical kings of Scotland, diamonds being emblematical of royalty. The term is also said to be an equivalent of the Cross of Scotland, the nine pips on the card orig. forming a St. Andrew's Cross.

Curtail (Cut-tail) dog, A : orig. the dog of a person not authorized to hunt ; later, a dog not used for sport. These dogs had their tails cut short, partly to identify them, and partly because a tail was thought to interfere with their running.

Curtain-lecture, A : a string of matrimonial censure and criticism delivered nightly by a nagging wife to her husband in bed, *i.e.*, within the curtains, when he wants to go to sleep. The term was popularized by Douglas Jerrold, *Mrs. Caudle's Curtain Lectures*, which first appeared as a serial in

Punch. The term forms the title of a little book by T.H. (? Thos. Heywood) published in 1637.

Curtain-raiser, A : a short preliminary theatrical piece that precedes the main play. Fr., *lever-de-rideau*.

Cushion, To miss (hit) the : to fail (succeed) in an undertaking. Metaphor drawn from archery. [Heywood, *Proverbes* (1546)]

Cushion, To set beside the : to ignore ; pass over with contempt. [Heywood, *Proverbes* (1546)]

Cuss, A : (1) a curse ; (2) a somewhat despised person.

Cuss, Not worth a : *see* Curse.

Customer, An ugly : one whose character gives justifiable cause for expectation of harm or difficulty.

Custos Rotulorum : Keeper of the Records of an English county, an office now practically merged in that of Lord Lieutenant.

Cut the cackle and come to the 'osses, To : to cut a long story short and come direct to the principal matter. Phrase attributed to Philip Astley (1742–1814), the circus-proprietor, when criticising an equestrian show which was being exhibited before him.

Cut a comb, To : to suppress a conceited person. A farmyard metaphor. [G. Harvey, *Pierce's Supererog.* (1593)]

Cut a dash, To : to swagger ; to dress so as to attract attention. [Foote, *Maid of Bath*, I (1771)]

Cut a person's claws, To : to deprive a person of his opportunities for mischief. [Peter Pindar, *The Rights of Kings*, Ode 1 (1791)]

Cut above .. A : a rank above ..

Cut acquaintance, To : without apparent reason to ignore a person previously known. [S. Rowley, *Noble Souldier*, II, i (1634)]

Cut and come again, To : to have at one's disposal an unfailing supply. Orig. of a joint of meat from which one can cut a helping and then return for a further portion. [Swift, *Polite Conversation*, Dial. ii (1738)]

Cut and run, To : to make off in a hurry. Properly, to cut the cable without waiting to weigh anchor.

Cut blocks with a razor, To : to ruin a valuable instrument where a cheaper one would serve better.

Cut both ways, To : of an argument, action, etc., that tells for and against one ; harms as well as benefits.

[Peter Pindar, *Farewell Odes*, Ode iv (1786)]

Cut no ice, To : to carry no weight ; to have no influence.

Cut of one's jib, The : one's personal appearance. A nautical metaphor.

Cut off one's nose to spite one's face, To : to do oneself a considerable injury for the sake of gaining a minor end.

Cut off with a shilling, To : to disinherit. Under Roman law a man was compelled to bequeath a portion of his estate to his natural heir ; to leave him a shilling or a similar trivial amount is practically to disinherit him.

Cut one's eye-teeth, To : *see* Cut one's wisdom-teeth.

Cut one's coat according to one's cloth, To : *see* Coat.

Cut one's sticks, To : to depart ; escape. In reference apparently to the cutting of a staff preparatory to a journey.

Cut one's wisdom- (eye-) teeth, To : to arrive at the years of discretion.

Cut out, To : to supersede or supplant a rival.

Cut out for, To be : to be specially fitted for.

Cut the ground from under a person's feet, To : to destroy the basis of a person's argument, project, etc.

Cut the knot, To : to solve a serious difficulty. *See* Gordian Knot.

Cut the painter, To : *see* Painter.

Cut up rough, To : to show ill-temper or displeasure.

Cut-and-dry (-dried) : completely ready for attention. A metaphor from the timber-trade.

Cut-purse, A : a pickpocket ; a thief. Lit., one who steals by cutting purses, which used to be worn at the girdle.

Cut-throat competition : fierce competition that is reckless of consequences.

Cutlers' poetry : doggerel verse. From the lines formerly engraved on knife-blades. [Shakespeare, *Merchant of Venice*, V, i (1596)]

Cutler's Law : never to let another want so long as one has means of alleviating his distress. The practice of cut-purses and other criminals.

Cutty stool, A : the stool of repentance ; formerly in Scotland, the seat in church on which offenders sat while they were publicly rebuked by the pastor.

Cycle of Cathay, A : *see* Cathay.

Cycle of the moon, A : a period of 19 years, after which the date of the moon recurs.

Cycle of the sun, A : a period of 28 years.

Cyclic Poets, The : epic poets subsequent to Homer who wrote of the Trojan War, keeping within the circle of a single subject.

Cyclopean : gigantic ; fierce. After the Cyclops, a mythological race of Sicilian giants.

Cymerian darkness : *see* Cimmerian.

Cynic ; cynical : sneering ; suspicious of good. The Cynics were a school of Grk. philosophers who, holding virtue and knowledge as the sum of goodness, were contemptuous of all else. From Grk, *kuōn*, a dog ; on account of their morose tenets.

Cynosure : a centre of attraction. From the name of the constellation of the Lesser Bear, to which the eyes of mariners are often directed.

Cynthia's lamp : the moon. After Cynthia, one of the names of Diana, the goddess of the Moon, who was born on Mount Cynthus, in Delos.

Cyprian, A : a harlot. From Cyprus, once a centre of the worship of Venus. Also used as an adjective.

Cyprian Goddess, The : Venus ; *see* Cyprian.

Cyprian Trade, The : prostitution ; *see* Cyprian.

Cyrano, A : a large nose. After Edmond Rostand's *Cyrano de Bergerac*.

Czar : the title borne by the Emperor of Russia and the Kings of Bulgaria. From Cæsar. First assumed in Russia by Ivan III (1472).

Czar Liberator, The : Alexander II of Russia, who liberated the serfs in 1861.

D.T. : *delirium tremens.*

Da capo (*Ital.*, from the beginning) : to repeat precisely. A musical term.

Dab at .. To be a : to be thoroughly expert at .. A corruption of ' adept.' [Peter Pindar, *Lyric Odes to the Royal Academicians for* 1783, Ode VIII]

Daddy Long-legs, A : a popular name for the crane-fly. From its long legs.

Dædal ; dædalian : ingenious, intricate. After Dædalus, of Crete, a mythical craftsman, the personification of all handicrafts and of art.

Dædale earth : earth variously adorned. [Spenser, *Faerie Queene*, Bk. IV, canto x, st. 45 (1596)]

Daft days, The : the days of merriment at Christmas.

Dagger] 107 Dance

Dagger ale : ale. After 'The Dagger,' a celebrated 17th-cent. tavern in Holborn, London.

Daggers drawn, At : in a state of declared hostility.

Daggers at .. To look : to look at with an aspect of hostility.

Dago, A : an American or sailor's name for a Spanish, Portuguese or Italian immigrant or seaman. From Span., *Diego,* James, a common name among Spaniards.

Dagon, A : an idol. After the god of the Philistines.

Daguerrotype, A : an early method of photography ; a photograph so taken. After Louis J. M. Daguerrè (1789–1851), the French inventor.

Daily Telegraphese : a 'cheap' exaggerated 'journalese,' a literary style similar to that at one time used by regular writers in the (London) *Daily Telegraph.*

Daimio, A : a Japanese feudal noble. From Chinese *dai myo,* great name.

Daisy-cutter, A : (1) a horse that, when in motion, raises its feet but slightly from the ground ; (2) a cricket-ball bowled along the ground instead of being cast upwards.

Dalmatica, A : a robe worn on occasions by priests, and formerly by kings. After Dalmatia, whence it was introduced into Rome by the Emperor Commodus (d. 169).

Daltonism : colour-blindness. After John Dalton (1766–1844), Eng. chemist, who suffered from this infirmity.

Damascene, To : to inlay metal with gold or silver ; to variegate the appearance of steel blades. After Damascus, where such work was done.

Damasco, A : a sword of exceptional temper. Formerly manufactured at Damascus.

Damascus of the North, The : Bosna-Serai. On account of its numerous trees and gardens, for which Damascus is famous.

Damask : linen woven in raised figures ; formerly silk similarly woven. After Damascus, where the fabrics were woven.

Damask rose : a variety of rose native to Damascus.

Damask steel : *see* Damascene.

Dame Earth : *see* Mother Earth.

Dame Partington's broom : *see* Partington.

Damer, As rich as : John Damer, of Antrim, migrated to Tipperary, where he attained wealth, in the reign of George I.

Damiens' Bed of Steel : an instrument of torture to which Robert François Damiens was bound after his attempt on the life of Louis XV in 1757. [Goldsmith, *The Traveller,* 436 (1764)]

Dammarel, A : (Fr., *Damaret*) an effeminate man, fond of the company of the fair sex.

Dammy ; Dammy Boy, A : an unruly person. In allusion to the habit of the excessive use of the word 'damn' and general swearing by the man-about town of 16th and 17th cents.

Damn for .. Not to care a (twopenny) : to have not the smallest fear of or concern for .. From *dam,* a small Hindu coin worth less than a farthing. Orig. an Anglo-Indian phrase. A 'twopenny' damn arose from a folk-etymological association of the word with 'damn,' condemn.

Damn with faint praise, To : to praise so slightly, or in such an equivocal manner, that the unexpressed criticism condemns. [Pope, *Epistle to Arbuthnot* (1735)]

Damnosa hereditas (*Lat.*) : inheritance that brings loss instead of gain.

Damocles' sword, A : a threatening danger. Damocles (4th cent. B.C.) was a courtier of Dionysius of Syracuse, over whose head at a royal feast a sword was hung by a thread.

Damon and Pythias : two inseparable friends. They flourished at the Court of Dionysius of Syracuse in 4th cent. B.C. Their devotion to one another is proverbial.

Damson, A : a small variety of plum. After Damascus, whence it was introduced.

Dan to Beersheba, From : from one extreme limit of a country, etc., to the other ; the biblical formula for the limits of the Holy Land (Dan in the north, Beersheba in the south). [*Judges,* xx, i]

Dan Cornuto, A : *see* Cornuto.

Danai, A gift of the : a Greek gift (*q.v.*).

Danaid's work : futile and long drawn out work. From the punishment of the Danaides, daughters of Danaus, King of Argos, of eternally pouring water into sieves.

Dance attendance on .. To : to attend obsequiously on .. ; to be at the

beck and call of .. In allusion to the early practice of the bride being expected to dance with every guest who might ask her. [*Paston Letters*, No. 754 (1475)]

Dance of Death, The : a representation of Death leading people of all classes to the grave.

Dance (of) Macabre : *see* Dance of Death. Macabre is a form of St. Macarius, an Egyptian anchorite who appears in 13th cent. legend with which the representation of the Dance of Death became connected.

Dance on a volcano, To : to enjoy oneself with dire misfortune impending. Phrase used by the Comte de Salvandy (1796–1856) at a fete given by the Duke of Orleans to the King of Naples in 1830.

Dance the Tyburn jig, To : to be hanged. Tyburn was a former place of execution in London.

Dance to another tune, To : to suddenly change one's action.

Dance to another's piping, To : to have to act in accordance with another's demands. In allusion to the music of mythology which compelled all hearers to dance. [Heywood, *Proverbs* (1546)]

Dance, To lead a person a (pretty) : to give him a bad time, to cause him much unnecessary trouble. [*Paston Letters*, No. 1006 (15th cent.)]

Dance, To open (lead) (begin) the : to commence.

Dance, To teach an old woman to : *see* Teach.

Dance to the tune of .. To : to follow submissively the directions given or the wishes expressed or unexpressed. [Sir Thos. Overbury, *Characters : A Timist* (1616)]

Dance upon nothing, To : to be hanged (one's feet being in the air).

Dancing Chancellor, The : Sir Christopher Hatton (1540–91), Lord Chancellor of England, who first attracted the attention of Queen Elizabeth by his dancing.

Dancing Days : youth. [Shakespeare, *Romeo and Juliet*, I, v, ll. 32–3 (1592)]

Dander up, To get one's : to become angry. Probably from ' dander ' in the sense of ferment ; or possibly from ' dandruff ' as the equivalent of hair or fur of an animal.

Dandie Dinmont, A : a species of terrier. After a character in Sir W. Scott's

Guy Mannering (1815), the owner of two dogs of this species.

Dandies, The Prince of the : Beau Brummell (1778–1840), a famous beau.

Dandin, a George : one who marries above his station. After a character in a comedy of that title by Molière (1668).

Dandiprat, A : *see* Dandyprat.

Dando, A : a glutton, esp. one who cheats. After a personage of that description named Dando.

Dandy, A : a fop. Introduced from the Scottish Border (c. 1800). In use in the form Jack-a-dandy a century and a half earlier. Possibly a corruption of Andrew ; or from Dandin, George (*q.v.*).

Dandy-horse, A : an early form of bicycle, on which the rider propelled himself by treading the ground with alternate feet.

Dandy King, The : Joachim Murat, king of Naples.

Dandy-prat, A : a dwarf. Possibly from the name of a small coin minted in the reign of Henry VII.

Dane's skin : freckled skin. From the tradition that freckles denote remote Danish origin.

Daniel come to Judgment, A : an upright, just judge, impervious to all influence. From the description of Portia, given by Shylock, when he thought that she was deciding in his favour. [Shakespeare, *Merchant of Venice*, IV, i, l. 223 (1595)]

Danites, The : an Order in the Mormon Church, committed to support the leaders in all circumstances.

Dantesque : sombre and sublime. In allusion to the style of Dante's *Inferno*.

Daphne, A : a beautiful young girl unspoilt by society or fashion. After a nymph in Grk. mythology.

Daphnis, A : a young shepherd. After a Grk. mythological shepherd. Familiarised by a Grk. pastoral romance of 4th or 5th cent., *Daphnis and Chloe* ; by innumerable other romances ; by Beaumont and Fletcher, *The Faithful Shepherdess* (1609), etc.

Darbies : handcuffs. After a notorious usurer of the 16th cent. [Gascoigne, *Steel Glass*, I, 787 (1576)]

Darby and Joan, A : a couple devoted to one another after many years of married life. After a ballad by Henry Woodfall, published in *The Gentleman's Magazine*, Vol. V, 153 (1735).

Darby's bands : strict bonds by which a debtor bound himself. Possibly after the usurer : *see* Darbies. [*Marriage of Wit and Science*, IV, i (1570)]

Darbyiste, A : a member of the sect of Plymouth Brethren. After John Nelson Darby (1800–82), their first leader.

Dare-devil, A : a reckless person ; one ready to dare the Devil.

Dares, A : a pugilist. After the Trojan pugilist in Virgil, *Æneid*, V.

Dark, To be in the : to be without knowledge in some particular matter.

Dark Ages, The : the Middle Ages. On account of the intellectual darkness of that period. More narrowly (c. 814–c. 987).

Dark and Bloody Ground, The : the State of Kentucky, of whose name the term is said to be a translation of one of the Indian dialects. It is, however, more probably derived from the bloody warfare with the Indians of which the State was in early days the scene.

Dark Continent, The : Africa. On account of the unknown character of the continent until recent years. [Sir H. M. Stanley, *Through the Dark Continent* (1878)]

Dark as Erebus, As : *see* Erebus.

Dark, To keep : to keep secret.

Dark, To keep .. in the : to conceal from ..

Dark, A leap in the : *see* Leap.

Dark horse, A : a competitor of whose character or capabilities nothing is known by the public ; one who suddenly appears at the last moment without any previous warning, *i.e.*, has previously been kept in the dark. Orig. a racing term, applied to an unknown horse in a horse-race.

Darkness visible : extreme darkness. Phrase coined by Milton in *Paradise Lost*, Bk. I, l. 62 (1667).

Darling of the Graces, The : (1) Aristophanes (444–380 B.C.), so-called by Goethe, in his introduction to *The Birds* ; (2) Heine (1789-1856), German poet.

Dash, To cut a : *see* Cut.

Dash-buckler, A : a swaggerer. Related to swashbuckler. *See* Cut a dash.

Date, Up to : not behind the times ; wide-awake and fully acquainted with. Orig. a book-keeping phrase.

Daughter of Eve : a woman. [Shakespeare, *Merry Wives of Windsor*, IV, ii, ll. 23–5 (1600)]

Daughter of the horse-leech, A : one who is perpetually putting forward demands. [*Proverbs*, xxx, 15]

Daughter of Peneus, The : the bay-tree, which flourishes best on the banks of the River Peneus.

Daughter of the Sphere, The : the echo. [Milton, *At a Solemn Musick*, l. 2 (1630)]

Dauphin, The : the eldest son of the King of France. After the Dauphiné, a Fr. province. The name of the province was derived from the dolphin which the Seigneur, Guy VIII, Count of Vienne, wore as his cognizance.

David, A : a youthful hero. After the King of Israel.

David and Jonathan : two devoted friends. After the friendship of David and Jonathan (II *Samuel*, i, 26)]

David's sow, As drunk as : *see* Drunk.

Davy-Jones : the controlling genius of the ocean. Possibly a corruption of ' duffy,' a West-Indian negro's ghost, and ' Jonah,' the prophet.

Davy-Jones' locker : the sea as the final resting-place of the drowned. *See* Davy Jones.

Davy Jones' natural children : smugglers ; pirates. *See* Davy Jones.

Davy putting on coppers for parsons : indications of a coming storm at sea. *See* Davy Jones.

Davy-lamp, A : a lamp which may be used with safety in a coal-mine. After the inventor, Sir Humphrey Davy (1778-1829).

Davy's dust : gunpowder. After Davy Jones, the sailors' Devil (*q.v.*).

Davy's sow : *see* Drunk as David's sow.

Daw, To play the : to behave as a fool. From the popular belief that the daw is an exceptionally foolish bird.

Dawcock, A : an empty, chattering fellow. Properly, a male-daw. *See* Daw, To play the.

Dawk : travel by relays ; relays of men, horses or palanquins for travelling dawk. An Anglo-Indian term.

Day after the fair, A : too late. [Heywood, *Proverbs*, Pt. I, ch. viii (1546)]

Day after to-morrow, The : never, on the principle that to-morrow never comes.

Day of Doom, The : *see* Doomsday.

Day of Judgment, The : the last day of the life of the world, when all men will be judged.

Day of Wrath, The : the last day of the world, on which the Divine Wrath will be kindled against the wicked.

Day, To carry the : to win in a contest.

Day, To have had one's : to have been successful, powerful, wealthy, etc., in the past, but to be no longer so. From the proverb : 'Every dog has his day.'

Days of one, To make two : to delay.

Days to be numbered, One's : to be within a short distance of one's death.

Day's work, To be all in a : to be treated as a part of the ordinary routine. [Swift, *Polite Conversations*, Dial. I (1738)]

Day-dream, A : a reverie, esp. a pleasant one.

Daylight, To burn : to waste time. [Shakespeare, *Merry Wives of Windsor*, II, i, l. 54 (1600)]

Daylight (through ..) To see : to foresee the successful end of an arduous task or undertaking. Metaphor drawn from the passage through a long tunnel.

De die in diem (*Lat.*) : from day to day.

De facto (*Lat.*, by the fact) : in reality. [Bacon, *Essays : Of Great Place* (1625)]

De jure (*Lat.*, by law) : [Bradford, *Writings* (1550)]

De novo (*Lat.*, from a new [start]) : anew, afresh. [In Engl. about 1630]

De profundis : an expression of deep sorrow. The first two words of *Psalm* cxxx : 'Out of the depths.'

De proprio motu (*Lat.*, of one's own motion) : of one's own initiative ; spontaneously.

De trop (*Fr.*, too many) : in the way. [Lord Chesterfield, *Letters*, II (1752)]

Dead against, To be : to be directly opposed to.

Dead as Chelsea, As : not necessarily dead, but permanently incapacitated. The allusion is to Chelsea Hospital, the hostel for superannuated soldiers. The phrase is said to have originated with a grenadier at the Battle of Fontenoy, who applied it to himself when his leg was carried away by a cannon-ball.

Dead as a door-nail, As : absolutely-dead, as if one had been knocked on the head as is a door-nail or knob. [Will. *Palerme*, 628 (1350) ; Langland, *Piers Plowman*, A, I, 161 (14th cent.)]

Dead as Queen Anne, As : *see* Queen Anne.

Dead, To ask counsel of the : to refer to books. [Diogenes Laertius, VII, i, 3 ; Bacon, *Essays : Of Counsell* (1625)]

Dead cert (certainty), A : that which is certain to occur. Possibly corrupted from 'as certain as death.' A metaphor from the race-course.

Dead Fire : St. Elmos' Fire, superstitiously believed to foretell death.

Dead Hand : control by laws, regulations, etc., made in the past by those now dead. Translation of Fr., *mort main.*

Dead Hand of the Church, The : perpetual tenure of property by the Church, as distinguished from tenure by an individual.

Dead head, A : a person admitted to a public entertainment without payment. Said to have been derived from a toll-gate leading to a cemetery in Delaware. A physician on paying the toll once remarked that, in view of his profession, he ought to be permitted to pass free. The reply he received was : 'We can't afford that. You send too many deadheads through here as it is.'

Dead heat, A : a race or other competition in which two or more competitors are exactly equal, resulting in a 'tie.' A 'heat' is that part of a race that is run without stopping ; a 'dead heat' is therefore a futile heat having no result.

Dead as a herring, As : either from the belief that herrings die on leaving the water more quickly than most other fish, or because to the masses the herring is known only as a dead fish. [T. Nabbes, *Tottenham Court* (1638)]

Dead horse : work for which payment is made before it is completed. [Cartwright, *Siedge* (1651)]

Dead horse, To flog a : to exert oneself to no purpose.

Dead horse, To work on the : *see* Horse.

Dead language, A : a language no longer spoken.

Dead letter, A : (1) a post-letter which is undeliverable through an undecipherable address, etc. ; (2) a law that has, without being repealed, become obsolete. The Dead Letter Office is a former name of the Returned Letter Department of the (London) General Post Office, where 'dead' letters are dealt with.

Dead lift, To be at a : to be in a considerable difficulty. [G. Wilkins, *Miseries of Enforced Marriage*, IV, ll. 574–5 (1607)]

Dead as a log, As : motionless. [Benj. Franklin, *Poor Richard's Almanac for 1733 : April*]

Dead men's shoes, To wait for : to live in expectation of a legacy or other advantage from a man's death. [Heywood, *Proverbes* (1546)]

(Dead) nuts on .. To be : to be devoted to ..

Dead of night, The : at the stillest hour of the night ; at midnight. [Hall, *Chronicle* (1548)]

Dead pay : pay dishonestly drawn by officers after the death of the soldiers to whom it relates. [Dekker and Webster, *Northward Ho*, I, ii (1607)]

Dead reckoning, A : an estimate of a ship's position by calculations independent of astronomical observations.

Dead Sea fruit : *see* Apple, Dead Sea.

Dead set at .. To make a : to make a determined attack on .. Perhaps alluding to the setter dog.

Dead shares : pay made to naval officers based on the fiction of a complement larger than the reality.

Dead shot, A : an accurate marksman, certain to hit his objective.

Dead, To chastise the : *see* Chastise.

Dead, To paint the : *see* Paint.

Dead weight : a heavy inert mass, such as a dead body.

Deadlock, A : a situation in which the two opposing parties mutually prevent any advance towards or retreat from one another.

Deaf as an adder, As : from the legend that the adder, in order to safeguard himself from the charmer, presses one ear against the ground and inserts his tail in the other. [*Psalm*, lviii, 4 ; Shakespeare, 2 *King Henry VI*, III, ii, 76 (1593)]

Deaf as an ass, As : from the popular belief that the ass has no ear for music.

Deaf as a beetle, As : the beetle in this simile is generally believed to be a mallet, which is dull and consequently deaf and also dumb.

Deaf as a door-nail, As : absolutely deaf. [*Alexander*, 4747 (1420)]

Deaf as a (door) post, As : quite deaf, or so inattentive as to appear so.

Deaf as a stone, As : [Horace, *Epodes*, XVII, 53–5 ; Occleve, *De Regimine Principium* (1450)]

Deaf as a wave, As : [Euripides, *Medea*, 28 ; Milton, *Samson Agonistes*, 960–4 (1671)]

Deaf as a white cat, As : from the popular belief that white cats are deaf and stupid.

Deaf-nuts, To live on : to be dependent on the worthless or unsubstantial. A 'deaf' nut is a nut without a kernel. [Bp. Hall, *Sermons*, I *Sam.*, xii, 24 (1613)]

Death, In at the : present at the crowning of an undertaking. A fox-hunting metaphor.

Death bell, A : a passing bell ; a ringing noise in the ear, superstitiously believed to foretell a death.

Death or Glory Boys, The : the 17th Lancers. From their badge, a Death's Head and the words ' Or Glory.'

Death's door, To be at : to be at the point, or almost the point, of death. [Coverdale, *Spiritual Perle*, XVIII (1550)]

Death's-head, A : a human skull.

Death-watch, A : an insect whose ticking, usually on a window, is supposed to foretell a death.

Debatable Land, The : the borderland between two countries claimed by both ; esp. a tract between the Esk and the Sark on the border of England and Scotland.

Debt, Bad : *see* Bad.

Debt of honour, A : a gambling-debt, which cannot be legally enforced.

Debt of Nature, The : death. [Caxton, *Art and Craft How to Die* (1491)]

Decalogist, The : Rev. John Dod (1549–1645), Eng. Puritan divine, in allusion to his famous exposition of the Decalogue.

December and May : of a married couple, the husband old and the wife young.

Decimo, A man in : a hobble-de-hoy.

Decks, To clear the : to get minor matters out of the way preparatory to undertaking a more important engagement.

Decoration Day : May 30th, on which the graves of those who fell in the American Civil War (1861–5) are decorated with flowers.

Decoy duck, A : a person, animal, or inanimate object used as a means of enticing into a trap. Orig. a duck trained to decoy wild ducks into a trap.

Decretals, The False : Papal edicts, forged in 9th cent., in order to support the claims of the Papacy.

Dedalian : *see* Dædal.

Deeds not words : action instead of talk.

Deep waters, In : *see* Waters.

Defender of the Faith : a title borne by the kings of England, first conferred on Henry VIII by the Pope in recognition of his zeal in opposing the Reformers.

Deficit, Madame : Marie Antoinette. In allusion to the State deficits said to have been due to her extravagance.

Dekabrists, The : the conspirators concerned in the abortive Russian Revolution of 1825. From December, the month in which the rising occurred.

Delectable Mountains, The : the mountains from which the Celestial City was to be seen. Cf. Bunyan, *Pilgrim's Progress* (1678).

Delegations, The : the deliberative assembly representative of Austria and Hungary jointly, by which the common affairs of the two halves of the former Austrian Empire were governed.

Delenda est Carthago (*Lat.*, Carthage must be destroyed) : a quotation from Plutarch's life of Cato, stated to have been uttered in the Senate by Cato (234–149 B.C.) after a visit to Carthage during which he noticed its prosperity, strength and wealth.

Delian Problem, The : the problem of finding the cube-root of 2. From the answer of the oracle of Delos that a plague would be stayed when Apollo's altar, which was cubical, was doubled.

Delight of Mankind, The : the Emperor Titus (40–81).

Delilah, A : a temptress. After Delilah, the betrayer of Samson. [*Judges*, xvi]

Deliver the goods, To : to carry out one's undertaking ; to complete a contract by carrying out one's own side of it.

Della Crusca ; Della Cruscan (*Ital.*, of the chaff) : after the Accademia della Crusca, founded at Florence in 1582, celebrated for its dictionary of the Italian language and its endeavours to sift and purify the language. ' Della Cruscan ' is used by English writers to designate an artificial style in poetry. Robert Merry (1755–98), a writer of this character, adopted the signature ' Della Crusca ' on account of his membership of the Accademia.

Della Robbia : a kind of terra cotta. After Luca della Robbia (1399–1482), the inventor.

Delphic (Delphian) ambiguity : after the Oracle of Apollo at Delphi, in Greece.

Delphic sword, A : a two-edged sword. In allusion to the ambiguities of the Oracle of Apollo at Delphi. [Aristotle, *Politica*, I, 2]

Delphine editions : editions of the Greek and Latin classical authors prepared ' *in usum Delphini* ' (for the use of the Dauphin), the Dauphin (eldest son) of Louis XIV.

Delta, A : the land between two mouths of a river. After the triangular letter, *delta*, in the Grk. alphabet. Orig. applied to the land between the mouths of the Nile.

Deluge, The : the flood in the days of Noah.

Deluge, After us the : the future does not concern us. Translation of '*Après nous le deluge !* ' a remark made by Mme. de Pompadour to Louis XV when he was depressed after the defeat by Frederick the Great at Rossbach (1757).

Demijohn, A : a large bottle with a narrow neck. Probably from *Dame Jeanne* (Lady Jane), or from Damaghan in Persia, where glass-ware was made.

Demi-monde, The (*Fr.*, half-world, half-society) : immoral women and women ' of doubtful reputation ' as a class. The word was coined by Alexandre Dumas, fils. [*Fraser's Magazine*, LI, 579 (1855)]

Demi-rep, A : a woman of doubtful reputation. A contraction of demi-reputable, half-reputable.

Democritus, A : a philosopher who ridicules the world. After Demokritos of Abdera (460–357 B.C.), ' The Laughing Philosopher.'

Democritus, To dine with : to be deprived of one's dinner.

Democritus Junior : Robert Burton (1577–1640), author of *The Anatomy of Melancholy* (1621). Demokritos was a Grk. philosopher, surnamed ' the Laughing Philosopher ' probably on account of his advocacy of humour.

Demoivre, As sure as : very sure indeed. After Abraham de Moivre (1667–1754), a famous French mathematician, who settled in England. The phrase was coined by Alexander Pope.

Demon of Rebellions, The : Henri, Duc de Bouillon (1555–1623).

Demos : the people personified. Previously, the populace of Athens. Orig., the communalty of a Grk. town.

Demosthenes, A : an eloquent orator. After the greatest of Grk. orators (384–322 B.C.).

Demosthenes of the Pulpit, The : Dr. Thomas Rennell (1753–1840), Dean of Westminster. So-called by William Pitt.

Demy, A : a holder of a scholarship at Magdalen College, Oxford. Orig., he received half (*demi*) of a Fellow's allowance.

Denarius Dei (*Lat.*, God's 'penny') : payment made to complete a bargain.

Denarius Sancti Petri (*Lat.*, St. Peter's 'penny') : Peter's pence ; a voluntary tax paid by Catholics to the Pope.

Denim : a coarse fabric. A corruption of *serge de Nîmes* (Nîmes, in France).

Depth, Out of one's : speaking on topics with which one is not well acquainted. A swimming metaphor. [*The Spectator*, No. 105 (1711)]

Derby, The : the principal English horse-race ; founded by Edward Smith Stanley, Earl of Derby, in 1780.

Derby dog, A : an incident of little importance sure to occur at the last minute. From the proverbial dog on the Derby race-course after it has been cleared for the race.

Dernier cri, Le (*Fr.*, the latest cry) : the latest fashionable craze.

Dernier ressort, Le (*Fr.*, the last resort) : orig. the highest tribunal to which an appeal could be made ; later, any last resort. [Archbp. Williams, *Apologie for Bishops*, 89 (1641)]

Derrick, A : a contrivance for lifting heavy weights. After Derrick, a noted English hangman, c. 1600.

Derring-do, A deed of : a deed of desperate courage. 'Derring-do' is properly 'daring to do,' or 'daring deed.' The modern substantive is derived from a misprint in an early 16th-cent. edition of *Lydgate*.

Derwentwater's Lights, Lord : the Aurora Borealis, which is said to have been esp. brilliant on Feb. 24th, 1716, the night of the execution of James, Earl of Derwentwater.

Desobligeant, A (*Fr.*, disobliging) : a kind of chaise. Disobliging, because it holds only one person.

Desolation, The abomination of : *see* Abomination.

Despotism tempered by assassination : the government of Russia under the Czars. So-described after the murder of the Emperor Paul in 1801.

Destiny, The Man of : Napoleon I. In allusion to his belief in Fate.

Destiny, The shears of : *see* Shears.

Destiny, The web of : from the Fates, personified as the spinners of the web of life.

Desultory : rambling ; purposeless ; aimless. From *Desultor*, a Roman circus-rider who used to ride two horses at once, leaping from one to the other.

Deucalion's Son, A : from the Grk. legend of Deucalion, who, after the world had been destroyed by a flood, at the instance of the Oracle of Themis at Delphi, re-peopled the earth from stones.

Deuce, The : an expletive. From Germ., *das Daus*. Possibly connected with the Celtic, *dus*, a wood demon, and the Latin, *Deus*, a god.

Deuce (Devil) with .. To play the : to create havoc or mischief. [*Devil*, 1542 A.D.]

Deuce-ace : bad luck ; poverty. After a dicing term, meaning a throw of two and one.

Deus ex machina (*Lat.*, God from the machine) : an unexpected benefactor who extricates from a difficulty. An allusion to the mechanical contrivance by which the god was made to appear on the Grk. stage. The phrase first appeared in Greek. [Lucian, *Hermotimus*, 86]

Deutschland über Alles (*Germ.*, Germany above all, *i.e.*, Germany before everything) : the expression of German patriotism. It does not bear the meaning 'Germany above all other countries' put upon it by Germany's enemies during the World War of 1914–8.

Devil, A printer's : a printer's errand-boy. The boys so smeared themselves with ink that they were said to be 'as black as the Devil.' Printing used to be called 'the Black Art.' [Moxon, *Mechanic Exercises*, II (1683)]

Devil and the deep sea, Between the : between two desperate alternatives. [Monro, *Expedition with Mackay's Regiment*, II, 55 (1637)]

Devil blacker than he is, To paint the : to give an offender a worse reputation than he deserves. From the proverb, 'The Devil is not half so black as he is painted.'

Devil for .. To : to do subordinate work for a lawyer, editor, etc.

Devil his due, To give the : to allow all that can properly be said on behalf of an offender. [Shakespeare, 1 *Henry IV*, I, ii (1596)]

Devil is blind, When the : *i.e.*, never ; a time so remote as not to be worthy of consideration. [Simon Wagstaff (Jon. Swift), *Polite Conversations*, Dial. I (1738)]

I

Devil is dead, When the : when evil is entirely banished from the world. [Coryat, *Crudities* (1608)]

Devil loves apple-dumplings, As the : *i.e.*, not at all. From the practice at the University of Oxford early in 18th cent. of feeding the students on apple-dumplings on fast-days.

Devil loves Holy Water, As the : not at all. In allusion to the exorcism of devils in the Roman Catholic Church by means of Holy Water.

Devil overlooking Lincoln, Like the : alluding to a grotesque on Lincoln College, Oxford. [J. Heywood, *Proverbes* (1546)]

Devil, pull baker, Pull : *see* Pull.

Devil rebuking sin, The : an offender calling attention to the offence of another.

Devil take the hindmost, The : everyone must look after his own interests. [Horace, *Ars Poetica*, 417 ; Sir S. Tuke, *Adventures of Five Hours*, V (1663)]

Devil, To go to the : to be ruined, morally or materially. [*Paston Letters*, No. 512 (1465)]

Devil, To hold a candle to the : to assist an evil-doer. From the story of an old woman who lit a candle before St. Michael, and another before the Devil he was trampling under foot, and, when reproved, replied that as she did not know where she would go when she died, she wished to be safe in either event.

Devil to pay, The : suggesting a bad bargain made, with heavy retribution. In allusion to bargains made with wizards or with Satan.

Devil, To raise the : to create trouble ; to make a disturbance. [Vanbrugh, *Confederate*, V, ii (1705)]

Devil, To shame the : to tell the truth. [Henry Porter, *Two Angry Women of Abington*, 640–1 (1599)]

Devil was sick, The : of an insincere conversion. From an interpolation by Urquhart and Motteux in their translation of Rabelais, *Gargantua* (Bk. IV, ch. xxiv) :

' The Devil was sick,
The Devil a monk would be ;
The Devil was well,
The Devil a monk was he ! '

Devil with .. To play the : *see* Deuce.

Devil's advocate, The : the Promotor Fidei who is appointed to put forward the arguments against the canonization of a proposed Saint. Hence any debater who deliberately puts forward a weak case on behalf of his cause.

Devil's Bedpost, The : the four of clubs ; supposed to be an unlucky card.

Devil's Bible, The : playing-cards.

Devil's Blue : *see* Blue.

Devil's box, A : a dice-box with dice in it. [Etherege, *Comical Revenge*, II, iii (1664)]

Devil's book : *see* Devil's playbooks.

Devil's cushion, The : idleness.

Devil's daughter's portion : Deal, Dover, and Harwich. On account of the impositions practised on seamen at those ports.

Devil's dozen, A : thirteen, which is also a baker's dozen (*q.v.*). From the number of witches supposed to be necessary for a witches' Sabbath.

Devil's fourposter, A : a hand at whist which includes four clubs, and is said to be invariably unfortunate.

Devil's Island : an island off the coast of French Guiana, used as a penal settlement.

Devil's livery, The : black and yellow. Black for death ; yellow for the plague.

Devil's luck ; Devil's own luck : astonishingly good luck, which used to suggest a bargain with the Devil.

Devil's Mass : promiscuous swearing.

Devil's Own, The : (1) the 88th Foot ; so-called on account of their bravery in the Peninsular War ; (2) the Inns of Court Volunteer Regt. ; in allusion to lawyer's devils. The title is said to have been given to the Temple Company of Militia by King George III. *See* Devil for...

Devil's Parliament, The : the English Parliament of 1459, which was notorious for its attainders of Yorkists.

Devil's Paternoster, To say the : to grumble. [*Terence in English* (1614)]

Devil's play-books, The : playing-cards. So-called by the early Presbyterians.

Devil's snuffbox : a fungus which, when opened, contains dust.

Devil's tattoo, To beat the : to keep on repeating a monotonous tap or other simple sound.

Devoirs to..To pay one's : to pay one's respects to .. esp. socially. Fr., *devoir*, duty.

Devonshire C's, The three : the Crocker, Cruwys and Copplestone families, very ancient families of Devon.

Dewitt, To : to lynch. From Jan and Cornelius de Witt, Dutch statesmen, who were murdered by the mob in 1672.

Diamond cut diamond : a contest between two keen intellects, or practised contestants. [Simon Wagstaff, *Polite Conversation*, Dial. III (1738)]

Diamond of the first water, A : a person of superlative excellence. Lit., a diamond of the finest quality.

Diamond necklace, The : *see* Necklace.

Diamond, A rough : a person of great worth of character, but of unpolished manner or uncouth appearance ; like a diamond in its rough state. *See* Lord Chesterfield, *Letters to His Son* (1748).

Diamond State, The : Delaware.

Diana's livery, To wear : to remain a virgin. After Diana, the chaste goddess of the chase.

Diana's worshippers : midnight revellers. After Diana, the moon.

Diaspora, The : the Jews living outside of Palestine and dispersed throughout the world. Grk., *diaspore*, dispersion.

Dicers' oaths, Like : like oaths made to be broken, *i.e.*, oaths of gamblers never to touch dice again. [Shakespeare, *Hamlet*, III, iv (1602-3)]

Dick, To happen in the reign of Queen : not to happen at all, for there never was a Queen Richard.

Dick's hat-band, As cross as : in allusion to a character in some forgotten farce. ' Dick's hat-band ' is referred to in other sayings as fause, fond, tight, fine, queer, etc.

Dick-a-Tuesday : a hobgoblin.

Dick Talbot's truths : lies. After the habitual lying of Richard Talbot, Earl of Tyrconnell (1630-91).

Dickens ? What (Who) the : an emphatic form of inquiry. ' Dickens ' is a corrupt form of Nick (the Devil). [Shakespeare, *Merry Wives of Windsor*, III, ii, 19 (1600)]

Dickey, A : a shirt-front ; Germ., *decken*, to cover.

Dickon of the Broom : Richard I, Cœur de Lion. From the broom plant, the symbol of his family, the Plantagenets.

Dicky Sam : a native of Liverpool.

Dictator of Letters, The : Voltaire (1694-1778), Fr. philosopher and writer.

Dictionary, A Living : Wilhelm Leibnitz (1646-1716). So-called by George I.

Diddler, A : a mean cheat. After Jeremy Diddler, a character in James Kenney, *Raising the Wind* (1803).

Die in one's boots, To : to die a sudden and violent death. [*Dict. of Canting Crew* (1700)]

Die in the last ditch, To : to hold on in a contest until the last resource is expended. From the remark made by William III when asked whether he did not agree that the United Netherlands, of which he was then Stadtholder, was not on the verge of ruin. ' Nay, there is one certain means by which I can be sure never to see my country's ruin. I will die in the last ditch ! '

Die is cast, The : the decision is taken. Metaphor derived from the dice. From the phrase said to have been used by Julius Cæsar when about to cross the Rubicon.

Die-hard, A : an irreconcileable ; one who holds to his principles even though left alone in their support.

Die Hards, The : the 57th (now the West Middlesex) Regt. of Foot, whose colonel at the Battle of Albuera (1811) adjured his men, when surrounded, to die hard.

Diego, A Don : a Spaniard. Diego is a common name in Spain.

Dies non, A : a day that is not counted ; a non-legal day. Short for *dies non juridicus*, a day on which legal business is not transacted.

Dig, To : *see* Diggings.

Dig a pit, To : to lay a trap. [*Eccles.*, x, 8 ; *Ecclesiasticus*, xxvii, 26]

Dig the well at the river, To : to perform a futile and needless task.

Diggings : lodgings. Originated with the Galena lead-miners of Wisconsin who in winter lived underground in dug-outs.

Dignity, To stand upon one's : to show consciousness of one's own superiority, real or imaginary, in regard to others.

Dike-louper, A : one who breaks the laws of morality. A Scotticism : properly, a person or animal that leaps over fences.

Dilly, A : a wheeled vehicle. Orig. a stage-coach. A contraction of ' diligence.'

Dilution of Labour : the employment on work, supposed to require special training, of untrained labour mingled with trained labour.

Dimanche, Monsieur : a dun. After a character in Molière, *Don Juan* (1665).

Dime-cheap : very low in price. The American ' dime ' is worth 10 cents.

Dine with the Cross-legged Knights, To : to go dinnerless, but spend the dinner hour in the Round Church, in which are to be seen effigies of cross-legged knights.

Dine with Democritus, To : *see* Democritus.

Dine with Duke Humphrey, To : *see* Humphrey.

Dine with Mohammed, To : to die, and dine in Paradise.

Dine with St. Giles and the Earl of Murray, To : to go hungry. The Earl of Murray was buried in St. Giles Cathedral, Edinburgh, which starving people used to frequent.

Dine with Sir Thomas Gresham, To : not to dine, *i.e.*, to spend the dinner-hour in the Royal Exchange, London. Founded by Sir Thomas Gresham.

Diner-out of the first water : Sydney Smith, the wit (1769–1845). So-called by *The Quarterly Review*. A parody on ' a diamond of the first water.' The phrase ' A diner-out of the highest lustre ' was applied by Sydney Smith himself to George Canning.

Ding-thrift, A : a spendthrift. One who dings, or drives away, thrift.

Dingaan's Day : December 16. The anniversary of the defeat in 1838 of the Zulus under Dingaan by the Boers.

Dinner-bell, The : a sobriquet of Edmund Burke (1729–97), who was accustomed to speak at such length in Parliament that he encroached on the dinner-hour.

Diogenes' cell : *see* Diogenes and his tub.

Diogenes and his lantern : Diogenes (412–323 B.C.), the Grk. cynic philosopher is said to have once been found in the street with a lighted lantern, and, when asked his reason, replied that he was seeking an honest man.

Diogenes and his tub : Diogenes was reputed to have lived a part of his life in a tub feeling himself independent of the ordinary necessities of civilization.

Diogenes of four-legged brutes, The : the pig. So-called by Douglas Jerrold.

Diomedean swop, A : an exchange in which one party obtains a preponderant advantage. From an exchange of armour between Diomed and Glaucus described in Homer, *Iliad*, VI.

Diotrephes, A : one who seeks high office in church. After a character mentioned in *John*, iii, 9–10.

Diplomacy, Shirt-sleeves : *see* Shirt-sleeves.

Diplomatic cold, A : a feigned indisposition, invented in order to escape the necessity of committing oneself to a definite course of action or policy. First used in 1885 by Timothy Healy of the then Lord Hartington and W. E. Gladstone.

Dircæan Swan, The : Pindar (518–442 B.C.). From the fountain of Dirce in the neighbourhood of his birth-place.

Direct action : a strike or other industrial action taken not to secure industrial ends, but as a means of interference in the general government of the country or in its foreign policy.

Directory, The : the ruling Committee in France under the First Republic from 1795–1799. Fr., *Directoire*.

Dirleton, To doubt with : after Sir John Nisbet, of Dirleton, whose *Doubts* (1698) is considered a legal classic in Scotland.

Dirt, To eat : to submit to humiliation. From the proverb, ' Every man must eat a peck of dirt before he dies.'

Dirt-cheap : exceedingly cheap ; almost as cheap as dirt.

Dirty action, A : a mean action. [Sheridan, *The Rivals*, II, ii (1775)]

Dirty Half-hundred, The : the 50th Regt. of Foot (1st Batt. Royal West Kent Regt.), who in the Peninsular War wiped their faces with their black facings.

Dirty linen in public, To wash : to discuss or disclose scandals in the course of a public dispute. The phrase was used by Napoleon in a speech to the Legislative Assembly on his return from Elba, and previously by Voltaire in an address to the Encyclopædists.

Dirty Shirts, The : the 101st Foot (1st Batt. Munster Fusiliers), who fought in their shirt-sleeves at Delhi in 1857.

Dirty weather : stormy weather at sea.

Disciples of St. Antling : Puritans. After the Church of St. Antling, or Anthony, in the City of London, which Puritans used to frequent.

Discount, At a : not in demand, reduced in value.

Discretion, Years of : the age at which one is expected to have attained responsibility ; in English law this age is 14.

Disgruntled (To be) : (to be) sulky, grumpy, dissatisfied. [H. Cave, *History of Popery* (1682)]

Dish a person, To : to circumvent a person ; to upset his plans. From the cook's point of view the preparation of food is completed and disposed of when it is dished up.

Dish fit for the gods, A : a course at a meal most attractively prepared. [Shakespeare, *Julius Caesar*, II, i, l. 173 (1603)]

Dish the Whigs, To : to upset the plans of one's opponent by appropriating his programme. The phrase was used by Edward, 14th Earl of Derby, in reference to the Reform Bill of 1867.

Dish, To lay in one's : to charge a person with .. ; to accuse a person of .. [Phaer, *Virgil* (1600)]

Disjecta membra (*Lat.*, scattered remains) : From Horace, *Disjecti membra poetae*, limbs of a dismembered poet. [*Satires*, I, iv, 62]

Dismal Science, The : political economy. So-called by Thomas Carlyle.

Diss, To know nothing about : to take no interest in matters of slight importance. From the infrequency of the visits of travellers to Diss, in Norfolk.

Distaff side, On the : on the female side of a family. The distaff was the emblem of feminine industry.

Distaff-sisters, The : the Fates.

Distaff's (St. Distaff's) Day : the day following the Feast of Epiphany, on which women resumed their work.

Distance, To keep one's : to take up an attitude of reserve. [*Lady Alimony*, II, vi (1659)]

Distinction without a difference, A : no difference at all. [William Hazlitt, *First Acquaintance with Poets*]

Dithyrambic : wild, boisterous. From *Dithurambos*, a hymn in honour of Bacchus.

Dittany, To strew : to prepare the bridal chamber. Dittany is an aromatic plant, whose name is derived from Mount Dicte in Crete.

Ditto to Mr. Burke, To say : to have nothing further to add to a previous complete statement of your case. The speech on the hustings of a fellow-candidate of Edmund Burke, after an eloquent address by that orator, was : ' I say ditto to Mr. Burke.'

Dittoes : coat, waistcoat, and trousers, all of the same pattern. Frequently used for trousers only.

Ditty bag ; Ditty box, A : a bag or box used by seamen to hold small articles. Possibly from ' dittis,' the name of a

material of which they may originally have been made.

Diva Fortune (*Lat.*, the Goddess Fortune): games of chance.

Dives, A (*Lat.*, rich) : a rich man. From the parable of Dives and Lazarus in *Luke*, xvi.

Divide et impera (*Lat*, divide and rule) : introduce dissensions among your opponents, a maxim of Macchiavelli (1469–1527), the Italian political writer.

Divine Doctor, The : Jan de Ruysbroeck (1293–1381), Flemish mystic.

Divine lovers : platonic lovers (*q..v*).

Divine Pagan, The : Hypatia of Alexandria (d. 415), woman philosopher.

Divine plant, The : vervain or Herba Sacra. So-called by the Romans, who believed it to have almost miraculous powers.

Divine Right of Kings, The : the theory that kings are appointed by God, and that it is of the nature of blasphemy to attempt to frustrate their actions.

Divine Speaker, The : Tyrtamos (370–287 B.C.). So-called by Aristotle.

Dix-huit Brumaire : the Coup d'Etat of November 9, 1799 (18 Brumaire in the Republican calendar), when Napoleon appointed himself First Consul.

Dixie's Land : the Southern or Slave States of the United States ; the negro name for the land that was to them their home. The term arose in New York early in 19th cent. from a song, or popular story, of a kindly disposed slave-owner named Dixie whose slaves increased so that there was no room for them all on his estate. The surplus migrated, but continued to look on their birthplace, ' Dixie's Land,' as home, their earthly paradise. Another derivation is from the Mason and Dixon's Line, which separated the Slave States from the Free.

Dixit (Ipse dixit), A (*Lat.*, he [himself] has spoken) : a positive statement. Also *dixi*, I have spoken. [Earle, *Microcosmography : A Scepticke in Religion* (1628)]

Dizzy : Benjamin Disraeli, Lord Beaconsfield (1804–81). A corruption of his surname.

Do ut des (*Lat.*, I give that you may give): a suggestion of an agreement for mutual benefit. A Roman legal term, popularized by its use by Bismarck.

Do what is done, To : to act in a futile manner. From an ancient Grk. proverb.

Dobbin, A : (1) a faithful friend and patient lover, after a character in Thackeray, *Vanity Fair* (1847) ; (2) a steady old horse suitable for children to ride.

Doctor, A : a seventh son. From the belief that he had exceptional powers in curing certain diseases.

Doctor, The : the cook on board ship who doctors the food.

Doctor accounts, To : to falsify or manipulate accounts. A suggestion that the accounts are ill and require to be cured or drugged.

Doctor Brighton : Brighton, the famous watering-place in Sussex. This name is said to have been given it on account of its salubriousness by George IV, who spent much time there.

Doctor Dodipoll, As wise as : not at all wise. *See* Dodipoll. [*The Wisdome of Dr. Dodypole* (1600)]

Doctor, The Authentic : *see* Authentic.

Doctor, The Divine : *see* Divine.

Doctor Fell : Applied to a man whom one dislikes instinctively, without being able to give one's reasons for such dislike. After John Fell (1625–86), Dean of Christchurch, after he had expelled Tom Brown, the satirist, who wrote the following lines on him :

'I do not like thee, Doctor Fell,
The reason why I cannot tell ;
But this alone I know full well—
I do not like thee, Doctor Fell.'

Doctor Illuminatus : (1) Raymond Lully (1235–1315), Span. scholastic ; (2) Johannes Tauler (1294–1361), Germ. mystic.

Doctor Jekyll and Mr. Hyde : *see* Jekyll.

Doctor Mirabilis : Roger Bacon (1214–92), Eng. scholar and philosopher.

Doctor My-book : John Abernethy (1765–1830), who used continually to refer his patients to 'my' book, *Surgical Observations*.

Doctor Singularis et Invincibilis : William of Occam (d. c. 1349), Eng. Franciscan scholar and controversialist.

Doctor Syntax : a simple-minded, scholarly clergyman. After a character in *The Tour of Dr. Syntax* by William Combe (1813).

Doctors : false dice ; because they are doctored (faked).

Doctor's Commons : offices in London for the registration and probate of wills, granting of marriage-licenses, etc. Orig. the common buildings of the College of Doctors of Law engaged in the Ecclesiastical and the Admiralty Courts.

Doctrinaire, A : one who puts, or attempts to put, theories into practice. After a French political party which came into existence after 1815, considered by their opponents to be wedded to doctrines rather than to practice.

Doddy, A : (1) a stupid person ; a contraction of 'doddy poll' ; (2) (Scot.) a cow or bull without horns. The origin of the word from 'dodded,' hornless, is in both senses the same.

Dodger, An artful : *see* Artful dodger.

Dodipoll (Doddypoll), A : a stupid person. *See also* Doddy.

Dodipoll, As wise as Doctor : *see* Doctor Dodipoll.

Dodo, As dead as a : the dodo, a large bird of the island of Mauritius, which was specially stupid in appearance, has been extinct since 17th cent.

Doe and Richard Roe, John : imaginary personages introduced to illustrate an argument. Orig. so-used in legal documents.

Doe-faces : *see* Dough-faces.

Dog a bad name, To give a : to condemn a person from prejudice. From the proverb 'Give a dog a bad name and hang him.'

Dog, A dead : something of no value. (1 *Samuel*, xxiv, 14).

Dog, A dirty : an objectionable, usually lewd, fellow. From the dogs in the Near East, which are employed as scavengers.

Dog a person's footsteps, To : to follow a person like a dog. [*A Warning for Faire Women*, II, ll. 261–2 (1599)]

Dog and bones to one's ass, To give straw to one's : *see* Straw.

Dog and shadow, To be like : (of two persons) to be inseparable, one to be always following the other.

Dog and wolf, Between : dusk.

Dog in a doublet, A : a bold, determined man. From the practice in Germany and Flanders of clothing in doublets dogs employed in hunting the wild-boar.

Dog in the Manger, A : one who, unable himself to use an advantage, prevents others from doing so. From the fable of the dog that lay in a manger and prevented the ox from feeding.

[Lyly, *Euphues : Anatomy of Wit* (1579)]

Dog Latin : *see* Latin.

Dog life, To lead a cat-and- : (of people who live together) to be always quarrelling.

Dog, Love me, love my : if you love me you must love all that pertains to me ; do everything for my sake. [Heywood, *Proverbes* (1546)]

Dog, of God, The : the bear. So-called by the Laplanders.

Dog over a stile, To help a lame : to assist a person in a difficulty. [Heywood, *Proverbes* (1546) ; Marston, *Insatiate Countess*, II, ii (1605)]

Dog, The black : melancholy ; bad-temper.

Dog to bark, To teach : *see* Teach.

Dog, To be top : *see* Top dog.

Dog, To be under- : *see* Under-dog.

Dog, To wake a sleeping : to stir up trouble unnecessarily. From the proverbial saying, ' Let sleeping dogs lie.'

Dogs as you have bones to pick, To have as many : to have as many children as you can support. [J. M. Wilson, *Tales of the Borders : The Henpecked Man* (1835)]

Dog's death, To die a : to die like a dog, no one troubling himself in the matter.

Dog's life, To lead a : to live a life of wretchedness, like a dog which nobody wants. [Anth. Brewer, *Lingua*, II, iv (1607)]

Dogs, The : the 17th Lancers, whose crest is a Death's Head and ' Or Glory,' *viz.*, D.O.G.

Dog's letter, The : ' R,' whose sound is uttered by a dog when snarling.

Dogs lie, Let sleeping : *see* Dog, To wake a sleeping.

Dogs of war, The : famine, sword and fire. [Shakespeare, *Julius Cæsar*, III, i (1601)]

Dogs, To go to the : to go to the bad ; to fall to a very low moral or material level. In the East the remains of a feast are thrown to the dogs. Possibly, however, from the Dutch proverb : ' *Toe goe, toe de dogs*,' ' Money gone, credit gone.'

Dogs, To throw to the : to throw away as worthless. [Shakespeare, *Macbeth*, V, iii, 47 (1606)]

Dog-bolt, A : a term of reproach ; a servile follower. [*Paston Letters*, No. 533 (1465)]

Dog-cart, A : a small two-wheeled cart or trap in which sportsmen used to convey their dogs to the field.

Dog-cheap : very cheap. Swed., *dog*, very. [Shakespeare, 1 *Henry IV*, III, iii (1596–7)]

Dog days, The : the period about the rising of the Dog Star, the hottest of the year. It was a popular belief that at this time of year more than at any other dogs are liable to become mad.

Dog-eared : (of leaves of a book) turned down at the corners.

Dog-fall : a fall in which both combatants touch the ground. A wrestling term.

Dog-rose, A : a wild rose. From the popular belief that its root was an antidote for the bite of a dog.

Dog-sleep, A : a pretended sleep. From the popular belief that dogs sleep with one eye open.

Dog-tired : extremely tired ; as a dog after the chase.

Dog-whipping Day : October 18, on which a dog is once said to have eaten the consecrated wafer in York Minster.

Dogberry, A : a stupid, self-important official. After a character in Shakespeare, *Much Ado About Nothing* (1599).

Doggett's Badge : a prize in a rowing match on the Thames awarded annually on August 1. Instituted by the actor, Thomas Doggett, in 1716.

Doily : a small ornamental napkin ; formerly, ' doily napkin.' After Doily, a London linen-draper in the early 18th cent.

Doit for .. Not to care a : to place no value upon .. A doit was a small Scottish coin.

Dolce far niente (*Ital.*, sweet do-nothing) : pleasant idleness.

Doldrums, In the : a period of quietude and rest or dejection. After the name of a region of the ocean near the Equator, noted for its calms.

Dollar, A : a coin of varying value in the Amer. States. An abbreviation of Joachimsthaler. After Joachimsthal, Bohemia, whence the silver from which the coin was first minted in 1518 was obtained.

Dollar, The Almighty : *see* Almighty.

Dolly-shop, A : a rag-shop, which formerly had a black doll as a sign.

Dolly Varden, A : a kind of woman's dress or hat. After a character in Dickens, *Barnaby Rudge* (1840).

Domesday Book : an account of the division and ownership of the land of England, compiled in the reign of William I.

Dominican, A : a friar of the Order founded by Dominic de Guzman (1170–1221) ; a Black Friar, or Preaching Friar.

Dominie Sampson, A : a village schoolmaster. After a poor, modest, scholarly village schoolmaster in Sir W. Scott, *Guy Mannering* (1815).

Dominoes : a game with marked stones, invented by two French monks, the victor reciting the first verse of the Vesper service : ' Dixit Dominus Domino meo.'

Don Diego, A : *see* Diego.

Don Juan, A : a libertine. After a semi-mythical Spaniard, Don Juan Tenorio, who lived in 14th cent., and whose career has supplied the basis for several plays.

Don Quixote, A : a romantic, absurdly chivalrous person. After the hero of Cervantes, *Don Quichotte* (1604).

Donat ; Donet, A : an elementary grammar. After Ælius Donatus (fl. 356), Roman grammarian.

Donation of Constantine, The : a forgery, attributed to Constantine the Great, conveying the donation to the Papacy of temporal sovereignty over Rome and the neighbouring region.

Donation of Pepin, The : the basis of the temporal claims of the Papacy. In 755 Pepin gave the Pope the exarchate of Ravenna and the Republic of Rome.

Done to one's hand : already done ; completed.

Donkey, To ride the black : to be obstinate (as is a donkey.)

Donkey between two bundles of hay, To be like the : unable to make up one's mind between two alternatives. From the story of the donkey that died of starvation while hesitating whether to partake of the hay on his right or on his left.

Donnybrook Fair ; Donnybrook : a scene of disorder and not very serious riot. From the proceedings at the annual fair held until 1855 at Donnybrook, Co. Dublin.

Doom, The crack of : the end of the world ; the signal for the Last Judgment.

Doomsday, To wait till : to wait an indefinite time ; to wait for that which will never occur. Lit., to wait until the Day of Judgment at the end of the world.

Door of .. To lay a charge at the : to accuse of ..

Door of .. To lay at the : to attribute to ..

Door of .. To be left at the : to be left to be paid by ..

Door with an axe, To open a : *see* Open.

Doornail, As dead as a : *see* Dead.

Dopper, A : (1) in early 17th cent., an Anabaptist ; (2) a member of the Dutch South African Church. Dutch, *Dipper*, Baptist.

Dora : the initial letters (D.O.R.A.) of the Defence Of the Realm Act, the Act of Parliament by which the liberties of the English people were restricted or suspended during the period of the European War (1914–18).

Dorcas Society, A : an association of philanthropic women who make clothes for the poor. After the charitable Dorcas in *Acts*, ix, 39.

Dorchester butts, As big as : the butts of Dorchester were famous for their size.

Doric Dialect, The : a broad dialect, esp. those of the Scottish Lowlands and the North of England. After the dialect anciently spoken at Doris, in Greece.

Doric Reed, The : pastoral poetry. After Doris, a division of ancient Greece, and the reed (flute), the musical instrument of the pastoral poets.

Dormouse, As sleepy as a : the dormouse has been looked upon in England as the example of a heavy sleeper at least as far back as the early 16th cent.

Dosser, A : one who frequents doss-houses (*q.v.*).

Doss-house, A : a low-class lodging house. Perhaps from Lat., *dorsum*, the back.

Dosser-headed : silly ; empty-headed. Fr., *dosser*, a pannier.

Dot the i's and cross the t's, To : to be meticulously accurate.

Dotheboys Hall, A : a low-class boarding-school at which the boys are badly treated. After the school in Dickens, *Nicholas Nickleby* (1838).

Dotterel, A : a silly person ; a dupe. After the dotterel, a bird, formerly believed to be so exceptionally silly as to be easily caught.

Dotterel, To dor the : to cheat. From ' dor,' to outwit, and ' dotterel ' (*q.v.*).

Dotty (To be) : (to be) silly. Formerly 'doat' or 'dote.' [Dekker and Webster, *Northward Ho*, IV, i (1607)]

Douay Version, The : the Roman Catholic translation of the Bible into English, completed at the English College at Douay in 1609.

Double, A : a person who exactly or nearly exactly resembles another in appearance.

Double Dutch : *see* Dutch.

Double entendre (entente) (*O.-Fr.*, double meaning) : a remark capable of two interpretations, esp. when one of them is suggestive of indelicacy. [Dryden, *Mariage à la Mode*, III, i, 36 (1673)]

Double-faced : treacherous, deceitful. [Thos. Lodge, *Rosalind* (1590)]

Double First, A : two First-Class Honours certificates at Oxford or Cambridge University.

Double-headed Eagle, The : the emblem of the German Empire, formed by Charlemagne of a combination of the German eagle with its head turned to the left and the Roman eagle with its head turned to the right.

Double or quits : the alternative of the cancellation of a debt or the doubling of its amount. A gambling phrase.

Double-dealing : dishonourable, deceitful proceedings. [Skelton, *Dethe Erle Northumberland*, 174 (1529)]

Double-dyed traitor, A : a thorough traitor. Lit., one who has been twice dyed with treason.

Double-edged : cutting both ways, both the user and him against whom the argument or instrument is used.

Douceur, A (*Fr.*, sweetener) : a bribe ; a present. [Horace Walpole, *Letters*, IV (1763)]

Doudon, A : a short, fat woman.

Doughboy, A : an American private soldier. From the shape of the buttons on his tunic.

Dough-faces : Northern politicians believed to be easily influenced by those of the Southern States ; whose faces could be worked upon as if they were made of dough.

Doukhobors, The (*Russ.*, spirit-fighters) : a Russian nonconformist sect.

Dover and Calais meet, When : *i.e.*, never.

Doverco(ur)t, A : a Babel. Probably from the confusion caused by the many frequenters of the Church at Dovercourt, Essex, which once possessed a miraculous Cross that spoke.

Dowager Princess Albert of Saxe-Coburg, The : the Legitimist designation of Queen Victoria.

Dowlas ; Mr. Dowlas : (1) a kind of calico, made in imitation of a linen, formerly manufactured at Daoulas in Brittany ; (2) a linen-draper, one who sells dowlas.

Down, A bed of : *see* Bed.

Down a person, To : to force him down ; to defeat him. [Mrs. Piozzi, *Anecdotes of Dr. Johnson* (1786)]

Down in the dumps : *see* Dumps.

Down on .. To be : to be severe upon ..

Down on one's luck, To be : to be unlucky.

Down in the mouth, To be : to be low-spirited, dejected. [Bp. Hall, *Epistles*, I, 6 (1608)]

Down tools policy, A : a strike on the part of workmen, *i.e.*, a policy of laying down tools.

Down train, A : a train proceeding away from the railway headquarters. *See* Up train *and* Go up, To.

Downing Street : the British Government of the day. After the street in which the Prime Minister of the day resides. It was named after Sir George Downing, M.P. (1624–84), who lived there in the reign of Charles II.

Downright Dunstable : *see* Dunstable.

Downy cove (etc.), A : a sharp individual, awake to every subterfuge.

Dozen, To talk nineteen (sixteen) to the : to talk very quickly ; to gabble ; to utter nineteen words in the normal time for twelve.

Dozen, Thirteen to the : over-full measure. [*Panegyricke Verses upon Coryat and His Crudities* (1611)] *See* Baker's dozen.

Draconic ; Draconian : extremely harsh and cruel. After Draco (fl. 624 B.C.), an Athenian law-giver who made every crime a capital offence.

Draft on Aldgate Pump, A : a worthless cheque or bill-of-exchange. A pun on 'draft' (on a bank) and 'draft' (a drawing of water). [Fielding, *Essay on Character of Men* (1762)]

Draggle-tail (Dratchel, Drazel), A : a slut ; an untidy woman, whose skirts are dragged in the mud. [Nashe, *Saffron Walden*, 143 (1596)]

Drago doctrine, The : a doctrine enunciated (1902) by Luis Drago (1859-1921), Argentine minister for foreign affairs, that no power had any right to use force against another power in order to collect debts due to its nationals.

Dragoman, A : an interpreter attached to embassies in the Near East. Arab., *Tarjuman*, interpreter.

Dragon, A blind : a chaperon ; one who plays propriety in the presence of two young people of opposite sexes.

Dragons' teeth : causes of civil dissension. From the legend of dragons' teeth sown by Cadmus, from which irrepressible fighting men sprang to life.

Dragon's teeth, To sow : to stir up civil strife ; to lay the seeds of future trouble. *See* Dragons' teeth.

Dragonnade, A : a devastating incursion. From the persecution of Fr. Protestants by soldiery under Louis XIV, in which dragoons were quartered on the sufferers.

Dragoon, A : a cavalry soldier armed with a ' dragoon ' (musket), so-called because, like a dragon, it breathes fire.

Dragoon, To : to oppress and ill-treat. *See* Dragonnade.

Dramatic Unities, The : according to Aristotle : one catastrophe, one locality, one day.

Dram-drinking : intemperance ; tippling. From ' dram,' a small liquid-measure

Drang nach Osten (*Germ.*, pressure towards the East) : the political policy of the German Empire (before 1918 !) to extend its influence in the direction of the East.

Drat it ! : a corruption of the oath ' May God rot it ! '

Draw a blank, To : to secure no result for one's efforts. In allusion to drawing a blank in a lottery.

Draw a person, To : to obtain information from a person who is unaware that he is furnishing it.

Draw a person out, To : to entice a person to show that of which he is best capable.

Draw a waggon, To take a hair to : *see* Take.

Draw it mild, To : to request another to be moderate. Orig. in reference to a barmaid's drawing mild, as opposed to strong, beer.

Draw the King's Picture, To : to coin false money.

Draw the line at, .. To : not to go beyond an imaginary line in matters mental and spiritual as well as material.

Draw the long bow, To : *see* Bow.

Draw the teeth of .. To : to deprive of the opportunity of doing mischief.

Draw water with a sieve, To : to act in a futile manner. From an ancient Grk. proverb.

Drawcansir, A : a blustering bully. After a character in George Villiers, Duke of Buckingham, *The Rehearsal* (1672).

Drawn battle, A : a contest in which neither party has the advantage. Possibly the original form was ' withdrawn battle,' indicating the withdrawal of both armies.

Dreadnought, A : a man-of-war of very great power, after the name of the first of the class.

Dreamer, The Immortal : John Bunyan (1628–88), author of *The Pilgrim's Progress* (1678).

Dred Scott Decision, The : the decision of the Federal Court of the United States (1856) that a slave had no rights as a person but was a property, and as such to be protected by the State. After Dred Scott, a slave around whom the litigation centred.

Dree one's weird, To : to suffer one's fate.

Dreikaiser Bund, The (*Germ.*, three Emperors' alliance) : an informal alliance between the Emperors of Germany, Austria and Russia between 1872 and 1879.

Dresden shepherdess, A : a girl dainty in dress and appearance. From the style of the shepherdesses in Dresden china.

Dressed up to the knocker : dressed in the height of fashion. In allusion to the time when door-knockers were affixed as high as possible on doors so as to prevent them from being wrenched off and stolen (a common practice).

Drink like a fish, To : to drink much ; to be addicted to intemperance. [Gray, *Letters*, LX, (1747)]

Drink at Freeman's Quay, To : to enjoy a free drink. At one time carmen, etc., who called at Freeman's Quay, nr. London Bridge, were entertained with free drinks.

Drink in one's own glass, To : to follow one's own bent.

Drink up the sea, To : to attempt the impossible. [Naevius, *Fragmenta*, verse 52]

Drinks on a person, To have the : to have the advantage of a person.

Dripping Pan, The Queen of : *see* Queen.

Drive] [Drunk

Drive a coach-and-four (-six) through .. To : to find ready means of evading a (law or regulation). Daniel O'Connell (1775–1847), the Irish orator and agitator, boasted : ' I can drive a coach-and-six through any Act of Parliament,' in allusion to the loose manner in which parliamentary bills were drafted. Earlier, Sir Stephen Rice (1637–1715), Irish judge, had boasted, before he was raised to the bench, that he would ' drive a coach and six horses through the (Irish) Act of Settlement.'

Drive a hard bargain, To : to exact more than the value. [Sam. Butler, *Characters : A Traveller* (1670)]

Drive pigs to market, To : to snore, like the grunting of a pig.

Drive too many omnibuses through Temple Bar, To : to attempt too many undertakings simultaneously.

Droit d'Aubaine : the right of the French king (abolished in 1819) to all the movable property of aliens dying in his kingdom.

Dromios, The Two : two (brothers) very much alike in appearance. After the characters in Shakespeare, *Comedy of Errors* (1589).

Drone among the bees, A : an idler among the active. [*Paston Letters*, No. 1004 (1465)]

Drop an acquaintance, To : to cease to acknowledge an acquaintance. [In early 18th cent.]

Drop o' the Cratur, A : *see* Cratur.

Drop in the ocean, A : that which bears an insignificant proportion to its surroundings.

Drop too much, To take a : to drink more than is good for one ; to become drunk.

Drown the miller, To : to pour an excessive amount of water into tea, etc. A suggestion that the excess is so great as to drown the miller who uses the water-wheel.

Drug in the market, A : a commodity that is unsaleable or saleable only with difficulty ; a superfluity, not desired by anybody. The use of ' drug ' in this sense probably arose out of a play on words in 17th cent. Its original meaning is an ingredient used in chemistry, pharmacy, etc. ; it is also derived from Fr., *drogue*, rubbish.

Drum, A : an evening party. Either (1) from the noise made by the card-players, or (2) a corruption of ' drawing-room.' [18th and early 19th cents.]

Drum Ecclesiastic, The : the cushion of the pulpit on which some preachers are accustomed to thump. [Butler, *Hudibras*, Pt. I, canto i, l. 11 (1663)]

Drum's entertainment, John (Tom) : ill-treatment ; possibly derived from a forgotten story or incident. There was a short early 17th cent. play entitled *Jacke Drum's Entertainment.* Or the expulsion of an unwelcome guest who is, as it were, drummed out of the Army.

Drum-sticks : cooked legs of a chicken. On account of their resemblance to drum-sticks proper. [Foote, *Mayor of Garrat*, I (1763)]

Drumhead Court Martial, A : a summary military trial. Held in the open field, with a drum as a table.

Drummer, A : a commercial traveller, whose function it is to drum up customers as if they were recruits. An American term.

Drunk as a cobbler, As : exceedingly drunk. From as early as 15th cent. in England cobblers were proverbial for drunkenness.

Drunk as a fiddler, As : very drunk. The intemperance of professional fiddlers at evening parties was proverbial. [*The Puritan* (1609)]

Drunk as a lord, As : very drunk. Alluding to the intemperance of many members of the Upper Classes until the beginning of 19th cent. [Middleton and Rowley (1623)]

Drunk as a Pope, As : very drunk. In allusion to the reputation for drinking acquired by Pope Benedict XII (d. 1342).

Drunk as Chloe, As : very drunk. In allusion to the cobbler's wife of Linden Grove, to whom the poet Prior was attached, and who was notorious for her intemperance.

Drunk as David's sow, As : from the wife of one David Lloyd of Hereford, whose wife was found drunk in his pig-stye, when his friends came to view a freak sow that he owned. This explanation cannot be traced earlier than 1711 [*British Apollo*, I, 527] although the phrase appears in Ray, *English Proverbs* (1670).

Drunk as the Devil, As : impudently drunk. [14th cent.]

Drunk as a tinker at Banbury, As : *see* Banbury.

Drunkard's cloak, A : a contrivance like a large wooden crinoline, placed on a drunkard's shoulders in order to restore him to sobriety.

Drunken Deddington : unconscious through drink. A play on the word ' dead.'

Drunken Parliament, The : see Parliament.

Drunkenness, The seven degrees of : ape-drunk, because the subject leaps and sings ; lion-drunk, because he is quarrelsome ; swine-drunk, because he is sleepy ; sheep-drunk, because he is conceited but speechless ; martin-drunk, because he has drunk himself sober again ; goat-drunk, because he is lascivious ; fox-drunk, because he is crafty.

Dry as a bone, As : [Taylor, *Western Voyage to the Mount*, 7 (1649)]

Dry goods : merchandise consisting of hosiery, textile fabrics, etc. Orig. an American term.

Dry lodgings : sleeping accommodation without food.

Dry-as-dust, A : a pedant and antiquary. After Dr. Dryasdust in Sir W. Scott's Prefaces. The word as a common noun was popularized by Carlyle. [*Wit Revived, or a New and Excellent Way of Divertisement*, by Asdryasdust Tossofacan (1674)]

Dub up, To : to pay. From the practice of dubbing (touching a man on the shoulder) when about to arrest him for debt.

Dubbed a Knight, To be : said of one who has drunk deeply to his mistress in a kneeling posture.

Ducat, A : a European coin, no longer current. First struck by Roger II, Duke of Apulia. The name is derived from the legend (' Sit tibi, Christe, datus, quem tu regis, iste ducatus ') which appeared on the first ducats.

Duchess of Devonshire fashion, In the : in the style of dress of the Duchess of Devonshire in Gainsborough's famous portrait of her.

Duchess, A regular old : a middle-aged or elderly woman of extremely dignified appearance.

Duchy, The : (1) the Duchy of Cornwall, belonging to the Prince of Wales ; (2) of Lancaster, pertaining to the British Crown.

Duck, A lame : a disabled person, esp. one who cannot meet his financial obligations. Orig. a Stock Exchange colloquialism. [Horace Walpole, *Letters to Sir Horace Mann* (1761)]

Duck in a thunderstorm, Like a dying : very ' down-in-the-mouth,' or lackadaisical.

Duckling, An ugly : the unpromising child in a family who ultimately surpasses the others. From one of Hans Andersen's fairy-tales of that title.

Duck's egg, A : a score of naught. From the resemblance of the symbol O to a duck's egg.

Ducks and drakes with, To play : to squander ; to scatter carelessly. From the game of duck and drake, which consists of so casting a pebble along the surface of water that it keeps on dipping into and then rising out of the water. The phrase was used in the figurative sense as early as 1600. [Shakespeare, *Timon of Athens*, V, v, (1607–8)]

Dud, A : a shell that fails to burst, or any expected excitement which fails to mature.

Dudman and Ramhead meet, When : *i.e.*, never. Dudman and Ramhead are capes on the Cornish coast.

Dug-out, A : an underground refuge from shells or bombs ; a retired military officer recalled on the occasion of war to active service.

Duke of Exeter's Daughter, The : an instrument of torture said to have been introduced by Duke of Exeter in 1447.

Duke, The Great : the Duke of Wellington (1769–1852).

Duke Humphrey : see Humphrey.

Duke's Walk, To meet a person in the : to fight a duel. From a promenade frequented by the Duke of York (afterwards James II) in the neighbourhood of Holyrood Palace, where duels were frequently fought.

Dukeries, The : a part of Nottinghamshire in which are to be found seats of several dukes.

Dulcarnon, A (*Arab.*, two-horned) : a dilemma ; a person in a dilemma. [Chaucer, *Troilus and Cressida*, Bk. III, ll. 930–1 (14th cent.)]

Dulcarnon, To send a person to : to puzzle him. *See* Dulcarnon.

Dulce Domum (*Lat.*, ['tis] sweet [to return] home) : from a school breaking-up song, said to have originated at Winchester School.

Dulcinea, A : a sweetheart. After Don Quixote's mistress, Dulcinea del Toboso.

Dull as ditchwater, As : exceedingly dull. From the stagnancy of water in ditches.

Dumb as a fish, As : silent. [Dekker, *The Seuen Deadly Sinnes: Sloth* (1606)]

Dumb as a stone, As : [*Cursor Mundi* (1340) ; Chaucer, *House of Fame*, II, 148 (14th cent.)]

Dumb-waiter, A : an article of dining-room furniture on which dishes, plates, etc., are placed, which in a sense serves the purposes of a waiter.

Dum-dum bullet, A : a soft-nosed bullet. After Dum-dum, near Calcutta, India, where they were originally made.

Dump, To ; Dumping : lit., to cast down in a disordered heap. Dumping is the exportation to a foreign country of goods in large quantities at prices less than they can be sold at by the foreign manufacturers, generally for the purpose of destroying the foreign industry.

Dumps, To be (down) in the : to be depressed, dejected. 'Dump' was formerly a term for a melancholy strain in music. [Nich. Grimald, *The Garden* l. 22 (1557)]

Dun a person, To : to press a person for payment of a debt. After Joe Dunn, a famous bailiff in the reign of Henry VII. [Bacon, *Apophth.* (1626)]

Dun out of the mire, To draw : to help a person out of a difficulty. In allusion to a medieval English game in which 'Dun' apparently represented a dun-coloured horse. [Chaucer, *Prologue to Maunciple's Tale* (14th cent.)]

Dunce, A : an ignorant person ; a dullard. Orig. a nickname given by the followers of Thomas Aquinas to the disciples of Johannes Duns Scotus (c. 1265–1308), the leader of the school-men.

Dunce-comb, A : an ignoramus. Apparently invented by John Taylor, the Water Poet (1630).

Dundrearies : a style of wearing the whiskers. After Lord Dundreary, a character in Tom Taylor, *Our American Cousin* (1858), as played by Edw. Askew Sothern.

Dundreary, A Lord : a fop: see Dundrearies. Caricaturing an English nobleman.

Dunedin : Edinburgh (in poetry).

Dunghill, To sprinkle incense on a : see Sprinkle.

Dunkers, The : a sect of German-American Baptists. Germ., *tunken*, to dip.

Dunmow bacon, To eat : to live together in conjugal amity. *See* Dunmow flitch, The.

Dunmow Flitch, The : a flitch of bacon awarded annually to a married couple that had had no dispute during the preceding year. The custom was instituted at Great Dunmow, Essex, by Robert Fitzwalter in 1244.

Dunstable, As plain as the road to : *see* Dunstable, Downright. [Heywood, *Proverbes* (1546)]

Dunstable, Downright (Straight) : straightforward. The Roman road from London to Dunstable is proverbial for its flatness and straightness. [Ray, *Proverbs* (1670) ; Fuller, *Worthies* (1662).

Durance vile, In : under close restraint. [W. Kenrick, *Falstaff's Wedding* (1766)]

Duresley, A man of : a liar and swindler. After Dursley in Gloucestershire.

Durham mustard, As peppery as : the city of Durham was formerly famous for its mustard.

Dust beneath one's feet, As : of no account.

Dust, To bite the : (1) to be knocked over and fall to the ground ; (2) to humble oneself; (3) to die. [Homer, *Iliad*, Bk. II, ll. 416–8 ; Ovid, *Metamorphoses*, Bk. IX, ll. 59–61]

Dust in the eyes of .. To throw : to mislead ; to confuse. From the Mohammedan practice of throwing dust in the air in order to mislead or 'confound' their enemies. [Aulus Gellius, *Tragi-Comedy of Calisto and Melibaea*, ll. 484–7 (1519)]

Dust a person's jacket, To : to thrash him. [Early 17th cent.]

Dust off one's feet, To shake the : to leave, with a feeling of contempt. [*Acts*, xiii, 51]

Dust, To write in : to make but a temporary record, soon to be obliterated. [Sir Hy. Wotton, *Elegy of a Woman's Heart* (1602)]

Dutch Auction, A : a method of sale whereby the price of an article is successively reduced until a purchaser is forthcoming.

Dutch Bargain, A : (1) a one-sided bargain. From the couplet :—
'In matters of commerce the fault of the Dutch
Is giving too little and asking too much.'

(2) a bargain concluded by the parties drinking together.

Dutch Comfort : comfort derived from the knowledge that affairs might be worse than they are.

Dutch Concert, A : a great commotion and uproar, such as that made by a company of intoxicated Dutchmen.

Dutch Courage : physical courage induced by intoxication. From a practice said to have been employed by the Dutch in the course of their wars with the English in the reign of Charles II.

Dutch Defence, A : a pretended defence.

Dutch, Double : gibberish; unintelligible language. 'Dutch' was at one time taken to mean 'foreign.' 'Double Dutch' is therefore 'excessively foreign.' [Marlowe, *Faustus*, IV (1604)]

Dutch Feast, A : an entertainment at which the host gets drunk first.

Dutch Gleek : drinking. Gleek is an old game. The suggestion is that the favourite game of the Dutch is drinking.

Dutch Nightingales : frogs.

Dutch, To beat the : to make a statement apparently incredible. Introduced in the course of the wars with the Dutch, when they gained a bad reputation in England.

Dutch Treat, A : hospitality in which each participant pays his own expenses.

Dutch Uncle, To talk like a : to reprove sharply. The Dutch were reputed to exercise severe discipline. An uncle has always been considered an unsatisfactory substitute for a father.

Dynamite Saturday : Jan. 24, 1885. On this day the Fenians attempted to blow up the Houses of Parliament and the Tower of London.

E pur si muove (*Ital.*, and yet it moves) : the remark attributed to Galileo Galilei (1564-1642), the Ital. astronomer, said to have been made immediately after his recantation of the teaching that the earth moved round the sun, a doctrine which was deemed heretical.

Eagle of Brittany, The : Bertrand du Guexlin (1320-80), Constable of France.

Eagle of Divines, The : Thomas Aquinas (1227-74), Ital. Scholastic theologian.

Eagle of Meaux, The : Jacques Bénigne le Bossuet (1627-1704), Bp. of Meaux, orator and writer.

Eagle of the Doctors of France, The : Pierre d'Ailly (1350-1425), astrologer.

Eagle, The Theban : Pindar (518-442 B.C.), who was partly educated at Thebes.

Eagles in one's eyes, To have : to be very keen-sighted. [Peter Pindar, *Sir Joseph Banks and the Emperor of Morocco* (c. 1794)]

Ear, To give : to listen. [*That Few Wordes Shew Wisdome*, ll. 3-4 (1557)]

Ear and out at the other, In at one : of a thing heard yet making no impression on the mind or memory. [*Romaunt of the Rose* (c. 1400); Chaucer, *Troilus and Cressida*, Bk. IV, ll. 432-4 (1369)]

Ear, To turn a deaf : to refuse to listen ; to ignore. [Publilius Syrus, 123]

Ear, To win a person's : to gain his favourable consideration.

Ears of .. To tickle the : to flatter.

Ears, To be all : to be closely attentive. [Milton, *Comus*, l. 574 (1634)]

Ears, To go (fall) together by the : to fight with fists and nails. [Rob. Arnim, *A Nest of Ninnies* (1608)]

Ears, To have long : to be inquisitive. [Lilly, *Compaspe*, III, iv (1584)]

Ears, To hear a thing both sides of the : to be spoken to insistently. [Foote, *The Author*, II, i (1757)]

Ears, To hold by the : to have securely. In allusion to dogs fighting.

Ears, To listen with all one's : to listen most intently.

Ears, To prick up one's : to give sudden and intense attention ; like a startled horse. [Virgil, *Æneid*, I, ll. 151-2 ; Chapman, *All Fools*, III, i (1605) ; Shakespeare, *The Tempest*, IV, i (1609-10)]

Ears, To set by the : to create discord between people. In allusion to a dog-fight. [Anth. Brewer, *Lingua*, IV, i (1607)]

Ears in .. Up to the : overwhelmed by .. Lit., immersed up to the ears. [Shakespeare, *Merry Wives of Windsor* (1598-9)]

Ear-mark, To : to mark as a means of identification ; to set aside for a definite purpose. From the practice of marking a sheep on the ear to show its ownership.

Ear-rent : (1) the call on the patience of a person who has to listen to a tedious discourse ; (2) loss of ears in the pillory.

Ear-shot : the distance the voice will carry. [Beaumont and Fletcher, *Woman Hater*, I, iii (1607)]

Earl of Mar's Grey Breeks : the 21st Regt. of Foot (Royal Scots Fusiliers). On account of the colour of their breeches when under the command of the Earl of Mar (1678–86).

Early bird, An : an early riser ; the first in the field. From the proverb : ' 'Tis the early bird that catches the worm.'

Earnest money (penny) : money, orig. a penny, paid to seal a contract, to show one's good faith.

Earthly Paradise, An : a place of delight. The title of a collection of poems (1868–71) by William Morris. The term had been used previously in 1844 by A. W. Kinglake in reference to Damascus. [*Eothen*, ch. xxvii]

East Indies and be drowned in the Thames, To come safe from the : to survive many difficulties only to succumb when on the point of completing one's journey.

Easily as a fox eats fruit, As : very easily. [Plautus, *Mostellaria*, l. 559]

East Indies for Kentish pippins, To send to the : to take on a long journey when a short one would serve the purpose equally well.

East, The Far : the extreme eastern regions of the world, *i.e.*, Japan, China, etc.

East, The Middle : India, Persia, and their neighbouring countries.

East, The Near : the former Western dominions of the Turkish Empire.

Easterlings : the German Hanseatic traders in England.

Eastern Empire, The : the Greek or the Byzantine Empire ; the eastern half of the Empire when it was divided into two in 364. The Eastern Empire comprised, at its greatest period, South-Eastern Europe, Western Asia, Northern Africa, part of Italy and the Eastern islands. The Eastern Empire came to an end with the capture of Constantinople by the Turks in 1453.

Eastern Question, The : the problems of international politics that centred around the Turkish Empire before 1919.

Eastern States, The : Maine, New Hampshire, Vermont, Massachusetts, Rhode Island and Connecticut, the New England States of the American Union.

Easy Street, In : in easy circumstances.

Easy, To take things : not to permit oneself to be worried.

Eat a person out of house and home, To : to live at the expense of another so as to endanger his resources. [*Paston Letters*, No. 607 (1469) ; Shakespeare, *2 Henry IV*, II, i, 80 (1597–8)]

Eat one's cake and have it too, To : see Cake.

Eat dirt, To : see Dirt, To eat.

Eat its head off, To : (of an animal) to cost more to keep than it produces. [*The Country Farmer's Catechism* (1703)]

Eat one's heart out, To : to suffer from silent annoyance or vexation which it is beyond one's power to remove. [Homer, *Iliad*, Bk. VI, ll. 200–2 ; Lyly, *Anatomy of Wit : Euphues and His Ephoebus* (1579) ; Spenser, *Prosopopoia*, ll. 903–4 (1591)]

Eat one's terms, To : to go through the prescribed course for the English bar-examinations. The course includes the eating of a certain number of dinners during certain terms in hall.

Eat one's words, To : to withdraw one's words ; to retract. [Lyly, *Euphues and His England* (1580)]

Eat the leek, To : to submit to humiliation. From the incident narrated in Shakespeare, *Henry V*, V, i, 10 (1599).

Eat the mad cow, To : to be reduced to extremities, so as to eat even a cow that has died of madness. From the French.

Eatanswill : a corrupt parliamentary constituency. After a borough in Dickens, *Pickwick Papers* (1836) at which an election is held.

Eavesdropper, An : one who listens secretly. Lit., one who hides under the eaves of a house in order to listen.

Ebb, To be at an : to be in difficulties. [Heywood, *Proverbs* (1546)]

Ebony, An ; A son of Ebony : a negro. On account of his complexion. Thomas Fuller (1608–61) used the expression, ' God's image done in ebony.'

Ecce Homo ! (*Lat.*, Behold the Man !) : a picture of Christ as presented to the people by Pilate. From the words of Pilate : ' Behold the man ! ' [*John*, xix, 5]

Echo answers the voice, As the : as effect follows cause. From a Japanese proverb.

Echo, To applaud to the : to applaud so loudly as almost to call forth an echo. [Shakespeare, *Macbeth*, V, iii, 53 (1606)]

Echo a person's opinions, To : to share or imitate a person's opinions.

Echo verses : verses in which each line repeats the final syllables of the preceding one without destroying the sense.

Eckhardt, A faithful : a very faithful man. After a character in a Germ. legend.

Ecstatic Doctor, The : the Divine Doctor (*q.v.*).

Eden, An : a place of delightful scenery. After the Garden of Adam and Eve. [*Genesis*, ii, etc.]

Eden of Germany, The : Baden. On account of its splendid scenery.

Edge of one's appetite, The : the first keenness of one's appetite.

Edge off, To take : to deprive of zest.

Edge, To set one's teeth on : to grate upon one. [*Ezekiel*, xviii, 2]

Edge upon, To set an : to sharpen, intensify. [Lyly, *Euphues and His England* (1580)]

Edge upon, Not to put too fine an : not to conceal anything or subdue one's ardour; to speak plainly.

Edged tools, To play with : to amuse oneself with, or to employ, something that may cause one serious harm. [Ascham, *The Schoolmaster*, Bk. II ; *True Tragedy of Richard III* (1594)]

Edinburgh of America, The : Albany, New York. On account of its magnificent buildings and situation.

Edwin and Angelina : a pair of lovers. It forms the title of a ballad by Oliver Goldsmith (1764).

Eel, An : a New-Englander.

Eel, A salt : a rope's end. An eel's skin was formerly used as a lash.

Eel by the tail, To hold an : to have a precarious hold over .. [Heywood, *Proverbes* (1546) ; Hy. Porter, *Two Angry Women of Abington*, ll. 2410–2 (1599) ; *Terence in English* (1614)]

Eel by the tail, To skin an : to go the wrong way about a business.

Eel of science by the tail, To hold the : to have an elementary knowledge of a subject which is quickly lost.

Eel, To get used to it like a skinned : to get inured to trouble or hardship. [Peter Pindar, *Ode to Townsend* (1792)]

Eel-skins, A merchant of : a rag and bone collector. [Heywood, *Proverbes* (1562)]

Egalité, Philippe : Philippe, Duke of Orleans (1747–93), who assumed the name on his adhesion to the French Revolution.

Egeria, An : a source of inspired wisdom. After Egeria, the Roman nymph who is said to have instructed Numa Pompilius, the second king of Rome.

Egg, A bad : a person or project that results in disappointment ; one who is commercially or morally liable to suspicion. After Thomas Egg, an American, who, having committed crime, was known by his neighbours as Bad Egg.

Egg, A Nuremberg : a watch. From their invention at Nuremberg, about 1500. They were orig. egg-shaped.

Egg dance, An : a task of extreme difficulty. Properly, a dance blindfold with eggs scattered around.

Egg Feast (Saturday) : the Saturday before Shrove Tuesday, when the students of Oxford are provided with Pasch eggs.

Eggs, As like as two : exactly alike. [Seneca, *Apocolocymtosis*, ch. 11 ; Shakespeare, *Winter's Tale*, I, ii (1611)]

Eggs for money, To take : to be imposed upon ; to be bullied into taking something worthless at a relatively high price. [Shakespeare, *Winter's Tale*, I, ii, 161 (1611)]

Egg in a person's pocket, To break the : to spoil his plan.

Egg, In the : in embryo ; in the earliest stage.

Egg Saturday : *see* Egg Feast.

Eggs in one basket, To put all one's : to risk all on one venture. [Cervantes, *Don Quixote*, ch. ix (1605)]

Eggs is eggs, As sure as : absolutely sure. Perhaps a corruption of the logician's formula : x is x.

Eggs on the spit, To have : to have business in hand.

Eggs, To teach one's grandmother to suck : to attempt to instruct one who is better informed than oneself.

Eggs, To tread upon : to walk cautiously, as if eggs were on the ground.

Egg-trot, An : a quiet trot, as if one were carrying eggs.

Eglantine, As sweet as : eglantine is the sweet-briar.

Egyptian, An : a gypsy ; a pseudo-gypsy. Formerly supposed to have come from Egypt.

Egyptian bondage : harsh bondage ; like that of the Israelites in Egypt.

Elephant, A white : *see* White.

Eleusinian Mysteries : the Mysteries of Demeter, which were celebrated at Eleusis in Attica.

Eleventh hour, At the : at the latest possible moment. [*Matthew*, xx, 1]

Elf-locks : tangled hair. Orig. it was supposed that they were entangled by elves, and that the straightening of them would cause misfortune.

Elgin Marbles, The : the Grk. sculptures from the Parthenon brought to England by the Earl of Elgin in 1801–3. They comprise the finest extant examples of sculpture.

Elijah's Mantle : succession to office. From the mantle cast by Elijah over Elisha in order to designate him as his successor as prophet in Israel. [I *Kings*, xix, 19]

Eliott's Light Horse : *see* Eliott's Tailors.

Eliott's Tailors : the 15th Hussars. The regt. originated in a number of tailors recruited by a Colonel Eliott in 1759.

Elixir vitae (*Lat.*, elixir of life) : a supposititious drug long sought for by the alchemists of the Middle Ages ; it was supposed to prolong life indefinitely.

Elizabeth, The spacious days (times) of : the illustrious period of Queen Elizabeth's reign (1558–1603).

Elizabethans, The (Great) : the company of great men — poets, dramatists, statesmen, etc., who flourished during the reign of Queen Elizabeth (1558–1603).

Elm City, The : New Haven, Connecticut. On account of the number of its elm-trees.

Eloquent Doctor, The : Peter Aureolus (14th cent.), Archbishop of Aix.

Eloquent, The Old Man : (1) Isocrates (436–338 B.C.), Grk. orator ; (2) William Ewart Gladstone (1809–98), Eng. statesman.

Eltchi, The Great : Lord Stratford de Redcliffe (Sir Stratford Canning) (1786–1880), British Ambassador to the Porte. Turk., *elchee*, ambassador.

Eltham motion : a perpetual-motion machine exhibited at Eltham. Alluded to by Ben Jonson and others.

Elysian Fields, The ; Elysium : a place of delight. After the mythical abode of the Blessed after death.

Elzevir : a style of printing-type as used by the Elzevir family at Leyden and Amsterdam (1583–1712). ' Elzevir Editions ' of the classics were at one time prized by book-collectors.

Emathian Conqueror, The : Alexander the Great. After Emathia (Macedonia and Thessaly).

K

Embarras de richesse (*Fr.*, embarrassment of riches) : an excess of wealth, resources. [Lord Chesterfield, *Letters*, II (1750)]

Ember Days : four religious periods of fasting : early in Lent, Whitsunday, Holy Cross Day, St. Lucia's Day. Anglo-Sax., *ymbren*, circuit.

Ember Weeks : the weeks in which the Ember Days fall.

Emberings : the fasts of the Ember Weeks.

Embryo, In : in an early, undeveloped stage. [*Verney Papers* (1636–7)]

Emerald Isle, The : Ireland. On account of the predominant greenness of the land. First used by William Brennan (1754–1820), Irish poet, in *Erin* (1798).

Emerald, To look through an : to look in a spirit of happiness and contentment. [Lyly, *Euphues and His England* (1580)]

Emergency man, An : one who can be employed in an emergency, esp. to assist in evictions in Ireland.

Emigrés (*Fr.*, emigrated [ones]) : Royalist refugees from France during the period of the first Revolution.

Empire City, The : *see* Empire State.

Empire Day : May 24, the birthday of Queen Victoria ; a British imperial festival.

Empire State (City), The : New York, as the most important of the States and cities of the Union. The title was given to the state by George Washington in reply to an address by the common council of New York City (Dec. 2, 1784).

Empire State of the South, The : Georgia.

Empress of the North, The : Edinburgh, so-called by Sir Walter Scott. [*Marmion*, ca. 4, st. 32 (1808)]

Enceladus, An : a giant. After a giant in Grk. mythology.

Enclave, An : a piece of territory under the jurisdiction of one Power surrounded by territory under the jurisdiction of another.

Encourager les autres, Pour (*Fr.*, to encourage the others) : from Voltaire, *Candide* (1759), in allusion to the shooting of Admiral Byng for his failure to relieve Minorca (1757).

Encyclopædia, A walking : *see* Walking.

Encyclopædists, The : Diderot, d'Alembert, Voltaire, Rousseau, Montesquieu, and others, who edited and wrote the famous French *Encyclopédie* (1751–65).

End, At a loose : with no definite occupation.

End goes forward, Not to care which : to be negligent or reckless. [Withal, *Dictionarie* (1608)]

End of one's tether, To come to the : to reach one's limit. In allusion to a goat tied to a stake.

End of the chapter, To : until the end.

End up, To keep (hold) one's : to do one's part on terms of equality.

Ends meet, To make both : to fit one's expenditure to one's income.

Ends, To burn the candle at both : to overwork by encroaching on time that should be devoted to rest or recreation.

Endymion, An : a beautiful youth. After Endymion of Grk. legend.

Endymion's sleep : endless sleep. From the Grk. legend of Endymion, on whom Jupiter conferred eternal youth in the form of unbroken sleep.

Enemy but his own, Nobody's : one who by weakness of character, while attempting to benefit others generally fails, and seldom does anything of advantage to himself. The phrase was originated by Anacharsis, the Scythian (fl. 592 B.C.), one of the sages of antiquity.

Enemy ? How goes the : what is the time ? 'Time' in the sense of the enemy, the destroyer, of man. [Dickens, *Nicholas Nickleby*, ch. xix (1838)]

Enemy of mankind, The : Satan.

Enfant de la Fortune, L' (*Fr.*, the child of fortune) : André Masséna (1756–1817), Fr. marshal ; the title given to him by Napoleon after the battle of Rivoli (1807).

Enfant gâté, An (*Fr.*) : a spoilt child.

Enfant terrible, An (*Fr.*, terrible child) : a person habitually getting those responsible for him into trouble.

Enfants de Dieu (*Fr.*, children of God) : a name assumed by the Camissards (Fr. Protestants) who revolted in 1702.

England, Young : *see* Young.

England's darling : Hereward the Wake (d. 1072), a Saxon hero.

English Aristophanes, The : Samuel Foote (1722–77). After Aristophanes (448–385 B.C.), the famous Grk. comedian.

English as she is spoke : colloquial English.

English Attila, The : Oliver Cromwell (1599–1658). After Attila (d. 453), the conquering king of the Huns.

English Diana, The : Queen Elizabeth (1533–1603). After Diana, the Roman goddess of the chase, the moon, etc.

English Ennius, The : Layamon (fl. 1200). After Quintus Ennius (239–170 B.C.), an early Roman poet.

English Garrison, The : the landlords of Ireland. So-called by the Irish Land League.

English Hobbema, The : John Crome, the elder (1769–1821), leading painter of the Norwich School of landscape-painters. After Meindert Hobbema (1638–1709), the Dutch landscape-painter.

English Homer, The : *see* Homer, The British.

English Justinian, The : *see* Justinian.

English Juvenal, The : John Oldham (1653–83). After Juvenal (60–140), the Roman satirist.

English Mersenne, The : John Collins (1625–83). After Marin Mersenne (1588–1648), Fr. philosopher and mathematician.

English Naples, The : Bournemouth.

English Pale, The : *see* Pale.

English Petrarch, The : Sir Philip Sidney (1554–86). After Francesco Petrarch (1304–74), the Ital. poet. So-called by Sir Walter Raleigh.

English Pindar, The : (1) Abraham Cowley (1618–67), so-called by George, Duke of Buckingham (1628–87) ; (2) Thos. Gray (1716–71), so-called on the tablet to his memory in Westminster Abbey. After Pindar (522–443 B.C.), the famous Theban lyric poet.

English Poussin, The : Richard Cooper (d. 1806). After Nicholas Poussin (1594–1665), the Ital. painter.

English Rabelais, The : (1) Jonathan Swift (1667–1745), so-called by Voltaire ; (2) Laurence Sterne (1713–68) ; (3) Thomas Amory (1691–1788). After François Rabelais (1490–1553), the Fr. satirist.

English St. Sebastian, The : St. Edmund, the martyr-king of East Anglia. After St. Sebastian (d. 288). In both cases the martyrdom (shooting by arrows) was similar.

English Sappho, The : Mrs. Mary Darly Robinson (1758–1800), Eng. actress, novelist, and poet. After Sappho (fl. 611–592 B.C.), the early Grk. poetess.

English Seneca, The : Joseph Hall (1574–1656), Eng. bishop and author. After

Seneca (3 B.C. to 65 A.D.), Roman philosopher and statesman.

English Solomon, The : (1) Henry VII (1457–1509), so-called by John Skelton, the poet, and by Lord Bacon ; (2) James I (1566–1625).

English Terence, The : Richard Cumberland (1732–1811). After Terence (194–159 B.C.), the Roman dramatist. So-called by Oliver Goldsmith.

English, To get to one's : to get into a passion.

English Virgil, The : *see* Virgil.

Englishman's castle, An : his house, into which by law the bailiff cannot enter without permission of the occupier. From the proverb, ' An Englishman's house is his castle ! '

Englishman's meal, The : tea. So-called by Mr. J. W. Lowther, Speaker of the House of Commons, in June, 1920.

Enlightened Doctor, The : Raymund Lully, of Palma (1234–1315).

Enniskilliners, The : the 6th Dragoon Guards. On account of their origin from among the defenders of Enniskillen in 1689.

Ennuis, The English, The French, The Spanish : *see* English, French, Spanish.

Enoch Arden, An : a man who returns after a long disappearance to find his wife happy as the wife of another man. From a poem so-entitled by Alfred, Lord Tennyson (1864).

Ensign, The Blue : the flag of the Royal Naval Reserve.

Ensign, The Red : the flag of the British merchant-service.

Ensign, The White : the flag of the Royal Navy and of the Royal Yacht Squadron.

Entelechy : the realization of an ideal. After the kingdom of Queen Quintessence in Rabelais, *Gargantua and Pantagruel* (1532).

Entente, An : a friendly understanding, less definite than an Alliance, between Powers in relation to foreign affairs.

Entente Cordiale, The : the friendly understanding between England and France, entered into in 1905, which later developed into a formal Alliance. The friendly relations between France and England were first thus described by Louis Philippe in a speech from the throne in January, 1843.

Entire : ale, as distinguished from ' Cooper,' which is half ale and ha f porter.

En-tout-cas, An (*Fr.*, in all cases): a light umbrella serving also as a sunshade.

Entre nous (*Fr.*, between ourselves): in confidence. [Christopher Anstey, *Poetical Epistles*, Letter I (1767)]

Eparchy, An: (1) an administrative division in Greece; (2) a diocese of the Russian Orthodox Church.

Ephesian, An: a drunkard; a boon companion. [Shakespeare, 2 *Henry IV*, II, ii (1597–8)]

Ephesian Poet, The: Hipponax (fl. 540 B.C.), who was born at Ephesus.

Ephesus, Letters of: bribes. The original *Letters of Ephesus* were magical writings that assured success.

Epicure, An: one who is an expert in taste of food and drink. After Epicurus (340–270 B.C.), the Grk. philosopher.

Epicurean, An: one devoted to refined pleasures; luxurious.

Epicurus of China, The: Tao-tse (6th cent. B.C.). After Epicurus (342–270 B.C.), Grk. philosopher.

Epimenides' sleep: a lengthy sleep which induces wisdom. After the miraculous sleep of 57 years' duration of Epimenides, of Crete, as told by Diogenes Laertius, in his *Lives of the Greek Philosophers*.

Epiphany: Jan. 6, a Church festival held in celebration of the appearance of Christ to the Wise Men of the East.

Epitaph, To lie like an: from the reputation attaching to epitaphs as a class of exaggerating or inventing the virtues of their subjects. [Ben. Franklin, *Poor Richard's Almanac* (1742)]

Equality State, The: Wyoming. The first State in which women were granted the suffrage.

Eques Auratus, An (*Lat.*, gilded knight): a knight-bachelor, who was formerly entitled to wear gilded armour.

Era of Good Feeling, The: 1817 to 1824, in Amer. history, when there were no strong political divisions. The phrase was coined as the title of a leading article in the Boston *Sentinel* on July 12, 1817.

Erebus, As dark as: in mythology, Erebus is the place of darkness between earth and Hades. [Shakespeare, *Merchant of Venice*, V, i, 87 (1596)]

Erin: a poetical name for Ireland. Celtic, *eri*, western.

Ermine, To wear the: to be a judge. From the ermine trimmings on the official robes of British judges.

Erotic School, The: the Amer. school of poets and novelists, Amélie Rives, Edgar Saltus, Gertrude Atherton and others, who treat of the passion of love. The phrase first appeared in Amer. newspapers in 1888. From Eros, the Grk. god of Love.

Erra Pater, An: an almanac. After a medieval astrologer.

Erudite of the Romans, The most: Marcus Terentius Varro (116–27 B.C.), Roman man-of-letters.

Erythrœan Main, The: the Indian Ocean. Its classical name.

Esculapian: medical. After Esculapios, a physician, mentioned by Homer.

Esperanto: the name of an artificial universal language invented by Dr. L. Zamenhoff (1887) under the *nom-de-plume* of 'Dr. Esperanto.'

Esprit d'escalier (*Fr.*, staircase wit): a happy afterthought that occurs to one's mind too late for useful expression to be given to it, *e.g.*, when one is already descending the staircase on departing from the gathering at which it could have been utilized.

Esprit de corps (*Fr.*, spirit of the body): devotion of an individual to the moral interests of the body of which he is a member. [Horace Walpole, *Letters*, II (1780)]

Esprit fort, An (*Fr.*, a strong mind): one who is superior to common prejudices; a freethinker. [*Tavernier's Travels*, II, p. 154 (1684)]

Esses, A collar of the: *see* Collar of the SS.

Essex Junto: a political group in U.S. history at the end of 18th and beginning of 19th cents. After Essex County, Massachusetts, with which several of the leaders were connected.

Essex lion, As valiant as an: timorous. Calf and sheep abound in Essex. A proverbial saying. An Essex lion is a calf. [Ray, *Proverbs* (1670)]

Essex man (woman), An: a simpleton. [Killigrew, *The Parson's Wedding*, III, v (1663)]

Essex stile, An: a ditch. On account of the number of marshes in Essex.

Estate, The Fifth: *see* Fifth estate.

Estate, The Fourth: *see* Fourth.

Estate, The Third: *see* Third.

Estates, The Four: the Lords Spiritual, the Lords Temporal, the Commons, the Press. The fourth is added humorously, or sarcastically. Its earliest use is attributed to Edmund Burke. *See also* Third Estate, Fourth Estate, Fifth Estate.

Estates, The Three ; Estates of the Realm : the Lords Spiritual, the Lords Temporal, the Commons.

Et tu, Brute (*Lat.*, you, too, Brutus) : a reproof conveying a charge of base ingratitude. Attributed to Julius Cæsar after Brutus had stabbed him. [Shakespeare, *Julius Cæsar*, III, i (1601)]

Eternal City, The : Rome. The phrase in the form of ' Eternal Rome,' was first used in literature by Tibullus, the Rom. poet (54–19 B.C.). In Virgil, *Æneid* (I, 79) Rome's eternal empire is given by Jupiter.

Ethiopian white, To wash the : *see* Wash.

Eton Montem : *see* Montem.

Ettrick Shepherd, The : James Hogg (1770–1835), the Scottish poet and shepherd.

Eucrates, More shifts than : full of shifts. After Eucrates, one of the archons of Athens, who was famous for his shiftiness.

Eumæus, A Second : after Eumæus, the faithful swineherd of Ulysses.

Euphrosyne, An : a happy young woman. After one of the three Graces, the goddess of Joy.

Euphues, To speak (talk) : to use flowery language : *see* Euphuism.

Euphuism : florescence of language. After Lyly, cultivator of a new style, in his works, *Euphues, or the Anatomy of Wit* (1579) and *Euphues and His England* (1580).

Eurasia : Europe and Asia, regarded as one continent.

Eurasian, A : a child of mixed European and Asiatic parentage.

Eureka ! (*Grk.*, I have found it !) : an exclamation of success. Attributed to Archimedes (287–212 B.C.), on discovering the law of specific gravity.

Euripus, A : a dangerous fluctuation of affairs. After a dangerous strait between Bœotia and Eubœa.

Euterpean : relating to music. After Euterpe, the muse that presided over wind-instruments.

Evangelic Doctor, The : John Wycliffe (1324–84), precursor of the Reformation.

Evening of one's age, The : old age, esp. a placid one. [Bacon, *Spurious*

Essays : Essay on Death (early 17th cent.)]

Ever-sworded, The : the 29th Regt. of Foot, now the Worcestershire Regt. From an instruction issued, after the surprise and massacre of a part of the regiment by the French in 1746, that they should always wear their swords.

Ever-victorious Army, The : the army of Charles George Gordon, with which he suppressed the Taeping Rebellion in 1864.

Everglad State, The : Florida. On account of its wide tracts of grass-land and water.

Everlasting staircase, The : the treadmill.

Evil days, Fallen on : subject to misfortune ; reduced in circumstances.

Evil eye, The : the supposed magical gift of causing harm to others merely by looking at them. This belief is very widespread and of great antiquity. It was prevalent among the Greeks and Romans and a reference to is to be found in *The Wisdom of Solomon*.

Evil Eye, An : a harmful glance ; a look of hatred. [*Matthew*, xx, 15.]

Evil genius, An : one who influences another for evil. Properly, the evil one of the two spirits—the other one is the good—which are supposed to accompany everyone through life.

Evil May Day : Mayday, 1517, when the London Apprentices attacked the foreign residents.

Evil principle, The : the devil.

Evovae : an abbreviation of the last two words of the doxology sEcUlOrUm-AmEn to be found in Latin psalters.

Ewe-lamb, A : an unique and much prized possession. [II *Samuel*, xii, 1–14]

Ewig-weibliche, Das (*Germ.*, the eternal feminine) : [Goethe, *Faust*, Pt. II, v]

Ex cathedra (*Lat.*, from the chair) : (speaking) with authority. The ' chair' is the throne of the Pope.

Ex libris, An (*Lat.*, from the books) : a book-plate.

Ex luce lucellum (*Lat.*, out of a light a little gain) : motto suggested by Robert Lowe, Lord Sherbrooke (1811–92), on the occasion of his abortive proposals for a tax on matches (1871).

Ex officio (*Lat.*, by virtue of office). [More, *Apology* (1533)]

Ex oriente lux (*Lat.*, light from the East).

Ex parte (*Lat.*, out of a part) : one-sided ; partisan. Orig. a legal term. [A. C., *Answer to a Letter of a Jesuited Gentleman*, p. 4 (1601)]

Ex pede Herculem (Herclem) (*Lat.*, from the foot, Hercules) : judgment by sample. From the legend that Pythagoras calculated the height of Hercules by comparison of the length of the Hercules stadium at Olympia with that of an ordinary stadium.

Ex post facto (*Lat.*, from after the deed) : of a law adopted to deal with an offence already committed ; of a conclusion arrived at theoretically after the result is known.

Ex uno omnes (*Lat.*, from one, all) : of a general inference drawn from a solitary example. [Virgil, *Æneid*, Bk. II, ll. 65–6]

Ex voto (*Lat.*, from a vow) : of a thank-offering made in fulfilment of a vow.

Exalt one's horn, To : to offer resistance. From the biblical sense of 'horn' as a symbol of power or means of defence. [*Psalms*, lxxv, 5, 10]

Excalibur, An : a trusty sword. After the magical sword of King Arthur.

Excelsior State, The : New York. On account of its motto 'Excelsior' (Higher).

Exchange wench, An : a woman who kept a stall at an Exchange. The reputation of this class of women was low.

Exclusionists, The : the supporters of the Bill to exclude the Duke of York, afterwards James II, from the English throne.

Exellers, The : the 40th Regt. of Foot. From the Roman numerals XL (forty).

Exeter Hall : the Evangelical Party in the Church of England. After the former locale in London of their May Meetings (*q.v.*).

Exeter Hall, The Bray of : the opposition of the Evangelical Party to the May-nooth College Endowment. From a speech by Lord Macaulay in the House of Commons, April, 1845.

Exeter's Daughter, The Duke of : *see* Duke.

Extinct volcano, An : a person who has lost his former power or force.

Extinguish the fire, To take oil to : *see* Take.

Extol to the skies, To : to praise extravagantly.

Extra pull, An : an advantage. A drinking metaphor from the extra pull at the handle of the beer machine.

Eye for an eye and tooth for a tooth : the law of retaliation. [*Exodus*, xxi, 24]

Eye of a needle, To put a rope to an : *see* Put.

Eye of day, The : (1) the Sun ; (2) the daisy, which opens with the sun. [Chaucer, *Legende of Good Women*, Prologue, ll. 182–5 (14th cent.)]

Eye of Greece, The : (1) Corinth ; (2) Athens. *See* Eyes of Greece.

Eye of heaven, The : the sun. [Spenser, *Faerie Queen*, I, iii, 4 (1590–6)] *See also* Eyes of heaven.

Eye of the Baltic, The : Gottland.

Eye of the night, The : the moon. [Pindar, *Odes : Olympia*, III, 33–6 ; Rich. Glover, *Leonidas*, Bk. III (1737)]

Eye of the Storm, The : an opening between storm-clouds.

Eye of the World, The : (1) literature ; so-called by Carlyle ; (2) the sun.

Eye of .. To catch the : to attract the attention of .. [*The Spectator*, No. 224 (1711)]

Eye on .. To keep an : to keep under observation.

Eye parley : communication by means of interchange of looks.

Eye, The apple of one's : *see* Apple.

Eye to eye, To see : to be in perfect agreement.

Eye, To see with half an : of something that is obvious. [Northbrooke, *Treatise against Dicing* (1577)]

Eye to the main chance, To have an : to keep one's own advantage always before one. A dicing metaphor. [Lyly, *Euphues : Anatomy of Wit* (1579) ; Rob. Wilson, *Three Ladies of London*, II, l. 1253 (1584)]

Eye upon .. To have (keep) an : to keep under one's observation. [Dryden, *Sir Martin Marr-all*, IV, i (1668)]

Eyes and ears of an army, The : the cavalry.

Eyes and ears of the State, The : the ambassadors. So-called by Sansovino. [*Concetti Politici*, 276]

Eyes at a person, To make : to ogle ; to look lovingly at a person.

Eyes at the back of one's head, To have : to be mentally very alert. [Apostollius, *Proverbia*, xii, 94]

Eyes in .. Up to one's : immersed in ; fully engaged in.

Eyes of a fleet, The : (1) cruisers ; (2) airships.

Eyes of Greece, The : Athens and Sparta. [Milton, *Paradise Regained*, IV, 240 (1671)] *See also* Eye of Greece.

Eyes of heaven (night), The : the stars. [Shakespeare, *Hamlet*, II, ii, 540 (1602–3)] *See also* Eye of heaven.

Eyes of the world, In the : in public opinion.

Eyes open, To have (keep) one's : to be wideawake, fully alert.

Eyes open, To sleep with one's : to be always on the *qui vive*. [Lyly, *Euphues and His England* (1580)]

Eyes, The Almond : the Chinese. From the shape of their eyes.

Eyes, The King's : the principal officers of the state.

Eyes to draw straws, To have : to be nearly asleep ; from the appearance of candlelight through eyelids almost closed.

Eyes to the blind : a staff. In allusion to the staff given by Athena to Tiresias in place of the eyes of which she had deprived him.

Eyes to .. To close one's : to refuse to see or acknowledge .. [*The History of Hamlet, Prince of Denmark*, ch. 3 (1608)]

Eye-opener, An : that which suddenly casts light on something hitherto concealed, or indefinite ; a surprise.

Eye-sore, An : that which offends the eye. [Lyly, *Euphues and His England* (1580)]

Eye-teeth, To cut one's : to pass out of childhood.

Eye-teeth, To draw a person's : to moderate his self-confidence.

Eye-teeth, To have one's : to be well awake to current events and their meaning.

Eye-wash : means of deceit ; 'bunkum.'

F, To be branded on the forehead with an : to have the appearance of a rogue. From the letter F (felon) at one time branded on convicted criminals who had obtained the Benefit of Clergy (*q.v.*).

F's The three : Fair rents, Fixity of tenure, and Free sale. An Eng. political claim (1880–90) for agriculturists.

Fabian, A : a member of the Fabian Society, founded in 1884 for the promulgation of socialist ideas. After Quintus Fabius Maximus, a Roman General (275–203 B.C.), whose delaying tactics, avoiding battle while harassing the enemy, earned him the cognomen 'Cunctator' (the 'Delayer.').

Fabian tactics : delaying tactics. After those adopted by the Roman General Quintus Fabius Maximus (275–203 B.C.) in his battles with the Carthaginians.

Fabius, The American : George Washington (1732–99).

Fabius, The French : Anne, Duc de Montmorency, Constable of France (1493–1567).

Fabricius, As simple (contented) as : very honest and frank. After Fabricius Luscinus Caius (fl. 285–278 B.C.), Roman Consul and General, famous for his incorruptibility.

Face against, To set one's : to oppose. In allusion to the expression of one's face when determined on opposition.

Face it with a card of ten, To : to adopt an impudent demeanour. Apparently a metaphor derived from a card-game. A card of ten was a tenth card. [Ben Jonson, *The New Inne*, I, iii (1631) ; Shakespeare, *Taming of the Shrew* (1596)]

Face of Europe, To change the : to alter the boundaries of the European states.

Face of it, On the : apparently.

Face out a thing, To : to carry oneself through a difficult situation by means of effrontery. [Wever, *Lusty Juventus*, l. 683 (1560)]

Face the music, To : to appear before one's judges, usually the public, and explain one's actions. Four possible derivations have been suggested. From (1) the actor, who in facing the music faces the public, his critics ; (2) the difficulty in training army-horses to remain quiet in the company of a regimental band ; (3) the drumming-out of men dismissed by the U.S. army ; (4) the muster of militia men who are drawn up in ranks facing the band.

Face to face : in the presence of one another. [*Marriage of Wit and Science*, II, ii (1570)]

Face, To pull a long : to look discontented or disappointed. [Peter Pindar, *Expostulatory Odes*, Ode xv (1789)]

Face to .. To have the : to have the impudence to .. [1600]

Face, To show one's : to put in an appearance.

Face upon .. To put a good : to make the best of .. [Heywood, *Proverbes* (1546)]

Faces, To make : to pull grimaces.

Faces under one hood, To keep two : to be deceitful or double-faced. [Heywood, *Proverbes* (1546)]

Facer, A : a situation, or a problem, almost hopeless of solution. From a ' facer,' a blow in the face, in the slang of the Ring.

Facile princeps (*Lat.*, easily first) : [Cicero, *De Divinatione*, II, 42]

Facilis descensus Averni (*Lat.*, the descent of the Avernus is easy) : it is easy to degenerate or fall. From Virgil, *Æneid*, vi, 126. Avernus, a lake in Italy, was supposed to be the entrance to Hades.

Facing-both-ways, Mr. : an insincere man who pretends agreement with both parties. After a character in Bunyan, *Pilgrim's Progress* (1678).

Facings, To put one through his : to call to account ; to examine searchingly. A military-drill metaphor.

Façon de parler (*Fr.*, manner of speaking) : customary mode of speech.

Factotum, A : one who performs a variety of services for another. From ' Dominus fac totum .. ' (Lord, do everything ..). [Greene, *Groat's Worth of Wit* (1592)]

Fad, A : a personal (generally unconventional) view or pursuit of little consequence to which one devotes exaggerated importance ; a hobby.

Faddist, A : a person possessed by, or possessing, a fad (*q.v.*).

Fag end of .. The : the very last portion of .. A contraction of ' fatigued ' (spent) end. [Rob. Tailor, *The Hog Hath Lost His Pearl*, I, i (1614)]

Faggot : *see also* Fagot.

Faggot stitch, A : a fancy stitch in needlework in imitation of a faggot.

Fagin, A : a trainer of young thieves and receiver of their stolen articles. After a character in Dickens, *Oliver Twist* (1838).

Fagot (Faggot), A deceitful : a term of abuse applied to a woman.

Fagot (Faggot) vote : a qualification for the franchise specially created by the division of one qualifying property into several smaller ones. In 18th cent. a person hired to fill a vacancy in a regiment or muster was termed a ' fagot.'

Fainéant, Le Roi (*Fr.*, King Do-nothing) : the occupant of an office who leaves all the power and responsibility to another. The Rois Fainéants of history were Clovis II of Neustria

(d. 656) and his ten successors ; they left the government to the Mayors of the Palace, who ultimately usurped the throne.

Faint-hearted, To be : to be easily discouraged. [Marlowe, *Tamburlaine*, Pt. II (1590)]

Fair and square : straightforward. [Fr. Bacon, *Proph.* 443 (1604)]

Fair City, The : Perth. On account of its beautiful situation.

Fair day's work, A : a full day's work. [John Still, *Gammer Garton's Needle*, I, iii (1566)]

Fair game : *see* Game (Fair).

Fair Maid of February, The : the snowdrop, which blooms in February.

Fair Maid of Kent, The : Joan Plantagenet, daughter of the Earl of Kent.

Fair Maid of Norway, The : Margaret, daughter of Eric II of Norway, and heiress to the crown of Scotland (d. 1290).

Fair play : just behaviour as between competitors or enemies.

Fair Quakeress, The : Hannah Lightfoot, wife of George III before his accession to the throne.

Fair sex, The : the female sex. Fr., *le beau sexe*. [Dryden, *Preface* to Wm. Walsh, *Dialogue Concerning Women* (1691)]

Fair trade : (1) smuggling [18th cent.] ; (2) the protection of home-trade by the imposition of import duties.

Fairest jewel in the Imperial Crown, The : India.

Fair-weather friends : supposed friends who desert one in time of trouble.

Fairy ring (circle), A : a circular mark in the grass, popularly supposed to be caused by the night-dancing of fairies ; really due to the growth of fungi.

Fait accompli, A (*Fr.*, accomplished fact) : [De Quincey, *On Murder Considered as a Fine Art* (1827)]

Fake, To : to disguise, or alter, with a fraudulent intention. Orig. thieves' slang. From Germ., *fegen*, to clean, to sweep ; or from Fakir (*q.v.*).

Fakir ; Fakeer, A (*Arab.*, poor man) : an Oriental begging monk.

Falk Laws : Prussian anti-Catholic legislation, adopted between 1872 and 1879 at the instance of Paul Falk (1827-1900).

Fall, The : the autumn ; the period of the year in which the leaves fall. An Amer. revival of an Eng. meaning of the word which had become obsolete.

Fall foul of .. To : to quarrel with .. A nautical metaphor. [*Newes from Sea* (1616)]

Fall of the leaf, The : the autumn. *See* Fall, The.

Fall into line with .. To : to agree with .. ; to agree to follow the same course as ..

Fall, To ride for a : *see* Ride.

Fall to the ground, To : to fail.

Fall upon one's feet, To : to escape from trouble with the assistance of good-luck.

Fall with .. To try a : to enter into a contest with .. A wrestling metaphor.

Falls City : Louisville, Kentucky, which overlooks the falls of the Ohio River.

Fallen woman, A : a woman who has fallen, or descended from the level of chastity.

Falling sickness, The : epilepsy. [*Look about you*, I, ii (1600)]

False as a fox, As : utterly false. [Montgommery, *Cherry and Slae* (1597)]

False as a Greek, As : *see* Græca Fides.

False as God is true, As : utterly false. [Heywood, *Proverbes* (1546)]

False as hell, As : utterly false. [Shakespeare, *Othello*, IV, ii, 40 (1604)]

False as the wind, As : utterly false. The instability of the wind has from early times made it a symbol for falseness.

False as Waghorn, As : utterly false. Waghorn, according to a Scottish proverb, was nineteen times falser than the devil and was crowned King of Liars.

False Colours : *see* Colours.

Falstaff, A : a self-indulgent, free-living, jolly, elderly man. After a character in Shakespeare, *Henry IV* (1596–8) and *Merry Wives of Windsor* (1598–9).

Familiar, A : (1) a servant of the Holy Inquisition ; (2) an assistant to a magician.

Familiar spirits : demons supposed to be in close connection with man.

Familist, A : a member of a Dutch religious sect, ' The Family of Love,' which taught love for all people. Founded by David George (d. 1556).

Family circle, The : the family at home. ' Circle ' refers to the Norman period, when the fire was in the centre of the living-room.

Family man, A : a man of domestic habits.

Family of Love : *see* Familist.

Fan with a feather, To : to employ wholly inefficient means to achieve one's end. From an ancient Grk. proverb.

Fancy, The : pugilists ; the prize-ring. From ' fancy ' as the equivalent of ' sports.'

Fancy Franchise, A : an out-of-the-ordinary qualification for a vote, such as an educational standard, the number of one's family, etc.

Fancy price, A : a price far above the intrinsic value.

Fancy-free : not yet affected by the sentiment of love ; not yet engaged to be married.

Fandango, A : a Spanish and Spanish-American dance ; probably of negro origin.

Fanfaron ; Fanfaronade : a boaster ; boasting. One who behaves as if announced by a fanfare of trumpets. Span., *fanfarron*, a bully.

Fantee, To go : to relapse into barbarism.

Fantique (Fantigue), To be in a : to be anxious or excited. [Geo. Colman, jun., *Sylvester Daggerwood*, II (1795)]

Far and away : very much. [Heywood, *Proverbes* (1546)]

Far-fetched : (of an argument, story, etc.) scarcely credible. Lit., fetched from afar. [Greene, *Selimus*, Pt. I, l. 306 (1594)]

Fare : (1) a person conveyed ; (2) the price charged for conveying him. [(1) Thos. Kyd, *Jeronimo*, Pt. I (1591)]

Farmer George : George III. On account of his dress and habits, and also of the profits he made out of farming at Windsor.

Farmer's Alliance, The : an American political association (1873–91), formed to watch over the interests of agriculturists ; ultimately merged in the People's Party.

Faro : a gambling card-game. Pharoah's effigy is said once to have been borne by one of the cards.

Farrago of nonsense, A : a medley of humorous anecdotes, etc. ; a nonsensical tale. Lat., *farrago*, a mixture or medley.

Farrant-like, Auld : *see* Auld.

Fasces : authority. From the name of the bundle of rods surrounding an axe carried before the superior magistrates in Rome as an emblem of their authority.

Fash one's beard, To : to take trouble. ' Fash,' to afflict.

Fast and loose with .. To play : to act in a reckless, usually dishonest, way with .. Two derivations are possible : (1) from a 16th-cent. cheating game, mentioned by Shakespeare, Drayton and others ; (2) from the idea of treating a person as ' fast ' to one when he is of use and as ' loose ' when he is no longer so. [Lyly, *Euphues and His England* (1580)]

Fast as a Kentish oyster, As : hermetically sealed. Kentish oysters are proverbially good and consequently fast closed. [Greene, *Tu Quoque*, ll. 3008–10 (1614)]

Fast as one's legs can carry one, As : very quickly.

Fastern's E'en : Shrove Tuesday ; the eve of the fast of Lent. A Scotticism.

Fastingong : Shrove Tuesday.

Fat and drink the sweet, To eat the : to feast. [*Nehemiah*, viii. 10]

Fat from one's lips, To lick the : to deprive one of his living ; to take the bread out of one's mouth. [Rich. Edwards, *Damon and Pithias*, l. 178 (1567)]

Fat to be in the fire, The : all the ingredients for a noisy quarrel to be now ready. A cooking metaphor. [Heywood, *Proverbes* (1546)]

Fat of the land, To live on the : to have every luxury at one's call. [Earle, *Microcosmography : A Cooke* (1628)]

Fat as a porpoise, As : [Swift, *Polite Conversation*, 294 (1731)]

Fata Morgana, A (*Ital.*, Fairy Morgana) : an atmospheric phenomenon whereby distant objects become inverted, or distorted. The Fairy Morgana, according to medieval romance, was the sister of King Arthur.

Fatal Sisters, The : the Fates (*q.v.*). [Arth. Brooke, *Tragical History of Romeus and Juliet* (1562)]

Fates, The : Clotho, the spinner of the thread of life ; Lachesis, the disposer of lots, who fixed its length ; and Atropos, who severs the thread of life.

Father Abraham : Abraham Lincoln (1809–65), President of the United States.
Father Adam : Adam, the first man, the father of humanity.
Father Neptune : the ocean. After Neptune, the Roman god of the seas.
Father Nile : the Nile, personified.
Father of a 'chapel,' : *see* Chapel.
Father of America, The : Samuel Adams (1722–1803), American statesman and revolutionist.
Father of Angling, The : Izaak Walton (1593–1683).
Father of Believers, The : Mahomet.
Father of Botany, The : Joseph Pittou de Tournefort (1656–1708), Fr. botanist.

Father of British inland Navigation, The : Francis Egerton, Duke of Bridgewater (1736–1803), who planned and financed the Bridgewater Canal system.
Father of Business efficiency, The : Frederick Winslow Taylor (d. 1915).
Father of Chemistry, The : Arnauld de Villeneuve (1238–1314).
Father of Comedy, The : Aristophanes (448–385 B.C.).
Father of Dutch Poetry, The : Jakob Maerlant (1235–1300).
Father of Ecclesiastical (Church) History, The : Eusebius of Cæsarea (264–349).
Father of English Botany, The : William Turner (1520–68).
Father of English Cathedral Music, The : Thomas Tallis (1510–85).
Father of English Poetry, The : Geoffrey Chaucer (1340–1400).
Father of English Printing, The : *see* Printing.
Father of English Prose, The : (1) Wycliffe (1324–84) ; (2) Roger Ascham (1515–68).
Father of Epic Poetry, The : Homer (10th cent. B.C.).
Father of Equity, The : Heneage Finch, Earl of Nottingham (1621–82), Lord Chancellor.
Father of French Drama, The : Etienne Jodelle (1532–73).
Father of French History, The : André Duchesne (1584–1640).
Father of French Prose, The : Geoffroi de Villehardouin (1167–1212).
Father of French Satire, The : Mathurin Regnier (1573–1613).
Father of French Sculpture, The : *see* Sculpture.
Father of French Surgery, The : *see* Surgery.
Father of French Tragedy, The : (1) Rob. Garnier (1545–1600) ; (2) Pierre Corneille (1606–84).
Father of Geology, The : (1) Avicenna (980–1037), Arabic scientist ; (2) Nicolas Steno (1631–87), Danish-Italian geologist ; (3) Wm. Smith (1769–1840).
Father of German Literature, The : Gotthold Ephraim Lessing (1729–81).
Father of Good Works, The : the Sultan Mahomet II (1430–81).
Father of Greek Drama, The : (1) Æschylus (525–456 B.C.) ; (2) Thespis (fl. 535 B.C.).
Father of Greek Music, The : Terpander (fl. 676 B.C.).
Father of Greek Prose, The : Herodotus (c. 484–424 B.C.).
Father of Greek Tragedy, The : Æschylus (525–456 B.C.).
Father of his Country, The : a title borne by many patriots throughout the course of history. The first was Cicero, on whom it was conferred by Cato.
Father of His People, The : (1) Louis XII of France (1462–1515) ; (2) Christian III of Denmark (1503–59). *See also* Father of the People.
Father of Historic Painting, The : Polygnotos of Thaos (fl. 463–435 B.C.).
Father of History, The : Herodotus (484–408 B.C.). So-called by Cicero.
Father of Iambic Verse, The : Archilochus of Paros (fl. 700 B.C.).
Father of Inductive Philosophy, The : Francis Bacon, Lord Verulam (1561–1626).
Father of International Law, The : Hugo Grotius (1583–1645), Dutch jurist.
Father of Italian Prose, The : Boccaccio (1313–75).
Father of Jests, The : Joseph Miller (1684–1738), English wit.
Father of Jurisprudence, The : Ranulph de Glanville (d. 1190), author of *Tractatus de Legibus et Consuetudinibus Angliae* (1181).
Father of Landscape Gardening, The : André Lenôtre (1613–1700), French architect and landscape gardener.

Father of Letters, The : Francis I of France (1494–1547), a patron of literature.

Father of Lies, The : Satan. [*John*, viii, 44].

Father of Medicine, The : (1) Aretæos of Cappadocia ; (fl. 70) ; (2) Hippocrates of Cos (460–357 B.C.).

Father of Modern Oil Painting, The : Jan van Eyck (1385–1440), Flemish painter.

Father of Modern Prose Fiction, The : Daniel Defoe (1663–1731).

Father of Modern Scepticism, The : Pierre Bayle (1647–1706), philosopher.

Father of Moral Philosophy, The : Thomas Aquinas (1227–74), Italian Scholastic theologian.

Father of Music, The : Giovanni Pierluigi da Palestrina (1525–94), Italian composer.

Father of Musicians, The : Jubal. [*Genesis*, iv, 21]

Father of Navigation, The : Don Henrique, Duke of Viseo (1394–1460), one of the greatest of Portuguese travellers.

Father of Ornithology, The : George Edwards (1693–1773).

Father of Orthodoxy, The : Athanasius, Bp. of Alexandria (293–373).

Father of Parody, The : Hipponax (5th cent. B.C.), Grk. iambic poet.

Father of Peace, The : Andrea Doria (1466–1560), Genoese admiral and condottiere. Title given to him by the Senate of Genoa.

Father of Philosophy, The : (1) Roger Bacon (1214–94), Eng. philosopher and scholar ; (2) Albrecht von Haller (1708–77), Swiss physiologist, anatomist, botanist and poet.

Father of Poetry, The : (1) Orpheus, a semi-legendary Grk. poet ; (2) Homer.

Father of Reform, The : John Cartwright (1740–1824), Eng. radical politician and publicist.

Father of Ridicule, The : François Rabelais (1490–1553), Fr. satirist.

Father of Rivers, The : (1) the River Apidanus in Thessaly, so-called by Euripides in *Hecuba* (ll. 446–52) ; (2) the River Lydias in Macedonia, so-called by Euripides in *Bacchæ* (ll. 571–5).

Father of Roman Philosophy, The : Cicero (106–43 B.C.).

Father of Roman Satire, The : Caius Lucilius (180–103, B.C.).

Father of Satire, The : Archilochus of Paros (700 B.C.).

Father of Scotch Landscape Painting, The : John Thomson, of Duddington (1778–1840).

Father of Swedish Eloquence, The : Nordenhjelm.

Father of Symphony, The : *see* Symphony.

Father of the Church, A : one of the writers of the Early Church, whose teachings are accepted as authoritative.

Father of the Faithful, The : the Patriarch Abraham. [*Romans*, iv].

Father of the House of Commons, The : the living member who has sat there continuously for the longest period.

Father of the Human Race, The : Adam.

Father of the People, The : (1) a title assumed by the Absolutist kings of Denmark ; (2) Gabriel du Pineau (1573–1644), Fr. lawyer. *See also* Father of his People.

Father of the Potteries, The : *see* Potteries.

Father of the Spanish Drama, The : Lope Felix de Vega Carpio (1562–1635).

Father of the Vaudeville, The : *see* Vaudeville.

Father of Tragedy, The : (1) Æschylus (525–456 B.C.) ; (2) Thespis (fl. 535 B.C.).

Father of Waters, The : (1) the Irrawaddy ; (2) the Mississippi · (3) the Nile, so-called by Samuel Johnson in *Rasselas* (1759).

Father on a person, To : to impute to a person.

Father Thames : the River Thames.

Father, The Little : *see* Little Father.

Father, The Thoughtful : Nicholas Catinat (1637–1712), Marshal of France. So called by his soldiers.

Father Tiber : the River Tiber, personified.

Father Time : time, personified ; generally depicted as an old man with a scythe.

Fathers of Christian Doctrine The Founder of the : Cæsar de Bus (1544–1607).

Fathers of the Church, The : (1) the Apostolic Fathers, contemporaries of the Apostles, *viz.*, Clement of Rome, Barnabas, Hermas, Ignatius and Polycarp ; (2) the Primitive Fathers, who lived in the first three centuries of the Christian era, *viz.*, Justin, Theophilus of Antioch, Irenæus, Clement of Alexandria, Cyprian of Carthage, Origen, Gregory Thaumaturgus, Dionysius of Alexandria, Tertullian ; (3) *see* Fathers of the Greek Church.

Fathers of the Greek Church, The : Eusebius, Athanasius, Basil the Great, Gregory Nazianzenus, Gregory of Nyssa, Cyril of Jerusalem, Chrysostom, Epiphanius, Cyril of Alexandria, and Ephraim of Edessa.

Fathers of the Latin Church, The : Origen, Tertullian, Clement of Rome, Ignatius, Justin, Irenæus, Cyprian, Hilary of Poitiers, Ambrose, Optatus, Jerome, Augustine, Leo the Great, Prosper, Vincent of Lerins, Peter Chrysologus, Cæsarius of Arles, Gregory the Great, Isidore of Seville, Bede, Peter Damian, Anselm, Bernard.

Father's son, To be one's : to resemble one's father, morally or physically. [Thos. Lodge, *Wounds of Civil War*, V, i, ll. 2213–4 (1594)]

Fathers, The Last of the : *see* Last of the Fathers.

Fatted Calf for .. To kill the : to welcome back one who has absented himself and returns to his old relationships and environment. From the parable of The Prodigal Son (*Luke*, xv, 30).

Fauna : the animals of any given region or period. After Fauna, a nymph of the Liris, near Minturnæ, and the sister and wife of Faunus, a mythical Ital. king, afterwards deified, represented as a Satyr and identified with Pan.

Fauntleroy, Little Lord : *see* Little.

Faute de mieux (*Fr.*, for lack of something better) : [Lord Chesterfield, *Letters*, II, No. 175 (1766)]

Fauteuil, The (*Fr.*, armchair) : symbolizing membership of the French Academy.

Faux pas, A (*Fr.*, false step) : a wrong move, leading to an awkward, or unpleasant, situation ; a slip. [Wycherley, *Plain Dealer*, V (1676)]

Favonius : the West Wind, in Roman mythology.

Favour, To curry : to seek diligently for approval or favourable notice. [Lyly, *Euphues and His England* (1580)]

Favourite son, A : a politician respected or admired in his own State, but not much regarded outside it.

Faye, The way to : a crooked path. After the road which leads to the village of Faye in France.

Fear Babes : a bugbear. Used for frightening children.

Feast one's eyes on .. To : to gaze with pleasure or longing on ..

Feast of Fools, The : a burlesque Church festival celebrated in the Middle Ages on New Year's Day.

Feast of Reason, A : the intercourse of wits and wise men. [Pope, *Imitations of Horace*, II, i (1733–7)]

Feastings Even : properly, Fastern's E'en (*q.v.*).

Feather, An oiled : friendliness of manner and address. Metaphor drawn from the trade of a locksmith who uses an oiled feather to persuade a stubborn lock.

Feather, Birds of a : people of similar character, habit, or taste. From the proverb, ' Birds of a feather flock together.'

Feather, In full (grand ; high ; fine) : in excellent condition. Metaphor drawn from bird-life.

Feather in one's wing, The : the most valuable of one's belongings, *e.g.*, children. [R. Cumberland, *The Fashionable Lover*, II (1772)]

Feather in the cap, To have a : to have scored a success. From the world-wide practice of inserting in one's head-dress a feather for every enemy slain, or other exploit.

Feather, Not to care a : not to care at all. [Sheridan, *School for Scandal*, III, iii (1777)]

Feather one's nest, To : to make full provision for one's material future. Metaphor drawn from bird-life. [Jas. Howell, *Familiar Letters*, Bk. III, Letter xvii (1647) ; Greene, *Francesco's Fortunes* (1590)]

Feather, To fan with a : see Fan.

Feather, To knock down with a : so to surprise a person as to take him completely off his guard.

Feather, To show the white : to display cowardice. In allusion to the fact that a white feather in a game-bird's tail is a mark of impure strain.

Feather-bed publicist (etc.), A : a publicist (etc.) who, from a position of comfort, criticizes those who are undergoing hardships.

Feather-brained (-headed) : foolish ; silly. With brains metaphorically as light as a feather.

Feather-heads, The : the Republican supporters of President Garfield in New York State in his efforts for the reform of the Civil Service. Also called ' Half-breeds.'

February face, A : a face that betokens worry or depression.

February, On the 30th of : *i.e.*, never.

February Fill-dyke : a popular name for the month of February, referring to the prevalence of rain or snow.

Federalists ; Federals : supporters of the Northern States in the American Civil War (1861–5). An earlier American political party of the same name flourished from 1787 until about 1812 : it was formed to support the Federal Constitution.

Feed the fishes, To : see Fishes.

Feet of .. At the : devoted to .. ; as if kneeling at the feet of ..

Feet, To carry a person off his : to carry a person away with enthusiasm or excitement, so that he is temporarily free from the guidance of reason.

Feet, To fall (light) on one's : to achieve a successful end in spite of difficulties, usually with some assistance from good-fortune.

Feet, To have at one's : to have subservient to one.

Feet, To set a person on his : to establish him, to enable him to start afresh. From the idea of raising a man who has fallen down. [Geo. Cavendish, *Life and Death of Wolsey* (1557)]

Feet, To stand on one's own : to be independent of the assistance of others. [Jos. Hall, *Characters : A Happy Man* (1608)]

Fehmic Court : see Vehmgericht.

Félibrige : a literary society, founded in 1854, to preserve the Provençal language and literature. Lat., *Filii Ecclesiae*, sons of the Church.

Fell, Doctor : see Doctor Fell.

Fellowship Porter, A : a member of the Fellowship of Porters of Billingsgate, one of the City of London Guilds.

Fellowship with .. To make a : to band together with others for mutual assistance.

Felo de se (*Low-Lat.*, a felon from himself) : a suicide.

Fen nightingale, A : a frog. It ' sings ' in the fens.

Fence, To sit on the : to adopt such an attitude as commits one to neither party in a controversy. Orig. an Americanism.

Fencible Regiments : regiments (1759–1802) liable for defensive service at home.

Fenian, A : a member of an Irish revolutionary organization active from 1858 to 1885. From *Fene*, a name of the Irish people, and the Fians, a mythical band of followers of Finn MacCool.

Feringhee, A : an Indian name for a European or Eurasian. Persian, *Farangi*, a corruption of Frank.

Ferment, To be in a : to be agitated.

Ferney, The Patriarch of : Voltaire, who spent the last years of his life at Ferney, near Geneva.

Fescennine verses : scurrilous and coarse verse. After Fescennia, in Etruria, famous for the jeering verses written there.

Festive Season, The : Christmastide.

Fête Champêtre, A (*Fr.*, an outdoor entertainment).

Feu de joie, A (*Fr.*, fire of joy) : a bonfire. [Bp. W. Barlow, *Answer to a Nameless Catholic's Censure*, II (1609)]

Feudal System, The : the system of land-tenure under which the whole of the land of the country was vested in the Crown, and the actual holders were under obligations to perform military service as rent. Introduced into England by William the Conqueror.

F.F.V's : the First Families of Virginia, descendants of the original settlers in the State. After the initial letters.

Fiacre, A (*Fr.*, cab) : a French hackney cab. From the Hôtel de St. Fiacre, in Paris, the first station for carriages for hire (c. 1650). St. Fiacre (d. 670) is the patron of Gardeners.

Fib, A : a falsehood of a minor character. An abbreviation of ' fable.' [Congreve, *Double Dealer*, IV, iii (1694)]

Fiddle about (Fiddle about with ..), To : to behave (deal with) in an aimless, perfunctory, inefficient manner. [T. Wright, *Passions*, IV, ii § 3 (1530)]

Fiddle, As fit as a : in excellent condition. [Wm. Haughton, *Englishmen for My Money*, IV, i (1597)]

Fiddle, The Scotch : the itch. From the resemblance between playing the fiddle and scratching oneself.

Fiddle, To hang up one's : to withdraw from business ; to resign.

Fiddle, To have a face as long as a : to have a very dismal look.

Fiddle, To play second : to occupy a subordinate position.

Fiddle when one comes home, To hang up one's : to reserve one's gifts of entertainment for the amusement of strangers.

Fiddle while Rome is burning, To : to interest oneself in trivialities, while events of great importance are transpiring. In allusion to the Emperor Nero (37–68) who is said to have continued to amuse himself with his violin while his capital, Rome, was burning before his eyes.

Fiddler's fare (pay) : meat, drink and money. [Lewis Machin, *The Dumb Knight*, III, i (1608)]

Fiddler's Green, A : a sailor's elysium, composed of wine, women and song.

Fiddler's money : a threepenny-bit, the payment at one time made by each dancer to the fiddler at a party.

Fiddler's news : stale news ; such as that formerly circulated by itinerant fiddlers.

Fiddle-de-dee : nonsense. [Johnson, in Boswell's *Life* (1791)]

Fiddle-faddle : trifling ; trivial. A duplicative word. The earlier form was fiddle-cum-faddle. [Bullinger, *Decades*, 103 (1577)]

Fiddler, As drunk as a : *see* Drunk.

Fiddlesticks : nonsense.

Fides Carbonarii : implicit faith. A carbonaro being asked what he believed, replied, ' What the Church believes ' and being asked once again, what the Church believes, replied, ' What I believe.'

Fides Punica : *see* Punic Faith.

Fidus Achates : *see* Achates.

Field, The : (1) the riders in a hunt ; (2) the horses in a race ; (3) the scene of sports.

Field of Blood, The : the battlefield of Cannae, in Italy, where in 216 B.C. Hannibal overwhelmed the Roman army.

Field of the Cloth of Gold, The : the scene in the Pas-de-Calais, France, of the meeting between Francis I, of France, and Henry VIII, of England, in 1520, famous on account of its splendour.

Field of the Forty Footsteps, The : an open space behind Montagu House, Bloomsbury, London, built over about 1800, the legendary scene of a duel between two brothers on whose forty footprints nothing would ever grow. In reality a district abandoned to vice and crime.

Field-day, A : a day of important or exciting events. Orig. the day of a military review.

Field-Marshal's baton in one's knapsack, To carry a : to have the opportunity of rising to the height of one's ambition. From a saying attributed to Napoleon : ' Every French soldier carries in his knapsack the baton of a Marshal of France,' but in reality based on an utterance of Louis XVIII to the students of St. Cyr in Aug., 1819.

Fiery Cross, To send the : to summon to battle. In the Scottish Highlands the clansmen used to be summoned to battle by means of a cross dipped in blood and sent from village to village.

Fifteen, The : (1) the Jacobite Rebellion of 1715 ; (2) the Scottish Court of Session, consisting originally of fifteen judges.

Fifteener, A : a book printed in the 15th century.

Fifth Estate, The : (humorously) the Ladies.

Fifth Monarchy Man, A : a member of an Eng. politico-religious party at the time of the Commonwealth which believed in the early establishment of the fifth universal monarchy with Christ at its head. The four previous monarchies were believed to be Assyria, Persia, Macedon, and Rome.

Fifth wheel of the coach, The : something quite superfluous. [Dekker, *Match Me in London* (1631)]

Fig for .. Not to care a : to have neither fear nor respect for .. *See* Fig, To give the, from which phrase it is probably derived.

Fig Sunday : the Sunday before Easter, in allusion to Christ's desire to eat the fruit of a fig tree on his way to Bethany on the day following the entry into Jerusalem.

Fig to .. To give the : to jeer at .. ; insult ; by thrusting the thumb between two fingers or into the mouth. A phrase of Ital. origin, said to have been derived from a contemptuous punishment inflicted on the Milanese by the Emperor Frederic Barbarossa in 1162.

Fig's end, A : something worthless.

Figs where only brambles grow, To seek : *see* Seek.

Figaro, A : a clever and ingenious rogue. After characters in *Le Barbier de Séville* and *Le Mariage de Figaro*, by Beaumarchais.

Fight shy of .. To : to avoid conflict or association with .. Perhaps orig. to lose courage in battle.

Fight the tiger, To : to gamble. An Americanism.

Fight with foot and horse, To : to contend with the assistance of all of one's forces. [Cicero, *De Officiis*, III, 33, 116]

Fight with shadows, To : to contend against imaginary opposition.

Fight with the gloves off, To : to fight in earnest. A boxing metaphor.

Fight with the gloves on, To : to fight in a perfunctory manner, being careful to do one's adversary no damage. A boxing metaphor.

Fighting chance, A : a slight chance, which may be brought to fruition after a desperate struggle.

Fighting cock, To live like a : to live in the lap of luxury. Game-cocks were always generously fed in order to encourage their pugnacity.

Fighting Fifth, The : the 5th Regt. of Foot, now the Northumberland Fusiliers. On account of their prowess in the Peninsular War (1808–14).

Fighting Prelate, The : Henry Spenser, Bp. of Norwich (d. 1406).

Figure, To cut a (fine) : to make oneself conspicuous : often ironically said. [Francis Coventry, *Hist. of Pompey the Little*, ch. 9 (1751)]

Figure-Flinger, A : a term of contempt for one who pretends to astrology, or foretells the future by means of figures. [Bacon, *Wisdom of the Ancients*, no. xviii (1619).

Filbert, A : the nut of the hazel-tree. After St. Philibert, whose feast (August 22nd) is in the nutting-season.

Filia Dolorosa (*Lat.*, the grieving daughter) : the Duchess of Angoulême, daughter of Louis XVI of France (1778–1851).

Filibuster, To : to obstruct business in Parliament, etc., esp. on the part of a minority. Orig. an American political term. Dutch, *vrijbueter*, freebooter.

Filioque Controversy, The : a religious controversy between the Eastern and Western Churches arising out of the word ' *Filioque* ' (' and from the Son ') in the Western version of the Nicene Creed. The question was whether the Holy Ghost proceeded from the Father and the Son, or from the Father only.

Fill up the cup, To : to complete a series of offences, etc., so that at their conclusion a very severe punishment will be justified.

Filthy Lucre : dishonourable gain ; also money. [Tindale, *Titus* I, ii (1526)]

Fin de Siècle (*Fr.*, end of century) : up-to-date ; ultra-modern. The suggestion is that civilization degenerates morally, intellectually, politically— as the end of a century approaches, to be revivified with the opening of a new century. The term originated in Paris about the year 1890 and was derived from the title of a play by Micard and de Jouvenot which was produced in Paris in 1888.

Finality John : Lord John Russell, who always referred to the Reform Act of 1832 as ' a finality.'

Findon haddock, A : a haddock smoked with green wood. After Findon, a village near Aberdeen, where haddocks are prepared in this manner.

Fine as fivepence, As : excellently. A fivepenny-piece was the ancient Saxon silver coin. *See* Fivepence.

Fine by degrees and beautifully less : gradually diminishing in size. [Prior *Henry and Emma* (1718)]

Finger in, To have a : to have some interest or concern in ; to interfere in. [*A Warning for Faire Women*, II, ll. 421–3 (1599)]

Finger in the pie, To have a : to take part, esp. an officious one, in any affair. [Cervantes, *Don Quixote*, xxii ; Shakespeare, *Henry VIII*, I, i, ll. 52–3 (1613)]

Finger in behalf of .. To raise a : to make the slightest effort on behalf of .. [Cicero, *Pro Caecina*, xxv, 71]

Finger, The Index : the first finger of the hand because it is used as a pointer.

Finger, The Marriage : the finger on which the wedding-ring is placed.

Finger, The Medical : the third finger of the hand. It was formerly believed that this finger had a direct connection with the heart and that a noxious drug could not touch it without giving direct warning. This finger was therefore used for stirring medical and other mixtures.

Finger, The Ring : the third finger of the hand.

Finger, To twist round one's (little) : to make subservient to one's will. [Lewis Machin, *The Dumb Knight*, II, i (1608)]

Finger, With a wet : easily, without any trouble. [Heywood, *Proverbes* (1546)]

Fingers, To burn one's : to suffer through interfering in other people's affairs, or through rash speculation.

Fingers' ends, At one's : of knowledge with which one is thoroughly acquainted. [Rabelais, Bk. IV, ch. 54 ; Heywood, *Proverbes* (1546)]

Fingers, To slip through the : to escape against all expectation.

Fingers at .. To snap one's : not to care the least about .. Snapping one's fingers was formerly the manner of summoning a slave.

Fingers are all Thumbs : of a clumsy person. [Udall, *Roister Doister*, I, iii (1534) ; Heywood, *Proverbes* (1546)]

Finger-tips, To the : to the minutest point. [Horace, *Ars Poetica*, ll. 291–4]

Finger-tips, With the : faint-heartedly ; reluctantly.

Finger-tips, To stand on one's : to be proud.

Fingle-fangle : something unimportant or fantastic.

Finishing school, A : a school at which young ladies are taught social deportment preparatory to their admission into society.

Fire, To take oil to extinguish the : *see* Take.

Fire and water, To go through : to undergo hardships and difficulties. In allusion to the ordeals by fire and water. [Shakespeare, *Merry Wives of Windsor*, III, iv, 109–11 (1598–9] A military metaphor.

Fire in one hand and water in the other, To carry : to say one thing and mean another. [Heywood, *Proverbes* (1546)]

Fire, To go through the : to experience trouble or anxiety. In allusion to the ordeal in the fiery furnace of Shadrach, Meshach and Abednego. [*Daniel*, iii]

Fires, Between two : faced by alternative difficulties.

Fire water : alcoholic spirits. An American-Indian term.

Firebrand, A : one who causes excitement and disturbance. In allusion to a piece of wood kindled at the fire. [Shakespeare, *Troilus and Cressida*, II, ii (1606–7)]

Firebrand of the Universe, The : Timur Tamerlane (1336–1405), the Tartar Conqueror.

Fire drake, A : a fiery dragon, a man always prone to fight.

Fire-eater, A : a fire-drake (*q.v.*).

Fire-eaters, The : extreme supporters of the claims of the Southern States before the outbreak of the Civil War.

Firk of law : a legal quibble or trick. [*Ram Alley* in Dodsley, *Old Plays*, V, 467]

Firm as hodge-wife, As : *see* Hodge-wife.

First born of Egypt, The : according to Dr. Johnson, people of aristocratic birth.

First catch your hare : *see* Hare.

First cause, The great : according to the students of evolution, God. [Pope, *Universal Prayer* (1738)]

First Christian kingdom, The : France.

First fruits : the first production of animal or vegetable ; the earliest results of one's efforts ; a tax representing the first year's income ; formerly an offering consisting of the first production of the harvest.

First Gentleman of Europe, The : George IV (1762–1830), king of England. So-called by his admirers.

First Grenadier of France, The : Theophilus de Latour d'Auvergne (1743–1800). So-called by Napoleon.

First of June, The glorious : the anniversary of the naval battle in 1794 in which the French were defeated by Lord Howe off Ushant.

First rate : (orig. a nautical term) of the highest degree of excellence. In allusion to a warship of the highest rating.

First water, A diamond of the : *see* Diamond.

Fish to bite, To teach a : *see* Teach.

Fish that comes to his net, All is : whatever comes along is welcome and made use of.

Fish for compliments, To : to pay a compliment in the expectation of receiving a greater one in return. [Jane Austen, *Mansfield Park*, ch. 29 (1814)]

Fish, He eats no : he is not a Papist or Roman Catholic and is therefore to be trusted. The phrase dates from the time of Queen Elizabeth when all Roman Catholics were under suspicion.

Fish of one and flesh of another, To make : to make unjustifiable distinctions. [Jonathan Swift, *Polite Conversation*, Dial. ii (1738)]

Fish, flesh nor fowl, nor good red herring, Neither : without the particular qualities of one thing or the other. Derived from a proverb current in the 16th cent. Other forms of the phrase are ' Neither fish nor flesh,' ' Neither fish nor fowl.' The suggested allusions are fish (food for the monks), flesh (for the laity generally), red herring (for the poorer classes). [Heywood, *Proverbes* (1546) ; Roy,

Rede me and be not Wrothe, I, iii (1528)]

Fish to fry, To have other : to have other business to attend to.

Fish with a golden hook, To : to offer bribes. [Suetonius, *De Vita Cæsarum : Augustus Octavianus*, 25 ; Arth. Brooke, *Tragical History of Romeus and Juliet* (1562)]

Fish to the Hellespont, To send : to perform a work of supererogation.

Fish, A loose : a person of loose habits.

Fish in the middle of the ocean, To go netting for : to do something foolish or unprofitable. [Plautus, *Asinaria*, l. 100–1]

Fish, A pretty (nice) kettle of : a muddle. The phrase is probably derived from the kettle or kiddle-nets which when drawn from the water, full of fish, furnish an excellent illustration of flurry, confusion, disorder and muddle. [Samuel Richardson, *Pamela*, III, 308 (1741)]

Fish, A queer : a curious person, not altogether to be understood.

Fish, To cry stinking : *see* Stinking.

Fish story, A : a grossly exaggerated and practically invented story ; like the proverbial tales told by amateur fishermen of their catches.

Fish in troubled waters, To : to seek one's own advantage in other people's troubles. From the French. [La Fontaine, *Contes et Nouvelles : Belphégor* (1665)]

Fish out of water, A : a person who is uncomfortable because he is out of his element. [Wycliffe, *English Works*, p. 449 (14th cent.) ; Chaucer, *Prologue to the Canterbury Tales*, 177 (14th cent.)]

Fish well and catch a frog, To : to obtain little result after great effort. [Heywood, *Proverbs* (1546)]

Fishes, To feed the : (1) to be drowned ; (2) to be sea-sick.

Fishes, To make clothes for : *see* Make.

Fishday, A : a fast day. A day on which fish instead of meat is eaten.

Fisher of men, A : one who preys upon humanity. [Cowley, *Essays : Dangers of an Honest Man* (17th cent.)]

Fisher of souls, The great : the Devil.

Fisher's Folly : a fishing or shooting box. [Braithwait, *Survey of History* (1638)]

Fishing question, A : a question intended to elicit information on which further questions may be based.

Fishy : doubtful, subject to suspicion. Perhaps as slippery as a fish. *See also* Fish Story, A.

Fishy Story, A : a story that arouses doubt or suspicion. *See* Fishy.

Fist, To be brought to : to be compelled to fight. [Shatterley Marmion, *The Antiquary*, IV, i (1641)]

Fist, To write a good (bad) : to be a good (bad) calligrapher. [Udall, *Ralph Roister Doister*, III, v, l. 48 (1550)]

Fit : in good health and spirits. [*Hamlet* V, ii (1602–3)]

Fit as a fiddle, As : *see* Fiddle.

Fit as a fiddler, As : in excellent condition. Probably ' Fiddler ' was introduced merely for alliteration.

Fit as a pudding for a Friar's mouth, As : appropriate ; welcome. [Fulwell, *Like will to Like*, 212 (1568)]

Fits and starts, By : spasmodically.

Fittest, Survival of the : phrase coined by Herbert Spencer [*Principles of Biology*, § 164 (1864)] to express the results of the struggle for existence.

Five alls, The : a publichouse sign consisting of a king in his regalia (I govern all), a bishop in his vestments (I pray for all), a lawyer in his gown (I plead for all), a soldier in his uniform (I fight for all), a labourer with his tools (I pay for all).

Five-minute clause, A : a clause, sometimes inserted in a deed of separation, to the effect that if the parties remain together for five minutes after the deed has been signed it will become null and void.

Five Nations, The : the five tribes that comprised the Iroquois confederacy.

Five per cent patriotism : patriotism which displays itself in remunerative investments. In allusion to the five per cent. War Loan raised to finance Great Britain during the European War of 1914–1918.

Five senses, The : sight, hearing, smell, taste and touch.

Five wits, The : commonsense, imagination, fantasy, estimation and memory.

Fivepence, As fine as : emphatically fine. [R.B., *Appius and Virginia*, l. 161 (1563)] *See* Fine.

Fiver, A : a five-pound note.

Fix, To be in a : to be in a difficulty.

Flabbergasted, To be : to be astounded and confused. Appeared first in 1772 as fashionable slang. [*Annual Register : On new words* (1772)]

Flag, A black : the emblem of piracy.

Flag day, A : a day set apart for money collections in the street on behalf of some charitable institution, after the little flags with which donors are presented to wear in their buttonholes.

Flag, To get one's : to be promoted to the rank of admiral, and thus be entitled to fly one's flag.

Flag half mast high : an emblem of mourning.

Flag, To hang the red : to issue a defiance. The Red Flag was the Roman battle signal.

Flag, To hang the yellow : to announce the presence of contagious illness. From the signal used on such occasions on board ship.

Flag, To hoist the white : to surrender, to admit defeat. From the flag of truce, raised by one of the parties to a fight when a cessation of hostilities, temporary or permanent, is desired.

Flag, To lower one's : to submit to, to surrender. A nautical term.

Flag rank : naval rank not lower than that of commodore, entitling the holder to fly his flag.

Flag, To strike the : to give up one's office or command. A nautical term.

Flag, To unfurl the black : to declare war. The Moslem flag is black, *i.e.*, the colour of the curtain that hung before the door of Ayeshah, Mahomet's favourite wife, which was taken as the battle-flag of his followers. *See also* Flag, a black.

Flag, The yellow : the signal used to announce the existence of contagious disease.

Flagellants : members of a rel. sect who in the 13th and 14th cents. taught that flogging was a virtue and rel. duty.

Flagellum Dei (*Lat.*, The Scourge of God) : Attila, King of the Huns.

Flagrante Delicto (*Lat.*, while the offence is flagrant) : caught in the very act.

Flame, A (*Lat.*, *flamma*, love) : a sweetheart ; prob. from the burning passion of love. [Cowley, *Mistress* (1647)].

Flanders babies : wooden dolls.

Flanders, To pass over the sandbanks of : to pass safely through a difficulty. In allusion to the sandbanks at the mouths of the Scheldt and the Meuse which caused difficulty to Spanish navigators. [Cervantes, *Don Quixote*, II, 21]

L

Flank of .. To turn the : to circumvent a person. A military metaphor.

Flannel, A : a Welshman ; in allusion to the manufacture of flannel in Wales. [Shakespeare, *Merry Wives of Windsor*, V, v, 172 (1598–9)]

Flannelled fools : individuals who devote an undue amount of time to sport, *i.e.*, in wearing flannel suits. Phrase coined by Rudyard Kipling. [*The Islanders* (1902)]

Flapper, A : a girl of about 16 or 17. Perhaps in allusion to the flapping of their plaits of hair as they move rapidly.

Flare up, A : a sudden fit of anger, like a flare or blaze of fire.

Flash : a shallow, showy person or behaviour, like a sudden, brief flash of light.

Flash : counterfeit. In allusion to the glitter of cheap flash jewellery, also to Flash, a district in the North Midlands frequented by swindling hawkers.

Flash men : dishonest sporting men. *See also* Flash.

Flash notes : false bank notes.

Flash in the pan, A : a failure after a well-advertised preparation. In allusion to a gun that fails to explode when fired.

Flashy : empty but showy. *See* Flash.

Flat as a Flounder, As : flattened out ; depressed. [Beaumont and Fletcher, *Women Pleased*, II. iv (1620)]

Flat as a Pancake, As : dull. [Henry Porter, *Two Angry Women of Abington*, ll. 1127–9 (1599) ; Middleton and Dekker, *Roaring Girl*, II, i (1611)]

Flat, To fall : (of a play, etc.) to prove unattractive.

Flattering unction to your soul, Lay not that : do not lull yourself into a state of false security by means of that supposition. [Shakespeare, *Hamlet*, III, iv (1602–3)]

Flax to the fire : a ready cause of excitement. [Heywood, *Proverbes* (1546)]

Flea in one's ear, To go away with a : to suffer a sudden and quite unexpected reproof or rebuff. [Rabelais, *Pantagruel*, III, ch. vii (1533) ; Heywood, *Proverbes* (1546)]

Flea-bite, A mere : a trouble or annoyance of very slight consequence. [Heywood, *Proverbes* (1546)]

Fleece, To : to cheat a person as a sheep is deprived of its fleece. [Nashe, *Christe's Teares* (1593)]

Fleet Book evidence : no evidence. The books of the Fleet Prison could not be produced in proof of a marriage.

Fleet of the Desert, A : a caravan.

Fleet Marriages : secret or hasty marriages, celebrated in the Fleet Prison by clergymen of doubtful reputation. These marriages were brought to an end by the Marriage Act of 1754.

Fleet Street : the London newspaper world. The offices of most of the principal London newspapers are in or about Fleet Street.

Flemish Account, A : an account that shows an unwelcome deficit. In allusion to the value of an Antwerp livre or pound, *viz.*, 12s.

Flesh, After the : resembling in physical appearance.

Flesh creep, To make one's : to make one nervous and expectant of evil.

Flesh one's sword, To : to use one's sword for the first time. [Thos. Hughes, *Misfortunes of Arthur*, II, ii (1587)]

Flesh, The way of all : death. In allusion to 'the way of all the earth.' [*Joshua*, xxiii, 14 ; Heywood, *The Golden Age* (1611)]

Fleshly School, The : a nineteenth cent. school of Eng. poets—Swinburne, William Morris, D. G. Rossetti and others—so-called by Robert Buchanan ('Thos. Maitland') in the *Contemporary Review* of October, 1871.

Fleshpots of Egypt, The : good things of this world formerly at one's disposal, but no longer so. [*Exodus*, xvi, 3]

Fleur de Luce : Fleur de Lys (*q.v.*).

Fleur de Lys (Lis) : the royal insignia of France, the heraldic lily, the iris.

Flibbertigibbet : an idle chatterer; the name of a devil in Shakespeare, *King Lear*, and of a character in Sir W. Scott, *Kenilworth*. The fiend was invented by the Jesuits about the time of the Span. Armada. [Heywood, *Proverbes* (1546)]

Flighty, To be : to be frivolous, esp. of a girl.

Flim flam : nonsense ; a trifle. A duplication of flam, a lie. [Heywood, *Proverbes* (1546)]

Flimsy, A : a bank note ; in allusion to the thinness of its paper.

Flinch one's glass, To : to avoid emptying one's glass. Flinch, to draw back. [Arbuthnot, *History of John Bull*, Pt. II, ch. 6 (1713)]

Fling at, To have a : to gibe at. [*Wily Beguiled*, ll. 423–4 (1592)]

Fling oneself at someone's head, To : to place oneself unreservedly at the disposal of .. ; (in affairs of the heart) for a woman to make unmistakable advances without securing her retreat.

Fling, To have one's : to pursue pleasure singlemindedly until satisfied. [Beaumont and Fletcher, *Rule a Wife*, III, v (1624)]

Flint, To bleed (skin) the : of a miser, to be exacting to the last farthing. [Rob. Greene, *Menaphon* (1589)]

Flint, A heart of : *see* Heart.

Flint against .. To set one's face like a : to be rigidly averse from .. [Bunyan, *Pilgrim's Progress*, Pt. I (1678)]

Flintlock, A : an obsolete kind of handgun which was fired by means of a flint attached to the hammer.

Flirt, To : to make love or be coquettish without serious intention. Orig. to flit inconstantly from one object to another. According to Lord Chesterfield (1694–1773) first used by Lady Frances Shirley early in the 18th cent. The term is apparently derived from that of flirting, or moving with a quick sharp motion, a fan.

Floaters : in Amer. politics, voters not attached to either party and open for purchase.

Flog a dead horse, To : to attempt to revive an interest that has passed away.

Flood, To take .. at the : to make the most of an opportunity, like a vessel using a flood to assist its progress. [Shakespeare, *Julius Cæsar*, IV, iii (1601)]

Floor, To : a sporting metaphor, to knock to the floor ; to confound ; to nonplus.

Floorer, A : that which floors. *See* Floor, To.

Flora : the vegetables of a certain district or period. After Flora, the goddess of flowers.

Florence, The German : Dresden.

Florence of the North, The : Dresden.

Florimel from the false, To distinguish the true : to recognize one's true affinity in contrast to temporary attractions. In allusion to Florimel, a damsel-character in Spenser, *Faerie Queen*, Bks. III and IV (1590–6).

Florimel's Girdle : the test of chastity and true wifehood. In allusion to the cestus or girdle of Venus and to Florimel, the type of virgin modesty in Spencer, *Faerie Queen*, Bks. III. and IV. (1590–6).

Florin, A : a coin of varying value in different periods and countries. In allusion to Florence in which city it was introduced.

Flos Regnum (*Lat.*, the Flower of Kings): King Arthur. So-called by John of Exeter.

Flotsam and jetsam : orig. a legal term : wreckage floating on the sea and cast ashore ; odds and ends.

Flower of Chivalry, The : (1) Sir Philip Sidney (1554–1586); (2) William Douglas, Lord of Liddesdale (c. 1300–53); (3) Chevalier de Bayard (1476–1524).

Flower of Fishes, The : the grey ling. So-called by Isaac Walton.

Flower of the flock, The : the flower of the garland (*q.v.*).

Flower of the garland, The fairest : the most beautiful or choicest member of the party. [Heywood, *Proverbes* (1546)]

Flower of Kings, The : Arthur. So-called by John of Exeter.

Flower of the Levant, The : the Island of Zante. In allusion to its beauty and bounteous products.

Flower of one's age, The : early manhood. [Tyrtæus, VII, 29 ; Virgil, *Eclogues*, VII, ll. 4–5 ; *A Complaint of the Losse of Libertie by Loue*, ll. 17–8 (1557)]

Flower of the Poets, The : Geoffrey Chaucer (1328–1400).

Flowers, A Battle of : *see* Battle.

Flowers of Rhetoric : flowers of speech (*q.v.*). [Dunbar, *Golden Targe* (1508)]

Flowers of Speech : ornaments of speech.

Flowery Kingdom, The : one of the native names for China. Properly the Flower of Kingdoms.

Fluke, By a : by a piece of luck. Orig. a billiard term.

Flummery : empty flattery ; properly a sweet dish made of milk, eggs, etc. [Peter Pindar, *Subjects for Painters : The Soldier and the Virgin Mary* (18th cent.)]

Flummux, To : to confound ; to nonplus.

Flush of money : with plenty of money. [Dekker, *Batchelor's Banquet*, ch. viii (1603)]

Flute, To teach a pig to play on a : *see* Teach.

Flutter, A : a venture in earnest ; a small gamble or bet.

Flutter the dovecots, To : to cause a mild excitement in society. [Shakespeare, *Coriolanus*, V, vi, 116 (1607)]

Flux, To be in a : to be in a state of uncertainty or fluctuation. [Bacon, *Essayes : Of Vicissitudes of Things* (1625)]

Fly, To be : to be wideawake.

Fly in amber, A : something surprisingly out of place, like the flies occasionally found imbedded in amber.

Fly on the coach-wheel, A : a person of little consequence who considers himself of great importance. From one of Æsop's *Fables*, later popularized by La Fontaine in his fable, *Le Coche et la Mouche.*

Fly into an elephant, To change a : *see* Change.

Fly in the face of .. To : to oppose ; to attempt to prevent ; rashly to seek danger. [Francis Coventry, *History of Pompey the Little*, ch. 5 (1751)]

Fly high, To : to nurse an extravagant ambition.

Fly a kite, To : (1) to borrow money by means of accommodation bills ; (2) to write a begging letter.

Fly at .. To let : to strike at. A cock-fighting metaphor.

Fly-by-night, A : a person who decamps in the night, generally to avoid his creditors ; a sedan chair on wheels, in use at the beginning of the 19th cent.

Fly, To rise to the : to be taken in ; to be deceived.

Fly, To take a spear to kill a : *see* Take.

Fly on the wheel, To crush a : to devote much energy to little purpose.

Flying colours, To come off with : to score a public success.

Flying Dutchman, The : a spectre ship supposed by superstitious seamen to haunt the seas around the Cape of Good Hope. The legend was the subject of an opera by Wagner, *Der Fliegende Hollaender*, and of a novel by Frederick Marryat, *The Phantom Ship* (1839).

Flying fishes, To talk of : to tell travellers' tales, *i.e.*, tales based for the most part on the imagination.

Fobbed off, To be : to be put off under false pretences. [Shakespeare, 2 *Henry IV*, II, i, 37 (1597–8)]

Foeman worthy of one's steel, A : a competitor whose qualities necessitate the employment of all one's powers in the contest. [Scott, *Lady of the Lake* (1810)]

Fogey, An old (*Scot.*, an old invalid or garrison soldier) : an old-fashioned person.

Fogrum, An old : an old fogey (*q.v.*). [R. Cumberland, *The Mysterious Husband*, I, i (1783)]

Follower, A : a man who courts a maid-servant. [Dickens, *Nicholas Nickleby*, ch. xv (1838)]

Folly, To fill up the measure of one's : to complete the sum of one's foolishness. [*Matthew*, xxiii, 32 ; *Genesis*, xv, 16]

Folly as it flies, To shoot : to detect folly as soon as it shows itself. [Pope, *Essay on Man*, Epistle I, 9 (1732–4)]

Fons et origo (*Lat.*, fountain and origin) : the original cause.

Food for Acheron : *see* Pabulum Acherontis.

Fool for one's pains, A : one who labours to no purpose.

Food for powder : recruits for the army. [Shakespeare, 1 *Henry IV*, IV, ii (1596–7)]

Food for worms : a dead body. [Rob. Arnim, *A Nest of Ninnies* (1608)]

Fool in Christendom, The most learned (wisest) : James I of England, so-called by Henri IV of France, who, however, himself derived the term from the Duc de Sully.

Fool's chair, A : a chair with a leg missing, on which fools attempt to sit and consequently fall.

Fools Day, All : *see* April Fool.

Fool's errand, A : a profitless undertaking. [Swift, *Polite Conversation*, Dial. I (1738)]

Fools, Feast of : *see* Feast.

Fool's Fire : the will-o'-the-wisp.

Fool's Paradise, A : a state of happiness or satisfaction resting on no reliable basis. [*The Paston Letters* (1462)] According to the Schoolmen, one of the divisions of the region which was on the outskirts of paradise was *Limbus Fatuorum* or the 'Border' of Fools.

Foolish as a Daw, As : in the 16th cent. a 'daw' was a silly, chattering person. [*Trial of Treasure*, l. 344 (1567)]

Foolish as a Woodcock, As : in allusion to the proverbial foolishness of wood-cocks. [Bacon, *Works* (1564)]

Foolometer, A : a pretended standard of measurement of folly.

Foolosopher, A : a foolish pretender to philosophy. [Chaloner, *Erasm Moriæ Enconium*. (1549)]

Foolscap : a size of paper. From the fool's cap which orig. served as the watermark, said to have been introduced by Sir John Spielmann or Spilman, a German who built a paper mill at Dartford in 1580. Also possibly a corruption of (Ital.) *foglio capo*, folio-sized sheet.

Foot it, To : to pay an account ; lit., to pay the amount stated at the foot.

Foot, To show the cloven : *see* Cloven hoof.

Foot in, To get one's : to get accustomed to an occupation.

Foot in the grave, To have one : to be very ill ; to be near death. The phrase is attributed to the Emperor Julian (331–63). [Lucian, *Apologia*, I ; Massinger and Field, *Fatal Dowry* (1632) ; Thos. Lodge, *Rosalind* (1590)]

Foot by one's own Last, To measure another's : to judge another by one's own standard.

Foot, To know the length of one's : to discover a person's weaknesses so as to be able to manage him. [Lyly, *Euphues and His England* (1580)]

Foot down, To put one's : to repress firmly, to adopt a determined attitude.

Foot foremost, To put one's best : to throw oneself energetically into an undertaking. [Shakespeare, *King John*, IV, ii (1596)]

Foot in it, To put one's : to make a blunder. The phrase is said to be an abbreviation of ' The bishop has put his foot in it,' used when soup or milk is burnt. The cook is supposed to have neglected her duty in order to run out and see the bishop pass. Tyndale gave another explanation : ' If the pottage be burnt .. we say the Bishop hath put his foot in the pot, or the Bishop hath played the cook. Because the Bishops burn who they lust and whosoever displeases them.' [*Obedience of a Crysten Man* (1528)]

Foot in, To get one's : to make oneself acquainted with the task to be undertaken.

Football of fortune, A : a plaything of fortune ; a person who is apparently subject to the whims of chance and has no control over his own fortunes.

Footing, To be on a good : to have a good reputation. The translation of a French phrase.

Footing, To pay one's : to pay (not necessarily in money) for admission into a circle, profession, etc. Properly, to pay for one's footing.

Footlights, The : the stage ; in allusion to the row of lights at the edge of the stage level with the feet of the performers.

Footman's Inn : a poor lodging. [*Penniles Parliament of Threed-bare Poets* (1608)]

Footpad, A : an unmounted highway robber, whose boots were originally padded so as to deaden the sound of his approach.

Forbidden fruit : unlawful indulgence. An allusion to the fall of Adam and Eve in the garden of Eden.

Forbidden Land, The : Thibet, from which country all foreigners were rigidly excluded.

Force the hand, To : to compel a person to show his case or to take action which he would prefer to defer. A whist-playing metaphor.

Forced march, A : a march in which troops are compelled to exert themselves beyond the ordinary limit of endurance. A military term.

Forefathers' Day : December 21st, observed in the New England States as the anniversary of the landing of the Pilgrim Fathers.

Foreign Office, The : the British dept. of state which deals with foreign affairs.

Forest Cantons, The : the cantons of Lucerne, Schwyz, Uri, and Unterwalden, in the Swiss Federation.

Forest City, The : Cleveland, Ohio. In allusion to its numerous trees.

Forest of Fools, The : the world. [Dekker, *Gull's Horn Book* (1609)]

Forfeits in a barber shop : *see* Barber shop.

Forget-me-nots of the angels, The : stars. [Longfellow, *Evangeline* (1847)]

Fork, To pass under the : to admit defeat. In allusion to the fork or yoke at Caudi under which the Roman army had to pass on the occasion of their defeat in 321 B.C.

Forked radish, A : man. [Shakespeare, *2 Henry IV*, III, ii (1597–8)]

Forlorn Hope, A : (Dutch, *verloren hoop*, lost troop) (1) a small body of troops used as a sacrifice to gain an advantage for the main army ; (2) a task practically impossible of fulfilment. [Tonstall, *Sermons* (1539)]

Form, Bad (Good) : *see* Bad (Good) form.

Forma pauperis, In (*Lat.*, in the guise of a pauper): of a suitor too poor to engage counsel.

Fortiter in re (*Lat.*): determined in action.

Fortuitous concourse of atoms, A : an accidental collection of objects. First used by Richard Bentley (1692): applied by the *Quarterly Review* to Sir Robert Peel's Administration (LIII, p. 270). [Cicero, *De Natura Deorum*, Bk. II, 37]

Fortunate Islands, The ; Islands of the Blest, The : orig. mythical islands in the Atlantic, the abode of the supremely happy. When the Canary Islands were discovered the name was attached to them.

Fortunatus' purse : the purse whose contents are never exhausted. After the medieval legend of Fortunatus.

Fortunatus' wishing cap : the hat which transports the wearer to any destination he wishes. From the medieval legend of Fortunatus.

Fortune, Dame : the personification of fortune or luck.

Fortune hunter, A : a person who seeks to marry an heiress for her money. *See* the comedy of that title by J. Carlisle (1689).

'Forty-five, The : the Jacobite Rebellion of 1745–6.

Fortyniners, The : the argonauts of 'Forty-nine (*q.v.*).

Forty stripes save one : the Thirty-nine Articles.

Forty winks : a short sleep, esp. after dinner.

Forum, A : a place or opportunity for public discussion. In allusion to the Forum, the place at Rome where public business was transacted.

Forward, To be : to be the opposite of diffident or retiring.

Forwards, Marshal : name borne by Marshal Blücher (1742–1819) during the campaign of 1813. In allusion to his continual exhortations to his troops to advance.

Foul of .. To fall : to come into collision with .. A nautical metaphor. [Sir Thos. Overbury, *Newes from Sea* (1613)]

Foul Fiend, The : Satan.

Foul play : unfair play ; treachery. [Lyly, *Euphues* (1579)]

Foul weather Jack : Admiral John Byron (1723–86). In allusion to his ill-luck at sea.

Founder of the Fathers of Christian Doctrine, The : Cæsar de Bus (1544–1607).

Fountain-head, To go to the : to go to the original source. [T. Washington, Transl. of *Nicholay's Voyages*, I, viii (1585)]

Fountain of human liberty, The : knowledge, according to Daniel Webster.

Fountain of Life, The : Alexander of Hales (d. 1245), Eng. theologian and philosopher.

Fountain of Youth, The : a mythical spring which is supposed to give those who bathe in it perpetual youth. It has been located at different times in many places.

Four Apprentices (Prentices), The : four mythical heroes, Godfrey, Grey, Charles and Eustace, sons of an Earl of Boloign, who, rejecting trade for war, performed prodigies of valour in the Holy Land and elsewhere. Their exploits are narrated in *The Foure Prentises of London : With the Conquest of Jerusalem* (1615).

Four-bottle man, A : a man who customarily drinks four bottles of wine at a sitting.

Four in hand, A : coach with four horses.

Four Hundred, The : the élite of New York society.

Four walls, Within : *see* Walls.

Fours, On all : in complete agreement.

Fours, To go on all : to proceed on hands and feet like a quadruped.

Fourierism : a scheme for the organization of mankind in small communities, invented by François Charles Marie Fourier (1772–1837).

Fourteen hundred : the cry uttered on the London Stock Exchange when the presence of a stranger is detected. It is supposed to be derived from the fact that the number of members of the Exchange was for long limited to 1399.

Fourth dimension, The : a supposed or assumed dimension whose relation to the recognized dimensions of length, breadth, and thickness is analogous to that borne by any one of these to the other two. The conception has been used to explain certain super-physical phenomena, which seem otherwise inexplicable.

Fourth Estate, The : the Press. The suggestion, made by Edmund Burke, is that its power is greater than that of the three estates of the realm. *See also* Estates.

Fourth of July, The : the day of the declaration of American Independence in 1776, observed as a national holiday in the United States.

Fourth Party, The : a party in the House of Commons consisting of Lord Randolph Churchill, Sir Henry Drummond Wolff, Sir John Gorst and Mr. Arthur J. Balfour, active during the Parl. of 1880. The other three parties were the Conservative, Liberal and Irish.

Four-wheeler, A : a four wheeled hackney carriage, distinguished from a hansom cab (two wheels).

Fox, An old : (1) a good blade ; after the design of a fox, which was once customarily engraved, as a sort of trade-mark, on the best Toledo and other blades ; (2) a sly person. [Shakespeare, *Merry Wives of Windsor*, III, iii, 71–3 (1598–9) ; Letter of Queen Elizabeth to James VI of Scotland (June, 1585)]

Fox, The old : Marshal Soult (1769–1851), so called on account of his strategic gifts.

Fox that has lost his tail, A : a person who having himself met with misfortune endeavours to involve others in similar troubles. From the fable of the fox, which having lost his own tail, tries to persuade his fellows to sacrifice theirs.

Fox's sleep, A : pretended indifference to what is transpiring. In allusion to the proverbial cunning of the fox.

Foxes to the plough, To yoke : to act foolishly and to no purpose.

Francis's distemper, St. : impecuniosity. The members of the Order of St. Francis are vowed to poverty.

Franc-tireur, A (*Fr.*, free-shooter) : an irregular soldier, esp. on the French side during the Franco-Prussian War of 1870–1.

Frank, A : a European in Turkey and other Moslem lands ; from France. The term originated in the period of the Crusades and was first applied to the French only.

Frank pledge : the system of common responsibility for each individual member of a body.

Frankenstein, A : (1) one overpowered by his own creation ; (2) the monster of one's own creation which overpowers. After the title of a novel (1818) by Mary Wollstonecraft Godwin (Shelley) (1797–1851).

Frankum's night, A : a night in June fatal to apple or pear blossom ; from the story of Frankum who offered a sacrifice in order to secure esp. favourable weather for his orchard but was cursed by a blight instead.

Frazzle, Beat to a : beaten to ribbons or fragments.

Freddy, A pretty : a swell ; a dandy.

Free as air, As : [Marston, *The Insatiate Count* (1613)]

Free as the sun, As : [Dekker, *The Honest Whore* (1604)]

Free Breakfast Table, A : a fiscal system in which no import duties are levied on tea, coffee, cocoa, sugar, and other common articles of diet. The phrase was coined by John Bright, Eng. statesman and orator (1811–1889) in an address to the Edinburgh Chamber of Commerce in 1868.

Free Church, A : an independent church, esp. the Presbyt. Church that seceded from the Est. Church of Scotland in 1893. (The Free Kirk).

Free Churches, The : the Eng. Nonconf. Churches.

Free Company, A : a band of mercenary soldiers, available for hire by any ruler or state.

Free and easy, A : a social gathering at which one is freed from the trammels of society conventions. [Lister, *Journey to Paris*, 41 (1699)]

Free fight, A : a melée in which every man's hand is against everyone.

Free hand, To have a : to be untrammelled. To have full liberty of action.

Free house, A : a public-house not " tied " or bound to purchase its beer from any particular brewer.

Free Kirk, The : *see* Free Church.

Free labour : labour unattached to any Trade Union.

Free lance, A : (1) a member of a Free Company (*q.v.*) ; (2) a person unattached to any party, class, etc. ; (3) a journalist unattached to any periodical but contributing to several.

Free with, To make : to take liberties with.

Free Soilers : an Amer. polit. party in the middle of the 19th cent., formed to oppose the extension of slavery to the Territories. Merged in 1854 in the Republican Party.

Free States, The : those states of the American Union in which slavery had been abolished prior to the outbreak of the Civil War of 1861.

Free Trade : the principle of the interchange of commodities between different states, unhindered by customs duties, except for purposes of revenue.

Free Trade, The Apostle of : Rich. Cobden (1804–1865).

Freeman, Mrs. : see Mrs. Morley and Mrs. Freeman.

Freestone State, The : Connecticut, U.S.A. In allusion to the freestone found within its borders.

Freeze out, To : to force out of a business, company, etc., either by boycott or by intense competition. An Americanism.

French Aristides, The : Albert Grévy (1813–91), President of the French Republic. After Aristides the Just (c. 530–468 B.C.), the Athenian statesman and general.

French Aristophanes, The : Molière (1622–73). After Aristophanes (c. 448–385 B.C.), the famous Grk. comedian.

French Cream : brandy. In allusion to the Fr. practice of taking it with coffee.

French Crown : baldness caused by the French disease (q.v.). [Shakespeare, *Midsummer Night's Dream*, I, ii, 99 (1590)]

French Disease, The : venereal disease ; from its prevalence in France (early 16th cent.).

French Ennius, The : (1) Guillaume di Lorris (1235–65) ; (2) Jehan de Meung (1260–1320), French poet. After Quintus Ennius (239–170 B.C.), the early Roman poet.

French leave, To take : to act without permission. After the custom in France in the 18th cent. of leaving a social gathering without taking leave of the host or hostess. Another origin is from the practice of the Fr. soldiery in the 16th cent. of seizing whatever they required.

French Lycophron, The : Jean Dorat (1504–88), philologist and poet. After Lycophron (fl. 285–247 B.C.), the father of the anagram in Greece.

French Ovid, The : Joachim de Bellay (c. 1524–1560). After Ovid (B.C. 43 to A.D. 18), the Rom. poet.

French Phidias, The : (1) Jean Goujon (1515–1568) ; (2) Jean Baptiste Pigalle (1714–1785). After Phidias (c. 500–432 B.C.), the famous Grk. sculptor.

French Pindar, The : (1) Jean Dinemandy (Dorat) (1504–1588) ; (2) Ponce Denis Lebrun (1719–1807). After Pindar (c. 522–443 B.C.), the famous Theban lyric poet.

French Raphael, The : Eustache Le Sueur (1616–1655). After Raphael da Urbino (1483–1520), the great Ital. painter.

French of Stratford atte Bowe : Cockney French. [Chaucer, *Canterbury Tales : Prologue*, 120–2 (14th cent.)]

French Tibullus, The : see Tibullus.

Fresh as flowers in May, As : very fresh. [*The Worlde and the Chylde*, l. 133 (1522)]

Fresh woods and pastures new : a new field of activity. [Milton, *Lycidas*, 193 (1637)]

Fresh-water soldier, A : a raw recruit. [Florio, *A Worlde of Wordes* (1598)]

Friar Rush : a will o' the wisp. In Germ. folklore Friar Rush was an evil spirit who in particular led monks and friars astray.

Friar Tuck : a vagabond friar in medieval Eng. folklore.

Friday, A : a man Friday (q.v.).

Friday-faced : sad looking. In allusion to Friday as a fast-day in the Roman Catholic Church. [John Day, *Blind Beggar*, III, ii (1592)]

Friday, Long : see Long.

Friday, A man : a faithful personal attendant. In allusion to a character in Defoe, *Robinson Crusoe* (1719).

Friday tree, A : a trouble or misfortune. In allusion to the tree or cross on which Jesus was crucified on the original Good Friday.

Fridays come together, When two : never.

Friend at Court, A : one who is in a position to use his influence on behalf of another. Properly one who attends in a court of law to watch for and point out irregularities. [*Romaunt of the Rose* (c. 1400)]

Friend in need, A : a friend who has been tested and found reliable. From the proverb, ' A friend in need is a friend indeed.'

Friend of God, The : (1) Abraham ; (2) any pious man.

Friend of man, The : (1) Victor, Marquis de Mirabeau (1715–89), author of *L'Ami des Hommes*, The Friend of Men (1756) ; (2) the robin. ; (3) the dog.

Friends of Ireland : an organization founded by Daniel O'Connell in 1830, afterwards merged in the Irish Volunteers.

Friends of the People : a Whig society formed at the end of the 18th cent. to secure parl. reform.

Fritz, A : a Germ. soldier. So-called in the British Army, during the war of 1914–18. After a common personal name in Germany.

Fritz, Unser (*Germ.*, Our Fritz) : the Emp. Frederick of Germany (1831–88). So-called by the Germans.

Froebel, The Italian : Antonio Rosmini-Serbati (1797–1855).

Froebel System, The : a system of education for young children, invented by Frederick Wilhelm August Froebel (1782–1852), German educationist.

Froebelism : *see* Froebel System.

Frog, A : a Frenchman, or more properly a Parisian. In allusion either to the device of the City of Paris, three frogs or toads, or to the gastronomical use of frogs in France.

Frog, To catch a : to obtain little result to great exertions. [Heywood, *Proverbes* (1546)]

Frog, Nic (Nicholas) : a Dutchman. So-called in John Arbuthnot, *Law is a Bottomless Pit* (1712).

Frog's march, A : the carrying of a man face downwards by four bearers, one holding each limb.

Fronde (*Fr.*, a sling) : the French political party that rebelled against the govt. of Mazarin during the minority of Louis XIV (1648–53). Hence any violent political opposition. *Frondeur*, a member of the party ; also a political opponent concerned with party advantage alone.

Frondeur, A : a spiteful critic ; a scandalmonger. *See* Fronde.

Frost and flowers, To suit like : to be quite unsuitable.

Frost Saints : St. Mamertus, St. Pancratius, St. Servatius, St. Boniface, whose days fall in 'the blackthorn winter' (May 11th–14th).

Frowning cloth, To wear one's : to be displeased. From an imaginary covering of the eyes (frowning cloth).

Frozen music : architecture. So-called by Carl Wilhelm Friedrich von Schlegel (1772–1829).

Fruit, Forbidden : *see* Forbidden.

Fry, The common : young or unimportant people in general. From ' fry ' in the sense of the young of human beings or fishes, collectively.

Fry, Small : people of little consequence, lit. newly spawned fishes.

Frying-pan into the fire, Out of the : out of one trouble into a greater one. [Cervantes, *Don Quixote*, Pt. I, Bk. III, ch. iv ; Heywood, *Proverbes* (1546)]

Fuchsia : a flowering plant, native to S. and C. America. After Leonard Fuchs, Germ. bot. (1501–66).

Fudge (*Germ.*, *futsch*, a term of contempt) : nonsense. Apparently invented by Oliver Goldsmith in the *Vicar of Wakefield* (1766).

Fuel to the fire, To add : to act or speak so as to increase a person's anger. [Horace, *Satires*, Bk. II, iii, 32 ; Ingeland, *Disobedient Child*, l. 317 (1560) ; Thos. Kyd, *Spanish Tragedy* (1592)]

Fugger, As rich as a : very wealthy. In allusion to the Fuggers, a family of rich 16th cent. German merchants.

Fulhams : loaded dice. After the district of London which was notorious in the 17th cent. for its bad characters.

Full of meat as an egg, As : of prime quality. [John Still, *Gammer Gurton's Needle*, V, ii (1566) ; Shakespeare, *Romeo and Juliet*, III, i, 21 (1591)]

Full swing, In : with the utmost energy.

Fum the Fourth : George IV of England.

Fume, In a : in a temper. From the former sense of fume, vapour given off by bodies when heated.

Fun of, To make : to ridicule. Phrase apparently invented by Horace Walpole (1717–97). *See* his *Correspondence*.

Fun at, To poke : to ridicule. Phrase apparently invented by Thos. Hood (1799–1845)]

Funds, The : the stock of a national debt.

Funk, To be in a : to be frightened ; poss. from (Walloon) *fonk*, smoke. [Peter Pindar, *Subjects for Painters* (18th cent.)]

Funny bone, The : the extremity of the elbow. A verbal play on the Lat. equivalent, *humerus*.

Furnace, To roast snow in a : *see* Roast.

Fussy as a hen that has one chick, As : *see* Busy as a hen, etc.

Fustian : (1) bombast ; (2) a coarse cotton fabric. From Fostat, a dist. of Cairo, where the fabric was orig. obtained. [Gosson, *Ephemerides of Phialto* (1579) ; Lyly, *Euphues and his England* (1580)]

Futures, To deal in : to purchase shares in the expectation that their value will rise before the purchaser is called on to pay for them.

G.O.M., The : the Grand Old Man, Wm. Ewart Gladstone (1809–98), British statesman. The epithet, ' The Grand Old Man,' is said to have been first applied to him by Sir Stafford Northcote (1818–87), 1st Earl of Iddesleigh. The initial letters were first applied to Gladstone by Lord Rosebery on the 26th of April, 1882. Still earlier Walter Farquhar Hook (1798–1875), Dean of Chichester and author, used the term on at least two occasions, in reference to Handel, the composer, and to Theodore, Archbishop of Canterbury.

G.O.M. of Athens, The : Pericles (490–429 B.C.), Athenian statesman. So-called by Frederick Apthorp Paley in his *Fragments of Greek Comic Poets* (1888).

G.T.T. : gone to Texas ; decamped.

Gab, The gift of the : the power of eloquence and persuasive talking ; from *gab* (Ang.-Sax.), speech, (Scot.) the mouth. [Godwin, *Caleb Williams* (1794)]

Gaberlunzie man, A : a wandering beggar. From gaberlunzie, a coarse woollen gown, a costume worn by licensed beggars.

Gabrielle, La belle : Gabrielle d'Estrées (1571–1599), Mistress of Henry IV of France.

Gabriel's hounds : wild geese. From the noise they make when flying and from the legend that they are the souls of unbaptized children doomed to wander until the Day of Judgment.

Gaff, To blow the : to divulge a secret.

Gaff, A penny : a low class theatre. After the name of the first Drury Lane theatre, built on the site of a cockpit. The gaff was the iron hook with which cocks were goaded to the fight.

Gag, A : an interpolation in the dialogue of a play by the actor. Properly a mining term for a piece of timber pushed in hurriedly to prevent others from settling.

Gag, The : the closure, the power given to the majority in the House of Commons to close a debate.

Gage d'Amour (*Fr.*, a love token) : [Sterne, *Sentimental Journey* (1768)]

Galanty Show, A : a shadow pantomime.

Galaxy, A : orig. the Milky Way ; a brilliant concourse of persons. Grk., γαλαξίας, milky.

Galen, A : a physician. After a celebrated physician of Pergamus (2nd cent.).

Galen says no and Hippocrates says yes, When : when doctors disagree. Galen (2nd cent.) and Hippocrates (460–357 B.C.) were famous physicians of antiquity.

Galena : salt pork ; from Galen, Illinois, a pork packing centre.

Galenist, A : a herb doctor. *See* Galen.

Galère ? Que faites vous dans cette : *see* Que.

Galère, Vogue la : *see* Vogue.

Galilean, A : (1) a Christian, after Galilee one of the scenes of Jesus' activities ; (2) a telescope, after the inventor, Galileo (1564–1642).

Galilee, A : a church porch. After Galilee as an outlying province of the Holy Land.

Gall of Bitterness, The : extreme bitterness of spirit. According to the ancients the gall was the seat of grief and joy. [*Acts*, viii, 23]

Gall, Full of : full of bitterness. [Jas. Puckle, *The Club : The Buffoon* (1711)]

Gall, To be turned to : to be changed into sorrow. [Gray, *William Shakespeare to Mrs. Anne*, ll. 11–2 (1765)]

Gall and Wormwood : that which causes mental pain and bitterness. Gall and wormwood are both synonyms for bitterness. [Wycliffe, Transl. of the Bible (14th cent.)]

Gallantee Show, A : *see* Galanty Show.

Gallery, To play to the : of a leader, speaker, etc., to lower his views or the expression of them to the level of the mob. A theatrical metaphor :— to act as to satisfy the crude desires of the occupants of the gallery.

Gallicanism : the movement within the R.C. Ch. in France which is opposed to Ultramontanism and the encroachments of the Papal authority.

Galligaskins : (1) a style of trousers ; (2) leather gaiters worn by sportsmen. Old Fr., *garguescans*, from *grechesco* (Ital.) greekish, a term in use in Venice. Another suggested der. is from Galley and Gascons, the suggestion being that such garments were worn by galley seamen of Gascony. [Thomas Nashe, *Pierce Penilesse* (1592)]

Gallio, A : an easy-going person ; one who does not interfere outside of his official duties. After Gallio, the Rom.

pro-consul, ' who cared for none of those things.' [*Acts*, xviii.].

Gallomania : a passion for things and fashions French.

Galloway, A : a horse of small size, bred in Galloway, Scotland.

Gallowglasses : Scot. and Irish heavily armed mercenary foot troops in the time of Elizabeth. Irish, *galloglach*, foreign soldier.

Gallows, To cheat the : of a criminal, who dies otherwise than on the gallows.

Gallows-bird, A : one who deserves to be hanged.

Galley-breeches : *see* Galligaskins.

Gally-Gaskins : *see* Galligaskins.

Gally-pot baronet, A : a physician-baronet.

Galore (*Irish, go leór*): in abundance.

Galvanism : a branch of the science of electricity. From Luigi Galvani, Ital. physicist (1737-98).

Galway Jury, A : a courageous, just jury. From the action of a Galway jury in deciding against the King in a case heard in 1635.

Gamaliel, A : a pedant ; a distinguished teacher. After the Jewish teacher of St. Paul.

Gamaliel Ratsey, A : a highwayman. After one who flourished in the 16th and 17th centuries.

Game, To be : to be ready and fully prepared, esp. for a fight or mischief. A cockfighting metaphor.

Game, To die : to remain resolute until the last. A cockfighting metaphor.

Game, Fair : a legitimate object of attack, ridicule, etc. A hunting metaphor.

Game leg, A (*Irish, gam*, bad, crooked): an injured leg.

Game, One's little : one's dodge or trick.

Game of .. To make : to ridicule [Ros, *Belle Dame sans Mercy*, 226 (1460)]

Game, To play a losing : *see* Losing.

Game, To play the : to act straight-forwardly. A gambling metaphor. [Dryden, *Epistle to Mr. Lee*, ll. 5–6 (1677)]

Game, Two can play at that : of sharp or incorrect practice ; others can act similarly. A gambling metaphor.

Game is up, The : an admission of defeat. A gambling metaphor. [Shakespeare, *Cymbeline*, III, iii (1610)]

Game is not worth the candle, The : *see* Candle.

Game's afoot, The : the enterprise has commenced. [Shakespeare, *Henry V*, III, i (1599)]

Gamin, A (*Fr.*) : a street Arab.

Gammon : nonsense ; idle chatter. Orig. thieves' slang. To keep in gammon is to keep the attention of a person while a confederate is robbing him. [14th cent.]

Gamp, A : a large shabby umbrella. After Mrs. Sairey Gamp, a character in Dickens, *Martin Chuzzlewit* (1843), who always carried such a one.

Gamp, Sarah (Sairy) (Mrs.) : a middle-aged, unqualified, drinking midwife. After a character in Dickens, *Martin Chuzzlewit* (1843).

Gamps and Harrises : workhouse or other low-class nurses. After characters in Dickens, *Martin Chuzzlewit* (1843).

Gang agley, To (*Scot.*) : to go wrong.

Gang days, The : the Rogation days ; three days preceding Ascension Day, on which processions take place.

Gang one's own gait, To : to go one's own way. Scot., *gang*, to go, *gait*, a course.

Gang Monday : Monday in Rogation Week. *See* Gang days.

Gang Week : Rogation Week. *See* Gang days.

Ganymede, A : (1) a beautiful youth ; (2) a pot-boy. After the cupbearer of Jupiter, ' the most beautiful boy ever born.'

Ganymede, The birds of : eagles. From the legend of Ganymede riding to Olympus on the back of an eagle.

Gaol bird, A : a criminal, esp. one who is frequently in prison. [Earle, *Micro-cosmography : A Vulgar-spirited Man* (1628)]

Gape's nest, To seek a : to stare about open-mouthed. Devonshire phrase.

Gape seed, To look for : to stare open-mouthed. [Florio (1598)]

Gaps with one bush, To stop two : *see* Stop.

Gaps with rushes, To stop : *see* Stop.

Garcias ; Garcias, The Soul of Pedro : money. According to a statement made in the preface to Le Sage, *Gil Blas* (1715), two scholars of Salamanca discovered a tombstone with the inscription ' Here lies the soul of the licentiate Pedro Garcias.' In the tomb they found only a purse of gold.

Garden of Armida : *see* Armida.

Garden City, The : Chicago.

Garden of Cymodoce, The : the island of Sark. So-called by Swinburne in a poem of that name (1880).

Garden of England, The : (1) Kent ; (2) Worcestershire ; (3) the Isle of Wight.

Garden of Erin, The : Carlow.

Garden of Europe, The : (1) Italy ; (2) Belgium.

Garden of France, The : (1) Touraine ; (2) Amboise in Indre et Loire.

Garden of Helvetia, The : Thurgau.

Garden of India, The : Oude.

Garden of Ireland, The : Carlow.

Garden of Italy, The : Sicily.

Garden of South Wales, The : South Glamorganshire.

Garden of Spain, The : Andalusia.

Garden State, The : (1) Kansas ; (2) New Jersey.

Garden of the Sun, The : the East Indian Archipelago.

Garden of the West, The : (1) Kansas ; (2) Illinois.

Garden of the World, The : (1) Italy ; (2) London ; (3) the region of the Mississippi.

Gardenia : a genus of evergreen shrub. After Alex. Garden, Amer. bot. (c. 1730–91).

Gargantua, A : a person with an insatiable appetite. *See* Gargantuan.

Gargantuan : (1) gigantic ; (2) threatening. After the giant king in Rabelais, *The Life of Gargantua* (1532).

Gargantuan course of studies, A : a course of studies covering all subjects. *See* Rabelais, *Pantagruel*, ii, 8 (1532).

Garibaldi, A : a blouse, orig. red, the colour of Garibaldi's red shirts ; from the name of the Ital. revolutionist Giuseppe Garibaldi (1807–82). *See next entry.*

Garibaldi's red shirt : the uniform adopted by Garibaldi and his men in the liberation of Italy (1859–66). From the garment worn by Amer. merchant-seamen, first adopted by Garibaldi when he took command of the merchantmen at Baltimore.

Garter, The Order of the : England's highest order of knighthood ; established about 1349. The foundation and name of the Order are attributed to the finding of a garter of the Countess of Salisbury by the King, Edward III.

Garters untied, To go with one's : in the reign of Elizabeth, an outward expression of being in love, being too

much engrossed to trouble about one's personal appearance.

Garvies : sprats. After Inch Garvie in the Firth of Forth where they are caught.

Gas, To : to talk at great length but without any value.

Gascon, A : a boaster. *See* Gasconade.

Gasconade, A : boasting. After Gascony in France whose people were reputed to have a tendency in that direction.

Gascoyne Bride, The : Moll Cutpurse (*q.v.*), who assumed male attire. *For* Gascoyne *see* Galligaskins.

Gaspipe cavalry : military cyclists.

Gate, The : the money taken at the gate for admission to a cricket or football match or other sporting display.

Gate of Horn : *see* Horn Gate.

Gate of Ivory : *see* Ivory Gate.

Gate of the mind, The : the face. [Rob. Johnson, *Essayes : Of Travell* (1607)]

Gate money : *see* Gate.

Gate of Tears, The : the entrance to the Red Sea. So-called by the Arabs on account of the number of shipwrecks that occur there.

Gath ! Tell it not in : publish not the news abroad ! [II *Samuel*, i, 20]

Gathers, Out of : in distress. Like a woman's dress whose gathers or pleats have become unfastened.

Gathered to one's fathers, To be : to die. A biblical phrase. [*Genesis*, xxv, 8 ; *Judges*, ii, 10]

Gatling-gun, A : a species of machine-gun. After Rich. Jordan Gatling, the Amer. inventor (1818–1903).

Gauche (*Fr.*, left-[handed]) : clumsy ; tactless.

Gaucho, A : a mixed Spanish and Indian inhabitant of S. America, esp. skilled in horsemanship.

Gaudy days (nights) (*Lat.*, *gaudere*, to rejoice) : days (nights) of rejoicing ; gala days. [16th cent.]

Gauntlet, To run the : to undergo punishment ; to run the risk of punishment or danger from two or more sides. Properly to run the gantlope, a military and naval punishment in which the sufferer, stripped to the waist, ran between two rows of men armed with whips. [Smollett, *Peregrine Pickle*, ch. 80 (1751)]

Gauntlet, To throw down the : to challenge. From the practice of chivalry of throwing down a gauntlet or glove as a challenge.

Gautier and Garguille : everybody in general. Gautier-Gargouille was a 17th cent. French clown who made fun of everybody.

Gavelkind : an Anglo-Saxon system of inheritance whereby all the sons shared alike.

Gay deceiver, A : a libertine ; a man who, with no real intentions of matrimony, sponges on families where there are marriageable daughters. [Smollett, Transl. of *Gil Blas* (1749)]

Gay dog, A : a gallant.

Gay as the king's candle, As : showily dressed. In allusion to a candle of many colours, formerly burnt in France on the Vigil of the Kings. (Jan. 6).

Gay Science, The : (1) poetry ; (2) belles lettres, generally ; (3) minstrelsy.

Gazet, Not worth a : of practically no value. From gazet, a Venetian coin worth less than a farthing.

Gazette, A : a newspaper. After the gazet or gazzetta, the Venetian coin that was paid for permission to read the manuscript newspaper which recorded the events in the war with Soliman the Magnificent (c. 1522).

Gazing-stock, A : anything that is gazed at or attracts idle attention. [Miles Coverdale, Transl. of the Bible (1535)]

Geese are swans, All his : he is given to exaggeration. [Robert Burton, *Anatomy of Melancholy*, Pt. I, Sect. II, memb. 3, sub-sect. 14 (1621)]

Gehenna : Hell. Lit., the Valley of Hinnom, near Jerusalem, the place of sacrifice of children to Moloch, and later the receptacle of the refuse of the city which was consumed by fire. Heb., *Ge*, valley, and *Hinnom*.

Gelert, As faithful as : devoted. In allusion to the dog Gelert, the hound of Llewellyn, famous in Welsh legend for its devotion to its master.

Gem of the ocean, The : Ireland. So-called by Thomas Moore.

Gemini ! Oh : a 17th cent. oath invoking the Gemini or twin-gods, Castor and Pollux.

General, The : the mob. So-used by Shakespeare.

General Janvier and General Fevrier (*Fr.*, General January and General February) : the rigours of winter which destroyed the army led by Napoleon into Russia (1812).

General post, The : the first postal delivery of the day ; orig. the mail that arrived from the General Post Office in London.

Generous as Hatim, As : Hatim was a Bedouin chief who lived during the generation before Mahomet.

Geneva : (1) Calvinism, after the Swiss town formerly the centre of the cult ; (2) gin ; an alcoholic spirit flavoured with juniper berries. (Fr., *genièvre*, the juniper tree).

Geneva bands : white neckbands orig. worn by Calvinists and subsequently by clergymen of that denomination. *See* Geneva (1).

Geneva Bible, The : the Eng. translation of the Bible, printed at Geneva in 1560.

Geneva Bull, The : Stephen Marshall (c. 1594–1655), a Calvinist divine, who possessed a very loud voice.

Geneva Convention, The : the Convention between the Powers (1864) by which was regulated international usage in warfare as regards the wounded and sick. The Red Cross is the badge of those who work under it.

Geneva courage : valour induced by alcohol. In allusion to Geneva as a synonym for gin.

Geneva Cross, The : a red cross on a white ground, worn by doctors, nurses, and others connected with the service of the wounded and sick in the army. *See* Geneva Convention.

Geneva Doctrines : Calvinism. After John Calvin, the reformer, who lived at Geneva from 1541 onwards.

Geneva gown, A : a black gown with bands worn by Calvinist and other clergymen, similar to those worn by the Calvinists in Geneva.

Geneva hat, A : a hat of the style worn by Puritan clergymen. *See* Geneva gown.

Geneva print, To read : to drink gin or other spirit. *See* Geneva.

Geneva Weaver, A : a puritan. In the 16th cent. weavers were celebrated for their psalm-singing : Geneva was a centre of Puritanism.

Genius, One's evil : he who has a bad influence over one.

Genius loci (*Lat.*, genius of the place) : the presiding spirit ; the associations and inspirations that gather round a place. [Dryden, *Epistle to Dr. Charleton*, ll. 53–6 (1663)]

Gentle craft, The : (1) angling ; (2) shoemaking. [Greene's *George-a-Greene* (1592)] In the former case the phrase turns on the gentle or maggot used as a bait; in the latter the allusion is to the Romance of Prince Crispin who was a cobbler.

Gentle People, The : fairies.

Gentle Shepherd, The : George Grenville (1712–1770), Eng. statesman; so called by William Pitt, Earl of Chatham.

Gentleman in black, A : a scholar. [Sir Thos. Overbury, *Characters : A meere Scholar* (1616)]

Gentleman in Black, The : the Devil.

Gentleman in black (brown) velvet, The : a mole. So called by the Jacobites who believed that a mole was the cause of the death of King William III.

Gentleman-commoner, A : a specially privileged undergraduate of Oxford or Cambridge.

Gentleman of fortune, A : (1) a pirate; (2) an adventurer.

Gentleman of the four outs, A : one without manners, without wit, without money, without credit.

Gentleman of the jacket, A : a sailor. [Henry Fielding, *Voyage to Lisbon* (1755)]

Gentleman at large, A : one of the unemployed; orig. one attached to the Court without any specific duties.

Gentleman of the long robe, A : a barrister or clergyman. In allusion to the costume worn by members of those professions when on duty. [*The Spectator*, No. 197 (1711)]

Gentleman, The old : the Devil.

Gentleman of the pad, A : a highwayman. [Farquhar, *Beaux Stratagem*, II, ii (1706)]

Gentleman of paper and wax, A : a newly created Knight; one made a 'gentleman' by patent and seal.

Gentleman of the Press, A : a journalist. Phrase coined by Lord Beaconsfield in a speech in the House of Commons (18th Feb., 1853).

Gentleman ranker, A : a private soldier of superior social station; generally one who enlists after failure to pass the examination for a commission and is speedily promoted.

Gentleman in red, A : a soldier. In allusion to the former colour of the ordinary Brit. military uniform.

Gentleman of the Road, A : a highwayman.

Gentleman of the Short staff, A : a constable.

Gentleman of the three outs, A : ' Without money, without wit, without manners ' (Grose's *Dict. of the Vulgar Tongue*), ' out of pocket, out of elbows, out of credit ' (Lytton, *Paul Clifford*).

Gentleman's gentleman, A : a valet. [Defoe, *Everybody's Business* (1725); Goldsmith, *Citizen of the World*, Letter cxx (1760)]

Genus omne, Et Hoc : *see* Hoc.

George, Farmer : *see* Farmer.

George-a-Green, As strong (good) as : George-a-Green was a popular hero of the old ballad poetry. As pinner or pindar (pound-keeper) of Wakefield he defeated all comers at quarterstaff. He was the subject of *The Pindar of Wakefield* by R. Greene (1599). [*Wit's Recreations* (1640)]

German comb, The : the four fingers and thumb. In allusion to the former German practice of adjusting the hair with the fingers.

German Florence, The : Dresden.

German Literature, The father of : Gotthold Ephraim Lessing (1729–81).

German Plato, The : Fredrich Heinrich Jacobi (1743–1819). In allusion to Plato (427–347 B.C.), the Grk. philosopher.

German Pliny, The : Konrad von Gesner (1516–65). In allusion to Pliny, the Elder (23–79), Roman naturalist.

German silver : an alloy that looks like silver; first made in Germany.

German Voltaire, The : *see* Voltaire, The German.

German's lips, As just as : *see* Jerman's Lips.

Germanophobia : unreasonable hatred of Germany, Germans or things German.

Germany, Young : *see* Young.

Gerrymander, To : so to arrange the electoral divisions as artificially to secure a majority. After Elbridge Gerry, Gov. of Massachusetts (1744–1814), who was given to this practice. The word was coined by Benjamin Russell, Editor of *The Continent*, in 1812.

Get at a person, To : to obtain influence over improperly or corruptly.

Get one's back up, To : to estrange; to render antagonistic. In allusion to the atittude of a cat when faced by an enemy.

Get out of bed on the wrong side, To : to be irritable and bad tempered. In allusion to the proverb ' To rise on the right side is accounted lucky.'

Get into one's good graces, To : to get into a person's favour.

Get on one's nerves, To : to affect one so as to make one irritable.

Get on in the world, To : to advance in fortune, to make progress.

Ghetto, A (*Ital.*) **:** orig. the quarter of a medieval continental city in which the Jews were confined ; now any district of a city largely inhabited by Jews.

Ghibellines, The : the Imperial party in med. Italy ; the opponents of the Guelphs.

Ghost, A : a person who does literary or artistic work on behalf of another and in his name.

Ghost Book, A : a book that has been announced but has never been published.

Ghost of a chance, The : a very slight chance.

Ghost, To give up the : to die. [*Job*, xiv, 10 ; Earl of Surrey, *Complaint of a diyng louer* (1557)]

Ghost Word, A : a word that had never any real existence but owed its origin to the blunder of a printer, copyist or editor. Term invented by W. W. Skeat. [*Transactions Philological Society*, p. 371 (1886)]

Ghoul, A : a person who seeks profit of the dead. After an oriental demon who was supposed to devour human beings.

Giant Despair : the owner of Doubting Castle in Bunyan, *Pilgrim's Progress* (1678).

Giant gooseberry, A : a marvellous story. After the wonderful accounts of giant gooseberries, etc., with which newspapers used to fill their columns in the slack season.

Giant of Literature, The : Dr. Samuel Johnson (1709–83).

Giant, To stand on the shoulders of a : of a mediocrity who has the advantage of the discoveries of the great men who have preceded him. [Sir Isaac Newton to Rob. Hooke, 5 Feb. 1675–6]

Giants, Battle of the : *see* Battle.

Gib, The cut of one's : a person's facial appearance. A nautical metaphor.

Gib, To hang one's : to be angry. The gib is the lower lip of a horse.

Gib, To play fy : to threaten. From Gib, a cat, a diminutive of Gilbert, the cat in the fable of *Reynard the Fox*.

Gib, To play the : to behave like a cat.

Gibberish : unintelligible nonsense. After Geber (fl. c. 800), an Arabian alchemist, who spoke an unintelligible jargon in order to protect himself against prosecution for heresy.

Gibelines : *see* Ghibellines.

Gibeonite, A : a menial. After the Gibeonites who were made in perpetuity hewers of wood and drawers of water to the Israelites. [*Joshua*, ix, 27]

Gibeonites' work, To do : to be a slave. *see* Gibeonite.

Gibraltar of .. The : an impregnable outpost of a country or fortress, like Gibraltar.

Gibraltar of America, The : Quebec.

Gibraltar of the New World, The : Quebec, or more properly, Cape Diamond in the Province of Quebec.

Gibson girl, A : a style of girl as depicted in the drawings of Mr. Chas. Dana Gibson (b. 1867), Amer. artist.

Gibus, A : an opera-hat. After the name of the inventor.

Giddy goat, To play the : to live a fast, happy-go-lucky life.

Gift of the gab : *see* Gab.

Gift horse in the mouth, To look a : to criticise a gift. From the proverb, ' Never look a gift horse in the mouth,' which was current at least as early as the 4th cent.

Gigantomachia, A : a superhuman contest or battle. After the battle of the giants against the gods, of Grk. legend.

Gigmanity ; Gigmanic : respectability ; respectable. Word invented by Thomas Carlyle to express the respectability of a man as proved by his keeping a gig. [*Essay on Boswell's Life of Johnson* (1832)]

Gilbertian : humorously absurd. After Sir William Schwenck Gilbert (1836–1911), Eng. humorous librettist.

Gild the pill, To : to soften the asperity of a course of action. From the practice of gilding a pill so that it may be the more easily swallowed. [Dekker, *Satiromastix* (1602)]

Gild refined gold, To : *see* Gold.

Gilded Chamber, The : the House of Lords.

Gilded youth, A : a wealthy young man of fashion and of much leisure. After the *Jeunesse Dorée* (gilded youth) who assisted in the overthrow of Robespierre.

Gilderoy's kite, To be hung higher than : to be punished most severely. Patrick Macgregor, otherwise Gilderoy (Red-headed Gillie), was a famous Highland brigand who was caught and hanged on a gallows higher than those of his associates at Edinburgh in June, 1636.

Gilead, Balm in : *see* Balm.

Giles, Hopping (Hobbling) : *see* Hopping Giles.

Gillian of Brentford : a noted witch.

Gillie-wet-foot, A : a follower of a Highland chief, among whose duties was the carrying of his master across streams. So-called in derision by Lowlanders. Gaelic, *gille*, a servant.

Gilt off the gingerbread, To take the : to destroy the illusion. It was once the custom to gild gingerbread, esp. when it was made up into fancy shapes.

Gilt-edged Securities : Stock Exchange securities of the highest class. The term was introduced during the last quarter of the 19th cent. from the U.S.

Gimlet eye, A : a crossed eye ; a piercing eye.

Gin : an alcoholic drink. An abbreviation of Geneva (*q.v.*).

Gin palace, A : a public house made esp. attractive in appearance. [*Oxford Univ. Magazine* (1834)]

Ginger : an appellation applied to red-haired people. After Guinevere, Queen of King Arthur, who is said to have had red hair.

Gingerbread, To take the gilt off the : *see* Gilt.

Gingham, A : a cheap umbrella. After the name of the cotton material of which they are made. Malay, *ging-gang*, striped, or from Guingamp in Brittany.

Giotto's O, As round as : stupid. In allusion to a story told of Giotto who sent an O as a specimen of his work to the Pope.

Gipsy : from Egypt, once believed to be the country of origin of the wandering race of gipsies.

Girdle, To give up one's : to become bankrupt. In allusion to the old French practice of giving up one's girdle when deprived of one's property. The girdle held one's keys, money, dagger, arms, etc.

Girl of all work, A : a maid-servant ; esp. one not of a very high class. [Jane Austen, *Sense and Sensibility*, ch. 38 (1811)]

Girl at ease, A : a prostitute.

Girl-graduates, Sweet : a phrase derived from Tennyson, *Princess*, Prologue, 142 (1847–50)]

Girondins ; Girondists, The : the moderate party in the Fr. Revolution. After the Dept. of the Gironde whose deputies led the party.

Gist of the matter, The : the pith ; the central point of the matter.

Give a person away, To : to betray a person ; intentionally or unintentionally.

Give oneself away, To : to make a confidential communication to the wrong person ; to tell a story against oneself ; to disclose one's foibles on the slightest provocation.

Give as good as one gets, To : to return blow for blow. [*The Spectator*, No. 605 (1714)]

Give and take, To : to compromise ; of two persons or parties, to give way on both parts.

Give straw to one's dog and bones to one's ass, To : to do precisely the wrong thing.

Gizzard, To stick in one's : to annoy one ; prove unpleasant. Pepys (1633–1703) used gizzard in this sense.

Glad eye, The : the glance of a girl intended to attract a strange man.

Gladstone : cheap claret. After William Ewart Gladstone (1809–98), who reduced the import duty on Fr. wines in 1869.

Gladstone bag, A : a small portmanteau. After William Ewart Gladstone, British statesman (1809–98).

Gladstone's umbrella : a reference to the discordant political elements which united in support of Gladstone at the General Election of 1885.

Gladstonize, To : to talk at great length without saying much of consequence. After the manner of William Ewart Gladstone (1809-98), Brit. statesman.

Glasgow capon, A : *see* Capon.

Glasgow magistrate, A : a herring. After the practice of sending specimen herrings to the Baillie of Glasgow.

Glasshouse, To live in a : to lay oneself open to criticism. From the proverb, ‘ They who live in glasshouses should not throw stones.’

Glassite, A : a member of a Scot. religious sect founded by John Glass (1695–1773) in 1728.

Glaucus, A second : one who ruins himself by horseracing. After Glaucus who was killed by his horses.

Glaucus swop, A : an exchange in which one party obtains a considerable advantage. In allusion to the exchange of armour between Glaucus and Diomedes.

Globe-trotter, A : a traveller in foreign lands for his own pleasure.

Gloriana : Queen Elizabeth. From the name of the Faerie Queen in Spenser's poem so-entitled (1590–6).

Glorious first of June : *see* First of June.

Glorious John : John Dryden (1631–1701), Eng. poet and man of letters.

Glory Demon, The : war. So-called by C. Thomson.

Glove, To bite one's : to determine on revenge. A practice derived from the borderland of England and Scotland.

Glove money : a bribe or gratuity given nominally for the purchase of gloves.

Glove, To take up the : to accept a challenge. From the feudal practice of challenging by means of a glove. [Gosson, *Ephemerides of Phialto* (1579)]

Glove, To throw down the : to issue a challenge. Metaphor derived from chivalry. [Shakespeare, *Troilus and Cressida*, IV, iv (1606)]

Gloves, To go for the : *see* Go.

Gloves, To win a pair of : to kiss while asleep, the forfeit being nominally a pair of gloves. [Jonathan Swift, *Polite Conversation*, Dial. III (1738)]

Gloves off, With the : very severely ; unmercifully. A pugilistic metaphor.

Glue chalk, To : to act foolishly. From an ancient Grk. proverb.

Gnat and swallow a camel, To strain at a : to object to a trifle while accepting something of greater consequence. [*Matthew*, xxiii, 24 ; J. King, *On Jonas* (1594)]

Go, All the : the fashion.

Go for the gloves, To : to initiate an offensive after having succeeded while on the defensive.

Go further and fare worse, To : to lose an opportunity in the baseless expectation of securing a better one. [Heywood, *Proverbes* (1546)]

Go, Great : *see* Great Go.

Go, Little : *see* Little Go.

Go one better, To : to surpass a previous effort or competitor.

Go to pieces, To : suddenly to lose all power of resistance or cohesion.

Go, To have plenty of : to have plenty of energy.

Go too far, To : to exceed a person's patience.

Go up, To : to proceed from the country or a smaller town to the principal one. After the biblical phrase ' to go up to Jerusalem.'

Go to the wall, To : *see* Wall.

Go without saying, To : to be self-evident. From the Fr. phrase, ' Ça va sans dire.'

Go wrong, To : to commit a crime ; of a woman, to surrender her chastity.

Goat's Wool : a figment of the imagination. [Udall, *Demonstr. Discipl.* (1588)]

Go-by, To give a person the : to ' cut ' or ignore a person. [Earl of Bristol, *Elvira*, IV, i (1667)]

Go-off, At the first : in the first instance.

Gobelin : tapestry made at the factory founded by Jean Gobelin of Paris (d. 1476).

Gobemouches, A (Fr., *gober*, to swallow, *mouche*, a fly) : one who is easily deceived.

God, An act of : an action of uncontrollable natural forces resulting in damage or injury. A legal term.

God in the machine, The : *see* Deus ex machina.

Gods, Among the : in a theatre gallery. In allusion to the pictures of classical gods on the ceiling of Drury Lane Theatre. The gallery of a theatre is of course close to the ceiling.

God's acre : *see* Acre, God's.

God's blessing into the warm sun, To go out of : to make a change for the worse. Derived from a proverbial expression. [Heywood, *Proverbes* (1546)]

God's image cut in ebony : a negro. So-called by Thos. Fuller in *The Good Sea-Captain*.

God's mark : a mark placed on a house infected by plague.

God's Sunday : Easter Sunday.

Goddem, A : an Englishman. In allusion to the English propensity to swearing. Corruption of ' God damn.'

Goddess of Beauty, The : Venus.

Goddess, The capricious : fortune.

Godsend, A : an unexpected benefit.

Gog and Magog : two gigantic statues in the Guildhall, London, which date from the reign of Henry V. According to *Ezekiel* xxxviii and xxxix, Gog was king of the land of Magog. The two figures in London are supposed to represent Gogmagog, a legendary king of the giants, and Corineus, a hero and giant of Cornwall, by whom he was killed.

M

Goggle-eyed : with staring, outstanding eyes. [Ascham, *Toxophilus*, Bk. II (1545)]

Gogmagogical : gigantic ; monstrous. [Taylor, *Workes* (1630)] *See* Gog and Magog.

Golconda, A : a very rich mine. After the diamond mines of Golconda, near Hyderabad, India.

Gold, To gild refined : to attempt to improve perfection. [Shakespeare, *King John*, IV, ii, ll. 11–6 (1596)]

Gold, Mannheim : an alloy of copper and zinc, invented at Mannheim, Germany.

Gold Mine, A : a source of wealth or fortune. [H. Peacham, *Worth of a Penny* (1664)]

Gold of Nibelungen, The : wealth that brings misfortune. In allusion to the legendary Nibelungen hoard.

Gold Purse of Spain, The : Andalusia, the richest province of the kingdom.

Gold Stick in Waiting : a court official who carries a gilt stick on formal occasions.

Gold of Tolosa, The : ill gains that bring no prosperity. Caepio, the Roman Consul, on his invasion of Southern Gaul, appropriated the sacred gold and silver of Tolosa (Toulouse), but was shortly afterwards severely defeated by the Cimbrians (106 B.C.).

Gold, Worth its weight in : of very great value.

Goldbugs : supporters of monometallism or the gold standard in the U.S.

Golden Age, A : the period of the greatest literary and artistic excellence in a nation's history.

Golden Age, The : (1) the fabulous period when happiness was universal ; (2) youth.

Golden Age of China, The : 626–684.

Golden Age of Egypt, The : 1336–1224 B.C.

Golden Age of England, The : 1558–1603.
Golden Age of France, The : 1640–1740.
Golden Age of Germany, The : 1519–58.
Golden Age of Portugal, The : 1383–1578.
Golden Age of Prussia, The : 1740–86.
Golden Age of Russia, The : 1672–1725.
Golden Age of Spain, The : 1474–1516.
Golden Age of Sweden, The : 1523–1632.

Golden Apple, A : a tomato.

Golden Ball, A : Ball Hughes (fl. 1802–30), Eng. dandy, famous for his extravagance.

Golden Book, A : a register of noble or distinguished persons ; esp. that of the nobility of the Venetian Republic.

Golden Bowl is broken, The : one's strength is exhausted and death arrives. [*Ecclesiastes*, xii, 6]

Golden Bridge, A : an easy means of retreat. From a Fr. proverb, ' Make a golden bridge for your enemy.'

Golden Bull, A : a medieval charter of great importance, sealed with a golden bulla. Esp. that issued by the Emp. Charles IV in 1357, which laid down the rules for the election of the king of the Romans.

Golden Calf, The : money. [*Exodus*, xxxii]

Golden calf, To worship the : to be devoted to material interests. [*Exodus* xxxii]

Golden City, The : San Francisco, on account of its proximity to the gold-fields.

Golden Fleece, The : one of the great orders of knighthood of Spain and Austria, founded by Philip, Duke of Burgundy. In Grk. mythology the fleece of the ram on which Phrixus and Helle fled to Colchis.

Golden Fleece of the North, The : the fur and peltry of Siberia.

Golden Hind among Adventurers, A : a pioneer.

Golden Horde, The : the body of Tartars who overran Russia in the 13th cent. (*Sir Orda*, the golden camp, the gorgeous tent of their leader, Batu.)

Golden Kite, The : the chief military order of Japan.

Golden Legend, The : a collection of lives of the saints made by Jacopus de Voragine (Giacoma da Varaggio) (1230–1298).

Golden Mean, The : a policy of moderation, avoiding extremes. Derived from one of the maxims of Cleobulus (fl. 580–76 B.C.), poet and king of Lindus. [Earl of Surrey, *Praise of Meane and Constant Estate* (1557)]

Golden Medicine, The : the elixir of life.

Golden Mountains, To promise : *see* Promise.

Golden Mouth : Chrysostom (347–407), Grk. Church father. On account of his eloquence.

Golden Number, The : (1) the number of any year in the Metonic lunar cycle of 19 years, in allusion to its importance in calculating the date of Easter ; (2) any number that brings good luck.

Golden Opinions, To earn : to earn respect and praise. [Shakespeare, *Macbeth*, I, vii, ll. 32–3 (1606)]

Golden Rose, The : a jewel, in the form of a cluster of roses, awarded by the Pope every year to the queen who has earned it by her work for the Church.

Golden Rule, The : (1) ' Whatsoever ye would that men should do to you, do you even so to them : for this is the law and the prophets,' (*Matthew*, vii, 12) ; (2) in mathematics, the Rule of Three.

Golden Shoe, A : a large amount of money.

Golden Shower, A : a bribe. In allusion to the legend of Jupiter gaining access to Danae in the disguise of a shower of gold.

Golden State, The : California. In allusion to its gold mines.

Golden Time, The : youth. [Lyly, *Euphues and His England* (1580)]

Golden Town, The : Mainz, so-called in the Carlovingian period.

Golden Wedding, A : the fiftieth anniversary of a wedding.

Golden World, The : the golden age (*q.v.*).

Golgotha, A : (1) a place of martyrdom ; (2) a charnel-house. From the place of the Crucifixion. Aramaic, *gulgalta*, a skull.

Golgotha, The City : Temple Bar, London, on which the heads of traitors used to be exhibited.

Goliard, A : a wandering continental student of the 12th and 13th cents. under an imaginary patron, St. Golias (? Goliath).

Goliath, A : a giant. After the giant in the first book of *Samuel*.

Gombeen Man, A (*Celtic*, *kmbion*, change) : in Ireland, a moneylender.

Gondola of London, The : a hansom cab. So-called by Lord Beaconsfield.

Gone on .. To be : to be enamoured of ..

Gone under : failed financially ; sunk in the social scale. A drowning metaphor.

Gone up the country : insolvent. A colonial expression. When a man in one of the colonial towns became bankrupt he used to go prospecting into the country to seek a change of fortune.

Goneril, A : an unnatural daughter. After a character in Shakespeare, *King Lear* (1605–6).

Good and all, For : finally.

Good Books : *see* Books.

Good Earl, The : Anthony Ashley, 7th Earl of Shaftesbury (1801–85), philanthropist.

Good Form : good breeding ; good behaviour. A cricketing metaphor.

Good Friday : the Friday before Easter Day, kept as the anniversary of the Crucifixion.

Good as Gold, As : generally of children, submissive and well-behaved. This simile is of quite modern creation.

Good Grace, With a : willingly. [Bacon, *Essayes : Of Discourse* (1625)]

Good, To make : to succeed.

Good Money after bad, To throw : to venture still more in a speculation that has already proved unfortunate.

Good Mother, A : a mother-in-law ; or step-mother.

Good come out of Nazareth ? Can any : what good is to be expected of such surroundings ? [*John*, i, 46]

Good for nothing : worthless. [Bacon, *Essayes : Of Goodnesse* (1625)]

Good Parliament, The : *see* Parliament.

Good as a Play, As : phrase attributed to King Charles II of England on hearing a debate in parl. on Lord Ross's Divorce Bill.

Good Regent, The : James Stuart, Earl of Moray (1533–70), Regent of Scotland.

Good Samaritan, A : one who befriends another who has no claim on him. [*Luke*, x, 30–7]

Good Turn, To do a : to do a kindness. [*Paston Letters*, No. 706 (1472)]

Good as one's Word, To be as : to keep one's word strictly. [Fulwell, *Like Will to Like*, l. 622 (1568) ; Stanyhurst, *Description of Ireland* (1577)]

Good one's Word, To make : to fulfil one's undertaking. [*Knack to Know a Knave*, l. 66 (1594)]

Goose, A : a foolish person. In allusion to the supposed stupidity of geese. [Shakespeare, *Romeo and Juliet*, II, iv (1591–3)]

Goose, To ; Goose, To give the : to hiss. From the sounds uttered by geese. Theatre slang.

Goose, To cook a person's : to punish a person. In allusion to the story told of Eric, King of Sweden, who, when approaching an enemy's town, was received in derision by a goose hung over the wall. He subsequently took the town and burnt it.

Goose Fair : a fair held about Michaelmas when geese are a seasonable dish.

Goose File : single file.

Goose and give the giblets in alms, To steal a : to amass wealth and to salve one's conscience by giving a small portion of it in charity. [Howell (1659)]

Goose that lays the golden eggs, To kill the : to overreach oneself and thereby destroy a source of profit. From the Grk. fable of the goose that laid the golden eggs.

Goose Quill, A : a pen. In allusion to the former use of goose quills for their manufacture.

Goose, To shoe the (gray) : to spend one's time uselessly. [Inscription on one of the stalls of Whalley Church (1434) ; Skelton, *Colin Clout* (1510)]

Goose, To be sound on the : to be staunch to one's party. Orig. to be a strong advocate of slavery. An Americanism.

Goose Step, The : elementary military drill.

Goose among Swans, A : *see* Swans.

Goose, A Tailor's : a tailor's iron. In allusion to the resemblance of its handle to the neck of a goose, or from the practice of roasting it.

Gooseberry, Giant : *see* Giant.

Gooseberry, Old : the devil.

Gooseberry Picker, A : a chaperon ; *see* Gooseberry, To play.

Gooseberry, To play : to play propriety ; to act as chaperon.

Gooseberry, To play old : to cause havoc. *See* Gooseberry, Old.

Gooseberry Season, Big : *see* Big.

Goose-cap, A : a stupid person. *See* Goose.

Goose-flesh ; Goose-skin : a rough condition of the skin resembling that of a plucked goose.

Gordian : complicated. *See* Gordian knot.

Gordian Knot, A : a difficult, almost insoluble, problem. Gordius, a king of Phrygia, tied a knot in such a manner that it was impossible to unloose it. The legend grew up that he who could solve it would gain the empire of Asia. Alexander the Great cut the knot with his sword. [Gosson, *Playes Confuted* (1582)]

Gordian Knot, To cut the : to solve a difficult practical problem. *See* Gordian Knot.

Gorgon, A : a very ugly or horrible object. After the three Gorgons, famous in mythology for their intense

ugliness, whose eyes (according to Æschylus the three sisters had only one eye, which they were able to pass from one to the other, between them) turned to stone all on whom they gazed.

Gorgon's Head, A : an object that terrifies ; *see* Gorgon. [*Life and Death of Capt. Thos. Stukeley*, ll. 2104–5 (1605)]

Gormogon, A : a member of a society formed early in the 18th cent. in imitation of the Freemasons. An invented word.

Goshen, A : a long-desired goal. After the bountiful district in Egypt in which the Israelites sojourned, previous to the Exodus.

Gosling, A : a simpleton ; *see* Goose.

Gospel Truth : a statement to be depended on with as much reliance as the Gospel. [17th cent.]

Gospel of Wealth, The : the theory that it is money alone that matters and that the acquisition of it should be the principal aim of man.

Gospeller, A hot : an ardent Protestant. The name was first given in derision in the 16th cent.

Goth, A : a barbarian ; one heedless of the claims of the arts and sciences. After the people that overran and devastated the Roman Empire in the 3rd and 5th cents.

Goths and Vandals : uncultured people who pay no heed to the claims of art or literature.

Gotham : a name for New York City, given by Washington Irving in *Salmagundi* (1807). *See* Gotham, Fools of.

Gotham, Fools of : Gotham, a village near Nottingham, England. The simplicity of its inhabitants has been proverbial since at least early in the 15th cent., when it was referred to in the *Towneley Mysteries*. This simplicity is said to have been simulated orig. in order to turn aside the wrath of a king.

Gotham College : an imaginary institution for the training of simpletons. [*The Last Will and Testament of Charyng Crosse*, p. 6 (1646)]

Gotham, A man of : a simple person. *See* Gotham.

Gothamites : inhabitants of New York. *See* Gotham *and* Gotham, Fools of.

Gothenburg System, The : a system of the sale of intoxicants by the municipality, as introduced at Gothenburg, Sweden, in 1865.

Gothic : (1) of a medieval style of architecture ; (2) uncouth. The term was first applied to the style of architecture contemptuously to indicate barbarism. *See* Goth.

Gourd and Fullam : two names for false dice. *See* Gourds. Fullam, because the dice are full or loaded. [Shakespeare, *Merry Wives of Windsor*, I, iii, ll. 93–4 (1600)]

Gourds : loaded dice. From (Old Fr.) *gourd*, a swindle, or because the dice were hollowed like gourds before being filled with a heavy substance to give them a bias.

Government of the People, by the People and for the People : the watchword of the English Liberal Party. The phrase is American in origin and was coined by Theodore Parker (1810–60). In a slightly different form, ' The people's government, made for the people, made by the people, and answerable to the people,' it was uttered by Daniel Webster (1782–1852) in 1830.

Gowk, To hunt the : to go on a fool's errand. Scottish, *gowk*, a foolish person.

Gowk (Gouk) storm, A : a storm of brief duration, esp. in the spring (the time of the cuckoo). Gowk, a cuckoo.

Gown, To wear the : to be a clergyman. [Wm. Combe, *Tour of Dr. Syntax* (1812)]

Gownsman, A : a member of a univ. ; as distinguished from townsman, a non-univ. resident in a univ. town.

Gracchus, The Modern : Count Honoré de Mirabeau (1749–91), Fr. revol. and orator. After Tiberius Sempronius Gracchus (163–133 B.C.) and Gaius Sempronius Gracchus (153–121 B.C.), who were famous Rom. tribunes and reformers.

Grace Card, The : In Kilkenny, the six of hearts, the card on which a member of the Grace family of Courtstown indignantly rejected the invitation of William III to desert to him.

Grace Cup, The : the last cup ; the loving cup ; formerly passed round the table after grace.

Grace Darling : the daughter of Wm. Darling, lighthouse-keeper on one of the Farne Islands, who on the 7th September, 1838, heroically assisted her father to rescue a shipwrecked crew.

Grace Darling of America, The : Ida Lewis (Mrs. W. H. Wilson), the daughter of the lighthouse-keeper in Newport Harbour who on five occasions rescued or assisted in rescuing persons from drowning.

Grace, To take heart of : to take courage from indulgence. [Heywood, *Proverbes* (1546)]

Gradasso, A : a bully. After a character in Ariosto, *Orlando Furioso* (1516).

Gradgrind, A : a ' practical ' man devoted to materialism. After a character in Dickens, *Hard Times* (1854).

Gradus, A ; Gradus ad Parnassum, A (*Lat.*, steps ; steps to Parnassus) : a Grk. or Lat. dictionary showing the quantities of vowels as an aid to the writing of Latin verse.

Graeca Fides (*Lat.*, Greek faith) : in allusion to the proverbial reputation of the Greeks for untrustworthiness.

Grahamize, To : to open letters in the post. After Sir James Graham (1792–1861), who, when Home Secretary in 1844, authorized the opening of Mazzini's letters by the Post Office.

Grail, The Holy ; the San Graal (*Medieval Fr.*) : the receptacle in which Joseph of Arimathea is said in medieval legend to have received the blood of Christ while on the Cross. The grail was lost and could be recovered only by a knight of irreproachable character.

Grain, Against the : uneasily ; against one's disposition. As cutting wood, etc., against the grain. [Wm. Cartwright, *The Ordinary*, II, iii (1651)]

Grain of mustard seed, A : a small seed out of which something great may develop. *See Matthew*, xiii, 31, where the black mustard which grows to a great height is probably intended.

Grain of salt, With a : with reservations. A translation of the Lat. phrase, *Cum grano salis*.

Gramercy, To get for : to get for nothing, merely for the thanks. Fr., *grand merci*, great thanks.

Grammarians, The Prince of : Appolonios of Alexandria (fl. 40-30 B.C.). So-called by Priscian.

Grampus, A : a person given to puffing and blowing, like the grampus, a sea-animal.

Grampus, To blow the : to drench a person with water. [Fred. Marryat, *Frank Mildmay* (1829)]

Grampus, To blow like a : *see* Grampus. [Peter Pindar, *Subjects for Painters : The Gentleman and His Wife* (1797)]

Granary of Europe, The : Sicily. On account of its fertility.

Grand Alliance, The : (1) England, Holland and the Empire against France and Spain, 1701 ; (2) England, Prussia, Russia, Austria and Sweden, against Napoleon, in 1813 ; (3) England, France, Russia, Japan, and afterwards Italy and the United States as well as smaller powers, against Germany and her allies, 1914.

Grand Corruption : Sir Rob. Walpole (1676–1745), Prime Minister, on account of his practice of bribery.

Grand Monarque, Le (*Fr.*, the Great Monarch) : Louis XIV of France.

Grand Monde, Le : *see* Great World, The.

Grand Old Man, The : *see* G.O.M.

Grand Old Man of India, The : Dadabhai Naoroji (1825–1917), Indian political reformer. ' The father of Indian nationalism,' the first Indian member of the House of Commons.

Grand Old Party, The ; G.O.P., The : the Republican Party in the United States. The phrase was adopted in the full form by members of the party and in the contracted form as a term of derision by the Democrats, about 1880.

Grand Sérieux, Au : *see* Sérieux.

Grand Signior, The (*It.*, *Gran signore*, great lord) : the Sultan of Turkey.

Grand Tour, The : an extended tour on the continent, a necessary completion of a young gentleman's education in the 18th and the first half of the 19th cent.

Grande Armée, Le (*Fr.*, the Great Army) : the army led by Napoleon against Russia in 1812.

Grande Passion, La (*Fr.*, the great passion) : passionate love.

Grandisonian : chivalrous, formally courteous and somewhat platitudinous. After Sir Charles Grandison, the hero of Richardson's novel so entitled(1754).

Grandmother, This beats my : this causes me great surprise.

Grandmother to suck eggs, To teach one's: to attempt to instruct an expert in his own subject.

Grandmother's child, A : a spoilt child. [Scott, *Marmion*, Canto III (1808)]

Grangerize, To : to add pictorial illustrations, etc., to a book already complete. After James Granger (1723–76), author of a *Biographical History of England*, written for the special purpose of extra illustrations, etc.

Grangers, The : an American secret political society active between 1870 and 1880 ; also known as the Order of Husbandry, or Patrons of Husbandry.

Granite City (Capital), The : Aberdeen.

Granite Redoubt, The : the Grenadiers of the Consular Guard of France who withstood the Austrians as a wall of granite at the battle of Marengo in 1800.

Granite State, The : New Hampshire. On account of the considerable amount of granite found within its borders.

Grape-monger, A : a wine-tippler. [Dekker, *The Seuen Deadly Sinnes : Candlelight* (1606]

Grapes, Sour : an object not desired because it is unobtainable. From Æsop's fable, *The Fox and the Grapes*.

Grasp the nettle, To : to face a difficulty resolutely.

Grass, To cut one's own : to earn one's own living.

Grass from under a person's feet, To cut the : to thwart a person.

Grass, To give : to admit oneself beaten. [Servius, *To Virgil, Æneid*, VIII, 128]

Grass, Gone to : dead. In reference to the grass that grows on graves.

Grass grow under one's feet, To let no : to display energy. [Udall, *Ralph Roister Doister*, III, iii, 179 (1550)]

Grass to know where the wind sits, To pluck the : to make full use of one's powers of observation.

Grass widow, A : a woman permanently or temporarily separated from her husband but not divorced from him. Corruption of ' grace widow,' a widow by grace of courtesy. Orig. an unmarried mother. [Sir John Kaye, *English in India* in *Calcutta Review* (1844)]

Grasshopper, To sing like a : in allusion to the sounds made by grasshoppers when moving.

Grattan's Parliament : the Irish parl. of 1782 to 1801 in the course of which Henry Grattan secured its independence of the English parliament.

Grave as a judge, As : sedate and serious. [Wesley, *Maggots* (1685)]

Grave as an owl, As : very solemn in appearance.

Grave, To make a person turn in his : to do that which would cause him deep distress if he were still living.

Gravelled : confounded ; nonplussed. Metaphor drawn from the grounding of a ship. [Shakespeare, *As You*

Like It, IV, i (1600) ; Ascham, *The Schoolmaster*, Bk. I (1570)]

Gray : *see* Grey.

Grease a person's palm (fist), To : to bribe. [Nat. Woodes, *Conflict of Conscience*, III, iii (1581)]

Grease the wheels, To : by gifts or otherwise, to remove difficulties. [15th cent.]

Greaser, A : a contemptuous name for Mexicans and other Latin Americans current in the U.S. The term originated during the first war with Mexico, and is supposed to have been derived from the habits of the Mexicans.

Great Cham of Literature, The : Samuel Johnson (1709–84). So-called by Tobias Smollett.

Great Commoner, The : William Pitt the elder (1708–78). Pitt had himself termed Sir John Barnard (1685–1764), one of the members for the City of London, the Great Commoner.

Great cry and little wool : *see* Cry.

Great Duke, The : the first Duke of Wellington (1769–1852).

Great Elchee, The : Stratford Canning, Viscount Stratford de Redcliffe (1786–1880), British amb. to Turkey. Turk., *ilchi*, ambassador.

Great Elector, The : Frederick William (1620–88), Elector of Brandenburg.

Great Frederick, The : Frederick II (1712–86), King of Prussia.

Great Go : the popular name for the B.A. degree examination at Cambridge ; formerly the same as Greats (*q.v.*).

Great Gun, A : *see* Gun.

Great Hundred, A : 120.

Great King, The : Cyrus, King of Persia (6th cent. B.C.). Self-styled.

Great Magician, The : Sir Walter Scott (1771–1832). So-called by John Wilson.

Great Marquis, The : (1) James Graham, Marquis of Montrose (1612–50), Scottish royalist hero ; (2) Dom Sebastiano Jose de Carvalho, Marquis de Pombal (1699–1782), Portuguese statesman.

Great Million, A : a billion.

Great Mogul, The : the head of the Mogul Empire.

Great Moralist, The : Dr. Samuel Johnson (1709–84).

Great Mother, The : (1) Demeter, the goddess of vegetation and protectress of social order and of marriage ; (2) the Earth, according to the Delphic Oracle.

Great Perhaps, The : the future state, according to Rabelais (1485–1553).

Great Powers, The : the principal powers. Orig. Britain, France, Prussia, Austria and Russia ; later with the addition of Italy and the substitution of Germany and Austro-Hungary, for Prussia and Austria ; still later with the addition of the United States and Japan and the omission of Austro-Hungary.

Great Scot(t) : an euphemism for Great God.

Great Tom : the great bell of the Tom Gate, Christ Church, Oxford.

Great Unknown, The : (1) Sir Walter Scott (1771–1832), anonymous author of *The Waverley Novels* ; term applied by Jas. Ballantyne, his publisher ; (2) Death.

Great Unpaid, The : English justices of the peace or honorary magistrates.

Great Unwashed, The : the lower classes. Term first applied by Edmund Burke (1729–97).

Great World, The (Fr., *Le grand monde*) : aristocratic society.

Greats : the final honours examination (as a rule in classics) at Oxford University.

Greatest happiness of the greatest number, The : a political maxim adopted by Jeremy Bentham in *Liberty of the People* (1821). The phrase has been traced back in English to Hutcheson, *Inquiry Concerning Moral Good and Evil*, sect. 3 (1720), but it appears also in Plato, *Republic*, IV, i.

Greatheart, A : a philanthropist and benefactor. After Mr. Greatheart in Bunyan, *Pilgrim's Progress* (1678).

Grec, Un (Fr., a Greek) : a cheat. After a Grk. knight who was discovered cheating at cards in the palace of Louis XIV.

Grecian, A : a member of the highest classical form at Christ's Hospital.

Grecian bend, The : an affected pose of the body, fashionable in England about 1875.

Greco, The (It., Greek) : the north-east wind.

Gree, To bear the : to carry off the prize ; to be pre-eminent. [Rob. Ferguson, *Elegy on the Death of Scots Music*, ll. 49–52 (1772)]

Greedy as a cow in a clover-field, As : [R. Cumberland, *The Fashionable Lover*, I, i (1772)]

Greedy as a hawk, As : *see* Hungry as a hawk, As.

Greedy-guts, A : a greedy person. [Heywood, *Proverbes* (1546)]

Greek, A : a swindler. *See* Grec.

Greek to me, It is : it is unintelligible. [Shakespeare, *Julius Cæsar*, I, ii, 87 (1603)]

Greek Calends, On the : *see* Greek Kalends.

Greek Commentator, The : Fernan Nunen de Guzman (1470–1553), Spanish Hellenist.

Greek Cross, The : *see* Cross, Greek.

Greek Drama, The Founder of the : Æschylus (525–456 B.C.).

Greek Ease : laziness. In allusion to the proverbial laziness of the Greeks.

Greek Faith : *see* Græcca Fides.

Greek Fire : material used for setting fire to hostile ships, etc. So-called because first used by the Greeks of the Eastern Empire.

Greek Gift, A : a gift presented to conceal treachery. After the gift of a wooden horse presented by the Greeks to the Trojans, which being filled with men led to the capture of Troy. [Virgil, *Æneid*, II, 49]

Greek as a Greek cobbler, To know as much : to have a paltry knowledge of the Greek language. The simile was used by Bentley (1662–1742), the classical scholar, in allusion to Joshua Barnes (1654–1712), the Regius Professor of Greek at Cambridge.

Greek meets Greek, When : when two well-matched combatants meet. The phrase is derived from the proverb, 'When Greek meets Greek, then comes the tug of war,' which itself first appeared, in a slightly different form, in Nathaniel Lee, *The Rival Queens*, IV, ii (1677).

Greek Kalends, On the : never. There were no kalends in the Grk. calendar. The Emp. Augustus (B.C. 63–A.D. 14) used to say he would pay on the Greek kalends when he wished to intimate that a person would not pay at all. The Rom. kalends was the usual pay-day. Queen Elizabeth used the phrase in a reply to the envoys of the King of Spain.

Greek Life, The : a sound mind in a healthy body. In allusion to the cult of the 'Games' by the ancient Greeks.

Greek, As merry as a : drunk. Possibly a corruption of 'As merry as a Grig' (*q.v.*). *See also* Merry Greek, A. The Romans used to refer to the Greeks as fond of good living and excessive drinking and they used the word, *graecari*, to express the idea of good feeding and drinking.

Greek, To play the : (1) to drink to excess. *See* Greek, As merry as a, *and* Grec, Un ; (2) to cheat, esp. at cards.

Greek without knowing it, To speak : to use medical language. [Earle, *Microcosmography : A Meere Dull Phisician* (1628)]

Green : young ; inexperienced ; foolish. From the sense of immature. [Earl of Surrey, *Restlesse State of a Lover* (1557); Shakespeare, *Hamlet*, I, iii, 101 (1602–3)]

Green, The : R.C. Ireland. In allusion to the Irish national colour.

Green Apron : *see* Apron.

Green Cloth, The Board of : a department of the Lord Steward's office in the British royal household. From the green-covered table at which its business used to be conducted.

Green Dogs : any extinct race.

Green Dragoons, The : the 13th Dragoons now the 13th Hussars. In allusion to the green facings of their uniforms.

Green in one's eye, To see any : to see indications of gullibility. *See* Green.

Green-eyed Monster, The : jealousy. [Shakespeare, *Merchant of Venice*, III, ii, 110 (1596)]

Green Glasses, To look through : to be jealous.

Green Goose, A : a young goose.

Green as grass, As : easily deceived. [Shakespeare, *Midsummer Night's Dream*, V, i, 326 (1590)] *See* Green.

Green Hand, A : a sailor of the lowest class of capacity.

Green Head, A : a young, inexperienced person. [Udall, *Diotrephes* (1588)]

Green Horse, The : the 5th Dragoons. In allusion to their green facings.

Green Howards, The : the 19th Regiment of Foot (Princess of Wales's Own) whose colonel, from 1738 to 1748, was the Hon. Charles Howard and whose facings were green.

Green Island (Isle), The : Ireland. On account of its verdure.

Green, To keep a thing : to keep a thing fresh (in one's memory). [Bacon, *Essays : Of Revenge* (1625)]

Green Labour : the lowest paid labour, esp. in the tailoring trade. *See* Greener.

Green Linnets, The : the 39th Regiment of Foot, now the Dorsetshire Regiment. In allusion to the green facings of their uniforms.

Green Men : savages. Orig. wild men of the woods ; later, American-Indians.

Green Mountain Boys : troops from Vermont raised in 1775. *See* Green Mountain State.

Green Mountain State, The (*Fr., vert mont,* green mountain): Vermont.

Green Ribbon Day : in Ireland, March 18th, St. Patrick's Day, when green ribbon is worn as a badge by Irishmen.

Green Room, The : the rest room for actors at the theatre. The room at Drury Lane appropriated to that purpose by Garrick had green walls.

Green Room, To talk : to gossip about the theatre. *See* Green Room.

Green Rushes for Strangers : a symbol of hospitality. From the former practice of strewing fresh rushes as a carpet when about to entertain a distinguished guest. [Jno. Heywood, *Proverbes* (1546)]

Green Sea, The : the Persian Gulf. In allusion to the colour of a strip of water near the Arabian Coast.

Green Sleeves, A : a flirt ; an inconstant girl lover. [*A New Northern Ditty of the Lady Green Sleeves* (1580)]

Green Thursday : Maundy Thursday.

Green Wound, A : a recent, unhealed wound. [Richard of Gloucester (1297)]

Greenback, A : a U.S. currency note, with its back printed in green. The name is said to have been invented by Salmon Portland Chase (1808–73), Amer. statesman.

Greenback Party, The : an Amer. political party (1874–84) which advocated the payment of the American National Debt in paper money. *See* Greenback.

Greenbacker, A : an advocate of the issue to an unlimited extent of paper money. *See* Greenback.

Greenbag, A : a lawyer. In allusion to the bag in which legal papers used to be carried.

Greener, A (*Germ., ein grüner,* a green or foolish one): one who is inexperienced ; esp. a recently arrived alien workman. [*Daily Chronicle,* April 18, 1888] *See* Green.

Greengage, A : a green plum introduced into England by Sir Wm. Gage (c. 1725).

Greenhorn, A : a raw youth. An allusion to the undeveloped horns of a male calf.

Greening for .. To have a : to have a liking for ..

Greenlandman's Galley : the extreme of bad language. In allusion to the customary obscenity of Greenland seamen.

Greenwich Barber, A : one who sells sand from the Greenwich pits. Greenwich barbers are said to ' shave the pits.'

Greenwich Time : standard time in accordance with the meridian of Greenwich.

Grego, A (*Port.,* Greek): a kind of short cloak or jacket, such as those worn by Greeks in the Levant.

Gregorian, A : a wig. After Gregory, a barber in the Strand, who first made them in England.

Gregorian Calendar, The : the calendar in general use, introduced by Pope Gregory XIII in 1582.

Gregorian Chant, A : a plain chant used in church services and introduced by Pope Gregory I in the 6th cent.

Gregorian Tones : *see* Gregorian chant.

Gregorian Tree, The : the gallows. From Gregory (sen.), Gregory (jun.) and Gregory Brandon, three successive hangmen of London in the reign of James I.

Gregorian Water : Holy water. After Pope Gregory I who strongly advocated the use of it.

Gregorian Year, A : a year according to the Gregorian Calendar (*q.v.*).

Gregory, A : a school feast. After St. Gregory's Day, March 12, a scholars' festival.

Gregory, A : a hangman. *See* Gregorian tree.

Gregory knights (St. Gregory's Knights) : contemptible boasters ; sham soldiers. After the children who played at soldiers on St. Gregory's Day.

Gregory Powder : a medical drug. After James Gregory (1758–1822), Scot. physician.

Grenadiers : orig. troops employed in throwing hand grenades.

Gresham, To dine with Sir Thomas : *see* Dine.

Gretchen, A : an unsophisticated Germ. girl. After the heroine of Goethe's *Faust.*

Gretna Green : a village just over the Scot. border, famous for the celebration of runaway marriages, which could not be effected in England. Such marriages were prevented by legislation in 1856.

Gretna (Gretna Green) Marriages : *see* Gretna Green.

Grey Cloak, A : an alderman who has served as mayor. In allusion to the colour of the fur on his costume.

Grey Coat, A : a Cumberland yeoman. In allusion to the colour of the home-spun clothing of that county.

Grey Friars : Franciscans or Friars of the Order of St. Francis. In allusion to the colour of their clothing.

Grey Goose wing, A : an arrow, which used to be winged with grey goose feathers.

Grey Groat, A : an object of little value.

Grey hairs with sorrow to the grave, To bring down one's : to cause pain and sorrow to an old man. [*Genesis*, *xlii*, 38]

Grey Mare, A : a wife who rules her husband. In allusion to the proverb, ' The grey mare is the better horse.'

Grey of the Morning, The : the twilight. [Shakespeare, *Romeo and Juliet*, III, v, 19 (1591–3)]

Greybeard, A : (1) an old man ; (2) a large earthenware jug or jar for spirits.

Greycoat, A : a Russian soldier. In allusion to the colour of his coat.

Greycoat Parson, A : an impropriator or tenant who hires the tithes.

Grief, To come to : to meet with mis-fortune, in material affairs.

Griffin, As rich as a : in allusion to the fabulous animals, the griffins, which, according to Grk. legend, used to keep watch over the gold of Scythia.

Griffin, A young : a cadet from India, half English, half Indian. In allusion to the fabulous monster, the griffin, half lion, half eagle.

Griffiths, A : a safe man. A pun, in allusion to the firm of C. H. Griffiths and Sons, safe manufacturers (19th and 20 cents.).

Grig, As merry as a : the term ' grig ' has, or has had, many meanings. It is in one place or another a synonym for a short-legged hen, a young eel, a grasshopper, a cricket, a tadpole, a gnat dancing in the sun, a bantam, a young child, a wandering dancer and tumbler ; in fact, anything that moves with a light, lively motion. It has also been suggested that the phrase is a corruption of ' As merry as a Greek ' (*q.v.*). *See also* Merry Greek, A. [Vanbrugh and Cibber, *The Provoked Husband*, V, i (1728)]

Grig, To swim like a : in this phrase ' grig ' is employed as a synonym for an eel.

Grille, The : the lattice in front of the Ladies' Gallery in the House of Commons, abolished in 1917.

Grim Death, Like : doggedly. [Shakespeare, *Taming of the Shrew*, Ind., i, 35 (1596)]

Grim, The Giant : a giant. [Bunyan, *Pilgrim's Progress* (1678)]

Grimalkin : (1) an old cat, lit., grey malkin (a dimin. of Maud or Matilda) ; (2) a fiend supposed to resemble a grey cat.

Grim-gribber : legal proceedings. The name of an imaginary estate referred to in a legal discussion in Steele, *Conscious Lovers* (1722).

Grin and bear it, To : to show no other sign of impatience than a grin in sub-mitting to unpleasantness.

Grind a person down, To : to deal harshly with ; to oppress. [Bacon, *Advice to Villiers* (1626)]

Grind for an examination, To : to study intently for an examination. Meta-phor derived from a mill.

Grind the face of .. To : to oppress ; to deal harshly with .. [*Isaiah*, iii, 15]

Grind, To take a : to take a walk ; to take part in a steeplechase. Univ. slang.

Grinder, To take a : to make an offensive gesture with the hand and the nose. [Dickens, *Pickwick Papers*, xxxi (1836)]

Grindstone, To hold (tie) a person's nose to the : *see* Nose.

Gringo, A : a Mexican name for an inhabitant of the United States.

Griselda ; Grisilda, A : a patient, faithful wife ; from the name of a character in one of Boccaccio's *Decameron*. [Geo. Cavendish, *Life and Death of Wolsey* (1557)]

Grisette, A : a young Frenchwoman of the working classes ; orig. a cheap, coarse dress of grey cloth worn generally by working women. Fr., *gris*, grey.

Grist to the mill, To bring : to afford one an advantage or an opportunity of profit. [Golding, *Calvin on Deut.*, cxxiii, 755 (1583)]

Groaning Cake, A : a cake provided for visitors to a woman after childbirth. [Groaning (dial.), lying in]

Groaning Chair, The : the chair in which a woman recovering from childbirth receives her friends. *See* Groaning Cake.

Groaning Cheese : see Groaning Cake.

Groaning Malt : liquid refreshment provided for visitors to a woman after childbirth. See Groaning Cake.

Groat, An old Harry : see Harry Groat.

Groats in kail, To get : to be paid in one's own coin.

Grobian, A : a boor; a clown. After Grobianus, an imaginary person referred to by Germ. writers in the 15th and 16th cents. as the type of boorishness. See Grobianus et Grobiana, books of rules how to be boorish (1549–58) by Dedekind.

Grog : a mixture of rum or other spirit and water. From ' Old Grog ' (Adm. Edw. Vernon (1684–1757) who wore a grogram cloak, and diluted the sailors' rum with water (1740).

Groggy : intoxicated; unsteady or staggering, more or less resembling one of the symptoms of intoxication. See Grog.

Grograms, Blood of the : see Blood.

Grolier, A : bookbinding in a highly decorative style. From Jean Grolier (1479–1565), Fr. statesman, patron of learning and book collector.

Grosbec (Fr., gros bec, large nose) : Napoleon III. A nickname given on account of his large nose.

Ground, To break : to commence an undertaking.

Ground, To bring to the : to overthrow.

Ground from under, To cut the : to deprive of one's basis or support.

Ground, To be dashed to the : (of hopes), to fail to be realized; to come to naught.

Ground, Down to the : completely. [Judges, xx, 21, 25]

Ground, To fall to the : (of schemes), to fail to become realized.

Ground, To gain : to make progress in an undertaking.

Ground, To hold one's : to maintain one's position.

Ground, To lose : to be out-distanced in competition; to fall away instead of maintaining one's position.

Ground, To meet a person on his own : to contend or argue with a person on a matter or in circumstances of his own choice.

Ground, To stand one's : to maintain one's position in argument or otherwise.

Ground-floor, To get in on the : to obtain an opportunity for a fortunate speculation or investment in advance of others or of the general public.

Groundling, A : an uncultivated spectator of a play, or reader. In allusion to those who occupy the ground or pit of a theatre. [Shakespeare, Hamlet, III, ii, 12 (1602–3)]

Grouse's Day, St. ; Grouse, Festival of St. : Aug. 12th ; the day on which grouse shooting commences.

Grout-head, A : a stupid person. [Bale, English Votaries, II, E iii (1550)]

Growler, A : a four-wheeled hackney-carriage. In allusion to the proverbial bad temper of their drivers.

Grub Street : unattached writers for journals and publishers as a body, as a rule underpaid. After Milton Street, formerly Grub Street, in London, where such writers used to congregate.

Gruel, To get one's : to receive punishment.

Gruel, To give a person his : to punish (defeat) a person.

Gruelling, A : a punishment. From the phrase, ' To get one's gruel,' to receive punishment.

Grumbletonians : a name of the Country Party in Great Britain, borne at the end of the 17th cent. An invented word.

Grundy, Mrs. : an imaginary censor of public and private morals. After a character in Thomas Morton, Speed the Plough (1798), who was set up by one of the other characters in the play as a standard of propriety.

Grundyism, A : conventionalism ; prudery. See Grundy, Mrs.

Guam, To clear out for : see Clear.

Gudgeon, A bait to catch a : anything that will deceive a credulous person. For ' Gudgeon ' as a synonym for a credulous person, see Shakespeare, Merchant of Venice, I, iii (1596).

Gudgeon, To play the : to deceive ; to cheat. In allusion to the use of a gudgeon as a bait.

Gudgeon, To swallow a : to be easily deceived. See Gudgeons, To gape for. [Lyly, Euphues : The Anatomy of Wit (1579)]

Gudgeons, To bite like : to show oneself credulous. See Gudgeon, A bait to catch a. [Peter Pindar, Lyric Odes to the Royal Academicians, IX (1783)]

Gudgeons, To gape for : to be easily deceived. In allusion to the attractiveness of a gudgeon as a bait. [Holinshed, II, 91–2 (1577)]

Guelph Fund, The : the sum agreed to be paid by Prussia to the King of Hanover as compensation for the cancellation of his sovereign rights in 1866. This sum was afterwards seized by Prussia and used for subventioning the Germ. press.

Guelph or Ghibelline, Either : one party or the other. The Geulphs and the Ghibellines were the Papal and Imperial parties respectively in medieval Italy. [Ascham, *The Schoolmaster*, Bk. I (1570)]

Guerre des Amoureux, Le (*Fr.*, War of the lovers) : the war between Henry III of France and Henry of Navarre in 1580, which arose out of a court intrigue.

Guevarist, A : a writer in a very ornate or euphuistic style. After Antonio de Guevara (c. 1490–1544), Span. writer.

Guillotine, The : (1) a machine for decapitating criminals and other offenders ; (2) a system of closure of parl. discussion on a measure by means of time-limits for the consideration of different clauses or groups of clauses. After Jos. Ignatius Guillotin (1738–1814), a Fr. physician, who advocated its adoption in place of the rack and other instruments of torture during the French Revolution.

Guinea, A : an obsolete Eng. gold coin ; the sum of 21 shillings. Orig. coined from gold from the Guinea Coast of Africa, which was captured from the Dutch in 1666.

Guinea-pig, A : (1) a midshipman in the East Ind. Service : just as a guinea-pig is neither a pig nor has any connection with the Guinea Coast, so a midshipman is neither an officer nor a sailor ; (2) a director of a public company who accepts the office merely for the fees attached to it : in allusion to a guinea, the standard fee paid to directors for attendance at a meeting ; (3) a special juryman who is paid a guinea a case ; (4) a military officer on special duty who receives an allowance of a guinea a day ; (5) a clergyman of the Church of England acting as a substitute, who receives payment of a guinea a sermon.

Guinever, A : a wanton. After the Queen of King Arthur.

Gules of August, The : the 1st of August. Lat., *gula*, the throat *or* entrance into.

Gulf between, A great : a separation or division almost impassable.

Gulf States, The : Florida, Alabama, Mississippi, Louisiana and Texas ; the states of the Union which border on the Gulf of Mexico.

Gum tree, Up a : at the end of one's tether. An Americanism.

Gummed velvet, To fret like : velvet was formerly occasionally treated with gum to make it stiff and then quickly fretted itself out.

Gun, A great : a person of distinction or importance. Prob. a transfer from the ordnance sense as distinguished from a small gun or musket. [Peter Pindar, *Progress of Knowledge* (1792)]

Gun money : money coined by James II in Ireland from gun-metal.

Gun, Son of a : (1) a somewhat contemptuous designation, applied orig. to boys born aboard ship, the child of a naval officer or officer of the mercantile marine ; (2) a jovial fellow. In allusion to 'gun' in the sense of a flagon of ale.

Guns, To blow great : see Blow.

Guns, To run away from one's own : see Run.

Guns, To stand (stick) to one's : see Stand.

Gunner's daughter, The : the gun to which a seaman was bound while he received punishment. A naval term.

Gunter, According to : correctly and systematically. After Edmund Gunter (1581–1626), Eng. mathematician and inventor.

Gutter-blood, A : a person of low birth. [Scott, *Fortunes of Nigel*, ch. 7 (1822)]

Gutter snipe, A : a child of the lowest class, brought up in the gutters ; one who rakes among the refuse of the gutter for rags, etc.

Guy, A ; Guy Fawkes, A : a person of ludicrous appearance. In allusion to the effigy of Guy Fawkes, conspirator, conveyed through the streets on the 5th November, in commemoration of his abortive plot.

Gyges, As rich as : very wealthy. Gyges was King of Lydia from 716 to 678 B.C.

Gypsy : *see* Gipsy.

Hab or nab (*Med. Eng.*, Have or not have) : win or fail ; at random. [Heywood, *Proverbes* (1546)]

Habeas Corpus : one of the foundations of British liberty ; the Act of Parliament (1679) which requires a jailer to produce every prisoner for trial.

(Lat.) You are to produce the body, the opening words of an old writ in English law calling upon the custodian of a prisoner to produce his charge in court.

Habeas Corpus Act of Rome, The : the *Lex Valeria de Provocatione* (509 B.C.).

Habitans : the Fr.-Canad. farmers in the Province of Quebec.

Hack, A : a hired horse or carriage ; a literary or other drudge. Abbreviation of hackney (*q.v.*). [Chaucer, *Canterbury Tales* (14th cent.)]

Hack, A literary : *see* Hack.

Hack writing : *see* Hack.

Hackney (horse), A (*Fr.*, *haquenée*) : a saddle-horse, not thoroughbred ; a hired horse. [*Paston Letters*, No. 446 (1462)]

Hackney coach (carriage) : a hired coach. Fr., *haquenée*, any horse that is not thoroughbred ; hence a hired coach-horse.

Hackney woman, A : a prostitute ; one who hires herself out.

Hackneyed : of an expression, etc., so frequently used as to have lost its freshness.

Haddock to paddock, To bring : to waste all one's possessions. [Heywood, *Proverbes* (1546)]

Hades : the infernal regions. After the name of the Grk. god of the lower regions.

Hagiographa, The : the third Jewish division of the Old Testament, *viz.*, Chronicles, Ruth, Esther, Ezra, Nehemiah, Job, Psalms, Proverbs, Song of Songs, Ecclesiastes, Lamentations and Daniel.

Hague Congress, The : a congress of the Powers, held at The Hague in 1899, to consider the question of international disarmament. Out of the Congress arose an international court of arbitration.

Hail fellow well met, A : one on intimate and friendly terms. From the greeting ' Hail Fellow ! '

Hair, Against the : against the grain ; lit., contrary to the direction in which an animal's hair lies naturally. [T. Usk, *Testament of Love*, II, iv (1387)]

Hair, To a : exactly. [Ben Jonson, *Cynthia's Revels*, II, i (1600)]

Hair curl, To make a person's : *see* Make.

Hair to draw a waggon, To take a : to act foolishly and to no purpose. From an ancient Grk. proverb.

Hair and hide (1) **; Hair and hoof** (2) **:** entirely. [(1) St. Cuthbert (1450) ; Jean Irvine, *Collection of Dying Testaments* (1705)]

Hair to make a tether of, A : an excuse for much fuss.

Hair in one's neck, A : a cause of annoyance. [*Rate's Ravine*, III (1450)]

Hair, Not to turn a : to remain undisturbed despite surrounding excitement. Lit. of a horse, not to sweat and roughen its hair in consequence of fear or disturbance.

Hair of .. Within a : within very little of ..

Hair's breadth, A : the minimum of narrowness. [Heywood, *Proverbes* (1546) ; Lilly, *Gallathea*, II, iii (1592)]

Hairs, To split : to enter into and to give undue importance to minutiæ.

Halcyon days : days of peace and restfulness ; the days immediately preceding and succeeding the shortest day, which are supposed to be free from storms. From ' halcyon,' a name for the kingfisher which is supposed to lay her eggs during the halcyon days.

Half, One's better : one's wife.

Half-lights, At : indistinctly. [Bacon, *Essays : Of Simulation* (1625)]

Halfseas over : intoxicated. A nautical term for a ship in full sail rushing before the wind. From a resemblance between the movements of the man and of the ship if the wind is subject to changes. Said to have been derived orig. from Dutch, *op zee zober*, over sea beer. [*The Spectator*, No. 616 (1714)]

Half-breeds : *see* Featherheads.

Half-done, as Elgin was burnt : in the Scottish civil war of 1452, the Earl of Huntley burnt the half of the town of Elgin that belonged to the Douglases, but spared the other half which was his own property.

Half-hearted : not thorough ; not having the whole of one's heart, energies, or interest in the matter.

Halfway house, A : a building, generally an inn, situated approximately halfway between two towns, or stages in a journey.

Halfway, To meet : to make a compromise with .. [Nashe, *Unfortunate Traveller* (1594)]

Halgaver, Summoned before the Mayor of : for an offence against the laws of tidiness. The mayor was a personage in the Carnival held in July on the Moor of Halgaver in Cornwall.

Halidom, By my (*Germ.*, *Heiligtum*) : an oath. Halidom = anything considered holy.

Halifax Law : capital punishment for a relatively trivial offence. In allusion to the Halifax Gibbet Law which laid down death as the punishment for the theft of anything of the value of 13½ pence or over.

Hall Sunday : the Sunday before Shrove Tuesday. A corruption of Hallow (Holy) Tuesday.

Hallelujah lass, A : a girl member of the Salvation Army.

Hallmark, A : a stamp of genuineness and quality. Orig. only the stamp impressed on gold and silver plate by the Goldsmith's Company at their Hall.

Hallow Mass Day : properly All Hallow Mass Day. The feast of All Hallows or All Saints.

Hallow Mass Eve : All Hallow Mass Eve : *see* Hallow Mass Day.

Hallstadt : relating or belonging to European prehistoric civilization. In allusion to Hallstadt in Austria where a collection of weapons, etc., illustrating the transition from the bronze to the iron age was found.

Halves, To go : to share equally.

Ham, A child of : a negro. In allusion to the supposed descent of the inhabitants of Africa from Ham, the son of Noah.

Hamaco, As mad as : Hamaco was a term used for a fool in Turkey. [Scott, *St Ronan's Well*, ch. 37 (1824)]

Haman's, A gibbet higher than : in allusion to the gallows on which Haman was hanged. *See* the *Book of Esther.*

Hamilton, The Reek of Mr. Patrick : Patrick Hamilton (1504–28) was burnt to death by Cardinal Beaton. His martyrdom was one of the contributing causes of the Reformation in Scotland.

Hamilton, Single-speech : William Gerard Hamilton (1729–96), Eng. politician. His maiden speech in the House of Commons was a remarkable success and gained for him the sobriquet.

Hamlet, A : an introspective, philosophical man of dreams rather than of action. In allusion to the hero of Shakespeare's play of that name (1602–3).

Hamlet with the part of the Prince left out : with the principal character omitted ; just as Shakespeare's

Hamlet would be if the character of the Prince of Denmark were lacking.

Hammer, The : Judas Maccabæus. Maccabæus = a hammer.

Hammer and anvil, Between : caught between two opposing forces. [Rabelais, *Pantagruel*, IV, 29 ; *Second Maiden's Tragedy*, I, ii (1611)]

Hammer away at .. To : to devote oneself energetically to ..

Hammer, To be brought under the : to be sold by auction. In allusion to the auctioneer's hammer.

Hammer, To go under the : to be sold by auction. In allusion to the auctioneer's mallet.

Hammer of Heretics, The : (1) Pierre d'Ailly (1350–1420), Fr. Cardinal and President of the Council of Constance ; (2) John Faber (1470–1541), from the title of his work, *Malleus Hereticorum,* the hammer of heretics.

Hammer of the Monks, The : Thomas Cromwell (1490–1540), Eng. religious reformer and suppressor of the monasteries.

Hammer of the Scots, The : Edward I of England. So-called in his epitaph on his tomb in Westminster Abbey (*Malleus Scotorum*).

Hammer and Tongs : violent disputing. A corruption of hammer and tongues.

Hammered, To be : to be declared a defaulter on the Stock Exchange. The procedure is for the head Stock Exchange waiter to strike three strokes with a mallet on the side of a rostrum in the Exchange before making formal declaration of the default of a member.

Hampden, A village : a local patriot. After John Hampden, Eng. patriot, who lived from 1594–1643. [Gray, *Elegy in a Country Churchyard* (1751)]

Hân, Sons of : the Chinese. After Hân, the founder of the 26th dynasty.

Hanaper, The Clerk of the : an officer of the Hanaper Office.

Hanaper Office, The : the dept. of Chancery, abolished in 1832, which collected fees for the sealing and enrolment of documents. After the hanaper (hamper) or wicker basket in which such documents were kept until the fees were paid.

Hand, To bear (lend) a : to assist.

Hand, Done to one's : *see* Done.

Hand that feeds one, To bite the : *see* Bite.

Hand over fist : with great rapidity.

Hand and foot, To be bound : to be strictly controlled.

Hand and foot, To wait on a person : to be devotedly attentive to a person.

Hand gallop, A : a gallop during which the horse is kept easily in hand or under control.

Hand in, To get one's : to become familiar with (an occupation). [Dekker and Webster, *Westward Ho*, II, i (1607)]

Hand and glove : in close intimacy ; as close as hand and glove are to one another. [Cowper, *Table Talk*, l. 173 (1782)]

Hand at .. To be a good : to be an expert at ..

Hand grips with .. To be at : to be engaged in a close contest with ..

Hand in hand with .. : in close co-co-operation with .. [Chapman, *Monsieur D'Olive*, I, i (1606)]

Hand over hand : with great rapidity.

Hand to hand contest, A : a contest at close quarters. Also Hand with hand, Hand by hand, Hand of hand, Hand for hand. [Early 13th cent.]

Hand in .. To have a : to take part in .. [Shakespeare, *Julius Cæsar*, III, ii (1601)]

Hand and heart, To offer one's : to propose marriage. [Shakespeare, *The Tempest*, III, i, 89–90 (1609–10)]

Hand know what one's right hand does, Not to let one's left : to act secretly, esp. in the performance of good deeds. [*Matthew*, vi, 3]

Hand to mouth, From : thriftlessly ; without preparation or reserves. Like one who consumes all the available food as soon as he receives it.

Hand, An old : a person with much experience.

Hand, An old Parliamentary : a politician well versed in parliamentary procedure and able to take full advantage of all its opportunities. Phrase applied by W. E. Gladstone to himself in a speech in the House of Commons on Jan. 22, 1886.

Hand, Out of : (1) immediately [Heywood, *Proverbes* (1546)] ; (2) beyond control.

Hand for all it is worth, To play one's : *see* Play.

Hand to the plough, To put one's : to undertake a task ; to enter upon a course of life or undertaking. [*Luke*, ix, 62]

Hand in one's pocket, To put one's : to pay money.

Hand at .. To be a poor : to be unskilful at ..

Hand and seal, Under : confirmed in writing. When writing was an uncommon accomplishment, a signature to a document took the form of the impression of the hand (later the thumb only) dipped in ink together with the impression of a seal.

Hand, To shew one's : to disclose one's intentions. A card-playing metaphor derived from the game of poker.

Hand, By the strong : by force. [*Exodus*, vi, 1]

Hand, The upper : the advantage ; precedence. [Ascham, *Toxophilus* (1545)]

Hand, A young : a person with little experience.

Hands, Off one's : out of one's charge. [Rutherford, *Letters*, I, ccx (1636)]

Hands, To change : to pass from the possession of one person into that of another.

Hands, Clean : a clear record, above suspicion. [Wycliffe, Transl. of *Job* (1380)]

Hands of .. To fall into (be in) the : to fall into (be in) the power of .. [Cicero, *Brutus*, xxxv, 133]

Hands full, To have one's : to be fully occupied. [Heywood, *Proverbes* (1546)]

Hands, With full : lavishly.

Hands on .. To lay : to do violence to .. [Bp. Hall, *Characters : The Wise Man*, Bk. I (1608)]

Hands of .. To play into the : to act, unknowingly, for the advantage of another person. [*The Spectator*, No. 423 (1712)]

Hands of .. To strengthen the : to support and assist. [*Ezra*, i, 6]

Hands, To strike : to make an agreement. In allusion to the practice of clasping hands on such an occasion. [*Proverbs*, vii, 1]

Hands of .. To wash one's : to decline to have anything to do with .. After Pontius Pilate's washing of his hands at the trial of Jesus.

Handfasting : betrothal. In allusion to the practice of joining hands as an indication of betrothal.

Handful, To be a : to be rather more than can comfortably be dealt with or managed.

Handgrips with .. To be at : to contest with .. In allusion to a hand-to-hand struggle. [Bunyan, *The Holy War* (1682)]

Handkerchief to .. To throw the : to hint one's preference for a man, to invite his attention. After a children's game known as 'Kiss in the Ring' and by other names.

Handle to .. To give a : to give some justification for a suspicion.

Handle to one's name, A : a personal title of honour.

Handle without gloves, To : to deal with very severely, unmercifully. A pugilistic metaphor.

Handsel : see Hansel.

Handsome Englishman, The : John Churchill, Duke of Marlborough (1650–1722). So-called by the French troops.

Handsomely, To act : to be generous, liberal.

Handsuppers : Boers who surrendered to the British in the course of the Boer War of 1899–1902.

Handwriting on the wall : a warning of an approaching calamity. [*Daniel*, v]

Handy man, A : a sailor. Since the bombardment of Alexandria, after which a naval force was landed in Egypt, a variety of duties, apart from those relating to ships, have been imposed on the British naval forces.

Hang back, To : to display unwillingness to come forward. [Geo. Pettie, *Guazzo's Civile Conversation*, II (1581)].

Hang on, To : to keep attached to after one's company is no longer desired.

Hang out, To : to lodge. [*Lexicon Balatronicum* (1811)]

Hang together, To : of people, to keep united in a company. [Shakespeare, *Merry Wives of Windsor*, III, ii (1598)]

Hang in the bell ropes, To : to defer a marriage after the banns have been called in church.

Hang, Not to care a : to be quite indifferent.

Hangdog look, A : a guilty appearance that would justify hanging like a dog.

Hang fire, To : to delay the accomplishment ; to come to no decisive result. A military metaphor.

Hang of .. To get the : to make oneself familiar with the working or use of ..

Hang by a thread, To : to be in a very critical condition. In allusion to the story of the sword which was suspended by a hair over the head of Damocles at a feast to which he was invited by Dionysius of Syracuse. [Cicero, *Tusculanae Disputationes*, V, 21 ; Horace, *Odes* III, i, 17]

Hang upon the lips of .. To : to listen intently to the words of .. [Ovid, *Heroides : Penelope Ulixi*, l. 30 ; Jos. Hall, *Characters : The Flatterer*, Bk. II (1608)]

Hanged for a sheep as a lamb, As well be : once one has committed an offence involving punishment one need not hesitate to commit further offences which will involve no greater penalty.

Hanger-on, A : an extra-subservient dependant. [B. Jonson, *Cynthia's Revels*, V, iii (1600)]

Hanging judge, A : a very severe judge ; who theoretically is always ready to condemn the guilty to death by hanging. [Maxwell Gray, *The Silence of Dean Maitland*, Bk. I, ch. 16 (1886)]

Hanging look, A : a personal appearance that suggests a tendency towards crime and therefore a justification for hanging. [Shakespeare, *Measure for Measure*, IV, ii, 34–5 (1603)]

Hanging matter, A : a serious matter ; one which theoretically may involve the punishment of hanging. [Shakerley Marmion, *The Antiquary*, V, i (1641)]

Hangman's Day : Friday. In allusion to the former custom of executing criminals on that day.

Hannibal, A : a great general. After Hannibal (249–183 B.C.), Carthaginian general and statesman.

Hannibal is at the gates : great and urgent danger threatens. After the fear aroused in Rome of the Carthaginians under Hannibal (*q.v.*).

Hans en kelder (*Dutch*, Jack in cellar) : an unborn child. [Cleaveland, *Character of a London Diurnall* (1647)]

Hans von Rippach : an imaginary personage ; one who does not exist. Rippach is a village in Saxony.

Hansa : see Hanse Towns.

Hansard : the official reports of the British Parliamentary proceedings. After the name of the firm of printers who printed the reports during the 18th and 19th cents.

Hanse Towns, The ; Hanseatic League, The : (*Hansa*, association), a federation, for commercial and defence purposes, of a number of North German towns. It held for a time the position of one of the Powers of Europe. The League arose out of a treaty between Lübeck and Hamburg in 1241 and lasted in name until its incorporation in the German Empire in 1871.

Hansel (*Ang.-Sax.*, *handselen*, to deliver into the hand) : (1) a bribe ; (2) a gift ; (3) the first money received for the sale of goods and as a consequence considered an indication of fortune (good or bad).

Hansel Monday : the first Monday in the year, when it was the practice to present gifts to servants.

Hansom cab, A ; Hansom, A : a two-wheeled hackney-cab. After Jos. Aloysius Hansom (1803–82), the inventor.

Happy as a clam at high tide, As : exceedingly happy. At high tide a clam or bivalve mollusc is quite safe from enemies. [Dow, *Sermons* (? 1636)]

Happy as a king, As : (1) contented ; (2) slightly drunk. [*Tragical History of Guy, Earl of Warwick* (1661)]

Happy despatch, The : suicide, or rather Hara-kiri (*q.v.*).

Happy hunting grounds, The : life after death. In accordance with the North American Indian conception.

Happy Valley, The : the garden of peace in Johnson, *Rasselas* (1759), which it was almost impossible either to enter or to leave.

Hara-kiri (*Jap.*, stomach-cutting): suicide in honourable circumstances. Orig. by means of an opening in the stomach.

Harcourt's Round Table : the meeting of the Liberal leaders in Sir William Harcourt's house in January, 1887, to ascertain whether an agreement between them on the Irish Question was not possible.

Hard at hand : close by. [Marlowe, *Tamburlaine*, II, iii (1590)]

Hard as iron, As : very hard. [Propertius, I, xvi, 30 ; Thos. Lodge, *Wit's Miserie and Worlde Madnesse* (1596)]

Hard as nails, As : exceedingly hard ; hard-hearted.

Hard as the nether millstone, As : obdurate ; hard-hearted. The lower or nether millstone is supposed to be the harder of the two. [*Job*, xli, 24]

Hard as steel, As : hard-hearted. [*Towneley Mysteries*, 288 (14th cent.) ; Shakespeare, *Two Gentlemen of Verona*, I, i, 135 (1590)]

Hard as a stone, As : [Wycliffe (1382) ; *Pety Job*, 318 (1400) ; Ovid, *Ars Amatoria*, Bk. I, 475]

Hard up : in financial straits. Orig. a slang term for ' Hard put to it.'

Hard with .. To go : to cause annoyance or difficulty to .. [Cyril Tourneur, *The Revenger's Tragedy*, II, i (1607)]

Hardouin would not object, E'en : a phrase used in apology for a statement to which exception might be taken on the ground of its authenticity. Jean Hardouin (1646–1729), librarian to Louis XIV, archæologist and numismatist, was notable for his extreme scepticism in matters of archæology and history.

Hardshell : (1) in 1850, a supporter of Senator Benton in his advocacy of ' hard money ' ; (2) in 1852 *et seq.* the more conservative faction of the Democratic Party in New York State ; (3) the stricter section of Baptists.

Hard swearing : perjury ; keeping tenaciously to one's statements under oath, heedless of the truth.

Hardy Annual, A : a measure that comes frequently before parliament but is never adopted.

Hare, First catch your : make sure of the preliminaries before you begin to consider the next step. The phrase is attributed to Mrs. Hannah Glasse, *The Art of Cookery* (1747), but it is not to be found there. The basis of the phrase is probably the instruction ' Take your hare when it is cased,' *i.e.*, skinned.

Hare in a hen's nest, To seek a : to attempt a task that is almost impossible. [Porter, *Two Angry Women of Abington*, ll. 2407–9 (1599)]

Hare and hunt with the hounds, To hold with the : to endeavour to secure the favour of both parties in a controversy or contest. [15th cent.]

Hare of .. To make a : to cover with ridicule.

Hare, To start a : to open a subject that will temporarily absorb the attention of the company. [*Paston Letters*, No. 721 (1473)]

Hare with a tabor, To catch (hunt for) a : to undertake an almost impossible task. [Langland, *Richard Redeles* (1399)]

Hare, To set the tortoise to catch the : to undertake a practically impossible task. In allusion to Æsop's fable of *The Hare and the Tortoise*.

Hare without a hound, To seek a wild : to undertake an impossible task. [*Second Maiden's Tragedy*, III, i (1611)]

Hares afoot, To have : to enter into too many undertakings.

Hare's foot (head) (Hare pie) against the goose giblet, To set the : to place one

N

thing as a set-off against another. [*A Match at Midnight*, V, i (1633)]

Hare's foot, To kiss the : to be late, esp. for dinner. Possibly to miss the dish of hare and have an opportunity of seeing only the foot. [*Health to Servingmen* (1598)]

Hare's foot to lick, To get the : to obtain a small return for one's undertaking.

Hares with foxes, To take : to undertake an apparently impossible task.

Hares, To hunt (run after) two : to undertake too many projects. From the proverb, 'He who hunts two hares leaves one and loses the other.' [Plautus, *Casia*, II, viii, 39–40 ; Lyly, *Euphues and His England* (1580)]

Hare-brained : with no more brains or intelligence than a hare. [Geo. Gascoigne, *The Steel Glass* (1576)]

Hari-kari : *see* Hara-kiri.

Harlequin, A : a male character in the pantomime ; a buffoon. After the name of a Teutonic demon.

Harley Street : the medical profession. In allusion to the thoroughfare in London in whose houses many of the most distinguished London physicians practice.

Harm's way, To keep out of : to avoid danger or risk. [Smollett, *Peregrine Pickle*, ch. 11 (1751)]

Harmless as a dove, As : the dove is an emblem of innocence and is quoted as such in *Matthew*, x, 16.

Harmonia's necklace : an unlucky possession. In allusion to the necklace that proved fatal to whoever possessed it, which was given to Harmonia, the daughter of Mars and Venus, by one of the Grk. gods on her marriage.

Harness, To die in : to die while fully employed, before retirement from work. 'In harness,' in the sense of engaged in one's daily work.

Haro (Harrow), To cry : to denounce (anyone). 'Ha-row' was the Norman hue and cry.

Haroun- (Harun-)al-Raschid : Caliph of Baghdad (786–809), around whose name innumerable romantic stories centre in *The Arabian Nights*.

Harp on a .. To : to repeat a remark so as to bore ; as playing continuously on one string of a harp. [Heywood *Proverbes* (1546)]

Harpagon, A : a miser. After a character in Molière, *L'Avare*.

Harpocrates, To be a : to be silent. In allusion to Harpocrates, the god of silence.

Harpy, A : a hateful, vulture-like woman. In Grk. mythology, half-woman, half bird of prey, with the attributes of the latter, a minister of divine vengeance.

Harridan, A (*Old Fr., haridelle*, a worn-out horse) : a hateful old woman.

Harrington, A : a farthing. After the Lord Harrington who received from James I the patent for making brass farthings.

Harris, Mrs. : an imaginary person, frequently referred to but never seen. After a character in Dickens, *Martin Chuzzlewit* (1843).

Harrow, To cry : *see* Haro.

Harrow, Under the : suffering persecution or torture, like a toad confined by and at the same time threatened by a harrow.

Harry Groat, A : a groat coined in the reign of King Henry VIII which bore his effigy.

Harry, Old : (1) the Devil. A corruption of Old Hairy. In *Leviticus*, xvii, 7, the Hebrew for 'Hairy ones' is translated devils ; (2) Henry VIII of England.

Harry with .. To play Old : to harm ; torment ; ruin. *See* Harry, Old.

Harry Sovereign, A : a sovereign of the reign of Henry VII or Henry VIII.

Harry Twitcher : Henry, Lord Brougham (1778–1868), orator, statesman, jurist and scientist. In allusion to his habit of twitching the face.

Harry of the West : Henry Clay (1777–1852), Amer. statesman and orator.

Harrys : second-rate playing cards.

Hartford Convention, The : a secret convention held at Hartford, Connecticut in 1814–15 which protested against the actions of the Federal Government. It was suspected of treason.

Harvest ears, To hear with one's : not to listen or pay attention. [Heywood, *Proverbes* (1546)]

Harvest Home, The : the end of the harvest ; the celebration of the conclusion of the harvest.

Harvest for a little corn, To have a large (make a long) : to get little return for great preparations. [Heywood, *Proverbes* (1546)]

Harvest moon, The : the moon near the full at the time of the harvest in England.

Hash of .. To make a : to spoil in the course of an unsuccessful attempt to deal with ..

Hash, To settle a person's : to reduce a person to silence or powerlessness.

Hasty pudding, A : a species of pudding or porridge, made with little trouble. So-called by H. Buttes (1599) ' for .. in so great haste I composed it.' *See however* Wm. Haughton, *Englishmen for My Money,* II, i (1597).

Hat covers his family, His : he is alone, unmarried.

Hat in Friesland, Not to wear a brown : to tolerate the prejudices of those in whose midst one finds oneself. After the story of the insults received by the wearer of a brown hat in Friesland where such hats are or were unfashionable.

Hat in hand, To go : to be obsequious ; begging for a favour.

Hat, To hang up one's : of a man who marries a wife who has already a home into which he is admitted.

Hat on a hen, To put a : *see* Put.

Hat money : a payment made to a master of a vessel in recognition of his care of the freight.

Hat, To pass (send) round the : to make a collection of money, generally for a charitable object. [Goldsmith, *Life of Beau Nash* (1762)]

Hat, To be a (shocking) bad : on one occasion at a race at Newmarket a little man pushed himself into the Duke of York's (Fred. Augustus) circle and offered to bet. The Duke enquired who the man was and was informed, ' Walpole.' His reply, referring to the shape of Walpole's hat, was, ' Then the little man wears a shocking bad hat.'

Hat, Only fit to wear a steeple-crowned : ought to be burnt as a heretic. In allusion to the style of hat worn by Puritans.

Hat, A white : a radical. In allusion to the white hat worn by Henry (Orator) Hunt (1773–1835) during the administration of Wellington and Peel.

Hatch before the door, To have a : to remain silent ; to have a means of concealing one's actions. [Heywood, *Proverbes* (1546)]

Hatch, Match and Despatch Column, The : the births, marriages and deaths advertisements in a newspaper.

Hatchet, To bury the : to make peace. From a practice formerly prevalent among the N. Amer.-Indians of burying a tomahawk on the conclusion of a peace.

Hatchet after the helve : *see* Helve.

Hatim, As generous as : *see* Generous.

Hatted dame, A : a peasant woman. In the 17th cent. they were accustomed to wear hats.

Hatter, As mad as a : *see* Mad.

Haul over the coals, To : to subject to cross-examination and reproof. In allusion to the medieval ordeal by fire.

Haussmannize, To : to rebuild a city on improved lines. After Baron George Eugene Haussmann (1809–91) who rebuilt Paris.

Haut ton (*Fr.,* high tone) : the fashionable ranks of society.

Have it out, To : to continue a contest or dispute to the finish. Properly, to cause to come out to a duel.

Haves and the Have-nots, The : those who have property and those who have none. [Cervantes, *Don Quixote,* II, 20]

Havoc, To cry : orig. to order an army to set about pillaging.

Haw, Not worth a : of no value at all ; a haw being the fruit of the hawthorn. [1000]

Hawk about, To : to offer for disposal in the manner of a hawker.

Hawk and buzzard, Between : (1) between two equally dangerous enemies ; (2) of doubtful social status, not the equal of the members of the family and yet above the level of the servants.

Hawk Eye State, The : Iowa. After an Indian chief with whom the early colonists had many battles.

Hawk from a handsaw, To know : to distinguish one thing from another. Handsaw is a corruption of hernshaw or heron. [Shakespeare, *Hamlet,* II, ii (1602)]

Hawk's meat : one easily tricked by a swindler. A play on hawk in the sense of a rogue. [Thos. Preston, *King Cambyses,* ll. 1488–90 (1561)]

Hawker's news : stale news.

Hawse Hole, To creep through the : to rise in the Navy from the lowest rank. The hawse hole is the hole through which the cable of a vessel runs.

Hay and grass, Between : (1) too late for one purpose and too early for another ; (2) between boyhood and manhood ; (3) neither one thing nor the other.

Hay on the horns, To carry : to be bad-tempered and consequently a source of danger. In allusion to the practice of binding the horns of vicious oxen with hay. See Horace, ' Fenum habet in cornu.' (*Satires*, I, iv, 34).

Hay of .. To make : to throw into disorder ; (of arguments) to pull to pieces.

Hay, To look for a needle in a bundle (bottle) of : see Look for.

Hay while the sun shines, To make : to take full advantage of every opportunity when engaged in an undertaking. [Barclay, *Ship of Fools*, II, 45 (1509)]

Head, Over a person's : (1) superseding another one who has a prior claim [9th cent.] ; (2) beyond one's understanding. [Bacon, *Holy War* (1622)]

Head in the clouds, To have one's : to be in a mental state of unreality. [Bunyan, *Pilgrim's Progress*, Pt. II (1684)]

Head cook and bottle washer : a person in authority, esp. one who makes a great show of that authority. Properly a general servant.

Head, To do on : to act rashly. [Cooper, *Thesaurus* (1565)]

Head and ears, Over : completely ; desperately. [Fleming, *Panoplie of Epistles* (1576)]

Head off, To eat one's : to be in a condition of powerless inaction. A metaphor drawn from an animal whose food is a source of unrequited expense.

Head, To fly at the : to attack. [*Terence in English* (1614)]

Head to foot, From : completely. [Pliny, *Natural History*, VII, 77 ; *Cursor Mundi* (1300)]

Head and front of .. The : the principal leader ; the chief point. Used by Shakespeare in sense of highest point.

Head high, To carry one's : to be proud ; to display a proud mien. [Arbuthnot, *History of John Bull*, ch. 15 (1713)]

Head, To let him have his : to give a person freedom to follow his course, just as a horse when his head is freed from the reins.

Head over heels : upside down. More properly, Heels over head. [14th cent.]

Head, To keep one's : to retain one's self-control despite alarm or difficulty.

Head in the lion's mouth, To put one's : to enter a situation of great peril. [*Psalms*, xxii, 21 ; II *Timothy*, iv, 17]

Head, To lose one's : to lose one's self-control. [Chaucer, *The Knight's Tale* (14th cent.)]

Head against .. To make : to make one's way against opposition. [Sir Thos. Overbury, *The Remedy of Love*, Pt. I, ll. 33–6 (1620)]

Head, Off one's : out of one's mind.

Head, To run on : to incite. [Heywood, *Spider and Flie* (1556)]

Head against, To run one's : to attempt the impossible with hurt to oneself ; as if one tried to push a wall down with one's head. [*The Spectator*, No. 307 (1712)]

Head on one's shoulders, To have a : to be shrewd.

Head, Swollen : a state of self-conceit.

Head or tail of, Not to make : to be unable to understand. A gambling metaphor. [Vanbrugh, *Journey to London*, IV (1728)]

Head, To take one in the : to occur to one's mind.

Head off, To talk a person's : to talk to a person until he is so wearied as to be unable to reply.

Head of .. To throw oneself at the : of a woman, to show a man unmistakably that she is willing to marry him.

Head of .. To turn the : to make vain or unreasonable. [*The Spectator*, No. 201 (1711)]

Head for washing, To give one's : to submit without resistance. [Beaumont and Fletcher, *Cupid's Revenge*, IV, 3 (1615)]

Head above water, To keep : to retain one's solvency, generally by a struggle.

Heads together, To lay : of persons, to confer. [Chaucer, (14th cent.) ; Gosson, *Schoole of Abuse* (1579)]

Heads I win, tails you lose : whatever happens I am bound to gain. Phrase drawn from the practice of gambling by means of tossing.

Healing art, The : the practice of medicine.

Heap, To be struck all of a : to be overcome and (metaphorically) paralyzed by surprise. [Shakespeare, *Titus Andronicus*, II, iii (1594)]

Hear ! Hear ! : an exclamation of approval. Orig. ' Hear him ! ' a call for silence. The phrase came into use about the end of the 17th cent.

Hear as a hog in harvest, To : to give one's hearing but not one's attention. Giles Firmin (*Real Christian*, 1670) said, ' If you call hogs out of the harvest stubble, they will just lift up their heads to listen and fall to their shack again.'

Heart, The : in medieval philosophy the heart was considered to be the seat of the affections and feelings.

Heart, An affair of the : a love affair.

Heart, With all one's : with all one's energies and devotion. [*Paston Letters*, No. 14 (1430)]

Heart bleed, To make one's : to arouse in one a deep feeling of pity. [Chaucer, *Troylus*, IV, Prologue, 12 (14th cent.)]

Heart in one's boots (hose), With one's : with fear and timidity. In allusion to the metaphorical sinking of the heart at sorrow or despair. [*Thersites*, ll. 381–3 (1537)]

Heart, To break a person's : see Break.

Heart, From the depth (bottom) of one's : with all sincerity. [Horace, *Satires*, I, i, 66–7 ; *New Custom*, III, i (1573)]

Heart out, To eat one's : to grieve silently.

Heart of England, The : Warwickshire. On account of its central position.

Heart of flint (stone), A : a person devoid of feeling or compassion. [Tibullus, Bk. I, i, 63–4 ; *A Praise of M. M.*, ll. 25–6 (1557) ; *Ezekiel*, xi, 19]

Heart to be full, The : to be deeply moved by emotion. [*Seliman and Perseda* (1599)]

Heart good, To do one's : to gladden and strengthen one. [Shakespeare, *Midsummer Night's Dream*, I, ii, 73 (1590)]

Heart of grace, To take : see Grace.

Heart, With half a : half-heartedly ; not very willingly.

Heart to heart talk, A : an intimate conversation.

Heart, To lay to : to remember.

Heart, To learn by : to commit to memory. [Chaucer, *Troylus*, V, 1494 (14th cent.)]

Heart of Midlothian, The : the Tolbooth, an Edinburgh prison, demolished in 1817.

Heart in one's mouth, With one's : filled with fear. A suggestion that the trembling of the heart with fear brings it almost into one's mouth. [*Thersites*, ll. 396–7 (1537)]

Heart of oak : (1) courage ; (2) a stout heart ; (3) a man of enduring valour. [Munday and Chettle, *Death of Robert, Earl of Huntington*, IV, iii (1601)]

Heart, Poor : an expression of pity.

Heart at rest, To set one's : to render one easy in mind.

Heart is in the right place, One's : one is well-meaning and has good intentions.

Heart upon .. To set one's : to desire most earnestly. [Bacon, *Essays : Of Empire* (1625)]

Heart upon one's sleeve, To wear one's : to advertise one's sentiments and emotions to the world. [Shakespeare, *Othello*, I, i, 64 (1604)]

Heart, Smoker's : an affection of the heart caused by excessive smoking.

Heart and soul, With : thoroughly ; devotedly. [*Deuteronomy*, vi, 5]

Heart strings, One's : one's deepest feelings or emotions. [Spenser, *Faerie Queen*, IV, vi, 29 (1590)]

Heart, To take to : to take very seriously ; to grieve deeply over .. [*Cursor Mundi* (1300)]

Heart, To take : to take courage. [Shakespeare, *Julius Cæsar*, IV, iii (1601)]

Heart's content, To one's : as far or as much as one desires. [Chapman, *Blinde Beggar of Alexandria* (1598)]

Heart's ease, To wear : to live a contented life. [Bunyan, *Pilgrim's Progress*, Pt. II (1684)]

Hearth money : a tax imposed in 1663 on fire hearths.

Heathen Chinee, The : a designation of a Chinaman ; invented by Bret Harte (1839–1902).

Heathen, The Great : Johann Wolfgang von Goethe (1749–1832), Germ. poet. So-called by Heine (*Norderney*).

Heather on fire, To set the : to create uproar and excitement. [Scott, *Rob Roy*, ch. 35 (1818)]

Heather, To take to the : to flee from justice ; to become an outlaw.

Heaven and earth, To move : to make every possible effort. [Scott, *Guy Mannering*, ch. 31 (1815)]

Heaven on earth, A : a condition of great happiness. [Chapman, *All Fools*, I, i (1605)]

Heaven, The nine-fold : the heaven of the Muses. [Nich. Grimald, *The Muses*, ll. 18–9 (1557)]

Heaven, To be in the seventh : to be supremely happy. According to the Cabbalists there are seven heavens, each more blissful than its immediate inferior.

Heavens, The five : the planetary heaven, the heaven of the fixed stars, the crystalline heaven, the primum mobile and the seat of God and the angels, according to the Ptolemaic system.

Heavens, The nine : the orbits in which nine of the celestial bodies, *viz.*, the Moon, Venus, Mercury, the Sun, Mars, Jupiter, Saturn, the Firmament and the Crystalline, move.

Heavens, The seven : the number of heavens according to the Mahometan system.

Heavens, The three : the air, the starry firmament, the dwelling-place of God, according to the Jewish system.

Heavenly City, The : *see* City.

Heaven-sent Minister, The : William Pitt, the younger (1759–1806).

Heavies, The : the Dragoon Guards or Heavy Cavalry.

Heavy friend, A : an evil friend ; an enemy.

Heavy hand, To have a : of a cook, to sprinkle condiments, etc., too freely. [Jonathan Swift, *Polite Conversation*, Dial. II (1738)]

Heavy hand, To rule with a : to oppress.

Heavy Hill : the road leading to the place of execution at Tyburn, consequently (fig.) the road to the gallows.

Heavy as a log, As : a dead weight. [Lilly, *Endimion*, III, iii (1591)]

Heavy man, The : the actor who plays a serious or tragic part.

Heavyweight, A : a boxer of the heaviest class, *i.e.*, over 11 stone in weight.

Hebe, A : a waitress. After the goddess of youth.

Hecate, A : a witch. After the Grk. goddess of sorcery.

Heck and Manger, To live at : to live in luxury.

Hector, A : (1) an heroic leader ; (2) a swaggerer, a street bully. After one of the Trojan heroes in the Trojan War. [*Lady Alimony* in Dodsley's *Old Plays* (1659)]

Hector, To : to swagger ; to bully. *See* previous entry.

Hector, The British : Nennius (fl. 796).

Hector of Germany, The : Joachim II of Brandenburg (1505–71).

Hector, To play the : to bully and boast. *See* Hector.

Hector's cloak, To wear : to be punished in the manner of one's own offence. From the betrayal of Thomas Percy, Earl of Northumberland in 1569 by Hector Armstrong, in whose house he took refuge. From that time Armstrong's fortunes began to decline.

Hecuba, On to : to the main point of the story. The story of Hecuba was the centre of many of the Grk. tragedies.

Hedge alehouse, A : an inn of a poor character.

Hedge priest, A : an itinerant Irish priest attached to no parish and probably devoid of educational qualification for his office.

Hedge school, A : an open-air school in Ireland in a poor district.

Hedge schoolmaster, A : *see* Hedge school.

Hedge, To be on the right (wrong) side of the : to be in a right (wrong) position.

Hedge, To sit on the : to sit on the fence (*q.v.*).

Hedgehog, To play the : to go through the world careless of other people's feelings. In allusion to the fable of the hedgehog which, being received into the den, drove out his host. [Sir Philip Sidney, *Defence of Poesie*, Pt. I, § 1 (1595)]

Heel, Down (Out) at : giving evidence of poverty or carelessness in personal appearance. [Shakespeare, *King Lear*, II, ii (1605–6)]

Heel of Italy, The : the south-eastern extremity of Italy, which in form resembles a heel.

Heel tap : the dregs.

Heels, To bless the world with one's : to be hanged. [Painter, *Palace of Pleasure* (1566)]

Heels, To cool the : to await another's pleasure. [*The Merry Devil of Edmonton*, ll. 151–3 (1608)]

Heels, To gather up one's : to run away. [Bunyan, *The Holy War* (1682)]

Heels of .. To have (get) the : to surpass in running.

Heels over head : *see* Head over heels.

Heels, To kick one's : to spend time waiting another's pleasure. [Ben Jonson, *Bartholomew Fair* (1614)]

Heels, To kick up one's : to die. [Dekker and Webster, *Westward Ho*, II, ii (1607)]

Heels, To lay (set) (clap) by the : to arrest ; imprison ; render powerless. Properly, to imprison in the stocks. [*Hickscorner*, l. 481 (1520)]

Heels in one's neck, To cast : to leap forward heedlessly. [Nashe, *Lenten Stuff* (1599)]

Heels of, To see the : to see for the last time. [*Interlude of Youth*, l. 191 (1554)]

Heels, To show a light (clean) (fair) pair of : to run away swiftly. [Heywood, *Proverbes* (1546)]

Heels, To take to one's : to run away. [Thos. Preston, *King Cambyses*, ll. 395–6 (1561)]

Heels of .. To tread upon the : to follow closely upon ..

Heeler, A : a political follower of low character; one who follows at the heels of his leader.

Heep, A Uriah : an ostentatiously humble hypocrite. After a character in Dickens, *David Copperfield* (1849).

Heir of the Republic, The : Napoleon I, who became Emperor after having been First Consul of the Republic.

Helen, A : a very beautiful woman. After the wife of Menelaos, King of Sparta.

Helen of one's Troy, The : the acme of one's ambition. After Helen who was the cause of the Trojan War. [Lord Brooke (1554–1628), *Treatise of Humane Learning*]

Helicon : the inspiration of poets; the home of poetry. After the mountain of that name in Bœotia which was sacred to the poets.

Heliconian Sisters, The Nine : the Muses (*q.v.*), who dwelt on Mount Helicon in Bœotia.

Heliogabalus, A : a monster of folly and debauchery. After the Roman Emperor (c. 205–222).

Hell on earth, A : a place of mental torture. [Rich. Breton, *Characters : War* (1615.)]

Hell, To move : to make every possible effort. [Thos. Campion, *When Thou Must Home* (1601)]

Hell of a time, To have a : to have a very lively time.

Hell and Tommy, To play : to ruin utterly. [Haliburton, *The Clock-maker* (1837)]

Hellebore, As sad as : very sad. In allusion to a character in Samuel Foote, *The Devil upon Two Sticks* (1768).

Helm, To be at the : to direct; control. [Wm. Penn, *Some Fruits of Solitude*, Pt. II, § 17 (1693)]

Helping hand, To hold out a : to offer assistance. [Marcus Seneca, *Controversiae*, I, i, 14; Gosson, *Speculum Humanum*, ll. 20–2 (1576)]

Helve, To send axe after : see Axe.

Helve after the hatchet, To throw the : to be reckless, esp. after heavy losses.

In allusion to the legend of the wood-cutter who threw the handle of his axe into the water in which the head had fallen.

Hemp in one's pocket, To have : to have luck on one's side. In allusion to the superstition that hemp brings good luck.

Hempen caudle, A : a hangman's rope. [Shakespeare, 2 *Henry VI*, IV, vii (1593)]

Hempen collar (cravat) (tie), The : the hangman's rope.

Hempen fever : death by hanging.

Hempen widow, A : the widow of one who has been hanged.

Hen to chuck, To teach a : see Teach.

Hen, To put a hat on a : see Put.

Henpeck, To : of a wife, to nag and rule her husband. In allusion to a hen that pecks feathers out of a cock. [Early 17th cent.]

Henry Dubb, A : the ideal workingman, in the opinion of the U.S. capitalist.

Hep, hep ! the cry by which an attack on the Jews used to be announced in Germany. Contraction for *Hierosolyma est perdita* (Jerusalem is destroyed), the inscription on the recruiting banners of the Crusaders.

Hepplewhite : a kind of domestic furniture. After Geo. Hepplewhite, Eng. cabinetmaker (d. 1786).

Heptarchy, The : the period of English history prior to the consolidation of the kingdom by Edward the Elder in 924. Previously the country was divided into several kingdoms.

Herb of grace, The : rue. In allusion to its use in the R.C. Church.

Herclem, Ex pede : see Ex pede.

Herculean : extremely difficult or dangerous; very powerful; gigantic. After Hercules, Grk. mythical hero, celebrated for his strength.

Hercules, A : a man of exceptional physical strength. After the mythical hero and god of that name.

Hercules' knot, A : a knot, extremely difficult to unravel. The invention of it was attributed to Hercules.

Hercules' labour, A : a very great task. In allusion to the twelve stupendous labours imposed on the god, Hercules. See Labours of Hercules.

Hercules of Music, The : Christopher Glück (1714–87).

Hercules, The Pillars of : Gibraltar and Ceuta, on either side of the Straits of Gibraltar. According to the ancient myth they were set up by Hercules as the Western boundary of the world. Hence any impassable limit.

Hercules Secundus : Commodus, Rom. Emperor (161–192). So-called by himself.

Hercules, To snatch a club from : to attempt an impossible or very difficult task. [Macrobius, *Satires*, Bk. V, iii § 16]

Herefordshire kindness, A : a good service rendered in return for another.

Hermaphrodite, A : an animal that combines in its own person both of the sexes. After Hermaphrodytus (Grk. myth.) who became combined with the nymph of the fountain, Salmacis.

Hermeneutic : relating to interpretation. After Hermes, the god of skill.

Hermes, A : a messenger. After the messenger of the gods in Grk. mythology.

Hermetic : (1) relating to chemistry ; (2) completely sealed or closed. After the Egyptian Hermes Trismegistus, the fabled inventor of alchemy.

Hermetic art, The : chemistry.

Hermit Nation (Kingdom), The : Corea. In allusion to the seclusion from the outer world practised by its governments until its virtual annexation by Japan.

Héro de la Fable, L' : Duke of Guise (1614–64).

Héro de l'Histoire, L' : le grand Condé, Duc d'Enghien (1621–87).

Hero of a Hundred Fights, The : the first Duke of Wellington (1769–1852). So-called in Tennyson, *Ode on the Death of the Duke of Wellington* (1852).

Hero of the Nile, The : Viscount Nelson (1758–1805), who won the Battle of the Nile.

Herod, To out-Herod : to exceed even Herod in cruelty, ferocity or violence. In the old morality and mystery plays King Herod was always depicted as of most ferocious temper and language. [Shakespeare, *Hamlet*, III, ii (1602–3)]

Herodotus of Old London, The : John Stow (1525–1605), author of the *Survey of London*. After Herodotus, famous Grk. historian, who lived from 484 to 425 B.C.

Heroic Age, The : the mythical age when the heroes are supposed to have lived.

Heroic medicine : medicine which either kills or cures.

Heroic poetry : epic poetry ; poetry celebrating the life of a hero.

Heroic remedies : violent remedies.

Heroic size, Of : in sculpture, greater than life-size.

Heroic verse : the verse in which heroic or epic poetry is written.

Herring-pond, The : the sea ; in particular the Atlantic Ocean. [*England's Path to Wealth* (1722)]

Herrings in a barrel, Like : very closely packed together. [Cervantes, *Don Quixote*, II, 43, 52]

Hesperia : the Western Land. According to the Greeks, Italy ; according to the Italians, Spain. *See* Hesperian *and* Hesperides.

Hesperian : western. After Hesperus, the evening star.

Hesperides : (1) the nymphs, daughters of Hesperus, who, with the aid of a dragon, guarded the garden of the golden apples in the extreme west of the world ; (2) the Fortunate Isles or Isles of the Blest in the far west beyond the Pillars of Hercules in which the golden apples grew ; (3) the Islands of Cape Verde or the Canary Islands. Grk., western ; daughters of the west.

Hesperus : the evening star.

Hessian, A : a mercenary soldier or politician in the U.S. In allusion to the Hessian soldiers who fought in the pay of England in the American Revolution.

Hessians : high boots. After the Hessian mercenary soldiers who introduced them into England.

Hew blocks with a razor, To : to employ fine powers or tools for an unworthy object. ' To endeavour to work upon the vulgar with fine sense.' [Pope, *Thoughts on Various Authors* (1741)]

Hewers of wood and drawers of water : slaves ; labourers of the lowest class. In allusion to the Gibeonites who were enslaved by the Israelites. [*Joshua*, ix, 21]

Hibernia : the Roman name for Ireland.

Hic jacet, A : an epitaph. After the two first words of Lat. epitaphs, ' Hear lies.' [Shakespeare, *All's Well that Ends Well*, III, vi (1601–2)]

Hiccius Doctius ; Hixius Doxius (*Imitation Lat.*) : a pretentious humbug. [Thos. Shadwell, *The Virutoso* (1676)]

Hickory, Old : Andrew Jackson (1767– 1845), Amer. general and President of the U.S. In allusion to the strength and toughness of his character, like hickory wood.

Hickory, Young : Martin van Buren (1782–1862), President of the U.S., on whose shoulders the political mantle of Old Hickory (Pres. Jackson) (*q.v.*) was said to have fallen.

Hickscorner, A : a scoffer. After the name of a character in an interlude of that name printed by Wynkyn de Worde (d. 1534).

Hide of land, A : an early Eng. measure of land sufficient to be tilled by means of one plough in the course of a year.

Hide-bound : narrow-minded ; obstinate. In allusion to the condition of ill-fed cattle whose skin clings tightly to the body. [*Return from Parnassus*, II, iv (1606)]

Hieroclean legacy, The : the legacy of jokes. After Hierocles (5th cent.), who was the original compiler of an anthology of jokes.

High brow, A : a person aggressively intellectual or supposedly so.

High Church : the party in the Church of England which attributes great importance to the Episcopate and to those doctrines and opinions generally which distinguish the Church from the Nonconformist bodies. Orig. (17th cent.) applied as a nickname to the Tory party in the Church.

High day, A : a solemn festival.

High and dry : left aside from the current of events. Metaphor drawn from the sea, as of a ship stranded high on the beach.

High falutin : bombastic pretence. Either corruption of high flighting, or from (Dutch) *verlooten*, stilted.

High game, To fly at : to have great ambitions.

High hand, With a : autocratically.

High horse, To ride the : to be arrogant. [Addison, *Freeholder* (1716)]

High in the instep : haughty. [Heywood, *Proverbes* (1546)]

High jinks : a noisy frolic ; properly, a game of forfeits.

High life : life in the upper ranks of society.

High and mighty : arrogant. Orig. an epithet of dignity.

High places : altars erected to heathen gods. From their elevated situation.

High ropes, On the : arrogant and disdainful. [Goldsmith, *She Stoops to Conquer*, II, i (1773)]

High Seas, The : the great ocean outside of territorial waters.

High spirits, In : jovial ; in good spirits.

High tea, A : a meat tea.

High words : angry words. [Sheridan, *School for Scandal*, V, ii (1777)]

Higher Criticism, The : a series of questions affecting the composition, the editing and the collection of the books of the Bible. The phrase was first used by Eichhorn in *Einleitung in das Alte Testament*, Bd. II, § 424, 295 (1787).

Higher Orders, The : the upper classes.

Highflier, A : (1) a High Churchman ; (2) in Scotland, an Evangelical ; (3) one whose ambitions are great ; (4) a pretentious beggar.

Highland bail : pugilistics.

Highlanders : playing cards of low quality. In allusion to the device on the wrappers of packs of such cards.

Hildebrand, A : an overbearing, powerful, strongminded pope ; of the character of Gregory VII (Hildebrand) (1013–85).

Hill, To go down : to be on the decline.

Hinc illae lacrymae (*Lat.*, Hence these tears) : the cause of the trouble. [Terence, *Andria*, I, i ; Whitgift, *Works*, I (1572)]

Hindustan Regiment, The : the second Battalion of the West Riding Regt., formerly the 76th. In allusion to the distinction gained in Hindustan.

Hip, On the : at a definite advantage. A metaphor drawn either from hunting or wrestling. [Heywood, *Proverbes* (1546)]

Hip and thigh, To smite : to attack without quarter. [*Judges*, xv, 8]

Hipped, To be : to be low-spirited ; from hypochondria.

Hippocras : a medicinal wine. After Hippocrates (4th cent. B.C.), the Father of Medicine, from whose prescription it is said to be made up.

Hippocratic face, A : the appearance of a face betokening death. After Hippocrates (4th cent. B.C.), by whom it was described.

Hippocrene : poetic or literary inspiration. After a fountain on Mount Helicon, sacred to the Muses.

Hippodrome, A : (1) a circus ; (2) a music hall ; (3) in America a fraudulent horserace. After the ancient Grk. course for horse and chariot races.

Hit the bull's eye, To : to have a neat and perfect success. A shooting metaphor.

Hit, A great : a considerable success. From the game of hit and miss.

Hit, To make a : to make a success.

Hit a man when down, To : to take advantage of a man when he is at one's mercy.

Hixius Doxius : *see* Hiccius Doctius.

Hobbema, The English : John Crome, the elder (1769–1821). After Meindert Hobbema (c. 1638–1709), a famous Dutch landscape painter.

Hobbema, The Scotch : Peter Nasmyth (1787–1831).

Hobbes' voyage : a leap in the dark. In allusion to the last saying of Thomas Hobbes (1588–1679), the philosopher, ' Now I am about to take my last voyage, a leap in the dark.'

Hobbling Giles : *see* Hopping Giles.

Hobby, A : a favourite pursuit. From ' hobby-horse,' orig. a pleasure-horse, afterwards a child's toy.

Hob's pound, To be in : to be in difficulties. Hob represents a rustic fool and the phrase therefore means to be in difficulties in consequence of one's own folly.

Hobson Jobson : a noisy festivity.

Hobson's Choice : no choice. Generally supposed to be in allusion to Thomas or Tobias Hobson, livery stable keeper of Cambridge (c. 1544–1630), who allowed his customers no choice. They had to take whichever horse was next due to go out. The phrase in the form of ' Hudson's Choice ' was, however, current as early as 1614 and was probably adapted to apply to Hobson of Cambridge.

Hoc genus omne (*Lat*, All this sort of people) : [Horace, *Satires*, I, ii]

Hock Day : Tuesday. *see* Hock Tide.

Hock Monday : *see* Hock Tide.

Hock Tide : a popular festival celebrated on the second Monday and Tuesday after Easter in commemoration of the expulsion of the Danes in 1074.

Hockey cake : *see* Hoky.

Hocus-pocus : charlatanism ; a conjuror's trick ; conjurer's gibberish. Said to be from Ochus Bochus, a celebrated It. wizard of the 17th cent., or from ' Hoc est Corpus ' of the Mass. ' Hokos-Pokos ' is the name of the juggler in Ben Jonson, *Magnetic Lady* (1632). *See also* Ben Jonson, *The Staple of News* (1625).

Hod, A : a bricklayer's labourer. From the implement used in his employment.

Hodge : a countryman. From ' hedger.' [Chaucer, *Coke's Prologue*, l. 12 (1386)]

Hodge-Podge : a mixture. Corruption of Hotch-potch (*q.v.*).

Hodge-wife, As firm as : very firm and secure. Hodge's wife is said to have been confirmed by a bishop several times.

Hodman, A : one who performs the drudgery in literature for the assistance of a writer of repute. Properly, a bricklayer's labourer.

Hog in armour, A : a clumsy person ; one obviously uncomfortable in his attire. [Howell, *English Proverbs* (1660)]

Hog and hominy : ordinary food. Pork and maize are among the cheapest of foods in the United States.

Hog, To go the whole : (1) to perform a business completely ; (2) to support one's party in everything without question. [Cowper, *Love of the World Reproved*]

Hogs to a fine market, To bring one's : to get one's affair into a bad state of mismanagement. [*Look About You*, I, xiii (1600)]

Hog's Norton, To be brought up at : to be badly behaved. Hook Norton, formerly Hoch Norton, in Oxfordshire, was proverbial for the clownishness of its inhabitants. [*Interlude of Youth*, l. 498–9 (1554)]

Hogan Mogan : *see* Hogen Mogen.

Hogarth of Novelists, The : Henry Fielding (1707–54). The original Hogarth (1695–1764) was called ' The Juvenal of Painters.'

Hogarth, The Scottish : David Allan (1744–96).

Hogen Mogen : (1) Holland ; (2) the Dutch ; (3) people of high rank. From the Dutch title of the States General, *Hoogmogendheiden*, High Mightinesses.

Hogsdon cask, Over a : in a very hurried and unceremonious manner. [*The Wizard* (1640)]

Hoi Polloi : *see* Oi Polloi.

Hoigh, On the : excitedly. [*Terence in English* (1614)]

Hoist with one's own petard : caught in his own trap. [Shakespeare, *Hamlet*, III, 4 (1602–3)]

Hoky ; Hockey cake : the seed cake distributed at a Harvest Home (*q.v.*).

Holborn Hill, To ride backwards up : to go to be hanged. The road to the gallows at Tyburn passed along Holborn Hill and criminals in former times used to be taken to execution with their backs to the horse.

Hold forth, To : to harangue. First used by the Nonconformists (c. 1642) in this sense.

Hold the candle to, Not to be worthy to : In allusion to the link boys who used to light their masters.

Hold one's hand, To : to forbear. [*Towneley Mysteries*, IV, 260 (c. 1350)]

Hold one's head high, To : to be proud and arrogant.

Hold a looking-glass to a mole, To : to act foolishly and to no purpose. From an ancient Grk. proverb.

Hold one's own, To : to maintain oneself in a contest. [R. Brunne, *Chronicle* (1330)]

Hold the serpent by the tail, To : to act foolishly. From an ancient Grk. proverb.

Hold one's tongue, To : to keep silent. [Scott, *Legend of Montrose*, ch. 4 (1819)]

Hold water, To : to come successfully through a test ; to bear inspection. [Mabbe, Transl. of Aleman, *Guzman d'Alfarache*, II, 79 (1622)]

Hole and corner : secret ; underhand. Lit., done in a hole and corner, *i.e.*, in a secret place. [Ascham, *Toxophilus*, Bk. I (1545)]

Hole in .. To pick a : to find fault with .. In allusion to the Rom. practice of dressing criminals in rags. [Chapman, *All Fools*, IV, i (1608)]

Hole in the water, To make a : to be drowned. From an It. proverb.

Holiday liking, A : a mere temporary, superficial friendship, intended perhaps merely for the period of a holiday. [Mrs. Cath. Crowe, *Light and Darkness : The Money Seekers*, ch. 6 (1850)]

Holiday speeches (words) (terms) : choice language. [Shakespeare, 1 *Henry IV*, I, iii (1596–7)]

Holland House Circle, The : the political and social circle that gathered round the 3rd Lord Holland (1773–1840) at Holland House, Kensington, London.

Hollantide : contraction of All-Hollantide, All Hallows, November 1st.

Hollow, To beat : to beat wholly, of which the phrase is a corruption. [Jas. Townley, *High Life Below Stairs*, I, ii (1759)]

Holy Alliance, The : the alliance between Russia, Austria and Prussia (1816–30) and subsequently joined by the other powers except Britain and Rome, for the preservation of the dynastic *status quo* or to regulate the affairs of Europe ' by the principles of Christian charity.'

Holy Boys, The : the 9th Regt. of Foot. In allusion to their practice, during the Peninsular War, of sacking monasteries and selling the bibles.

Holy City, The : of the Western Arabs, Fez ; of the Christians, Jerusalem ; of the Hindoos, Benares ; of the Incas, Cuzco ; of the Jews, Jerusalem ; of the Mahometans, Mecca, Medina ; of the Indian Mahometans, Allahabad ; of the Russians, Kief, Moscow.

Holy fire : erysipelas ; St. Anthony's fire.

Holy Grail, The : *see* Grail.

Holy of Holies, The : (1) the sanctuary of a church ; (2) anywhere especially sacred. Orig. the innermost sanctuary of the Temple at Jerusalem.

Holy Isle, The : (1) Lindisfarne, off the coast of Northumberland, on account of its monastery ; (2) Ireland, on account of its numerous saints.

Holy Land, The : among the Christians and Jews, Palestine, or more properly Judæa, the scene of the biblical narrative ; among the Mahometans, Mecca, the birthplace of the Prophet ; among the Chinese Buddhists, India, the native-land of the Buddha ; among the Greeks, Elis, the site of the Temple of Zeus.

Holy land of mountain adventure, The : the Alps.

Holy League, The : (1) the League between the Pope, Ferdinand of Aragon, Venice, and Switzerland in 1511, and later Henry VIII of England and the Emp. Maximilian directed against Louis XII of France ; (2) the league between the Pope, Venice and Spain against the Turks in 1571 ; (3) the association formed in France by the Duc de Guise in 1576 with the assistance of the King of Spain and the support of the Pope ' for the defence of the Holy Catholic Church against the encroachments of the Reformers,' but in reality to secure the succession to the throne of the Duc de Guise instead of Henry of Navarre, afterwards Henry IV ; (4) the league formed in 1684 by the Pope between the Emperor, Poland, Venice and Muscovy against the Turks.

Holy Mother of the Russias, The : the City of Moscow.

Holy oak, A : an oak that marked a parish boundary at which the Gospel was read at the beating of the bounds during the Rogation Days ; also known as Gospel Oak.

Holy Office, The : the Inquisition (*q.v.*).

Holy Orthodox Church, The : the Greek Church.

Holy Roman Empire, The : the successor to the (Western) Roman Empire, founded by Charlemagne in 800 and destroyed by Napoleon in 1806. It was succeeded by the Austrian Empire, which was dissolved in 1918.

Holy Saturday : the day before Easter Sunday.

Holy Thursday : Ascension Day.

Holy Wars, The : the Crusades, the Thirty Years War, and other wars of religion.

Holy Water, As the Devil loves : *see* Devil.

Holy Week : Passion Week ; the week immediately preceding Easter.

Holy Writ : the Bible ; formerly all writings on sacred subjects.

Home to .. To bring a thing : (1) to convict a person of .. ; (2) to say something that kindles the attention of ..

Home Counties, The : Middlesex, Surrey, Kent, Essex and Hertford, and sometimes Sussex, the counties bordering on London.

Home, To go : to die. [First quarter of the 16th cent.]

Home, To go to one's long : *see* Home, To go.

Home of Lost Causes, The : Oxford University, noted for its extreme conservatism. [Matthew Arnold, *Essays in Criticism* (1865)]

Home, Man's long : the grave.

Home Office, The : the Ministry of the Interior in the United Kingdom ; the department of state concerned with home as distinct from foreign affairs.

Home, To pay : to press hard in combat.

Home, To press a thing : to pursue a course until it is completed to the full. [Dryden, *Annus Mirabilis*, st. 127 (1667)]

Home Rule : self-government. The phrase was apparently invented by George Brodrick in *The Times* on the 9th of February, 1871.

Home Rulers : a British political party which advocates autonomy for Ireland.

Home Secretary, The : the Minister of the Interior in the United Kingdom

Home to .. To speak : to tell plain truths to .. [Foote, *The Author*, II, (1757)]

Home, To strike (hit) : to touch a person where he is most vulnerable.

Home, To touch : to give a mortal wound to.

Homer, The British : (1) Geoffrey Chaucer (1340–1400), so-called by Ascham ; (2) John Milton (1608–74) so-described on Gray's monument in Westminster Abbey.

Homer, The Celtic : Ossian (fl. 300).

Homer of Dramatic Poets, The : Shakespeare. So-called by Dryden.

Homer of Ferrara, The : Ariosto (1474–1533). So-called by Tasso.

Homer of the Franks, The : Angilbert (fl. 814). So-called by Charlemagne.

Homer of the French Drama, The : Peter Corneille (1606–84). So-called by Sir Walter Scott.

Homer of History, The : Herodotus (c. 484–425 B.C.), Grk. historian.

Homer of Human Nature, The Prose : Henry Fielding (1707–64). So-called by Byron.

Homer sometimes nods : even the most trustworthy sometimes fails. [Horace, *Ars Poetica*, 359]

Homer, The Oriental : Firdusi (904–1020), the Persian poet.

Homer of Philosophers, The : Plato (429–347 B.C.).

Homer, The Prose : Henry Fielding (1707–64). So-called by Byron.

Homer, The Scottish : William Wilkie (1721–72), author of *Epigoniad*, ' the Scottish *Iliad*,' which is written in heroic couplets based on the 4th book of the *Iliad*.

Homeric laughter : unquenchable, long drawn out laughter. In allusion to the laughter of the gods in the *Odyssey*, VIII, 326.

Homeric question, The : the question of the authorship, etc., of the poems of Homer.

Homeric verse : hexameters. In allusion to the metre in which Homer wrote.

Homespun lass, A : a country girl ; one whose clothing material is spun at home. [*Grim, the Colier of Croydon*, IV, i (1662)]

Honest Abe : Abraham Lincoln (1809–65), President of the United States.

Honest Broker, The : Prince Otto von Bismarck (1815–98), in view of his chairmanship of the Berlin Congress of 1878, where he endeavoured to bring Austria and Russia to an agreement. *See* his speech in the Reichstag of Feb. 19, 1878.

Honest George : George Monk, Duke of Albemarle (1608–70).

Honest-man, King : Victor Emanuel II of Italy (1820–78), who fulfilled in times of prosperity the promises of constitutional reform made by his father and himself in a period of adversity.

Honest penny, To earn an : to earn one's money by honest work.

Honest penny, To turn an : to earn money legitimately. [Wycherley, *Plain Dealer*, III (1676)]

Honey to the beehives, To send : to perform a labour of supererogation. Of Spanish origin.

Honey for a halfpenny, To sell : to estimate at a low price. [Nash, *Pierce Penilesse* (1592)]

Honey Island : an ancient name for Britain.

Honeyed speech (words) : flattery. [Homer, *Iliad*, vi, 212–4 ; Ausonius, *Epistulae*, ii ; Heywood, *Proverbes* (1546)]

Honeyed tongue, A : a flatterer. [Homer, *Iliad*, Bk. I, 247–9 ; Thos. Lodge, *Wounds of Civil War*, I, 283–5 (1594)]

Honeymoon, A : the first month after marriage. From the Scand. practice of drinking diluted honey during it. Moon = month.

Hong merchant, A : a Chinese merchant (native or foreign). *Hong*, a foreign warehouse or factory at Canton.

Honorificabilitudinitatibus : honourableness. The longest word in the Eng. language. [Nashe, *Lenten Stuffe* (1599)]

Honoris causa (*Lat.*, For the sake of honour) : honorary (esp. of a Univ. degree).

Honour, An affair of : a duel or a dispute leading up to one. Duels were governed and prescribed by the Laws of Honour.

Honour bright ! : an asseveration of sincerity.

Honour, A court of : a tribunal for the decision of matters of honour ; a successor to the medieval court of chivalry.

Honour, A debt of : a gambling or other debt that cannot be enforced by law, but is dependent on one's sense of honour.

Honour, The Fountain of : the King of England, with whom titular honours originate.

Honour, Laws of : laws of etiquette, which govern polite society.

Honour, A point of : an obligation, binding not on account of law but out of self-respect or on account of conscience.

Honour, One's word of : a statement or promise made on one's honour.

Honours, To do the : to preside at a social function.

Honours are easy : both sides have equal advantages. A cardplaying metaphor.

Honours of war, The : the right to retain arms and colours, granted to a defeated army by the victor.

Honoured in the breach than in the observance, More : of a custom or example that should not be followed. [Shakespeare, *Hamlet*, IV, iv (1602–3).

Hoodlum : an Amer. term for a street ruffian. Said to have been a corruption of Muldoon, a hooligan leader in San Francisco about 1868. Muldoon was re-arranged as Noodlum, which was misread as Hoodlum.

Hoodwink, To : to deceive. From the game of hoodman-blind or blind man's buff. [Thos. May, *The Heir*, IV, i (1633)]

Hook, Above one's : beyond one's capacity.

Hook or by crook, By : by one means or another. By the ancient Law of the New Forest, every Forester-born has the right to remove fallen branches, etc., ' with hook and crook.' A popular but baseless derivation is from Hook and Croke, two successful advocates, one or other of whom was generally retained by litigants in the early 17th cent. Yet another derivation is from Hook and Crook, two places in the port of Waterford, by one or the other of which, Strongbow, when he invaded Ireland in 1172, is said to have sworn that he would capture the city. [*Colin Clout* (1240) ; Wycliffe, *Controversial Tracts* (1370)]

Hook, To fish with a golden : to bribe.

Hook, On one's own : self-dependent.

Hooligan, A : a street ruffian. Either a perversion of hoodlum (*q.v.*), or from the name of a prominent street ruffian in South London about the year 1898. [*Daily Mail*, Jan. 9, 1899)]

Hoosier, A : a native of the state of Indiana. *See* Hoosier State.

Hoosier State, The : Indiana. After Husher, a bully (Amer. colloq.), one who hushes his opponents.

Hop o' my Thumb, A : (1) a dwarf ; (2) a term of contempt used figuratively for one small enough to hop over a thumb. Introduced in the 16th cent.

Hop the twig, To : to run away from one's creditors as a bird escapes from the fowler.

Hope against hope, To : not to lose hope despite overwhelming disappointments.

Hopeful, A young : a male child.

Hopping Giles, A : a lame man. After St. Giles, the patron saint of cripples.

Horace of England, The : (1) Ben Jonson (1573–1637), so-called by Dekker ; (2) Abraham Cowley (1618–67), so-called by the Duke of Buckingham. Horace, famous Rom. poet, lived from 65 to 8 B.C.

Horace of France, The : (1) Jean Macrinus (1490–1557) ; (2) Pierre Jean de Beranger (1780–1857).

Horace of Portugal, The : Antonio Ferreira (1528–69).

Horace of Spain, The : (1) Lupercio Argensola (1559–1613) ; (2) Bartolme Argensola (1562–1631).

Horn in the bog, To stick one's : to get into a difficult position. [Scott, *Rob Roy*, ch. 18 (1818)]

Horn Book, A : an elementary treatise ; a school book. Orig. in the 16th cent. a child's book protected by a covering of horn.

Horn and corn : cattle and provisions.

Horn, To exalt (lift up) one's : *see* Exalt.

Horn Gate, The : in Grk. legend, one of the two gates of dreams, though which those which are to be fulfilled pass. After a pun between the Grk. words *keras*, horn, and *krano*, to bring to an issue.

Horn nor hoof, Neither : without trace.

Horn, To come out at the little end of the : to get the worst in a contest or dispute ; to be swindled. [Ben Jonson, *Eastward Ho* (1605)]

Horn mad : raving mad ; so mad or angry as to toss as with the horns of an ox. [Burton, *Anatomy of Melancholy : To the Reader* (1621)]

Horn, To put to the : to denounce as a rebel ; to outlaw. In allusion to the

former practice in Scotland of blowing a horn three times before announcing a sentence of outlawry.

Horn of Salvation, The : God. [II *Samuel*, xxii, 3]

Horn, To be squeezed through a : to get the worst of a contest or dispute. [Fletcher, *A Wife for a Month* (1624)]

Horn Thumb, A : a pickpocket. In allusion to the practice, when bags were worn as purses, of wearing horn thimbles so as to protect the thumb from the knife used to cut away purses.

Horns of the Altar, To the : to the uttermost. In allusion to the Roman custom of holding the horns of the altar when swearing.

Horns, To take the bull by the : *see* Take.

Horns of a dilemma, On the : between two alternative difficulties.

Horns, To draw in one's : to modify one's demands or expectations. In allusion to the snail which draws in its horns when disturbed.

Hornet's nest about one's ears, To bring a : to bring much petty annoyance, esp. the remonstrances of individuals, upon oneself. [Peter Pindar, *Odes of Condolence : The Churchwarden* (1792)]

Hornets' nest, To stir up a : to cause oneself trouble and petty annoyance. The bear, which is very fond of honey, occasionally inserts his snout in a hornet's nest instead of one of bees.

Hornie, Auld : In Scotland, the Devil. In allusion to his supposed horns.

Horrors, The : the Delirium Tremens.

Hors de combat (*Fr.*, out of fight) : disabled from the contest. [Lord Chesterfield, *Letters*, Bk. II, No. cxii (1757)]

Horse to an ass, To come from a : *see* Ass.

Horse, To go from an ass to a : *see* Ass.

Horse of another colour, A : a different matter.

Horse, A dark : a candidate of whose capacity and qualifications little or nothing is publicly known. A racing metaphor.

Horse, To flog a dead : *see* Dead horse.

Horse and foot : completely ; with all one's might. In allusion to the former two branches of an army. [Chapman, *An Humerous Daye's Myrth* (1599)]

Horse Guards, The : the headquarters of the Commander-in-Chief of the British forces ; formerly the office of the Horse Guards.

Horse and harness, To come for : to come in order to serve one's own ends.

Horse, To get upon one's high : to pretend to a dignity higher than that to which one is entitled.

Horse licks his ear, Before a : very promptly. [Heywood, *Proverbes* (1546)]

Horse to the pond, To lead a : to perform the easier half of an operation. From the proverb, ' You can lead a horse to a pond but you can't make him drink.'

Horse, To ride the high : *see* High.

Horse Latitudes, The : a portion of the Atlantic Ocean between 30° and 35° North, where calms were frequent and in consequence sailing vessels conveying horses used often to have to throw their cargoes overboard.

Horse Marines, The : a self-contradiction ; but a nickname of the 17th Lancers, two of whose men once had been previously in the Marines.

Horse to market, To run before one's : to reckon up one's profits prematurely.

Horse in the mouth, To look a gift : to criticize a gift. [Heywood, *Proverbes* (1546)]

Horse night-cap, A : a bundle of straw. [Greene, *Contention Between Liberality and Prodigality*, I, ii (1602)]

Horse play : rough play in which horses might participate. [Vanbrugh and Cibber, *The Provoked Husband*, II, i (1728)]

Horse sense : strong common sense.

Horse Tails, The : the Turks.

Horse, To talk : to boast. A racing metaphor.

Horse, A Trojan : a concealed danger. In allusion to the wooden horse left behind by the Greeks at Troy.

Horse, To ride the wooden : *see* Wooden horse.

Horse, To work on the dead : to do work for which payment has been made in advance.

Horses together, To set one's : to join forces ; to co-operate. [Walter Pope, *Life of Seth Ward, Bp. of Salisbury* (1697)]

Horses while crossing a stream, To change (swop) : *see* Swap.

Hortus Siccus, A (*Lat.*, dry garden) : a herbarium or collection of dried plants.

Hospitaller, A : a Knight Hospitaller or member of an order of military monks which was founded at Jerusalem (c. 1048) by It. merchants for the assistance of poor pilgrims. The Order was known variously as Brothers of the Hospital of St. John the Baptist, Knights of the Hospital of St. John of Jerusalem, Knights of Rhodes, Knights of Malta.

Host in oneself, To be a : to be above the average in value or use in a contest. The phrase was used by the Duke of Wellington in reference to Lord John Russell, in conversation in 1838 or 1839. A similar phrase, ' Himself a host,' had been used by Pope in his transl. of the *Iliad*, Bk. III, 293 (1715–20).

Host, To reckon without one's : to overlook a factor of great importance.

Hostages to fortune, To give : to handicap oneself, *e.g.*, by marriage, in the struggle for existence. [Bacon, *Essays : Of Marriage and Single Life* (1625)]

Hot blood, In : excitedly. [Bacon, *Essays : Of Death* (1625)]

Hot cakes, To sell like : *see* Sell.

Hot and cold, To blow : to be uncertain of mind or intention. An allusion to one of Æsop's *Fables*.

Hot as fire, As : intensely hot. [Barclay, *Ship of Fools* (1509)]

Hot for .. To get too : to become a centre of annoyance or persecution. *See* Hot for, To make it.

Hotfoot : rapidly ; hastily. [Map, *Body and Soul* (1300)]

Hot (and strong), To give it a person : to punish severely ; to scold.

Hot Gospeller, A : a Puritan (after 1660). The original Hot-Gospeller was Edw. Underhill of Worcester who lived in the reign of Queen Mary.

Hot for .. To make it : to make a place or situation very uncomfortable. [Gosson, *Schoole of Abuse* (1579)]

Hot shot, A : a skirmishing soldier ; one who shoots hotly.

Hot as toast, As : comfortably warm. [*Two Cookery Books* (1430)]

Hot water, In : in trouble. In allusion to the ordeal by hot water. [*Lisle Papers*, XI, 100 (1537)]

Hotch-potch, To bring into : to group properties together preparatory to an equal division. Fr., *Hochepot*, the family pot (*hocher*, to shake ; *pot*, pot).

Hotch-potch : (1) a dish consisting of various ingredients ; (2) a mixture. *See also* previous entry. [Hall, *Satires* (1597)]

Hotel Dieu, A (*Fr.*, mansion of God) : a hospital.

Hotspur, A : a fiery-tempered person. In allusion to Harry Percy (Hotspur) (1364–1403).

Hound a person, To : to pursue a person relentlessly, as if with the assistance of a hound ; to persecute.

Hounds and run with the hare, To hunt with the : see Hare, To hold with the.

Houndsfoot trick, A : a rascally trick. Houndsfoot = a scoundrel.

Hour, The eleventh : the latest possible moment. See the Parable of the Labourers (*Matthew*, xx).

Hour, In an evil : acting under an unfortunate impulse. Phrase derived from astrology.

Hours, A Book of : a book of prayers to be said at the Canonical Hours (*q.v.*).

Hours, Canonical : Matins, Lauds, Prime, Terce, Sext, None and Vespers ; the seven periods of the day set apart for prayer in the Early Christian and Roman Catholic Churches.

Hours, To keep good : to be home or go to bed betimes at night. [Jos. Hall, *Characters*, Bk. II : *The Busybody* (1608)]

Hours, The small : one to three a.m.

House, The : the House of Commons.

House afire, Like a : very rapidly ; as quickly as a house would burn.

House, Atop of the : in a state of anger or other excitement.

House, To bring down the : to call forth so great applause as might possibly cause the building to collapse.

House of cards, A : see Cards.

House of Correction, A : a prison for minor offences.

House divided against itself, A : a party, family, etc., split by internal dissension. [*Matthew*, xii, 25]

House of God, The : a place of worship. [10th cent.]

House on one's head, To pull a : to get into trouble.

House and home, To eat one out of : to flourish at the expense of another so as to endanger his welfare. [Shakespeare, 2 *Henry IV*, II, i (1597–8)]

House in order, To set one's : to put one's affairs straight. [Dryden, *Absalom and Achitophel : To the Reader* (1681)]

House, The Lower : see Lower.

House, To keep open : to exercise general hospitality. [Thos. Nash, *Summer's Last Will and Testament*, ll. 1614–6 (1600)]

House of Rimmon, To bow down in the : to conform outwardly while opposed inwardly ; as Naaman did in the Temple of Rimmon after his conversion to Judaism. [II *Kings*, v, 18]

House, The Upper : see Upper.

House out of the windows, To throw the to throw everything into confusion. From the French. [Field, *A Woman is a Weathercock*, IV, ii (1612)]

Houses, As safe as : thoroughly safe.

Household gods : furniture and other domestic property. Metaphor drawn from the domestic gods of the Romans.

Household Troops : troops appointed to guard the Royal Household, *viz.*, the Life Guards, the Royal Horse Guards, the Grenadier, Coldstream, Scots and Irish Guards.

Household word, A : a proverbial saying familiar to everyone. [Shakespeare, *Henry V*, IV, iii, 51–5 (1599)]

Housemaid's knee : an affection of the knee, induced by kneeling.

House-tops, To cry from the : to announce loudly and publicly. In allusion to a custom prevalent in the East.

Housewarming, A : a social gathering held to celebrate the entrance into a new house. [Evelyn, *Diary*, Nov 28, 1661]

Houyhnhnms, The : a race of human horses described in Swift, *Gulliver's Travels* (1726).

Howard, The female : Mrs. Elizabeth Fry (1780–1844). In allusion to John Howard (1726–90), the philanthropist who devoted himself to the welfare of prisoners.

Howards, The : the British aristocracy. The Howard family (Duke of Norfolk) stands at its head.

Howe of the night, In the : in the middle of the night.

Howler, A : a glaring blunder ; that which metaphorically howls in the hearing of those who know what is correct.

Howling wilderness, A : an empty wilderness. [*Deuteronomy*, xxxii, 10]

Hub (of the Universe), The : Boston, Mass. In allusion to the following passage from Oliver Wendell Holmes' *Autocrat of the Breakfast Table*, ch. v (1859) : ' Boston State-house is the hub of the solar system.' The hub is the centre of a wheel.

Hub of the Universe (world), The : any centre considered by its inhabitants to be of great importance.

Hub, Up to the : entirely ; as far as possible. Like a cart sunk in the mud up to the hub of its wheels.

Hubert, Praise from Sir : see Praise.

Huckleberry, Above one's : out of one's reach.

Huckleberry above one's Persimmon, A : something beyond one's ability. In allusion to the preference in the Southern of the U.S. for the huckleberry above the persimmon fruit.

Hudibrastic : mock-heroic. In the manner of Butler's *Hudibras* (1663).

Hue and cry (*Fr.*, *huer*, to shout after) : general pursuit after a fugitive. [*A Warning for Faire Women*, II, ll. 778 (1599)]

Huff and ding, To : to bounce and swagger. [Arbuthnot, *History of John Bull*, ch. 15 (1713)]

Huggins and Muggins : a pretender to importance. Probably derived from Dutch, *Hoogmogende*, all-powerful, a title of the Dutch states-general. [Butler, *Hudibras* (1663)]

Huguenot, A : a French protestant. The name first appeared in France about 1560, having been introduced from Switzerland where it was in use as a political nickname. Germ., *Eidgenossen*, confederates.

Huguenot Pope, The : Philippe de Mornay (1549–1623), Fr. protestant statesman and writer.

Hull cheese, To eat : to get drunk. After Hull cheese, a strong beer formerly brewed at Hull. [Ray, *Proverbs* (1737)]

Hull, As strong as : very strong indeed. In allusion to the former fortifications of the City of Hull.

Hum and haw, To : to stammer and express hesitation in speech. In allusion to the meaningless sounds introduced between words by one who hesitates in his speech. [Rob. Arnim, *A Nest of Ninnies* (1608)]

Hum of men, The busy : a busy city or other resort of people. [Milton, *L'Allegro*, l. 120 (c. 1633)]

Human clay : see Clay.

Human probability, In all : with practical certainty. [*The Spectator*, No. 72 (1711)]

Humaner Letters : see Litterae humaniores.

Humanities, The : learning concerned with human culture, *e.g.*, the languages, literature, rhetoric.

Humble pie, To eat : to be subservient or obsequious, esp. to abandon a higher position. At hunting banquets the umbles (heart, liver, etc.) of venison were made into pies and reserved for the hunt servants, etc.

Humbug ; A humbug : deception ; a deceiver. Either It., *uomo brigiardo*, a lying man, or Irish, *uim bog*, soft copper, has been suggested as a derivation. In the second case there is a connection with the debased coinage, made of an alloy of copper, etc., which was issued from the Dublin mint by James II. [*The Student*, Vol. II, p. 41 (1751)]

Humming beer : strong beer, which causes the head of the drinker to hum.

Humming cup of sack, A : a frothing cup of sack.

Hump, To get the : to become ill-tempered and depressed. [Nashe, *Lenten Stuffe* (1599)]

Humphrey, To dine with Duke : to go hungry. The monument of Sir John Beauchamp in Old St. Paul's Cathedral was popularly believed to be that of Humphrey, Duke of Gloucester. Starving people used to frequent St. Paul's. Hence to dine with Duke Humphrey came to mean to have no dinner at all. Another explanation, current at Oxford, is derived from the Bodleian Library, orig. founded by Humphrey, Duke of Gloucester. When a student remained in the Library during the dinner-hour he is said to have dined with Duke Humphrey. The phrase, however, orig. meant ' to accept hospitality,' after the proverbial hospitality extended to allcomers by Humphrey, Duke of Gloucester (1391–1447).

Humpty Dumpty : (1) a short, stubby person ; (2) that which once damaged can never be repaired. From the nursery rhyme so-named.

Hundred Days, The : March to June, 1815. The period between Napoleon's escape from Elba and the Battle of Waterloo. The phrase was coined by the Comte de Chambord in addressing Louis XVIII.

Hundred miles away (off), Not a : a locution intended to indicate ' not very far away ' without indicating the exact place.

Hundred Years' War, The : the series of wars between England and France which lasted from about 1338 to 1453.

O

Hung up, To be : to be impeded, involved. [*The Spectator*, No. 551 (1712)]

Hungary Water : a perfume. After a Queen of Hungary to whom the recipe for it was given by a hermit.

Hunger Strike, A : persistent abstention from food on the part of political prisoners, so as to secure their release or gain come concession to which they consider themselves entitled. The government in many instances conceded the demands in order to avoid the odium of permitting the prisoners to die in prison. The practice seems to have originated in Russia, but was widely practised by women political prisoners in England who were agitating for the enfranchisement of their sex during the first and second decades of the 20th cent., and also by Irish political prisoners somewhat later.

Hungry Forties, The : the earlier half of the fifth decade of the 19th cent. in England immediately before the repeal of the Corn Laws.

Hungry (Greedy) as a hawk, As : very hungry. [Martial, *Epigrams*, Bk. IX, lv, 9–10 ; Taylor, *Short Relation of a Long Journey* (1652)]

Hungry as a hunter, As : very hungry. [Trapp (1650)]

Hungry as a wolf, As : since ancient times the wolf has been in all countries the frequent illustration of a voracious eater.

Hunkers : Conservatives ; Democrats in Amer. politics. Introduced c. 1845. Dutch, *honk*, home.

Hunks, An old : a stingy old man. [*Historie of Albino and Bellama* (1638)]

Hunt's dog, Like : self-willed ; one who will do neither one thing nor the other. Hunt, a Yorkshire labourer, had a dog which he left at home when he went to church on Sundays. The dog barked and howled so loudly as to disturb the congregation. He then determined to take it with him to church, but the dog declined to enter the churchyard.

Hunter, The mighty : Nimrod.

Hunter, Mrs. Leo : a lady whose principal occupation is the attraction of celebrities into the social circle of which she is the centre. After a character in Dickens, *Pickwick Papers* (1836).

Hunter's Mass, A : any hurried proceeding. Orig. a brief mass recited hurriedly by hunters eager to set off for the chase.

Hunter's Moon, The : the full moon of the middle or end of October, the beginning of the hunting season.

Huntingdon Sturgeon, A : an ass's foal. In allusion to a story told by Pepys in his *Diary* of the natives of Huntingdon mistaking a young donkey floating on the water for a sturgeon.

Hurdygurdy, A (onomatopoeic) : a hand organ or other primitive musical instrument. [Peter Pindar, *The Royal Tour* (1795)]

Hurly-burly, A : a noise ; disturbance. In allusion to the tumult of ancient battles, the hurling of spears, etc. [R. B., *Appius and Virginia*, l. 899 (1563)]

Husband's boat, The : the boat that used to leave London for Margate on Saturday afternoons in the summer. Many husbands used habitually to use it to join their families while on holiday.

Husband's tea : very weak tea.

Hush up, To : to suppress all mention of .. [Bunyan, *The Holy War* (1682)]

Hush-money : money paid to avoid exposure ; blackmail. [Richard Steele, *The Tatler*, No. 26 (1709)]

Husk from the grain, To separate : to separate the good from the bad. An agricultural metaphor.

Hussar, A : a light cavalry soldier. Orig. one of the national cavalry of Hungary and Croatia. (Magyar, *husz*, twenty, *ar*, price of). Matthias Corvinus, King of Hungary, enjoined every twenty families to support one soldier.

Hustle-cap, To play at : to play pitch and toss, a game in which coins are hustled or shaken together in a cap. [Scott, *Fortunes of Nigel*, ch. 11 (1822)]

Hyacinth, A : a plant and its flower. After a Laconian youth who was killed by Apollo and from whose blood the flower sprang.

Hybla, Bees of : the bees for which Hybla Minor in Sicily was famous in ancient times.

Hyblean : sweet. In allusion to Hybla in Sicily whose hills were famous for their honey.

Hydra-headed : many headed. In allusion to Hydra, a fabulous dragon of Grk. mythology, with nine heads, any one of which, if cut off, was instantly replaced by two new ones.

Hydra-headed multitude, The : the mob. [Dekker, *The Gull's Hornbook*, ch. 5 (1609)]

Hygiene : the science of health. From Hygeia, the goddess of health.

Hymeneal ; Hymenean : relating to marriage or a wedding. After Hymen, the god of marriage and nuptials.

Hymettus, Bee of : *see* Attic bee.

Hyperborean : most northerly ; extremely cold. Grk,, *hyper*, excessive, and *Boreas*, the north wind. The Hyperborei were a mythical people who dwelt beyond the North Wind.

Hyperion : (poetical) the sun. Properly, the father of the sun and moon.

Hyphenated American : an American citizen of foreign birth or parentage, such as an Irish-American or a German-American.

I.D.B. : illicit diamond buying (*q.v.*).

I.H.S. (*Lat.*, Jesus Hominum Salvator) : Jesus, Saviour of Men. Orig. a Grk. contraction for Jesus.

I.O.U. : a written admission of a debt. Contraction of ' I owe you.' [Breton, *Court and Countryman* (1618)]

I per se : the letter I by itself.

I's and cross the T's, To dot the : *see* Dot the I's, etc.

Iberia's Pilot : Christopher Columbus (1447–1506). In allusion to Iberia, the Grk. name for Spain and Portugal, the country of the Ebro.

Icarian : soaring ; adventurous. After Icarus, who flew with his father from Crete.

Ice, To break the : to initiate conversation on a difficult or unpleasant topic. Metaphor drawn from navigation in frozen waters. [Shakespeare, *Taming of the Shrew*, I, ii, 267 (1594)]

Ice, To cut no : *see* Cut.

Ice Saints : *see* Frost Saints.

Ice-brook temper, Sword of : a sword of the finest temper. The Spanish sword makers used to plunge the weapons while still hot into the ice-cold water of the Salo. [Martial ; Shakespeare, *Othello*, V, ii (1604)]

Ich dien (*Germ.*, I serve) : the motto of the Prince of Wales, acquired by Edward, the Black Prince, at the Battle of Creçy (Aug. 26, 1346), where he slew the King of Bohemia, the former holder of it.

Ichabod (*Heb.*, the glory has departed) : an exclamation of lamentation. After the name given to the son of Phinehas. [I *Sam.*, iv, 21]

Iconoclast, An : one who rejects everything that savours of idolatry ; one who is heedless of accepted prejudices. Lit. (Grk). a breaker of images. The original iconoclasts were a party of idol breakers who flourished on the Continent in the 8th and 9th cents. The name was afterwards applied to the Huguenots in France and to the Puritans in England.

Ideal Ward : Wm. Geo. Ward, of the Oxford Movement (1812–82).

Ides, The : the 15th of March, May, July and October and the 13th of the other months in the Roman calendar.

Ides of March, The : a fatal day. After the day foretold for the murder of Julius Cæsar. [Shakespeare, *Julius Cæsar*, I, ii (1601)]

Idiot, The Inspired : Oliver Goldsmith (1728–74). So-called by Horace Walpole.

Idleness, To eat the bread of : to live without labour. [*Proverbs*, xxxi, 27]

Idles, To be sick of the : to be lazy. [Withal, *Dictionary* (1634)]

Idols of the market-place : errors of belief arising from language and social intercourse ; catch phrases whose original meaning is no longer heeded. [Francis, Lord Bacon (1625)]

Ignis Fatuus, An (*Lat.*, foolish fire) : (1) a will of the wisp, apparent but unapproachable light floating over marshy ground ; (2) an Utopian scheme that cannot be realized. For the second sense *see* Francis Quarles, *Shepherd's Oracles*, 11th Éclogue (1646),

Iliad, An : a long series of struggles or troubles. After the title of Homer's great poem.

Iliad of Old English Literature, The : *The Knight's Tale* in Chaucer, *Canterbury Tales* (14th cent.).

Iliad, The French : *The Romance of the Rose* (1230–70) by Guillaume di Lorris and Jean de Meung.

Iliad, The German : *The Nibelungenlied*

Iliad of Ills (Woe), An : a number of troubles falling together. So-called by Cicero, *Ad Atticum*, VIII, ii.

Iliad, The Portuguese : *The Lusiad* (1572) of Camoens.

Iliad, The Scotch : *The Epigoniad* (1757) of William Wilkie which is written in heroic couplets, based on the 4th book of the *Iliad*.

Ilk, Of that (*Scot.*) : of the same, *e.g.*, Grant of that ilk, Grant of Grant.

Illicit Diamond Buying ; I.D.B. : the S. African offence of purchasing diamonds stolen by employees of diamond-mining companies.

Illiterate Parliament, The : *see* Parliament, The Lack-learning.

Ill-starred : unlucky ; born under unfavourable stars. An astrological metaphor.

Illuminated Doctor, The : (1) Raymond Lully (1235–1315), scholastic philosopher ; (2) Johann Tauler (1300–61), Germ. mystic.

Illuminati (*Lat.*, Lit up) : the name borne by several religious sects which flourished in Europe from the 15th to the 19th cents. They claimed to enjoy a light on their subject superior to that of other mortals.

Immortal Four of Italy, The : Dante, Petrarch Ariosto and Tasso, It. poets.

Immortal Maids, The : the nine Muses or goddesses of literature and music.

Immortal Three, The : Homer, Dante, Milton.

Immortal Tinker, The : John Bunyan (1628–88), author of *The Pilgrim's Progress*, who was a tinker by trade.

Immortals, The Forty : *see* Academy, French.

Imperial, An : a style of beard, as worn by the Emp. Napoleon III.

Imperial City, The : Rome.

Imperium in Imperio, An (*Lat.*, an empire within an empire) : an independent authority within the jurisdiction of a government. [Wm. Penn, *Some Fruits of Solitude*, Pt. I, § 354 (1693)]

Imperium et Libertas (*Lat.*, Empire and Liberty) : phrase used by Lord Beaconsfield at the Guildhall, London, on Nov. 9th, 1879, to describe the policy of his government. He had employed the same phrase in a speech on agricultural distress, Feb. 11th, 1851. The phrase had previously been used by Cicero in his peroration to 4th *Catiline*, and by Clarendon in his *History of the Rebellion*, I, 163 (1702).

Improve the occasion, To : to draw a moral lesson from an event.

In all conscience : as far as one can go without transgressing the laws.

In capite (*Lat.*, in chief) : holding direct from the crown. [Staunford, *King's Prerogative*, ch. 1 (1548)]

In esse (*Lat.*) : in actual existence. [W. Warner, *Albion's England*, Bk. V, xxviii (1589)]

In excelsis (*Lat.*, in the highest) : [W. Watson, *Quodlibets of Religion and State* (1602)]

In extenso (*Lat.*, in full) : [*Congress Debates*, II, ii, 1767 (1826)]

In extremis (*Lat.*, in the last) : at the point of death. [Ellis, *Original Letters*, 3rd Ser., I, lxxx, p. 199 (c. 1548)]

In flagrante delicto : *see* Flagrante.

In forma pauperis (*Lat.*, in the form of a pauper) : exempted from the payment of law costs. [*Soliman and Perseda* (1592)]

In loco parentis : *see* Loco parentis.

In medias res (*Lat.*, in the middle things) : into the middle of a narrative. [Horace, *Ars Poetica*, 148]

In nubibus (*Lat.*, in the clouds) : not yet practicable. [Babington, *Commandments* (1583)]

In partibus (infidelium) (*Lat.*, in the regions of the infidels) : part of the title of a bishop appointed nominally to a heathen or heretical country.

In petto : (*Lat.*, *in pectore*, in the breast), privately. [Swift, *Works* (1701)]

In petto, Cardinals : cardinals whom the pope intends to appoint, but whose names have not yet been disclosed. *See* In petto.

In posse : (*Lat.*, *posse*, to be able) possible but not actual ; the opposite of In esse (*q.v.*). [R. Burton, *Anatomy* (1621)]

In propria persona (*Lat.*, in one's own person) : not by deputy or in writing. [Congreve, *Double Dealer*, IV, i (1693)]

In re (*Lat.*) : in the matter of. [W. Watson, *Quodlibets of Religion and State* (1602)]

In statu quo (*Lat.*) : in the same state as .. ; generally, in the same state as formerly. [Mabbe, Transl. of Aleman, *Life of Guzman d'Alfarache* (1623)]

In toto (*Lat*) : entirely. [Wotton, *Reliq. : Survey of Education*, p. 293 (1651)]

Ins and outs of .. The : all the details of ..

Inaccessible as Abaton, As : *see* Abaton.

Incense on a dunghill, To sprinkle : *see* Sprinkle.

Inch of candle : a former method of sale by auction, according to which the bidding remained open while the candle burnt down an inch.

Inch and he will take an ell, Give him an : yield him a little and he will demand a lot. The ell varies from 27 to 54 inches. [Heywood, *Proverbes* (1546)]

Inch of .. Within an : to the very utmost of .. [Lilly, *Gallathea*, I, iv (1592)]

Incorruptible, The : Maximilian Robespierre (1758–94), Fr. revolutionary leader. So-called by Thos. Carlyle.

Increment, Unearned : *see* Unearned.

Incunabula : books printed before 1500 ; the earliest stages of anything. (Lat., swaddling clothes ; childhood.) The application of the word is derived from the idea that the 15th cent. was the period of the infancy of printing.

Indemnity Act, An : an act of parliament giving exemption from punishment incurred by illegal action.

Independence Day : the 4th of July ; the anniversary of the Amer. Declaration of Independence in 1776.

Index ; Index Librorum Prohibitorum : the official list of books forbidden by the R.C. Church to be read by faithful Catholics.

Index Constituency, An : a parliamentary constituency that polls early in a general election and thus gives some index or intimation of the probable general result.

Index Expurgatorius ; Index Librorum Expurgandorum : a list of books permitted by the R.C. Church to be read only after deletion of certain passages.

Index-learning : superficial knowledge gained from indexes and similar material, instead of from the books themselves. [Pope, *The Dunciad*, Bk. I (1728)]

Indian drug, The : tobacco. On account of its discovery among the N. American Indians.

Indian File : single file. Order adopted by N. American-Indians when on the march, in order to conceal or obliterate their tracks.

Indian gift, An : a reclaimed gift. In allusion to the expectation of the N. American-Indian when he makes a gift, either to receive one in return or to have his own restored to him.

Indian summer, An : a period of warm. pleasant weather in the late autumn, In allusion to the period of fine weather usual in November, of which the N. American-Indians take advantage in order to complete their harvest.

Indies, The wealth of the : proverbially great wealth. In allusion to that drawn by Spain from her Amer. colonies. A similar phrase was used by classical writers in allusion to India.

Indulgence, An : a remission of a punishment for sin, granted by the R.C. Church.

Indulgences to Rome, To send : to perform a labour of supererogation.

Inexpressibles : trousers, which may not be mentioned, or expressed in words, by the prudish. [Peter Pindar, *A Rowland for an Oliver : Ode to Affectation* (1790)]

Infallibility, His : (in ridicule) the Pope. In allusion to the doctrine of papal infallibility.

Infant prodigy, An : a child of precocious genius. [D. E. Williams, *Life of Sir Thomas Lawrence*, I, 51 (1831)]

Infernal machine, An : an explosive machine used by terrorists for the perpetration of outrages.

Infirmity of a noble mind, The last : *see* Last.

Infra dig. : a corruption of Lat., *infra dignitatem*, beneath one's dignity.

Inglorious arts of peace : *see* Peace.

Initiative, The : a political instrument whereby a certain number of electors can initiate proposals for consideration by the legislature.

Inkhorn mate, An : a dilettante in reading or writing. In allusion to the horn in which clerks used formerly to carry their pens, ink, etc. [Shakespeare, 1 *Henry VI*, III, i (1592)]

Inkhorn, To smell of the : to be pedantic. [Geo. Gascoigne, *Instruction in English Verse*, § 5 (1575)]

Inkhorn (Inkpot) terms ; Inkhornisms : studied expressions, which suggest careful preparation. [Wilson, *Art of Rhetoric*, II (1553) ; Jos. Hall, *Satires*, Bk. I, viii, 7-12 (1597)]

Inkpot, Sons and daughters of the : writers for the press.

Inkpot term, An : *see* Inkhorn term.

Inkslinging : reckless writing in the newspapers, etc.

Inkle-weavers, As great (thick) as two : extremely intimate. On account of the intimacy of the weavers of inkle (linen tape) who work very closely together. An alternative derivation is from the secrecy with which the Flemish weavers who introduced the industry into England in the 16th cent. guarded their craft. These weavers were few in number, and forming a close corporation amid alien surroundings, became proverbial for their mutual friendship. [*Dictionary of the Canting Crew* (1700)]

Inkling of .. To get (have) an : to get a hint or suspicion of .. [Heywood, *Proverbes* (1546)]

Inns of Court, The : the Inner Temple, the Middle Temple, Lincoln's Inn and Gray's Inn.

Inner man, The : the stomach.

Innocent as a babe unborn, As : quite harmless or innocent. [Middleton, *Family of Love* (1608)]

Innocent as a (sucking) dove, As : the dove is one of the emblems of innocence and is referred to as such in *Matthew*, x, 16. [Wm. Rowley, *A Woman Never Vexed*, IV, i (1632)]

Innocents' Day : December 28th. A Festival in commemoration of the slaughter of the Innocents by Herod.

Innocents, The Massacre of the : the announcement in the House of Commons, towards the end of a session, of the measures already introduced with which it is not proposed to proceed further.

Inquisition, The : a Roman Catholic tribunal, instituted in 1215 for the suppression of heresy, which became notorious for its extreme tyranny and cruelty.

Insane root, The : hemlock, which was formerly supposed to induce insanity.

Institution, The : slavery.

Instrument of Instruments, The : the hand. [Anth. Brewer, *Lingua*, IV, vi (1607)]

Insult to injury, To add : to offend as well as harm. [Cicero, *Pro Tullio*, XVII, 41 ; Horace, *Odes*, III, v, 26]

Intelligencia, The : the professional or educated class, derived as a rule from the lower class in the community, whose education has aroused ambitions or desires the realization of which are prevented by the circumstances in which they find themselves. This class, of its nature dissatisfied, has often taken a prominent part in recent continental political revolutions.

Intents and purposes, To all : practically. [Hazlitt, *Characteristics*, § 102 (1837)]

Inter canem et lupum (*Lat.*, between the dog and the wolf) : between two difficulties.

International, The : the international socialist organization founded by Karl Marx in London in 1864. Properly, The International Workingmen's Association.

Intransigeant, An ; Intransigent, An : an advanced Radical or Republican, steadfast in his opinions and averse from compromise. Lat., *in*, not, and *transigere*, to come to an agreement.

Invincibles, The : an Amer.-Irish revolutionary society, esp. active from 1880 to 1885.

Invincible Doctor, The : William of Occam (d. c. 1349), scholastic philosopher and Franciscan.

Invisible King, The : God.

Invita Minerva (*Lat.*) : with difficulty (esp. mental). Lit., Minerva (the goddess of Wisdom) being unwilling. [Cicero, *De Officiis*, I, 31 ; Horace, *Ars Poetica*, 385]

Io pæan : a pæan of joy. After Apollo Pæan, the healing god. *See* Io, To sing.

Io, To sing : to utter exclamations of joy. *Io* was the Lat. and Grk. exclamation of joy. [Jas. Shirley, *Poems: Io !* (1646)]

Ionic accomplishments : gesture and dress. Ionia was one of the divisions of ancient Greece.

Ipse dixit, An : Lat. transl. of (Grk.) Αὐτὸς ἔφα, Himself said it, a phrase used by the disciples of Pythagoras Zacynthius (fl. 540–510 B.C.). An *ipse dixit* has come to mean a statement which displays self-confidence. [*Paston Letters*, III, No. 808 (1477)]

Ipsissima verba (*Lat.*, the exact words) : [Southey, *Letters*, II (1807)]

Ipso facto (*Lat.*, by the very fact) : apart from all external considerations. [*Liturgical Services of Queen Elizabeth* (1559)]

Irish Agitator, The : Daniel O'Connell (1775–1847).

Irish apricots : potatoes.

Irish bulls : *see* Bull.

Irish of the East, The : the Burmese.

Irish Levellers : *see* Levellers.

Irish wedding, To go to an : to receive a black eye. In allusion to the quarrels supposed to break out as a rule at festivities among the Irish.

Irishman's crossing, An : a method of progress by frequent crossing and re-crossing of the street in order to avoid corners.

Iron Age, An : an age of suffering and wickedness.

Iron Age, The : the last and the worst of the periods of the world's life.

Iron, Blood and : *see* Blood.

Iron Chancellor, The : Prince Otto von Bismarck (1815–98). In allusion to his iron will.

Iron City, The : Pittsburg, U.S.A. In allusion to its iron manufactures.

Iron Cross, The : a Prussian decoration awarded for bravery on the battlefield.

Iron discipline : the strictest discipline.

Iron dogs of the air, The : church-bells. So-called by Heine.

Iron Duke, The : the Duke of Wellington (1769–1852). The term was first applied to a steamboat, named *The Duke of Wellington.*

Iron Emperor, The : Nicholas I of Russia (1796–1855).

Iron enters into his soul, The : he is the object of very hard usage or severe treatment. After the incorrect Vulgate version of *Psalm* civ, 18, which should have been translated, 'His person entered into the iron.'

Iron hand in a velvet glove, An : rigid firmness, accompanied by courtesy and politeness.

Iron horse, The : the railway engine.

Iron is hot, To strike while the : to take advantage of the opportunity that is offered. [Heywood, *Proverbes* (1546)]

Iron Maiden of Nuremberg, The : an instrument of torture, lined with spikes and constructed so as to embrace a man.

Iron, A man of : a man of very strong character.

Iron mask, The man in the : a mysterious prisoner in the Bastille in the reign of Louis XIV whose identity has never been disclosed.

Iron rations : emergency army rations, consisting of tins of meat and soup and hard biscuits.

Iron, To rule with a rod of : to rule tyrannically.

Iron to swim, To teach : *see* Teach.

Irons in the fire, Other : alternative courses of action. [Seneca, *Apocolocyntosis Claudii Caesaris*, 9; G. Harvey, *Pierce's Supererogation* (1593)]

Irons in the fire, To have too many : to be engaged in too many undertakings. [Sir W. Paget (1549)]

Irons, Just off the : just finished his training. [Scott, *Red Gauntlet*, Letter 13 (1824)]

Ironclad, An : a great armoured man-of-war.

Ironclad Oath, The : the oath of office instituted in the U.S. at the conclusion of the Civil War and intended to exclude all possible opponents of the Union.

Ironsides : Cromwell's troops. So-called from their invincible determination in battle.

Irony of fate, The : a development of events that induces a cause to have the opposite of its expected effect.

Irredentism : the political movement for the incorporation in a state of neighbouring territory inhabited by a population racially identical with the population of the state to be enlarged. Orig. the movement to incorporate in Italy the Italian-speaking territories of Austria. From the political cry, *Italia irredenta*, Italy unredeemed.

Irrefragable Doctor, The : Alexander of Hales (d. 1245), Eng. scholastic philosopher.

Irritable Genus, The : poets and other men of letters. [Horace, *Epistles*, II, ii, 102]

Irtish Ferry, To cross the : to be sent into retirement or exile. The ferry on the Irtish was crossed by political prisoners who went into exile in Siberia during the period of the Czars.

Irus, As poor as : very poor. In allusion to the beggar Irus, who acted as messenger between the suitors and Penelope during the absence of Ulysses at the Trojan War. [*Odyssey*, XVIII] The simile was current in Grk. and Rom. literature.

Irvingites : *see* Catholic Apostolic Church.

Ishmaelite, An : an outlaw. After Ishmael, 'whose hand was against every man.'

Island City, The : Montreal, Canada.

Island of Saints, The : Ireland. On account of the strong hold Christianity had on its inhabitants in early days.

Island of the Seven Cities, The : an imaginary earthly paradise, supposed to have been discovered by seven bishops who left Spain during the period of the Moors.

Islands of the Blest, The : the Fortunate Islands (*q.v.*).

Isle of Death, The : Norfolk Island, a convict settlement.

Isle of Lanterns, The ; Lantern-land : an imaginary land inhabited by pretenders to knowledge. [Rabelais, *Pantagruel*, V, 32–33)]

Isle of Mist, The : the Isle of Skye. In allusion to its customary weather.

Isle of Saints, The : see Island of Saints.

Isles, The Fortunate : see Fortunate Islands.

Isms : movements, doctrines and theories. In allusion to the termination 'ism,' denoting a movement, doctrine or theory.

Isocrates, The French : Fléchier (1632–1710), Bp. of Nismes. After Isocrates, the famous Athenian orator who lived from 436 to 338 B.C.

Issachar's ears : ass's ears. In allusion to the blessing of Issachar in *Genesis*, xlix, 14.

Italia Irredenta (*It.*, Italy unredeemed) : lands adjacent to Italy inhabited by an Italian-speaking population under alien rule. They now comprise part of Istria and Dalmatia in Jugo-Slavia, Ticino in Switzerland, Nice, Malta and Corsica.

Italian Froebel : see Froebel.

Italian Molière, The : Carlo Goldoni (1707–93). After Jean Baptiste Molière, the distinguished Fr. dramatist, who lived from 1622 to 1673.

Italian Pindar, The : Gabriel Chiabrera (1552–1637). After Pindar, Theban lyric poet, who lived from 522 to 443 B.C.

Italic : a kind of printing type invented by Aldus Manutius (c. 1500) and dedicated by him to the States of Italy.

Italiote, An : an Italian subject of Greek race.

Italy, Young : see Young Italy.

Itch for .. To have an : to have a great desire for .. [Greene, *Selimus*, Pt. I, ll. 188-9 (1594)]

Itch for gold, An : a great desire for money.

Itching ears, To have : to be inquisitive or eager for news. [II *Timothy*, iv, 3]

Itching palm, An : a great desire for money. [Shakespeare, *Julius Cæsar*, IV, iii, 10 (1603)]

Ivan Ivanovitch : the general name for a Russian.

Ivory, Black : African slaves. Both slaves and ivory were exported from the same region.

Ivory Gate, The : in classical mythology the gate of sleep through which false dreams enter. The phrase is based upon a Grk. pun, *elephas*, ivory, and *elephairomai*, to cheat with vain hopes.

Ivory, To touch : to play at dice or billiards.

Ivy bush, To beat the same : see Beat.

Ivy bush, Like an owl in an : with a sapient, vacant stare. Ivy bushes were supposed to be the favourite haunts of owls.

Ixion : disappointment following unjustified expectation. In allusion to the mythical king of Thessaly who, desiring Juno, was punished by being bound to a wheel kept in perpetual motion.

Ixion's wheel : the treadmill. In allusion to Ixion, King of Thessaly.

Jack, A : (1) a boy or lad ; (2) a worthless paltry fellow ; (3) an instrument that takes the place of a boy, *e.g.*, a boot-jack.

Jack of .. To be on the : to attack with violence. From Jack, a horse-soldier's upper garment.

Jack Adams, A : a fool.

Jack-boy, A : a stable boy or other boy employed as a menial. [*Pol. Poems* (1401)]

Jack-of-all-trades, A : a handy man, who can turn his hand to a variety of occupations. Often master of none. [*Lady Alimony*, II, ii (1633)]

Jack of both sides, A : a person who shifts his support from one party to another in a controversy. [Nashe, *Terrors of the Night* (1594)]

Jack of the bowl : a Swiss fairy ; for whose provision a bowl of refreshment was set in the house every night.

Jack Brag : a vulgar braggart. From a novel of that title by Theodore Hook (1837). But see Withal, *Dictionarie* (1608), for Jacke Bragger, in the same sense.

Jack, To be common : to be at everyone's beck and call. [Heywood, *Proverbes* (1546)]

Jack, Cousin : a Cornishman.

Jack-a-Dandy : a pert fellow. [Brome, *Northern Lass*, III, ii (1632)]

Jack-out-of-doors, A : a homeless person. [Withal, *Dictionarie* (1634)]

Jack-a-dreams : a dreamer, one who wastes his life.

Jack-a-drognes : a lazy, good-natured fellow. Dutch, *druilen*, to be listless.

Jack (John) (Tom) Drum's entertainment: the forcible expulsion of a person. In allusion to the drumming of a person out of the army. [Stephen Gosson, *Schoole of Abuse* (1579) ; *Jacke Drum's Entertainment* (1601)]

Jack Fletcher and his bolt, As like as : unlike. ' Jack Fletcher ' is Jack the fletcher, and ' his bolt ' the arrow which he has made. [Richard Edwards, *Damon and Pithias*, l. 105 (1567)]

Jack Fool, A : a Tom Fool. [*A Warning for Faire Women*, II, ll. 161–3 (1599)]

Jack Frost : the personification of frost.

Jack-gentlewoman, A : a woman of low birth or manners who pretends to be a lady.

Jack and Gill (Jill) : the boy and girl in Eng. nursery song. The story is derived from Icelandic mythology.

Jack in the green : a puppet character in the Eng. May-day games.

Jack-hold-my-staff : a servile attendant.

Jack Ketch : a hangman. From Richard Jacquett, the owner of Tyburn Manor, the place of execution near London.

Jack-o'-Lantern : the ignus fatuus (*q.v.*).

Jack-a-Lent : a puppet used as an object at which to throw missiles as an amusement during Lent.

Jack in the low cellar, A : an unborn child. Dutch, *Hans-en-kelder* (*q.v.*).

Jack among the maids, A : a gallant.

Jack, Every man : *see* Man.

Jack-meddler, A : a busybody. [Withal, *Dictionarie* (1608)]

Jack Nokes (Noakes) : *see* John-a-Noakes.

Jack of Norfolk : *see* Jockey of Norfolk.

Jack in office, A : a self-important official, generally of low rank.

Jack out of office, A : one who has ceased to be a Jack in office (*q.v.*). [Heywood, *Proverbes* (1546)]

Jack, To play the : to play the rogue ; to lead astray like a Jack-o'-Lantern. [Shakespeare, *The Tempest*, IV, i (1609–10)]

Jack Pudding, A : a showman's buffoon. [Milton, *Defence of the People of England* (1651)]

Jack Robinson, Before you can say : very promptly. Jack Robinson is said to have been an eccentric who made a practice of paying sudden and very brief visits to his neighbours. The phrase is a quotation from a comic song by Hudson (early 19th cent.).

Jack-sauce : an insolent male person.

Jack-snip : a tailor, esp. an inefficient one.

Jack Sprat : a dwarf. According to the nursery rhyme he could eat no fat. [*Marriage of Wit and Science*, IV, i (1570)]

Jack Straw : a man of straw ; a worthless man or one of no consequence. [*New Custom*, I, i (1573)]

Jack Tar, A : a seaman. Jack is the generic name for a man of the lower classes ; tar is from tarpaulin which formed part of the sailor's clothing in bad weather.

Jack-in-the-water, A : a loafer near the water's edge, willing to wet his feet for a gratuity.

Jackanapes, A : a saucy fellow ; combination of Jack and ape. [Rich. Edwards, *Damon and Pithias*, l. 925 (1567)]

Jack-boots : high leather boots. When first worn by cavalry the legs were protected by jacques or metal plates.

Jacob's ladder : a rope-ladder used on board ship.

Jacob's staff : a pilgrim's staff. In allusion to the pilgrimages to St. James of Compostella, or to the representations of the Apostle James with a staff.

Jacob's Stone : the Coronation Stone in Westminster Abbey. Said to be the stone on which the patriarch Jacob slept when he dreamt of the angels ascending and descending.

Jacobin, A : a member of a party of extreme Fr. revolutionists in 1789 ; a seditious demagogue. From the monastery of the Jacobin friars in Paris in which the Jacobin party used to hold their meetings. The friars derived their name from the Rue St. Jacques in Paris, where their monastery was situated.

Jacobite, A : a supporter of James II and his house after their expulsion. Lat., *Jacobus*, James.

Jacquard loom, A : a weaving loom invented by Jos. Marie Jacquard (1752–1834).

Jacquerie, La : the peasant revolt in France of 1358. After Jacques Bon-homme (James Goodman), the popular name for the Fr. peasant.

Jacques : a Fr. artisan or peasant.

Jacques Bonhomme (James Goodman) : the popular name for the Fr. peasant. Orig. applied in contempt by the nobles.

Jade, The : fortune. In reference to her proverbial fickleness.

Jaeger : hygienic woollen clothing. After the Germ. hygienist, G. Jaeger, who advocated all-wool clothing.

Jail bird, A : a prisoner or ex-prisoner. The earliest prison for malefactors in England was in the form of an open-air iron cage.

Jamie Duff (*Scot.*) : a mourner. After an eccentric of that name who delighted in attending funerals.

Jamrach, A : a dealer in wild animals. After Johann Christian Carl (Charles) Jamrach (1815–91), a London dealer in wild animals.

Janissary, A : a soldier forcibly recruited while a young child and kept under military control for a very long period. Esp. in Turkey (Christian) and Russia (Jew.). The Turkish Janissaries who formed a privileged class were disbanded in 1825. Turk., *Yeni Askary*, new soldier. Hence the mercenary soldier of a tyrant.

Jansenists : a religious sect prominent in France in the 17th and 18th cents. Suppressed in 1713. From Cornelius Jansen, Bp. of Ypres (1585–1638).

January : the first month of the year. After Janus, the Rom. god of doors and gates, to whom the month was sacred.

Janus, To play : to be deceitful and two-faced. In allusion to the two faces of the god, Janus. [Dekker and Webster, *Westward Ho, IV*, i (1607)].

Janus, The Temple of : a Rom. temple whose doors were kept open in times of war and closed in those of peace.

Janus, Two-headed : the two-faced god whose temple at Rome was always kept open during time of war and closed when the republic was at peace.

Japan, To : to varnish objects in the manner of the Japanese.

Jaquemart, A : a clock whose hours are indicated by the movements of figures of a man and woman. After Jean Jaquemart of Dijon, who invented that style of clock.

Jarkman, A : an Abram man (*q.v.*) ; a beggar possessed of some education of which he makes full use. From Jark, the seal of a forged document.

Jarnac, Le coup de (*Fr.*, Jarnac's thrust) : a peculiar blow in fencing similar to that given by Jarnac in a duel with La Chateignerail before Henri II in July, 1547.

Jarndyce suit, A : an interminable lawsuit. In allusion to the Chancery suit of Jarndyce and Jarndyce, described in Dickens' *Bleak House* (1852).

Jarvey, A : a hackney-coach driver. In allusion to Jarvis, the name of a notorious one who was hanged.

Jaundiced eye, A : a prejudiced eye.

Jaws of death, The : a position of extreme danger. [Shakespeare, *Twelfth Night*, III, iv, 394 (1601)]

Jay, A : a foolish young man who squanders his money. After the initial letter of Juggins, such a one who was notorious in England for a time in 1887.

Jay Hawker State, The : Kansas. In allusion to Colonel Jennison of New York, the commander of the troops there, who was known as the Gay Yorker.

Jeames (de la Pluche) : a footman or other flunkey. Corruption of James. [Thackeray, *Jeames's Diary* (1845)]

Jean Crapaud : *see* Johnny Crapaud.

Jean de la Suie : a Savoyard.

Jedburgh Justice : summary punishment with or without trial. From the measures taken in the reign of James I (VI of Scotland) to suppress border raiding in the neighbourhood of Jedburgh.

Jeddart Justice : Jedburgh Justice (*q.v.*).

Jedwood Justice : Jedburgh Justice (*q.v.*). Jedwood is the district of which Jedburgh is the centre.

Jee, On the : uncomfortable ; irritated. [R. L. Stevenson, *Catriona*, ch. xxiii (1893)]

Jeffries, As bad as : probably a reference to George Jeffreys (1648–89), the notorious Judge Jeffreys of Monmouth's Rebellion.

Jehoiada box, A : a box for savings. After Jehoiada, the priest, who placed a box at the gate of Jerusalem to receive money for the repair of the Temple. [II *Chronicles*, xxiv]

Jehu, A : a coachman, esp. a furious driver. In allusion to Jehu, King of Israel. [II *Kings*, ix, 20 ; J. Crouch, *Return of Charles II* (1660)]

Jekyll and Hyde : a person possessing two apparently distinct characters, one good and the other evil. From *The Strange Case of Dr. Jekyll and Mr. Hyde*, by Robert Louis Stevenson (1885).

Jellyby, A Mrs. : a lady who devotes herself to public philanthropy and neglects her domestic duties. In allusion to a character in Dickens' *Bleak House* (1852).

Jemmie Duff : *see* Jamie Duff.

Jemmy Jessamy (Jessamine) : foppish, effeminate. From Jemmy (a fop) and Jessamy (a fop who wears jessamine in his buttonhole).

Jenkins's ear : the ear alleged to have been cut off Robert Jenkins, the cause of the war between Britain and Spain of 1739.

Jenneting, A : a species of early apple. After St. Jean, whose day, June 14th, falls about the time of the ripening of the apple.

Jenny, A : a man who concerns himself with women's affairs. From the female name.

Jenny l'Ouvrière (*Fr.*, Jenny the working-woman) : an industrious seamstress. Name invented by Emile Barateau (1847).

Jeremiad, A : a tale of trouble and misfortune. From Jeremiah, the prophet and author of the *Book of Lamentations*.

Jeremiah, A : a prophet of woe. *See* Jeremiad.

Jeremiah, The British : Gildas (516–70), author of *Lamentations over the Destruction of Britain*. So-called by Gibbon.

Jeremy Diddler : *see* Diddler.

Jericho, Go to : Jericho was the name of a country manor of Henry VIII to which he used sometimes to retire. The phrase has also been derived from Thos. Heywood, who in his *Hierarchie*, Bk. IV, p. 208 (1635), used Jericho in the sense of a place of concealment or banishment. The allusion is to II *Samuel*, x, 5, where David bids his servants, who had had half their beards cut off, ' to tarry at Jericho till their beards were grown.'

Jericho, To walk to : to conceal oneself ; to go into hiding. From II *Samuel*, x, 5, where David bade his servants tarry in Jericho until their beards were grown.

Jerman's (German's) lips, As just as : apparently an allusion to the firm compression of the lips practised by Germans. [Heywood, *Proverbes* (1546)]

Jeroboam (of rum, etc.), A : a large bottle or bowl. In allusion to Jeroboam, King of Israel, ' a mighty man of valour,' ' who made Israel to sin.'

Jerry-builder, A : one who erects cheap badly-built houses for immediate sale. Said to be derived from Fr., *jour*, a day, suggesting temporary. The term came into use in Liverpool about 1830. There may also be a connection with Jericho, whose walls were unstable.

Jerry shop (Tom and Jerry shop), A : a low-class public house. From the one made famous in Pierce Egan, *Life in London* (1821).

Jerrysneak, A : a henpecked husband. In allusion to a character in Foote, *Mayor of Garratt* (1764).

Jerrymander : *see* Gerrymander.

Jerusalem artichoke, A : Jerusalem is a corruption of *Girasole* (It.), a sunflower, which it resembles.

Jerusalem (Jew's) Letters : inscriptions tattooed on the body. In allusion to the former practice of tatooing on the arm of visitors to Jerusalem, the name of the city, the date and the sign of the Cross.

Jerusalem pony ; Jerusalem, A : a donkey. In allusion to the one on which Christ entered Jerusalem.

Jerusalem pony, A : an impecunious clergyman who hires out his services to colleagues.

Jesse, To give a person : to give a person a sound thrashing, to abuse him severely . In allusion to the valour of Jesse, the father of David.

Jesse Tree, A : a genealogical tree exhibited in churches in the Middle Ages, in which was traced the descent of Christ from Jesse.

Jesse Window, A : a church window decorated with a Jesse Tree (*q.v.*).

Jests, The Father of : *see* Father.

Jesuit's bark : Cinchona. Introduced from S. America by Jesuit missionaries.

Jeu d'Esprit (*Fr.*, a play of wit) : a witticism. Used in Eng. in No. 305 of *The Spectator* (1712).

Jeu de mot, A (*Fr.*, a play on a word) : a pun. [Sir W. Scott, *Peveril of the Peak* (1822)]

Jeunesse dorée (*Fr.*, gilded youth) : the young men of Paris who attempted a counter-revolution in 1794. Also the young and wealthy class of society generally.

Jew, As rich as a : from the mistaken belief that all, or most, Jews are wealthy.

Jewish Plato, The : Philo Judæus (c. 20 B.C.—c. 40 A.D.), Alexandrian Jewish philosopher.

Jewish Socrates, The : Moses Mendelssohn (1729–86).

Jews' ears : a fungus that grows on the elder tree. Lat., *Auriculae Judae*, Judas's ears. From the tradition that Judas hanged himself on an elder tree.

Jew's]

204

[John

Jew's eye, To be worth a : to be of great value. From the practice of some of the medieval kings of England of threatening blinding as a method of extorting money from Jews.

Jew's harp, A : a primitive musical instrument, played with the teeth. Corruption of jaws' harp ; or from Fr., *jeu*, a game.

Jews' Letters : *see* Jerusalem Letters.

Jews' Tree, The : the Eucalyptus. So-called by the Arabs of Palestine, into which country it was introduced by modern Jewish settlers.

Jezebel, A : a brazen-faced, vicious woman. In allusion to the wife of Ahab, king of Israel.

Jezebel, A painted : a woman who paints her face. In allusion to Jezebel, the queen of Ahab, king of Israel. *See* preceding entry.

Jib, The cut of one's : one's personal appearance. Orig. a sailor's expression, drawn from the jib of a ship.

Jiffy, In a : (colloq.) in a very short time. [*Münchhausen's Travels*, XXIII, 96 (1785)]

Jill, A : a young woman. Contraction of Juliana.

Jim Crow : a nigger in the U.S. (colloq.). The name was derived from a song by Thomas D. Rice (1835).

Jim Crow car, A : a public conveyance set aside for negroes, esp. in the southern of the U.S.

Jim Dandy, A : a rare example, a fine specimen.

Jimson weed : a poisonous weed. From Jamestown.

Jingo, A ; Jingoism : an extreme blustering pseudo-patriot ; chauvinism, exaggerated patriotism. From the refrain of a music-hall song, ' We don't want to fight, but, by Jingo ! if we do,' supporting Lord Beaconsfield's foreign policy, and current in 1878.

Jingo, By : an oath. Jingo was a god of the heathen Basque mercenaries who were introduced into England by Edward I.

Jis, By : an oath. Probably a corruption of By Jesus.

Joan Cromwell's kitchen-stuff tub : kitchen perquisites. In allusion to a charge brought by Royalists against the wife of the Protector Cromwell.

Job, A : (1) a person of inexhaustible patience ; in allusion to the central figure of the Book of Job ; (2) an appointment or transaction made at the public expense from corrupt or semi-corrupt motives. So used by Pepys in his *Diary*. ' Whenever any emolument, profit, salary or honour is conferred on any person not deserving it, that is a job ; if from private friendship, personal attachment, or any view except the interest of the public, any one is appointed to any public office— that is a job.' (Sheridan).

Job, A bad (good) : an unfortunate (fortunate) event, business, etc. [*Dictionary of Canting Crew* (1700)]

Job lot, A : a miscellaneous collection of articles.

Job, As patient as : *see* Job (1).

Job, As poor as : in allusion to Job when deprived of all his wealth. [Gower (1390 ; T. Wilson, *Art of Rhetorike*, 210 (1553)]

Job's comforter, A : one whose attempts at consolation only increase the distress. In allusion to the friends of Job in the biblical book to which he gave the name.

Jobs' news : bad news. From the story of Job.

Job's post : a bearer of bad news. [*Job*, i, 13–19]

Job's pound : a prison.

Job's turkey, As poor as : in allusion to Job in his period of extreme misfortune and a N. Amer.-Ind. proverb which refers to the thinness of wild turkeys in periods of scarcity. An Americanism.

Jockey of Norfolk : Sir John Howard (c. 1430–85), the first Duke of Norfolk of the Howard family.

Joe, A : a Joe Miller (*q.v.*).

Joe Manton, A : a fowling piece made by Joseph Manton, a London gunsmith.

Joe Miller, A : a stale joke. From a jest-book attributed to the comedian Joseph Miller (1684–1738) and published after his death by John Mottley. This was for long the only printed collection of Eng. jokes extant.

Joey, A : a groat. After Joseph Hume (1775–1855), member of Parliament, who strongly supported the use of the coin.

John Audley there? Is : John Audley was a showman. This signal was given by the doorkeeper to bring the performance to a speedy conclusion in order that a second audience, already waiting, may be provided for.

John Barleycorn : see Barleycorn.

John Blunt : a plainspoken, frank man.

John Bull : the typical Englishman. From a character in John Arbuthnot, *The History of John Bull* (1713).

John Cheese : a clown. [Ascham, *The Schoolmaster*, Bk. I (1570)]

John Chinaman : in the U.S. the generic term for a Chinaman, first adopted into general use at the time of the Californian gold rush.

John Company : the Honourable East India Company. From Jan Kompanie, by which name the Dutch East India Company was known in the East.

John Doe and Richard Doe : two fictitious names inserted in Eng. writs of ejectment prior to 1852.

John Dory, A : an edible sea-water fish. Fr., *jaune*, yellow, and *dorée*, golden.

John Drawlatch : (1) a thief ; (2) an idler ; (3) a good-for-nothing.

John-a-dreams : a stupid, person unable apparently to concentrate his mind. [Shakespeare, *Hamlet* II, ii (1602)]

John Drum's entertainment : see Jack Drum's entertainment.

John Fool : see Jack Fool.

John o' Groats to Land's End, From : from the extreme north of Scotland to the extreme south of England. John of Groats and Land's End are the names of the extreme points. John o' Groat was a Dutchman who settled in Scotland in the reign of James IV.

John-hold-my-staff : a subservient parasite.

John Long, the carrier, To wait for : to wait a long time. [Jno. Heywood, *Proverbs* (1546)]

John-a-napes, A : a Jack-a-napes.

John-a-No(a)kes, A : a stupid, foolish rustic ; a fictitious name for a party in a legal action. [*Histrio-mastix*, IV, i, ll. 77–9 (1610)]

John-a-nods : John-a-dreams (*q.v.*).

John Roberts, A : a tankard holding sufficient liquor to last a man from Saturday to Monday. In allusion to John Roberts, M.P., at whose instance the Welsh Sunday Closing Act was adopted in 1886.

John, Sir : a priest (contemptuously).

John of Stiles (Nokes) : see John-a-Styles. *and* John-a-Noakes.

John-a-Styles : a fictitious name for a party in a legal action.

John Tamson's man : see John Thomson's man.

John Thomas, A : a flunkey ; a liveried servant.

John Thomson's man : (Scot.) a man ruled by his wife. Probably orig. Joan Thomson's man.

John Trot : a country bumpkin ; a stupid, uneducated person.

John in the wad, A : a will-o'-the-wisp.

Johnian Hog, A : a member of St. John's College, Cambridge.

Johnny, A : a dude, esp. one who spends his time about stage doors.

Johnny Crapaud : a Frenchman. So-called by the Eng. seamen during the Napoleonic wars. Fr., *crapaud*, a toad, which appears in the emblem of France.

Johnny Darby, A : a gendarme ; a handcuff.

Johnny Newcome, A : a newborn child.

Johnny Raw, A : a raw recruit in the army or elsewhere.

Johnny Rebs : Confederate soldiers during the Amer. Civil War. So-called by their opponents.

Johnstone's tippet, St. : a halter.

Joint account, To open a : to get married. [Thos. Morton, *Town and Country*, I, ii (1807)]

Joie de vivre (*Fr.*, joy of living) : the physical pleasure derived from a feeling of good health.

Jolly, A : a marine. So-called by sailors. Because he is of as much use to a ship as the jolly-boat that floats behind her.

Jolly god, The : Bacchus, the god of wine.

Jolly Roger, The : the black flag, the ensign of pirates.

Jolly as a sandboy, As : an allusion to a sandboy, a very lively insect found in the sand of the seashore.

Jonah, A : one who brings trouble to his associates who in self-defence are compelled to discard him. In allusion to the biblical prophet.

Jonathan, Brother : a nickname for the people of the U.S. From Jonathan Trumbull, a confidant of George Washington, who frequently alluded to him as Brother Jonathan.

Jonathan and David : see David and Jonathan.

Jonathan Wild : a highwayman or other criminal of distinction. From the name of a famous Eng. criminal who was hanged at Tyburn in 1725.

Jonathan's, At : Jonathan's coffee-house in Change Alley was the predecessor of the London Stock Exchange.

Jonathan's arrows : not intended to harm but only to give warning. [*I Samuel*, xx, 36]

Jorkins : *see* Spenlow and Jorkins.

Joseph, A : (1) a moral young man who resists temptation ; from the story narrated of the patriarch Joseph in *Gen.* xxxix, 7, *et seq.* ; (2) a long riding cloak worn by women. After the coat that Joseph left in the hands of Potiphar's wife.

Joseph Surface, A : a hypocrite. In allusion to a character in R. B. Sheridan's play, *The School for Scandal* (1777).

Josh, To : to banter. After Josh Billings (1818–85), Amer. humourist. An Americanism.

Journée des Anes : the defeat of the Papal Army near Bologna, in 1571, by the Bolognese and the French. Lit., Battle of the asses, from the great number of pack animals captured.

Jouvence, The fountain of : the source of youth or rejuvenation. A play upon the town of Jouvence, Saône-et-Loire, France and Fr., *jouvence*, youth.

Jove ! By : an asseveration. By Jupiter, a Rom. god.

Jove's bird (hound) : the eagle : consecrated to Jupiter (Jove).

Jove's servant in ordinary : the eagle.

Joyeuse science, The : minstrelsy. So-called by Sir Walter Scott in *The Talisman* (1825).

Judas, A : (1) a traitor, from Judas Iscariot, who betrayed Jesus Christ ; (2) a lattice or other opening useful for espionage.

Judas kiss, A : an apparently friendly action that betrays. From the kiss by which Judas betrayed Jesus.

Judas slits (holes) : peepholes in a prison door. *See* Judas.

Judas tree, A : a tree of the northern Mediterranean basin, *Cercis siliquastrum*, on which according to tradition Judas Iscariot hanged himself ; also the elder.

Judas-coloured hair : red hair. In allusion to the tradition that that was the colour of the hair of Judas Iscariot. The Eng. antipathy to red hair may, however, be due to hatred of the fair-haired Danes.

Judicial murder : an unjust, though legal, sentence of death.

Judicious bottle-holder, The : Lord Palmerston (1784–1865), who, in 1851, said to a deputation that waited on him to congratulate him on the success of his efforts to secure the liberation of Kossuth, that the crisis had required much generalship and a good deal of judicious bottle-holding. A bottle-holder is an attendant on a pugilist at a prize-fight.

Judicious Hooker, The : Richard Hooker (1553–1600), Eng. divine.

Juge de paix, A (*Fr.*, a justice of the peace) : a cudgel.

Juggernaut, A : that which or he who crushes whatever lies in his path. From the name of a Hindoo god, *Jagannatha*, Lord of the World, whose great car is dragged along the roads on the occasion of his festival by his worshippers. The mistaken idea was formerly held that on these occasions many of the worshippers in a religious frenzy cast themselves under the wheels of the car.

Juggins, A : a foolish fellow. From one of that name who squandered a fortune in betting about 1887.

Julian year : the year according to the calendar instituted by Julius Cæsar and in force until the introduction of that of Gregory XIII.

Jumbo, A : an elephant. From the name of a very large elephant exhibited in London about 1883.

Jump over the broomstick (two sticks), To : to marry in an unconventional manner.

Jump land (a claim), To : (Amer.) to take possession of .. by unlawful means.

Jumping cat, Cult of the : opportunism ; decision in favour of the winning side.

June : the sixth month of the year, the month of the Rom. family of Junius.

June, The glorious first of : the victory of the British fleet under Lord Howe over the French on June 1st, 1794.

Junker, A (*Germ., Jung Herr*, young master) : an extreme reactionary in politics. In allusion to the Junker or extreme conservative party in Germany which consists mainly of the land-owning classes.

Juno's (Junonian) bird : a peacock. Sacred to the goddess, Juno.

Junto, Essex : *see* Essex.

Jupiter Scapin : Napoleon I. So-called by the Abbé de Pradt. Scapin was a valet in Molière, *Les Fourberies de Scapin.*

Jupiter's bird : the eagle.

Jupiter's fools : women.

Jurisprudence, The Father of : *see* Father.

Jus divinum : (*Lat.*, divine right).

Jus gentium (*Lat.*, law of nations) : international law. [Hooper, *Early Writings* (1548)]

Jusqu'auboutiste, A (*Fr.*, *jusqu au bout*, to the end) : a whole-hogger ; one who is determined to pursue his object to the very end. The word came into use in the course of the European War of 1914–18, and was used to designate the advocates of the continuance of the war until the complete defeat of Germany.

Juste milieu, Le (*Fr.*, the proper mean) : phrase used by Louis Philippe to express his policy shortly after his accession to the throne of France. The phrase was not original, having previously been used by Pascal in his *Pensées* and by Voltaire in a letter to the Comte d'Argental.

Justice, Poetic : *see* Poetic justice.

Justinian, A : a renowned lawyer and jurist. In allusion to the Emperor Justinian (483–565), famous for his codification of the Laws of Rome.

Justinian, The English : Edward I (1239–1307). So-called by Edward Jenks, in the title of a book (1902).

Justitia, ruat cœlum, Fiat (*Lat.*, Let justice be done even though the heavens fall) : do justice heedless of the consequences. A passage in the judgment of Lord Mansfield (1705–93) in the case of John Wilkes (1768). Similar phrases appear in the writings of Martin Luther (1483–1546), the Emp. Ferdinand I (1503–64), and Corneille (1625–1709).

Juteopolis : Dundee, the centre of the jute industry.

Juvenal, The English : John Oldham (1653–83). After Juvenal (60–140), Rom. satirist and poet.

Juvenal of Painters, The : William Hogarth (1697–1764).

Juvenal, The Young : Thomas Lodge (1555–1625). So-called by Robert Greene.

J'y suis, j'y reste (*Fr.*, I am here, I remain here) : the reply of the Marshal MacMahon when warned after the, capture of the Malakoff (Sept. 9, 1855), that the evacuated fortress was probably mined.

K's, The Three : the King, the Church and the Constitution.

Kabbala : *see* Cabbala.

Kail thro' the reek, To give a person the : (Scot.), to behave unpleasantly to a person ; to abuse him violently. Kale (cabbage) becomes bitter when smoked.

Kailyard (School), The (*Scot.*, cabbage-garden school) : the Scot. dialect school of fiction dealing with home life. The principal members were Sir J. M. Barrie, Ian MacLaren and S. R. Crockett.

Kaiser Klas : a Germ. name for Napoleon I.

Kalends : *see* Greek Calends.

Kangaroo Closure, The : a system of closure in the House of Commons under which the Speaker is authorized to select amendments for discussion.

Kansas, Bleeding : *see* Bleeding.

Karun, The riches of : in allusion to Karun, the uncle of Moses, according to the Koran.

Katerfelto, A : a charlatan. In allusion to a quack doctor and pseudo-scientist of that name who practised in London about the year 1782.

Kathay : *see* Cathay.

Kedar's tents, In : in this world as opposed to the next. Kedar is Arabia Deserta.

Keen as a hawk, As : eager ; mentally acute. [Peter Pindar, *Ode upon Ode* (1785)]

Keen as mustard, As : mentally energetic.

Keep, To : (Camb. Univ.) to live. In general use in this sense in the 16th and 17th cents. [*Pol. Poems*, II, 65 (1401)]

Keep one's powder dry, To : to be prepared for eventualities. A military metaphor.

Kemp ; Kempery man, A : a soldier ; a champion.

Kendal green : cloth worn by foresters, made at Kendal.

Kennedy, A : a poker. In allusion to a man who was killed with a poker.

Kent, Men of : those who come from Kent east of the Medway. *See* Kentish.

Kent Street ejectment, A : ejectment for non-payment of rent by means of the removal of the front door. Practised formerly by landlords in Kent Street, Southwark.

Kentish fire : concerted clapping of hands and stamping of feet, spaced like a sort of Morse Code and sounding like the discharge of musketry. In allusion to the reception given to ' No Popery ' orators in Kent in 1828-9. The term was coined by the Earl of Winchelsea at an ' Orange ' meeting held in Dublin in 1834.

Kentish men : those who come from West Kent. *See* Men of Kent.

Ketherick's pie, As big as : Ketherick was the first mayor of Plymouth (1493). The pie made for his inaugural banquet is said to have been 14 ft. long.

Kettle of fish, A pretty : *see* Fish.

Key of Christendom, The : Buda in Hungary. In allusion to its position as a bulwark against the Turkish invasion.

Key beneath the door, To leave the : to vacate a house without paying rent. [Jno. Taylor, *Discovery by Sea from London to Salisbury* (1623)]

Key of the Gulf, The : Cuba. On account of its position at the entrance to the Gulf of Mexico.

Key of India, The : Herat in Afghanistan.

Key of the Mediterranean, The : Gibraltar, which commands the entrance thereto.

Key of Russia, The : Smolensk.

Key of Spain, The : Ciudad Rodrigo.

Key of the street, To get the : ironically, to be shut out.

Key upon one's shoulder, To have the : to be in authority. In allusion to the period when keys which were instruments of considerable size, were carried by the steward over the shoulder.

Keys of Knowledge, The : the time of the Day of Judgment, the time of rain, the sex of an animal before birth, the events of to-morrow, the place of one's death, all hidden from man ; according to the Koran.

Keys into the pit, To throw the : to disclaim a debt, esp. that of a deceased husband. From an ancient Fr. custom in which, where the estate left was insufficient to pay the debts, the widow cast a key into the grave.

Keys, The power of the : authority of the ministry in Christian churches over laymen. From the promise of Christ to Peter to give him ' the keys of the Kingdom of Heaven., [*Matthew*, xvi, 9]

Keystone State, The : Pennsylvania ; the central one of the 13 original states of the Union.

Kibes, To gall (tread) on one's : to annoy or irritate. A kibe is a chilblain.

Kibes of .. To tread (follow) on the : to follow closely on the heels of .. [Shakespeare, *Hamlet*, V, i, 153 (1602)]

Kibosh on it, To put the : (colloq.) to dispose of permanently.

Kick against, To : to rebel against. [Wycliffe, *Deuteronomy*, xxxii, 15]

Kick against the pricks, To : to resent treatment to one's own harm or discomfort ; as a horse resents the prick of the spur. [*Acts*, ix, 5 and xxvi, 14 ; Pindar, 2 *Pythian Victories*, V, 173 ; Æschylus, *Agamemnon*, 1624 ; Euripedes, *Bacchae*, 791 ; Terence, *Phormio*, I, ii, 27 ; Ovid, *Tristia*, II, 15 ; Jno. Heywood, *Proverbes* (1546)]

Kick the beam, To : to be outweighed. The beam = the balance in a pair of scales.

Kick the bucket, To : (colloq.) to die. From a manner of committing suicide, *viz.*, to kick away the supporting bucket after having adjusted a rope around one's neck, or from the bucket or beam by which dead pigs are suspended in the butcher-shop.

Kick downstairs, To : to eject from the house.

Kick one's heels, To : *see* Heels.

Kick up one's heels, To : to die. [Dekker, *Honest Whore* (1604)]

Kick down the ladder, To : to make use of people to enable oneself to rise in the world and then to ignore them.

Kick up a row, To : to create a disturbance. A suggestion that noise can be kicked up like dust. [Tobias Smollett, *Letter to Wilkes* (1759)]

Kick over the traces, To : to get free from restraints ; as a horse getting its leg over the traces is able to kick more freely.

Kicked upstairs, To be : to be promoted from a responsible position to a sinecure.

Kicks than halfpence, More : more pain than pleasure.

Kickshaws (*Fr.*, *quelque chose*, something): trifles, generally elegant. Orig. a fancy dish in cookery. [Shakespeare, 2 *Henry IV*, V, i (1597-8)]

Kidd, Captain : a pirate. Capt. James Kidd (b. in Scotland ; hanged 1701) was sent by the Amer. colonists to suppress piracy, but himself turned pirate.

Kidderminster poetry : rough, inferior verse, like the woollen manufactures of Kidderminster. Phrase coined by

Wm. Shenstone. In allusion to a Mr. C. of Kidderminster.

Kidney, Of the same : of the same nature or disposition. From the belief that the kidneys were the seat of the affections. [Shakespeare, *Merry Wives of Windsor*, III, v (1598-9)]

Kilkenny cats, To fight like : to fight to the point of mutual destruction. The story is told of some Hessian troops employed to suppress the Irish Rebellion of 1798 who when stationed at Kilkenny, amused themselves by tying the tails of two cats together and hanging them over a line there to fight with one another. The sport was interrupted by an officer who ordered the cats to be released. This order was carried out by cutting the cats free of their tails, which were left hanging on the line. When the officer returned and enquired the fate of the cats, he was told that they had devoured one another.

Kill a bee, To take a post to : *see* Take.

Kill two birds with one stone, To : *see* Birds.

Kill the goose that lays the golden eggs, To : *see* Goose.

Kill by inches, To : to kill slowly. In allusion to the several medieval methods of torture, long drawn-out and ending in death.

Kill one's mandarin, To : *see* Mandarin.

Kill time, To : to waste time. [Vanbrugh and Cibber, *The Provoked Husband*, I, i (1728)]

Killogie, Smoked like a (*Scot.*) : the killogie is the covered place in front of the fireplace of a kiln.

Kilmainham Treaty, The : the agreement between Wm. Ewart Gladstone and Charles Stewart Parnell in accordance with which the latter was released from Kilmainham gaol in May, 1882.

Kilmarnock cowls : nightcaps. After those manufactured at Kilmarnock.

Kindheart, A : a dentist. After the name of a member of that profession who flourished in the reign of Elizabeth.

King at Arms : one of the three Eng. chief heralds.

King of Bark, The : Christopher III of Scandinavia, who in time of famine had bark mixed with the bread.

King of Bath, The : Richard Nash (Beau Nash) (1674-1762), who was for over half a century Master of the Ceremonies at Bath, then a fashionable resort.

King of the Bean, The : the Twelfth Night King. In allusion to the bean in the Twelfth Night cake which decided the office.

King of beasts, The : the lion.

King of the beggars, The : Bamfylde Moore Carew (1693-1770 c.), also King of the gypsies.

King of birds, The : the eagle.

King Charles' Head : a monomania. After the topic which entered into every conversation of the slightly insane Mr. Dick in Dickens, *David Copperfield* (1849).

King Charles spaniel : a small species of dog, a favourite of King Charles I of England.

King of the Cockneys, The : *see* Cockneys.

King Cotton : cotton, the staple production of the southern of the United States and manufacture of Lancashire. Phrase first used by James H. Hammond in the U.S. Senate in 1858. Three years previously David Christy published *Cotton is King; or, Slavery in the Light of Political Economy*.

King of Dalkey : a burlesque king. Dalkey is a small island south of Dublin Bay.

King is dead, long live the King, The : the formula that expresses the theory that a throne is never vacant. It was the official formula for announcing a change in the occupancy of the Fr. throne from 1461 to 1824. *See* King never dies, The.

King Demos : *see* Demos.

King never dies, The : the theory that the throne is never vacant, that at the moment of the death of the occupant his successor becomes king.

King of dulness, The : Colley Cibber (1671-1757), poet laureate.

King, The Factory : Richard Oastler (1789-1861), advocate of the Ten Hours Factory Law.

King of the forest, The : the oak.

King of fresh-water fish, The : the salmon. So-called by Izaak Walton.

King of the jungle, The : the tiger.

King of Kings, The : (1) God ; (2) Jesus ; (3) Agamemnon, in Grk. legend, the most powerful ruler of Greece ; (4) Artaxerxes (465-425 B.C.), King of Persia.

King Log and King Stork : a king who is unable to exercise power and one who oppresses his subjects. From the fable of *The Frogs Desiring a King*. First Jupiter gave them a log and they

P

were dissatisfied because it showed no strength or other kingly quality. Then he sent them a stork which ate them up.

Kingmaker, The : Richard Neville, Earl of Warwick (1428–71). From his influence in securing the accession of Edward IV and the restoration of Henry VI.

King of Men, The : Agamemnon, king of Mycenæ ; also Jupiter.

King of metals, The : gold.

King Mob : the powerful crowd.

King of Painters, The : Parrhasios (fl. 400 B.C.).

King Pétaud : a king whose subjects are his equals, after the name of the 'king' of a company of Fr. beggars.

King Pétaud, The Court of : the board of a company, or a committee, whose members take little notice of the rulings of the chairman. *See* King Pétaud.

King of Preachers, The : Louis Bourdaloue (1632–1704), Fr. divine.

King of Prussia, The : *see* Roi de Prusse.

King, The Railway : George Hudson (1800–71), promoter of railways. So-called by Sydney Smith.

King of Reptiles, The : Germain Etienne de la Ville, Count Lacépède (1756–1825), author of *Histoire Naturelle des Reptiles*.

King of Roads, The : John Loudon Macadam (1756–1836), inventor of an improved process of making roads.

King, More royalist than the : *see* Royalist.

King of the sea, The : the herring.

King of shadows, The : Oberon, the king of the fairies.

King of shreds and patches, A : a literary hack writer. Orig., in the old mystery plays, Vice.

King, The Snow : Gustavus Adolphus of Sweden, who, according to the Viennese, melted away, or lost his power, as he came south.

King of Spain's trumpeter, The : a donkey. A pun on the Span. title don.

King Stork and King Log : *see* King Log and King Stork.

King of Terrors, The : death.

King over the water, The : (1) James II, after his deposition and escape to France ; (2) James Stuart, the Old Pretender ; (3) Charles Edward Stuart, the Young Pretender.

King of waters, The : the river Amazon.

King of Wisdom, The : Omar Khayyám (11th and 12th cents.), Persian poet and astronomer, famous for his *Rubaiyat*.

King, The Wise : Solomon, king of Israel. In allusion to the divine gift of wisdom conferred on him.

King of the world, The : the Roman Emperor.

King of Yvetot, The : (1) the king or reign of a happy people, from a song by Pierre Jean de Béranger (1813), popular throughout France among the people who had tired of military glory and its cost and were longing for peace and contentment ; (2) a man of great pretensions but small merits. In allusion to the tiny kingdom of Yvetot, near Rouen, which flourished from the 6th until the 14th cent.

Kings, The books (history) of four : a pack of cards.

Kings of Brentford : *see* Brentford.

King's candle, Gay as the : (of a showily dressed woman). From the French in allusion to the Eve or Vigil of the Kings, observed on the 6th of January by burning a candle of divers colours.

King's Champion, The : the official who challenges all opponents at the Coronation Banquet.

Kings (of Cologne), The Three : the three wise men of the East who visited the Infant Jesus. Reputed to have been buried at Cologne.

Kings, Divine right of : *see* Divine.

King's English, The : correct, pure English. [Shakespeare, *Merry Wives of Windsor*, I, iv (1598)]

King's evidence, To turn : for a criminal to give evidence, under promise of pardon, against his accomplices.

King's Evil, The : scrofula ; supposed to be curable by the touch of a king.

King's Friends (Men), The : royalists ; partisans of the king.

Kings, The game of : chess.

King's Hanoverian White Horse, The : the 8th Regt. of Foot, now the Liverpool Regt. In allusion to its services against the Old Pretender. Their badge was a white horse.

King's highway, The : the public roads. Formerly only those highways which were under the protection of the king.

King's Men, The : (1) the 78th Regt. of Foot ; after their motto, *Cuidich'r Rhi*, Help the King ; (2) King's friends (*q.v.*).

King's Own Men, The : the 78th Regt. of Foot, whose motto was (Gaelic) *Cuidich'r Rhi*, Help the King.

King's Shilling, The : the coin formerly given to a recruit, as a ratification of his implied engagement to enlist in the British army.

King's three cardinal errors, A : pity, placability and clemency. [Thucydides, *History*, III, 40, 2]

Kingdom Come : (colloq.) the next world. From the phrase ' Thy kingdom come,' in *The Lord's Prayer*.

Kingdom, The Most Christian : *see* Most Christian.

Kings, The sport of : *see* Sport.

Kingsley's Stand : the 20th Regt. of Foot, now the Lancashire Fusiliers. After the name of their colonel when they made their famous ' stand ' at Minden in 1759.

Kingston Bridge : a bent card. So as to guide him who cuts the pack.

Kingswood lions : donkeys. After the large number of them kept by the miners at Kingswood.

Kirke's Lambs: the forces of Colonel Kirke, which were put in command of the West of England after the suppression of Monmouth's Rebellion and became notorious for their cruelties. The badge of the regiment was a Paschal lamb, in allusion to the purpose for which they were first recruited, *viz.*, to fight the infidel in Morocco.

Kiss the book, To : to give evidence in a court of law, after having taken the oath and kissed the Bible. [Early 16th cent.]

Kiss the counter, To : to be confined in the stocks. From ' counter,' formerly ' compter,' the prison attached to a mayor's court. [Rowland, *Night Raven* (1620)]

Kiss the cup, To : to drink. [Early 15th cent].

Kiss the dust, To : to be defeated ; to be humiliated.

Kiss the ground, To : to cast oneself to the ground as an act of reverence ; to be humiliated.

Kiss the gunner's daughter, To : (naval slang) to be lashed to a gun preparatory to receiving punishment.

Kiss hands, To : to be endowed with high government office, by the sovereign whose hand is kissed on the occasion of the transfer of the seals of office.

Kiss the hare's foot, To : *see* Hare's foot.

Kiss of peace, The : a kiss given as a sign of friendliness, esp. as a token of Christian love in the course of a religious service.

Kiss the post, To : to be shut out. [Barclay, *Eclogues* (1515)]

Kiss the rod, To : to accept punishment submissively. [Sir Philip Sidney, *Arcadia*, II, 190 (1590)]

Kissing comfits : scented sweets, to perfume the breath.

Kit Callot : *see* Callot.

Kit-cat Club, The : a political club. Formed in 1703 to uphold the principles of the Revolution of 1688. It met at a tavern kept by Christopher Cat (d. 1773).

Kit-cat size : three-quarter length portraits on canvas, 29 in. by 36 in., adopted by Sir Godfrey Kneller in painting portraits of members of the Kit-cat Club (*q.v.*).

Kit-cats : mutton pies. After a dish for which Christopher Cat's tavern was renowned. *See* Kit-cat Club.

Kitchen Cabinet, The : the intimate political circle of Andrew Jackson during his term of office as President of the U.S. (1829–33).

Kitchen fee : dripping. Supposed to be the perquisite of the cook.

Kitchen love : affection displayed in the expectation of favours, esp. food.

Kittle Cargo, A : clergymen. A nautical phrase.

Kittle cattle to shoe : a difficult person to manage.

Knave of hearts, A : a flirt.

Knave of Sologne, A : one who is more knave than fool. Sologne forms part of the Departments of Loiret and Loire-et-Cher.

Knee to .. To bow (bend) the : to submit to ..

Knee to .. To give the : to pay homage to .. [Bacon, *Henry VII* (1622)]

Knee tribute : adoration or reverence displayed by bending the knee. [Milton, *Paradise Lost*, V, 782 (1667)]

Knees of the gods, On the : in the future ; beyond human control. [Homer, *Odyssey*, I, 267]

Knickerbocker City, The : New York. From the dress of the early Dutch settlers.

Knickerbockers : loose trousers ending at the knees, as worn in Holland, etc. After Diedrich Knickerbocker, pseudonymous author of Washington

Irving's *History of New York*, taken as the typical Dutchman.

Knife of Academic Knots, The : Chrysippos (280–207 B.C.), the keenest disputant of his age.

Knife at the throat of .. **To hold a :** to exercise compulsion towards ..

Knife, War to the : relentless warfare. Palafox's answer to the French general at the siege of Saragossa.

Knifeboard, The : the double-seat on the top of an old horse-omnibus.

Knight, An ale : *see* Ale knight.

Knight bachelor, A : orig. a knight who had forsworn marriage until he had performed some feat of outstanding valour ; a knight attached to no order.

Knight Banneret, A : a knight created on the battlefield, to whom a streamer hastily torn from a banner was given as ensignia of investiture.

Knight of the blade, A : a bully. In allusion to his frequent reference to his sword in the days in which it was fashionable to wear that weapon.

Knight of the brush, A : an artist.

Knight of the burning pestle, The : a mock heroic play by Beaumont and Fletcher (1613).

Knight, A carpet : a civilian knight ; one who has not earned the honour on the battlefield. [Michael de Montaigne, *Works*, Bk. I, chap. xxv ; Guillaume de Salluste du Bartas, *Divine Weekes and Workes*, 2nd week, 3rd day, Pt. I ; Geo. Whetstone, *Remembrance of George Gascoigne*, st. 9 (1577). ' Carpet knights are the men who are by the prince's grace and favour made knights at home .. They are called carpet knights because they receive their honours in the court and upon carpets.' Francis Markham, *Booke of Honour* (1626)]

Knight of the carpet, A : a knight created on Shrove Tuesday, when the recipient of the honour knelt on a carpet before the king. *See also* Knight, A carpet.

Knight of carpetry, A : *see* Knight, A carpet.

Knight of the chamber, A : a knight created in time of peace in the audience chamber instead of the battlefield.

Knight of the cleaver, A : a butcher.

Knight of the cloak, The : Sir Walter Raleigh. In allusion to the incident of his cloak and Queen Elizabeth.

Knight of the collar, A : one who has been hanged. [*Youth* in Dodsley, *Old Plays* (1554)]

Knight of the cue, A : a billiard-player.

Knight of the dice-box, A : a gambler.

Knight of the elbow, A : a cheating gambler.

Knight errant, A : a knight who wandered abroad in search of adventure.

Knight of the field, A : a tramp.

Knight of the forked order (order of the fork), A : a gardener ; a cuckold.

Knight of the grammar, A : a school-master.

Knight of the green cloth, A : a carpet knight (*q.v.*). ; a gambler.

Knight of the handcuff, A : a policeman.

Knight of industry, A (Fr., *Chevalier d'Industrie*) : a swindler.

Knight of the knife, A : a pickpocket ; a cutpurse. [Ben Jonson, *Bartholomew Fayre* (1614)]

Knight or a knitter of caps, To be either a : to be as happy as a prince or as wretched as a mourner. [Lyly, *Euphues and His England* (1580)]

Knight of La Mancha, The : Don Quixote de la Mancha.

Knight of the needle, A : a tailor.

Knight of the pen, A : a writer ; a clerk.

Knight of the pencil, A : a betting man. In allusion to his frequent use of a pencil.

Knight of the pestle, A : an apothecary.

Knight of the post, A : a false witness, who when discovered was whipped at the post. [Nashe, *Pierce Pennilesse* (1592)]

Knight of the quill, A : a writer.

Knight of the rainbow, A : a male domestic servant. In allusion to his gorgeous uniform.

Knight of the road, A : a highwayman. A pun on the knights of Rhodes. [R. Head, *English Rogue* (1671)]

Knight of the rueful countenance, The : Don Quixote. So-called by Sancho Panza.

Knight of St. Crispin, A : a shoemaker. After St. Crispin, who was a cobbler.

Knight (Clerk) of St. Nicholas, A : a thief. St. Nicholas was patron saint of thieves. [Rowley, *Match at Midnight* (1633)]

Knight of the shears, A : a tailor. A pun on knight of the shire.

Knight of the shire, A : a representative of a county or shire in Parliament. Orig. a knight.

Knight of the spigot, A : a publican.

Knight of the spur, A : a Knight Bachelor.

Knight of the stick, A : a compositor. In allusion to the stick used by him in setting type.

Knight of the tar-brush, A : a sailor.

Knight of the thimble, A : a tailor.

Knight of the Thistle, A : a member of a Scot. order of knighthood, said to have been ins. in 809, revived in 1540.

Knight of the vapour, A : a smoker.

Knight of the wheel, A : a cyclist.

Knight of the whip, A : a coachman.

Knight of the yardstick, A : (Amer.) a draper's assistant.

Knights, To dine with the cross-legged : see Dine.

Knights of Labour : one of the principal Amer. Trade Unions, founded in 1869.

Knight's service : good service ; service due from a knight under the Feudal System.

Knipper-doling, A : a religious fanatic. From Bernhard Knipperdolling (c. 1490–1536), Germ. Anabaptist leader and martyr.

Knock out, To : to put a person *hors de combat* or unable to continue the contest. Prize-ring metaphor.

Knock under, To : to submit ; admit oneself beaten. Properly, to knock under board, to fall under the table in a drinking bout.

Knock the bottom out of .. To : to deprive an argument or case of its basis.

Knock into a cocked hat, To : to beat out of recognition.

Knock on the head, To : to bring to naught. [W. Fulke, *Heskin's Parliament Repealed*, 327 (1579)]

Knock one's head against, To : to be stopped in one's course by inconvenient facts or conditions. [16th cent.]

Knock under, To : to submit. Possibly from to knuckle under (*q.v.*).

Knockabout man, A : (1) (Austral.) a handy man, a labourer ready to turn his hand to anything ; (2) (theatrical) an actor who plays a noisy, boisterous part.

Knockout, A : a conspiracy among frequenters of auction sales, not to bid against one another in public, but to share among themselves the difference between the sale price and the real value of the article.

Knot, To cut the : see Gordian.

Knot in a rush, To seek for a : to seek for

difficulties gratuitously. [Terence, *Andria*, V, iv, 38 (166 B.C.) ; *Ayenbite of Inwyte* (1340)]

Knot, To tie the : to perform the ceremony of marriage. [Thos. May, *The Old Couple*, V, l. 167 (1655)]

Knotty point, A : a matter involved in intellectual difficulties. [Pope, *January and May*, 140 (1702)]

Know, In the : (colloq.) possessed of information not yet public property.

Know a thing or two, To : to be wide-awake ; to be fully acquainted with what is transpiring.

Know the ropes, To : to be well acquainted with the conditions, circumstances, etc. Nautical metaphor.

Know which side one's bread is buttered, To : to recognise where one's interests lie.

Know-nothings : an Amer. political party founded in 1853. Its principal plank was the requirement of 21 years' residence as a qualification for naturalisation. *See* American Party. The programme of the party was for a time secret and the members denied all knowledge of it. Hence the name.

Knuckle under, To : to submit. Knuckle formerly meant to kneel. To knuckle under consequently means to kneel under.

Koepenick, A Captain of : an amusing rogue. After a swindler who, masquerading as a military officer, assured the municipal authorities of Koepenick (Germany) of his *bona fides* and was thus able to rifle the local treasury.

Koh-i-Noor, A : something of very great value. After the name of a very valuable and large diamond included in the British Crown jewels.

Kolis, The : the King's Own Light Infantry. From the initial letters.

Koran of Belfast, The : Paine's 'Rights of Man,' according to Wolf Tone.

Kriss Kringle (*Germ.*, *Christ Kindel*, the Christ child) : a young Santa Claus.

Ku Klux Klan : an organisation formed in the Southern States after the conclusion of the Civil War for the intimidation of the coloured population.

Kulturkampf, The : the struggle in Germany between the state and the Roman Catholic Church (1872–82). Lit., Culture-conflict. The phrase was popularized by Rudolph Virchow, the scientist and politician (1821–1902), who said that the contest was not merely a religious one, but involved man's entire intellectual and moral culture. It was coined by Ferdinand Lassalle (1825–64) in *Demokratische Studien*, II, 505.

L's, The Three : (nautical) lead, latitude and look out. Term invented by W. Clark Russell.

Laberius, A Second : after Decimus Laberius (c.105–43 B.C.), Rom. satirist.

Labour of love, A : work undertaken not for reward but for pleasure.

Labours of Hercules, The : (1) wrestling with the Nemean lion ; (2) destruction of the Lernean hydra ; (3) capture of the Arcadian hind ; (4) capture of the boar of Erymanthus ; (5) cleansing of the Augean stables ; (6) shooting of the Stymphalian birds ; (7) capture of the Cretan bull ; (8) capture of the man-eating mares of the Thracian Diomedes ; (9) seizure of the girdle of Hippolyte ; (10) leading of the oxen of Geryones from Erythia ; (11) bringing of the golden apples from the garden of the Hesperides ; (12) carrying Cerberus from Hades to the Upper World.

Labyrinth, A : a maze ; a complicated, tortuous condition of affairs. After Labyris, an Egyptian king of the 12th dynasty.

Lacedæmonians, The : the Duke of Cornwall's Light Infantry. Because while under heavy fire in 1777 they were addressed by their colonel on the virtues of Spartan discipline.

Lack-Latin, A : an uneducated person ; one who lacks Latin. [Sir F. Bygod, *Treatise Concerning Impropriations*, VI (1534)]

Lack-learning Parliament, The : *see* Parliament.

Laconic ; Laconian : concise ; sparing in words. From Grk., *Lakon*, a Lacedæmonian, proverbial for the affectation of brevity.

Lad o' wax, A : a shoemaker.

Ladder behind one's back, To kick down the : to disown friends of whom one no longer has need. [Shakespeare, *Julius Cæsar*, II, i (1601)]

Ladder, To climb up the : to advance socially or officially.

Ladder after oneself, To draw up the : to make oneself impossible of approach by others.

Ladder, To see through a : to discover the obvious.

Ladies' man, A : a man who pays much attention to the female sex.

Lady of Babylon, The : the Roman Catholic Church. In allusion to the scarlet woman of *Revelations*.

Lady Bell : the bell used in ringing the Angelus.

Lady Bountiful, A : the generous and charitable lady of the village. After the name of a character in Farquhar, *Beaux Stratagem* (1707).

Lady of the broom, A : a housemaid. [Peter Pindar, *The Diamond Pin* (1794–1801)]

Lady chair, A : a seat formed of the crossed hands of two people facing one another.

Lady Chapel, A : a chapel in a church dedicated to the Virgin Mary.

Lady Day : the 25th of March, the day of the Annunciation of the Virgin Mary.

Lady of easy virtue, A : a prostitute.

Lady of the frying-pan, A : a cook.

Lady Huntingdon persuasion, Of the : of the sect of Calvinistic Methodists founded by Selina, Lady Huntingdon, in 1779.

Lady of Kingdoms, The : Babylon. [*Isaiah*, xlvii]

Lady of the lake, A : a nymph ; a kept mistress. From Vivien, the mistress of Merlin.

Lady Nicotine, My : *see* My.

Lady of pleasure, A : a prostitute.

Lady of Rome, The : the Roman Catholic Church. In allusion to the scarlet woman of *Revelations*.

Lady-killer, A : a man possessing much influence over women.

Laetare Sunday : the fourth Sunday in Lent. After the first word of the Introit of that day.

Lafontaine, The Danish : Hans Christian Andersen (1805–75). After Jean de Lafontaine, a Fr. fabulist who lived from 1621 to 1695.

Lafontaine of the Vaudeville : Charles Francis Panard (1689–1765), Fr. poet and dramatist.

Lais, A : a prostitute. After a famous one of that name in ancient Greece.

Laissez faire (*Fr.*, leave it alone) : the doctrine of non-interference by the State in economic matters. From the reply of a Fr. merchant to Jean Baptiste Colbert, the Fr. statesman (1619–83), when asked how he could assist trade.

Lake Country, The : Cumberland, Westmorland and North Lancashire. After the lakes with which that region abounds.

Lake, The Great : the Atlantic Ocean. Term derived from the N. Amer.-Ind.

Lakeland : the Lake Country (*q.v.*).

Lake School, The : the group of Eng. poets — Wordsworth, Coleridge, Southey, etc.—who lived in or were connected with the Lake Country. So-called first by the *Edinburgh Review.*

Lake State, The : Michigan, situated on Lakes Michigan, Huron, Erie, Superior and St. Clair.

Lakin, By'r : by Our Lady the Virgin Mary. Lakin is a contraction of Ladykin or little lady.

Lamartinism : attribution of good motives. In allusion to the practice of Alphonse Lamartine (1790–1869), Fr. historian.

Lamb of God, The : Jesus Christ, typified by the Paschal Lamb.

Lame dog over a stile, To help a : to assist a person in a difficulty. [Marston, *Insatiate Countess*, II, ii (1605) ; Jno. Heywood, *Proverbes* (1546)]

Lame duck, A : a member of the Stock Exchange who is unable to meet his engagements ; a person who for one reason or another is below the average of capacity or prosperity.

Lame post, To come by the : to arrive late.

Lame as St. Giles Cripplegate : St. Giles was the patron saint of cripples. The congregation of cripples in and around the Church of St. Giles, London, gave the neighbouring city gate the name, Cripplegate.

Lammas Day (Eve) : August 12th, the Harvest Festival. From Ang.-Sax., *hlaf maesse*, loaf-feast, feast of first-fruits.

Lammas lands : lands thrown open to pasture after the harvest (Lammas Day).

Lammas, At latter : never. Lammas (Aug. 1st) was the day for the payment of accounts. Latter (last) Lammas never came. [Gascoigne, *Steele Glass* (1576)]

Lammermoor lion, A : a sheep.

Lamourette kiss : a shortlived reconciliation. From the speech of the Abbé Adrien Lamourette in the French Legislative Assembly on the 7th of July, 1792, in consequence of which political opponents were reconciled—for three days.

Lamp of Heaven, The : (1) the moon ; (2) the sun.

Lamp of Phœbus, The : the sun. Phœbus was the mythical personification of the sun.

Lamp, To smell of the : of a literary work, to show sings of most careful preparation. First applied to the orations of Demosthenes, which were prepared with great care late into the night.

Lancaster gun, A : after Charles William Lancaster (1820–78), the inventor.

Land of Beulah, The : Paradise. According to *The Pilgrim's Progress* (1678). [*Isaiah*, lxii, 4]

Land of Bondage, The : Egypt. According to *Exodus*.

Land o' cakes, The : Scotland. From the widespread consumption of oatmeal cakes. So-called by Robert Burns.

Land of Cockaigne, The : the land of sensual pleasures. After the title of a popular poem of the 13th cent., according to which the houses were made of barley sugar and cakes, the streets were paved with pastry, and the shops supplied goods without charge.

Land flowing with milk and honey, A : see Milk and honey.

Land of the golden fleece, The : Australia, in allusion to the wealth of wool produced there.

Land of inverted order, The : Australia.

Land League, The : an Irish political association, formed in 1879, to secure the land for the people.

Land o' the Leal, The (*Scot.*) : Heaven, the mythical land of happiness. Norm.-Fr., loyal.

Land lies, To see how the : to ascertain the state of affairs. A nautical metaphor.

Land of the living, In the : alive. [*Job*, xxviii, 13]

Land leaper (loper), A (*Dutch, land-looper*, one who runs up and down the land) : a vagabond.

Land of the midnight sun, The : Norway, in the northern regions where daylight lasts throughout the summer night.

Land of myrrh, The : Azab ; Saba.

Land of Nod, The : sleep. A pun on the country mentioned in *Gen.*, iv, 16.

Land of the nymphs, The : Ireland.

Land of Promise, The : (1) Palestine, promised to the Israelites by God ; (2) any country that offers attractions to the immigrant.

Land of roasted pigs, The : China. After the essay of Charles Lamb in which he narrated the discovery by the Chinese of the art of roasting pork.

Land of shadows, Gone to the : fallen asleep. Shadows = dreams.

Land shark, A : a boarding-house keeper in seaport towns who preys on seamen.

Land of stars and stripes, The : the United States of America. After the design on the national flag.

Land of steady habits, The : Connecticut. After the supposed moral character of its inhabitants.

Land of the two-legged mare, The : the gallows. [Fulwell, *Like Will to Like*, l. 612 (1568)]

Land's End, From Berwick to : *see* Berwick.

Landslide, A : an overwhelming movement of electors from one party to another in a general election.

Langue d'Oc : Provençal, the language of Southern France, in which tongue 'oc' signifies 'yes.'

Langue d'Oïl : the Walloon language, in which 'oil' signifies 'yes.'

Lantern, To bear the : to act as leader.

Lantern face, A : a long thin face with hollow cheeks.

Lantern jaws : lantern face (*q..v.*).

Lantern Land : *see* Isle of Lanterns.

Lantern of the night, The : the moon. [*That Nature Hath Made Women for our Comfort*, ll. 19–20 (1557)]

Lanterne, La : the extremists of the French Revolution or followers of Robespierre. After La Lanterne de la Grève or street-lamp at the Place de la Grève where several summary executions of political opponents had taken place.

Laodicean : lukewarm ; half-hearted. After Laodicea in Asia Minor. [*Rev.*, iii, 14, *et seq.*]

Laodicians, The sin of the : indifference in religion, politics, etc. *See* Laodicean.

Lapsus linguæ, A (*Lat.*, a slip of the tongue) : [Zeno, *Diogenes Laertius*, VII, i, 22, 26 ; Dryden, *Martin Marr-all*, III, i (1668)]

Lapwing, As cunning as a : from the reputed practice of the lapwing of crying in other places in order to attract her enemies away from her nest. [Ray, *Proverbs* (1670)]

Lares and Penates : the household gods ; one's cherished household possessions. The Lares familiares were the Roman gods of the household or family, the Penates those of the store-room.

Large as life, As : full-sized. [Wilson. *Art of Rhetoric* 102 (1580)]

Large, To set at : to set free. [Sir Thos. Overbury, *Characters : A Meere Common Lawyer* (1616)]

Lark, To rise with the : to rise from bed very early in the morning. [Lyly, *Endimion*, IV, i (1591)]

La Rochefoucauld of England, The : Philip Dormer Stanhope, Earl of Chesterfield (1694–1773), orator, wit and author of the famous letters. So-called by Sainte-Beuve. François, Duc de La Rochefoucauld (1613–80) was a Fr. statesman and moralist.

Larrikin, A (*Austral.*) : a young street rowdy. Introduced in the press about 1870. Possibly from Larry, an Irish diminutive of Lawrence, or a corruption of larking.

Larry Durgan's eye-water : blacking. From the name of a Dublin shoe-black.

Last argument of kings, The : force. The maxim was engraved by Richelieu (1585–1642) on the Fr. cannon. He derived it from Card. Francisco Ximenes (1436–1517).

Last infirmity of a noble mind, The : (1) love of fame ; from Milton, *Lycidas*, ll. 70–1 (1638) ; (2) ambition. [Ben Jonson, *Catiline*, III, ii (1611)]

Last of the Barons, The : Rich. Neville, Earl of Warwick (1428–71). From the title of a novel by Edward Bulwer, Lord Lytton (1843).

Last of the Dandies, The : Count Alfred Guillaume Gabriel D'Orsay (1801–52).

Last of the English, The : Hereward (fl. 1070), a rebel against the Norman conquerors of England.

Last of the Fathers, The : St. Bernard of Clairvaux (1091–1153). In allusion to the Church Fathers.

Last of the Goths, The : Roderick, King of the West Goths (d. 711).

Last of the Greeks, The : Philopœmen (253–184 B.C.). So-called by Plutarch.

Last of the Knights, The : Maximilian (1459–1519), Emp. of Germany.

Last legs, On his : at the end of his defence or resources. [Philip Massinger and Thomas Middleton, *The Old Law*, V, i (1656)]

Last Man, The : Charles I of England. So-called by the Puritans as an expression of their hope that he would be the last king of England.

Last minstrel of the English stage, The : James Shirley (1596–1666), English dramatist.

Last of the Mohicans, The : Uncas, a character in *The Last of the Mohicans* by James Fenimore Cooper (1826).

Last of the Romans, The : (1) Cola di Rienzi ; *see* Last of the Tribunes ; (2) Caius Cassius Longinus (d. 42 B.C.), so-called by Brutus ; (3) Ætius (c. 400–454), so-called by Gibbon ; (4) Bonifacius (d. 432), so-called by Gibbon. The term was also applied to François Joseph Terasse Desbillons (1751–89), on account of his elegant Latin style, by Pope, to the dramatist, Wm. Congreve (1670–1729), to Charles James Fox (1749–1806), Eng. statesman, and to Horace Walpole (1717–97), Eng. man of letters.

Last, Stick to one's : *see* Stick.

Last straw, The : *see* Straw.

Last of the Stuarts, The : Henry, Cardinal of York (1725–1807). The last legitimate male descendant of James I of England.

Last things, The four : (Theol.) death, judgment, heaven, hell.

Last of the Tribunes, The : Cola di Rienzi (1313–54), the hero of the Rom. rebellion of 1347.

Last of the Troubadours, The : Jacques, Jasmin, Provençal poet (1798–1864).

Last word, To have the : to make the last retort in an altercation. [Lilly, *Endimion*, II, ii (1591)]

Last-ditcher, A : an irreconcileable ; one who resists to the last. One who dies in the defence of the last ditch of an entrenchment. [Gilbert Burnet, *History of His Own Time*, I, 457 (1715)]

Lathe painted to look like iron, A : Robert Cecil, 3rd Marquis of Salisbury (1830–1903), British statesman. So-called by Prince Bismarck, in connection with the Berlin Congress of 1878.

Latin Church, The : the Roman Catholic Church as distinct from the Eastern or Grk. Church.

Latin Cross : *see* Cross, Latin.

Latin, Dog : uncouth, although grammatically accurate, Latin.

Latin, Low : *see* Low Latin.

Latin Union, The : a monetary agreement between France, Belgium, Italy, Greece and Switzerland. Belgium subsequently withdrew.

Latona's son : the god, Apollo.

Latter day saints : the Mormons. So-called by themselves.

Latter Lammas, At the : *see* Lammas.

Laudator temporis acti (*Lat.*, a praiser of past events) : one who idealizes the past. [Horace, *Ars Poetica*, 173]

Laugh and grow fat : an allusion to the Laughing Philosopher (*q.v.*), who was famous for his size as well as his laughter and his length of days.

Laugh in one's sleeve, To : to laugh to oneself. From the period when sleeves were worn very wide and it was easy to conceal the face with one. [Jno. Heywood, *Proverbs* (1546)]

Laugh on the wrong side of one's face, To : to cry ; to be grieved. [Scott *Rob Roy*, ch. 37 (1818)]

Laughing matter, No : not a matter for laughter. [Foxe, *Acts and Monuments*, II (1563)]

Laughing Philosopher, The : Democritus of Abdera (c. 460–357 B.C.). Because he laughed at the follies of mankind.

Laureate, Poet : the official poet of the country on whom is conferred a small court appointment. Orig. a degree in poetry conferred by the Universities. From *laurus*, the leaf of the bay, sacred to Apollo, with which poets and other men of letters were formerly crowned.

Laurels, To gain (win) : to earn honour. From the laurel with which in classic times those on whom honour was conferred were crowned.

Laurels, To look to one's : to take precautions lest one's position of eminence be endangered. *See* Laurels, To gain.

Laurence bids wages : idleness is attractive. *See* Laurence, A lazy.

Laurence, A lazy : an indolent person. Probably alliterative ; possibly an allusion to the hot season during which St. Laurence's Day (Aug. 10th) falls. From the Germ., *Der faule Lenz*, current in the 16th cent. There is also a tradition that the phrase is derived from a sneer by the executioner of St. Laurence, who attributed the latter's steadfastness under torture to his laziness. [*The Infamous History of Sir Lawrence Lazie* (1670)]. *See also* Lazy as David Laurence's dog, As.

Lavender, In : put away carefully, like domestic linen laid aside in lavender. [Earle, *Microcosmography : A Young Raw Preacher* (1628)]

Lavender, To lay in : to pawn ; because goods pledged with a pawnbroker used to be kept in lavender. [Florio,

Worlde of Wordes (1593) ; Greene, *Quip for an Upstart Courtier* (1592)]

Law, The : the Pentateuch, the Law of Moses.

Law of .. To have (take) the : to take proceedings against in a court of law. [*The Spectator*, No. 122 (1711)]

Law of arms, The : (1) the convention observed by professional soldiers ; (2) a thrashing.

Law to .. To give the : to force one's will upon ..

Law into one's own hands, To take the : to fill the combined roles of complainant, judge and inflicter of punishment.

Law, To lay down the : to adopt a dictatorial manner in argument.

Law, The letter of the : *see* Letter.

Law unto oneself, To be a : to follow one's own inclinations without reference to the law or other regulations. [Geo. Chapman, *Bussy d'Ambois*, II, i (1607)]

Law, The Unwritten : *see* Unwritten.

Laws of the Medes and Persians, The : that which is not subject to modification or alteration. [*Daniel*, vi, 12]

Laws of Nature, The : the bases of natural order.

Lawless Parliament, The : *see* Unlearned Parliament.

Lawrence : *see also* Laurence.

Lawrence on one's back, To have ; Lawrence, To have a touch of Old : to be unemployed. *See* Laurence, A lazy.

Lawyer's treat, A : refreshment in company at one's own expense.

Lay hands on, To : to seize ; to apprehend. [Shakespeare, *The Taming of the Shrew*, V, i (1596)]

Lay heads together, To : to consult. [Congreve, *The Double-dealer*, V, xx (1694)]

Lay by the heels, To : to deprive of power for action. An allusion to the punishment of the stocks.

Lay to a person's charge, To : to accuse a person of .. [*Deuteronomy*, xxi, 8]

Lay on the table, To : *see* Table.

Lazaroni : *see* Lazzaroni.

Lazarus and Dives : the poor and the rich. From the parable in *Luke*, xvi, 19 *et seq.* Lat., *Dives*, rich man.

Lazy as David Laurence's dog, As : from Laurence, the Scot. folk patron of the lazy. *See* Laurence, A lazy.

Lazy as Ludlam's dog, As : Ludlam, the sorceress of Farnham, had a dog which was too lazy to bark.

Lazy man's load, A : a load too great to carry at one journey, but under which the bearer struggles in order to avoid a second journey.

Lazzaroni : the beggars and street population of Naples. From the Hospital of St. Lazarus, the workhouse of that city.

Lead apes in Hell, To : the supposed fate of old maids, esp. those who were coquettes while alive. Ape was sometimes a synonym for fool. [Shakespeare, *Much Ado About Nothing*, II, i (1599–1600)]. *See also* Apes in Hell.

Lead a person a chase, To : to cause trouble by not following a clear line.

Lead a person a dance, To : to cause a person much trouble. [Heywood, *Woman Killed* (1607)]

Lead a person a life, To : to annoy and torment a person.

Lead by the nose, To : to cause to carry out one's wishes submissively. From an ancient Grk. proverb, in allusion apparently, to the leading and guiding of oxen by means of rings inserted in their noses. [Shakespeare, *Othello*, I, iii, 407 (?1604)]

Lead by the sleeve, To : to lead by the nose (*q.v.*).

Leaden sword (dagger), To fight with a : to undertake a task impossible of fulfilment. [Fulke, *Heskin's Parliament* (1579)]

Leading question, A : a question (esp. in law) that suggests the answer that is required.

Leading strings, To be in : to be under close direction, like a child. Leading-strings are the strings by which children are taught to walk.

Leaf out of a person's book, To take a : to follow another person's example. Perhaps an allusion to literary plagiarism.

Leaf, To turn over a new : to enter on a new line of conduct. A metaphor derived from book-reading. [Heywood, *Proverbes* (1546)]

League, The : formed in 1576 by the Guises to uphold Catholicism in France and incidentally to prevent the accession to the throne of Henry of Navarre.

League with .. To be in : to be in close co-operation with .. [Cooper, *Thesaurus* (1565)]

Lean as a rake, As : very thin. [Chaucer, *Canterbury Tales*, I, 289 (14th cent.)]

Leap in the dark, A : the description by the dissentient conservatives of the Conservative Reform Bill of 1867. First used in this connection by the Marquis of Salisbury, then Lord Cranbourne. Any decision which, carrying with it great uncertainty, is of the nature of a gamble. Also used by Thomas Hobbes (1588–1679), the Eng. philosopher, and subsequently by others in reference to death.

Leaps and bounds, By : with great rapidity.

Learned Blacksmith, The : Elihu Burritt (1810–79), Amer. philanthropist and linguist.

Learned fool in Christendom, The most : James I of England. Description applied to him by the Duke of Sully (1560–1641).

Learned Painter, The : Charles Lebrun (1619–90). From the accuracy of his costumes.

Learned Tailor, The : Henry Wild of Norwich (1684–1734), who knew Greek, Latin, Hebrew, Persian, Arabic, Syriac and Chaldaic.

Learned Theban, A : one who is expert at solving riddles. From Œdipus, King of Thebes, who solved the riddle of the Sphinx.

Learning, The New : Greek and other subjects of study revived in England during the 16th cent.

Leather and prunella : anything that arouses no interest in one. Prunella is the material used for the uppers of women's boots.
' Worth makes the man, and want of it the fellow ;
The rest is all but leather and prunella.'
[Pope, *Essay on Man*, IV, 204 (1732–4)] Leather represents the cobbler ; prunella (from which clerical gowns are made) the parson.

Leather-hunting : fielding, in cricket. In allusion to the leather of which the cricket-ball is made.

Leathering to .. To give a : to thrash. In allusion to the leather lash.

Leave, French : see French.

Leaves without figs : promise without fulfilment. In allusion to the barren fig-tree mentioned in *Luke*, xiii.

Led captain, A : a parasite. [Wycherley, *Love in a Wood*, I, i (1694)]

Leeds, The Austrian : Brünn in Moravia, formerly in the Austrian Empire. In allusion to its woollen manufactures.

Leek, To eat the : to accept humiliation submissively. From a passage in Shakespeare, *Henry V*, V, i, 10 (1599).

Left, The : the democratic or advanced party in a legislature. In allusion to the seats occupied by them on the left of the chairman.

Left eye, To see with the : to see imperfectly.

Left (shoulder), Over the : a suggestion that the statement is untrue ; not to be taken seriously. [*Records of Hartford County Court* (1705)]

Left hand of friendship, To give the : to treat in an unfriendly manner.

Left hand, To work with the : to work inefficiently.

Left shoulder, To go over the : to be wasted.

Left-handed compliment, A : a doubtful or ambiguous compliment.

Left-handed marriage, A : a morganatic marriage, in which the husband is said to give his left hand to his bride in the course of the marriage ceremony.

Left-handed oath, A : an oath when taken not intended to be kept.

Leg, To have a bone in one's : see Bone.

Leg, The boot is on the other : see Boot.

Leg up, To give a person a : to help a person over a difficulty, (metaph.) over a stile or other physical obstruction.

Leg, To make a : to make a bow. [*Rare Triumphs of Love and Fortune*, III, l. 77 (1589)]

Leg of mutton school, The : poetasters and parasites who write servile poetry for their living instead of their art or other mission. So-called by J. G. Lockhart (1794–1854) in a review of *Fleurs : A Poem in Four Books*.

Leg, To pull one's : to deceive, impose upon, a person.

Leg foremost, To put one's best : to throw oneself thoroughly into an affair ; to make every effort to attain the goal. [Dekker and Webster, *Northward Ho*, IV, ii (1607)]

Leg to stand on, Not a : with no support (generally metaph.) whatever. [De Quincey, *On Murder Considered as a Fine Art* (1827)]

Legs, To get upon one's : to get into a temper. Metaphor drawn from the rearing of horses.

Legs, One's last : see Last legs.

Legs, To set upon his : to establish in business ; to place a man in a position to support himself.

Legs, To stand upon one's own : to be self-supporting, self-reliant.

Legs, To take to one's : to run away.

Leg-up, To give a person a : to render a person assistance.

Legerdemain (*Fr.*, light of hand) : sleight of hand. [W. Roy and Jeremy Barlowe, *Rede Me*, etc. (1528)]

Legion of Honour ; Légion d'Honneur : the Fr. Order of Merit, founded by Napoleon I in 1802.

Legislator of Parnassus, The : Nicholas Boileau (1636–1711), a famous Fr. critic and poet. So-called by Voltaire, on account of his *Art of Poetry*. After Parnassus, a mountain ridge in Greece which was in mythology the seat of music and poetry.

Leipsic, To be one's : to be the occasion of one's disaster or ruin. After the Battle of Leipsic (1813) in which Napoleon was severely defeated.

Lemnian deed, A : a deed of unusual barbarity. From two ferocious massacres said to have been perpetrated in classical times by the inhabitants of Lemnos.

Lemnian Smith, The : Vulcan. From the legend that when flung out of heaven he fell on the Island of Lemnos.

Length of a person's foot, To know the : to understand his meaning or intentions fully. [Bunyan, *The Holy War* (1682)]

Lenson Hill to Pilsen Pin, As much akin as : not at all related. Lenson Hill and Pilsen Pin are two independent heights in Dorsetshire, which, viewed from the sea, appear as one.

Lent, A : a period of abstinence or depression. From the ecclesiastical period of fasting and penitence which precedes Easter.

Lent, Clean : the ecclesiastical Lent or period of forty weekdays of abstention and penitence which precedes Easter.

Lenten lover, A : one easy to feed.

Leo Hunter, Mrs. : *see* Hunter.

Leonidas of modern Greece, The : Marco Bozzaris, who defeated a Turkish-Albanian army three and a half times as large as his own at Kerpenisi in 1823. After Leonidas, the Spartan hero, who with 300 followers withstood the immense Persian army at Thermopylæ in 480 B.C.

Leonine contract, A (*Span.*, *Contrato Leonino*) : a contract which is unjustly one-sided. In allusion to the fable of *The Lion and His Fellow-hunters*.

Leonine verses (elegiacs) : verses whose ends rhyme with their middles. After Leo or Leoninus, a Canon of Paris in the 12th cent., who popularized them.

Lerna of ills, A : a very great evil. In allusion to Lake Lerna where Hercules destroyed the Hydra.

Lesbian : pliant, easily influenced. After the Lesbian rule, a mason's rule, which can be bent to fit into curves, mouldings, etc.

Lesbian Citizen, The : Alcæus (611–580 B.C.), of Mytilene in Lesbos. By some authorities considered the first of the lyric poets of Greece.

Lesbian kiss, A : an immodest kiss. In allusion to the licentiousness for which the ancient Lesbians were notorious.

Lesbian rule, The : making a rule conform to the thing ruled, instead of making the thing ruled conform to the rule. *See also* Lesbian.

Lèse Majesté (*Lat.*, *laesa majestas*, offended majesty): an offence against the dignity of the sovereign.

Lessian diet : strict temperance, as advocated by Leonhard Lessius (1554–1623), Dutch Jesuit.

L'Etat, c'est moi (*Fr.*, I am the state) : a remark falsely attributed to Louis XIV at a meeting of the parliament in 1655 when he was 17 years of age. It was, in fact, a crystallization of his policy as developed later in his reign.

Let down, To : to fail to fulfil one's engagements to ..

Let in, To be : to be deceived, trapped. [Wm. Haughton, *Englishmen for My Money*, II, ii (1597)]

Lethe : oblivion. After Lethe, one of the rivers of hell (Grk. mythology), a draught of which caused oblivion of the past.

Letter, A dead : *see* Dead letter.

Letter of the law, The : the law as literally interpreted.

Letter of Marque, A : a commission authorizing a private individual to seize enemy property on the seas, *i.e.*, to fit out privateers. Abolished by the Treaty of Paris in 1856. Marque is derived from the marches or border lands whose lords were authorized to exact reprisals on the population over the border.

Letter and the spirit, The : the nominal and the real. From the letter and the spirit of the law.

Letter of Uriah, A : a letter pretending friendship but in reality engineering betrayal. [II *Samuel*, xi, 14]

Letters, St. Agatha's : letters written on St. Agatha's Day (Feb. 5th) as a means of protection against fire.

Lettre de Cachet, A (*Fr.*) : an order committing to prison without trial, signed with the seal (*cachet*) of the French king. Abolished in 1790.

Lettre de Jérusalem, A : a blackmailing letter.

Levant, The (*It., Levante*, the eastern region) : the countries bordering on the Eastern Mediterranean.

Level best, To do one's : to do one's utmost.

Levellers, Irish : agrarian offenders in the latter half of the 18th cent. who levelled the fences by which common land was enclosed.

Lever de rideau, A (*Fr.*, raising of the curtain) : a short introductory play.

Leviathan of Literature, The : Dr. Samuel Johnson (1709–84).

Levitical Degrees : the degrees of relationship between which marriage is forbidden. From the *Book of Leviticus* in which the laws are laid down.

Lex non scripta (*Lat.*, the unwritten law) : the common law as distinguished from the statute or written law.

Lex talionis (*Lat.*) : the law of retaliation, based on the biblical law of an eye for an eye, a tooth for a tooth, etc.

Leyden jar, A : a jar so made as to be charged with electricity. Invented at Leyden, Holland.

Leze Majesté (Majesty) : *see* Lèse Majesté.

Libel from a lupine, Not to know a : to be entirely ignorant. Among the Romans a libel was a small silver coin, a lupine, a counter.

Liberal Arts, The : education suitable for a gentleman. Orig. those arts considered worthy of a free man.

Liberal education, A : an education in the Liberal Arts (*q.v.*).

Liberal Party, The : a British political party in favour of progress and democracy ; the successor of the Whig party. From the title of Lord Byron's periodical, *The Liberal* (1828).

Liberal Republicans, The : a political party, formed in the U.S. in 1872, to prevent Pres. U. S. Grant from securing election for a second term.

Liberal Sciences, The : sciences worthy of a free man. *See* Liberal Arts.

Liberal Science, The Eighth : warfare.

Liberal Unionist Party, The : a British political party formed of a secession from the Liberal party in 1886 in opposition to Home Rule for Ireland.

Liberation, The War of : the war waged against Napoleon in 1813–14 which resulted in the liberation of the Germ. states from French rule.

Liberator, The : Daniel O'Connell (1775–1847), the advocate of Catholic Emancipation and other Irish liberties. *See also* Libertador, El.

Liberator of the New World, The : Benjamin Franklin (1706–90).

Libertador, El : the Liberator Simon Bolivar (1783–1830), who led the revolt of the Amer. colonies from Spain.

Libertine, A chartered : *see* Chartered.

Liberty, The Apostle of : Henry Clay (1777–1852), Amer. statesman and orator, who supported the South Amer. states in their revolt from Spain.

Liberty, Cap of : *see* Cap.

Liberty, Equality, Fraternity : the watchwords of the French Revolution.

Liberty Hall : a place where one may do as one likes. [Oliver Goldsmith, *She Stoops to Conquer*, II (1773)]

Liberty man, A : a sailor who absents himself on leave from his ship.

Liberty Party, The : an Amer. political party founded in 1839 in opposition to slavery.

Liberum Veto, The : a provision in the old Polish Diet under which no law could be enacted in the absence of unanimity on the part of members of the Diet.

Libro d'Oro, A (*It.*, book of gold) : any list of titles of honour, etc. Orig. a register of noble families in Venice and other It. republics.

Licinian Laws : laws adopted in Rome about 370 B.C. in the interests of the Plebeians as against those of the Patricians. After C. Licinius Calvus (Stolo), the tribune of the people.

Lick a person, To : to thrash a person. Perhaps from the phrase ' an unlicked cub,' or from Welsh, *llach*, a slap.

Lick the dust, To : to fall in battle. [*Psalm*, lxxii, 9]

Lick a person's feet, To : to be obsequious. [Anth. Brewer, *Lingua* (1607)]

Lick into shape, To : to put into order ; to make presentable. In allusion to the long persistent superstition supported by Pliny and Aristotle, among others, that a bear's cub is born an amorphous mass and is licked into shape by its mother. [Burton, *Anatomy of Melancholy*, To the Reader (1621)]

Lick-spittle, A : a toady. [Davenant, *Albovine* (1629)]

Lick-trencher, A : a parasite. [Withal, *Dictionarie* (1608)]

Lie like a bulletin, To : in reference to military bulletins in general, and esp. to those of Napoleon during his Russian campaign.

Lie circumstantial, The : ' the lie with circumstance.' [Shakespeare, *As You Like It*, V, iv (1600)]

Lie direct, The : [Shakespeare, *As You Like It*, V, iv (1600)]

Lie with one's fathers, To : to die ; to be buried. [*Genesis*, xlvii, 30]

Lie, To give a person the : to accuse a person of untruthfulness. [Dekker, *The Seuen Deadly Sinnes : Lying* (1606)]

Lie in the lap of .. To : to be destined for, but not defined in advance ; like an unborn child.

Lie low, To : to conceal oneself or one's intentions. [J. C. Harris, *Uncle Remus* (1880)]

Lie quarrelsome, The : [Shakespeare, *As You Like It*, V, iv (1600)]

Lie for the whetstone, To : to exaggerate or deceive grossly. At Whitsun amusements in olden times a whetstone ' to sharpen his wit ' used to be given as a reward to the victor in a lying-match.

Lie, A white : a falsehood that does no harm and is considered morally justifiable.

Life, To the : perfectly counterfeited. [Lilly, *Campaspe*, I, ii (1584)]

Life dear, To sell one's : to defend oneself with the utmost energy.

Life in one's hand, To carry one's : to pursue an undertaking fraught with danger to one's life.

Life and soul of .. The : the centre of good spirits of .. ; the centre of life. [Fes. Coventry, *History of Pompey the Little*, ch. 16 (1751)]

Lift, To : to steal. [Ben Jonson, *The Devil is an Ass* (1616) ; Robert Greene, *James the Fourth*, III, i (1594)]

Lift, To have a person at a : to have a person in one's power. A wrestling metaphor.

Light of the Age, The : Maimonides (1135–1204), Hispano-Jewish philosopher.

Light under a bushel, To hide one's : to be modest ; not to trumpet forth one's qualifications. [*Matthew*, v, 15]

Light of one's eyes, The : a beloved one. [10th cent.]

Light as a feather, As : (1) of very light weight ; [Cicero, *Ad Atticum*, VIII, xv, 2 ; Heywood, *Proverbes* (1546) (2) very easily ; (3) worthless. [*The Man in the Moon*, 5 (1609)]

Light as gossamer, As : very light and flimsy. Gossamer has been used in this sense since the 14th cent.

Light as a kex (kyx), As : very light. A kex is a dry, hollow stalk. [Heywood, *Proverbes* (1546)]

Light o' love, A : a flirt, a woman of accommodating morals. From the title of an old tune. [Nashe, *Anatomie of Absurditie* (1589)]

Light of .. To make : not to treat seriously. [Bacon, *Rulers of Good and Evill*, § 8 (1597)]

Light, To stand in one's own : *see* Stand.

Light upon .. To throw : to give information regarding ..

Light as the wind, As: [*Interlude of Youth* ; Lyly, *Gallathea*, I, iv (1592)]

Light of the World, The : Jesus Christ. From the title of a painting by Wm. Holman Hunt. [*Matthew*, v, 14]

Lights, Before the : *see* Before.

Light-fingered : dishonest. Properly, having light or nimble fingers. [*Nice Wanton* (1560)]

Light-fingered gentry, The : pickpockets. *See* Light-fingered.

Lightning strike, A : a strike of workmen declared at a moment's notice, and therefore as sudden as a stroke of lightning.

Ligurian Arts, The : deception ; trickery.

Like as two peas, As : exactly alike. [Lyly, *Euphues : Anatomy of Wit*, Epistle Dedicatory (1579) ; Thos. Flatman, *Heraclitus Ridens* (1681)]

Lilburne, John would quarrel with : in allusion to John Lilburne (1618–57), a cantankerous schismatic of the period of the Commonwealth.

Lilliputian : of diminutive size. After Lilliput, the land of tiny men, described in Swift, *Gulliver's Travels* (1726).

Lily, To paint the : *see* Paint the lily, To.

Lily-livered : timorous. The liver was formerly considered the centre of passion and physical courage.

Limb of the law, A : a legal functionary. [Tobias Smollett, *Sir L. Greaves*, I, ii (1762)]

Limb of Satan, A : an imp of Satan.

Limb from Warburton, To tear : a play on the place named Lymm-cum-Warburton.

Limbo, In : in prison ; in confinement. From limbus, in scholastic theology, a place bordering on hell. [Lyndsay, *The Dreme*, I, 14 (1553)]

Limbus Fatuorum : a fool's paradise. [Milton, *Paradise Lost*, III, 495 (1667) *See* Limbo, In.

Limbus Infantum : the place where the souls of unbaptised infants go after death. *See* Limbo, In.

Limbus of the moon : the borders of Hell, according to Ariosto (*Orlando Furioso*, xxxiv, 70), situated in the moon. *See* Limbo, In.

Limbus Patrum : the place where the souls of good men who lived before Christ go after death. *See* Limbo, In.

Limbus Puerorum : the place where the souls of unbaptized children remained. *See* Limbo, In *and* Limbus Infantum.

Limehouse : unrestrained abuse of one's political opponents, similar to that employed by Mr. David Lloyd George in a speech at Limehouse, London, on the 30th of July, 1909.

Lime-juicer : (Amer.) a British sailor or ship. In allusion to the consumption of lime juice on board British vessels.

Limerick, A : a more or less nonsense verse of a certain character, in the metre popularized by Edward Lear in his *Book of Nonsense* (1846), said to have been derived from a refrain sung at gatherings at which the pastime of making limericks was followed.

Lime-twigs for .. To set : to lay a snare for .. In allusion to the twigs smeared with bird lime used for catching birds. [Joshua Cook, *How a Man May Choose a Good Wife from a Bad*, IV, ii, (1602)]

Linceus' sight, As sharp as : in reference to Lynceus, one of the Argonauts, famous for his keen sight. [Geo. Gascoigne, *The Steel Glass* (1576)]

Lincoln green, Clad in : Lincoln was formerly famous for the manufacture of green dye.

Lincolnshire bagpipes : the croaking of frogs. In allusion to their prevalence in the Lincolnshire Fens.

Lindabrides, A : a mistress. After the heroine of a romance called *The Mirror of Knighthood*, mentioned in *Don Quixote*.

Line of life, The : (Palmistry) one of the lines in the palm of the hand. [Shakespeare, *Merchant of Venice*, II, ii (1596)]

Line, The thin red : *see* Thin red line.

Lines, To read between the : to deduce a not obvious meaning from a written or spoken statement.

Linenopolis : Belfast. On account of its linen manufactures.

Lingua Franca : the commerical language used in the Near East. A mixture of Fr., It., Arabic, etc., [Dryden, *Limherham*, I (1679)]

Linseed Lancers, The : the Royal Army Medical Corps.

Linsey-woolsy million, The : the masses. From the supposition that they wear linsey-woolsy as opposed to broadcloth, the clothing of the classes. [Peter Pindar, *Benevolent Epistle to Sylvanus Urban* (1790)]

Lion, A : a person much sought after on account of his distinction. [Lady Mary Wortley Montagu, *Town Eclogues* (1715)] *See* Lionize.

Lion, The British : the emblem of Great Britain or the British nation.

Lion of Cotswold, A : a sheep.

Lion of God, The : the Caliph Ali (c. 602–661).

Lion of the North, The : Gustavus Adolphus (1594-1632), King of Sweden.

Lion Rouge, The (*Fr.*, *rouge*, red) : Marshal Ney (1769–1815). In allusion to his red hair.

Lion Sermon, The : an annual sermon preached in the Church of St. Katherine Cree, London, in commemoration of the escape of Sir John Gayer (d. 1649), who endowed the sermon, from a lion.

Lion of Sweden, The : Johan von Baner, Swed. general (1596–1641).

Lion in the way, A : an obstacle, real or imaginary. [*Proverbs*, xxvi, 13]

Lion's Heart, The : Richard I, King of England (1157-99). In allusion to his bravery.

Lion's mouth, To put one's head in the : to put oneself into a dangerous position. [*Psalms*, xxii, 21]

Lions of a place, The : the sights worth seeing, or the celebrities. *See* Lion, A.

Lion's provider, The : (1) the jackal ; (2) any person who offers himself as a foil to a person whom he considers more important than himself.

Lion's share, The : the principal share ; nearly the whole. In allusion to one of Æsop's *Fables*.

Lion's tail, To twist the : to subject England to petty annoyances or insults. The phrase was invented in the U.S. about 1886. *See* Lion, The British.

Lions of the Western World, The : the English. [*Soliman and Perseda*, I, ll. 99–100 (1599)]

Lion-hunter, A : one given to lionizing people. Popularized by Dickens in Mr. and Mrs. Leo Hunter. [*Pickwick Papers* (1836) ; Maria Edgeworth, *Helen*, ch. xii (1834)]

Lionize, To : to treat and exhibit as an object of interest. Orig. to take visitors to see the lions formerly kept at the Tower of London.

Lip homage : merely nominal homage.

Lip-service: pretended service, as of the lip but not of the heart. [*Isaiah*, xxix, 13]

Lit de Justice (*Fr.*, bed of justice) · a sitting of the Fr. States-general in the presence of the king at which laws were promulgated to which the States-general had refused their assent.

Litteræ Humaniores (*Lat.*, the more human letters) : the final classical examination in honours at Oxford University.

Little Britain School of Politicians, The : the Eng. school of politicians which is opposed to an imperialistic Jingo policy. So-called by their opponents.

Little Corporal, The : Napoleon I. Title given to him by his soldiers after the Battle of Lodi in 1796. In allusion to his stature.

Little Ease : the pillory ; the stocks. [Bp. Latimer (1490–1555), *Sermons*]

Little end of the horn, To come out of the : to get the worst of a bargain. [*Eastward Ho*, I, i (1605)]

Little Englander : an opponent of the further expansion of the British Empire ; one who considers the interests of the British Isles of more consequence than and sometimes opposed to those of the British Empire. The term is said to have been invented by the *Pall Mall Gazette* (July 30, 1884).

Little Father, The : the Czar of Russia.

Little Gentleman in Velvet, The : the mole that raised the hill on which the horse of William III of England stumbled when he was fatally injured (1702). In the subsequent reign the Jacobites used to drink to the Little Gentleman in Velvet.

Little Giant, The : Stephen Arnold Douglas (1813–61), Amer. statesman, small in stature, great in intellect.

Little Go : the first exam. for the B.A. degree at Cambridge University.

Little god, The : Cupid, the god of love. Depicted as a boy.

Little Lord Fauntleroy : a beautiful little boy, generally dressed in the style of the hero of Mrs. Frances Hodgson Burnett's novel of that name (1886).

Little Mac : George Brinton McClellan (1826–85), Amer. general.

Little Magician, The : Martin van Buren (1782–1862), President of the U.S.

Little Marlborough : Kurt Christoph, Count Schwerin (1684–1757), Germ. field-marshal. In allusion to John Churchill, Duke of Marlborough (1650–1722), British general.

Little Mary : the stomach. After the title of an allegorical play by Sir. J. M. Barrie.

Little Paris : (1) Brussels ; (2) Milan. In allusion to their gaiety.

Little Parliament, The : Cromwell's Parliament (Barebone's Parliament) of 1653. In allusion to the number (120) of its members.

Little Pedlington : a village or other small circle in which all the usual petty vices are prevalent. After the title of a story by John Poole (c. 1787–1872).

Little Rhody : Rhode Island, the smallest state of the Union.

Little Van : Martin van Buren (1782–1862), President of the U.S.

Little Venice : Arendal, Norway.

Little Witham : *see* Witham.

Live Oak State, The : Florida.

Liver vein, The : the style and manner of men in love.

Liverpool Landseer, The : William Huggins (1820–84), Eng. animal painter. Sir Edwin Henry Landseer (1802–73), was a distinguished Eng. animal painter.

Livery Company, A : one of the London City Companies. Orig. trade guilds, whose members formerly wore liveries.

Living wage, A : a wage sufficient to enable a worker to live comfortably. First used by Sir Andrew Clarke in 1892.

Livy of France, The : Juan de Mariana (1537–1624). In allusion to Titus Livius (Livy), the Rom. historian who lived from B.C. 59 to A.D. 17.

Livy of Portugal, The : Joao de Barros (1496–1570).

Livy, The Russian : Nicholas Michaelo-vitch Karamzin (1765–1826).

Lloyds : a London underwriting association. From Edw. Lloyd (fl. 1688–1726), at whose coffee-house merchants interested in shipping assembled and who published periodical shipping news.

Loaves and fishes : material advantage obtained under the guise of public or religious service. [*John*, vi, 26]

Lobby, To : to frequent the lobby of a parliamentary chamber in order to obtain support.

Lobelia : a genus of flowering plant. After Matthias de Lobel (1538–1616), Fr. botanist.

Lobster, A : a British soldier. In allusion to his red coat. First applied to Sir A. Hazilrigg's cavalry in 1642, which were completely armed with corslets.

Local option : the principle of extending to localities the decision whether to suppress the liquor traffic or not.

Local veto : the prohibition of the sale of alcoholic refreshment in localities. *See* Local option.

Lock Hospital, A : a hospital for sufferers from venereal disease. From Lock Lazar House, the name of a former hospital of this description in Southwark.

Lock and key, To keep under : to keep locked up.

Lock, stock and barrel : anything in its completeness. In allusion to the three parts which together compose a sporting rifle. A sporting metaphor.

Lock-out, A : a suspension of work at a factory, etc., due to a labour dispute originating with the employer, who 'locks out' the men.

Locksmith's daughter, The : a key.

Loco(-foco) : the radical wing of the Amer. Democratic party. At a meeting in 1835, an opponent suddenly cut off the gas, whereupon light was obtained from candles lit by ' locofoco ' matches.

Loco parentis, In (*Lat.*, in the place of a parent) : acting as a parent. [Lyly, *Campaspe*, II, i (1584)]

Locum tenens, A (*Lat.*, holding the place): a deputy or temporary substitute, generally for a physician.

Locus classicus (*Lat.*, classic place) : a passage in a book which is accepted as authoritative.

Locus standi (*Lat.*, place of standing) : right to appear (in court, ect.). Orig. a legal term.

Log or King Stork, King : *see* King Log.

Loggerheads, To be at : to quarrel; to dispute. [Cotton, *Virgil Travestie* (1678)]

Logic, To chop : *see* Chop.

Logrolling : co-operation between two or more individuals or political parties on the principle that one good turn deserves another. In allusion to the practice of the loggers of Maine of assisting one another to roll their logs to the river.

Log-rolling criticism : the practice of favourably reviewing one another's literary works.

Loi d'Amour (*Fr.*, Law of love) : the Fr. parliamentary repression of the Press of 1827.

Loi Bèrenger, The : a Fr. law (1891) under which sentence on first offenders may be suspended.

Loins, To gird up one's : to set to to a work. The ancient Hebrews used to wear loose garments and when preparing for work or a journey bound or girded them about their loins. [II *Kings*, iv, 2]

Lombard, A : a medieval banker or financier. After Lombardy, whence most of them spread over Europe.

Lombard Street : the London money market. From the name of the street in which many of the banks have their headquarters.

Lombard Street to a china orange : a formula for a wager in which there is a considerable difference between the value of the respective stakes. *See* Lombard Street. [Southey, *The Doctor*, X (1834) ; Arthur Murphy, *Citizen*, II, i (1786), ' All Lombard Street to an eggshell.']

Lombard Street man, A : a banker. *See* Lombard Street.

London-super-mare (*Lat.*, London on the sea) : Brighton, the principal watering-place of London.

London's dormitories : the outer suburbs, of London, from which so many of the workers come in the morning and to which they return at night.

Lone Star State, The : Texas. In allusion to the single star in its arms.

Long bow, To draw the : to exaggerate ; to tell incredible tales. [Urquhart, *Rabelais*, V, 30 (1453)]

Long chalk (chalks), To win by a : an allusion to the system of marking in the game of dominoes.

Long dozen, A : thirteen.

Long face, A : *see* Face.

Q

Long firm, A : a company of swindlers who make large purchases on credit on behalf of a non-existent firm.

Long Friday : Good Friday. From the length of its church services and of its fast.

Long home, To go to one's : to die.

Long hundred, A : one hundred and twenty.

Long innings, A : a long life ; a lengthy period of success. A cricketing metaphor.

Long, John : *see* John Long.

Long as a law-suit, As : in allusion to the proverbial dilatoriness of the law. [Dekker, *The Gull's Hornbook*, ch. 3 (1609)]

Long Parliament, The : the Parliament of 1640 which was not finally dissolved until after the Restoration in 1660.

Long Peter : Peter Aartzen (1507–73), Flem. painter. In allusion to his stature.

Long purse, A : wealth.

Long Robe, A Gentleman of the : *see* Gentleman.

Long run, In the : ultimately.

Long and the short of it, The : an epitome of the story. [*The Four Elements*, ll. 597–9 (1579)]

Long spoon, To need a : to need to take every precaution. From the proverb, ' one needs a long spoon wherewith to sup with the devil.'

Long Tom : *see* Tom.

Longshanks : King Edward I (1239–1307). In allusion to his long legs.

Longshore man, A : a wharfinger or one employed along the shore.

Long-winded, To be : to be tediously long in speech. [*Hay any Work*, 48 (1589)]

Lonsdale's ninepins, Lord : the nine boroughs in which the Earl of Lonsdale before the 1832 Reform Act, used to secure the election of his nominees to parliament.

Look before one leaps, To : to take at least elementary precautions before entering on an undertaking. From the proverb, ' Look before you leap.'

Look a gift-horse in the mouth, To : to criticize a gift. In allusion to the usual method of judging a horse by examining its teeth. [Butler, *Hudibras*, I, i (1663)]

Look for a needle in a bottle (bundle) of hay, To : to seek that which it is practically impossible to find. [Greene, *Upstart Courtier* (1592)]

Look for trouble, To : unnecessarily to put oneself in a position where difficulties may arise.

Look in, Not to have a : not to have a chance.

Looking-glass to a mole, To hold a : *see* Hold.

Look out, A bad : a bad prospect.

Loose, Out on the : unrestrained in behaviour ; dissolute.

Loose end, At a : *see* End.

Loose fish, A : a person of loose habits, who has escaped from moral restraints, like a fish that has got loose from the net.

Loose Girt Boy, The : Julius Cæsar.

Loose woman, A : a prostitute.

Lord Burghleigh's nod : a supposed indication of wisdom. After the nods vouchsafed by Lord Burleigh instead of words in Sheridan, *The Critic* (1779).

Lord of creation, The : man. [*Genesis*, i, 28–29]

Lord falls in Our Lady's lap, When Our : when Good Friday coincides with Lady Day.

Lord Harry ! By the : an oath sworn by Satan. See Harry, Old.

Lord of Lies, The : the Devil.

Lord of Misrule, The : the Abbot of Misrule (*q.v.*).

Lord's anointed, The : the king. In allusion to the theory of the Divine Right of Kings.

Los von Rom (*Germ.*, free from Rome) : an Aust. religious political movement at the beginning of the 20th cent. to withdraw its members from adhesion to the Church of Rome so that the incorporation of the Germ. parts of the Austrian Empire in the German Empire might thereby be facilitated.

Lose in the hake, but gain in the herring, To : to gain one way what one loses in another. Hakes drive herrings away but should be caught in their place.

Losing game, To play a : to be failing, but yet to continue on one's course. [Peter Pindar, *Bozzy and Piozzi*, Pt. II (1796)]

Loss, To be at a : to be unable to decide. [Jas. Puckle, *The Club : Dear Kinsman* (1711)]

Lothario, A gay ; Lothario, A : a fashionable and unscrupulous rake. After a character in Sir William Davenant, *The Cruel Brother* (1630).

Lothbury, To go by way of : to be unwilling. A pun on loth. [16th cent.]

Lotus-eater, A : in Grk. mythology one of a people (the followers of Ulysses) who ate of the lotus plant and were thereby rendered oblivious of their friends and home. Hence one who, careless of passing time and events, passes his life in idleness and pleasure.

Loud as a hog in a gate, As : very noisy. Possibly in allusion to the noise made by a pig caught in such a predicament. [Goldsmith, *She Stoops to Conquer*, II, i (1773)]

Loud as Tom of Lincoln, As : *see* Tom of Lincoln.

Louis d'or (*Fr.*, Louis of gold) : an obsolete Fr. gold coin. Orig. struck in the reign of Louis XIII.

Louisiana purchase, The : the purchase of New Orleans and the neighbouring lands, now the state of Louisiana, from France in 1803, for 15,000,000 dollars.

Loup the dike, To : *see* Dike-louper.

Love-child, A : an illegitimate child.

Love in a cottage : marriage on small or insufficient means.

Love lost between .. There is no : they are objects of mutual dislike. The meaning of this phrase has changed entirely from its former sense. The change took place about 1748 when Richardson used it in both senses in *Clarissa Harlowe*. [Ben Jonson, *Every Man Out of His Humour*, II, i (1600)]

Love or money, For : by any means possible. Lit. (to gain an end) either by the influence of affection or by payment. [Dekker, *The Gull's Hornbook*, ch. 6 (1609)]

Loving as a dove, As : doves are proverbially devoted to their mates and as early as Chaucer 'turtledove' was used as a term of endearment.

Loving cup, A : a cup of wine that is passed round among the guests at the table after the meal. The practice is a Jewish one as old as the period of the New Testament.

Low Church : the Evangelical branch of the Church of England, which gives a low place to matters of ecclesiastical organisation, etc.

Low Countries, The : Holland, Belgium and Luxemburg, which are low-lying.

Low-country men : soldiers. In allusion to the Eng. armies that fought in the Low Countries or Netherlands. [Bacon, *Essays : Of Seditions and Troubles* (1625)]

Low Dutch ; Low German : the language spoken in the low-lying lands of Germany.

Low Latin : the Latin of the Middle Ages.

Low life : life among the poorer classes.

Low Sunday : the first Sunday after Easter.

Low water, To be in : to be in financial straits. [17th cent.]

Lower House, The : the House of Commons.

Lower Middle Class, The : *see* Class.

Loyale Epée, La (*Fr.*, the loyal sword : Marshal MacMahon (1808–93), President of the Fr. Republic.

Lubber's hole : a lazy method of performing a task. In allusion to the name given by seamen to a part of the rigging through which boys clamber in order to avoid the more dangerous course.

Lubberland : ' Where the pigs run about ready roasted and cry, " Come, eat me." ' So-called because lubbers only believe in its existence.

Luce Lucellum, Ex : *ex luce lucellum* was the motto adopted by Robert Lowe (Viscount Sherbrooke) in 1871 on the new match-box for his proposed match tax, which was the subject of much press ridicule and never became law.

Lucifer (*Lat.*, light-bringing) : properly, the morning star. Through a misinterpretation of *Isaiah*, xiv, 12, applied to Satan.

Lucifer, As proud as : very haughty and overbearing. In allusion to Lucifer as an equivalent of Satan. In *Isaiah*, xiv, 12, the term was used in allusion to Nebuchadnezzar. [Barclay, *Ship of Fools*, II, 59 (1509) ; *Strange Metamorphosis of Man* (1634)]

Luck of a nigger, The : *see* Nigger.

Luck and throw him into the sea, To give a man : a lucky man is able to get safely out of any misfortune.

Lucky star, To thank one's : to feel grateful for one's good fortune. Astrological metaphor.

Lucullus feast, A : a magnificent banquet. From M. Lucinius Lucullus (d. c. 49 B.C.), Rom. consul and epicure.

Lucus a non lucendo : an absurd explanation. (Lat.) a grove, from not showing light, implying the absurd etymology of *lucus,* from *lucere*, to be light. [*The Spectator*, No. 59 (1711)]

Lud's Bulwark : Ludgate Prison. From a mythical King Lud.

Lud's Town : London. After Lud, a mythical king of Britain, after whom one of the gates of the City was named, Ludgate.

Luddites : rioters in the north of England who engaged in the deliberate destruction of machinery during the years 1811 to 1816. They took their name from a half-witted youth named Ned Ludd who set them the example.

Ludgat(h)ian, A : a bankrupt. After the debtor's prison, formerly situated near Ludgate.

Luke's bird, As light as : heavy. St. Luke's ' bird ' is usually represented as an ox.

Luke's summer, St. : the end of autumn, Oct. 9th to Nov. 11th.

Lumber : (1) useless portable property ; (2) timber sawn for use. Orig. a pawnbroker's shop or a pledge. After the Lombards, the medieval pawnbrokers.

Lumber State, The : Maine. On account of its numerous forests.

Lumping pennyworth, A : (dial.) plenty for one's money. [Arbuthnot, *History of John Bull*, ch. 20 (1713)]

Lundyite, A : a traitor. After Robert Lundy, Protestant governor of Londonderry in 1689, who attempted to surrender the city to the Catholic besiegers.

Lungs of London, The : London's parks and other open spaces. Phrase attributed to Lord Chatham by William Windham in a speech in the House of Commons (June 30th, 1808).

Lurch, To leave in the : to desert or leave in difficulties. A card-playing metaphor. [Nashe, *Saffron Walden*, 119 (1596)]

Lush : intoxicating drink. After Lushington, a brewer.

Lustrum, A : a period of five years. From the Lustrum or Rom. festival of purification, which used to be celebrated every five years.

Lusty-Juventus, A : a gay young man. From the title of an early morality play intended to illustrate the frailty of youth. Lat., *juventus*, youth. [*Trial of Treasure*, ll. 73–4 (1567)]

Lusus Naturæ (*Lat.*, a sport of Nature) : a natural production which departs considerably from the standard ; a freak of nature.

Lutestring, To speak in (*Fr., lustrine*, a glossy silk) : to speak in a stilted manner. First used in *The Letters of Junius* (1769–72).

Lycaonian tables : detestable food. In allusion to the human flesh placed before Jupiter by Lycaon.

Lyceum, A : a high school ; a literary institute. After the place in Greece at which Aristotle taught philosophy.

Lycurgus, A : a legislator. After a Spartan who flourished in the 9th cent. B.C. and is the reputed author of the laws and institutions of Sparta.

Lycurgus' State, A : *see* Lycurgus.

Lyddite : a high explosive. From Lydd in Kent where it is manufactured.

Lydford law : a trial in which the evidence is heard after judgment has been given. A satire on the people of Lydford, Devon. See the proverb,
' First hang and draw,
Then hear the cause by Lidford law.'

Lydian airs : soft and light musical airs. [Milton, *L'Allegro*, ll. 136–8 (1635)]

Lying Traveller, The : Sir John Maundeville (1300–72). On account of the marvellous adventures related by him.

Lynceus' eyed : *see* Lynx eyed. Lynceus was one of the Argonauts, famous for the keenness of his vision. [Greene, *Never Too Late* (1590)]

Lynch, To : to execute without formal trial. *See* Lynch law.

Lynch, Judge : *see* Lynch law.

Lynch law : summary punishment of an offender without regular trial. Prevalent in the Western States and afterwards in the Southern States of N. America. Derived from (1) Jas. Lynch of Piedmont, Virginia (fl. 1688) ; (2) John Lynch of Carolina (about the same date) ; and (3) Chas. Lynch of Virginia (1736–96).

Lynx eyed : keen sighted, like the lynx. Possibly, however, a corruption of Lynceus' eyed (*q.v.*).

Lyric poets, The : Pindar, Alcæus, Sappho, Stesidorus, Ibycus, Bacchylides, Simonides, Alcman, Anacreon.

M.B. waistcoat, An : a clerical waistcoat opening behind or at the side. Orig. worn only by Tractarian clergymen. These being suspected of a tendency towards Roman Catholicism, their opponents nicknamed the garment M.B., or Mark of the Beast, waistcoats.

M or N : in the Church Catechism. M = NN (names), N = name.

M under one's girdle, To have an : to be polite in one's method of address. In allusion to the frequent use of the

titles, Mr., Mrs., Miss and Master.
[Haughton, *A Woman Will Have Her
Will* (1597)]

M's, The Five : Mansa (flesh), Matsya
(fish), Madya (wine), Maithuna
(women), Mudra (gesticulation). Five
means of exercising Hindu ascetic-
ism.

Mab, Queen : the fairies' midwife ; *i.e.*,
the fairy whose function it is to deliver
the fancies of man and to produce
dreams. First mentioned in Shakespeare, *Romeo and Juliet*, I, iv, 53-4
(1591-3). Previously known in Irish
poetry as the Queen of Connaught.

Macaber (Macabre) dance : *see* Dance.

Macadam ; to macadamize : a specially
prepared road-surface ; to construct a
road of macadam. From John
Loudon McAdam (1756-1836), the
Scot. inventor.

Macaire, Robert : a Frenchman. In
allusion to the frequent use of the name
in the Fr. drama.

Macaronic Latin : invented hybrid
words, half modern, half Latin.
Like macaroni, a mixture.

Macaronic verse : satiric and other verse
written in invented words in a hybrid
language with Latin terminations.
From a poetical rhapsody entitled
Liber Macaronicorum, by Theophilus
Folengo of Mantua (1491-1544).
Macaroni means a medley.

Macaronies : fashionable dandies in
England during the latter half of
the 18th cent. The term was introduced from the Continent where
Macaroni clubs abounded. These were
formed for the cultivation of Macaronic
verse (*q.v.*).

Macaronies, The : a regiment, raised in
Maryland during the War of Independence. In allusion to their gay
uniforms.

Macaulay's schoolboy : an imaginary
schoolboy invented by Lord Macaulay
in his writings in order to illustrate the
ignorance of his opponents.

Macaulay's New Zealander : who will
at some future date ' take his stand on
a broken arch of London Bridge to
sketch the ruins of St. Paul's.' [*On
Ranke's History of the Popes* (1840)]

Macedonia's Madman : *see* Madman.

MacFarlanes's buat : the moon. The
men of the MacFarlane clan used to
sally out at night to ravage the lands
of their neighbours. Scot., *buat*, the
moon.

MacGirdie's mare : the amount of her
diet was gradually reduced to one straw
a day, when she inconsiderately died
and spoilt the interesting experiment.
[Scott, *Waverley* (1814)]

Machiavellian : unscrupulous and crafty
in matters of politics. After Niccolo
Machiavelli (1469-1527), Florentine
historian, statesman and philosopher,
who laid down a Machiavellian policy
in his book, *Del Principe*.

Machine, The : the organization of a
political party. First employed in
Amer. politics about 1876.

**Machines after the war is over, To bring
one's :** *see* Bring.

Mackerel sky, A : a sky, spotted to
resemble a mackerel.

Mackintosh, A : a waterproof outer
garment or waterproof material. After
Chas. Macintosh (1766-1843), Scot.
inventor.

Macreons, The Island of the : Great
Britain. According to Rabelais in
Pantagruel, long-lived, for no one is
there put to death for his religious
opinions.

Mad Cavalier, The : Prince Rupert of
Bavaria (1619-82), Eng. royalist
general. On account of his foolhardy
rashness.

Mad as a hatter, As : properly, mad as an
adder. ' Mad ' formerly represented
the idea of venomous. The phrase was
therefore orig. the equivalent of
' venomous as an adder.' There have
been several attempts to give the
phrase a literal explanation. In
addition it has been derived from
Fr., *huître*, an oyster, from the Fr.
phrase, ' He reasons like an oyster.'
The phrase, which became well known
as recently as about 1863, was popularized by Lewis Carroll in *Alice in
Wonderland* (1865).

Mad as a March hare, As : March is the
rutting season among hares which are
esp. wild then. [Heywood, *Proverbes*
(1546)] The phrase ' as brainless as a
March hare ' is found in *Blowbol's Test*
(15th cent.), ' as merry as a March
hare ' in Skelton, *Magnificance* (1526),
and as ' the mad March hare ' in
Skelton, *Replycation Against Certayne
Yong Scolers* (1520).

Mad Parliament, The : *see* Parliament.

Mad Poet, The : Nathaniel Lee (c.
1653-92), who wrote some of his best
poetry while confined in a lunatic
asylum.

Madame Veto : Marie Antoinette, who was believed to be largely responsible for her husband, Louis XVI's, veto of the acts of the Legislative Assembly.

Made man, A : a man whose good fortune is assured. [Marlowe, *Doctor Faustus*, IV, v (1604)]

Madman, Macedonia's : Alexander the Great (356–323 B.C.).

Madman of the North, The : Charles XII of Sweden (1682–1718).

Mæander : *see* Meander.

Maecenas, A : a generous patron of art or letters. After Gaius Cilnus Maecenas (c. 73–8 B.C.), Rom. statesman and patron of letters.

Maecenas, The last English : Samuel Rogers (1763–1855), poet and banker.

Maeonian Swan, The : Homer, after Maeonia (now Smyrna), one of the cities that claimed to be his birthplace.

Maffick, To ; A mafficker : to hold a riotous, unruly celebration of a victory or other joyful event. One who mafficks. From Mafeking, in South Africa, whose relief in the S. African War led to unruly rejoicings in the streets of London (1900). The word was coined by the *Pall Mall Gazette* (May 21st, 1900).

Mag to bless oneself with, Not a : penniless. Slang, mag, a halfpenny.

Magdalen ; Magdalene, A : a repentant prostitute. After Mary Magdalene or of Magdala. [*Matthew*, xxvii, 56, etc]

Magdalen Hospital, A : a place of detention for fallen women. *See* Magdalen.

Maggot bites, When the : when a strange idea seizes one. The idea was invented by Swift in *The Mechanical Operation of the Spirit.*

Magician, The Great : Sir Walter Scott (1771–1832). So-called by Christopher North on account of the wonderful attraction of his writings.

Magician of the North, The : (1) Johann Georg Hamann (1730–88), Germ. philosopher and theologian, so-called by himself ; (2) Sir Walter Scott. *See* Magician, The Great.

Magna Carta of .. The : the charter of freedom of .. After Magna Charta (1215), the charter of the liberties of England

Magnificat at Matins, To sing the : to act at the wrong time. The Magnificat (*Luke* i, 46–55) is sung at Evensong.

Magnum opus, A (*Lat.*, a great work) : a masterpiece. [Jonathan Swift, *Tale of a Tub* (1704)]

Magog : *see* Gog.

Mahogany, The : a dining-table. From the material of which it is generally constructed. [Dickens, *Master Humphrey's Clock* (1838–42)]

Mahomet and the mountain : after the story told by Francis Bacon in his *Essay : Of Boldness* (1625). ' Mahomet made the people believe that he would call a hill to him, and from the top of it offer up his prayers for the observers of his law. The people assembled. Mahomet called the hill to come to him, again and again ; and when the hill stood still he was never a whit abashed, but said, " If the hill will not come to Mahomet, Mahomet will go to the hill." '

Mahomet's coffin : according to legend, hangs midway between heaven and earth.

Mahomet's pigeon : trained to eat out of Mahomet's ear, believed by his followers to be a messenger from God.

Mahomet's tomb : *see* Mahomet's coffin.

Maia's son : the god, Hermes.

Maid of all work, A : a general servant, generally of a low class.

Maid of Norway, The : Margaret (1283–90), Queen of Scotland, who came from Norway.

Maid of Orleans, The : Joan of Arc (1412–31), who led the Fr. forces in the relief of Orleans.

Maid of Saragossa : Augustina Zaragossa, who shared in the defence of Saragossa against the French in 1808–9.

Maiden, The : (1) a sort of guillotine introduced into Scotland by the Regent, James Douglas, Earl of Morton, who was himself beheaded by it in 1581 ; (2) an instrument of torture in the shape of a woman which opened and enclosing the victim within impaled him on spikes.

Maiden : of a fortress that has never been taken by the enemy.

Maiden Assize, A : an assize at which there are no prisoners to be tried.

Maiden King, The : Malcolm IV of Scotland (1141–65). On account of his gentle disposition.

Maiden over, A : (cricket term) an over in which no runs are scored. [Florio, *Marcio* (1598)]

Maiden Queen, The : Elizabeth of England (1533-1603), who never married.

Maiden Speech, A : the first speech delivered by a Member in Parliament. [*Annual Register* for 1794]

Maiden sword, A : a sword that has never been used in warfare.

Maiden Town, The : Edinburgh, never captured after a siege. Also from the tradition that the maiden daughters of a Pictish king took refuge there.

Mailed Fist, The : military power. From a phrase used by the Emp. William II of Germany in 1897 in connection with Chinese affairs.

Main, The : the Spanish Main ; the mainland of S. America between the Orinoco and the Isthmus of Panama ; also the neighbouring sea, the Caribbean.

Main chance, The : the most probable line to success. Metaphor drawn from the game of hazard. *See also* Chance.

Main of cocks, A : a cock-fight. From the obsolete sense of main as match.

Maine Law : a law prohibiting the sale of intoxicants, adopted by the State of Maine, U.S.A., in 1851. The earliest alcohol prohibitory law in the U.S.

Maires du Palais : the prime ministers. Lit., Mayors of the Palace, of the later Merovingian kings of France, who were the *de facto* rulers and ultimately in the person of Charles Martel obtained the throne.

Majority, To join the : to die. In *Anthol. Palat.*, 11, 42, appears the phrase εὐτ᾽ ἂν ἵκηαι ἐς πλεόνων and in Plautus, *Trin*, II, ii, 14, ‘ penetrare ad plures,’ in the same sense. The Roman Legionaries in Britain are said to have employed the phrase ‘ abierunt ad multos.’ It appears first in Eng. literature in Young, *Revenge*, IV, 1 (1721).

Make one's bread, To : to earn one's living.

Make bricks without straw, To : to perform one's task under very great difficulties. [*Exodus*, v, 7]

Make clothes for fishes, To : to act foolishly and to no purpose. From an ancient Grk. proverb.

Make both ends meet, To : *see* Ends.

Make a person's hair curl, To : to astonish a person.

Make mountains out of molehills, To : to exaggerate difficulties.

Make much of .. To : to show great consideration for .. [*Paston Letters*, No. 465 (1463)]

Make ropes of sand, To : to act to no purpose. From an ancient Grk. proverb.

Make it up, To : to become friendly again. [Sheridan, *The Rivals*, I, ii (1775)]

Make a virtue of a necessity, To : [Chaucer, *Knight's Tale*, l. 3044 (14th cent.) ; Shakespeare, *Two Gentlemen of Verona* (1590) ; Dryden, *Palamon and Arcite* (1699)]

Make one's way in the world, To : to succeed.

Malade imaginaire, A (*Fr.*) : a person who imagines himself to be ill. From the title of one of Molière's comedies.

Malaprop, Mrs. ; Malapropism : a person who misuses words absurdly ; a ridiculous misuse of words. After Mrs. Malaprop a character in Sheridan, *The Rivals* (1775).

Malice prepense : premeditated malice.

Malignants : a name given to the Cavaliers by the Puritans during the Commonwealth.

Mall of Italy, The : Hannibal (247–183 B.C.).

Mall supper, A : a harvest feast. Ang.-Sax., *moel*, a feast.

Malt above the meal, With the : tipsy. [Heywood, *Proverbes* (1546)]

Maltese Cross, A : *see* Cross.

Malthusian : relating to the school of thought which advocates small families. After Thomas Robert Malthus (1766–1834), Eng. political economist.

Mamamouchi, A : a buffoon ; a mock title of consequence. After a mock-Turkish title conferred in Molière, *Le Bourgeois Gentilhomme*.

Mamelukes, The : a military class forming part of the Turk. army in Egypt until they were massacred by Mehemet Ali in 1811. Previously from 1250 to 1517 they formed the ruling class, supplying the dynasty, in Egypt. The Mamelukes were descended from captives, taken by Genghis Khan in the middle of the 13th cent. and sold by him as slaves in Egypt.

Mammon : the personification of worldliness and cupidity. From Mammon, the personification of riches, mentioned in *Matthew* and *Luke*. Syriac, *mamona*, riches.

Mammon of Unrighteousness : money. [*Luke*, xvi, 9]

Man of Belial, A : an evil man. [II *Samuel*, xvi, 7]

Man in black, A : a clergyman. From the colour of his clothing.

Man of blood, A : (1) a man guilty of bloodshed; (2) David; [II *Samuel*, xvi, 7] (3) Charles I, so-called by the Puritans on account of the Civil War.

Man of blood and iron, The : *see* Blood and iron.

Man in blue, The : *see* Blue.

Man in buckram, The : an imaginary person. [Shakespeare, 1 *Henry IV*, II, iv (1596-7), for 'four rogues in buckram' invented by Falstaff.]

Man of colour, A : *see* Colour.

Man of December, The : Napoleon III. In allusion to his *coup d'état* of December, 1851. He was also elected President of the Fr. Republic in December, 1848, and was made Emperor in December, 1852.

Man of Destiny, The : Napoleon I, who considered himself the instrument of destiny.

Man Friday, A : *see* Friday.

Man of Gath, A : an evil-doer; a man of violence. From Gath, one of the Philistine cities.

Man of iron, A : *see* Iron.

Man in the iron mask, The : *see* Iron mask.

Man Jack, Every : every individual. From Jack, the generic term for an ordinary man.

Man of Kent, A : *see* Kent, Men of.

Man, The late : Charles I of England. So-called by the Eng. Puritans after his execution.

Man of letters, A : an author, esp. one who devotes himself to literature.

Man of .. To make a : to put a male person on the road to success. [Greene, *Liberality and Prodigality*, III, ii (1602)]

Man of mettle, A : a man of courage. [*Life and Death of Captain Thomas Stukeley*, ll. 165-6 (1605)]

Man in the moon, The : (1) a fancied resemblance to a man's face to be seen at times in the moon; (2) an imaginary personage, esp. one who provides funds at election times. [Lilly, *Endimion, the Man in the Moone :* Prologue (1591)]

Man of motley, A : *see* Motley.

Man of parts, A : a man of capacity. [Farquhar, *The Stage-coach* (1704)]

Man of the People, The : Charles James Fox (1749-1806), Eng. statesman.

Man, To play the : to possess and display manly qualities. [Udall, *Ralph Roister Doister*, IV, vii, 7 (1550)]

Man of remnants, A : a tailor.

Man of Rome, The : the Pope.

Man of Ross, The : John Kyrle (1637-1724), Eng. philanthropist, immortalized by Pope in his *Moral Essays*, Ep. III (1732-5).

Man of salt, A : a man who cries salt tears. [Shakespeare, *King Lear*, IV, vi (1605-6)]

Man of Sedan, The : Napoleon III, who surrendered to the Germans at Sedan in 1870. So-called by Gambetta.

Man of silence, The : Napoleon III.

Man of Sin, The : [II *Thessalonians*, ii, 3] (1) according to the Roman Catholics, Anti-Christ; (2) according to the Puritans, the Pope; (3) according to the Fifth Monarchy Men, Oliver Cromwell; (4) the devil.

Man of straw, A : a person of neither means nor position who has nothing to lose and is therefore not worth proceeding against in the civil courts. A man of straw is usually used as a cover in proceedings of doubtful legality to shield the real author of the proceedings. There used to be a class of persons who attended the Law Courts, when at Westminster, and were prepared to give evidence in any cause to any effect for a consideration. To indicate their profession they displayed wisps of straw in their shoes. [*Return from Parnassus*, I, i, 231 (1599); Wycherley, *Country Life*, IV, iii (1675)]

Man in the street, The : the average man who has no source of information regarding current events beyond the newspapers, as compared with the man in the club. [Macaulay, *Essay on Southey's Colloquies on Society* (Jan. 1830); *The Greville Memoirs* (March 22nd, 1831)]

Man of the Third Republic, The : Napoleon III. According to Leon Gambetta.

Man about town, A : a man of pleasure. [17th cent.]

Man of valour, A mighty : a great soldier. A biblical term applied to successful soldiers. [*Judges*, vi, 12, etc.]

Man of wax, A : a model man, as if fashioned in wax. [Shakespeare, *Romeo and Juliet*, I, iii (1591-3)]

Man of whipcord, A : a coachman.

Man of the woods, A : a gorilla.

Man of his word, A : a person who is to be trusted, *i.e.*, who keeps his word. [*Wily Beguiled*, l. 1027 (1606)]

Man of the world, A : (1) a man who is expert in worldly affairs ; (2) an irreligious man.

Manana (*Span.*, to-morrow) : the crystallization of the precept, ' Never do to-day what you can manage to postpone until to-morrow.'

Manchester of America, The : Lowell, Mass. On account of its cotton mills.

Manchester of Belgium, The : Ghent.

Manchester goods : cotton fabrics. After Manchester, the centre of the Eng. cotton industry.

Manchester of Japan, The : Osaka.

Manchester line, In the : in the soft goods business. After Manchester, the centre of the cotton trade.

Manchester Martyrs, The : Allen, Larkin, and O'Brien, who were executed in 1867 for the murder of a policeman at Manchester while attempting the rescue of Fenian prisoners.

Manchester Massacre, The : a fatal riot in St. Peter's Fields, near Manchester, in 1819, when the military attempted to arrest some of the speakers at a Reform meeting. Also known as Peterloo, in travesty of the Battle of Waterloo.

Manchester of Prussia, The : Elberfeld.

Manchester poet, The : Charles Swain (1801–74).

Manchester School, The : the political school of Laissez Faire (*q.v.*), with headquarters in Manchester, which was instrumental in securing the adoption of Free Trade by Britain. The term is said to have been coined by Benjamin Disraeli.

Manchettes de Buffon, Les : an ornate literary style. In allusion to the lace ruffles habitually worn by the Fr. naturalist and philosopher, George, Ct. de Buffon (1707–88). Fr., *manchette*, ruffle.

Mandarin, To kill one's : to desire the death of another person. In allusion to the question put by Jean Jacques Rousseau (1712–78) whether if one had the power of merely by an effort of will and without any risk of detection of killing an unknown Chinese mandarin with great advantage to oneself, one would do so.

Mandeville, A : one who exaggerates grossly. After Sir John Mandeville (1300–72), a traveller of questionable veracity.

Mandrabul's offering, Like : Mandrabul, having discovered a gold mine, made an annual thank-offering to Juno, the value of which became every year less and after a few years ceased altogether.

Mandrake, To have eaten the : to be very indolent. In allusion to the supposed stupefying qualities of the mandrake.

Manes, To appease a person's : to act after a person's death in the manner he would have wished if he had still been living. Among the Romans the manes was the spirit of the departed.

Manlian Orders : excessive severity. After the capital punishment inflicted by Manlius Torquatus (fl. 352 B.C.), the Rom. consul, on his son for an offence that could almost be justified.

Manoa : the fabled capital of El Dorado (*q.v.*), a city whose streets were paved with gold.

Mantalini, A : a lazy, elegant man who allows his wife to support him. From a character in Dickens, *Nicholas Nickleby* (1838). Also a man-milliner ; same derivation.

Mantle, To assume the : *see* Assume.

Mantuan Swan (Swain) (Bard), The : Virgil, a native of Mantua.

Marah (*Heb.*, bitter) : bitterness. From a bitter spring in the Peninsula of Sinai.

Marah, Waters of : *see* Marah.

Maranatha : a curse. From anathema maranatha in I *Cor.*, xvi, 22 (Syriac).

Maranno, A : *see* Marranos.

March : the third month of the year. After Mars, the god of war.

March ale (beer) : a kind of ale, brewed as a rule in the month of March, which takes two years to mature.

March of events, The : the succession of events.

March hare, As mad as a : *see* Mad.

March on .. To steal a : to get an advantage of stealthily.

March with the times, To : to show adaptability to circumstances as they develop.

Marchington wake-cake, As short as : (used of a woman's temper) from the famous short cake made at Marchington, Staffordshire. A wake-cake is a cake connected with a local festival.

Mardi Gras (*Fr.*, Fat Tuesday) : Shrove Tuesday.

Mare clausum (*Lat.*, a closed sea) : a sea, such as the Black Sea, under the practical jurisdiction of one or a small number of powers. The opposite of mare liberum, a free or open sea.

Mare or lose the halter, To win the : to play for a great prize or an overwhelming loss.

Mare's nest, A : an imaginary discovery that brings ridicule on the finder, as would that of the nest of a mare. [Beaumont and Fletcher, *Bonduca*, V, ii (1647)]

Mareotic luxury : extreme luxury. In allusion to the white grapes, the favourite of Cleopatra, produced on the Arva Mareotica or shores of Lake Moeris.

Margarine substitute, A : an imitation, just as margarine is imitation butter.

Mariage de convenance, A (*Fr.*, a marriage of convenience) : a marriage arising out of avarice or ambition instead of love. [Thackeray, *Newcomes*, I (1854)]

Marine, The Female : Hannah Snell (1723–92) of Worcester, who fought in the attack on Pondicherry.

Marines, To tell to the : of a story or statement that does not carry conviction. From the reputation for gullability that the marines obtained among seamen.

Marionette, A : a puppet, acting on the motion of another; a figure in a puppet show. Lit., Little Mary, in allusion to the small figures of the Virgin Mary in It. puppet shows.

Mark, Beside (Wide of) the : out of the direct line. A metaphor drawn from shooting. [Stafford, *Pacata Hibernia*, I, v, 71 (1633)]

Mark of the Beast, The : a denunciation, esp. as unorthodox. [*Revelations*, xvi, 2]

Mark, To make one's : to attain success in life. To make ' one's mark ' on the page of history.

Mark ! Save the : an ironical exclamation. Orig. an archery term. [Shakespeare, 1 *Henry IV*, I, iii, 56 (1597)]

Mark Tapley, A : a person who retains his good humour in the most adverse circumstances. From a character in Dickens, *Martin Chuzzlewit* (1843).

Mark time, To : to take no action pending a favourable opportunity. Military drill metaphor.

Mark, Up to the : in average good health or spirits.

Marlin Tower, As high as : the tower of the Church of St. Mary Magdalen at Taunton.

Maroon, To : to put ashore on a desert island. From Maroons (*q.v.*), slaves who fled from civilization.

Maroons : fugitive slaves in the West Indies and South America, who became outlaws. After the Morony River in

Guiana in the neighbourhood of which large numbers of these slaves took refuge.

Marplot, A : a person who interferes harmfully in an undertaking. After a character in Mrs. Centlivre, *Busie Body* (1709).

Marquis, The Great : *see* Great Marquis.

Marranos (*Span.*, accursed ; from Maranatha) : Span. and Portuguese Jews, nominally Christians, but secretly obeying Jewish customs so far as they could. Their conversion, or that of their ancestors, to Christianity, was directly or indirectly forced.

Marriage of the Adriatic, The : *see* Adriatic.

Marriage of convenience, A : *see* Mariage de convenance.

Marriage à la mode (*Fr.*, marriage in accordance with fashion) : a marriage arranged entirely in accordance with the dictates of fashion. *See* Hogarth's painting of this title (1743).

Marrow Controversy, The : the struggle in Scotland between Puritanism and Presbyterianism. In allusion to *The Marrow of Modern Divinity* which was condemned by the General Assembly in 1720.

Marrow-bones, On one's : on one's knees. [More, *Confutacyon of Tyndale's Answere* (1532)]

Marry, Punch's advice to those about to : *see* Punch's.

Mars of Portugal, The : Alfonso de Albuquerque (1452–1515), Viceroy of India. After Mars, the Roman god of war.

Mars Year, The : 1715, that of the first Jacobite invasion.

Marseillaise, The : the song of the French Revolution. After Marseilles, whose inhabitants marching on Paris first sang it.

Marsh City, The : Petrograd, which is built on low-lying land intersected by streams of water and always liable to be flooded.

Marshal Forwards : *see* Forwards.

Martin of Cambray, Girt like : absurdly clad. In allusion to the costume of the figure of Martin in the great clock of Cambray.

Martin chain, A : an imitation gold chain. From St. Martin-le-Grand, London, where artificial jewellery was formerly made.

Martin drunk : a degree of drunkenness. After Martin, the monkey, in the fable of *Reynard the Fox*; or from the coincidence of St. Martin's Day (11th November) and the Festival of Bacchus.

Martin Marprelate : the pseudonym of a Puritan pamphleteer or body of pamphleteers at the end of the 16th cent.

Martin's summer, St. : fine weather about St. Martin's Day (Nov. 11th).

Martinet, A : a strict disciplinarian. After the Marquis de Martinet, an officer in the army of Louis XIV (d. 1672).

Martinmas : The Feast of St. Martin, Nov. 11th.

Martinmas beef : the meat of an ox salted at Martinmas, or the Feast of St. Martin (Nov. 11th).

Martyr King, The : Charles I of England who was executed by his subjects.

Martyr to Science, A : a person who dies or suffers in the cause of science. Claude Louis, Count Berthollet (1748–1822), ' The Martyr to Science,' died of an experiment on himself of the effect of carbolic acid on the human frame.

Marvellous Boy, The : Thomas Chatterton (1752–70), Eng. poet and literary forger.

Mary Ambree, A : *see* Ambree.

Mary Anne, A : a guillotine. *See* Mary Anne Association.

Mary Anne Association, A : a secret republican association in France in the time of Henri IV. Revaillac was inspired to assassinate the king by reading Mariana, *De Rege et Regio Institutione*.

Mary, Bloody : *see* Bloody.

Mary, Little : *see* Little Mary.

Mary-mas : the 25th of March ; Lady Day ; the Feast of the Annunciation of the Virgin Mary.

Mascot(te), A : a charm ; a source of good fortune. After E. Audran's opera, *La Mascotte* (1883). Previously the word was dialect in Provence and Gascony. It is supposed to be derived from *masqué*, masked or concealed, and to be equivalent to ' born with a caul,' which is popularly believed to be lucky.

Mask, To throw off the : to disclose one's intentions.

Mask, To wear a : to conceal one's motives.

Masochism : the tendency to carry pleasure so far that it becomes pain, a fascination thus being created for

inflicting pain on oneself. From Leopold von Sacher-Masoch (1836–95), Austrian-Germ. novelist, who depicted this form of cruelty.

Mason and Dixon's Line : the boundary between Maryland and Pennsylvania which became later the boundary between the slave and the free states, drawn in 1763–7 by Charles Mason and Jeremiah Dixon.

Massacre of the Innocents, The : the announcement by the Leader of the House of Commons towards the end of a session of the measures with which it is not proposed to proceed further. The phrase was first so applied in 1859.

Masses and Classes : *see* Classes.

Mast, To serve before the : to be a common sailor whose quarters are in the forepart of the vessel, before the mast.

Master Leonard : a chief of the demons.

Master of Love, The : Ovid (B.C. 43–A.D. 17). So-called by R. Bentley.

Master of the Mint, The : (pun) a gardener.

Master of Prussia, The : the Grand-Master of the Teutonic Order.

Master of the Rolls, The : (pun) a baker. [H. Peacham, *Worth of a Penny* (1641)]

Master of the Sentences, The : Peter Lombard (c. 1100–64), It. schoolman and bishop of Paris. In allusion to his work, *The Four Books of Sentences*.

Master of Stories, The : Petrus Comestor (d. 1198). From his work, *Historia Scholastica*.

Master of the Temple, The : the Grand-Master of the Knights Templar ; the clergyman attached to the Temple Church, London.

Master of those who knew, The : Aristotle (384–322 B.C.), the most famous of Grk. philosophers, according to Dante.

Mater Dolorosa (*Lat.*, sorrowing mother) : a name for the Virgin Mary.

Mathurin, The malady of St. : stupidity. After St. Mathurin, the patron saint of idiots.

Maudlin : silly through intoxication. After Mary Magdalene (pronounced Maudlen), who is depicted by painters with her eyes red with weeping.

Maunds, Royal : a royal charity, bestowed on Maundy Thursday. From maund, a basket.

Maundy, To make one's : to distribute one's charity as a duty.

Maundy money : money given by the reigning sovereign to the poor on

Maundy Thursday, the day before Good Friday. From *mandatum novum* (*John*, xiii, 34), the new commandment given by Christ when washing the feet of the disciples. Also from the *maund* (Ang.-Sax.), basket, in which the alms were carried.

Maundy Thursday : *see* Maundy money.

Mausoleum, A : a magnificent tomb. After that of Mausolus, King of Caria, who died 353 B.C.

Mauvais quart d'heure, Un (*Fr.*, a bad quarter of an hour) : an unpleasant interview of not very long duration. The phrase is attributed to Louis XIII of France in reference to the execution of the Marquis de Cinq-Mars, formerly a favourite of the King.

Mauvais sujet, Un (*Fr.*, a bad subject) : an undesirable person.

Mauvaise honte (*Fr.*, false shame) : [Lord Chesterfield, *Letters*, I, No. 79 (1746)]

May : the fifth month of the year. After Maia, the mother of Mercury, whose festival fell on the first day of the month.

May Bishop : (in derision) a titular bishop. In allusion to the May Day masquerades.

May Day : May 1st. Form. a people's festival of spring, now a red-letter day of Labour.

May and December : a young wife and an old husband. Chaucer has a poem on this theme entitled *January and May*. [Sir W. Raleigh, *Shepherd, What Is Love?* (1600)]

May Hill, To have climbed : to have passed the most dangerous period of the year.

May Meetings : meetings of religious societies held in London in or about the month of May every year. Hence a meeting of a religious organization.

May, Queen (Lady) of the : a girl treated as Queen in the May games.

May-game of .. To make a : to make a laughing-stock of .. In allusion to the merry-making and foolery of which the May games consisted.

Mayor of Banbury, As wise as the : *see* Wise.

Mayor of the Palace : *see* Maires du Palais.

Mazikeen ass, To swell out like the : in allusion to the story of an ass in a medieval Jewish legend.

Meadow, To pave the : *see* Pave.

Meal or malt, To pay in : to pay directly or indirectly ; in one way or another.

Meal Monday : a holiday at Scottish Universities. Orig. instituted to enable students to go home and fetch sufficient meal to last until the end of the session.

Meal of salt, A : a meal so slight as to be practically no meal at all.

Mean business, To : to engage oneself seriously in an affair.

Mean Whites, The : the poorer class of white men in the southern states of the Amer. Union and in South Africa.

Meander, To : to wander along leisurely, turning and twisting at frequent intervals. After the Maeander, a proverbially crooked river in Phrygia.

Measure other people's corn by one's own bushel, To : to judge other people by one's own standard.

Measure of one's foot, To take the : to guess at a person's character. An allusion to ' Ex pede Herculem ' (*q.v.*).

Measure one's length, To : to fall headlong on the ground. [Shakespeare, *Midsummer Night's Dream*, III, ii, 429 (1590)]

Measure swords, To : to enter into a contest with. Lit., the preparatory step in a duel. [Shakespeare, *As You Like It*, V, iv (1600)]

Measure the wind, To : *see* Wind.

Meat from the graves, To carry off : to be extremely poor, so poor as to steal the remnants of the feasts celebrated by the Grks. and Romans in honour of the dead, which remnants used to be left to regale the ghosts of the departed.

Mecca, A : the object of one's pious exertions. From Mecca in Arabia, the Holy City of the Moslems.

Meccas of the mind : the object to which one's most distant hopes are directed. From Mecca, the Holy City of Islam. [Fitz-Greene Halleck, *Burns* (1827)]

Medea's Kettle (Cauldron) : in which the old were boiled again into youth. Medea was a mythological sorceress.

Medes and Persians, Laws of the : laws that cannot be repealed or modified. [*Daniel*, vi, 12]

Medean : unchanging. In allusion to the laws of the Medes which were said not to be liable to modification.

Median Stone, The : which cured blindness.

Mediatized Princes : rulers of the smaller Germ. states who had been deprived of their sovereign rights, when their dominions were merged with those of more important neighbours.

Media, A via (*Lat.*) : a middle course.

Medicinal days : the sixth, eighth and other days of the progress of a disease on which, according to Hippocrates, no crisis can occur and medicine can be taken with safety.

Medicine, The Father of : *see* Father.

Medieval Haw and Heart, The : scholasticism and mysticism, which existed in the Middle Ages, side by side, distinct but yet not hostile.

Mediterranean, The Key of the : Gibraltar, which commands the entrance to the Sea.

Meek as a meacock, As : a ' meacock ' is a 16th cent. word, denoting an effeminate person. [R. B., *Appius and Virginia*, l. 162 (1563)]

Meek as Moses, As : very patient and mild-mannered. In allusion to the proverbial character of the Hebrew patriarch, Moses.

Meet a difficulty (troubles) halfway, To : to worry over a trouble in advance of its arrival.

Meg of Westminster, As long as : exceptionally tall. Meg of Westminster was a famous virago of the 16th cent., to whom allusion is frequently made in Elizabethan literature. In 1582 her *Life* was published as a penny storybook ; in 1594 *Long Meg of Westminster* was first performed. [Fuller, *Worthies*, II, 413 (1662)]

Megarian, As wise as a : stupid. In allusion to the Megarians, a people of ancient Greece who were proverbial for their stupidity.

Meissonier-like exactness : after Jean Louis Ernest Meissonier (1815–91), Fr. painter.

Meistersingers : wandering German minstrels of the 14th to 16th cents.

Melancholy as Fleet Street in the Long Vacation, As : in allusion to the legal vacation when the chambers near Fleet Street are unoccupied. [Dekker, *Northward Ho.* (1607)]

Melancholy as a hare, As : according to the medieval belief that the flesh of the hare induced melancholy. [Shakespeare, 1 *Henry IV*, I, ii (1596–7)]

Melancholy Jacques : Jean Jacques Rousseau (1712–78). After a character in Shakespeare, *As You Like It* (1600).

Melancholy as the man in the moon, As : melancholy in the former sense of mad. In allusion to the supposed influence of the moon over lunatics. [1609]

Melibean ; Meliboean : of verse (1) pastoral ; (2) alternately responsive. After a personage who sings the responses in Virgil's first *Eclogue*.

Meliboean dye : a purple dye. After the Syrian island of Meliboea, whence it was obtained.

Mell supper, A : a harvest supper.

Mellifluous Doctor, The : St. Bernard of Clairvaux (1091–1153).

Melting Pot, The : the United States, in which immigrants from all nations and races are fused into one new nation. First applied in this sense by Israel Zangwill, in the title of one of his plays (1908).

Melting tribe, The : poets. [*The Spectator*, No. 377 (1712)]

Memento mori (*Lat.*, remember to die) : a warning or reminder of death. [Nashe, *Summer's Last Will* (1592)]

Memnonian : giving forth music when touched by the dawn. After the alleged property of a statue believed to be that of Memnon at Thebes in Egypt.

Memory, The Bard of : Samuel Rogers (1762–1855), who wrote *The Pleasures of Memory* (1792).

Men of Lawn : bishops of the Church of England. In allusion to their official attire.

Men of La Vieille Roche : *see* Roche.

Men of light and leading : the leaders of opinion. [Burke, *Reflections on the Revolution in France*, III, 331 (1790)]

Mene Tekel : a warning of impending doom. From the words mysteriously written on the wall of Baalshazzar's palace. [*Daniel*, v, 25, 26]

Menechmians : two or more people very similar to one another in appearance. After the Menœchmi of Plautus.

Mentor, A : a wise and faithful councillor. From the name of the councillor of Telemachus and friend of Ulysses.

Mephistophelian : fiendish ; crafty. After Mephistopheles, one of the names of Satan.

Merchant of eel skins, To become a : to be drowned. [Ascham, *Toxophilus*, Bk. II (1545)]

Merchant Venturers (Adventurers) : a guild of merchants of Brabant origin who were granted privileges in England by Henry VII and Elizabeth.

Merciless Parliament, The : *see* Parliament, The Marvellous.

Mercurial : volatile ; changeable ; like the god Mercury, the messenger of the gods.

Mercury fig, A : a first fruit or first production. The first fig gathered from a fig tree was devoted by the Romans to Mercury.

Mercutio of Actors, The : William Thomas Lewis (1748–1811). After a character in Shakespeare, *Romeo and Juliet* (1591).

Merlin, The English : William Lilly (1602–81), the astrologer who assumed the name of ' Merlinus Anglicus.' After Merlin, the legendary Welsh bard and musician.

Merops, A son of : a conceited individual whose schemes end in failure. From Phaeton, the son of Merops, who attempting to drive the car of Phoebus almost set the world on fire.

Meroz, Curse of : [*Judges*, v, 23]

Merrie (Merry) England : properly, Illustrious England. Ang.-Sax., *moera*, famous.

Merry Andrew, A : *see* Andrew.

Merry as a cricket, As : the cricket, according to W. Jardine (Naturalist's Library), brings good luck. [Heywood *Proverbes* (1546) ; G. Harvey, *New Letter of Notable Contents* (1593)]

Merry Dancers, The : the Northern Lights. In allusion to their apparent waving motion.

Merry as the day is long, As : [Shakespeare, *King John*, IV, i, 18 (1595)]

Merry as a grasshopper, As : in allusion to the agility of grasshoppers.

Merry as a Greek, As : *see* Greek.

Merry Greek, A : a drunkard. *See* Greek, As merry as a *and* Grig, As merry as a. [Udall, *Ralph Roister Doister* (1550); Shakespeare, *Troilus and Cressida*, I, ii (1606) ; Ben Jonson, *New Inn*, II, ii (1630)]

Merry as a grig, As : *see* Grig.

Merry as maids, As : lighthearted. [Melbancke, *Philotimus*, 467 (1583)]

Merry as a marriage-bell, As : [Byron, *Childe Harold*, III, 21 (1816)]

Merry Monarch, The : Charles II of England. Famous for his wit and good humour.

Merry as a pie, As : a pie is a magpie. [Chaucer, *Shipm. Tale*, 209 (14th cent.) ; Heywood, *Proverbes* (1546)]

Merry as a popinjay, As : in allusion to the jay, decked with many colours, which was used as a target in archery, or to ' Captain Popinjay ' or ' The Captain of the Popinjay,' the victor in the archery contests. [Chaucer, *Shipmaster's Tale* (14th cent.)]

Mersenne, The English : John Collins (1625–83), mathematician. Marin Mersenne (1588–1648) was a Fr. mathematician, scholar and miscellaneous writer.

Mervousness : nervousness regarding Russian threats against the Indian Empire, especially about the year 1883, when the Russians occupied Merv in Central Asia. Word coined by the 8th Duke of Argyll (1823–1900).

Mesmerize, To ; Mesmerism : to hypnotize ; hypnotism. After Friedrich Anthony Mesmer (1733–1815), a Germ. physician.

Mesopotamia ring, The true : something high-sounding and pleasing but yet indefinite. In allusion to the proverbial old lady who told her pastor that ' she found great support in that comfortable [but to her vague] word Mesopotamia.'

Mess of pottage, To sell one's birthright for a : to exchange something of permanent value for a temporary pleasure. From the transaction between Esau and Jacob recorded in *Genesis*, xxv.

Messalina of Germany, The : Barbara of Cilley, wife of the Emperor Sigismund (15th cent.). Valeria Messalina, wife of the Emperor Claudius (10 B.C.–54 A.D.), was notorious on account of her vices.

Messalina, The Modern : Catherine II of Russia (1729–1796). On account of her cruelty and vice.

Metaphysical School of Poets, The : Donne, Cowley and others. So-called by Dr. Johnson on account of their fantastic language and literary style.

Metheglyn, As sweet as : metheglyn is a beer made of honey, brewed in Wales and the neighbouring counties. [Palsgrave's Trans. of W. Graphæus, *Acolastus*, R 4 (1540)]

Method in one's madness : a reason for apparently strange behaviour. [Shakespeare, *Hamlet*, II, ii (1602–3)]

Methodists : members of the religious sect founded by John Wesley (1738). In allusion to the methodical manner in which they observed their principles. The name was first applied by a student of Christ Church, Oxford.

Methuen Treaty, The : a commercial treaty between England and Portugal negotiated in 1703 by Paul Methuen.

Methuselah, A : a person of great age. After the longest-lived personage mentioned in the Bible, who is reputed to have lived 969 years.

Metonic Cycle, The : a lunar period of nineteen years. Discovered by Meton in 432 B.C.

Metropolis of Humidity, The : the brain. [Sir Thos. Browne, *Hydrotaphia*, III (1658)]

Meum and Tuum (*Lat.*, mine and thine) : an expression of the rights of property. [Bacon, *Henry VII* (1622)]

Micawber, A : an impecunious, well-intentioned individual, always waiting ' for something to turn up.' After a character in Dickens, *David Copperfield* (1849).

Michael (Michel) : the Germ. peasant.

Michael Angelo of Battle Scenes, The : Michael Angelo Cerquozzi (1600–60), It. painter of battle scenes. Michael Angelo Buonarotti (1474–1564) was one of the greatest of It. artists.

Michael Angelo of France, The : Jean Cousin (1500–90).

Michael Angelo of Music, The : Johann Christoph von Gluck (1714–87), Germ. musical composer.

Michael Angelo of Sculptors, The : (1) Pierre Puget (1623–94), Fr. sculptor ; (2) Réné Michael Slodtz (1705–64), Fr. sculptor.

Michaelmas Day : 29th Sept., the festival of St. Michael and All Angels.

Michel : *see* Michael.

Microcosm, The : man as the epitome of the universe.

Midas, A ; Midas-like : from the legend of Midas, King of Phrygia, to whom was given the supposed boon of turning to gold everything he touched. He was also endowed with ass's ears by Apollo for failure to appreciate his music.

Midas, The touch of : the touch which turns everything to gold. From the gift of Dionysus to Midas, a legendary king of Phrygia. *See* Midas.

Midas-eared : without discrimination or judgment. *See* Midas.

Middle Ages, The : the period of chronology ranging roughly from the fall of the Rom. Empire in 476 to the capture of Constantinople by the Turks in 1453. The earlier portion of the period until about the year 1200 is known as the Dark Ages (*q.v.*).

Middle Class, The : *see* Class.

Middle Kingdom, The : China. Either in allusion to the belief of the Chinese that their country is situated in the middle of the world, or from the situation of the Chinese royal domains in feudal times in the midst of the other states of the Empire.

Middle States, The : New York, New Jersey, Pennsylvania, Delaware, and (sometimes) Maryland, which lie between the New England states and the Southern States.

Middle Western States, The : West Virginia, Kentucky, Tenessee, Missouri, Kansas and Arkansas.

Midnight Appointments : (Amer. politics) appointments made by an administration at the end of its term of office.

Midnight oil, To burn the : to work late at night. [First half of the 17th cent.]

Midnight oil, To smell of the : of literary work, written obviously with great pains. *See* Midnight oil, To burn the.

Midnight Sun, The : the sun visible throughout the night during a portion of the summer in the Arctic regions.

Midsummer Ale : a festival held at Midsummer.

Midsummer madness : extreme madness. Apparently from the rabies supposed to be esp. prevalent about midsummer. [Shakespeare, *Midsummer Night's Dream*, III, iv (1590–1)]

Midsummer, To have but a mile to : to be slightly out of one's mind. *See* Midsummer madness.

Midsummer moon madness : *see* Midsummer madness. The Midsummer moon is the lunar month in which Midsummer Day falls.

Midwife of men's thoughts, The : (1) Socrates (469–399 B.C.), so-called by himself ; (2) Queen Mab of the fairies.

Midwife of men's thoughts, To play the : to edit a book which has not previously been published. [Ed. Blount, Introduction to Earle, *Microcosmography* (1628)]

Midwife of the Muses, The : a printer's devil. [Foote, *The Author*, I, i (1757)]

Might and main, With : with all one's energies. [*The World and the Child*, ll. 195–6 (1522)]

Mighty Hunter, The : Nimrod. [*Genesis*, x, 9]

Mighty man of valour, A : *see* Man of valour.

Milan Decree, The : a decree blockading British ports issued by Napoleon at Milan in 1807.

Milch-cow, A : a source from which gain is regularly and easily obtained, like milk from a cow. [J. Wheeler, *Treatise of Commerce*, 40 (1601)]

Mild as a dove, As : from the proverbial gentleness of the dove. [Shakespeare, *Passionate Pilgrim* (1589)]

Milesian fable (story), A : a short, witty but obscene story. From the collection of such stories made by Aristides (2nd cent. B.C.), which were very popular among the Milesians.

Milesian Republic, The : Ireland. After the two sons of Milesius, King of Spain, who are said to have conquered the country in the 13th cent. B.C.

Milesians, The : the Irish. After Milesius, a legendary King of Spain, whose sons are said to have conquered Ireland in 1300 B.C.

Milk and honey, A land flowing with : a land of plenty and prosperity. From a biblical description of Canaan in *Exodus*, iii, 8, etc.

Milk of Human kindness, The : compassion and kindness. [Shakespeare, *Macbeth*, I, v, 18 (1605–6).]

Milk again, To kick down all one's : to spoil the good work that one has performed. In allusion to the proverbial cow that gave a good bucket of milk and then kicked it over. [Killigrew, *The Parson's Wedding*, IV, ii (1663)]

Milk the market, To : so to manipulate the financial market as to have it completely under control.

Milk and water : weak, tasteless, powerless. Like milk diluted with water.

Milksop, A : an effeminate boy or youth ; compared with a piece of bread soaked or sopped in milk. [*35th Report, Dept. Keeper of the Records*, App. 17 (c. 1250)]

Milky Way, The : a broad band across the sky formed of myriads of stars.

Mill Boy of The Slashes, The : Henry Clay (1777–1852), Amer. statesman and orator, who early in life attended a mill situated in a district known as ' The Slashes.'

Mill, To bring grist to the : to be a source of profit. [Ayliffe, *Parergon* (1726)]

Mill, To go through the : to undergo a severe course of discipline, training or experience.

Miller, To drown the : to add an excessive amount of water to spirits, dough, etc. From the proverb, ' Too much water drowned the miller.' An Americanism.

Miller, A Joe : *see* Joe Miller.

Miller's eye out, To put the : to use too much water in cooking, esp. a pudding or thick soup.

Millinery of Bibliography, The : fine bindings, illustrations, etc., of books. So-called by Sir Herbert Maxwell (b. 1845).

Millstone, To look (see) into a : to fathom a secret. [Heywood, *Proverbes* (1546)]

Millstone, To look through a : to be sharp sighted. [Lyly, *Euphues and His England* (1580)]

Millstone about one's neck, To have a : to be weighed down by a heavy burden. [*Matthew*, xviii, 6]

Millstones, To weep : not to weep at all. [Shakespeare, *Richard III*, I, iii (1594)]

Milo's end : eaten by wolves while caught by the hand in a tree whose trunk he was attempting to rend asunder.

Milo, To carry a bull with : from the legend of Milo, the athlete of Crotona, who carried a four-year-old heifer across the stadium of Olympia.

Milton, The Anglo-Saxon : Caedmon (fl. 670). After John Milton, Eng. epic poet (1608–74).

Milton of Germany, The : Friedrich Gottlieb Klopstock (1724–1803). So-called by Coleridge.

Milton, A mute inglorious : a poet unconscious of his gift, to whom has never come the opportunity of delivering his message. [Gray, *Elegy in a Country Churchyard*, 15 (1751)]

Mince matters, Not to : to speak plainly and to the point. [Swift, *The Beast's Confession* (1732)]

Mincemeat of .. To make : utterly to destroy ; to cut to pieces. [Cowley, *Cutter Colman* (1663)]

Mind, To speak one's : to say plainly what one thinks. [Earle, *Microcosmography : A Blunt Man* (1628)]

Minden Boys, The : the 20th Regt. of Foot, which distinguished itself at the Battle of Minden (Aug. 1st, 1759).

Minds, To be of two : *see* Two.

Minerva, In spite of : contrary to one's natural inclination. In allusion to Minerva, the Rom. goddess of wisdom.

Minerva Press : ultra-sentimental novels, of the character of those issued from the Minerva Press, London, at the beginning of the 19th cent.

Minerva's bird : the owl, which appears in representations of Minerva, the goddess of wisdom.

Ministère] 241 [Moguls

Ministère de Trois Jours, La : the Ministry of Three Days ; that of the Duc de Bassano in France in 1834.

Ministry of All the Talents, The : Lord Grenville's ministry of 1806, consisting of a coalition of the leading men of all parties. It included Fox, Erskine, Fitzwilliam, Ellenborough, and Sidmouth.

Minor Prophets, The : (1) Hosea, Joel, Amos, Obadiah, Jonah, Micah, Nahum, Habakkuk, Zephaniah, Haggai, Zechariah, Malachi ; (2) their writings.

Mint, A : a place where money is coined. After Moneta or Juno in whose temple in Rome a mint was established.

Mint of money, A : a large amount of money. [Maria Edgeworth, *Castle Rackrent* (1799)]

Minute Men : the Massachusetts militia, formed on the outbreak of the Amer. Revolution, who undertook to be ready for service at a minute's notice.

Mirabeau of the Mob, The : Georges Jacques Danton (1759–94). After the Ct. de Mirabeau (1749–91), the Fr. Revolutionist leader.

Mirabile dictu (*Lat.*, wonderful to relate) : [Virgil, *Georgics*, II, 30]

Miracle of Nature, The : Christina, Queen of Sweden (1626–89).

Mirror up to Nature, To hold the : the function of the actor, according to Shakespeare, *Hamlet*, III, ii (1602–3).

Misrule, Lord (Abbot) of : *see* Abbot.

Miss Nancyism : effeminacy.

Missing link, The : the one point lacking to confirm a theory. Esp. the species required to connect man with the highest of the lower animals.

Mississippi Bubble (Scheme), The : a Fr. financial speculation based on a Mississippi concession, instituted by John Law, which ended in a panic in 1720.

Missouri Compromise, The : the U.S. Congress Act of 1821 prohibiting slavery north of 36° 30', the northern boundary of Missouri. The Act settled a controversy that had raged around the admission of Missouri into the Union.

Mistress of the Adriatic, The : Venice. In allusion to her former commercial importance as a centre of trade between Europe and the East.

Mistress Roper : a marine. In allusion to the ropes which he handles clumsily on board ship.

Mistress of the World, The : Ancient Rome.

Mitchelstown, Remember : the watchword of the Irish Land Leaguers. In the course of a political riot at Mitchelstown, Co. Cork, in August, 1887, the police fired upon the crowd and several were killed.

Mithridatism : artificially induced immunity from poison. After Mithridates Eupator, King of Pontus, who is said to have inadvertently rendered himself immune from poison. Term invented by E. Ray Lankester in *Nature*, June 13th, 1889.

Mittel-Europa : the doctrine of an economic union between the Germ. and Aust. empires.

Mitten, To give the : to jilt. From Lat., *mittere*, to send, or from the *mitaines* formerly presented in France to an unsuccessful wooer. An Americanism, of Fr.-Canadian origin.

Mixed Company : a company consisting of members of different social grades.

Mob, The : the crowd ; the lower classes. First used by the members of the Green Ribbon Club in the reign of Charles II. [Lat., *mobile* (*vulgus*), the fickle (crowd)]

Mob, King : *see* King.

Mobtown : Baltimore. In allusion to the reputation for lawlessness acquired by a section of its inhabitants.

Mock-beggar Hall (Manor) : a poverty-stricken mansion where no hospitality is practised ; a mansion fine without but neglected within.

Mode, à la : *see* à la mode.

Mode, All the : temporarily fashionable. [Evelyn (1664)]

Modern Athens, The : (1) Edinburgh ; (2) Boston, U.S.A.

Modern Babylon, The : London.

Modern Carthage, The : London.

Modern Gracchus, The : *see* Gracchus.

Mods : at Oxford, Moderations ; the first public examination by ' Moderators ' for the B.A. degree.

Modus operandi (*Lat.*, manner of operating) : the manner in which a person sets to work. [R. Whitlock, *Zootomia*, p. 222 (1654)]

Modus vivendi (*Lat.*, manner of living) : a working arrangement between two parties.

Moghul, The Great : *see* Cham.

Moguls : the best class of playing cards. In allusion to the design of the Great

R

Mogul which used to appear on their backs.

Mohair, The Men of : the citizens of France.

Mohammed : *see also* Mahomet.

Mohammed, To dine with : *see* Dine.

Mohock, A : an Eng. aristocratic hooligan of the 18th cent. A corruption of Mohawk, the name of a N. Amer.-Ind. tribe.

Mole, To hold a looking-glass to a : *see* Hold.

Molière, The Italian : Carlo Goldoni (1707-93). Jean Baptiste Molière, famous Fr. dramatist, lived from 1622 to 1673.

Molière, The Spanish : Leandro Fernandez Moratin (1760-1828).

Molinism : quietism. After Miguel Molinos (c. 1640-97), the founder of the Movement.

Moll Cutpurse, A : a woman of thoroughly vicious character. After Mary Frith, nicknamed Moll Cutpurse (1589-1664).

Moll Thomson's mark : (of a bottle) empty (M. T.). The initial letters of Moll Thomson.

Molly Coddle, A : a milksop or pampered person. From Molly, a diminutive of Mary, and coddle.

Molly fellow, A : an effeminate man or boy. From Molly, a diminutive of Mary.

Molly Maguires, The : members of the Ancient Order of Hibernians, an Irish politico-friendly society. In 1843 an Irish agrarian society, ' The Molly Maguires,' was formed for the purpose of refusing payment of rent. They took their name from Cornelius Maguire, an Irish leader in the Rebellion of 1641. The designation ' Molly ' referred to their practice of dressing as women when engaged in their raids. From 1867 to 1877 an Irish secret society of the same name operated in Pennsylvania with the object of gaining control of the State government by means of intimidation.

Moloch : a Palestinian idol, to which its worshippers used to sacrifice their children. Hence an evil to which people are willing to sacrifice either their own or other's welfare.

Mome ; Momus, A : a querulous, fault-finding person. From Momus, the carping god.

Momus, Daughter (Disciple) (Son) of : a buffoon. *See* Mome.

Momus' lattice (window) : the window that Momus (*q.v.*). suggested to Zeus should have been inserted in the breast of the man he created.

Monday, Black : (1) Easter Monday ; (2) (school slang) the Monday opening a new term.

Monday, Fat : the day before Shrove Tuesday.

Monday, Saint : Monday as a day of idleness among workingmen.

Money, To see the colour of one's : to be shown one's money. Of a person concerning whose trustworthiness there is doubt. [Fielding, *Tom Jones*, V, 8 (1749)]

Money on . . To put one's : to trust in ; to be prepared to risk something as a pledge of confidence in . . A betting metaphor.

Money out of a shoestring, To make : to make money without the advantage of preliminary capital.

Mongrel Parliament, The : *see* Parliament, Mongrel.

Monk Lewis : Matthew Gregory Lewis (1775-1818), author of *Ambrosio or The Monk* (1795).

Monkey sitting on one's shoulder, To have the black : to be in a bad temper.

Monkey up, To get one's : to become enraged. From monkey as a synonym for the devil.

Monkey's allowance : illtreatment ; more kicks than halfpence. In allusion to the ill-treatment of performing monkeys.

Monkey's money : service. From the Fr. law permitting a performing monkey to cross the Petit Pont at Paris without other payment than the performance of his tricks.

Monmouth cap, A : a soldier's or sailor's cap. Possibly from James, Duke of Monmouth (1649-85).

Monnaie de Basoche : worthless coin. From money with limited currency coined and circulated by the Clercs de la basoche, judges, lawyers, etc., of France.

Monroe Doctrine, The ; Monroism : the doctrine laid down in a message to Congress by President James Monroe in 1823 that none but Amer. powers were to intervene in the affairs of the Amer. Continent.

Monsieur : Philippe, Duke of Orleans (1674-1723), brother of Louis XIV.

Monsieur de Paris : the Fr. executioner.

Monsieur Vèto : Louis XVI of France (1754–93), in allusion to his right to veto the acts of the Legislative Assembly.

Monster, The Green-eyed : jealousy. [Shakespeare, *Othello*, III, iii (1604)]

Mont de Piété, A (*Fr.*, mountain of piety): a Fr. pawnbroker's shop. Originally established as charitable institutions.

Montague and Capulet : rival parties, esp. in society. From the names of the two rival families in Shakespeare, *Romeo and Juliet* (1591–3).

Montem : an Eton school festival. From the procession *ad montem* (*Lat.*, to the mound) on Whit Tuesday.

Montessori Method, The : a method of education introduced by Maria Montessori, It. teacher (20th cent.).

Montezuma's Realm : Mexico. After Montezuma, the last native emperor.

Month of Sundays, A : an indefinitely long period.

Month's mind, A : a great desire. Orig. a service held once a month in memory of a deceased person. ' By saying that they have a month's mind to a thing, they undoubtedly mean that, if they had what they so much longed for it would do them as much good as they believe " a month's mind," or service in the church said once a month, would benefit their souls after their decease.' According to another suggestion, the allusion is to a woman's longing during the first month of pregnancy. [Shakespeare, *Two Gentlemen of Verona*, I, ii (1590)]

Monumental City, The : Baltimore. In allusion to its numerous churches and other public buildings.

Moon, To bark at the : *see* Bark.

Moon, To cast beyond the : (1) to calculate deeply ; (2) to be ambitious ; (3) to attempt impossibilities. [Heywood, *Proverbes* (1546)]

Moon, To cry for the : to desire the unattainable. From the practice of some children of crying for the moon.

Moon, To find an elephant in the : to hoax oneself ; to discover a mare's nest. In allusion to the story of Sir Paul Neal (17th cent.) who claimed to have discovered an elephant in the moon but afterwards found that a mouse had crept into his telescope.

Moon is made of green (cream) cheese, To believe that the : to believe in an absurdity. A green cheese is a cream cheese, eaten green and fresh. [Heywood, *Proverbes* (1546)]

Moon, The Island of the : Madagascar.

Moon, To level at the : to be over-ambitious.

Moon, Man in the : *see* Man.

Moon, Minions of the ; Moon's men : nightwatchmen ; thieves. [Shakespeare, 1 *Henry IV*, I, ii (1596–7)]

Moon, To shoot the : to leave a house by night in order to avoid payment of the rent due.

Moonlight flitting, A : *see* Moon, To shoot the.

Moonlighters : an Irish agrarian secret society (1881 *et seq.*), guilty of many outrages at night. The orders issued by the Society were signed ' Captain Moonlight.'

Moonraker, A : a man of Wiltshire. In allusion to the silliness related of the people of that county who attempted or pretended to attempt to rake the reflection of the moon out of a pond.

Moonshine, All : nonsense ; as unsubstantial as moonshine. [Gabriel Harvey, *Pierce's Supererogation* (1593)]

Moonshine, Bottled : (1) illicit spirit, moonlight being a convenience for smuggling ; (2) a utopian scheme of benevolence. [A. Birrell, *Obiter Dicta* (1885)]

Moonstruck : mentally deranged. In allusion to the supposed influence of the moon over the human mind.

Moot point, A : a disputable point. From to moot, to discuss a point of law as an exercise. Ang.-Sax., *motian*, to debate. [Thos. Hughes, *Misfortunes of Arthur*, Introduction (1587)]

Moral or adorn a tale, To point a : to give force to a moral precept. [Samuel Johnson, *Vanity of Human Wishes* (1749)]

Moral certainty, A : a practical certainty which cannot however be proved by means of reason. [*Letter* by Earl of Glamorgan (1645) ; *Burd. Issach.*, II, 276 (1646)]

Moral victory, A : a defeat or an indecisive result, calculated to give the moral results of a victory. [Alison, *History of Europe*, V, xxxi, § 17 (1842)]

Moravians : a Prot. sect, originating in Bohemia and Moravia in the 16th cent. and expelled thence in 1627.

Morbleu ! : a Fr. oath. Corruption of *Mort de Dieu*, death of God.

Morbus Gallicus (*Lat.*, French disease) : an illness due to the practice of immorality.

Morbus Neapolitanus (*Lat.*, Neapolitan illness) : morbus Gallicus (*q.v.*).

Mordieu ! : Morbleu (*q.v.*).

More kicks than ha'pence : more pain than pleasure. An allusion to the treatment of performing monkeys.

More Scotico, To answer : to answer one question by asking another. [Scott, *The Abbot*, ch. 26 (1820)]

Morey letter, A : a forged letter intended to exercise influence in an election. The original Morey letter purported to be addressed by Pres. James Garfield to H. L. Morey, an alleged considerable employer of labour, but an imaginary personage, on the eve of the Presidential election of 1880. It advocated the free admission of Chinese labour.

Morganatic marriage, A : a marriage in which one party, generally the wife, is of lower degree, and she and her children are not entitled to inherit or to share the other party's dignities.

Morganize, To : to assassinate secretly in order to suppress information, as was said to have been done in the case of William Morgan in the U.S. in 1826.

Morglay : a sword. After the sword of Sir Bevis, in the Arthurian legends.

Morituri te salutant (*Lat.*, We, about to die, salute thee) : the cry with which the gladiators in the Rom. arena used to greet the Emperor before entering on the contest.

Morley, Mrs. : *see* Mrs. Morley.

Morning Star of the Reformation, The : John Wycliffe (1324–84).

Morocco men : agents for lotteries.

Morpheus, In the arms of : asleep. Morpheus was the Rom. god of dreams.

Morris dance, A : an Eng. folk dance. Orig. introduced from Spain, where it was of Moorish origin.

Mortal coil, To shuffle off this : to die. [Shakespeare, *Hamlet*, III, i (1602–3)]

Mortar-board, A : the peculiar cap worn by members of a university. From its resemblance to a board used by bricklayers for holding mortar.

Morton's Fork (Crutch) : the scheme for raising money devised by Archbp. John Morton (1410–1500). He obtained contributions from the rich on the ground of their wealth, and from others on account of their alleged thriftiness.

Moscow, To be one's : to be the turning point of fortune. In allusion to Napoleon's march to and retreat from Moscow in 1812. [Byron, *Don Juan*, XI, 56 (1823)]

Moses' horns : *Exodus*, xxxiv, 30, is translated in the Vulgate ' and his face was horned,' as compared with ' the skin of his face shone' in the A.V. In Lat. rays of light were called horns.

Moses to Moses there was none like Moses, From : said of Moses, the law-giver, and (1) Moses Maimonides (1135–1204), Span. Jewish philosopher ; (2) Moses Mendelssohn (1729–86), Germ. Jewish philosopher ; and (3) Sir Moses Montefiore (1784–1885), Eng. Jewish philanthropist.

Moses' rod : a divining rod. In allusion to the rod with which Moses performed his miracles.

Mossbacks : the extreme conservative branch of the Dem. party in the U.S. From the popular name of the snapping turtle.

Mosse took his mare, Napping, as : *see* Napping.

Mosstrooper, A : a freebooter. From the bands of these criminals who used to infest the ' mosses ' of the Scot. Border.

Most Christian Doctor, The : (1) John Charlier de Gerson (1363–1429), Fr. theologian and philosopher ; (2) Nicholas de Cusa (1401–64), Germ. cardinal, theologian and philosopher.

Most Christian Kingdom, The : France.

Most Learned Fool in Christendom, The : *see* Learned Fool.

Mot d'Ordre (*Fr.*) : word of command.

Mote and beam : *see* Beam.

Mother Ann : Ann Lee (1736–84), head of the Shakers.

Mother of Believers, The : Ayesha, the second wife of Mahomet.

Mother of Books, The : Alexandria, formerly famous for its great library, entirely destroyed under Theophilus, A.D. 391.

Mother Carey is plucking her geese : it is snowing. *See* next entry.

Mother Carey's chickens : stormy petrels. Mother Carey is a corruption of *Mater Cara*, dear mother.

Mother Carey's goose : the black petrel.

Mother Church, The : the principal church of a parish, city, country, etc.

Mother of Cities, The : Balkh, in Turkestan.

Mother Country, The : one's native country ; a country in relation to its colonies.

Mother of dreams, The : the earth. In allusion to the idea of the classical poets that dreams originated in Hades, *i.e.*, the recesses of the earth.

Mother of the gods, The : Cybele.

Mother of the Gracchi, The : one who so educates her sons as to fit them for an honourable and noble career. In allusion to Cornelia, the mother of Caius and Tiberius Gracchus, Rom. Tribunes of the 2nd cent. B.C.

Mother and Head of all Churches, The : the church of St. John Lateran of Rome.

Mother Hubbard : a woman's cloak. From the name of the heroine of a nursery rhyme.

Mother for a maid, To take one's : to be exceptionally simple.

Mother of Months, The : the moon.

Mother of Parliaments, The : the Eng. parliament. So-called by John Bright, orator and statesman (Jan. 18th, 1865).

Mother of pearl : the inner surface of an oyster's shell in which pearls are found.

Mother of Presidents, The : Virginia, from which state six of the Presidents of the U.S. came.

Mother of all the Russian cities, The : Kiev, which encloses the oldest cathedral in the Russian Empire.

Mother Shipton : the reputed author of Mother Shipton's Prophecies current in England in the 15th and later cents.

Mother of South-Western Statesmen, The : the state of Tennessee. From the number of statesmen it has produced.

Mother of States, The : Virginia. Either as the oldest of the N. Amer. colonies or because five other states— Kentucky, Ohio, Indiana, Illinois and West Virginia—separated from her at one time or another.

Mother wit : natural wit ; common sense. [Capgrave, *Life of St. Katherine*, V (1440)]

Mother's blessing, To have too much of his : to be excessively prudish for a youth.

Mothering Sunday : the fourth Sunday in Lent. Also known as Refreshment Sunday and Simnel Sunday. Mothering is supposed to have been orig. a visiting of the Mother Church. Afterwards it took the form of taking gifts to one's mother.

Motley, To go in : to behave as a mountebank. From the dress worn by professional fools.

Motley, Men of : fools. From the costume, variegated (motley), worn by professional fools. [Shakespeare, *As You Like It*, II, vii (1600)]

Mound City, The : St. Louis, which was built on several artificial mounds.

Mountain, The : the Jacobins or followers of Robespierre and Danton, the extreme revolutionists in France. From the upper seats which the party occupied in the Legislative Assembly.

Mountain dew : Irish whiskey. In allusion to the practice of illicit distilling in the mountains.

Mountain in labour brought forth a mouse : small results of great efforts. Saying of Agesilaus II, King of Sparta (c. 444–361 B.C.). [Horace, *Ars Poetica*, l. 136–9]

Mountain Men : the Cameron Highlanders.

Mountain out of a molehill, To make a : to exaggerate a difficulty. Phrase said to have been coined by Henry Ellis (1777–1869), *Original Letters*, 2nd Series, p. 312, *but see* Gabriel Harvey, *Letter-book* (1573).

Mountain, The Old Man of the : Imaum Hassan ben Sabbah el Homairi (d. 1174), Chief of the Assassins (*q.v.*), who lived in the mountains of Syria.

Mountains, To raise : to tell exaggerated stories. [Bunyan, *Holy War*, To the Reader, ll. 13–6 (1682)]

Mountebank, A : an antic fool. Orig. a travelling quack doctor who used to mount on banks or benches at fairs in order to advertise his skill. [Sir P. Sidney, *Defence of Poesie*, Pt. II (1595)]

Mouse, As poor as a church : *see* Poor.

Mouth, To laugh on the wrong side of the : to be sorry when pleasure was anticipated. Formerly to laugh in an obviously forced manner. [Scott, *Rob Roy*, ch. 37 (1818)]

Mouth water, To make a person's : to arouse a person's expectation of pleasure. [Petronius, *Satyricon*, ch. 48 ; Heywood, *Proverbes* (1546)]

Moutons, Revenons à nos (*Fr.*, Let us return to our sheep) : to return to the original subject. Quotation from the play *L'Avocat Patelin* by Blanchet.

Move the previous question, To : a convenient parliamentary method of avoiding a decision.

Mozart, The English : Sir Henry Bishop (1780–1855). Wolfgang Amadeus Mozart, famous Germ. musical composer, lived from 1756–91.

Mozart, The Italian : Cherubini (1760–1842).

Mrs. Grundy : *see* Grundy.

Mrs. Gummidge, A : 'a lone, lorn creetur' who is always lamenting the past. From a character in Dickens, *David Copperfield* (1849).

Mrs. Leo Hunter : *see* Hunter.

Mrs. Morley and Mrs. Freeman : Queen Anne and Sarah Jennings, Duchess of Marlborough. Names assumed in their private correspondence.

Mrs. Partington : the personification of impotent prejudice. From a personage invented by Sydney Smith in a speech at Taunton in 1831, who at a time of storm and high tide took out her mop in order to sweep away the Atlantic.

Much as one's life is worth, As : involving great risk to one's life.

Much of a muchness : practically no difference.

Mud, To throw (sling) : to abuse.

Mudlarks, The : the Royal Engineers.

Muff, A : a simple person, easily imposed upon. In allusion to the dandies in the 17th and 18th cents. who, carrying muffs, were unable to defend themselves if attacked by street bullies.

Mufti, In : in civil attire ; out of uniform. Apparently in allusion to the dress of a mufti or Mohammedan expounder of the law.

Mug, A : a face. In allusion to the portraits of celebrities that appeared on beer-house mugs during the 17th and 18th cents.

Mugwump, A : a member of parliament or other legislative assembly who attaches himself to no party. Orig. a member of the Republican Party in the U.S. in 1884 who declined to vote for the party nominee for the Presidency. From an Algonquin word meaning 'a chief.' This use of the word was introduced by the New York *Sun* (June 15, 1884).

Mugwump Press, The : independent organs of opinion. So-called by party men. *See* Mugwump.

Mule, To shoe one's : to misappropriate money held in trust. A Fr. idiom supposed to have been derived from the pretence that the money was expended on shoeing the mule. [*History of Francion* (1655)]

Mulligan Letters : letters sent by James G. Blaine, which came improperly into the possession of a clerk named Mulligan. They were used to discredit Blaine in his candidature for the Amer. presidency (1884).

Multitude, Hydra-headed : *see* Hydra-headed.

Multum in parvo (*Lat.*, much in little) : valuable material occupying small space

Mum's the word ! : Be silent ! From mum, the sound made when the lips are kept closed. [Farquhar, *The Stage-coach* (1704)]

Mumbo-jumbo : an object of superstitious worship ; supposed name of an African idol invoked by Central African natives to frighten their women. [Peter Pindar, *Epistle to the Pope* (1793)]

Mumping Day : St. Thomas' Day (Dec. 21st). In Herefordshire a day for begging. From *mump*, to beg.

Mumpsimus : an error, which the holder refuses to abandon. From the story of a monk who always used *mumpsimus* in place of the Lat. *sumpsimus* and when his error was pointed out to him replied that he had been taught it and he proposed to continue to use that word.

Münchhausen (Münchausen), A Baron : a romancing traveller. In allusion to Baron Karl Friedrich Hieronymus von Münchhausen (1720–97), a Germ. soldier in the Russian service whose adventures, narrated by Rudolph Erich Raspe, were too wonderful for credence.

Mundane Egg, The : the egg from which the world was hatched according to the Phoenician, Egyptian, Hindu and Japanese theologies.

Murray, To dine with St. Giles and the Earl of : *see* Dine.

Muscadin, A (*Fr.*, a dandy) : a member of the moderate party in the first Fr. Revolution, mostly young men of the upper middle class. In allusion to their dress.

Muscular Christianity : the religious school whose doctrines are laid down in the writings of Charles Kingsley (1819–75)—earnest Christianity combined with the cultivation of all clean pleasures.

Muse, The Tenth : (1) Marie Lejars de Gournay (1566–1645), Fr. writer ; (2)

Antoinette Deshoulières (1633–94), Fr. writer ; (3) Magdalen de Scuderi (1607–1701), Fr. romancist ; (4) Delphine Gay (1804–55), Fr. novelist and dramatist.

Muses, The : the nine goddesses who preside over the arts : Calliope (eloquence and epic poetry), Clio (history), Erato (erotic poetry), Euterpe (lyrics, music), Melpomene (tragedy), Polyhymnia (singing and rhetoric), Terpsichore (dancing), Thalia (pastoral and comic poetry), Urania (astronomy).

Museum, A Walking : Dionysius Cassius Longinus (213–273), Grk. philosopher and rhetorician.

Mushroom : something of sudden growth and therefore of doubtful permanence.

Mushroom Gentleman, A : one who has suddenly risen in the social scale.

Music, To face the : see Face the music.

Music, The Father of ; The Father of Greek : see Father.

Music, The Prince of : Palestrina (1529–94).

Music of the Spheres : in allusion to the globes imagined by the earlier astronomers to revolve round the earth, carrying with them the sun, moon, planets and fixed stars. [Shakespeare, *Twelfth Night*, III, i (1601)]

Musicians, The Father of : see Father.

Muster, To pass : to undergo examination successfully. A military metaphor.

Mutatis Mutandis (*Lat.*, With the necessary changes) : [*Egerton Papers*, p. 472 (1615)]

Mute as a fish, As : silent. [Rob. Burton, *Anatomy of Melancholy* (1621)]

Mute as a mouse, As : silent. In allusion to the customary quietness of mice. [Peter Pindar, *Lyric Odes to the Royal Academicians* for 1785, Ode 1]

Muttons, To return to one's : to recur to the subject-matter from which one has wandered. From Blanchet's play, *L'Avocat Patelin* (' Revenons à nos moutons ') (*q.v.*).

Mutton-chop whiskers : side-whiskers, supposed to resemble mutton chops.

Mutton-eating King, The : Charles II of England. *See* Mutton-monger.

Mutton-monger, A : a roué. From a mutton, an immoral woman, possibly as a lost sheep.

Mutual Admiration Society, A : a literary or social society whose members are supposed to devote an undue amount of time to singing one another's praises. Term invented by Oliver

Wendell Holmes in *The Autocrat of the Breakfast Table* (1857–8).

Muzzle the ox that treadeth the corn, To : to treat one's employees with meanness. [*Deuteronomy*, xxv, 4]

My Lady Nicotine : tobacco. From the title of a book by Sir James Matthew Barrie (1890).

Mynheer Closh : a Dutchman. Closh is a corrupt contraction of Nicholas, a common name in Holland. Mynheer is Dutch *mijn heer*, my lord.

Myrmidons of the Law : subordinate officials for the administration of justice. Properly soldiers or other loyal attendants. From the inhabitants of Myrmidon in Thessaly, whom Achilles led to the Siege of Troy.

Mystery of Religion, The Greatest : the Incarnation.

Mysteries, The Three Greater : the Trinity, Original Sin and the Incarnation.

Mysteries of woods and rivers, The : hunting and fishing.

Naboth's vineyard : the coveted possession of another. [I *Kings*, xxi]

Nadir, From Zenith down to : from the highest to the lowest. The Nadir is properly that point in the heavens (the lowest) which is opposite to the Zenith. (Arabic).

Naiad, A : a nymph of the water.

Nail, On the : on the spot ; immediately. The phrase appears in Lat. in this sense in a Scot. parliamentary deed of July 15, 1326. [Nashe, *Saffron Walden* (1596)]

Nail in one's coffin, To drive a : to hasten a person's death. [Peter Pindar, *Expostulatory Odes*, Ode XV (1789)]

Nail one's colours to the mast, To : to keep determinedly to one's purpose. A metaphor drawn from maritime warfare.

Nail, To go off at the : to get out of hand.

Nail on the head, To hit the : to succeed in one's aim ; to come clearly to the point. [Skelton, *Colin Cloute* (1529)]

Nail to the head (home), To drive the : to press a matter to its end. [Daus, Transl. of Sleidane, *Commentary*, 278 (1560)]

Nail a lie to the counter, To : publicly to expose a false statement. [Oliver Wendell Holmes, *Medical Essays* (1883)]

Nails, The : the 95th Regt. (now the Derbyshire) which gained the reputation in the Crimea of being ' as hard as nails.'

Nails, Not to part with the parings of one's : to be exceedingly mean. [Heywood, *Proverbes* (1546)]

Naked eye, The : the eye without any artificial assistance of telescope, microscope, etc. [Hy. Power, *Experimental Philosophy*, I, 17 (1664)]

Naked truth, The : the plain truth. In allusion to the fable of Truth and Falsehood going bathing, after which Falsehood stole Truth's garment, but Truth preferred to go naked rather than wear Falsehood's clothes. [Horace, *Odes*, I, 24, l. 7 ; Lyly, *Euphues : Anatomy of Wit* (1579)]

Namby pamby : sickly sentimental ; childish. In allusion to the poems of Ambrose Philips (c. 1675–1749). The nickname first appeared as the title of a parody on Philips by Henry Carey (1690–1743) and was immediately adopted by Pope.

Name the day, To : to appoint the day of one's marriage.

Name is Legion, My : an expression of a large number. [*Mark*, v, 9]

Nameless City, The : Ancient Rome. After the superstition that the utterance of its mystical name would involve death.

Nancy, Miss : an effeminate young man. *See* Miss Nancyism.

Nannygoats, The : the 23rd Regt. of Foot or Royal Welsh Fusiliers. In allusion to their pet, a goat.

Nap, To go : to stake everything on a venture. A cardplaying metaphor. The name of the game is a contraction of Napoleon III.

Napier's bones (rods) : narrow slips of bone or other material marked so as to be used to facilitate calculation in accordance with the system invented by John Napier of Merchiston (1550–1617).

Napoleon of the Drama, The : (1) Alfred Bunn (1796–1860), Eng. theatrical manager and dramatic author ; (2) Robert William Elliston (1774–1831), Eng. comedian.

Napoleon the Little : Napoleon III, Emperor of the French, so-called by Victor Hugo.

Napoleon of Oratory, The : William Ewart Gladstone (1809–98), British statesman.

Napoleon of Peace, The : Louis Philippe (1773–1850), Kg. of French, whose peaceful reign was a noticeable contrast to the warlike period of Napoleon.

Napping, To catch : to take unawares. [Lyly, *Euphues : Anatomy of Wit* (1579) ; Greene, *Tritameron* (1587)]

Napping, as Mosse took his mare : the mare is said to have been too nimble or cunning to be taken while awake.

Nappy ale : strong ale, that induces sleep. Nap=a short sleep. [Heywood, *Proverbes* (1546)]

Narikin, A : a parvenu ; a nouveau riche. After the Japanese term for a pawn in chess which by crossing the board may suddenly gain promotion.

Narrow Seas, The : the channels that separate England from France and Ireland. [*Sailing Directions* (15th cent.)]

Narrowdale noon, Till : indefinitely. After Narrowdale in Derbyshire, into which the sun does not penetrate throughout the winter.

Nash, Beau : *see* Beau.

Nathanael, A : one ' in whom there is no guile.' [*John*, i, 47]

Nation of Gentlemen, The : the Scottish. So-called by George IV when he visited Scotland in 1822.

Nation of Poets and Thinkers, The : the German. So-called by Lytton in the Introduction to *Ernest Maltravers* (1837).

Nation of Shopkeepers, The : *see* Shopkeepers.

Nations, The Battle of the : the Battle of Leipsic, Oct. 16–18, 1813. In allusion to the number of different nations— French, Austrian, Prussian, Russian and Swedish—that took part in it.

Natural man, A : a philosopher ; *viz.*, one devoted to or skilled in natural philosophy.

Nature, Dame : the personification of nature.

Nature, Debt of : *see* Debt.

Nature, In a state of : nude.

Nature's Darling : Shakespeare, according to Gray. [*The Progress of Poetry*, ll. 83–4 (1757)]

Navigation, The Father of : *see* Father.

Navigation, The Father of British Inland : *see* Father.

Navvy, A : a labourer engaged in the construction of roads, etc. From ' The Navigation Inn,' frequented by such labourers near a canal on the construction of which they were employed.

Nazareth? Can any good come out of: the suggestion that a person, family or place with a bad name will never change it. [*John* i, 46]

Ne plus ultra (*Lat.*, not further): the utmost limit. Phrase said to have been inscribed on the Pillars of Hercules as indicating the utmost limit beyond which mariners should not pass. [Peter Pindar, *Complimentary Epistle to James Bruce, Epistle Dedicatory* (1790)]

Neaera, A: a sweetheart. Used by Horace, Virgil and Tibullus.

Neat as wax, As: very carefully arranged. In allusion to the good order of the cells of bees.

Neck and crop: headlong. A sporting metaphor.

Neck and neck: equal in capacity or power. A horseracing metaphor.

Neck in the noose, To put one's: to put oneself in a dangerous situation or in the power of another.

Neck or nothing: complete success or total failure. A racing metaphor. [M. Davies, *Athenae Britannicae*, I, 321 (1716)]

Neck verse, The: the first verse of *Psalm* li, which had to be read by all condemned criminals who claimed benefit of clergy. Those who succeeded in reading it were handed over to the ecclesiastical authorities.

Necklace, The Affair of the Diamond: an incident that brought great discredit on the Court of Louis XVI. and Marie Antoinette through no fault on their part, in which the diamond necklace formerly owned by Madame du Barry and the Cardinal de Rohan figured prominently.

Neck-or-nothing Novelists, The Prince of: Charles Lever (1806–72), author of *Charles O'Malley, Harry Lorrequer*, etc.

Nectar, As sweet as: in allusion to nectar, the drink of the gods. [Ausonius, *Epistulae*, II]

Needam, To be on the high road to: to be on the road to ruin. *See* Needam's Shore.

Needam's Shore: penury. A play on the first syllable.

Needful, To do the: to find the money. [Scott, *Rob Roy*, ch. 2 (1818)]

Needle in a bottle of hay, To look for: *see* Look for.

Needle, To get the: to become irritated. Orig. a tailor's phrase to denote the feeling after having run a needle into the finger.

Needle, To put a rope to the eye of a: *see* Put.

Needle and thread, From: to the smallest detail. [Petronius, *Satyrion*, § 76]

Ne'er do weel, A: a worthless person; one who never does well.

Neiges d'Antan, The (*Fr.*, last year's snow): that which is passed.

Nemean lion, The: the lion killed by Hercules at Nemea.

Nemesis: retributive justice. After the goddess of divine retribution.

Nepenthe: a drink that induces oblivion of sorrow and trouble. After Nepenthes, such a drug, mentioned in Homer, *Odyssey*.

Neper's bones: Napier's bones (*q.v.*).

Nephelo-coccygia: an imaginary place. After the town in the clouds built by the cuckoos. *See* Aristophanes, *The Birds*.

Neptune: the ocean. After the Roman god of the seas.

Neptune, A son of: a sailor.

Neptune's Bodyguard: the Royal Marines.

Nereids: sea nymphs.

Neri: *see* Bianchi and Neri.

Nero, A: a cruel tyrant. After the Emp. Nero (37–68).

Nero of the North, The: Christian II of Denmark and Norway (1480–1559).

Nessus, The shirt of: a harmful gift. After the shirt of Nessus which, when given to Hercules and worn by him, pierced his body with poison of which he died.

Nest, To feather one's: *see* Feather.

Nest-egg, A: a sum set aside as savings, intended as a nucleus of a larger amount. After the parallel of the china egg placed in a hen's nest to encourage her to lay real ones.

Nestor, A: a wise and elderly adviser. After Nestor, the senior counsellor of the Grks. in the Trojan war.

Nestor of Europe, The: Leopold I (1790–1865), King of the Belgians, whose advice was frequently sought by monarchs junior to him in years.

Nestor, As old as: very aged. *See* Nestor. [Martial, *Epigrams*, Bk. II lxiv, 3–4]

Net, To catch the wind with a: *see* Catch.

Net for, To spread one's: to prepare to obtain advantage over. A fowling metaphor. [*Proverbs*, xxix, 5: Ovid,

Ars Amatoria, Bk. I, 263–4 ; Thos. May, *The Heir*, I, i (1633)]

Nettle, To grasp the : *see* Grasp.

Neutrality, An armed : *see* Armed.

New broom, A : a newly appointed and consequently energetic holder of an office. After the proverb, ' A new broom sweeps clean.' [Heywood, *Proverbes* (1546)]

New Christians, The : Spanish or Portuguese Jews of the 15th or 16th cent., forcibly converted to Christianity, who continued, or were suspected of continuing to practice Judaism in secret.

New College : Newgate Prison.

New departure, A : any radical reform or change of base, personal or political. The phrase was coined by Clement C. Vallandigham, one of the leaders of the Democratic Party, in a speech made in Montgomery County, Ohio, in May, 1871.

New England : the states of Maine, New Hampshire, Vermont, Massachusetts, Connecticut and Rhode Island, all colonized from England.

New England of the West, The : Minnesota, in which state a number of New Englanders have settled.

New Hampshire Grants : an early name of the state of Vermont.

New Jerusalem, The : paradise. [*Revelations*, xxi]

New Journalism, The : journalism in which undue emphasis is given to personal and sensational matters. Introduced into England from the United States about 1884.

New Law, The : the Gospel dispensation.

New Learning, The : *see* Learning.

New Model, The : the parliamentary army as reorganized after the Self-Denying Ordinance of 1645.

New Style : the reckoning of time according to the Gregorian Calendar ; adopted 1582, introduced into England 1752.

New Tipperary : an abortive attempt in 1890 by means of the creation of a new town to overcome the ground landlord of Tipperary in his struggle with his tenants.

New wine in old bottles : the inferior covered by the pretence of the superior.

New Woman, A : a progressive woman, who in the last two decades of the 19th cent., broke with convention to the extent of riding the bicycle, entering business or a profession, living away from home, etc.

New World, The : the Americas. The phrase was first used in this sense by Amerigo Vespucci in a letter to Lorenzo de Medici, written from Lisbon early in 1503.

Newcastle, To carry (send) coals to : *see* Coals.

Newcastle Cloak, A : a cask with apertures for the hands and head, into which drunkards were formerly placed as a punishment.

Newcastle hospitality : roasting a friend to death. From a proverb.

Newgate, A : a prison. After the former principal prison of the City of London.

Newgate Calendar, The : *see* Calendar.

Newgate fashion, To march : to march in twos as prisoners used to be conducted to Newgate.

Newgate fringe (frill), The : the remnant of whiskers remaining on the jaws after the face and chin have been shaven, which covers that portion of the neck which the hangman's noose touches.

Newgate knocker, A : a lock of hair as worn by costermongers. Formerly fashionable in Newgate prison.

Newton of Harmony, The : Jean Phillippe Rameau (1683–1764), author of *Dissertation on the Principles of Harmony*. After Sir Isaac Newton (1642–1727), the distinguished Eng. natural philosopher.

Next to nothing : hardly anything.

Niagara, To shoot : to run great risks, as a rule through ignorance of the consequences (esp. in political matters.) After an essay by Thomas Carlyle in *Macmillan's Magazine* (Aug., 1867).

Nibelungen Hoard, The : a hoard of gold and precious stones which, according to legend, Siegfried gave to his wife as a dowry. It was ultimately hidden in the Rhine and the owner being murdered, the place of concealment was lost.

Nice as ninepence, As : corruption of nice as ninepins. In allusion to the exactitude with which they are set up in preparation for the game.

Nice as a nun's hen, As : fastidious. [*Satirical Verses on Women* (1462) ; Heywood, *Proverbes* (1546)]

Niche in the Temple of Fame, A : immortality. Properly a place for setting up one's monument in the Pantheon or Temple of Fame of the Fr. Revolution.

Nicholas's Clerks : highwaymen. A pun on Old Nick, the devil, or from St. Nicholas, the patron saint of thieves.

Nicholas's Clerks, St. : scholars. After St. Nicholas, the patron saint of scholars.

Nick, the Bear : Russia. So-called in *Punch.*

Nick, Old : the Devil. After the Nickers, the water-fairies of the Germans.

Nick of time, In the : at the exact moment. In allusion to the former practice of marking time by means of nicks or notches on tallies. [Cicero, *Pro Quintio*, 19 ; *A Warning to Faire Women*, II, ll. 112–4 (1599)]

Nicka Nan Night : the night preceding Shrove Tuesday. A Cornish term. In allusion to the tricks played by boys on that night.

Nickel : a metallic element. Lit., little Nick, from a name of the devil. So-called by Paracelsus (1493–1541) on account of its impish properties. *See* Nick, Old.

Nicodemical : timid. After Nicodemus, the Jewish ruler, who came to Jesus by night. [*John*, iii]

Nicodemused into nothing : ruined by the oddity of one's name. After Nicodemus, a Christian name. [Laurence Sterne, *Tristram Shandy*, I, 19 (1759–67)]

Nicotine : an alkaloid yielded by tobacco. After Jean Nicot (1530–1600), who introduced tobacco into France.

Nigger, The luck of a : exceedingly good fortune. [Bret Harte, *Outcasts of Poker Flat* (1869)]

Niggerdriving : plying with work, like the continual driving of a nigger or slave.

Night into day, To turn : to work or enjoy oneself at night instead of resting.

Night, The eyes of the : stars.

Night hideous, To make : generally to disturb the slumbers of people by howling and other similar noises. [Shakespeare, *Hamlet*, I, iv, ll. 51–4 (1602)]

Night of it, To make a : to spend the night in carousal or other enjoyment. [*Twelfth Night Merriment* (1602)]

Night, Candles of the : *see* Candles.

Nightingale, An Arcadian : an ass.

Nightingale, The Cambridgeshire (Fen) : the edible frog, once common in the Cambridgeshire Fens.

Nightingale, The Italian : Angelica Catalani (1782–1849), vocalist.

Nightingale, The Liége : the edible frog.

Nightingale, The Swedish : Jenny Lind (1820–87), vocalist.

Nightmare of Europe, The : Napoleon I.

Nihilism : a Russian revolutionary movement which essayed to gain its objects by terrorism and outrages directed against the members of the governing class. The movement arose about 1840 and derived its name from Turgeniev, *Fathers and Sons.* ' A Nihilist is a man who bows before no authority, who accepts no principle without examination.' Lat., *nihil*, nothing.

Nil desperandum (*Lat.*, nothing to be despaired of) : [Horace, *Odes*, I, 7, 27]

Nile, The Hero of the : Lord Nelson (1758–1805). In allusion to his victory at the Battle of the Nile (1798).

Nimble as a Tailor, As : *see* Pert as a Tailor. [Peter Pindar, *Peter's Pension : The Royal Sleep* (1781)]

Nimrod, A : a great hunter. After Nimrod, the mighty hunter (*Gen.* x, 8). [Hakluyt, *Voyages*, II, i, 309 (1587)]

Nine Days' Wonder, A : an ephemeral excitement that agitates society. Said to be derived from the interest and excitement of children over the nine days' blindness of a newly born kitten. [Chaucer, *Canterbury Tales*, *Troilus and Creseide*, Bk. IV (14th cent.) ; Heywood, *Proverbs* (1546)]

Nine Gods, The : (1) (of the Etruscans) Juno, Minerva, Tinia, Vulcan, Mars, Saturn, Hercules, Summanus, Vedius ; (2) (of the Sabines) Hercules, Romulus, Æsculapius, Bacchus, Æneas, Vesta, Santa, Fortuna, Fides.

Nine Ladies, The : the Muses.

Nine Lives like a Cat : in allusion to the fable of *The Greedy and Ambitious Cat* by Bidpal, the Brahmin gymnosophist. [Heywood, *Proverbs* (1546)]

Nine Orders of Angels, The : Seraphim, Cherubim, Thrones, Dominions, Virtues, Powers, Principalities, Archangels, Angels.

Nine Points of the Law : possession. In allusion to the adage ' Possession is nine points of the law.' The nine points are said to be (1) plenty of money, (2) excessive patience, (3) a good cause, (4) a good adviser, (5) a good advocate, (6) reliable witnesses, (7) a friendly jury, (8) good luck.

Nine Sisters, The : the Muses.

Nine Spheres, The : the Moon, Mercury, Venus, the Sun, Mars, Jupiter, Saturn, the Firmament and the Crystalline.

Nine, The Tuneful : the Muses (q.v.)

Nine Virgins, The : the Muses.

Nine ways, To look : to squint.

Nine Worthies, The : Joshua, David, Judas Maccabæus, Hector, Alexander the Great, Julius Cæsar, King Arthur, Charlemagne and Godfrey of Bouillon. Three Hebrews, three heathens and three Christians : heroes of medieval romance.

Nine Worthies of London, The : Sir William Walworth, Sir Henry Pritchard, Sir William Sevenoke, Sir Thomas White, Sir John Bonham, Christopher Croker, Sir John Hawkwood, Sir Hugh Caverley, Sir Henry Maleverer.

Nines, To the : to perfection.

Ninth part of a man, A : a tailor. In allusion to the proverb, ' Nine tailors make a man.' This is a corruption of ' Nine tellers make a man,' the allusion being to the nine times a church bell was formerly tolled on the occasion of the death of a man.

Ninth degree, To the : completely, utterly. [Heywood, *Proverbes* (1546)]

Ninety-Eight, The : the Irish rebellion of 1798.

Niobe, A : a sorrowful, weeping woman ; the personification of female sorrow. After the daughter of Tantalus who was changed into stone while weeping for the loss of her children.

Niobe of Nations, The : modern Rome. So-called by Lord Byron. [*Childe Harold*, IV, 79 (1818)]

Nip in the bud, To : to suppress in its very earliest stage. [Rob. Wilmot, *Tancred and Gismunda*, I, iii (1591)]

Nitouche, A St. : a hypocrite. After the Fr., *Faire la Sainte Nitouche*, to pretend to great sanctity.

Nizolian paper-books : commonplace books. After Marius Nizolius (1498–1566), Ital. scholar, who was one of the first to publish such a book. [Sir Philip Sidney, *Defence of Poesie*, Pt. II (1595)]

No class : inferior in status. Properly, belonging to neither the upper nor the middle class.

No Man's Land : a borderland between two states or spheres of influence.

No Popery : an expression of hostility to Roman Catholicism ; popular at the time of the Gordon Riots (1780).

Nob of the first water, A : a great swell. First water is the highest degree of quality in a diamond. ' Nob ' is a contraction of ' nobleman.'

Noble to ninepence, To bring a : to dissipate money idly. [Fulwell, *Like Will to Like*, ll. 871–4 (1568)]

Noble Science, The : (1) fencing ; (2) boxing. [Tarlton, *Jests* (1588)]

Noblesse oblige : the doctrine that the nobleman should act nobly. Phrase coined by Peter Marc Gaston, Duc de Lévis (1764–1830), Fr. royalist writer, in 1808, as the best maxim for the nobility as a class.

Nod, The land of : the land of sleep. The Land of Nod is mentioned in *Genesis* as the land whither Cain fled after the murder of Abel. [Swift, *Polite Conversation* (1608)]

Nodding acquaintance, A : a slight acquaintance which has not passed beyond mutual nods on meeting.

Noggin-staves, To beat to : to beat to pieces. From noggin, a wooden cup made of staves.

Noisy god, The : Bacchus. In allusion to the noisy revelry of his worshippers.

Nolens volens (*Lat.*, willing or unwilling) : [Peele, *Edward I* (1593)]

Noli me tangere (*Lat.*, touch me not) : a person or thing not to be interfered with ; a warning against interference. [*John*, xx, 17 (Vulgate) ; Trevisa, *Bartholomaeus de Proprietati, Rex VII*, LIX (1398)]

Nom de guerre, A (*Fr.*, war name) : a pseudonym. [Dryden, *Kind Keeper*, I, i (1675)]

Nom de plume, A (*Fr.*, pen name) : a pseudonym. The phrase does not exist in French but is an English invention.

Non compos mentis (*Lat.*, not controlling one's mind) : being out of one's mind. [Congreve, *Love for Love*, IV, xii (1695)]

Non expedit, A (*Lat.*, it is not expedient) : a Papal decree prohibiting participation in political elections.

Non olet (*Lat.*, it does not smell) : a phrase used by the Emperor Vespasian in allusion to the proceeds of a tax on urinals.

Non possumus (*Lat.*, we cannot) : a refusal. The formula used by the Popes to express a refusal. Used by Clement VII to Henry VIII of England in declining to grant him a divorce from Catharine of Aragon.

Non sequitur, A (*Lat.*, it does not follow) : a conclusion that does not follow from the premisses. [Wynkyn de Worde,

A Treatyse of this Galaunt, ll. 141–2 (early 16th cent.)]

Nonce word, A : a word coined and used on one occasion only. Term coined by Sir J. A. H. Murray in the *New English Dictionary* (1888 *seq.*).

Nonconformist Conscience, The : the strain of Puritanism in the Liberal party, to be found for the most part among the Nonconformist members of that party, which manifests itself especially in requiring a high moral standard from public men.

Nonconformists : seceders from the Church of England and their spiritual descendants. In allusion to the two thousand clergymen who in 1662 refused to conform to the conditions of the Act of Uniformity.

Nones : (1) in the Rom. calendar, the ninth day before the Ides ; (2) in the R.C. Church a time of prayer, orig. 3 p.m. (the ninth hour), but subsequently changed to mid-day. Hence noon. Lat., *nona hora*, the ninth hour.

Nonjurors : the members of the clergy of the Church of England who refused to take the oaths of supremacy and allegiance to William and Mary on their accession.

Nonplus (*Lat.*, no further) : a mental state in which there is no knowledge of the step next to be taken. [Rob. Wilson, *Three Lords and Three Ladies of London*, l. 91 (1590)]

Non-plussed, To be : to be brought to a mental standstill. [Earle, *Microcosmography : A Bold Forward Man* (1628) *See* Nonplus.

Nonsense from .. To stand no : not to allow anyone to humbug or prevaricate.

Nooning, To take a : to rest. After noonday, the period of rest and refreshment.

Norfolk dumpling, A : a native of Norfolk. After a favourite dish in the county. [Rob. Arnim, *A Nest of Ninnies* (1608)]

Norfolk Howard, A : a bug. After one Joshua Bugg who advertised in *The Times* of the 26th of June, 1862, the change of his surname to Norfolk Howard.

Norfolk tumbler, As active as a : a Norfolk tumbler is a small greyhound of a species formerly employed in catching rabbits. [Dekker and Webster, *Westward Ho*, II. i (1604)]

North for .. To be too : to be too clever for .. In allusion to the reputation for shrewdness of Yorkshiremen.

North Country compliment, A : a gift, neither needed by the recipient nor valued by the donor.

North East Passage, The : a passage practicable for ships from the Atlantic to the Pacific, *via* the north of Europe and Asia.

North Star State, The : Minnesota. In allusion to its motto, ' L'Etoile du Nord,' The North Star.

North West Passage, The : a passage practicable for ships from the Atlantic to the Pacific, *via* the north of America.

Northamptonshire Poet, The : John Clare (1793–1864).

Northern Bear, The : Russia.

Northern Harlot, The infamous : Elizabeth Petrovna (1709–61), Empress of Russia.

Northern Herodotus, The : Snorre Sturleson (1188–1241), Icelandic historian. After Herodotus, Grk. historian, who lived 484 to 425 B.C.

Northern Semiramis, The : Catharine II of Russia.

Northern Victor, The : Gustavus Adolphus (1594–1632), King of Sweden, victor over Russia, Poland and the Empire.

Nose in air, With : disdainfully.

Nose off, To bite (snap) a person's : to answer shortly and peevishly. [Nashe, *Lenten Stuffe* (1599)]

Nose, To follow one's : to go straight ahead without thinking. [Earl of Bristol, *Elvira*, IV, i (1667)]

Nose to the grindstone, To keep one's : to keep a person hard at work, pressed like a knife or tool while being ground. [Heywood, *Proverbes* (1546) ; North, *Plutarch* (1578)]

Nose, To hold up one's : to be proud.

Nose out of joint, To put one's : to supplant a person in another's favour. [Riche, *Farewell* (1581)]

Nose, To be led by the : to be easily influenced. [*Isaiah*, xxxvii, 29]

Nose, To lead by the : to be able to control completely. [Shakespeare, *Winter's Tale*, IV, iv (1611) ; Bacon, *Essays : Of Suitours* (1597)]

Nose, To pay through the : to pay excessively. In the 9th cent. the Danes imposed a tax on the Irish, with nose-slitting as a penalty for non-payment.

Nose, To take pepper in the : to take offence. [*Optick Glasse of Humors*

(1639); Florio, *Worlde of Wordes* (1598)]

Nose into .. To poke one's : to interfere or display curiosity in a matter with which one has no business.

Nose upon his sleeve, To wipe a person's : to insult a person. [Heywood, *Proverbes* (1546)]

Nose to spite one's face, To cut off one's : to harm oneself in obtaining revenge on another.

Nose at .. To turn up one's : to be disdainful at .. [Peter Pindar, *Lyric Odes to the Royal Academicians for* 1785, Ode ii]

Nose of .. Under the : of an action performed in a manner in which it should have been witnessed, although the prospective witness, through negligence or other failure, neglected to notice it. [Dekker and Webster, *Westward Ho*, V, iii (1607) ; Sir Thos. More, *Hist. of Edward V and Richard III* (c. 1557)]

Nose of wax, A : a person easily influenced. [Tindale, *Exposition of Matthew*, vi, 23 (1532)]

Nose of .. To wipe one's : (1) to deprive of .. [*Terence in English* (1614)] ; (2) to offend. [Randolph, *Jealous Lovers* (1646)]

Nosey : the Duke of Wellington. In allusion to the large size of his nose. So-called affectionately by his troops.

Nostradamus, A : an astrologer ; a fortune-teller. After Michel de Nostredame (1503–66), a Fr. physician, who published a book of prophecies.

Nostradamus, As good a prophet as : so obscure in one's meaning as to be unintelligible. In allusion to the extremely obscure prophecies left by Nostradamus.

Nostradamus of Portugal, The : Gonçalo Annes Bandana (d. 1556), a poet-cobbler.

Not half : (colloq.) not at all. A sarcastic use of the term. Literary Eng. in the 16th to 19th cents.

Notes, To compare : to exchange views. [Mrs. Centlivre, *Busie Body* I (1708)]

Nothing of .. To make : to think no trouble of .. [*Joe Miller's Jests*, No. 31 (1739)]

Nottingham lambs : Nottingham bullies.

Nottingham Poet, The : Philip James Bailey (1816–1902). Born near Nottingham.

Nouveau Riche, A (*Fr.*, new rich) : a person newly attained to wealth, but

devoid of breeding. [Lord Lytton, *Pelham*, XXIII (1828)]

Noyades, Les (*Fr.*, the drownings) : the massacre, by means of drowning, of the Vendean refugees who fled to Nantes in 1793.

Nth, To the : to the utmost degree. In allusion to the mathematical formula of ' n.'

Nulli secundus (*Lat.*, second to none) : incomparable. [Burton, *Anatomy of Melancholy* (1621)]

Nulli Secundus Club, The : the Coldstream Guards.

Number, The Golden : *see* Golden.

Number One : oneself. [Peter Pindar, *Odes of Importance : The Wolf and the Lion* (1792)]

Number the waves, To : to act foolishly and to no purpose. From an ancient Grk. proverb.

Number 666 : the number of the Beast. From *Revelations*, xiii, 18.

Nuremburg eggs : watches, which are made to a considerable extent at Nuremburg, and were originally shaped like eggs.

Nut to crack, A hard : a difficult problem to solve.

Nut has no shell, To prove that a : to prove the impossible. [Horace, *Epistles*, II. i, 31]

Nuts aside, To lay one's : to abandon one's youthful follies. In allusion to the Roman marriage ceremony according to which the bridegroom scattered nuts in order to intimate that he thus abandoned his boyish pursuits.

Nutcrack Night : All Hallows Eve (October 31st), when it was formerly the practice to crack nuts by the heat of the fire as a method of divination.

Nutcrackers, The : the 3rd Regt. of Foot, now the East Kent Regt. In allusion to their boast of having broken the heads of the Polish Lancers at the Battle of Albuera.

Nutmeg State, The : Connecticut. On account of its supposed considerable production of wooden nutmegs and other frauds.

Nutshell, To lie in a : to be capable of brief explanation.

O tempora, O mores ! (*Lat.*) : What times ! What manners ! An expression of regret at the change. [Cicero, *In Catilinam*, I, i, 2 ; Jas.

Townley, *High Life Below Stairs*, I, ii (1759)]

O Yes, O Yes, O Yes! Oyez, Oyez, Oyez! (*Norm.-Fr.*, *oyez*, listen !) : the preamble of a town crier before uttering his proclamation.

O's, The Christmas : the seven antiphons, each beginning with O, sung on the nine days before Christmas.

O's, The Fifteen : fifteen prayers, each beginning with the letter O.

O.K. : correct ; quite right. The initial letter of ' Orl Korrect,' a corruption of ' All Correct.' Contraction said by his political opponents to have been used by Pres. Andrew Jackson (1767–1845) of the U.S.

Oak shall bear olives, When the : never. [Nich. Grimald, *A True Loue* (1557)]

Oak, To sport one's : to shut one's door as an indication of being engaged. The phrase originated at the Universities. Most rooms in college have two doors, the outer one being of oak, which is closed when the occupant is absent.

Oar in every man's barge, To have an : to interfere in other people's affairs. [John Redford, *Long Have I Bene a Singing Man* (1540)]

Oar, To put in one's : to interfere in another person's affairs. [Heywood, *Proverbes* (1546) ; Florio, *Worlde of Wordes* (1596)]

Oars, To rest on one's : to take a rest or respite. A boating metaphor.

Oats, To sow one's wild : *see* Wild.

Obadiah, An : a Quaker.

Obiter dictum, An (*Lat.*, something said by the way) : an incidental remark. Properly, ' An expression of opinion on a matter of law, given by a judge in Court in the course of either argument or judgment, but not forming an essential part of the reasons determining the decision, and therefore not of binding authority.' [N.E.D.]

Obiter, To speak : to speak by the way, in passing. *See* Obiter dictum. [Burton, *Anatomy of Melancholy* (1621)]

Occam's razor : the axiom, ' Entities are not to be multiplied,' by which William of Occam (1270–1349), the Eng. Franciscan controversialist, examined every question.

Ocean greyhound, An : a swift Atlantic liner. The term is said to have been invented by T. Dykes in the *New York Herald.*

Ocean Shepherd, The : Sir Walter Raleigh (1552–1618), explorer, courtier, man of letters and statesman.

Ocnus, The Rope of : labour without profit. In allusion to the rope which Ocnus twisted and which the ass consumed as fast as it was produced.

O'Connell's Tail : Daniel O'Connell's following in the House of Commons in the Reformed Parliament of 1832.

October Club, The : a club of extreme Tories formed about 1690. After the October ale for which the Club was celebrated.

October States : those states of the Amer. Union which hold their elections in October in advance of the other states and thus give some hint of the prospects of the wider elections that are to follow.

Octobrists : a Russian political party. After October, 1905, the date of the Czar Nicholas' manifesto promising a parliamentary constitution.

Odds and evens, To be at : to differ in opinion.

Odds, To give a person : to give a person an advantage. [Milton, *Arcades*, I, 20–5 (1633)]

Odds, By long : incomparably ; by a big advantage. A racing metaphor.

Odds, To make no : to make no difference. A betting metaphor.

Odin, A vow (promise) of : one made before the Stone of Odin (in the Orkneys), which has a hole in it large enough for the hand to be put through. [Scott, *The Pirate*, ch. 23 (1821)]

Odium Theologicum (*Lat.*, Theological hatred) : the bitterness of religious dissension.

Odour of sanctity, In the : in good repute. It was formerly believed that the bodies of saints gave out a pleasant odour, a belief probably derived from the excessive use of incense in the last rites.

Odyssey, An : a narrative of travel and adventure. After the title of Homer's poem, narrating the adventures of Odysseus after the capture of Troy.

Œdipus, An : one who is clever at solving riddles. After the Theban hero who solved the riddle of the Sphinx.

Œil de bœuf, An (*Fr.*, bull's eye) : a small round window.

Off colour : disreputable ; not in the best of health.

Ohio Idea, The : the proposal of Democratic leaders in 1868–76, esp. popular in the state of Ohio, to pay U.S. bonds in greenbacks.

Oi Polloi (*Grk.*, the common people) : undergraduates who take ordinary degrees without honours.

Oil to the City of Olives, To send : to perform a work of supererogation.

Oil to the fire (flames), To add (put) : to aggravate strife and turmoil. [Hall, *Chronicle* 820 (1548)]

Oil, To burn the midnight : *see* Midnight.

Oil to extinguish fire, To take : *see* Take.

Oil of palms : money. A pun on palm.

Oil, To smell of : to show signs of deep study. *See* Midnight oil.

Oil, To strike : to be suddenly and greatly successful in business. In allusion to the fortunes made by the discovery of the Pennsylvania and other oil springs.

Oil on troubled waters, To pour : to compose a disturbance or dispute. In allusion to the effect of oil poured on the waters on the occasion of a storm. [Bede, *Ecclesiastical History* (735)]

Old Abe : Abraham Lincoln (1809–65), President of the U.S.

Old Bags : Lord Eldon (1751–1838), Lord Chancellor. In allusion to his practice of carrying about, in separate brief bags, particulars of the cases in which his judgment was pending.

Old Bendy : the Devil, who is willing to bend to anyone's inclination.

Old Bona Fide : Louis XIV, King of France.

Old Boy : an expression of familiarity addressed to a man. [Shakespeare, *Twelfth Night*, III, ii (1601)]

Old Bullion : Thomas Hart Benton (1782–1858), Amer. statesman. In allusion to his advocacy of bimettalism.

Old Catholics : the Germ. Rom. Catholics who rejected the doctrine of Papal infallibility in 1870 and seceded under Johann Joseph Ignaz von Döllinger.

Old Colony, The : Eastern Massachusetts.

Old Country, The : England. So-called in the imperial dominions.

Old as a crow, As : [Aristophanes, *Birds*, 609 ; Ovid, *Amores*, Bk. II, vi, 35–6]

Old Dessauer, The : Leopold, Prince of Anhalt-Dessau (1676–1747), Prussian general.

Old Dominion, The : Virginia ; as the original of the Eng. colonies in N. America and in allusion to its former official description as ' The Colony and Dominion of Virginia.'

Old as an eagle, As : extremely old. [Terence, *Heautontimorumenos*, III, ii, 9]

Old England : first used generally in 1641, in contradistinction from the colony of New England, but employed in 1633 in the correspondence with Sir Edward Coke.

Old Ephraim : a grizzly bear.

Old Fogs : the 87th Regt. of Foot, now the Royal Irish Fusiliers. In allusion to its battlecry, *Fag-an-Bealach*, clear the way.

Old Fox : Marshal Soult (1769–1851). On account of his cunning strategy.

Old Fritz : Frederick the Great (1712–86). So-called (*Der Alte Fritz*) by his soldiers.

Old Gentleman, The : the Devil.

Old Glorious : William III of England.

Old Glory : the United States national flag.

Old Grog : Admiral Edward Vernon (1684–1757), who introduced grog into the British navy.

Old Harry : *see* Harry.

Old head on young shoulders, An : a person wise beyond his years.

Old Hickory : *see* Hickory.

Old as the hills, As : very aged.

Old Lady of Threadneedle Street, The : the Bank of England, which is situated in Threadneedle Street, London. So designated by John Gilray in a caricature (1797), and by Wm. Cobbett (1762–1835) on account of its conservatism.

Old Law, The : the Mosaic Dispensation ; the books of the Old Testament.

Old Line State, The : Maryland. In allusion to the Mason and Dixon line which separated it from Pennsylvania.

Old maids' children : ideal children whose behaviour is ideal.

Old Man Eloquent, The : a name applied to several persons : (1) Socrates (436–338 B.C.) by Milton ; (2) S. T. Coleridge (1772–1834) ; (3) John Quincy Adams (1767–1848) ; (4) W. E. Gladstone (1809–98), etc.

Old Man of the Mountain, The : Sheikh al-Jabal, the chief of the Assassins (Arab., *Hashashin*), a fanatical Moslem sect which flourished in Persia and Arabia in the twelfth and thirteenth centuries and murdered its opponents.

Old man of the sea, An : any person of whose company it is very difficult to rid oneself. In allusion to the monster who leapt on to the back of Sindbad in *The Arabian Nights* and refused to be dislodged.

Old Morality : William Henry Smith (1825–91), Eng. statesman.

Old Nick : *see* Nick, Old.

Old Noll : Oliver Cromwell. So-called by the Royalists. Noll is a contraction of Oliver.

Old North State, The : North Carolina, the northern of the two Carolinas.

Old Pam : Lord Palmerston (1784–1865), British statesman.

Old Port School, The : the old-fashioned party, who drink old port, and support Toryism in politics and strict orthodoxy in religion.

Old Pretender, The : James Edward Stuart (1688–1766), son of James II of England.

Old Public Functionary, The : James Buchanan (1791–1868), Pres. of the U.S.

Old Put : Israel Putnam (1718–90), Amer. general.

Old Reliable : George Henry Thomas (1816–70), Amer. general.

Old Rough and Ready : Zachary Taylor (1784–1850), Pres. of the U.S. So-called by his troops during the war with Mexico.

Old Rowley : Charles II. After the name of a favourite racehorse.

Old Salt, An : an experienced sailor.

Old Scratch : the Devil. After Schratz, a Scand. demon.

Old song, To go for an : to be sold for a nominal price. [*The Spectator*, No. 597 (1714)]

Old Style : the Julian method of reckoning time ; abandoned in England in 1752, in Russia in 1918.

Old Tom : an excellent brand of gin. After Thomas Chamberlain who used to distil it.

Old Toughs, The : the 23rd Regt. of Foot.

Old wives' tale, An : an unconvincing story. [Tyndale, *Translation of the Bible* (I *Tim.*, iv, 7) (1534) ; Peele, *Old Wives' Tale* (1590)]

Old woman, An : a timid, fussy person, supposed to resemble an old woman in character.

Old woman to dance, To teach an : *see* Teach.

Old World, The : Europe, Asia and Africa.

Old Zach : James Buchanan (1791–1868), President of the U.S.

Olibrius, An : a person in an unsuitable situation. After Olibrius, a Rom.

senator, who was in 472 proclaimed emperor without any special qualification.

Olive branch, To hold out the : to make approaches for peace or a reconciliation. Anciently the olive-branch was a symbol of peace. The vanquished in a fight, suing for peace, held out an olive-branch.

Olive branches : children. After *Psalm*, cxxviii, 3 : 'thy children like olive plants round thy table.'

Oliver asking for more, Like : in allusion to Oliver Twist, in Dickens' novel so entitled (1838).

Oliver, A Roland for an : *see* Roland.

Oliver Twist, An : one who is not satisfied with his portion but wants more. After the hero of the novel so entitled, by Dickens (1838).

Olla Podrida : a miscellaneous assortment. After an Ital. dish consisting of chopped meat and vegetables. Span., putrid pot.

Olney Doctrine, The : an extension of the Monroe Doctrine (*q.v.*), put forward in a dispute with Great Britain in 1895, by Richard Olney (1835–1917). It claimed that Great Britain, apart from her Amer. colonies, had no right to take any action on the American continent.

Olympiad, An : a period of four years ; that being the interval between two celebrations of the Olympic games.

Olympian : heavenly ; majestic. After Olympus (*q.v.*).

Olympic games : public games on a considerable scale. After the famous games of ancient Greece held in honour of Olympian Zeus.

Olympus : the abode of the gods. After the mountain on the borders of Macedonia and Thessaly where Jupiter held his court.

Omega : the last of a series ; the end of a discussion. After the last letter in the Grk. alphabet.

Omega, Alpha and : *see* Alpha.

Omnibus Bill, An : a parliamentary bill whose clauses treat of several miscellaneous matters. The Omnibus Bills in Amer. history were that of 1850, by which a series of compromises was enacted, and that of 1888 whereby several territories were in the one measure authorized to qualify for admission to the Union as states.

Omnium gatherum, An : a miscellaneous collection. Lat., *omnium*, of all

s

things, and *gatherum*, mock Latin. [Croke, *Letter to Cranmer* (1530)]

On dit, An (*Fr.*, they say) : a rumour.

Once in a blue moon : *see* Blue moon.

One-horse : mean ; petty. Apparently in allusion to people who keep a private conveyance but can afford to drive only one horse.

One o'clock, Like : very rapidly, energetically. Apparently from the rapidity with which the end of the workmen's customary dinner-hour (mid-day to one o'clock) arrives.

One too many for .. To be : to outwit.

Only, The : Jean Paul Richter (1763–1825), Germ. novelist and humorist.

Onus probandi, The (*Lat.*) : the responsibility for proving (a case).

Open arms, To receive with : to give a hearty welcome to ..

Open the ball, To : to commence a discussion or undertaking. A dancing metaphor.

Open court, In : publicly ; openly. Properly before a court to which the public has easy access.

Open door, The : the principle of free trade.

Open door policy, The : a policy of equal opportunities for all, esp. in matters of foreign commerce. Introduced in 1899.

Open a door with an axe, To : to act foolishly and to no purpose. From an ancient Grk. proverb.

Open ear, An : close attention. [Early 13th cent.]

Open hand, With : liberally ; generously.

Open house (table), To keep : to entertain generously with and without formal invitation. [Palsgrave, 597 (1530)]

Open question, An : a subject on which members of a political party are released from discipline and permitted to follow their own line.

Open secret, An : news that is not yet publicly announced, but is none the less known to the public. [Goethe, *Gespräche mit Eckermann*, III, 143 ; Carlyle, *Jean Paul Richter* (1830)]

Open Sesame, An : a means of obtaining immediate attention and satisfaction. After the magical formula in the *Arabian Nights'* tale of *Ali Baba and the Forty Thieves*.

Ophir, The gold of : fine gold. After the biblical region of Ophir whence gold was obtained. [*The Spectator*, No. 218 (1711)]

Opium eater, The English : Thomas de Quincey (1785–1859). After his *Confessions of an English Opium Eater* (1822).

Opium War, The : the war waged by Great Britain in 1840–2 to compel China to permit the importation of opium.

Opportunism : the policy of acting as is expedient, not in accordance necessarily with logical principles ; the policy that depends upon the opportunity. In Fr. history the opportunists were the party, led by Gambetta and Ferry, who adapted their policy to current exigencies.

Opposition, His Majesty's : the formally constituted party in opposition to the Government in parliament.

Oracle, An : an exceptionally wise person ; a decision that implies great wisdom. Properly the answer of a Pagan god to a question put to him by one of his believers.

Oracle of the Church, The : Saint Bernard (1091–1153).

Oracle, Sir : *see* Sir Oracle.

Oracle, To speak like an : to give utterance to words of wisdom. After the Oracles, in Grk. and Rom. antiquity, which were supposed to give utterance to the words of the gods. [Congreve, *Love for Love*, I, ii (1695).]

Oracle, To work the : to influence a powerful agency in one's favour ; to raise money by stratagem. In allusion to the Oracle at Delphi where Pythia uttered the revelations of Apollo.

Orange, The : Protestant Ulster. *See* Orangemen.

Orange blossoms, To gather : to seek a wife. In allusion to the orange blossoms generally worn by brides at their weddings, a custom derived from Syria.

Orange Lilies, The : the 35th Regt. of Foot, now the 1st Royal Sussex Regt. In allusion to the colour of the facings on their uniform and the white plumes gained by them at the Battle of Quebec.

Orange Lodges (Clubs) : societies of Orangemen (*q.v.*).

Orange Peel : Sir Robert Peel (1788–1850). In allusion to his strong anti-Catholic prejudice displayed when Chief Secretary for Ireland.

Orangemen : a body of Ulster Protestants, very determined in their opposition to Catholicism. After William III of Orange, the Protestant king.

Orator of the Human Race, The : Jean Baptiste (Anacharsis) Cloots (1755–94), Fr. revolutionary leader. So-called by himself.

Orbilian stick, The : the birch. After Pupıllus Orbilius (113–13 B.C.), Rom. schoolmaster.

Orbilius, An : a very strict schoolmaster. After one mentioned by Horace in *Epistles*, II, i, 71. *See* Orbilian stick.

Orchard of Ireland, The : County Armagh.

Order, To call to : to recall a speaker to the subject under discussion.

Order of the day, The : the agenda set down for consideration in a legislative body or other debating assembly.

Order reigns in Warsaw : the announcement made by Marshal Horace Sebastiani, Foreign Minister, in the French Chamber after the suppression of the Polish rebellion in 1831. It was the order of the cemetery.

Order, A tall : a considerable demand on one's credulity, patience, etc.

Orders : the ranks of (1) bishop, priest, deacon, sub-deacon, acolyte, exorcist, reader and doorkeeper in the R.C. Church ; (2) bishop, priest and deacon in the Anglican Church ; (3) bishop, priest, deacon, sub-deacon and reader, and sometimes also singer in the Eastern churches.

Ordnance map, An : a map prepared by the Ordnance Survey (*q.v.*).

Ordnance Survey, The : the official survey of the United Kingdom. Formerly carried out by the Ordnance Department of the War Office.

Ore rotundo (*Lat.*, with round mouth) : loudly ; elegantly. [Horace, *Ars Poetica*, 323 ; Swift (1720)]

Orestes, As mad as : in allusion to Orestes, son of Agamemnon and Clytæmnestra, who went mad after having avenged his father's death. [Burton, *Anatomy of Melancholy* (1621)]

Orestes and Pylades : inseparable and self-sacrificing friends. After two Grk. heroes, Orestes, the son of Agamemnon and Pylades, the son of Strophius.

Organic Statute, The : the Russian ukase of 1832 which deprived Poland of self-government.

Organized Hypocrisy, An : a Conservative government. So described by Lord Beaconsfield (1804–81) in the House of Commons (March 17, 1845).

Organizer of Victory, The : Lazare Nicolas Carnot (1753–1823), Fr. statesman. So-named in an anonymous interjection in the course of his speech in the French Convention on the 27th May, 1795.

Orgoglio : the personification of pride. After a giant in Spenser, *Faerie Queene* (1590–6).

Oriana, The peerless : Queen Elizabeth. Oriana was the legendary mistress of Amadis of Gaul.

Orientation : position in regard to a centre of influence or attraction. Properly, turning or indication towards the East as the religious centre.

Oriflamme, The : the ancient standard of France, until 1415. Orig. the banner of the Abbey of St. Denis. Late Lat., *auriflamma*, flame of gold.

Original sin : the doctrine of the natural evil tendency of man.

Orleans comment, Like an : rendering obscure instead of clarifying. After the long-winded commentaries of Orleans College.

Orleans, The Maid of : *see* Maid.

Ormus, The wealth of : in allusion to Ormus or Hormuz, an ancient and medieval city of Persia, famous for its commerce and wealth and in particular for its pearl fisheries. [Milton, *Paradise Lost*, Bk. II (1667)]

Ormusd ; Ormuzd : the angel or principle of light and goodness, according to the Magian system.

Ornithology, The Father of : *see* Father.

Orphan of the Temple, The : the Duchesse d'Angoulême, daughter of Louis XVI and Marie Antoinette. In allusion to her imprisonment by the Revolutionaries in the Temple prison.

Orpheus : a Grk. mythical personage able to exercise miraculous influence by means of his lute.

Orpheus of the Eighteenth Century, The : Handel (1685–1759), the musical composer.

Orpheus of the Green Isle, The : Furlough O'Carolan (1670–1738), the Green Isle being Ireland.

Orpheus of Highwaymen, The : John Gay (1685–1732), author of *The Beggar's Opera* (1727).

Orphic : mysterious ; esoteric. After Orpheus, the mythical poet, who was able to move inanimate objects by the music of his lyre.

Orson, As wild as : after Orson, who was brought up by a bear among its cubs in the early medieval romance of *Valentine and Orson*.

Orton in his shop, As sure as Job : Job Orton (d. 1717) was a grocer of Shrewsbury who was famous for his attention to business.

Ossa, To heap Pelion upon : to add difficulty to difficulty. After the attempt of the giants to reach to heaven by placing Mount Pelion on top of Mount Ossa. [Homer, *Odyssey*, Bk. XI ; Dekker, *The Gull's Hornbook*, ch. 6 (1609)]

Ostend, To hold out as long as : in allusion to the siege of Ostend which lasted for three years and ten weeks (1601-4). [Dekker and Webster, *Westward Ho*, I, i (1607)]

Ostrich, To hide one's head like an : *see* Ostrich policy.

Ostrich, To play the : *see* Ostrich policy.

Ostrich policy, An : a policy of closing one's eyes and imagining that nobody can see one. In allusion to the supposed practice of the ostrich of hiding its head when in danger.

Ostrich stomach, An : a stomach that can digest anything. In allusion to the practice of the ostrich of swallowing pieces of iron, etc., when stones to assist in the digestion of its food are not available.

Othello's occupation's gone : one is no longer to be the centre of attraction. [Shakespeare, *Othello*, III, iii (1604)]

Otium cum dignitate (*Lat.*, idleness with dignity) : the phrase ' cum dignitate otium ' was used by Cicero in the *Oration for Sextus*, xlv, 98, and was introduced into Eng. by Lord Bolingbroke in a letter to Swift (Nov. 19, 1729).

Out of the blue : quite unexpectedly.

Out at elbows : shabbily dressed.

Out of harness : retired from work.

Out of joint, The time is : the times are unsettled. [Shakespeare, *Hamlet*, I, v (1602-3)]

Out and outer, An : one who is thorough or extreme.

Out of pocket, by .. To be : to suffer financially from ..

Out of sorts : somewhat indisposed.

Out of the wood, Not to be : not yet to be clear of a difficulty. In allusion to the time when brigands infested the woods to the danger of travellers.

Out-Herod Herod, To : *see* Herod.

Outlander, An : an alien inhabitant ; esp. one who suffers disabilities.

[Verstegan, *Restitution of Decayed Intelligence* (1605)]

Outrun the constable, To : to live extravagantly ; properly, to avoid the law and its officers. [T. Powell, *Tom All Trades* (1631) ; Butler, *Hudibras*, Pt. I, Canto iii (1663)]

Overland Route, The : the route from England to India through France and Italy and thence from Brindisi by sea.

Overshoot the mark, To : to go further than was ' intended. An archery metaphor. [Fraunce, *Lawier's Logike* (1588)]

Ovid, The French : *see* French Ovid.

Owl light : dusk ; twilight.

Owl in an ivy bush, Like an : *see* Ivy bush.

Owl shall match the nightingale, When the : never.

Own, On one's : independently.

Ox goeth to the slaughter, As an : foolishly and helplessly. [*Proverbs*, vii, 22]

Ox on one's tongue, To have an : to have been bribed to silence. After the representation of an ox on Athenian coins.

Oxford Blues, The : the Royal Horse Guards. After the colour of their uniform and from the fact of their having been raised by Aubrey, Earl of Oxford.

Oxford Movement, The : a movement, originating among members of the University of Oxford in 1833, to effect a rapprochement between the Church of England and Rome. It was also known as the Tractarian Movement from *Tracts for the Times*, the volume in which the views of the founders of the movement were first set forth, and its members as Puseyites, from Edward Bouverie Pusey (1800-82), one of the founders.

Oxford School, The : the theological school of thought representative of the Oxford Movement (*q.v.*).

Oxymoron, A living : one who contradicts himself. After a figure of speech which is superficially self-contradictory.

Oyster part, An : a part of an actor which consists of one short sentence only. Like an oyster, he opens his mouth but once.

P.P.C. (*Fr., pour prendre congé*, to take leave) : initials put on a visiting card as a substitute for a farewell visit.

P's and Q's, To mind one's : to be careful. A reference to the pints and quarts chalked up in country public-houses against credit customers. Orig. a warning to the customer not to allow his account to mount too high. Other suggestions are from (1) the writing-master's injunctions to distinguish between p and h and q and g ; (2) '*pieds*,' deportment, and '*queues*,' tails of hair, both very important matters in the France of Louis XIV and Louis XV.

P's, The Five : William Oxberry (1784–1824), who was printer, poet, publisher, publican and player.

Pabulum Acherontis (*Lat.*, food for Acheron): a dead body. *See* Acheron.

Pace, To go the : to live a fast, extravagant life. [Beginning of 18th cent.]

Paces, To put through one's : to exhibit one's accomplishments. A metaphor drawn from the stable.

Pacific blockade, A : *see* Blockade.

Pack the cards, To : so to arrange the cards as to secure an undue advantage to oneself. [16th cent.]

Pack a jury, To : so to select a jury as to be assured of a verdict in one's own favour. [16th cent.]

Pack up one's traps, To : to depart. In allusion to the packing of one's personal belongings before departing from a place.

Packing, To send : to dismiss a person, to send him about his business. [R.B., *Appius and Virginia*, l. 216 (1563)]

Pack-rag Day : May Day. So-called in Lincolnshire, because servants being hired from that day for a year, packed up their rags or clothes preparatory to removing to their new homes. In some counties the term was similarly applied to Michaelmas Day.

Pacolet's horse ; A horse of Pacolet : a very swift horse. In allusion to the enchanted steed of Pacolet in the romance of *Valentine and Orson*.

Pacta Conventa : the agreement between the Polish nobles and their kings made on the occasion of the election of the latter.

Pactolian : golden. After the fabulous golden sands of the River Pactolus in Lydia.

Pactolus, As rich as the River : *see* Pactolian.

Pad, To go out in the : to tramp. From ' pad,' a path.

Pad the hoof, To : to tramp.

Pad in the straw, A : anything wrong ; a concealed danger. [Palsgrave (1530) ; Heywood, *Proverbes* (1546)]

Paddington Fair : a public execution at Tyburn which is within the Borough of Paddington. These executions were abolished in 1868.

Paddle one's own canoe, To : to rely on oneself and one's own exertions. Orig. an American phrase.

Paddy : an Irishman. After St. Patrick, the patron saint of Ireland.

Paddy-whack, A : an Irishman. After Patrick, the patron saint of Ireland, and wag, one who makes jokes.

Pæan, To sing the : to exult ; to sing in triumph. The pæan in Grk. antiquities was a hymn of thanksgiving addressed to Apollo.

Pæonian : medical. After Pæan, the physician of the gods.

Page of State to the Muses, The : Edmund Spenser (1552–99). So-called by Wm. Wordsworth in *The Prelude*, Bk. III (1850).

Paget's Irregular Horse : the Fourth Hussars. In allusion to its irregular drill after its return from India.

Paignton pudding, As big as a : Paignton, Devon, is famous for the immense size of the puddings made there to celebrate exceptional occasions.

Paint black, To : to attribute evil to . . [Lodge, *A Margarite of America*, 84 (1596)]

Paint-brush Baronets : artist baronets.

Paint the dead, To : to act foolishly and to no purpose. From an ancient Grk. proverb.

Paint the lily, To : to perform a work of supererogation. [Shakespeare, *King John*, IV, ii, ll. 11–6 (1596)]

Paint the town red, To : to create a disturbance ; to enjoy oneself in a rollicking, semi-riotous manner. An Americanism.

Painted sepulchre, A : a hypocrite ; one whose real thoughts belie his fair pretence. [*Matthew*, xxiii, 27, according to the version of the *Great Bible* (1539)]

Painted sheath, A : beauty. [Heywood, *Proverbes* (1546)]

Painter, To cut the : to dissociate oneself from . . ; esp. in allusion to the secession of colonies from the mother-country. A naval metaphor.

Painter of the Graces, The : Andrea Appiani (1754–1817), the best fresco painter of his age.

Pair, To : in Parliament, to arrange with a political opponent for a mutual abstention from voting for a limited period.

Pair, Au (*Fr.*) : phrase used in respect of exchanges of accommodation in two families residing in different countries.

Paladin, A : an eminent champion. Properly, a member of a band of knights in the service of Charlemagne, at whose head was the Count Palatine. Orig. an official of the palace at Byzantium.

Palaver, The National : parliament.

Palamedes, A : a clever, ingenious person. After the son of Nauplius, who invented many ingenious contrivances and penetrated the assumed madness of Ulysses.

Palatine, A : a county over which an earl, bishop or duke had royal jurisdiction. In England the counties palatine were Chester, Durham and Lancaster. Lit., belonging to a palace.

Pale, The ; The English Pale : the district in Ireland which was colonized by Eng. settlers in the reign of Henry II. It comprised orig. the districts of Cork, Drogheda, Dublin, Waterford, and Wexford, but it gradually became reduced to the Dublin district only.

Pale as death, As : exceedingly pale. [Beaumont and Fletcher, *Knight of the Burning Pestle* (1610)]

Pale Face, A : a European or a person of European descent. So-called by the Amer.-Indians.

Pale as a ghost, As : white in the face. [Chaucer, *Canterbury Tales, Prologue*, 205 (14th cent.)]

Pale, To leap the : to live beyond one's income. [*The Man in the Moone* (1609)]

Pale as a lily, As : *see* White as a lily, As.

Pale of Settlement, The Jewish : fifteen governments of Western Russia in the towns of which the Jews of Russia were confined in accordance with the oppressive policy of the Czarist regime.

Paley's watch : the watch used as an illustration to prove the argument of design, by William Paley in his *Natural Theology* (1802).

Palinody, A : a recantation. After the name of the ode which was composed by Stesichorus as an apology for his attack on Helen.

Palinurus, A : a pilot. After the steersman of Æneas.

Palladio, The English : Inigo Jones (1573–1653). After Andrea Palladio (1518–80), a famous Ital. architect.

Palladium, A : any object that affords protection. After the Palladion, the statue of Pallas, that afforded protection to Troy.

Palladium of Scotland, The : the Coronation Stone ; formerly of Scone.

Pallas : the Grk. goddess of wisdom.

Pallas' bird : the owl. After one of the attributes of the goddess, Pallas Athene.

Pallium, The : the cloak of office, the presentation of which by the Pope authorizes high church functionaries to enter on their office. Orig. the outer garment generally worn by men in ancient Rome.

Palm off, To : to persuade a person to accept goods or a statement of an inferior or fraudulent character. A conjuring metaphor.

Palm, To bear the : to carry off the prize. In allusion to the palm leaves with which in classical times the victor was crowned. [Nat. Woodes, *Conflict of Conscience*, III, i (1581)]

Palm, To give (yield) the : to suffer or admit defeat. *See* Palm, To bear the. [Lyttelton, *Dialogues of the Dead*, Dial. xi (1760)]

Palm, An itching : a hand ready to receive a bribe. In allusion to the superstition that if one's hand itches one is about to receive money. [Shakespeare, *Julius Cæsar*, IV (1601)]

Palm oil : a bribe ; that with which the palm is greased or made easy. A pun. [*Hickscorner*, ll. 268–9 (1520)]

Palm Sunday : the Sunday immediately preceding Easter, commemorative of the triumphant entry of Jesus into Jerusalem. [*John*, xii]

Palm Sunday, Sad : Palm Sunday in 1463, the day of the Battle of Towton, when 37,000 Englishmen are said to have been killed.

Palmetto State, The : South Carolina. In allusion to the palmetto tree in its arms and also to the number of those trees which grow in the state.

Palmy Days (of the drama, etc.), The : the splendid period whose leading representatives would, if they had been living in classical times, have been awarded palms of merit.

Palmyra of the North, The : Petrograd.

Palsy, The gentleman's : ruin through gambling.

Paltock's Inn : a poverty-stricken place. [Gosson, *Schoole of Abuse* (1579)]

Pam : Lord Palmerstone. A contraction.

Pamphlet, A : a small book, generally in paper covers. After *Pamphilus seu Amore* (*Pamphilet*), a 12th cent. Lat. poem. More remotely from Pamphylla (fl. 58 A.D.), a Grk. female historian ; or from Pamphilus, a comic writer of the 12th cent.

Pan : the personification and deification of nature.

Pan out, To : to show results. Orig. an Amer. gold miner's phrase.

Pan, The Great : Voltaire (1694–1778).

Panacea, A : a universal cure. After Panacea, the daughter of Æsculapius, the god of medicine.

Panama : the great Fr. financial scandal of 1892 which arose out of the company formed to cut the Panama Canal. Hence a financial scandal.

Panama hat, A : properly Palmata hat, from the leaf of the Cardulavia Palmata out of which it was made.

Pan-Americanism : the movement for close political co-operation between all the states of the Amer. continent.

Panamino : An Ital. financial scandal of 1893. Lit., the little Panama, in allusion to the Fr. Panama scandal of the previous year.

Pan-Anglican : embracing the whole of the Anglican Church in all countries and in all its developments.

Pancake Tuesday (Day) : Shrove Tuesday. In allusion to the pancakes eaten on that day.

Pandarus, To play Sir : to act as a procurer. *See* Pander. [Ben Jonson, *The New Inn*, I (1630)]

Pander, A : one who acts as procurer for the gratification of lust. After Pandarus, the Trojan, who acted as the intermediary between Troilus and Cressida.

Pandora's box : a box which contained the blessings of life, given to Pandora, the first woman, by the gods. She opened the box and the blessings escaped.

Panem et circenses (*Lat.,* bread and games) : food and amusement at the public expense. In allusion to the bread and games supplied free in the years of decline of the Rom. Empire.

Pan-Germanism : the movement for the extension of Germ. influence in general, in particular for the incorporation in the Germ. Empire of the Germ. districts of Austria.

Panhandle State, The : West Virginia. In allusion to its shape.

Pan-Islamism : a movement for the co-operation of all Mohammedans directed towards their freedom from Christian rule.

Panjandrum, The Great : a self-important, pretentious official. After a word invented in the nonsense verses of Samuel Foote (1720–77), to test the memory of Macklin.

Pan-pipes : the shepherd's flute. After the god, Pan, who is said to have invented it.

Pan-Slavism : a Russian movement for the incorporation in the Russ. Empire of all the neighbouring Slav populations.

Pantables, To stand upon one's : *see* Pantofles.

Pantagruelian : coarse and extravagantly satirical. After Rabelais, *Pantagruel.*

Pantagruelian herb, The : hemp. In allusion to its application to hanging by Pantagruel in Rabelais, *Pantagruel,* Bk. II.

Pantaloon, To play : to act invariably as subservient to another. In allusion to the pantaloon or buffoon in pantomime.

Pantheon, A : a church or other building employed as a burial-place for national heroes ; the whole body of the gods. After the Grk. temple which was dedicated to all the gods.

Pantheon, The British : Westminster Abbey.

Panthera bone, To wear a comb of : to be perfect. After the comb of panthera bone worn by the queen in H. von Alkmar, *Reynard the Fox* (1498). The panthera was an imaginary beast of the Orient.

Pantile shop, A : a nonconformist place of worship. After the pantiles with which formerly they were often roofed.

Pantofles (Pantables), To stand upon one's : to stand upon one's dignity. Pantofle is a slipper, from Dutch, *pantoffel.* [Saker, *Narbonus*, II, 99 (1580)]

Panton gates, As old as : in allusion to Pandon Gates, Newcastle on Tyne (1649).

Panurge asked if he should marry, As : asking advice with no intention of following it. In allusion to Panurge's procedure as narrated in Rabelais, *Gargantua and Pantagruel*, Bk. III, 9.

Pap with a hatchet, To give : to do a kind action in an unkind manner. *See* title of a book by John Lyly (1589).

Paper, On : in writing or print.

Paper blockade, A : *see* Blockade.

Paper house, A : a theatre whose audience has to a large extent been admitted free of charge, *i.e.*, with paper passes.

Paper King, The : John Law of Lauriston (1671–1729), financier. In allusion to the paper prospectuses which set forth his financial schemes.

Paper minister, A : a preacher who reads his sermons.

Paphian queen (goddess), The : Venus. After Paphos in Cyprus, which city was dedicated to her.

Par : *see* Above par *and* Below par.

Par excellence (*Lat.*, *per excellentiam*, by virtue of its excellence) : pre-eminently. [Tofte, *Alba* (1598)]

Par nobile fratrum (*Lat.*, a noble pair of brothers) : [Horace, *Satires*, II, iii, 243]

Paradise of exiles, The : Italy. In allusion to its large population of foreign rentiers.

Parbleus, The : the French. After the Fr. oath, Parbleu, corruption of *Par Dieu*, by God.

Parc aux Cerfs : Louis XV's harem at Versailles.

Parcæ, The : the Fates—Clotho, Lachesis, Atropos. Lat., *pars*, a lot.

Pardon Bell, A : the Angelus bell (*q.v.*). In allusion to the pardon gained by reciting the Angelus.

Pari mutuel (*Fr.*, mutual bet) : a form of mechanical betting in which the total amount wagered is divided among the successful.

Pari passu (*Lat.*, with equal pace) : simultaneously. [De Quincey, *On Murder Considered as One of the Fine Arts* (1827)]

Parian verse : spiteful satire. After Archilocos (fl. 650 B.C.), of Paros.

Paribanou, Like a Fairy : in allusion to the fairy in the *Arabian Nights'* tale, *Prince Ahmed and Pari-Banou*, who presented Ahmed with a tent which when folded would go into his pocket and when opened would cover a whole army.

Paridel, A : a wealthy, young, pleasure and interest seeking man of leisure. After a character in Spenser, *Faerie Queen*, III, x, *and* IV, i (1590–6).

Paris garden, A : a scene of disorder. In allusion to the place of popular resort, so-called, formerly situated in Southwark, London. The name was derived from Robert de Paris who founded it at the end of the 14th cent.

Paris of Japan, The : Osaka. So-called by Gibson in the *Gallery of Geography*.

Paris, Little : (1) Bucharest ; (2) Brussels ; (3) the Galleria Vittorio Emanuelo of Milan.

Paris Matins : the massacre of St. Bartholomew in 1572.

Parish, To come upon the : to be dependent for support on the Poor Law. In allusion to the parish as an area for the administration of poor relief. [Fcs. Coventry, *History of Pompey the Little*, ch. 10 (1751)]

Parisian Wedding, The : the massacre of St. Bartholomew, which was perpetrated in the course of the wedding festivities of Henri of Navarre and Marguerite of France (1572).

Parliament, The Addled : *see* Addled Parliament.

Parliament, Barebones : the parliament of 1653 in which Praise God Barbon (Barebones) sat for the City of London.

Parliament of Bats, The : the parliament of 1426 to which the members, being forbidden to wear swords, came armed with bats or bludgeons.

Parliament, The Black : the parliament held by Henry VIII in Bridewell.

Parliament, The Devil's : that of 1459 by which the Duke of York, the Earl of March and their principal followers were attainted.

Parliament, The Drinking (Drunken) : the Scot. parliament of 1661, the members of which, according to Burnet, were almost perpetually drunk !

Parliament of Dunces, The : the parliament of 1404, because lawyers were disqualified from membership.

Parliament, The Good : the reforming parliament of 1376.

Parliament, The Lack-learning (Illiterate) (Lay) : that of 1404 from which lawyers were excluded.

Parliament, The Little : *see* Little.

Parliament, The Long : *see* Long.

Parliament, The Mad : the parliament of 1258. In allusion to its opposition to King Henry IV.

Parliament, The Marvellous (Merciless) : that of 1388 which condemned the favourites of Richard II.

Parliament, The Mongrel : that held at Oxford in 1681, in which Whigs and Tories combined to pass the Exclusion Act.

Parliament, The Pacific : the parliament of 1710 which approved the Treaty of Utrecht, thus terminating a war of eleven years' standing.

Parliament, The Pensioner (Pensionary) : see Pensioned Parliament.

Parliament, The Rump : the Long Parliament of 1640, after it had been purged by Cromwell.

Parliament, The Running : the Scot. parliament, which frequently changed its place of meeting.

Parliament, The Short : that which sat from April 13 to May 5, 1640.

Parliament Soldiers : those of General Monk, who restored Charles II to the throne.

Parliament, The Unlearned : the parliament of Dunces (q.v.).

Parliament, The Unmerciful : the Marvellous Parliament (q.v.).

Parliament, The Useless : that of June 18 to Aug. 12, 1625.

Parliament, The Wonderful (Wonderworking) : the Marvellous Parliament (q.v.).

Parliamentary language : language which does not transgress the law of orderly discussion in parliament.

Parliamentary train, A : a train for third-class passengers at not more than a penny a mile (now 1¾d.), run in accordance with parliamentary statute.

Parnassian : sacred to the Muses ; in particular relating to a Fr. school of poets of the mid 19th cent. After Parnassus, the sacred mountain of the Muses.

Parnassus : the domain of poetry. See Parnassian.

Parnassus, To climb : to write poetry. [Marriage of Wit and Science I (1570)] See Parnassian.

Parnellism : the political movement led by Charles Stewart Parnell (1846–91) after the split in the Irish Nationalist Party of 1890.

Parnellite juice, To stew in : a phrase used by Sir William Harcourt (1827–1904) in allusion to the supporters of Home Rule for Ireland, in the period of Parnell and before the policy had been adopted by the Liberal Party as a whole.

Parolles in a pedagogue's wig, A : a vain pretender ; a man of words but not of deeds. Fr., parole, a word.

Parr, Old : Thomas Parr, an agricultural labourer, said to have been born in 1483 and to have died in 1635.

Parody, The Father of : see Father of Parody.

Parricide, The Beautiful : Beatrice Cenci (d. 1599).

Parsley, To need nothing but : to be dead. In allusion to the parsley with which the tombs of the Greeks used to be decked.

Parson Runo, A : a simple-minded clergyman. In allusion to the proverbial simplicity of the Lutheran clergy of the Isle of Runo.

Parson's barn, As big as a : a parson's barn is a tithe barn, which was often of very great size.

Parson's nose, The : the rump of a fowl.

Part, In good ; In bad : willingly ; unwillingly. [Sir Thos. Wyatt, The Louer Suspected of Change (1557)]

Part and parcel : an essential part of anything.

Parthian fight, A : a fight in which one party continues to fight while apparently fleeing. In allusion to the practice of the Parthians of discharging their missiles backwards while apparently fleeing.

Parthian glance, A : a final look from one withdrawing. See Parthian fight.

Parthian retreat, A : See Parthian fight. [Jasper Fisher, Fuimus Troes, III, v (1633)]

Parthian shot (shaft), A : a final pointed retort. See Parthian fight.

Parti pris (Fr., side taken) : bias.

Partibus infidelium, Bishops in : Rom. Catholic bishops holding imaginary sees without any catholic community. Lat., in the lands of the unbelievers.

Parting of the ways, At the : at the point at which one must make up one's mind as to the choice of two alternative courses.

Partington, Mrs. : a personage invented by Sydney Smith in a speech at Taunton on the Reform Bill in 1831. She proposed to sweep the Atlantic out of her house with a mop.

Partington's broom, Dame : see Partington, Mrs.

Partlet, Dame : a hen. [Chaucer, Nonnes Pr. Tale (14th cent.)]

Partridge's Day, St : September 1st, the day on which partridge shooting commences in England.

Parturiunt montes (Lat.) : see Mountain in Labour.

Party man, A : one who slavishly carries out the behests of his party. [Sydney Smith, *Peter Plymley's Letters*, I (1808)]

Parvenu, A (*Fr.*, arrived) : one who has risen suddenly or quickly in the social scale. The word in this sense was first popularized by the title of a work by Pierre Carlet de Chamblain de Marivaux (1688–1763), *Paysan Parvenu*.

Pas, To yield the (*Fr., pas*, step): to give precedence to . . [*Spectator*, No. 529, 1712]

Pascal's Abyss : an imaginary gulf. After an hallucination from which Blaise Pascal (1623–62), Fr. mathematician and religious philosopher, suffered as the result of an accident. He imagined there was always an abyss by his side.

Pasch (Pasque) egg, A : an Easter egg. *Pascha*, the Passover, which as a rule coincides with Easter.

Pasquinade (Pasquin) (Pasquil), A : a political lampoon. After the satires composed by the cobbler, Pasquino, against the Rom. government (15th cent.). The original pasquins or pasquinades were affixed to a mutilated statue which was found buried near Pasquino's shop.

Pass, To sell the : *see* Sell.

Passer le temps, Pour (*Fr.*, to pass away the time).

Passing-bell, The : a church bell rung to announce the passing of a soul.

Passion flower, The : a species of twining plant. After a fancied resemblance to the instruments of Christ's Passion and also from the fact that it remains open for three days, the period between the Last Supper and the Resurrection.

Passion Play, A : a dramatic representation of the incidents in the life of Jesus.

Passive Resistance : opposition, none the less determined though it refrains from action. Phrase coined by Hans Victor von Unruh, President of the National Assembly at Berlin on Nov. 10, 1848, when armed protection was offered to that body by the National Guard and Guilds of Berlin.

Past praying for, To be : to be deaf to influence against the course proposed to be followed, or so far on the road as no longer to be drawn aside from it.

Pat : an Irishman ; a diminutive of St. Patrick, the patron saint of Ireland.

Pat on the back, To : to praise ; to encourage ; to express approval of . .

Pat, To stand : to decline to alter one's position, though having the option of doing so. A poker term.

Patch upon it, Not a : not to be compared to it ; bearing the same relation in excellence as between the patch on a lady's cheek and the cheek itself.

Patelinage : buffoonery. From Patelin, a stock character in Fr. farce. [Blanchet's comedy, *L'Avocat Patelin*]

Pater Noster, The : the Lord's Prayer. From the two first words in Lat. (Our Father), also every tenth bead in a rosary, at which the Lord's Prayer is recited.

Paternoster line, A : a fishing line with leads and hooks at equal intervals, resembling a rosary of beads with which prayers are said. *See* Paternoster.

Patient as Griselda, As : *see* Griselda.

Patmos, To be one's : to be one's place of exile. After the island to which St. John was banished.

Patres Conscripti (*Lat.*, Conscript Fathers) : the Roman Senate.

Patriarch of Ferney, The : Voltaire (1694–1778), who spent the latter part of his life at Ferney near Geneva.

Patter : quick and thoughtless speech, esp. the chatter invented by a comedian on the stage. From Pater Noster, the Lord's Prayer.

Paul Pry, A : an impudent, meddlesome person. After a character in a comedy of that name by John Poole (1825).

Paul's man, A : a braggart. After St. Paul's Walk, London, formerly the haunt of such characters.

Paul's Pigeons : the boys of St. Paul's School, London.

Paul's Tide, St. : Jan. 25 and approximate dates, the festival of the Conversion of St. Paul.

Paul's walkers : idlers who frequented St. Paul's Cathedral, a resort of fashion during the period of the Commonwealth.

Paulo post futurum tense, In the : in the immediate future. After a tense in the passive voice of Grk. verbs. [De Quincey, *On Murder Considered as One of the Fine Arts* (1827)]

Pave the meadow, To : to act foolishly and to no purpose. From an ancient Grk. proverb.

Pax, To cry (*Lat., pax*, peace): to announce the cessation of the game or dispute.

Pax Romana (*Lat.*, Roman peace) : peace preserved by the incorporation of all countries in the Rom. Empire.

Pax vobiscum (*Lat.*, peace be with you !) : a greeting.

Pay a person in his own coin, To : to behave to a person in a manner similar to that in which he has behaved ; esp. to punish him. [Sir Walter Raleigh (1618)]

Pay through the nose, To : to pay an absurdly high price.

Pay with the roll of the drum, To : not to pay at all. A soldier cannot be arrested for debt when on the march.

Pay off old scores, To : to revenge oneself.

Paying guest, A : a boarder, *i.e.*, a guest who pays for his entertainment.

Peace, To hold one's : to keep silent. (14th cent.)

Peace with honour : the phrase used by Lord Beaconsfield to describe the results of the Berlin Congress of 1878. The phrase was used as early as the 12th cent. by Theobald, Count of Champagne, in a letter to Louis le Gros, by Burke in his second great speech on conciliation with America (1775), and by Lord Beaconsfield himself in the *Runnymede Letters* (1835).

Peace, The inglorious arts of : [Andrew Marvell, *Upon Cromwell's Return from Ireland* (1650).

Peace, Retrenchment and Reform : the watchword of the Liberal Party, introduced by Charles, Earl Grey, on becoming Prime Minister in 1830.

Peace, To smoke the pipe of : *see* Pipe.

Peacemakers, The : the Bedfordshire Regt., which had no battles on its colours.

Pear of Confession, The : an instrument of torture, shaped like a pear.

Pearl of the East, The : Zenobia, Queen of Palmyra (3rd cent., A.D.).

Pearl in price, Above a : of very great value. [Earl of Surrey, *The Louer Excuseth Himself of Suspected Change* (1557)]

Pearl of the West Indies, The : Cuba.

Pearls before swine, To cast : to waste an object of beauty on a person unable to appreciate it. [*Matthew*, vii, 6 ; Heywood, *Proverbes* (1546) ; *New Custom*, I, i (1573)]

Peasant Bard, The : Robert Burns (1759–96).

Peasant's War, The : the insurrection of the peasants of South Germany in 1524–5.

Peasant-boy Philosopher, The : James Ferguson (1710–76), Scot. astronomer and mechanician.

Peccavi, To cry (*Lat.*, I have sinned) : to admit an offence. [*Marriage of Wit and Science*, II, i (1570)]

Peck of troubles, A : a quantity of trouble. [*Archaeologia*, XXV, 97 (1535)]

Pecker up, To keep one's : to preserve one's courage and face events bravely. Pecker is a slang term for mouth, from to peck.

Peckham, To go to : to go to dinner. A pun on peck.

Pecksniff, A : a sanctimonious hypocrite. After a character in Dickens, *Martin Chuzzlewit* (1843).

Pecksniffian : *see* Pecksniff, A.

Peculiar Institution, The : in America, Negro slavery. The full title was ' The peculiar domestic institution of the South.' The phrase was used first in the South Carolina *Gazette* (c. 1852).

Pedlar's French : the jargon used by thieves, tramps, etc. A Frenchman was formerly a synonym for a foreigner.

Peel district, A : a clerical district formed in consequence of legislation initiated by Sir Robert Peel.

Peeping Tom, A : an inquisitive person. After Peeping Tom of Coventry, celebrated in the legend of Lady Godiva.

Peep o' Day Boys : an Irish Presbyterian agrarian secret society, active from 1785 to 1790, which committed outrages against the Rom. Catholic population, generally at daybreak.

Peg away, To : to continue determinedly on one's course. A camping metaphor.

Peg a person back, To : to interrupt a person.

Peg out, To : to die.

Peg, To take down a : to put a braggart to shame. In allusion to the lowering of a ship's colours which used to be moved up and down by means of pegs. [Butler, *Hudibras*, II. ii (1663)]

Pegasus : poetic inspiration. After the mythical horse, Pegasus, the stamping of whose hoof caused the fountain of the Muses to flow.

Pegasus, To ride : to indulge in poetry. *See* Pegasus. [Walpole, *Letter to George Montagu*, May 5, 1761]

Peine forte et dure (*Fr.*) : severe punishment or hardship. Properly, a manner of torture in the form of crushing to death. [*Dialogue on Laws of England*, II, xli, 133 (1554)]

Pelican State, The : Louisiana. After the pelican in its arms.

Pelion upon Ossa, To heap : see Ossa.

Pellean Conqueror, The : Alexander the Great, born at Pella in Macedonia.

Pelops, The Ivory shoulder of the sons of : a distinguishing mark. After the legend of the ivory shoulder supplied to Pelops by Demeter in place of that which had been eaten.

Pen to paper, To set : to write. [Bunyan, *Pilgrim's Progress*, Pt. I, Author's Apology (1678)]

Pen and inkhorn clerk, A : a pedant. [Chettle and Munday, *Downfall of the Earl of Huntingdon*, I, iii (1601)]

Penang Lawyer, A : a club ; properly, made from the stem of the dwarf palm of Penang. Humorously suggested as the means of settling disputes in Penang.

Penates : one's most valued household property. After Penates, the household gods of the ancient Latins.

Penelope, A (As faithful as) : the type of a faithful and domesticated wife. After the wife of Odysseus. [Pettie, Transl. of Guazzo, *Civile Conversation*, III (1581)]

Penelope, The web of : an endless work. In allusion to the story of Penelope who, in order to put off her suitors until she had completed her weaving, used to unravel at night all that she had woven during the day. [Sir Thos. Overbury, *Characters : A Melancholy Man* (1616)]

Peninsular State, The : Florida.

Penitential Psalms, The : *Psalms* vi, xxxii, xxxviii, li, cii, cxxx, cxliii.

Pen-name : see Nom de plume.

Penny to bless himself with, Not a : no money at all. [Heywood, *Proverbes* (1546)]

Penny Dreadful, A ; A Penny Blood : a cheap, blood-curdling story of exciting adventure.

Penny gaff, A : see Gaff.

Penny, To give one's life for a : to abandon hope of escape from death. [Bunyan, *Pilgrim's Progress*, Pt. I (1678)]

Penny, in for a pound, In for a : since one must be involved in the difficulty it matters not how deeply one is immersed in it.

Penny readings : popular readings or other literary entertainments, for admission to which the charge is a penny.

Penny, To cost a pretty : to cost an indefinite but considerable sum of money. In allusion to the former sense of penny as an indefinite amount.

Penny, To turn an (honest) : to earn a modest reward for honest work. [Foxe, *Acts and Monuments*, IV (1510)]

Penny, To turn up (come back) like a bad : said of something you had cleverly passed on which comes back to you at par value.

Penny Wedding, A : a rural wedding to which all are invited but expected to bring contributions, the smallest, that of a child, being a penny.

Penny the worse, Not a : no worse off.

Penny-a-liner, A : an unattached journalist of a low grade. Lit. one who writes for payment at the rate of a penny a line. [Thackeray, *Paris Sketch Book* (1840)]

Penny-father, A : a miser. [More, *Utopia*, II, vi (1516)]

Penny wise and pound foolish : unwise thrift, of the nature of miserliness. [Burton, *Anatomy of Melancholy*, To the Reader (1621)]

Pennyworth, To get one's : to get full value for one's money. [*Paston Letters*, No. 757 (1475) ; Chapman, *All Fools*, II, i (1605)]

Pensée d'escalier : see Esprit d'escalier.

Pensioned (Pensioner) (Pensionary) Parliament, The : the parliament of 1661–79. In allusion to the large number of its members who were in the enjoyment of pensions.

Pentarchy, The : the five great powers of Europe before the rise of Italy.

Pentateuch, The (*Grk.*, five books) : the five Books of Moses.

People's Charter, The : formulated by the Chartists in 1848 :—(1) Manhood Suffrage ; (2) Annual Parliaments ; (3) Vote by Ballot ; (4) Abolition of Property qualification for Parliament ; (5) Equal Electoral districts.

People's Friend, The : Dr. William Gordon of Hull (1800–49), philanthropist.

Pepper a person, To : to punish sharply. Attributive from the sense of applying pepper. [*Life and Death of Capt. Thomas Stukeley*, ll. 199–201 (1605)]

Pepper to Hindustan, To send : to perform a work of supererogation. A Persian phrase.

Pepper in the nose, To take : to take offence. [Langland, *Piers Plowman* (1362)]

Pepper and salt : of clothing, a light grey speckled mixture of colours.

Peppercorn rent, A : rent of a nominal amount.

Per saltum : a promotion or preferment awarded without following the customary course. [Bacon, *Essays : Of Envy* (1625)]

Perdu, To lie : to be concealed. Orig. a military phrase.

Père des Lettres, The (*Fr.*, Father of Letters) : Francis I of France.

Perfidious (Perfide) Albion : a designation applied to England on the Continent. The term is probably derived either from a sermon preached by Jacques Bossuet (1627–1704), or from a remark by Mme. de Sévigné (1626–96).

Perfumed terms of the time : euphemisms. So-called by Ben Jonson.

Pericles' boast : that no Athenian ever put on mourning through his severity, *i.e.*, that he had never put an Athenian unjustly to death. Pericles, Athenian statesman, lived from 490 to 429 B.C.

Perpetual motion : an imaginary machine which, once started, goes on continuously until stopped by some external force.

Persian Alexander, The : Sandjar (1117–58).

Persian Horace, The : Omar Khayyám (11th and 12th cents.). After Horace, the famous Rom. poet who lived from 65 to 8 B.C.

Persian King, The : Cyrus (d. 529 B.C.).

Persona grata (*Lat.*) : an acceptable person.

Persona gratissima (*Lat.*) : one who enjoys the greatest favour.

Pert as a pyet, As : *see* Pyet.

Pert as a sparrow, As : lively ; cheeky. [*Christmas Prince*, II (1607)]

Pert as a tailor at a wedding, As : very lively. The tailor was formerly expected to see his employer through the wedding, and was consequently very much at home during the accompanying festivities. [Dekker, *The Seuen Deadly Sinnes : Lying* (1606)]

Peru, To long for : to desire great wealth. In allusion to the fabulous wealth of Peru. [Sir Thos. Browne, *Religio Medici*, II (1643)]

Peru, That is not : that is of not much account. In allusion to the belief that Peru was identical with El Dorado.

Petard, Hoist with one's own : caught in one's own trap. [Shakespeare, *Hamlet*, ii, 4 (1602–3)]

Pètaud, The Court of King : a place of turmoil and confusion. King Pètaud was the king of beggars. Lat., *Peto*, I beg.

Peter, Blue : the blue flag flown as a signal of recall in the British Mercantile Marine. Prop., Blue Repeater.

Peter boat, A : a boat with bow and stern built alike so that it may be run into the water rapidly. Dutch, *pethur*, to hurry.

Peter Funk, A : the confederate of an auctioneer among the audience.

Peter the Packer : Peter, 1st Lord O'Brien (1842–1914), Lord Chief Justice of Ireland. In allusion to his supposed practice of packing or carefully selecting his juries.

Peter to pay Paul, To rob : *see* Rob.

Peter's pence : orig. a voluntary tribute paid to the Pope, later claimed as a due. Not paid in England after 1365.

Peterloo : the meeting of workers which was held in St. Peter's Field, Manchester in August, 1819, and was dispersed by armed force. The name was a coined resemblance to Waterloo.

Peter-man, A : a fisherman. In allusion to the occupation of St. Peter.

Peter-see-me : a Span. wine. From the Span. Cardinal, Pedro Ximenes (1514–95), who introduced the grape into Spain.

Petit Bleu, A (*Fr.*, little blue) : a letter sent by pneumatic post. In allusion to the colour (blue) of the envelopes employed for these missives in the Fr. Post Office.

Petit Caporal, Le : *see* Caporal.

Petit maître, A (*Fr.*, little master) : a fop. [Smollett, *Peregrine Pickle*, ch. 71 (1751)]

Petits Chevaux (*Fr.*, little horses) : a mechanical gambling game played with toy race-horses.

Petitio principii, A : a begging of the question. [Tyndale, *Exposition of I John*, v, 1–3 (1531)]

Petition of Right, A : a legal means of demanding redress against the Crown.

Petitioners and Abhorrers : the forerunners of the Whigs and Tories ;

those who petitioned the throne in 1680 to summon parliament and those who abhorred the presumption of the other party in doing so.

Petrarch, The English : Sir Philip Sidney (1554–86). So-called by Sir Walter Raleigh. After Francesco Petrarch, Ital. poet, who lived from 1304 to 1374.

Petrarch of Spain, The : Garcilaso de la Vega (1503–36).

Petrel, A : a sea-fowl. After the apostle Peter. In allusion to his walking on the sea, as, to the casual observer, the petrel appears to do.

Pétroleuses : Parisian women who in the last days of the Commune scattered about the City, setting fire to public buildings. After the petroleum which they used.

Petticoat Government : a system of government in which a woman or women have supreme influence or control.

Petticoat influence : female influence.

Pewter, To scour the : to work hard.

Phaeton, A : a four-wheeled open carriage. After Phaeton, the son of Phoebus, who attempted to guide the chariot of the Sun.

Phaeton's bird : the swan. After the legend of Cyenus, grieving over the fate of Phaeton, and being metamorphosed into a swan.

Phaeton's Car : the chariot of the Sun.

Pharaoh, A : a harsh, oppressive ruler. After the Pharaoh of the Exodus.

Pharaoh's chicken : a vulture. In allusion to its frequent appearance in Egyptian hieroglyphics.

Pharian Fields, The : Egypt. After Pharos, the lighthouse on its coast.

Pharisaical : hypocritical. After the Pharisees as portrayed in the N.T.

Pharisaism : hypocrisy in religion. *See* Pharisaical.

Pharisee, A : *see* Pharisaical and Pharisaism.

Pharos, A : a lighthouse. After an island off Alexandria, on which Ptolemy Philadelphus erected his famous lighthouse.

Pheasant, A Billingsgate : *see* Billingsgate.

Phidias, The French : *see* French Phidias.

Philadelphia Lawyer, A : an exceptionally shrewd lawyer.

Philander, To : to make love as an amusement. After the lover in Ariosto, *Orlando Furioso* (1516),

Beaumont and Fletcher, *Laws of Candy* (1647), and other early plays.

Philemon and Baucis : a pair of fond and constant lovers. After a mythical couple who after their simultaneous death at a ripe old age were changed by Jupiter into trees. [Ovid, *Met.*, 8]

Philip drunk to Philip sober, An appeal from : an appeal for second thoughts or a revised opinion given with deliberation. Philip of Macedon, when drunk, condemned a woman who, on his recovery of sobriety, appealed against his decision. ' I would appeal to Philip, but when he is sober.' She gained the object of her petition.

Philip of Macedon, As rich as : After Philip II of Macedon who captured the gold mines of Amphipolis.

Philippe Egalité : Louis Philippe, Duke of Orleans (1747–93), cousin of Louis XVI. The name adopted by him when he adhered to the Fr. Revolution.

Philippi, To meet at : to keep a critical appointment unfailingly. In allusion to the rendezvous with Brutus appointed at Philippi by the ghost of Julius Cæsar.

Philippic, A : a speech filled with invective. After the nine orations of Demosthenes against Philip of Macedon.

Philistine, A : an ignorant, self-satisfied individual, generally of the middle classes, impervious to the influence of art or of anything else above the material. Term so applied by Matthew Arnold in the *Cornhill Magazine.* Possibly derived from Philister, a policeman or watchman in Germ. university towns with whom the students frequently came into conflict.

Philistines, To have been among the : to be drunk. A pun on ' fill.'

Philistinism : indifference to all except the material in life. *See* Philistine.

Philomel : the nightingale. After Philomela, daughter of Pandion, King of Athens, who is fabled to have been changed into a nightingale.

Philosopher of China, The : Confucius (c. 551–478 B.C.).

Philosopher of Ferney, The : Voltaire (1757–1820), who spent the latter period of his life at Ferney near Geneva.

Philosopher with the golden thigh, The : Pythagoras (fl. 540–510 B.C.), Grk. philosopher.

Philosopher of Malmesbury, The : Thos. Hobbes (1588–1679), Eng. philosopher.

Philosopher of Persia, The : Abou ibn Sina of Shiraz (d. 1037).

Philosopher of Samosata, The : Lucan (39–65), the Rom. poet.

Philosopher of Sans Souci, The : Frederick the Great (1712–86), King of Prussia. *See* Sans Souci.

Philosopher of Wimbledon, The : John Horne Tooke (1736–1812), Eng. politician.

Philosopher's stone, The : an imaginary substance capable of transmuting other objects into gold.

Philosophy, The Father of : *see* Father of Philosophy.

Philosophy, The Father of Inductive : *see* Father.

Philosophy, The Father of Roman : *see* Father.

Phlegrian size, Of : gigantic. After the Phlegræan Plain in Macedon, where the giants fought with the gods.

Phocensian despair : despair that ends in victory. In allusion to the exploits of the men of Phocis when surrounded by enemies on an occasion in the 4th cent. B.C.

Phoebe, As fair as : in allusion to Phoebe, the moon ; the sister of Phoebus (*q.v.*). [Spenser, *The Shepheard's Calendar :* April, ll. 64–5 (1579)]

Phoebus : the sun ; one of the names of Apollo, the sun-god.

Phoebus' Lamp : the sun.

Phoenix, A : that which reappears after apparent destruction ; the emblem of immortality. After the fabulous bird which after destruction arises again from its ashes.

Phoenix among .. A : unique among .. Because only one phoenix was supposed to exist at one time. [Shakespeare, *Cymbeline*, I, vii (1610)]

Phoenix period (cycle), A : the period between the appearances of the phoenix, according to different authorities ranging from 1500 to 300 years.

Phylactery, A : a symbol of righteousness ; an amulet. Properly a small box containing quotations from the Law worn by Jews while praying, in accordance with *Deuteronomy*, xi, 18.

Phylactery, To make broad the : to advertize one's righteousness. [*Matthew*, xxiii, 5]

Phyllis, A : a country girl, esp. in pastoral poetry. So used by Virgil, Horace and other classical poets.

Phyllise the fair, To to philander (*q.v.*).

Physic to a dead man, To bring : to bring help too late. [Propertius, *Elegies*, II, xiv, 15–6]

Physicians, The Prince of : Avicenna (980–1037), the Arabian.

Pick and choose, To : to be fastidious. [Wm. Combe, *Tour of Dr. Syntax* (1812)]

Pick a person's brains, To : *see* Brains.

Pick a hole in a person's coat, To : to find fault with a person. [Bunyan, *Pilgrim's Progress*, Pt. I (1678) ; Peter Pindar, *Epistle to John Nichols* (c. 1794)]

Pick a quarrel, To : to seek an opportunity for quarrelling. [*Paston Letters* (1449)]

Pick straws, To : to display signs of fatigue.

Pick up the thread of .. To : to recover a lapsed acquaintance with ..

Pickle, In a : in trouble ; in a scrape. [Greene, *Liberality and Prodigality*, IV, iv (1602)]

Pick-me-up, A : anything, esp. refreshment, likely to stimulate one's energies.

Pickwickian sense, In a : not to be taken literally, of words which would be insulting if they were taken so. In allusion to an incident narrated in Dickens, *Pickwick Papers* (1836). This incident was based on an occurrence in the House of Commons on the 17th April, 1823, when Henry (Lord) Brougham referred to George Canning's conduct as ' the most incredible specimen of monstrous truckling, for the purpose of obtaining office, that the whole history of political tergiversation could furnish.' Whereupon Canning retorted, ' That is false,' and declined to withdraw the remark. The incident was, after some heated discussion, closed by Brougham stating that he was referring to Canning's official character and Canning announcing that his retort was made under the mistaken impression that his personal character was being impugned.

Picture hat, A : an elaborate woman's hat, copied from one depicted in a painting.

Pidgin (Pigeon) English : broken English mixed with Chinese, spoken by Chinese in their intercourse with Englishmen and Americans. Lit. (in this dialect), business English.

Pie, In spite of the : obstinately. The pie is the book of rules of service in the Rom. Catholic church. [Withal, *Dictionarie*, p. 390 (1608)]

Pie's nest, To be in a : to be in a difficult situation. In allusion to the inaccessible situation in which the magpie builds its nest.

Pie's nest, To look for a : to seek for that which cannot be found. In allusion to the inaccessible position in which the magpie builds her nest.

Piece of one's mind, To give a : to tell a person unpleasant truths. [Goldsmith, *The Goodnatured Man*, IV, i (1768)]

Pièce de résistance, A (*Fr*) : the principal item in a group or series.

Pieces, To go to : *see* Go.

Pied à terre, A (*Fr.*, a foot on the ground) : a resting place.

Pied de la lettre, Au (*Fr.*, at the foot of the letter) : literally.

Piedmont, A : the nucleus, from which a state is built up. After Piedmont from which the kingdom of Italy grew.

Pie powder, A : a hawker ; a chapman ; a travelling merchant. After the Court of Piepowders, formerly held at fairs and markets to administer justice among them. Lat., *pede-pulverosus*, dusty footed.

Pierce Penniless, A : a person without money.

Pierian Spring, The : the inspiration of music and poetry. After Pieria in Thessaly, the legendary birthplace of Orpheus and the Muses.

Pig with .. To : to crowd with in uncomfortable surroundings.

Pig iron : iron in the piece. Molten iron is run off into a vessel called a sow. A play on words.

Pig loves marjoram, As a : not at all.

Pig in a poke, To buy a : to purchase a bargain without examining it. Poke = pocket. [Heywood, *Proverbes* (1546) ; Chaucer, *Reeve's Tale*, 358 (1386)]

Pig to play on a flute, To teach a : *see* Teach.

Pigs, An it please the : a reference to the boys of St. Anthony's School, Threadneedle Street, London, applied to them by their rival scholars of St. Paul's School. The application is derived from the story of St. Anthony preaching to the pigs. Other derivations are from the pyx in which the Host is kept in Rom. Catholic churches, when the phrase means, ' If it please God,' and from the pixies or fairies. Yet another suggested derivation is from *piga* (Sax.), a virgin. The phrase would in this case mean, ' With the permission of the Virgin Mary.'

Pigs to market, To bring one's : to do business. [Wm. Cartwright, *The Ordinary*, IV, iii (1651)]

Pigeon English : *see* Pidgin English.

Pigeon and hit a crow, To shoot at a : to make an intentional blunder. [*The Louer Forsaketh His Unkinde Loue*, l. 8 (1557)]

Pigeon pair, A : a boy and girl, the former not more than two years older than the latter. Possibly from the constancy of pigeons proverbial among birds, or from the belief that a pigeon always hatches only two young, male and female.

Pigeon, To pluck a : to cheat a simple, gullible person. [Peter Pindar, *Brother Peter to Brother Tom* (1797)]

Pigeons, To fly the : to steal coal while on the road to its destination.

Pigeon's milk : an imaginary object which fools are sent to fetch. The idea is said to have originated with Aristophanes.

Pigskin, In the : riding in a horse-race. In allusion to the material of which horse-saddles are made.

Pig-tails, The : the Chinese. In allusion to the manner in which they wear their hair.

Pike, To trail a : to serve as a soldier. [Churchyard, *Chippes* (1565)]

Pikes, To pass the : to pass through difficulties and dangers.

Pikestaff, As plain as a : *see* Plain.

Pilate voice, A : a rough, loud voice, like that adopted by Pontius Pilate in the Mysteries. [Chaucer, *Canterbury Tales*, 3126 (14th cent.)]

Pilate's Bodyguard : *see* Pontius Pilate.

Pile, To make one's : to make a fortune. The phrase originated in America in the piles of coin that collect around a winner at a gaming table.

Pilgrim Fathers, The : the Puritan refugees from England who founded the colony of New England, subsequently merged in the U.S. of America in 1620.

Pill to cure an earthquake, To take a : to take altogether ineffective efforts to meet a considerable emergency. From a metaphor employed by John Bright (1811–89), Eng. statesman.

Pill, To gild the : *see* Gild.

Pill to swallow, A bitter : a disagreeable person or experience. [Udall, *Luke*, iv (1556)]

Pillar to post, To drive from : to keep a person perpetually moving. In allusion to the practice of moving an offender, followed generally by a jeering crowd, from pillory to whipping-post. Other derivations are from (1) the riding school in the centre of which was placed a pillar and around it a number of posts ; or from (2) the Germ. *von Pilatus zu Pontius* (from Pilate to Pontius), *i.e.*, from one to another for advice without any satisfaction. [Heywood, *Proverbes* (1546)]

Pillars of Heaven, The : the Atlas mountains. So-called by the Moors.

Pillars of Hercules, The : *see* Hercules.

Pillory, To : to expose to public scorn or indignation. In allusion to the pillory, the instrument of punishment in which offenders were confined in public.

Pillow lace : lace made with the assistance of pins stuck in a cushion or pillow.

Pilot balloon, A : in politics. a hint thrown out to ascertain the tendency of public opinion.

Pilot Jack : the Union Jack when used as a signal for a pilot.

Pilot who weathered the storm, The : William Pitt (1759–1806), who guided the state successfully through the critical period of the Napoleonic War. So-called by George Canning.

Pin, Not to care a : to care nothing at all. [Jas. Howard, *All Mistaken*, III (1672)]

Pin to choose between, Not a : no difference between. [Earle, *Microcosmography : A Scepticke in Religion* (1628)]

Pin, Not worth a : quite worthless. [R. Wever, *Lusty Juventus*, l. 387 (1560)]

Pin's head, As big as a : *see* Big.

Pinch, At a : in an emergency.

Pinchbeck : imitation gold. After the inventor, Christopher Pinchbeck (c. 1670–1732), an Eng. watchmaker.

Pindar, The British : Thomas Gray (1716–71). From his epitaph. After Pindar (c. 522–443 B.C.), the greatest of Grk. lyric poets.

Pindar of England, The : George, Duke of Buckingham (1628–87). So-called by Cowley.

Pindar, The French : *see* French Pindar.

Pindar, The Italian : Gabriello Chiabrera (1552–1637).

Pindaric verse : lyric poetry.

Pine-tree State, The : Maine. In allusion to its pine forests, and the pine-tree in its coat of arms.

Pink of perfection, The : the acme of perfection. Pink, a point.

Pin-money : the allowance of a husband to his wife for personal expenditure. At one time pins were very expensive.

Pinpricks, A policy of : a policy of petty annoyances, generally as applied by one state to another. First used in *The Times* on Nov. 16, 1898. ' Pinpricks ' was, however, used in this sense almost a century earlier. In the official account of the meeting between Napoleon and the Czar Alexander at Tilsit on the 22nd of June 1807, Napoleon is reported to have said, ' For the maintenance of peace nations should avoid the pinpricks which forerun cannon shots.'

Pious fraud, A : a deception practised for a supposed worthy object, *e.g.*, for the furtherance of religion. The phrase formed a mot by Lord Bute in 1763 in reference to a political action by Lord Shelburne. Fox, who was adversely affected, retorted, ' I can see the fraud plain enough, but where is the piety ? ' [Foxe, *Acts and Monuments*, III, 898 (1563)]

Pipe one's eye, To : to weep. Orig. nautical slang.

Pipe of peace, To smoke the : to come to an agreement. In allusion to the N. Amer.-Ind. practice of smoking a pipe with a person with whom one wishes to be on good terms.

Pipe and smoke it, To put a thing in one's : addressed to a man to whom a rebuke or other unpleasant remark has been spoken.

Pipes, To play on the still : to be silent.

Pipeclay : routine. In allusion to the former use in the British army of pipeclay for the cleansing of accoutrements, etc.

Piper while others call the tune, To pay the : to bear the expense or loss while another person has the power of incurring it. [T. Flatman, *Heraclitus Ridens*, No. 29 (1681)]

Piper for others to dance, To pay the : *see* Piper while others call the tune. [Molière, *La Comtesse d'Escarbagnas*, Sc. xxi]

T

Piper, To pay the : to pay the cost. In allusion to the legend of the Pied Piper of Hamelin concerning the payment for whose services a dispute arose. [Congreve, *Love for Love*, II, v (1695)]

Piping hot : like water that pipes or sings when it is about to boil. [Chaucer *Canterbury Tales : Miller's Tale*, 3377–8 (14th cent.)]

Piping times of peace, The : an era of peace celebrated by music (of the pipes). [Shakespeare, *Richard III*, I, i (1594)]

Pippa passes : a casual, passing influence sometimes produces valuable results. As the innocent songs of the light-hearted Pippa, in Rob. Browning's poem, *Pippa Passes* (1842) exert here and there a beneficial influence on those who hear them.

Pis-aller, A (*Fr.*, go worst) : the worst choice and generally also the last choice. [Etheridge, *Man of Mode*, I, i (1676)]

Pisgah, A : an outlook hill. After the mountain in Moab, from which Moses viewed the Promised Land.

Pisgah sight, A : a view from afar.

Piso's justice : a moral injustice. According to Seneca, Piso on one occasion had three men unjustly executed, in each instance making out a sort of justification for his action.

Pistol in the air, To discharge one's : to make a pretence of fighting or opposing.

Pit, The : the back portion of the ground-floor of a theatre. Because the original Drury Lane Theatre was built on the site of a cockpit.

Pitch black : intensely black ; as black as pitch. [Marston, *The Scourge of Villanie*, II, v, 197 (1599)]

Pitch and pay, To : to pay on the spot. Probably ' to throw down one's money in payment.' [Shakespeare, *Henry V*, II, iii (1599)]

Pitchfork into . . To : to thrust a person arbitrarily into an office.

Pitfall, A : a hidden trap. Properly a pit (concealed) into which one may easily fall.

Pitt Diamond, The : the Regent diamond brought to Europe by Thomas Pitt and sold to the Regent of Orleans in 1717 for £133,000.

Pitt's mark : the printer's imprint on a book, rendered necessary by William Pitt's Act of Parliament of 1799.

Pitt's pictures : blind windows. Introduced on the occasion of the increase of the Window Tax by William Pitt in 1784.

Place Bill, The : the Act of Parliament of 1743, whereby holders of offices of profit under the Crown vacated their seats in parliament.

Place aux dames (*Fr.*, room for the ladies) : give way to the ladies. [Laurence Sterne, *A Sentimental Journey* (1768)]

Place in the sun, A : a share in the economic and political advantages derived from colonies and dependencies. A phrase used by William II, Emperor of Germany, at Hamburg, Aug. 27, 1911. The phrase was used previously by Pascal in his *Pensées*, § 73 (1669).

Placebo, To sing : to endeavour to curry favour. From placebo, the Rom. Catholic vesper hymn for the dead. [Chaucer, *Summoner's Tale*, I, 367 (14th cent.)]

Placebo, A song of : *see* Placebo, To sing.

Plack and baubee (*Scot.*) : to the last penny.

Plague on both your houses ! A : an expression of annoyance with both parties to a dispute. [Shakespeare, *Romeo and Juliet*, III, i (1591–3)]

Plain, The : the Girondists in the Fr. Revolutionary Convention, who occupied seats lower than those of the Jacobins, or the Mountain (*q.v.*).

Plain as the nose on one's face, As : very obvious. In allusion to the nose as a prominent feature of the face. [Borrough, *On Hosea*, p. 25 (1652)]

Plain as a pikestaff, As : obvious. In allusion to the pikestaff which clearly denoted the status of the pilgrim who carried it. [Richard Shacklock, *Hatchet of Heresies* (1565)] In 1542, in Thomas Becon, *Boke of Matrimony*, the phrase appeared as ' plain as a packstaff.' A pikestaff (now only Scot.) was a long staff with a sharp pike in it. A packstaff is a staff on which a pedlar supports his pack while resting.

Plain as print, As : manifest on the face of it. [Peter Pindar, *Pindariana : Song* (1794)]

Plain dealing : honesty. [*Appius and Virginia*, l. 961 (1563)]

Plain sailing : an easy and straightforward course. A nautical metaphor.

Plan of campaign, The : a combination of Irish tenants between 1880 and 1888, formed to support one another in the refusal to pay rent.

Planet, To be born under a lucky : to be fortunate. A metaphor from astrology.

Plank in a platform, A : a principle in the programme of a political party.

Plaster of Paris : gypsum. So-called from the quantity quarried near Paris.

Platform, A : the programme of a political party. Term recently revived in the U.S., but in use in England in the 16th cent. [Lyly, *Discovery of the New World* (1581)]

Platine States : the S. Amer. states which border on the River Plate, *viz.*, the Argentine, Uruguay and Paraguay.

Plato, The German : Friedrich Heinrich Jacobi (1743–1819). After Plato (427–347 B.C.), the distinguished Grk. philosopher.

Plato, The Jewish : Philo Judæus (c. 20 B.C. to 40 A.D.).

Plato, The Puritan : John Howe (1630–1706).

Plato's year : a cycle of 25,000 years, in the course of which the stars all resume their original positions in the firmament.

Platonic love : friendship, as distinct from love, between individuals of opposite sexes. After Plato (427–347 B.C.), the Grk. philosopher, who advocated it.

Platonic Puritan, The : John Howe (1630–1706), nonconformist divine.

Plautine : in the style of the Rom. comic poet, Plautus (d. 184 B.C.).

Play one's cards well, To : to make excellent use of one's instruments and opportunities.

Play false, To : to deceive ; to betray. [Thos. Kyd, *Jeronimo*, Pt. I, l. 796 (1591)]

Play fast and loose, To : to be undecided and irregular in one's negotiations and dealings. From the game of prick the belt, or prick the garter.

Play on a flute, To teach a pig to : *see* Teach.

Play the fool, To : to behave foolishly. [I *Samuel*, xxvi, 21]

Play to the gods, To : to vulgarize or prostitute one's talent. *See* Gods.

Play one's hand for all it is worth, To : to avail oneself of one's opportunities to the fullest extent.

Play into the hands of .. To : *see* Hands.

Play one's part, To : to act for oneself. [Bacon, *Essayes : Of Friendship* (1611)]

Play on words, A : a use of words to create ambiguity or give a double meaning.

Played out : out of date ; exhausted.

Playwrights of the gutter : writers for the irresponsible sensational press. A phrase coined by Mr. Herbert Henry Asquith in the House of Commons, July 13, 1917.

Pleased as Punch, As : *see* Punch.

Plebeian : vulgar, relating to the common people. After Plebs, the Rom. class of the common people.

Pledge, To take the : to enter into an engagement to abstain from intoxicating drink. In America often used with regard to tobacco also.

Pleiad, The : a group of seven Fr. poets who flourished in the 16th cent.— Ronsard, Dorat, Du Bellay, Remi-Belleau, Jodelle, Baif and Thiard. After the Pleiades, the seven daughters of Atlas and Pleione, who were changed into stars.

Pleiad of Alexandria, The : Callimachos, Appolanios of Rhodes, Aratos, Philiscos, Lycophron, Nicander and Theocritos.

Pleiad of Charlemagne, The : Alcuin, Angilbert, Adelard, Biculfe Charlemagne, Varnefrid and Eginhard.

Pleiad, The second French : Rapin, Commire, Larue, Santeuil, Ménage, Duperier and Petit.

Plentiful as blackberries : very numerous. [Shakespeare, 1 *King Henry IV*, II, iv, 230 (1596–7)]

Plimsoll line ; Plimsoll mark : *see* Plimsoll's Act.

Plimsoll's Act : the Merchant Shipping Act of 1876 which requires a certain standard of safety in ships permitted to put to sea. The Plimsoll Line or Mark is the waterline of a fully-loaded ship in accordance with the Act, The Act was adopted as a consequence of the untiring efforts of Samuel Plimsoll, 'The Sailor's Friend' (1824–98).

Pliny, The German : Konrad von Gesner of Zurich (1516–65). After Pliny, the Elder (23–79), a famous Roman naturalist.

Plon-plon : Prince Napoleon (1822–91), son of Jerome Buonaparte. The name is intended as an equivalent for *craint-plomb*, fear bullet, and was given to him during the Crimean War in derision of his supposed cowardice.

Plough, To : *see* Ploughed, To be.

Plough the air, To : to act foolishly. From an ancient Grk. proverb.

Plough, To put (set) one's hand to the : to undertake a task or course of action. [*Luke*, ix, 62]

Plough a lonely furrow, To : to follow a course without associates.

Plough Monday : the Monday after Epiphany on which men are supposed to resume work.

Plough before the oxen, To put the : to act opposite to the natural order. [*Ayenbite of Inwit*, 243 (1340)]

Plough a rock, To : to act foolishly. From an ancient Grk. proverb.

Plough the sand, To : to undertake fruitless labour. [Ausonius, *Epistulae*, IV, 3 ; Jeremy Taylor, *Liberty of Prophesying* (1647)]

Ploughed, To be : to fail in an examination. 'Plough' is apparently a corruption of 'pluck' (*q.v.*).

Plover, To live like a : to live on nothing. After the supposition that a plover needs no food.

Pluck : courage. Properly the heart, liver, etc., which are plucked away from the carcase of a sheep or hog. The heart and liver were formerly considered to be the seat of the quality of courage.

Pluck, To : to cause to fail in an examination. Apparently from the analogy of plucking a magpie of its feathers. Chaucer, *Romaunt of the Rose*, 5983 (14th cent.)]

Pluck a person's goose for him, To : to expose a conceited individual. Suggested comparison with the plucking of a goose.

Pluck a pigeon, To : to rob a person who is easily swindled. After 'pigeon' in the sense of an innocent, harmless creature.

Pluck at straws, To : to trust to hopes that are practically without foundation.

Pluck up heart (courage), To : to arouse one's courage. [R. Wever, *Lusty Juventus*, l. 1018 (1560)]

Plugson of Undershot : a typical Radical. Term invented by Thomas Carlyle.

Plum, A (*Span.*, *pluma*, wealth) : £100,000.

Plum bed, A : a soft bed. Devonshire dialect.

Plums of office, The : the good things (advantages) of office.

Plums out of the pudding, To pick the : to select the good things and leave the inferior ones for others. [Sydney Smith, *Peter Plymley's Letters*, Letter IX (1808)]

Plumed Knight, The : James Gillespie Blaine (1830–93), Amer. statesman. So-called by R. G. Ingersoll in supporting his nomination for the Presidency (1876).

Plumes, In borrowed : with adopted but undeserved honours. In allusion to the fable of the jackdaw that bedecked itself with peacock's feathers.

Plump, To : to give all one's votes to one candidate ; or to vote for one candidate only, not using one's other vote or votes.

Plunge, To take the : to take a definite step, after more or less hesitation.

Plus Royaliste que le Roi (*Fr.*, more royalist than the king) : extravagantly royalist. An expression used by Louis XVIII with reference to the émigrés (*q.v.*).

Plush, John : a footman. In allusion to the material out of which his uniform breeches are made.

Plush, To take : to accept a subordinate position in a ministry. *See* Plush, John.

Plutarch, The Modern : Francis Vayer de la Mothe (1586–1672). After Plutarch (c. 46–120), a famous Grk. biographer.

Pluto : the grave. After the Grk. god of the dead.

Plutocracy, A : government by the wealthy classes ; wealthy people as a class. *See* Plutocrat.

Plutocrat, A : one who enjoys wealth while avoiding its responsibilities. After Plutus, the god of wealth.

Plutonian : igneous ; infernal ; relating to the centre of the earth. After Pluto, the god of Hell.

Plutonist, A : one who holds the opinion that the world was evolved by means of a cooling-down process. *See* Plutonian.

Plutus, As rich as : *see* Rich.

Plymouth Brethren, The : an English Nonconformist sect, founded at Plymouth in 1830.

Plymouth cloak, A : a cudgel. 'Because we use a staff in cuerpo (when we are nude), but not when we wear a cloak.' Plymouth used to be a landing place for the indigent.

Pocket, To be in (out of) : to profit (lose) by . .

Pocket, An appeal to the : an argument based on or reinforced by cupidity.

Pocket Borough, A : *see* Borough.
Pocket edition, A : a small copy of anything. Lit., an edition of a book small enough to go into one's pocket.
Pocket an insult, To : to submit to an insult without apparent resentment. [*Rare Triumphs of Love and Fortune* II, l. 72 (1589)]
Pocket Veto, A : automatic veto of a measure of the President of the U.S. by delaying a decision beyond a certain term.
Poco a poco (*It.*, little by little).
Podsnap, A ; Podsnappery : a self-confident, self-opinionated individual. Self-sufficiency combined with ignoring of the unpleasant. After a character in Dickens, *Our Mutual Friend* (1864).
Poet of France, The : Pierre Ronsard (1524–85).
Poet of Greta Hall, The : Robert Southey (1774–1843), who passed the last forty years of his life at Greta Hall, Keswick.
Poet of Haslemere, The : Alfred, Lord Tennyson (1809–93), who lived at Haslemere.
Poet Laureate : *see* Laureate.
Poet, A minor : a poet of minor importance. [Ben Jonson, *Time Vindicated* (1623)]
Poet of Poets, The : Percy Bysshe Shelley (1792–1822).
Poet of the Poor, The : George Crabbe (1754–1832).
Poet, The Quaker : *see* Quaker Poet.
Poet Sire of Italy, The : Dante Alighieri (1265–1321).
Poet's Poet, The : Edmund Spenser (c. 1552–99). From the admiration of him by contemporary and subsequent poets.
Poets, The Prince of : Edmund Spenser (1553–99). So-called on his monument.
Poets, The Prince of Spanish : Garcilaso de la Vega (1503–36). So-called by Cervantes.
Poetic Justice : the reward of the virtuous and the punishment of the guilty as described by popular novelists and other similar imaginative writers.
Poetic Licence : the liberty to break the laws of grammar and prosody taken by poets when the needs of their art demand it.
Poetry, The Father of ; The Father of Dutch ; The Father of English ; The Father of Epic : *see* Father.
Poetry of motion, The : dancing.
Poilu, A (*Fr.*, hairy) : a Fr. private soldier on active service. In reference

to the unshaven appearance of the soldiers in the trenches.
Point d'appui, A (*Fr.*, point of support) : a base of operations.
Point, To carry one's : to have one's way.
Point of .. To make a : to consider it a matter of duty to ..
Point, To stretch a : *see* Stretch.
Point of the sword, At the : under compulsion.
Points, To give : to allow an advantage (to a rival or competitor). A card-playing or sporting metaphor.
Point blank : direct, without disguise. A gunnery metaphor. [*The Merry Devil of Edmonton*, ll. 168–71 (1608)]
Poire, La (*Fr.*, The Pear) : King Louis Philippe, whose face was generally represented by caricaturists in the shape of a pear.
Poisson d'Avril (*Fr.*, fish of April) : an April fool (*q.v.*).
Poker pictures : pictures drawn on wood by means of a red-hot poker.
Poker talk : fireside chatter.
Poles asunder : widely separated.
Poles, As wide apart as the : *see* Wide.
Pole star to the North, As true as the : *see* True.
Policy of pin pricks, A : *see* Pinpricks.
Policy shop, A : an Amr. gambling office.
Polish Byron, The : *see* Byron.
Polish Franklin, The : Todeusz Czacki (1765–1813), writer and promoter of education among the Poles. After Benjamin Franklin, Amer. statesman of the revolution (1706–90).
Political arithmetic : statistics relating to a state.
Political prisoner, A : a person imprisoned for a political as distinguished from a moral offence.
Politics of the parish pump, The : local affairs, as contrasted with the greater ones of the state.
Polyphemus of Literature, The : Dr. Samuel Johnson (1709–84). After Polyphemus, in Grk. mythology, the most famous of the Cyclopes or monstrous giants.
Polypus, As grasping as a : a reference to the polypus, an octopus. [Plautus, *Aulularia*, l. 198]
Pombodita : the land where the impossible happens.
Pompadours, The : the 56th Regt. of Foot, now the 2nd Essex Regt. After the colour of the facings of their

uniform, purple, the favourite of Mme. de Pompadour.

Pompey, A : a black footman.

Pons asinorum (*Lat.*, asses' bridge) : the 5th proposition of the first book of Euclid. Because it is the first difficult proposition, at which most learners stumble.

Pontius Pilate's Bodyguard : the 1st Regt. of Foot (Royal Scots), the oldest in the British service. In allusion to an alleged boast of antiquity by one of its colonels.

Pontypool waiter, As round as a : in allusion to the japanned waiter-trays formerly manufactured at Pontypool, Mon., the original place of manufacture of japanned ware.

Pooh Bah, A : an incompetent, foolish official who holds one or more offices. After the name of a character in Gilbert and Sullivan, *Mikado* (1885).

Poor as a church mouse, As : since a church is one of the few buildings that contain no food. [1731 ; Peter Pindar *Ode Upon Ode* (1785)]

Poor as Job, As : *see* Job.

Poor John : salted and dried hake. Apparently because it is considered a type of poor fare. [Shakespeare, *The Tempest*, II, ii (1609–10)]

Poorer than Irus : *see* Irus.

Pop the question, To : to propose marriage. In allusion to the suggestion that the proposal is always sudden and unexpected. [Smollett, *Gil Blas*, 113 (1797)]

Pope, The Black : the general of the Jesuits.

Pope, To drink like a : in allusion to the intemperate wine drinking of Pope Benedict XII.

Pope of Geneva, The : John Calvin (1509–64), one of the founders of Protestantism, who lived at Geneva.

Pope of Philosophy, The : Aristotle (384–322 B.C.).

Pope, The Red : the Prefect of the Propaganda of the Church of Rome.

Popes, The Age of the : *see* Age.

Popes, Boy : John XII (938–964), elected pope at the age of 18, and Benedict IX (1023–54), elected at the age of 10.

Pope's nose, The : the parson's nose (*q.v.*).

Pope-Figs : Protestants. A term applied to the Gaillardets in Rabelais, *Pantagruel*, IV, 45, for saying ' A fig for the Pope.'

Poplin : a silk and worsted fabric (Fr., *popaline*), made at Avignon, the residence of the popes.

Popular Chamber, The : the House of Commons, as contrasted with the House of Lords.

Populists, The : the people's party. An Amer. political party formed in 1891.

Porch, The : the philosophical school of Stoics. After the Porch Poecile in which their founder Zeno used to lecture.

Porkopolis : (1) Chicago ; (2) Cincinnati. In both cases great pork packing centres.

Porridge, To keep one's breath to cool one's own : to reserve one's advice for one's own use.

Port Royal : a religious and literary community formed in Paris at the end of the 16th cent.

Porte, The Sublime ; Porte, The : the Turkish government. After the building in which its headquarters are situated. This building was orig. the gate of the Sultan's palace, Sublime Porte being a Fr. translation of *Babi Ali* (Arab.), High Gate.

Porterhouse steak, A : a steak cut from near the sirloin, such as that supplied at porter-houses, public-houses for the sale of porter.

Portfolio, A : the office of a minister of state. After the portfolio or despatch box he is supposed to carry.

Portia, A : a female advocate. After a character in Shakespeare, *Merchant of Venice* (1596).

Portland stone : a building stone, quarried in the Isle of Portland.

Portmanteau word, A : an invented word which combines two others. Term invented by the Eng. humourist Charles Ludwidge Dodgson, ' Lewis Carroll ' (1832–98).

Portuguese Cid, The : Nunez Alvarez Pereira (1360–1431). The Cid is the favourite but almost mythical hero of Spain.

Portuguese Horace, The : Antonio Ferreira (1528–69). After Horace, famous Rom. poet (65–8 B.C.).

Posse, In : *see* In posse.

Posse of .. A (*Lat.*, to be able) : a force or armed body of ..

Posse comitatus, A (*Lat.*, Force of the county) : a levy en masse of the men of a county.

Possess one's soul in patience, To : to exercise great patience. [Sir S. Tuke,

Adventures of Five Hours, V (1663);
The Spectator, No. 610 (1714)]

Possum, To play : to pretend ; esp. to
malinger. In allusion to the habit of
the opossum of pretending to be dead
when in danger of attack.

Post haste : rapidly ; quickly. A
survival from the days of the post-
chaise, which was then the quickest
means of travelling. [Chapman, *The
Gentleman Usher*, I, i (1606)]

Post obit, A (*Lat., post obitum*, after
death) : an agreement to repay a
loan with heavy interest after the
death of a third person.

Pot boiling, To keep the : to keep a
business, proceeding, game, etc., in
action with unabated energy.

Pot calling the kettle black : blaming
another while as much at fault oneself.
[Wm. Penn, *Some Fruits of Solitude*,
Pt. I, § 446 (1693)]

Pot companion, A : a fellow drinker.
[Bishop Latimer, *Third Sermon before
Edward VI* (c. 1550)]

Pot, To go to : to fail ; to fall to pieces.
In allusion to the receptacle into which
worthless odds and ends are thrown.
[*The Life and Death of Jacke Straw*
(1593) ; Nat Woodes, *Conflict of
Conscience*, III, ii (1581)]

Pot and kettle, To call each other : to
accuse one another, both being equally
offenders. After the proverb ' The
pot calls the kettle black.'

Pot luck : a meal composed of whatever
food may happen to be available
without special preparation. [Nashe,
Summer's Last Will, ll. 1105–8
(1600)]

Pot pourri (*Fr.*, putrid pot) : a mixture
or medley. Properly a mixture of
dried flowers or herbs.

Pot quarrel, A : a drunken quarrel.
[Hy. Porter, *Two Angry Women of
Abington*, ll. 195–8 (1599)]

Pot to the roses, To betray the : to let a
secret be published.

Pot shots at, To take : to aim for the
sake of amusement at anything that
happens to come within range. Orig.
to fire at anything within range in
order to provide a meal.

Pot valiant : courageous in consequence
of alcoholic stimulant.

Pots, Brazen and earthen : the upper and
the lower classes. After the fable of
the *Brazen and Earthen Pots*.

Potato bogle, A : a scarecrow : the head
is generally formed of a potato.

Potatoes and point : a very meagre
meal. At times of scarcity of salt
parents used to tell their children to
point their potatoes at the empty
salt-cellar and imagine that they have
the desired flavour. [Carlyle, *Sartor
Resartus*, Bk. III, ch. 10 (1831)]

Pot-boiler, A : a work of art or literature, created in a hurry for immediate
sale so as to obtain means both to
boil the pot and to supply contents
for it.

Pothooks : hooked strokes, formed by
children when learning to write. In
allusion to their resemblance to hooks
for suspending pots over the fire.
[Cotgrave (1611)]

Pothooks, The : the 77th Regt. of Foot,
now the 2nd Middlesex Regt. In
allusion to the fancied resemblance of
the figure " 7 " to a pothook.

Potsdam : military and bureaucratic
control in its severest form as practised
under the German Empire. After
Potsdam, one of the cities of residence
of the Kings of Prussia and German
Emperors.

**Pottage, To sell one's birthright for a
mess of :** see Birthright.

Potter, The Great : God. [Cowley,
Essays : The Garden, ii (17th cent.)]

Potteries, The Father of the : Josiah
Wedgwood (1730–1795).

Potwallopers : electors before the Reform
Act of 1832 whose qualification rested
on having boiled a pot in the constituency for six months.

Pound of flesh, To have one's : to
demand one's full bargain. In allusion
to one of the central points of Shakespeare, *Merchant of Venice* (1596).

Pound water (in a mortar), To : to undertake a useless task. From an Ital.
proverb.

Pour encourager les autres : see Encourager.

Pour rire (*Fr.*, to laugh) : not to be taken
seriously.

Pour-boire (*Fr.*, to drink) : a gratuity ;
a tip.

Pourparler, A (*Fr.*, to speak) : an
informal conversation as a preliminary
to formal negotiations.

Poussin, The British : Richard Cooper
(c. 1730–1820). After Nicolas Poussin
(1594–1665), a distinguished French
painter.

Pouting place of princes, The : Leicester
Square ; because George II. and
afterwards his son Frederick, Prince

of Wales, used to retire to his house there when either quarrelled with his father.

Poverty, The badge of : see Badge.

Powder dry, To keep one's : see Keep.

Powder and shot, Not worth : of little value ; not worth the cost of shooting.

Powers, The (Great) : Britain, France, Germany, Austria, Italy, Russia and more recently Japan and the United States.

Powers that be, The : the authorities.

Poyning's Law : an Irish Act of Parliament of 1495, making all English legislation effective in Ireland, passed at the instance of the Lieutenant of Ireland, Sir Edward Poyning.

Practical joke, A : a trick played on a person not only in order to make him an object of ridicule but also at the risk of causing him injury or damage.

Practical politics : a subject of practical as opposed to academic discussion. [Disraeli, *Vivian Gray*, Bk. II, ch. 14 (1826)]

Praetorian, Pretorian, A : a supporter of an established system. *See* Pretorian Guard.

Praetorian Guard : see Pretorian Guard.

Prague, The Articles of : the confession of faith of the Hussites, published in 1420.

Prairie State, The : Illinois, on account of its vast extent of prairie lands.

Prairie value : the value of land as if it were a prairie or unused. The phrase was first used by John Bright (1811–89), English statesman.

Praise from Sir Hubert : genuine unalloyed praise. ' Approbation from Sir Hubert Stanley is praise indeed.' [Thomas Morton, *A cure for the heartache*, V, ii (1810)]

Praise to the skies, To : to praise very highly. [Peter Pindar, *Lyric Odes to the Royal Academicians for* 1785, Ode xiv]

Pramnian Mixture, The : an intoxicating drink. After the Pramnian grape.

Prayer-book parade : Church parade (q.v.).

Preacher, The : King Solomon, reputed author of *Ecclesiastes* or *Koheleth* (The Preacher).

Preacher, The Glorious : St. Chrysostom (347–407).

Preacher, The Little : Samuel de Marets (1599–1663), Protestant controversialist.

Preacher, The Unfair : Isaac Barron (1630–1677), so called by Charles II. because he always exhausted his subject and left nothing to anyone else to say.

Précieuse, A : a woman who affects literary taste, esp. one who is over refined. From the title of Molière's comedy, *Les Précieuses ridicules*. Molière's satire was directed against ' Les Précieuses,' a Parisian society of pseudo-savants, of both sexes, of the 17th cent.

Precious school, The : the school of poetical euphuists who succeeded John Lyly (1533–1606).

Predominant partner, The : Great Britain as compared with Ireland, in the partnership of the United Kingdom. Term used by Lord Rosebery in the House of Lords (March, 1894) and at Edinburgh (March 17th, 1894).

Pre-exilic : dating from before the exile of the Jews to Babylon.

Preliminary canter, A : a minor matter that precedes the real business of the occasion. Racing metaphor.

Première, A (*Fr.*, first) : the first night of a play. [1884]

Premier pas qui coûte, Ce n'est que le (*Fr.*) : it is only the first step that costs.

Pre-Raphaelites, The : the Eng. 19th cent. school of painters who reverted to the style of art in force before the era of Raphael. The orig. members were Holman Hunt, D. G. Rossetti and Sir John Millais, who were afterwards joined by W. M. Rossetti, Thomas Woolner, F. G. Stephens and James Collinson.

Presbyterian true blue : in allusion to the blue aprons which Puritan preachers used to place on their improvised pulpits.

Presents, By these : by the documents present. A legal term. [Chapman, *Monsieur d'Olive*, V, i (1606)]

Preston and his mastiffs, To oppose : to be foolhardy. In allusion to the bear garden kept by Christopher Preston at Hockley in the Hole in the reign of Charles II.

Pretender, The Old : James Francis Edward Stuart (1688–1766), son of James II of England.

Pretender, The Young : Charles Edward Stuart (1720–88), son of the Old Pretender.

Pretorian Guard, The : the guard of the Rom. emperors which ultimately secured the power of deciding the succession to the throne.

Pretty kettle of fish, A : *see* Fish.

Pretty penny, A : a relatively large amount of money.

Preux Chevalier, A (*Fr.*) : a gallant knight.

Priam, As old as : in allusion to Priam, the last king of Troy.

Price, Not at any : in no circumstances.

Pricks, To kick against the : *see* Kick.

Prick-eared Cur, A : a Roundhead. Because the Roundheads wore skull caps on their short hair, thus leaving their ears exposed.

Pride of place : precedence. Orig. a falconry term.

Pride in one's pocket, To put one's : to suppress one's pride for the time being.

Pride's Purge : the action of Colonel Thomas Pride and his men in 1648 of forcibly excluding from the House of Commons all who were suspected of royalist tendencies.

Priest of the blue bag, A · a barrister. In allusion to the colour of the bag in which he carries his gown, etc.

Priest of Nature, The : Sir Isaac Newton (1642–1727), Eng. natural philosopher.

Prima donna, A (*It.*, first lady) : the leading lady vocalist in an opera.

Prima facie (*Lat.*, in the first face) : on the face of it, without careful consideration. (Geo. Cavendish, *Life and Death of Wolsey ·* Prologue (1557)]

Primitive Fathers, The : the fourteen church fathers who lived in the first three centuries.

Primrose Dame, A : a lady member of the Primrose League (*q.v.*).

Primrose Day : the 19th of April, the anniversary of the death of Lord Beaconsfield (1804–81), whose favourite flower the primrose is said to have been.

Primrose League, The : an Eng. Conservative League, founded in memory of Lord Beaconsfield (1804–81), whose favourite flower is said to have been the primrose.

Primrose path (way), The : the pleasant road. [Shakespeare, *Macbeth*, II, iii (1605–6)]

Primrose Sphynx, The : Benjamin Disraeli, Earl of Beaconsfield (1804–81). In allusion to the sphinx-like impenetrability which he practised, and his fondness for primroses.

Primum Mobile (*Lat.*, the first moving thing) : in medieval astronomy, the outermost sphere, supposed to revolve round the earth ; an original cause of motion.

Primus inter pares (*Lat.*) : first among equals.

Prince of the Air, The : Satan. [Milton, *Paradise Lost*, X, 185 (1667)]

Prince of Alchemy, The : Rudolph II (1552–1612), Emp. of Germany.

Prince of Angels, The : Michael. [Milton, *Paradise Lost*, VI, 281 (1667)]

Prince of Apostles, The : St. Peter.

Prince of the Blood, A : *see* Blood.

Prince of Celestial Armies, The : Michael. [Milton, *Paradise Lost*, VI, 44 (1667)]

Prince of Dandies, The : *see* Dandies.

Prince of Darkness, The : Satan. [*Epistle to the Ephesians*, vi, 12]

Prince of Denmark, The : Hamlet. After the principal character in the play of that name by Shakespeare.

Prince of Destruction, The : Timur Tamerlane (1333–1405), the Tartar conqueror.

Prince of the Devils, The : Satan. [*St. Matthew*, xii. 24]

Prince of Gossips, The : Samuel Pepys (1632–1703). In allusion to his gossiping diary.

Prince of Grammarians, The : *see* Grammarians.

Prince of Hell, The : Satan.

Prince of Hypocrites, The : the Emperor Tiberius (42 B.C.–37 A.D.).

Prince of the Kings of the Earth, The : Christ. [*Revelations*, i, 5)]

Prince of Liars, The : Fernando Mendes Pinto (c. 1509–83), Portuguese traveller. So-called by Cervantes.

Prince of Light, The : Christ.

Prince of Music, The : *see* Music.

Prince of the Ode, The : Pierre de Ronsard (1524–85), Fr. poet.

Prince of Painters, The : (1) Parrhasius (fl. 400 B.C.), Grk. painter, so-called by himself ; (2) Apelles (fl. 330 B.C.), Grk. painter.

Prince of Peace, The : the Messiah. [*Isaiah*, ix, 6]

Prince of Physicians, The : Avicenna (980–1037), Arab. physician and philosopher.

Prince of Poets, The : (1) Virgil (70–19 B.C.) ; (2) Edmund Spenser (1553–99), Eng. poet, so-called on his monument.

Prince of the Power of the Air, The : Satan. [*Epistle to the Ephesians*, ii, 2]

Prince of Princes, The : Christ.

Prince Rupert's drops : playthings consisting of drops of glass, invented or introduced into England by Prince Rupert (c. 1640).

Prince of Soot, The : Satan.

Prince of Spanish Poetry, The : Garcilasso de la Vega (1503–36). So-called by Cervantes.

Prince of the vegetable kingdom, The : the palm tree. So-called by Linnæus.

Prince of this World, The : Satan. [*John*, xiv, 30]

Prince's peers : men not belonging to noble or gentle families who are raised to the peerage.

Prinkled in all one's finery, To be : to be elaborately attired (to prinkle = to sparkle).

Printer's devil, A : *see* Devil.

Printing, The Father of English : William Caxton (1412–91).

Priscian's head, To break : to outrage the rules of grammar. After Priscian (fl. 500–25), a famous Lat. grammarian. [Butler, *Hudibras*, II, 2 (1664)]

Prisoner of the Vatican, The : Pope Pius IX, after the incorporation of Rome in the Kingdom of Italy, whereupon he refused to leave the Vatican and tread on Italian as distinct from Papal soil.

Pro and con : for and against. Contraction of Lat., *pro* and *contra*. [*Beryn*, 2577 (1400)]

Pro bono publico (*Lat.*, for the public good) : [Gilbert, *Cases in Law and Equity* (1760)]

Pro lege, rege et patria (*Lat.*) : for the law, for the king and for the country.

Pro tanto (*Lat.*, for so much) : as an instalment.

Pro tem : temporarily ; for a short time. Contraction of Lat., *pro tempore*, for the time. [Evelyn, *Diary*, May 21, 1645]

Procès Verbal, A (*Fr.*) : a detailed official statement.

Procris, Unerring as the dart of : in allusion to the unerring dart given to Procris by Diana.

Procrustean bed, A ; A bed of Procrustes : a forcible method of instituting conformity. Procrustes, of Attica, was a famous robber who used to tie his victims to a bed and cut down their length if they were too tall or torture them by stretching if they were too short.

Proctor, The King's : an official of the Divorce Court who has the right to intervene in divorce suits. Orig. an official of an ecclesiastical court.

Prodigal (son), A : one who spends his time in pleasure and extravagance, but afterwards repents and is forgiven. [*Luke*, xv ; Nat. Woodes, *Conflict of Conscience*, II, iii (1581)]

Prodigy of France, The : Guillaume Budé (1467–1540), Hellenist. So-called by Erasmus.

Prodigy of Learning, The : Samuel Hahnemann (1755–1843), Germ. physician and author of homœopathy.

Profanum vulgus (*Lat.*, the profane crowd) : the lower classes.

Profound Doctor, The : Thomas Bradwarden (c. 1290–1349), Archbishop of Canterbury.

Profound Doctor, Most : Aegidius de Columna (fl. 1287), Sicilian schoolman.

Prohibitionist, A : an advocate of prohibition of the manufacture and sale of intoxicating drink.

Proletariat, The : the lower classes ; the people generally. Proletarii, the sixth class of Servius Tullius in Rome.

Promethean : inspiring. After Prometheus, who in mythology stole fire from heaven in order to enable himself to create men from clay.

Promethean fire : *see* Promethean.

Promise golden mountains, To : to act foolishly. From an ancient Grk. proverb.

Promised Land, The : Palestine. In allusion to the divine promise to Abraham and his descendants.

Pronunciamento, A (*Span.*, a proclamation) : a revolution in Spain or Span.-America effected by a general with the support of his troops.

Propaganda, The College of the : a papal council, the Congregatio de Propaganda Fide, formed to propagate the Rom. Catholic faith in distant lands. It has control over all Rom. Catholic foreign missions.

Prophecy upon velvet, To : to prophecy that which is certain.

Prophet, The : Mohammed.

Prophet's mantle, The : the succession to an important office. In allusion to the mantle cast by Elijah on Elisha as the former ascended to heaven.

Propria persona, In (*Lat.*) : in one's own person.

Prose, The Father of English : *see* Father of English Prose.

Prose, The Father of French ; The Father of Greek ; The Father of Italian : see Father.

Prosperity Robinson : Frederick Robinson, Earl of Ripon (1782–1859). On account of his references to British prosperity immediately before the financial crisis of 1825. So-called by Cobbett.

Protean : see Proteus, A.

Protection : the economic system of imposing import duties in order to ' protect ' home productions.

Protectionist, A : an advocate of Protection (q.v.).

Protestant, A : orig. one of a party in the church who adhered to Martin Luther in protesting against the decree of the Emperor Charles V. Now a member of the Reformed Church.

Protestant Duke, The : the Duke of Monmouth (1649–85), who abandoned Rom. Catholicism for Protestantism.

Protestant Hero, The : Frederick the Great of Prussia (1712–86). So-called by the English.

Protestant Martyr, The : Sir Edmundbury Godfrey (1621–78), a London magistrate, murdered, as it was thought, as a part of the Popish Plot.

Protestant Pope, The : Clement XIV (1708–74), who suppressed the Jesuits.

Proteus, A : a person who readily changes his form or appearance. After Proteus, a sea-god who assumed different shapes.

Proto Martyr, The : Stephen, the first martyr. [Acts, v, 7]

Proud as a peacock, As : peacocks have always been proverbial for their pride. [Ovid, Metamorphoses, XIII, 801–2 ; Chaucer, Reeve's Tale, 3926 (14th cent.)]

Proud Duke, The : Charles Seymour, 6th Duke of Somerset (1662–1748), who would not allow his children to be seated in his presence and who refused to speak to servants.

Province of Brick, The : London. So-called by Madame de Stael (1766–1817).

Prudent tree, The : the mulberry, which never puts forth its leaves until winter is well over. So-called by Pliny.

Prudhomme, A Monsieur : a self-satisfied person. After Joseph Prudhomme, a character in Henri Monnier, Les Memoires de Joseph Prudhomme (1857).

Prudhommes, A Council of : in France a committee composed of employers and workmen appointed to settle disputes.

Prunella : see Leather and Prunella.

Prusse, To work for the Roi de : see Roi de Prusse.

Prussian blue : because it was discovered by a Prussian, Diesbach, in 1710.

Pry, A Paul : a person who interferes in the affairs of others. After the title of a novel by John Poole (1825).

Psaphon's birds : flatterers. After the story of Psaphon training innumerable birds to pronounce his name and then setting them free in the world.

Psyche's task, A : a heavy, exhausting task. In allusion to the task imposed on Psyche, the oppressed slave of Venus.

Ptolemaic System of Cosmogony, The : the system taught by Claudius Ptolemæus (fl. 139–161), Egyptian mathematician, astronomer and geographer, that the earth is fixed and that the heavens revolve around it.

Pucelle, La (Fr., The Virgin) : Joan of Arc.

Pudding for a friar's mouth, As fit as a : see Fit.

Pudding time, To come in : to come opportunely. In former times the pudding was the first course of a dinner. [Heywood, Proverbes (1546)]

Puff a thing, To : to praise unjustifiably. [Chesterfield, Letters (1749) ; Pope, Satires, Prologue, 232 (1735)] In allusion to the old pictures of Fame puffing forth praises from a trumpet or to the puffing out of the carcases of beasts or birds to make them appear more agreeable as food.

Puff oneself out like a frog, To : to swell with self-conceit until, like the frog in the fable which desired to emulate the size of an ox, one bursts.

Puffed up : conceited. [I Corinthians, iv, 6 ; Gosson, Schoole of Abuse (1579)]

Pull bacon, To : to make an offensive gesture, by spreading the fingers out from the nose.

Pull devil, pull baker : an incitement to effort.

Pull one's leg, To : to impose upon ; to humbug.

Pull the strings (wires), To : to direct or control without making oneself prominent ; like the man who pulls the strings which cause the marionettes to move.

Pull up stakes, To : to abandon one's home.

Pullman, Pullman car, A : a railway saloon carriage containing restaurant or hotel accommodation. From the Amer. inventor, George Mortimer Pullman (1831–97).

Pulver Wednesday : Ash Wednesday. Pulver = dust.

Pump a person, To : to obtain information from a person. [Earle, *Microcosmography : A Pretender to Learning* (1628)]

Pumps : dancing shoes. After the Pump Room at Bath and other spas, or from 'pomp.' [Nashe, *Piers Penniless* (1592)]

Punch, As pleased as : very pleased and joyful. In allusion to the marionette, Punch, who fills in all his leisure with song. Punch is from Punchinello, a character in Neapolitan comedy.

Punch, A Suffolk : a carthorse.

Punch's advice to those about to marry : 'Don't.' [*Punch Almanac*, January 1845]

Pundit, A : a learned person, used somewhat contemptuously. Properly, a learned Hindu.

Punic Faith : treachery. After the character attributed to the Puni or Carthaginians by the Romans.

Puritan, A : (1) a seceder from the Reformed Church, who claimed that his form of religion was purer than that which he had left ; (2) a prude.

Puritan Anthem, The : the hundredth psalm.

Puritan City, The : Boston, U.S.A.

Puritan Plato, The : *see* Plato, The Puritan.

Puritanical : overstrict in morality ; rigidly and narrowly religious. From the Puritans or early Eng. nonconformists.

Purple, The : the rank of cardinal. In allusion to the scarlet colour of the official dress of that office. Purple was a badge of distinction in early Rome.

Purple, In : in luxury. In allusion to the imperial colour. [Dekker, *The Seuen Deadly Sinnes : Politick Bankruptisme* (1606)]

Purple, To assume the : to attain to the imperial dignity. After the colour of the dress of Rom. emperors, etc.

Purple, Born in the : *see* Born.

Purple, Born to the : born of high rank ; *see* Purple, To assume the.

Purple deeds : bloody deeds. [*Second Maiden's Tragedy*, III, i (1611)]

Purple and fine linen : magnificence and splendour. [*Exodus*, xxvi, 1 ; *Esther*, i, 6, etc.]

Purple leaves of war : *see* Unclasp.

Purple patch, A : a 'splendid' or gorgeous literary passage. [Horace, *Ars Poetica*, 15]

Purple tyrants : in allusion to purple, the imperial colour.

Purse strings, To hold the : to control expenditure.

Puseyite, A : *see* Oxford Movement.

Push an open door, To : to exert pressure where no resistance is offered.

Push-pin player, A : one who wastes his time in trivialities. In allusion to the child's game of push-pin.

Pussyfoot, A : an extreme advocate of the prohibition of the manufacture and sale of alcoholic drink. The word was introduced from the United States about 1919. Three or four years earlier, however, the word 'pussyfooting' had been used to indicate very careful speech and action on the part of a politician in order to avoid committing himself to a definite policy. In allusion to a pussy or cat walking among china or other objects of a fragile nature.

Put a girdle round, To : to travel round. [Shakespeare, *Midsummer Night's Dream*, II, i, 175 (1590)]

Put one's hand in one's pocket, To : *see* Hand.

Put a hat on a hen, To : to act foolishly. From an ancient Grk. proverb.

Put one's pride in one's pocket, To : *see* Pride.

Put a rope to the eye of a needle, To : to act foolishly and to no purpose. From an ancient Grk. proverb.

Put to the touch, To : *see* Touch.

Putney, Go to : an expression of impatience. Putney was formerly considered outside of the pale of society.

Put-up job, A : something concocted or arranged beforehand.

Pyet, As pert as a : from pyet, a magpie. [Scott, *Ivanhoe*, ch. 32 (1819)]

Pygmæus, As small as : from Pygmæus, the name of an African race of dwarfs.

Pylades and Orestes : two friends whose friendship has become proverbial.

Pyrrhic Dance, The : the most famous war-dance of antiquity. After Pyraichos, a Dorian.

Pyrrhic victory, A : a victory as costly to the victor as to the vanquished. From the victory gained by Pyrrhus

(318–272 B.C.), King of Epirus, over the Romans at Asculum in 278 B.C. He is said to have exclaimed after the battle, ' One more such victory over the Romans and we are lost.'

Pyrrhonism : scepticism. After Pyrrho, founder of the Sceptics (360–270 B.C.).

Pythagoras, As silent as : in allusion to Pythagoras (6th cent. B.C.), Grk. philosopher. [Marston, *Satires*, I, iii (1599) ; Smollett, *Roderick Random*, 357 (1748)]

Pythagorean, A : one who has been transformed. In allusion to the doctrine of the transmigration of souls, attributed to Pythagoras of Samos (6th cent. B.C.).

Pythagorean letter, The : the Grk. γ, used by Pythagoras (582–500 B.C.), as a symbol of the two divergent paths of virtue and vice.

Pythagorean System, The : the philosophy taught by Pythagoras (582–500 B.C.), that the sun is a movable sphere, around which the earth and planets revolve.

Q.E.D. (*Lat., quod erat demonstrandum*, what was to be proved): the legend with which all theorems in Euclid conclude.

Quack, A : a charlatan ; an imposter ; an empiric. In allusion to the sound made by itinerant peddlers at fairs in order to attract customers. Orig., ' quacksalver,' shortened to ' quack.' [Wycherley, *Love in a Wood* (1671)]

Quadrilateral, The : the four fortresses of Northern Italy—Peschiera, Mantua, Legnago and Verona.

Quadrilateral, The Bulgarian : the four fortresses—Varna, Silistria, Rustchuk and Schumla.

Quadrilateral, The Prussian : the four fortresses—Luxemburg, Coblentz, Sarrelouis, and Mayence.

Quadrivium, A : a medieval course of studies in four subjects—arithmetic, astronomy, geometry and music.

Quadruple Alliance, The : (1) the alliance of 1674 between Germany, Spain, Denmark and Holland against France ; (2) the alliance of 1718–9 between Great Britain, France, Austria and the Netherlands, against Spain ; (3) the alliance of 1834 between Great Britain, France, Spain and Portugal, against the Pretenders, Don Miguel of Portugal and Don Carlos of Spain.

Quai d'Orsay, The : the Fr. Foreign Office. After the quay in Paris on which it is situated.

Quaker, A : a member of the Society of Friends. Orig. a nickname in allusion to the ' quakings ' which their preachers underwent in the course of their religious enthusiasms. According to George Fox, the name was given to the sect by Justice Bennet of Derby (1650), who had been bidden by Fox to ' quake and tremble at the word of the Lord.'

Quaker City, The : Philadelphia, which was founded by Quakers.

Quaker Poet, The : (1) in England, Bernard Barton (1784–1849) ; (2) in America, John Greenleaf Whittier (1807–92).

Quaker's bargain, A : a business offer that may be accepted or rejected but not modified.

Quaker-coloured : drab or grey. In allusion to the simple, plain attire of the Quakers.

Quality, The : the upper class socially. [Shakespeare, *Henry V*, IV, viii (1599)]

Quantité negligeable, A (*Fr.*, a negligible quantity) : that which may be ignored.

Quarantine : segregation of a person or ship in consequence of infectious disease. (Lat., *quadraginta*, forty.) In allusion to the forty days during which a ship, suspected of harbouring disease, was forbidden to have intercourse with the shore.

Quarrel over a bishop's cope, To : to quarrel over a matter that is of no consequence.

Quart d'heure, Un mauvais (*Fr.*, a bad quarter of an hour) : a brief period of trouble or annoyance.

Quartier Latin, Le (*Fr.*, The Latin Quarter) : the university quarter of Paris.

Quashee, A : a negro. From Quassi, the name of one.

Quatorzienne, A (*Fr.*, Fourteener) : a member of polite society who is willing at a moment's notice to accept an invitation to dinner so that the company shall not number thirteen.

Quattrocentist, A : a writer or painter of the Quattrocento (*q.v.*).

Quattrocento, The : the 15th cent., as a period of art and literature. Ital., Four hundred, in allusion to the cent. commencing 1400 A.D.

Que faites vous dans cette galère ? : properly, ' Que diable allait-il faire dans cette galère ? ' (*Fr.*, What the devil is he doing in that galley) ? What are you doing in such company ? The phrase appears in Molière, *Les Fourberies de Scapin*, II, vii (1671), but was borrowed by him, together with the whole of the scene from Cyrano de Bergerac, *Le Pédant Joué*, II, iv (1654).

Queen of the Adriatic, The : the City of Venice.

Queen Anne is dead : the news is very stale. Possibly in allusion to the excitement and great interest with which the news of the death of Queen Anne was awaited in view of the doubt regarding the succession. The constant repetition of the news of the death made it ultimately very stale.

Queen Anne's Bounty : a fund set aside by Queen Anne in 1704 for supplementing the emoluments of small benefices. It was derived from the church property which had been confiscated by Henry VIII.

Queen Anne's fan : an offensive gesture, made by the thumb and fingers spread out from the nose.

Queen Anne's Great Captain : John Churchill, Duke of Marlborough (c. 1650–1722).

Queen of the Antilles, The : Cuba.

Queen of Cities, The : (1) Rome ; (2) Bagdad.

Queen City of the Lakes, The : Buffalo. In allusion to its situation at the junction of the Erie Canal with Lake Erie.

Queen City of the Mississippi, The : St. Louis.

Queen City of the Mountains, The : Knoxville, Tennessee.

Queen City of the Plains, The : Regina, Canada.

Queen City of the South, The : Sydney, N.S.W.

Queen City (Queen) of the West, The : Cincinnati.

Queen Dick : Richard Cromwell (1626–1712), Lord Protector of England. In allusion to his weak character.

Queen Dick, That happened in the reign of : that never happened at all.

Queen of the dripping-pan, A : a cook. [Peter Pindar, *Pindariana : Tom and Dolly* (1794)]

Queen of the East, The : (1) Antioch in Syria ; (2) Batavia in Java ; (3) Zenobia, Queen of Palmyra (3rd cent.).

Queen of the Eastern Archipelago, The : Java.

Queen of Festivals, The : Easter Day.

Queen Fortune : the personification of fortune.

Queen of Hearts, The : Elizabeth of Bohemia (1596–1662), daughter of James I of England. In allusion to her great popularity.

Queen of Heaven, The : (1) in Phoenicia, Astarte ; (2) in Greece, Hera ; (3) in Rome, Juno ; (4) in Egypt, Isis ; (5) among Roman Catholics, the Virgin Mary.

Queen of Love, The : Venus.

Queen Mab hath been with you : you have been dreaming. In allusion to Mab, Queen of the Fairies. [Shakespeare, *Romeo and Juliet*, I, iv (1591–3)]

Queen of the May, The : a village girl who presided over the May-day festivities.

Queen of the Mississippi Valley, The : the City of St. Louis.

Queen of the Night, The : the moon. [Lyndesay, *Monarche* (1552)]

Queen of the North, The : Edinburgh.

Queen of the Northern Seas, The : Elizabeth, Queen of England, during whose reign the Navy prospered and grew.

Queen of Parley, The : the echo. [Milton, *Comus*, ll. 238–43 (1637)]

Queen Passion, The Great : love. [Peter Pindar, *Portfolio : Dinah* (c. 1790)]

Queen of Professions, The : divinity. [Burton, *Anatomy of Melancholy : To the Reader* (1627)]

Queen of Queens, The : Cleopatra, Queen of Egypt. So-called by Marc Anthony.

Queen Sarah : Sarah, Duchess of Marlborough (1660–1744). In allusion to the influence she exercised over Queen Anne.

Queen of the Sciences, The : theology.

Queen of the Sea, The : Tyre.

Queen of Sheba, A : an oriental queen ; a woman whose magnificence is oriental. After the Queen of Sheba who visited Solomon.

Queen of Shepherds, The : Queen Elizabeth. So-called by Spenser in *The Shepheard's Calendar :* April, ll. 33–4 (1579).

Queen of Song, The : Angelica Catalini (1782–1849), ' The Italian Nightingale.'

Queen Square Hermit, The : Jeremy Bentham (1748–1832), the economist, who lived at No 1, Queen Square, Bloomsbury, London.

Queen of the suds, A : a laundress. [Peter Pindar, *Lyric Odes to the Royal Academicians* for 1783, Ode ii]

Queen of Tears, The : Mary of Modena, wife of James II of England.

Queen of watering-places, The : Scarborough.

Queen's bus, The : a prison van.

Queen's English, The : correct English. [Nashe, *Strange Newes* (1593)]

Queen's Evidence : *see* King's Evidence.

Queen's heads : postage stamps, bearing the effigy of Queen Victoria.

Queen's Own, The : government property.

Queen's pipe, The : the furnace at the Victoria Docks, London, in which contraband tobacco, etc., was formerly destroyed.

Queen's shilling, The : the shilling formerly accepted (in the reign of Queen Victoria) by a recruit on enlistment in the Army.

Queen's weather : splendid weather. In allusion to the esp. fine weather with which Queen Victoria's appearances in public were generally favoured

Queer card, A : an unconventional person. *See* Card.

Queer one's pitch, To : to upset one's arrangements and cause annoyance. Said to be derived from the metaphor of street artists who have recognized pitches for their performances.

Queer Street : financial difficulties. The term ' Queer Street ' was formerly used to designate something wrong.

Querelle d'Allemand, A (*Fr.*, a German quarrel) : a dispute about a trifle.

Querpo, In (*Span., cuerpo,* the body): in shirt sleeves.

Question, To beg the : to assume that which requires to be proved.

Question, To move the previous : to take steps in parliament to avoid a decision on an inconvenient topic.

Question, To put to the : to seek a decision in a matter. A parliamentary metaphor.

Qui vive, To be on the : to be wide awake, on the alert. In allusion to the sentinel's challenge, ' *Qui vive ?* ' Fr., Who lives ? [Coningsby, *Siege of Rouen* (1591)]

Qui vivra verra (*Ital.*) : who shall live shall see.

Quick, To cut to the : to keenly hurt ; a reference to the quick underneath the fingernails, which is very sensitive. [*The Spectator*, No. 16 (1711)]

Quick as fire, As : very quickly ; as quickly as fire spreads.

Quick as lightning, As : with great rapidity. [Shakespeare, *King Richard II*, I, iii, 79 (1593) ; Butler, *Hudibras*, II, ii, 1065 (1663)] The metaphor is to be found in many of the literatures of the world.

Quick as a stag, As : in Rome, fugitive slaves (*servi*) were called *cervi* (stags), partly as a pun, partly in allusion to the speed of the stag. [Spenser, *Faerie Queen*, II, xi, 23 (1590)]

Quick as thought, As : immediately· [*Coventry Mysteries* (15th cent.) ; Shakespeare, *Winter's Tale*, IV, iv, 565 (1611)]

Quick as tinder, As : in allusion to the rapidity with which tinder ignites. [Peter Pindar, *A Rowland for an Oliver* (1790)]

Quick work of .. To make : to settle out of hand. [*The London Chanticleers*, vii (1659)]

Quid pro quo, A (*Lat.*, what for what) : an equivalent or compensating gift or payment. [Calfhill, *Answer to Martiall* (1565)]

Quidnunc, A (*Lat.*, what now) : one curious regarding other people's affairs. Popularized by a character in Murphy's farce, *The Upholsterer, or What News* (1758), but used previously by Sir Richard Steele in *The Tatler* (1709).

Quietists : a Fr. sect, dating from the end of the 17th cent., which preached a contemplative rather than an actively religious life.

Quill-drivers : clerks. From the time when quill pens were generally used.

Quits, To cry : to agree to a mutual settlement. [Chapman, *All Fools*, II, i (1605)]

Quiver full of them, To have one's : to have several children. In allusion to a quiver full of arrows. [*Psalms*, cxxvii, 5]

Quixote, A : a person extravagantly romantic or chivalrous beyond limit. From Don Quixote, the hero of Cervantes' romance bearing that title.

Quixote of the North, The : Charles XII of Sweden (1682–1718).

Quixotic : *see* Quixote.

Quiz, A : (1) one who causes amusement by puzzling or teasing others. The word is said to have arisen out of a wager that an invented word would be the talk of Dublin within twenty-four hours of its coinage. The wager was won by the chalking of the four letters (unintelligible in combination) Q U I Z on all the walls of the city ; (2) (Amer. univ.) the examination of the members of a class by means of verbal questioning.

Quodlibet, A (*Lat.*, whatever pleases one) : a subject for philosophical or theological discussion. [Sir P. Sidney, *Defence of Poesie*, Pt. II (1595)]

Quorum, A (*Lat.*, of whom) : the minimum number of persons attending a meeting which can constitute that meeting. The term was derived from the rule, generally adopted, which ran somewhat as follows : The committee shall consist of — members, of whom (quorum) — shall constitute a meeting. [Evelyn, *Diary*, II (1669)]

Quorum pars magna fui (*Lat.*, of which I was a great part) : [Virgil, *Æneid*, II, 6]

Quos ego, A : a threat of punishment for disobedience. In allusion to the words uttered by Neptune to the rebellious winds. [Virgil, *Æneid*, I, 135]

R months, The : September to April ; those in whose names the letter r appears, during which oysters are in season.

R's, The Three : reading (w)riting, (a)rithmetic (reckoning). Phrase said to have been originated in the form of a toast by Sir Wm. Curtis, Lord Mayor of London.

Rabelais, The English : (1) Jonathan Swift (1667–1745), so-called by Voltaire ; (2) Laurence Sterne (1713–68) ; (3) Thomas Amory (c. 1691–1788). After François Rabelais (c. 1490–1553), perhaps the greatest of French satirists.

Rabelais of Germany, The : Johann Mentzer Fischart (c. 1545–1614).

Rabelais, The Modern : William Maginn (1794–1842).

Rabelais' dodge : to get oneself arrested so as to avoid paying hotel and travelling charges. In allusion to an anecdote related of Rabelais.

Rabelaisian : coarse, extravagant in humour and satire. After the manner of the Fr. humourist François Rabelais (c. 1490–1553).

Rabshakle, A : a profligate. [II *Kings*, xviii, 17]

Rachel, A : a quakeress.

Racine of Italy, The : Pietro Antonio Metastasio (1698–1782). After Jean Racine (1639–99). the distinguished Fr. dramatist.

Racine of Music, The : Antonio Gaspare Sacchini of Naples (1735–86).

Rack and manger, To lie (live) at : to live in luxury. A metaphor derived from the stable. [Chapman, *All Fools*, I, i (1605)]

Rack Rent : the full rental value of a building, as distinguished from that on which rates and taxes are calculated.

Rack and ruin : utter destitution. A corruption of wreck and ruin.

Racket, To make (kick up) a : to be very noisy. In allusion to the noise made in the game of racquets.

Radicals : an Eng. political party, dating from early in the 19th cent., comprising the more advanced members of the Liberal party. The term was first applied in 1818 to Henry Hunt and others who advocated a radical reform.

Radish, A forked : *see* Forked radish.

Rag, A : (1) a disorderly orgy of practical joking ; (2) a term of contempt applied to a newspaper.

Rag, Red : *see* Red rag.

Rags of Antisthenes, The : the costume worn by Antisthenes (444–365 B.C.), founder of the Cynic School at Athens.

Ragamuffin, A : a ragged, unclean individual. Properly the name of a demon.

Ragtime : music in which no sense of time or rhythm is kept. (Amer.). Also cheap, ephemeral music. From ragged.

Raiffeisen bank, A : a co-operative agricultural bank. After the German originator, Friedrich Wilhelm Raiffeisen (1818–88).

Rail Splitter, The : Abraham Lincoln (1809–65), Pres. of the U.S., who for a time earned his living by splitting rails

Rails, Off the : in error. A railway metaphor.

Railroad City, The : Indianopolis, situated at an important railway junction

Railway King, The : George Hudson (1800–71), notorious railway speculator. So-called by Sydney Smith.

Rain cats and dogs, To : to rain very heavily. From the influence exercised by cats over the rain, according to

Scand. mythology, and from the dog as the sign of the wind in the same. [Swift, *Polite Conversation*, Dial. II (1738)]

Rainbow chase, A : a useless quest. From the fable of the pot of gold buried where the rainbow touches the earth.

Rainbow chaser, A : a doctrinaire politician.

Rainbow touches the ground, Where the : nowhere.

Rainy day, A : bad times ; a period of need. [J. Jefferie, *Bugbears*, III, ii (1580)]

Raise the wind, To : to obtain funds. A nautical metaphor.

Raison d'être (*Fr.*) : reason for existence.

Raj, The British : the British Empire of India. From (Hindi) *raj*, rule.

Rake, A : a contraction of rake-hell (*q.v.*). [Farquhar, *Constant Couple*, I, i (1699)]

Rakes, To carry heavy : to be proud and overbearing. [*Terence in English* (1614)]

Rake's progress, A : a reckless course of proceedings.

Rake-Hell, A : a man of dissolute habits ; a wild disorderly person. [*Alliterative Poems* (1360)]

Ralliés : Fr. monarchists who rallied or gave their adhesion to the Republic in 1890.

Ram's horn, A : a loud, unpolished speaker.

Raminagobris : (1) a cat, after the name used by La Fontaine in his *Fables* ; (2) an incompetent poet, from the use of the name by Rabelais as a satire on Guillaume Crétin (d. c. 1525).

Ramp, A : an ill-mannerly woman or girl. From to ramp, to rage. [Halle, *Henry VI* (1548)]

Ramshackle Empire, The : Austro-Hungary. So described by Mr. Winston Churchill after the outbreak of the European War of 1914–18.

Rank and fashion : the upper class of society.

Rank and file, The : the common people ; the undistinguished mass. A military metaphor.

Ranks, To rise from the : to rise in social status from a low degree. A military metaphor.

Rap, Not worth a : a rap was an 18th cent. Irish coin of very little value.

Raphael of Cats, The : Gottfried Mind (1768–1814), Swiss painter. After

Raphael Sanzio, the great Ital. painter (1483–1520).

Raphael, The Flemish : Frans Floris (1520–70).

Raphael, The French : *see* French Raphael.

Raphael of Holland, The : Martin van Hemskerck (1498–1574).

Rapier and Rosette Tories : the followers of Lord Randolph Churchill in the Parliament of 1880–5. So-called by Sir Herbert Maxwell in *Sixty Years a Queen*, ch. xvi (1897).

Rapparee, A : one of a band of Irish robbers who molested the Protestants early in the 18th cent. From an Erse word for a disorderly person.

Rara avis, A (*Lat.*, a rare bird) : something or somebody exceptional. [G. Wilkins, *Miseries of Enforced Marriage*, I, ll. 159–61 (1607) ; Horace, *Satires*, II, ii, 26 ; Juvenal, *Satires*, VI, 165]

Rare Ben : Ben Jonson (1574–1637), the dramatist. So-called by Shakespeare.

Rare as a white crow, As : *see* White crow.

Raree show, A : an exhibition ; esp. a small object or collection of objects of interest carried about in a box. From ' rare.'

Rat, To : to desert a party which is getting into trouble. In allusion to the belief that rats desert unseaworthy vessels.

Rat in one's garret, To have a : to be out of one's mind ; to suffer from delirium tremens. From the Fr. phrase, ' avoir des rats dans la tete.'

Rat, To smell a : to have strong suspicions of something being wrong. In allusion to a cat smelling the proximity of a rat. [*Image of Ipocrycy* (1529)]

Rational dress : a female costume, approximating to that of men, adopted by women cyclists about the end of the 19th cent. ; Bloomers (*q.v.*).

Ratten, To : to molest a fellow workman or employer by removing his tools or injuring his machinery.

Raven, To have the foresight of a : in allusion to the former belief that ravens had the power of forecasting death.

Raw Lobster, A : a policeman. Lobsters before they are boiled are dark blue (the colour of the police uniform) in colour. The term was first applied by the *Weekly Despatch* in derision.

Raw, To touch one on the : to revive an unpleasant or unhappy memory ; from the care of an ostler to avoid a sore place on a horse's back.

Razor, To cut blocks with a : to use an excellent tool for an inferior purpose. [Oliver Goldsmith, *Retaliation* (1774)]

Razzia, A (*Arab., Ghaziah,* a battle, war or hostile attack on infidels) : a raid ; a hostile incursion.

Razzle-dazzle, On the : in a state of excitement, noise and bustle.

Re Galantuomo (*Ital.,* King Honestman) : the title given to Victor Emanuel II (1820–78), by the people of Italy.

Reach-me-downs : (1) ready-made clothing ; (2) anything not specially prepared for the occasion.

Reach the end of one's tether, To : *see* Tether.

Read between the lines, To : to discern a hidden meaning.

Read while one runs, To : to understand without difficulty. [*Habakkuk,* ii, 2]

Reap as one sows, To : to suffer or enjoy the consequences of one's actions. [*Galatians,* vi, 7 ; Ingeland, *Disobedient Child,* l. 760 (1560)]

Rebec face, A : a very ugly face. Like those cut in a rebec or three-stringed fiddle.

Rebeccaites : rioters in South Wales in 1843 who demanded the abolition of toll gates. They were led by a man dressed in woman's clothes and derived their name from *Genesis,* xxiv, 60 : ' And they blessed Rebekah, and said unto her … let thy seed possess the gate of those which hate them.'

Rechabite, A : a member of a total abstinence society. After the Rechabites who in *Jeremiah,* xxxv, refused to drink wine.

Reciprocity : an agreement between two states for mutual tariff concessions.

Reck one's own rede, To : to trust to one's own opinion. [Shakespeare, *Hamlet,* I, iii, ll. 47–51 (1602)]

Reckon without one's host, To : to arrive at a conclusion without taking into account some important factor. [Rabelais, *Gargantua* ; Caxton, *Blanchardyn,* lii, 202 (1489)]

Reckoning, The Day of : the time of settlement. In reference to the sense of the time of divine judgment.

Reckoning, A Dutch : ' Wherein if you dispute the unreasonableness and exorbitance of the bill, the landlord shall bring it up every time with new additions.'

Reculer pour mieux sauter (*Fr.*) : to withdraw in order to jump forward the better.

Recumbentibus, To give a person a : to give a knock-down blow. From recumbent, lying down. [*Laud Troy Book.* 7400 (1400)]

Red Book, A : a peerage or court guide.

Red Button, A : a Chinese mandarin of the first class. After his badge of office.

Red Coats, The : British soldiers. In allusion to the scarlet uniforms they formerly wore. [1485]

Red cock will crow in his house, The : his house will be set on fire. [Scott, *Guy Mannering,* ch. iii (1815)]

Red Crescent, The : the Turkish equivalent of the Red Cross (*q.v.*), the emblem of which is a crescent instead of a cross.

Red Cross, The : the badge of those who work under the Geneva Convention (*q.v.*) ; the hospital, ambulance, etc., service of an army   Orig. the badge of the Crusaders.

Red Cross Knights : the Knights Templars who wore a red cross on their arm.

Red Cross Society, The : the international society (founded in 1864) for the succour of the wounded in war. The badge of the society is a red cross.

Red Eagle, The : a Prussian order of knighthood.

Red Ensign, The : the flag of the British Mercantile Marine.

Red Feathers, The : the 2nd Batt. Duke of Cornwall's Light Infantry which used to wear red feathers as a distinguishing mark.

Red as fire, As : red. [*Robert of Gloucester* (1297)]

Red Flag, The : (1) the emblem of international socialism ; (2) a signal used to indicate danger. In the Rom. Empire it signified a call to arms.

Red Friar, A : a Knight Templar.

Red Gown, A : a student of St. Andrew's University.

Red Hat, A : a cardinal. [Lyttelton *Dialogues of the Dead,* Dial. xxii (1760)]

Red Hat, The : the emblem of office of a cardinal.

Red herring across, To draw a : to distract the attention to a side-issue. In allusion to the practice of drawing a red herring across the trail in order to lead the hounds astray.

Red Knights, The : the Cheshire Regt. which was supplied with a red costume in 1795.

Red lane, Down the : down the throat. [Udal, *Roister Doister*, I, iii (1566)]

Red Laws, The : the civil code of ancient Rome which was written in red.

Red Letter Day, A : a joyful occasion. Orig. a saint's day or other festival marked in the calendar in red.

Red man, A : a red or N. Amer.-Indian.

Red Neck, A : a term of derision or contempt applied to British soldiers by S. African Boers. Probably a reference to the colour of the British soldier's uniform in the 7th and 8th decades of the 19th cent.

Red, To paint : *see* Paint.

Red Prince, The: Prince Frederick Charles of Prussia (1828–85), Field-Marshal.

Red rag, A : anything that causes passion or angry excitement, as does a red rag on the part of a bull.

Red Republicans : extreme Republicans. Red being used in the sense of fierce or violent.

Red Ribbon, The : the ribbon of the Order of the Bath or of the Legion of Honour.

Red right hand of Jove, The : lightning. [Horace, *Odes*, I, ii, 2–4 ; Milton, *Paradise Lost*, II, 172–4 (1667)]

Red as Rotherham College, As : *see* Rotherham.

Red Shanks : Scottish highlanders. In allusion to the ruddy complexion of their bare legs. Properly, one who has red legs.

Red Shirt, A : a revolutionist. After the colour of the shirts worn by Garibaldi's Ital. revolutionists.

Red Shirts, The : the followers of Giuseppe Garibaldi in the wars of Italian unity (1859–67).

Red Squadron, The : one of the three squadrons into which the British Navy was formerly divided.

Red Sultan, The : Abdul Hamid II (1842–1918), Sultan of Turkey.

Red Tape : official, bureaucratic formality. After the colour of the tape with which official documents are tied. The phrase was introduced by Lord Lytton, in *Alice* (1838), but in a letter dated August 31, 1775, Sir Gilbert Elliot refers to ' rules, tape and packthread ' in a similar sense.

Red Tapery ; Red Tapism : unintelligent adherence to rules and formalities. *See* Red Tape.

Red as a turkey cock, As : [Lodge, *Wit's Misery* (1596)]

Red, White and Blue, The : the British flag. In allusion to its colours.

Redbreast, A : *see* Robin Redbreasts.

Redbreasts, The : the 5th (Royal Irish) Lancers.

Red-handed, Caught : caught in the very act. Lit., with the hands still red with the blood of the victim of the murder.

Red-hot : highly excited or enthusiastic. [Middleton, *The Familie of Love*, III, iii (1608)]

Red-lattice phrases : publichouse language. In allusion to the red lattice windows formerly distinctive of an alehouse. [Shakespeare, *Merry Wives of Windsor*, II, ii (1598–9)]

Redskins : N. Amer.-Indians. So-called by the first white settlers.

Reductio ad absurdum, A (*Lat.*, reduction to the absurd) : an argument that leads to an absurdity.

Reed, A broken : a support not to be relied upon. [*Isaiah*, xlii, 3 ; II *Kings*, xviii, 21]

Reed, A bruised : an unreliable support. [II *Kings*, xviii, 21]

Reed shaken by the wind, A : a person moved by every passing influence. [*Matthew*, xi, 7]

Reef, To take in a : to reduce one's expenditure. A nautical metaphor.

Reek of Mr. Patrick Hamilton, The : *see* Hamilton.

Reel, Right off the : completed without intermediate stop. In allusion to the unwinding of cotton, etc., off a reel.

Referendum, A : a provision for referring proposed legislation to the entire body of electors.

Reformation, The : the religious movement in the 16th cent. which developed into the secession of Protestants from the Church of Rome.

Refreshment Sunday : *see* Mothering Sunday.

Regent Diamond, The : the Pitt Diamond (*q.v.*).

Regicides, The : the signatories to the death-warrant of Charles I.

Régime de la Calotte : government by ecclesiastics. In allusion to the *calotte* or skull-cap worn by churchmen.

Regius Professor, A : a holder of certain professorships at Oxford or Cambridge which was orig. endowed by Henry VIII.

Regulars, The : the British Army, apart from the Territorial Troops and the Volunteers.

Rehoboam, A : a clerical hat.

Rehoboam of claret (rum), A : an eight-fold measure, a double Jeroboam (*q.v.*), usually of champagne.

Reign of Terror, The : the period, March, 1793 to July, 1794, in Fr. history during which under the direction of Robespierre and the Revol. Tribunal there was a continuous succession of political executions.

Reins to .. To give : to let go un-restrained. A driving metaphor. [Rob. Johnson, *Essayes : Of Education* (1607)]

Reins of government, The : the control of government. [Wm. Penn, *Some Fruits of Solitude*, Pt. I, § 364 (1718)]

Reins of .. To hold the : to have control over. [*Hickscorner*, l. 25 (1520)]

Reins, To take the : to take command. A driving metaphor.

Reine Blanche, La (*Fr.*, The White Queen) : (1) Mary, Queen of Scotland, on account of the white mourning she wore ; (2) the title given to the Queen of France during the first six weeks of her widowhood, during which she dressed entirely in white.

Relic Sunday : the third Sunday after midsummer on which, in the R.C. Church, relics are specially venerated.

Rembrandt, A : an etching in the style of Rembrandt van Rhyn (1607–69), Dutch painter and engraver.

Renaissance, The : the revival of learning in Italy in the 15th cent.

Renard : *see* Reynard.

Rentier, A : a person who lives on dividends or interest derived from investments. Lit., one whose income is derived from *Rentes*, Fr. government securities.

Repealers : advocates of the repeal of the Union between Great Britain and Ireland under the leadership of Daniel O'Connell.

Repenter curls : a lady's long curls. Fr., *repentie* is a Lock or Magdalen Hospital. Mary Magdalen is depicted as having long hair. Hence the origin of the phrase.

Reptile Fund, The : the indemnity payable to the King of Hanover by Prussia as compensation for the loss of his sovereign rights, which was confis-cated on the ground of his continued opposition to Prussia. The fund was devoted to the payment of press subsidies.

Reptile Press, The : those German news-papers which received subsidies from the Reptile Fund (*q.v.*).

Republic of Letters, The : (1) the sphere of literature ; (2) authors and men of letters as a class. The phrase was first used by Joseph Addison (1702), but see Anthony Brewer, *Lingua*, III, v (1607), for 'Commonwealth of Letters,' and Gottlieb Friedrich Klopstock (1724–1803), Germ. poet, for 'Gelehrten Republik' (Learned Republic).

Republican Party, The : one of the two great existing political parties in the U.S., that which advocated the abolition of slavery in the controversy that led to the Civil War.

Republican Queen, The : Sophie Charlotte, wife of Frederick I of Prussia.

Res angusta domi (*Lat.*, the narrow affairs of home) : domestic poverty. [*Juvenal*, 3, 164 ; Nashe, *Have With You*, III (1596)]

Respecter of persons, No : a person who is not to be influenced by wealth, social standing, honours, etc. [*Acts*, x, 34 ; Thos. Lodge, *Rosalind* (1590)]

Resurrection man, A : a bodysnatcher ; a grave-robber. First used in 1829 in reference to William Burke and William Hare. ' Resurrection women' was, however, used by Sir Walter Scott in *Guy Mannering* (1815).

Resurrection pie : a dish made of remnants of cooked meat.

Revels, Master of the : the official appointed to direct the revels at court or in the Inns of Court.

Revenons à nos moutons (*Fr.*, let us return to our sheep) : let us return to the matter under discussion. From Blanchet's comedy, *L'Avocat Patelin*.

Rex, To play (Lat. *rex*, a king): to handle roughly. [Warner, *Albion*, I, vi (1586)]

Reynard : a fox. After the name given to that animal in Teutonic fables, poems, etc.

Reynard's ring, To have possession of : to bear a charmed life. In allusion to the imaginary magic ring mentioned in Alkmar's *Reynard the Fox* (1498).

Rhadamanthine ; Rhadamanthean : severe in the extreme. *See* Rhada-manthus.

Rhadamanthus, A : an extremely strict or severe master or judge. After one of the judges of the Lower World in Grk. mythology.

Rhetorical question, A : one which requires no answer.

Rhine, The Irish : the River Black-water. On account of its magnificent scenery.

Rhodian Master, The : Quintus Ennius (239–169 B.C.), Rom. epic poet who was born at Rudiæ.

Rhodomontade : *see* Rodomontade.

Rhone of Christian Eloquence, The : St. Hilary (300–68). In allusion to the vehemence of his eloquence, in that resembling the River Rhone.

Rhone of Latin Eloquence, The : St. Hilary (300–68). So-called by St. Jerome.

Ribbon dodge, The : persecution by means of secret threatening letters as practised by the Catholic Association or Ribbonmen of Ireland.

Ribbon Society, The : a secret association formed in Ireland about 1808 in opposition to the Orange Association. It soon became an agrarian movement directed against the landlord class. The name was derived from a green ribbon worn by the members.

Ribbons, To take the : to drive horses.

Ribbonism : an agrarian movement in the south and west of Ireland during the greater part of the 19th cent. The members of the secret society were known as ribbonmen and did not hesitate to have recourse to outrage to further their ends.

Ribbonmen : members of the Ribbon Society (*q.v.*).

Rice Christians : people whose religion is a source of profit. In allusion to the natives in the East who profess Christianity in return for food, etc., (rice).

Rich as a Griffin, As : *see* Griffin.

Rich as a Jew, As : very wealthy. In allusion to the proverbial wealth of the Jews of England in the 12th cent.

Rich as a new-shorn sheep, As : penniless. [*Cock Lorel's Bote* (1510)]

Rich as Plutus, As : very wealthy. After Plutus, in Grk. mythology, the personi-fication of wealth.

Richard is himself again : a phrase interpolated in Shakespeare, *Richard III*, by John Kemble, who derived it from Colley Cibber.

Richmonds in the field : rivals in active work. [Shakespeare, *Richard III*, V, iv (1594)]

Ride abroad with St. George, but at home with St. Michael, To : to be braggart abroad but a coward at home. St. George is depicted riding a war horse ; St. Michael is accompanied by a dragon, far more difficult to manage.

Ride for a fall, To : to set out with the intention of failing, esp. of a govern-ment which desires a parliamentary defeat. A racing metaphor.

Ridicule, The Father of : François Rabelais (1495–1553), Fr. satirist. So-called by Sir William Temple.

Rift within the lute, A : a small defect which spoils the general effect.

Rig out, To : to clothe ; to fit out. A nautical metaphor. [Ben Jonson, *Staple of News*, II, i (1625)]

Right, The : in politics, the conservative party or parties in a legislature. In allusion to the part of the chamber which it is accustomed to occupy.

Right Boys : an agrarian revolutionary society in South West Ireland (1785–6). After Captain ' Right,' its leader.

Right, Divine : *see* Divine.

Right foot foremost : (1) energetically ; (2) auspiciously. The second is the earlier sense.

Right as a glove : absolutely trust-worthy. According to Sir Walter Scott (*The Antiquary*) the phrase is derived from the custom of pledging a glove as a token of irrefragable faith. It may, however, also be derived from the phrase, ' to fit like a glove.'

Right hand, To be a person's : to be an invaluable assistant to a person. In allusion to the usefulness of one's right hand. [Thos. Nash, *Summer's Last Will and Testament*, ll. 804–5 (1600)]

Right hand know what the left hand doeth, Not to let the : to act secretly, esp. in matters of charity.

Right as a line, As : straightforward, in a direct course. [Heywood, *Proverbes* (1546)]

Right man in the right place, The : a person fitted for his employment. The phrase is said to have been coined by Talleyrand (1754–1838), the Fr. states-man, but was first used in England by Sir Austen Henry Layard in the House of Commons, Jan. 15, 1855.

Right of search : the right claimed by a belligerent to search neutral vessels for enemy's property. Declared illegal by the Treaty of Paris, 1856.

Right side of a man, To get the : to secure the favour and good opinion of a man.

Right as a trivet, As : *see* Trivet.

Rights of Man, Declaration of the : the principles adopted by the Fr. National Assembly of 1789.

Right-about, To send to the : to dismiss ; to put to flight. A military metaphor.

Right-hand man, A : a valuable assistant. *See* Right hand, To be a person's.

Rigmarole, A : a long incoherent statement. Corruption of Ragman's Roll, a list or catalogue. From Ragman, the name by which the statute, 4, Edward I, was known.

Rig Veda, The : the oldest of the four portions of the Veda or ancient sacred literature of the Hindoos.

Rimmon, The House of : *see* House.

Ring, The : the circle formed by the spectators at a prize fight.

Ring one's own bell, To : to announce one's own successes.

Ring the changes, To : a method of swindling by obtaining change for the same coin twice. [Butler, *Hudibras*, III, iii (1663–78)]

Ring hollow, To : to sound insincere. In allusion to the sound of a false coin.

Ring, To make a : to combine with other dealers so as to keep up or raise the price of a commodity.

Ring, The Prize : *see* Ring, The.

Ring true, To : to sound genuine. In allusion to the ringing of coins.

Ring, To have the true : to be genuine ; to possess unquestionable merit. In allusion to the ' ring ' of coins.

Ringing Island, The : (1) the Rom. Catholic Church, which is isolated from the world and is almost always within sound of church bells ; (2) a foreign name for England ' as having greater, more, and more tuneable bells than any one country in Christendom.' [Fuller, *Worthies*]

Ring-leader, A : a leader in a game or in mischief. Orig. the one who led a dance which opened with a ring.

Riot, To run : to act in a disorderly manner. [Chapman, *All Fools*, I, i (1605)]

Ripaille, To live at : to idle away one's time. After the retreat of Amadeus VIII of Savoy at Ripaille, where he lived a life of carelessness and pleasure.

Rip van Winkle, A : a person who reappears on the scene after a long period of retirement and finds everything changed. From the legend of Rip van Winkle who slept for twenty years, told by Washington Irving in his *Sketch Book* (1819–20).

Riphæan Rocks : a cold, mountainous country. After the fabulous Riphæan Mountains of Scythia.

Ripon Rowels, As true steel as : absolutely steadfast. Ripon spurs were proverbial as early as the 17th cent. [Drayton, *Polyolbion*. II (1612–22)]

Rise to the occasion, To : to show one-self worthy of the opportunity.

Rise out of .. To take a : to obtain an advantage over .. A fly-fishing metaphor. [Kemp, *Dance to Norwich* (1600)]

Risorgimento, The (*Ital.*, Re-birth) : the 19th cent. political movement for the union of Italy.

Ritsonism : severe and unjust criticism. After Joseph Ritson (1752–1803), Eng. antiquary.

River of Paradise, The : St. Bernard of Clairvaux (1090–1153), one of the most illustrious of preachers and monks.

River of Swans, The : the Potomac, U.S.A.

River, To dig the well at the : *see* Dig.

Rivers, The King of the : the Tagus.

Roar, To set in a : to cause to laugh immoderately. [*Paston Letters*, No. 422 (1461)]

Roar, To teach a bull to : *see* Teach.

Roaring Boys ; Roarers : street ruffians in the 16th and 17th cents.

Roaring Forties, The : the stormy part of the Atlantic Ocean between 39 and 50 degrees north and south latitudes.

Roaring game, The : the game of curling. So-called by the Scotch.

Roaring Meg : anything loud, efficient or extraordinary. After a very famous piece of ordnance of the 16th cent.

Roaring trade, To drive (do) a : to do a brisk retail business.

Roast a person, To : *see* Roasting.

Roast, To rule the : to take the lead ; to domineer. ' Roast ' is probably a corruption of ' roost,' and in that case the phrase is a poultry-yard metaphor. [14th cent. ; *Carpenter's Tools* (15th cent.) ; Skelton, *Colyn Cloute* (1518)]

Roast snow in a furnace, To : to act foolishly and to no purpose. From an ancient Grk. proverb.

Roasting, To give a : to treat severely, generally verbally. [Earl of Ailesbury *Memories* (1728)]

Rob Peter to pay Paul, To : to benefit one at the expense of another. In 1550 the Abbey Church of St. Peter, Westminster, was reduced from the status of a cathedral and its revenues appropriated for the repair of the Cathedral of St. Paul's. [Heywood, *Proverbes* (1546) ; Rabelais, *Works*, Bk. I, ch. xi]

Rob Roy, A : a kind of canoe. After the nom de plume of John MacGregor (1825–92), author of *Rob Roy on the Baltic*, and other canoeing books.

Robert Macaire, A : a highwayman. After the hero of a comedy so entitled by Frédéric Lemaître and Benjamin Antier.

Robert's men : bandits. After Robin Hood.

Robespierre's weavers : the women who joined the Parisian Guard in 1793.

Robin Goodfellow : Puck, a mischievous fairy.

Robin Hood, A tale of : an improbable story. After the legends that centre around Robin Hood.

Robin Hood wind, A : a cold thaw wind. In allusion to the objection which Robin Hood is said to have had to it.

Robin Hood's pennyworth, To sell : to sell goods below their value, as was the practice of Robin Hood.

Robin Mutton, A : a simpleton.

Robin Redbreasts : Bow Street runners, (*q.v.*). In allusion to the colour of their uniform waistcoats.

Robin Ruddock : *see* Ruddock.

Robinson Crusoe, A : a person shipwrecked or marooned on a desert island. After the title character of Daniel Defoe's story (1719).

Roc's egg, A : something unattainable. From Roc, a gigantic fabulous bird that appears in the story of *Sindbad* in the *Arabian Nights* and elsewhere.

Roche, Men of La Vieille : men of old-fashioned ideas. A geological metaphor.

Roche's bird, Like Sir Boyle : *See* Sir Boyle.

Roch Day : the day after Twelfth Day, when women resumed their work. Germ., *roche*, a distaff.

Rock, To plough a : *see* Plough.

Rocket and come down like a stick, To go up like a : to start a career with extraordinary success and to end it in failure. The phrase is attributed to J. W. Croker (1780–1857), who is said to have used it in allusion to Dickens.

Rococo jewellery : over decorated, florid, garish jewellery. From the rococo style of architecture and furniture.

Rod for one's own back, To make a : to provide trouble for oneself. [Heywood, *Proverbes* (1546)]

Rod of iron, To rule with a : to govern very strictly. [*Psalm*, ii, 9 ; *Revelations*, ii, 27]

Rod, To kiss the : to be submissive to ill fortune or punishment.

Rod in pickle, To keep a : to have a scolding in reserve. In allusion to the former practice of soaking birches in brine so as to keep them supple. [Chapman, *Monsieur d'Olive*, I, i (1606)]

Rod and spoil the child, To spare the : to refrain from corporal punishment and thereby allow the child to grow up spoilt and unruly. *Proverbs*, xiii, 24 : ' He that spareth his rod hateth his son.'

Rodomontade : empty and loud boasting. After Rodomonte, a character in Ariosto, *Orlando Furioso*. [Sir Thos. Browne, *Religio Medici*, Pt. I (1643)]

Roe and John Doe, Richard : two fictitious names formerly employed in legal documents. The term dates back to the reign of Edward III.

Rogation Days : the Monday, Tuesday and Wednesday of Supplication before Ascension Day. Lat., *rogatio*, supplication.

Rogation Week : *see* Rogation Days.

Roger Bontemps : *see* Bontemps.

Roger, The Jolly : the emblem of pirates.

Roi des Barricades, Le (*Fr.*, the king of the barricades) : Louis Philippe, King of the French, immediately before whose accession to the throne barricades were erected in the streets of Paris.

Roi Bourgeois, Le (*Fr.*, the Citizen King): Louis Philippe of France.

Roi Citoyen, Le (*Fr.*, the Citizen King) : Louis Philippe of France.

Roi Fainéant, A : a king or other person who either through incapacity or lack of interest, neglects his duties. The Rois Fainéants (sluggard kings) of history were the last of the Merovingian line in France (7th and 8th cents.), who devolved all their power and responsibilities on the Mayors of the Palace, who ultimately supplanted them.

Roi est mort ! Vive le Roi ! Le (*Fr.*, The King is dead ! Long live the King !) : an exclamation intended to convey that although individual kings die, the institution of monarchy is perpetual.

Roi Parade, Le (*Fr.*, the strutting king) : Louis XVIII of France.

Roi de Prusse, To work for the : to perform a hard, unprofitable or little profitable work. In allusion to Frederick William I (1688–1740), King of Prussia, proverbial for his harshness, meanness and rigid discipline. *Fr.*, the King of Prussia.

Roi du Roi, Le (*Fr.*, King of the King) : Card. Richelieu (1585–1642), who was the practical ruler of France in the reign of Louis XIII.

Roi Soleil, Le (*Fr.*, the Sun King) : Louis XIV of France.

Roi d'Yvetot, Le : *see* King of Yvetot.

Roland, To die like : Roland, a paladin of Charlemagne, who died in circumstances of great bravery at the Battle of Roncesvalles in 778.

Roland, Faire le (*Fr.*, to play the Roland): to swagger, *i.e.*, to imitate Roland, the Paladin.

Roland for an Oliver, To give a : (1) in a dispute or contest to return as much as one receives, after the contest of Roland and Oliver, both paladins of Charlemagne, as narrated in medieval romance ; (2) to cap one lie with another, from the incredible stories told of the valour of the paladins, Roland and Oliver.

Roland's horn, Like the blast of : the horn of Roland, one of the paladins of Charlemagne, which he won from the giant Jutmundus, could be heard at a distance of twenty miles.

Rolling mountains : waves.

Rolling stone, A : a wanderer ; one who frequently changes his occupation. From the Grk. proverb, ' A rolling stone gathers no moss.' [*Vision of Piers Plowman* (1326)]

Roman birds : eagles, which were the ensign of the Rom. Legions.

Romans, The Last of the : *see* Last.

Romance, A : a novel or work of fiction. The first romances were written in the Romance, or mixed Latin, dialects.

Romance languages, The : the languages derived from Latin, *viz.*, French, Spanish, Portuguese, Italian and Roumanian.

Roman-Dutch Law : Roman Law as based on the Institutes of Justinian and modified in Holland. In force in S. Africa.

Romantic School, The : a circle of young poets and prose writers in Germany early in the 19th cent. who wished to devote their talents to portraying romance. A quarter of a century later the school was introduced into France by Victor Hugo, Lamartine and Dumas.

Rome, All roads lead to : there are many ways of accomplishing an end.

Rome was not built in a day : patience is necessary. [Queen Elizabeth, *Speech Before University of Cambridge*, Aug. 9, 1564]

Rome does, When at Rome do as : follow the local conventions. The phrase is supposed to be based on the reply of St. Ambrose (340–97) to St. Augustine who enquired his practice in fasting when at Rome : ' When I am here I do not fast on Saturday ; when I am at Rome I fast on Saturday.' (St. Augustine, *Epistle*, XXXVI). [Hy. Porter, *Two Angry Women of Abington*, ll. 1104–7 (1599)]

Rome of the North, The : Cologne.

Rome of the West, The : Aix la Chapelle, the favourite capital of Charlemagne.

Romeo, A : a devoted lover. From the hero of Shakespeare, *Romeo and Juliet* (1591–3).

Romulus to account for Rome, To need no : to need no hypothetical history to account for a plain fact.

Rooden Lane, All on one side like : the village of Rooden, in Herefordshire, lies all on one side of the road.

Roof of the world, The : the Pamirs, a pleateau north of India.

Rook, A ; Rook, To : a cheat ; to cheat. [*Nottingham Records* (1577)]

Rookie, A : a raw recruit. After the rookery or the quarters in barracks occupied by subalterns. A military term.

Room to his company, To prefer a person's : to desire to be rid of a person. [Munday and Chettle, *Death of Robert, Earl of Huntington*, II, ii (1601)]

Room to swing a cat, Not enough : very restricted accommodation. In allusion to the former sport of swinging a cat to the branch of a tree as a target. [Smollett, *Letter to Dr. Lewis*]

Roorback, A : a political forgery. After the title of an alleged book, *The Travels of Baron Roorback*, from which extracts were published for political purposes in 1844. An Americanism.

Roost, To come home to : of an undertaking, when the time for fulfilment arrives. From the proverb, ' Curses are like young chickens : they always come home to roost.'

Root of all evil, The : (1) money ; [Ovid, *Metamorphoses*, I, 140 ; Spenser, *The Faerie Queen*, II, vii, 12 (1595)] (2) drunkenness. [James I, *A Counterblaste to Tobacco* (1604)]

Root and branch man, A : a radical in politics, one who advocates thorough reforms.

Root, To take : to stay in a place a long time.

Rope enough, To give a person : to give a person sufficient latitude so that he may commit himself. [Bp. Browning, *Sermons*, I, iii, 42 (1659)] Eight years earlier Abel Redivivus used ' chain ' in the same sense.

Rope to the eye of a needle, To put a : *see* Put.

Rope in the house of one who has been hanged, To talk of a : to remind a person, intentionally or otherwise, of an unpleasant incident in his career. [Cervantes, *Don Quixote*, I, 25]

Rope of Ocnus : *see* Ocnus.

Rope in one's pocket, To carry a : to be lucky at cards. From the Fr. superstition that a piece of the rope by which a man has been hanged brings good luck to card-players.

Rope round one's neck, To fight with a : to fight with the knowledge that defeat involves death or ruthless punishment.

Rope to .. To throw a : to give assistance to .. A nautical metaphor.

Rope's end, To give a person the : to flog a person. A nautical metaphor.

Ropes, To fight back to the : to fight to the bitter end. A pugilistic metaphor.

Ropes, To be on one's high : to be haughty in temper. In allusion to a tight-rope walker who looks down on the company.

Ropes, To know the : to be acquainted with the technicalities of .. Nautical metaphor.

Ropes of sand, To make : *see* Make.

Roquelaure, A : a cloak which buttons from top to bottom in front. From the Duc de Roquelaure, by whom it was introduced.

Rosa, Sub (*Lat.*, under the rose) : secretly. From the consecrated roses placed above Rom. Catholic confessionals. According to legend Cupid gave Harpocrates a rose as a bribe not to tell of the amours of Venus. The rose consequently became the symbol of silence. This was independently the case among the Teutons, and a sculptured rose often formed part of the decoration in dining-rooms as a hint to the guests not to repeat the conversation that passed at table.

Roscian, A ; Roscius, A : an actor. After Quintus Roscius (d. c. 62 B.C.), the greatest of Rom. comic actors.

Roscius, The African : Ira Aldridge (d. 1867), a negro actor.

Roscius Britannicus ; The English (British) Roscius : (1) Richard Tarlton (d. 1588) ; (2) Thomas Betterton (1635–1710) ; (3) David Garrick (1717–79).

Roscius of France, The : Michel Boyron (1653–1729).

Roscius, The Irish : Spranger Barry (1719–77).

Roscius, The Young : William Henry West Betty (1790–1874), a boy actor.

Rose, Under the : *see* Rosa, Sub. [Dymocke, *Letter to Vaughan* (1546)]

Rose, The Golden : a golden ornament, blessed by the Pope on the fourth Sunday in Lent, and sent by him as a reward and mark of distinction to some prince, church, or other individual or institution.

Rose, The Little Black : Ireland.

Rose, To mount the : to blush.

Rose Sunday : the fourth Sunday in Lent, when the Pope blesses the Golden Rose (*q.v.*).

Roses, A bed of : *see* Bed.

Roses, The Wars of the : the Eng. Civil Wars of 1455–85 in which the Lancastrians fought under the emblem of a red rose and the Yorkists under that of a white one.

Rose-coloured spectacles : favourably disposed or optimistically inclined eyes.

Rosicrucian, A : a member of a secret and mystical society, said to have been instituted by Christian Rosenkreuz in 1484.

Rosinante, A : a broken-down, worn-out horse. After the name of the steed in *Don Quixote*.

Rostrum (*Lat.*, a beak) : a pulpit or platform. From the name of the platform for public speakers which was erected on the Forum of Rome and was adorned with the prows or beaks of ships.

Rotherham College, As red as : in allusion to Rotherham College in Yorkshire, one of the first brick buildings to be erected in England since the Roman period.

Rothschild, A : a very wealthy man. From the proverbial wealth of the Rothschild family.

Rotten in the state of Denmark, Something : something is amiss. [Shakespeare, *Hamlet*, I, iv (1602–3)]

Roué, A (*Fr., roué*, broken on the wheel) : a licentious person. First applied to the associates of the Duke of Orleans (c. 1720), whose behaviour seemed to justify such a punishment.

Rough diamond, A : *see* Diamond.

Rough and Ready, Old : Zachary Taylor (1784–1850), Pres. of the U.S.

Rough and tumble : disorderly. Boxing term.

Rough-rider, A : a member of the first U.S. Volunteer Cavalry organized by Theodore Roosevelt and General Leonard Wood for service in the Span.-American War. The term was, however, at least a century old at the time. [Peter Pindar, *The Rights of Kings*, Ode 5 (1791)]

Roughshod over .. To ride : to proceed, heedless of another's feelings.

Rouncival : large ; powerful. After Roncesvalles, where gigantic bones, alleged to be those of the companions of Roland, used to be exhibited.

Round on a person, To : to betray a person.

Round numbers, In : a complete sum without fractions, *e.g.*, in pounds, ignoring the odd shillings, etc. ; or ten or a multiple thereof, ignoring all smaller numbers.

Round peg in a square hole, A : a person entrusted with an office or a task for which he is unsuited. Term invented by Sir Austen Henry Layard in an address to the Administrative Reform Association in 1855. The phrase ' a square person has squeezed himself into a round hole' was coined by Sydney Smith (1771–1845) in a lecture delivered before the Royal Institution about the year 1824.

Round Robin, A (*Fr., rond ruban*, round ribbon) : a petition so arranged that no signature heads the list. The first one, prepared by sailors, appeared in 1626.

Round Table (Conference), To hold a : to hold a conference between political opponents on equal terms where neither side has the advantage of the other. The table being round, no one can claim preference in seating. The historic Round Table Conference was that of 1887 in which leaders of the two divisions of the Liberal Party which had split on the subject of Home Rule for Ireland, met but failed to come to an agreement.

Rounder than Giotto's O : of impossible perfection. In allusion to the circle drawn with a pencil by Giotto (c. 1267–1337) as a specimen of his work to be placed before the Pope.

Roundheads : the Puritan party in the time of the Eng. Civil War. So designated on account of their closely cropped hair, as compared with the flowing locks of their opponents, the Cavaliers.

Roving commission, A : an indefinite mission, allowing the bearer a wide course.

Row beyond one's reach, To : to attempt beyond one's power. [*They of the Meane Estate Are Happiest* l. 24 (1557)]

Row to hoe, To have a hard (long) : to have a difficult (long) task to perform.

Row, To hoe one's own : to do one's own work. Agricultural metaphor.

Rowland for an Oliver, A : *see* Roland.

Rowley, Old : *see* Old Rowley.

Rowton House, A : a cheap hotel, intended for members of the working classes. From Montagu Corry, Lord Rowton (1838–1903), by whom these lodging-houses were introduced.

Roxburgh : a form of binding books. After the 3rd Duke of Roxburgh (1740–1804), a book collector.

Royal Goats, The : the Royal Welsh Fusiliers. In allusion to their regimental pet, a goat.

Royal Martyr, The : Charles I of England.

Royal Oak, The : the oak tree at Boscobel in the foliage of which Charles II hid after his defeat at Worcester in 1651.

Royal road to learning, The : a supposed easier method of obtaining learning available to the influential or powerful. From the reply of Euclid, the Grk. geometer of Alexandria (fl. 300 B.C.), ' There is no royal road to geometry,' when asked by Ptolemy whether there was no easier method of acquiring the science.

Royalist than the king, More : more devoted to a man's interests than he is himself.

Rub, There's the : there's the difficulty or hindrance. [Shakespeare, *Hamlet* III, i, 65 (1602–3)]

Rub up the wrong way, To : to cause annoyance to .. Metaphor derived from rubbing the fur of a cat or other animal the wrong way.

Rubber, To win the : to succeed in two efforts out of three. Cardplaying metaphor.

Rubicon, Napoleon's : Moscow.

Rubicon, To pass (cross) the : to take decisive action committing oneself to a definite policy. The Rubicon is a small Ital. river which formed the boundary between Cisalpine Gaul and the remainder of Italy. In 49 B.C. Julius Cæsar, after halting on its bank, decided to cross it and thereby rendered a civil war inevitable.

Rubric, A : an ecclesiastical ordinance ; formerly a Roman law. (Lat., *rubrica*, vermilion), from the colour in which the Rom. ordinances were written.

Ruddock, Robin (Red) : (1) Robin Redbreast ; (2) money ; from the longstanding idea that gold is red.

Rudolphine Tables, The : tables of astronomical calculations, named after the Emperor Rudolph II, under whose patronage they were prepared by Kepler in 1627.

Ruff, The Wooden : the pillory. The ruff was a stiff frill or ruffle worn around the neck.

Ruffle a person's feathers, To : to anger or discompose. Metaphor derived from the bird world.

Rugby : a form of football, orig. played at Rugby School.

Rule of the road, The : the regulation or custom which governs the order of traffic in the public streets.

Rule the roost (roast), To : to be in control. From the cock which decides which hen is to roost near him.

Rule of thumb : measurement by guess work or instinct. [Goldsmith, *She Stoops to Conquer*, III, i (1773)]

Rump, A : the last surviving members of a party or other body, after it has lost its most prominent members. *See* Rump Parliament.

Rump and a dozen, A : a rump of beef and a dozen of claret or oysters. A common wager early in the 19th cent.

Rump Parliament, The : *see* Parliament.

Run amuck, To : *see* Amok.

Run against the point of a spear, To : to act to no purpose. From an ancient Grk. proverb.

Run away from one's own guns, To : to abandon one's principles.

Run before one can walk, To try to : to attempt a task before one is fitted for it. [Jno. Heywood, *Proverbes* (1546)]

Run down a person, To : to depreciate, abuse a person.

Run a foil, To : to puzzle, to lead astray. A hunting metaphor, derived from the quarry which returns on its foil or trail in order to mislead its pursuers.

Run of the house, The : free access to the house and its hospitality.

Run on wheels, To : to proceed easily and quickly. [Jno. Heywood, *Proverbes* (1546)]

Run one's ship on the sands, To : *see* Ship.

Run upon the rocks, To : to encounter disaster. [Lyttelton, *Dialogues of the Dead*, Dial. 1 (1760)]

Runs may read, So that he who : easily understood. [*Habakkuk*, ii, 2]

Running fire, A : a rapid and lengthy series of questions, interruptions, etc.

Running, Out of the : with no chance of success. A horse-racing metaphor.

Running Parliament, The : *see* Parliament.

Running Thursday : Thursday, Dec. 13, 1688, on which day a terrible panic, in the course of which many of the inhabitants of London ran into the country, arose on the rumour of an invasion by French and Irish.

Rupert of Debate, The : Edward, 14th Earl of Derby (1799–1869), Eng. statesman. Name given to him by Edward, Lord Lytton, in *The New Timon*, and previously by B. Disraeli in the House of Commons (April, 1844). In allusion to Prince Rupert, the impetuous Royalist Cavalry leader in the Eng. Civil War.

Rupert's balls : Prince Rupert's drops (*q.v.*).

Rus in urbe (*Lat.*, country in the town).

Rush, Not worth a : in allusion to the former practice, before carpets were in general use, of strewing the floor with rushes. [Langland, *Piers Plowman*, 2421 (1362) ; Googe, *Heresbach's Husbandrie*, I (1577)]

Rushes for .. To strew green : *see* Green.

Russel, Dan (*Old Fr., roussel*, red-haired) : a fox. In allusion to the fox in Chaucer, *Nonnes Preestes Tale* (14th cent.).

Russel's wagon, As big as : Russel's wagon, which plied between Cornwall and London, was so big as to be drawn by from six to ten horses.

Russian Byron, The : Alexander S. Puschkin (1799–1837). Lord Byron, Eng. poet, lived from 1788 to 1824.

Russian Murat, The : Michael Milorado-vitch (1770–1820). Joachim Murat, who was the son of an innkeeper, and as one of Napoleon's marshals became King of Naples, lived from 1767 to 1815.

Rusticated, To be : to be temporarily expelled from a university as a punishment. Lit., to be sent into the country.

S, To cross one's : to cheat. In Old French the long ' s ' stood for sous and the ' f ' for francs. A franc equalled twenty sous.

S.O.S. : ' Save our souls,' the message sent out by wireless telegraphy from a vessel in distress.

S. P. Q. R. (*Lat., Senatus Populusque Romanus*, the Roman Senate and People) : the inscription on the Roman standards.

SS, Collar of the : *see* Collar.

SS which all true lovers possess, The four : sapience, solitude, solicitude and secrecy, according to Cervantes, *Don Quixote*, I, 34. (*Sabio, solo, solicito, secreto.*)

Sabbath, Not to be born on a : to be wide awake, not to be stupid.

Sabbath day's journey, A : a distance of about a mile ; that from the Ark in the wilderness to the extreme limit of the encampment. [*Exodus*, xvi, 29]

Sabbatical year, A : every seventh year, when, according to the Mosaic code, the land should lie fallow.

Sabellan Song : incantation. From the magic arts and incantations for which the Sabelli were famous.

Sables, A suit of : an expensive attire which, according to legislation adopted in the reign of Henry VIII, no one below the rank of earl was permitted to wear. [Shakespeare, *Hamlet*, III, ii (1602–3)]

Sabotage (*Fr., sabot*, a workingman's wooden shoe), deliberate hampering by workmen of the production of work.

Sabreur, Le Beau (*Fr.*, the handsome swordsman) : Joachim Murat (1767–1815), one of Napoleon's marshals.

Saccharine principle in things, The : the adaptation of living beings to their environment, the acquisition of callousness to one's own sufferings, conciliation with one's unattractive duties, according to R. W. Emerson.

Saccharissa turns to Joan : after once the novelty of the object has passed away one's opinion of its value deteriorates. Saccharissa is the type of faultless woman, Joan that of the ordinary average one. [Fenton, *The Platonic Spell*]

Sack, To give the : to dismiss. Said to be derived from the sack in which a workman kept his tools. On engagement the sack was placed in the care of the employer who returned it on the termination of the employment.

Sackcloth and ashes, In : in mourning. [*Esther*, iv, 1, etc.]

Sacred Isle, The : (1) Ireland, on account of its numerous saints ; (2) Mount Athos, on account of its monasteries ; (3) Guernsey, on account of its monks.

Sacred Nine, The : the Muses.

Sacrifice to the Graces, To : to make oneself pleasing to others, esp. by means of courtesy, suavity of manners and care in one's attire. The allusion is to the three Graces of mythology. The original use of the phrase is attributed to the philosopher, Plato (427–347 B.C.) when addressing his fellow-philosopher Xenocrates (396–314), who was noted for his uncouthness.

Sacripant, A : a bully and boaster. After a character in Alexander Passoni, *The Rape of the Bucket.*

Saddle, To be in the : to be in charge, in control. A riding metaphor.

Saddle on the right horse, To put the : to put the blame or praise where it is deserved. [Dekker and Webster, *Westward Ho*, V, ii (1607)]

Saddle, To seek the skirts of one's : to depart, withdraw. [*Paston Letters*, No. 146 (1451)]

Saddled with .. To be : to be burdened with .. [*The Spectator*, No. 551 (1712)]

Sadducee, A : a materialist. After the name of a Jewish sect active at the time of Christ.

Sadism : pleasure in inflicting pain on others. After Donatien, Marquis de Sade (1740–1814), Fr. novelist and dramatist, whose novels exploit cruelty of man to woman.

Saffron, To sleep on a bed of : to be light-hearted. From the exhilarating effect of saffron.

Sage of Auburn, The : Wm. Hy. Seward (1801–72), Amer. statesman.

Sage of Chappaqua, The : Horace Greeley (1811–72), Amer. statesman and man of letters.

Sage of Chelsea, The : Thomas Carlyle (1795–1881), Scottish man of letters and philosopher, who lived in Chelsea from 1834 until his death.

Sage of Concord, The : Ralph Waldo Emerson (1803–82), who lived at Concord, Mass.

Sage Hens : inhabitants of Nevada. From its wild fowl and sage bushes.

Sage of Monticello, The : Thomas Jefferson (1743–1826), President of the U.S., who lived at Monticello, Virginia.

Sage of Samos, The : Pythagoras (fl. 540–510 B.C.), Grk. philosopher, who was born at Samos.

Sage-brush State, The : Nevada, on which territory the sage-brush grows in profusion.

Sail than ballast, More : more show than substance. [Wm. Penn, *Some Fruits of Solitude*, Pt. I, §§ 259–60 (1693)]

Sail close to the wind, To : to be guilty of practices almost criminal. A nautical metaphor.

Sail under false colours, To : to live a life of deceit. In allusion to pirates.

Sail, To hoist : to depart. A nautical metaphor. [Shakespeare, *Twelfth Night*, I, v (1601)]

Sail, To put on all : to make every possible effort. A nautical metaphor. [Plato, *Protagoras* ; Cicero, *De Domo*, X, 24]

Sail with the wind, To : to prosper. A nautical metaphor. [Greene, *Liberality and Prodigality*, II, iv (1602)]

Sails, To haul in one's : to retire from the contest. [Cicero, *Ad Atticum*, I, xvi, 2]

Sails, To take the wind out of one's : to deprive suddenly of the basis of one's argument or case.

Sailor King, The : William IV, who, before his accession, was an officer in the Royal Navy.

Sailor's Friend, The : Samuel Plimsoll (1824–98), the author of Plimsoll's Act (*q.v.*).

Saint Agnes' Eve : the night of January 20th, when it is said that a girl, provided that she observes certain ceremonies, can see her future husband in a vision.

Saint Andrew, Order of : the oldest Russ. Order of Knighthood.

Saint Andrew's Cross : *see* Cross.

Saint Andrew's Day : Nov. 30th. St. Andrew is the patron saint of Scotland.

Saint Anthony's Fire : erysipelas. From the tradition that recovery from the disease, when it raged as a plague in 1089, was due to intercession to St. Anthony.

St. Anthony's pig : the smallest pig of a litter. St. Anthony, a swineherd, was the patron saint of pigs.

Saint Augustin's summer, A : a fine September.

Saint Barnabas Day : the 21st June, the day which is followed by the shortest night.

Saint Bartholomew : the massacre of the Huguenots in Paris on St. Bartholomew's Day, 1572.

Saint Bernard : a breed of large dogs. From the Abbey of St. Bernard where they were bred and trained to find travellers lost in the snow.

Saint Catherine's tresses, To braid : to live a virgin.

Saint Crispin, A Son of : a shoemaker. After St. Crispin, the patron saint of the craft.

Saint Crispin's holiday : *see* Crispin's.

Saint Crispin's lance : a shoemaker's awl. After St. Crispin, the patron saint of shoemakers.

Saint Cuthbert's duck : the eider duck.

Saint Distaff's Day : *see* Distaff's Day.

Saint Domingo Fever : yellow fever. From St. Domingo in the West Indies.

Saint Elmo's Fire : *see* Saint Hermes' Fire.

St. Francis' Distemper : impecuniosity. In allusion to the vow of poverty taken by the members of the Order of St. Francis.

Saint Geoffrey's Day : never. There is no saint of that name in the calendar.

Saint George's Cross : the flag of the British Navy.

Saint George's Day : April 23rd.

St. Giles's, Cripplegate, As lame as : St. Giles was the patron saint of cripples to whom a church near Cripplegate, London, was dedicated. Cripplegate derived its name from the number of cripples who used to congregate in its vicinity.

St. Giles and Earl of Murray, To dine: with : *see* Dine.

Saint Grouse's Day : the 12th of August, on which grouse shooting legally commences.

Saint Helen's Fire : St. Hermes' Fire (*q.v.*)

Saint Hermes' Fire : properly St. Elmo's Fire ; the ball of fire that often appears at mastheads during a storm ; a will-of-the-wisp.

Saint James' Tide (Day): July 25th. St. James is the tutelar saint of Spain.

Saint John's evil : epilepsy.

Saint Johnstone's tippet : the hangman's rope. From Johnstone, an executioner.

Saint Julian was he deemed : he was a great epicure. After St. Julian, the epicurean of saints.

Saint Lawrence, The fiery tears of : *see* Saint Lawrence's tears.

Saint Lawrence's tears : shooting stars which are generally seen in profusion about St. Lawrence's Day (Aug. 10). St. Lawrence was roasted to death on a gridiron.

Saint Lubbock's Day ; St. Lubbock, The Feast of : the first Monday in August, a bank holiday, instituted through the efforts of Sir John Lubbock, Lord Avebury (1834–1913).

Saint Luke's bird, As light as : as heavy as an ox. After the ox that generally appears in representations of St. Luke.

Saint Luke's little summer : the month of October, in which the weather is frequently pleasant. St. Luke's Day falls on the 18th of the month.

Saint Marget's ale : water.

Saint Martin's bird : the goose. From eating which bird St. Martin is said to have died.

Saint Martin le Grand : the administration of the British Post Office. From its headquarters built on the site of the ancient collegiate church of St. Martin le Grand.

Saint Martin's beads : imitation jewellery. From St. Martin le Grand where it was once made and sold.

Saint Martin's evil : drunkenness. *See* Martin drunk.

Saint Martin's jewellery : cheap or counterfeit jewellery. From that formerly on sale in the parish of St. Martin le Grand.

Saint Martin's lace : imitation gold lace ; tinsel. *See* St. Martin's beads.

Saint Martin's ring, A : a copper-gilt ring. *See* St. Martin's beads.

Saint Martin's summer : a period of fine weather between October 18 (St. Luke's Day) and November 11 (St. Martin's Day).

Saint Mathurin's malady : stupidity. After St. Mathurin, the patron saint of idiots and fools.

Saint Monday : the holiday kept by workingmen on Monday, to recover from the week-end rest. [Ben. Franklin, *Autobiography*, III (1771)]

Saint Nicholas's clerks (clergymen): thieves. From the story of St. Nicholas and the thieves.

Saint Partridge's Day : the 1st of September, the day on which partridge shooting legally commences in England.

Saint Patrick, Order of : an Irish order of knighthood, instituted in 1783.

Saint Roche (*Fr.*, Saint Peter) : a play on Fr., *Pierre*, a rock, and also Peter, and Fr., *roche*, a rock.

Saint Roch and his dog : two inseparable companions. In allusion to St. Roch and his dog, who are always depicted together.

Saint Simonian ; Saint Simonite ; Saint Simonist : a disciple of Saint Simonism (*q.v.*).

Saint Simonism : a political philosophy of socialism instituted by the Comte Claude de St. Simon (1760–1825).

Saint Stephen, The crown of : the royal crown of Hungary.

Saint Stephen's : the British House of Commons, which formerly met in the Chapel of St. Stephen, Westminster Abbey.

Saint Stephen's loaves (bread) : stones. In allusion to the stoning of St. Stephen.

Saint Swithin's Day : the 15th of July, the day of the attempted reinterment of St. Swithin within the church, contrary to his dying wish. The attempt was frustrated by rain on forty successive days and was then abandoned. Hence the popular belief that if it rains on St. Swithin's Day it will rain also on the forty subsequent days.

Saint Tammany : *see* Tammany.

Saint Tib's Eve, On : never ; the eve of the day of judgment. St. Tib is a corruption of St. Ubes, but there is no such saint in the calendar.

Saint Valentine's Day : the 14th of February, sacred to lovers. Bishop

Valentine was martyred on that day in the year 278, but it had already for long been a festival of young people from the belief that birds began to pair on that day.

Saint Vincent's Day : January 22nd. St. Vincent was the patron saint of drunkards, in accordance with the proverb :
' If on St. Vincent's Day the sky is
    clear,
More wine than water will crown the
    year.'

Saint Vitus' Dance : a hysterical disease (*chorea*). Formerly a dancing mania prevalent in Germany and the Netherlands. The connection with St. Vitus is due, either to the chapel of this saint at Ulm to which the religious enthusiasts used to jump and skip on Tuesday in Whit Week, or to the supposed power of the saint to control and cure nervous and hysterical affections.

Sainte Ampoule, La : *see* Ampoule.

Saints, The : the anti-slavery party in England.

Salad days : the period of inexperienced youth, when people are as green as salads. [Shakespeare, *Anthony and Cleopatra*, I, v (1606–7)]

Salamander's wool : asbestos. From the fable of the salamander which could live in fire.

Salamis of Britain, The : the Spanish Armada. The Greeks gained a great naval victory over the Persians at Salamis in 480 B.C.

Salary, A : fixed payment for services of a non-manual or non-mechanical character. Lat., *sal*, salt, and *salarium*, the money allowance to Rom. soldiers for the purchase of salt.

Sale by the candle : *see* Candle.

Salic Law, The : a law, first promulgated about the year 500, by which women were prohibited from inheriting land. It was afterwards extended to prevent a woman from inheriting a throne. Its prevalence in Hanover led to the disassociation of the British and Hanoverian crowns in 1837.

Sallust of France, The : César Vichard (1639–92), Abbé de St. Réal. So-called by Voltaire. Sallust, Rom. historian, lived from 86 to 34 B.C.

Sally, An Aunt : *see* Aunt.

Sally Lunn, A : a tea-cake. After the hawker who used to cry them in the streets of Bath (c. 1800).

Salmacis : effeminacy. After the fountain of Salmacis in Halicarnassus which rendered effeminate all who bathed therein.

Salmagundi : a dish composed of chopped meat, fish, etc. From the name of a lady of the court of Marie de Medici.

Salon, A (*Fr.*, drawing-room) : a social and intellectual gathering.

Salon, The : the annual exhibition of contemporary art in Paris. Orig. held in one of the salons of the Louvre.

Salt, A Covenant of : an absolutely binding agreement. From the incorruptibility of salt. [*Numbers*, xviii, 19]

Salt on the crown of . . To put : to imbue with judgment or discretion. [Cervantes, *Don Quixote*, I, 37]

Salt of the earth : of supreme excellence. [*Matthew*, v, 13]

Salt with . . To eat : to accept the hospitality of . . [Lyly, *Euphues : Anatomy of Wit* (1579)]

Salt, To eat a man's : to accept a man's hospitality. From the practice among the Arabs of accepting salt as a bond of friendship. [Lyly, *Euphues : Anatomy of Wit* (1579)]

Salt an invoice, To : to claim the highest obtainable price, so as to leave plenty of margin for a discount or other reduction.

Salt, An old : an experienced seaman.

Salt, With a pinch (grain) of : (to accept) with reservations. From the Lat., *cum grano salis.*

Salt to one's porridge, Not to earn : to earn practically nothing.

Salt River, To row up : of a political party which has suffered defeat. From the name of a river in Kentucky, small but difficult to negotiate. In early colonial days Salt River was infested by pirates who, taking their plunder up the turnings and windings of the stream, were practically secure from pursuit there. A second explanation offers an allusion to the salt-workers on the river, a set of brawny, athletic men alway ready with their fists. Hence if it was desired to punish anyone all that was necessary was to row him up Salt River. Yet another explanation is derived from an incident in the Presidential Election of 1832. Henry Clay, one of the candidates, had an appointment to speak at Louisville, but his boatman, who happened to be a political opponent, rowed him up the Salt River instead of the Ohio, and thus caused him to lose his appointment and the election.

Salt, To sit above the : to be entertained with honour. From the former practice of placing a large salt-cellar midway on a long dining-table, the guests and others whom it was desired to honour being seated above the salt ; menials and those whom it was desired to mortify below the dividing line.

Salt, To sit below the : see Salt, To sit above the.

Salt, To sow with : to render unfruitful. [*The Spectator*, No. 189 (1711)]

Salt, Not to be made of sugar or : to be unaffected by wet weather.

Salt on his tail, To put : to snare ; to catch. [Lyly, *Euphues* (1580)]

Salt, True to his : faithful. *See* Salt, To eat a person's.

Salt, Not worth his : not worth the cost of keeping him alive.

Salvation Army, The : a militant religious organization founded by 'General' William Booth in 1878.

Salvator Rosa, The English : John Hamilton Mortimer (1741–79). Salvator Rosa (1615–73) was an Ital. painter of brigands, etc.

Sam, A Dicky : a Liverpudlian.

Sam, To stand : to pay for the party. In allusion to Uncle Sam (the United States), who pays all the expenses of American soldiers.

Sam, Uncle : see Uncle Sam.

Samaritan, A : a benevolent person who is active in charity. From the parable of the good Samaritan in *Luke*, x, 30–37.

Samaritan, A good : see Samaritan.

Sambenito, The (*Span.*, St. Benedict): the garment worn by persons condemned by the Holy Inquisition.

Sambo (*Span.*, *zambo*, crook-legged) : a nickname for a negro. Properly the offspring of a negro and a mulatto or Indian.

Samian letter, The : Υ. Used in illustration by Pythagoras, the Samian sage, of the divergent paths of virtue and vice.

Samian Poet, The : Simonides (c. 556–469 B.C.), who was born at Samos.

Samian Sage, The : Pythagoras (fl. 540–510 B.C.), Grk. philosopher, who was born at Samos.

Samiel wind, The : the Simoon.

Sammy, A : an Amer. private soldier. After Uncle Sam (*q.v.*), the generic name for an American.

Samosatian Philosopher, The : Lucian of Samosata (120–180), where he was born.

Sampford ghost, The : a ghost supposed to have haunted a house in Sampford Peverell early in the 19th cent.

Sampson, A Dominie : a humble, old-fashioned, pedantic scholar. After a character in Sir Walter Scott, *Guy Mannering* (1815).

Samson, A : a man of great strength. After the biblical character. [*Judges* xiii]

Samson, The British : Thomas Topham (1710–53).

Samson, The Kentish : Richard Joy (1675–1742).

Samson's crown : a mighty achievement which involves the death of him who performs it. After Samson's last great exploit.

San Benito, The : see Sambenito.

Sance-Bell ; Sanctus Bell, The : a bell rung in the church at the Sanctus at Mass ; in Reformed churches, rung as the last summons to the congregants to come to church.

Sancho Panza, A : a magistrate. From the behaviour of Sancho Panza in *Don Quixote* as judge in the Island of Baratria.

Sanctuary : the right claimed by the church to afford protection to refugees from justice. Abolished in England in 1697.

Sanctuary men : men who have taken refuge from the law or from an enemy, in a sanctuary.

Sanctuary, To take : to take refuge. Properly in a sanctuary.

Sanctus Sanctorum (*Lat.*, Holy of holies): a private room of an individual. In allusion to the chamber in the Temple at Jerusalem into which the High Priest alone was permitted to enter. [Scott, *Old Mortality*, ch. 40 (1816)]

Sand, To build on the : to build on insecure foundations. [Rob. Davenport, *The City Night-cap*, III (1661)]

Sand, To plough the : see Plough the sand.

Sand, To make ropes of : see Make.

Sand, To sow on the : see Sow.

Sand, To weave a rope of : to undertake a useless task. [*Columella*, 10 Praef. 4]

Sand, To write in the : to engage in a labour that will soon be undone.

Sands, To count the : to undertake an endless task. [Calpurnius, *Eclogues*, II ; Shakespeare, *Richard II*, II, ii (1593)]

Sands of life (time), The : in allusion to the sands of the hour-glass.

Sands are run out, One's : the end of one's life is at hand. In allusion to the sand in the hour-glass.

Sandals, A man without : a prodigal. From the practice among the ancient Hebrews for the vendor to give his sandals to confirm the transaction.

Sandwich, A : a slight repast consisting of meat, etc., between two slices of bread which can be eaten without necessitating cessation of one's immediate employment. After John Montagu, Earl of Sandwich (1718–92), who invented them so that he might continue his gaming without interruption.

Sandwich, To : to insert between two other objects or ideas, as in a sandwich.

Sandwichman, A : a man who parades the streets, bearing advertisement boards back and front. *See* Sandwich.

Sandy, A : a Scotsman. Contraction for Alexander, a common Scot. name. *See* Sawney.

Sang froid (*Fr.*, cold blood) : coolness of temperament ; indifference. [Arbuthnot, *History of John Bull*, ch. 19 (1713)]

Sangrael : *see* Grail, Holy.

Sanguinary James, A : a sheep's head not singed. After James I of England who introduced the dish from Scotland.

Sanhedrim ; Sanhedrin, The : the ecclesiastical council of the Jews in Jerusalem.

Sanitas sanitatum, omnia sanitas (*Lat.*, health of healths, all is health) : a play on the biblical phrase, *Vanitas vanitatum, omnia vanitas*, Vanity of vanities, all is vanity. The phrase is attributed to Gilles Menage (1613–92). the Fr. savant, but was used by his fellow countryman, Jean Louis de Balzac (1594–1654). It was popularized by Lord Beaconsfield.

Sans Culottes, The (*Fr.*, without breeches) : the revolutionary rabble of Paris. So-called by the Royalists, because they wore trousers instead of knee breeches.

Sans Culottides, The : the five surplus days in the Fr. Revol. calendar, devoted to Genius, Labour, Actions,

Rewards and Opinion respectively. *See* Sans Culottes.

Sansculottism, Literary : literature of a second-class character. *See* Sans Culottes.

Sans Gêne, Madame : the Duchess of Dantzig, wife of one of Napoleon's marshals, formerly a laundress. The name (Fr., Madame Careless or Unrestrained) was given to her on account of her unconventional manners at court.

Sans peur et sans reproche : *see* Bayard, A.

Sans Souci (*Fr.*, without care) : a palace of retirement and rest. The name of a country house built by Frederick the Great near the Palace at Potsdam. The name was derived from his remark on looking at the royal tombs close at hand, ' Oui, alors je serai sans souci.' ' Yes, then I shall be without care.'

Sans Souci, The Philosopher of : Frederick the Great. So-called by Voltaire.

Santa Claus (*Dutch*, St. Nicholas) : Father Christmas, the patron saint of all children.

Santo Benito : *see* Sambenito.

Sappho, A : a poetess. After Sappho of Lesbos (fl. 611–592 B.C.), famous poetess.

Sappho, The English : Mary Robinson, *née* Darby (1758–1800).

Sappho, The French : Magdalen de Scudéri (1607–1701).

Sappho, The Scottish : Catharine Cockburn (1679–1749).

Sappho of Toulouse, The : Clémence Isaure (c. 1450–1500).

Saracen wheat : buck wheat. Introduced into Europe by the Saracens or Moors.

Sarah Gamp, A : *see* Sarey Gamp.

Saratoga trunk, A : an Amer. travelling trunk. After Saratoga Springs, a seaside resort in New York State, at which it was first used by visitors.

Sardanapalus, A : a self-indulgent tyrant. After Sardanapalus (d. 817 B.C.), King of Nineveh.

Sardinian herb, The : sardonic ; the herb which produces sardonic laughter. After Sardis in Asia Minor.

Sardinian laugh (smile) (grin), A : an expression of pain instead of pleasure. *See* Sardonic.

Sardinians, As cheap as the : *see* Cheap.

Sardonic : (of laughter) bitter and scornful. From the *herba Sardonia* or

Sardinian herb, which when eaten was supposed to cause in agony an appearance of laughter in the face.

Sarey Gamp, A : a large untidy-looking umbrella. From a character in Dickens, *Martin Chuzzlewit* (1843) who was accustomed to carry one.

Sassenach : Gaelic corruption of Saxon. An Irish and Highland Scot. term for an Englishman.

Satan, Calling in Beelzebub to cast out : using one evil to cure another. [*Matthew*, xii, 24 ; *Luke*, xi, 18]

Satan, A limb of : *see* Limb of Satan.

Satanic School, The : Byron, Moore, Shelley, Lytton, Paul de Kock, Victor Hugo and others. So-called by Southey on account of their supposed non-Christian or anti-Christian writings.

Satire, The Father of ; The Father of French ; The Father of Roman : *see* Father.

Saturnalia : a period of licence ; an orgy. From the Rom. Saturnalia, a licentious festival in honour of Saturn.

Saturnian days : days of dulness. After Saturn, the designation of lead among the ancients.

Saturnine : dull and heavy ; symptomatic of those born under the planet Saturn, the equivalent of lead.

Satyr, A : an ancient fabulous monster, half goat, half man.

Sauce for the goose is sauce for the gander : treatment suitable for one person is equally suitable for another. [Otway, *Venice Preserved* (1682)]

Sauce, To serve the same : to retaliate. [*The Man in the Moon* (1609)]

Sauce-box A : a saucy or impertinent person. [Wm. Haughton, *Englishmen for My Money*, III, ii (1597)]

Saucer eyes : big, round, staring eyes. [Arbuthnot, *History of John Bull*, Pt. II, ch. 16 (1713)]

Saul also among the prophets ? Is : a suggestion of the conversion to and public support of a policy by one not hitherto identified with it. [I *Samuel*, x, 11]

Saut Lairds of Dunscore : noblemen or gentlemen possessing little but their names. From the proverbial poverty of the Lairds of Dunscore in Scotland.

Sauve qui peut, A (*Fr.*, Let him save himself who can) : a general rout after a battle in which everyone thinks first of his own safety.

Save appearances, To : to keep up an appearance (of virtue, etc.) after the reality has passed away.

Save one's face, To : to preserve one's self-respect despite disappointment or defeat.

Saviour of the Nations, The : the Duke of Wellington. So-called after the Battle of Waterloo.

Savoir faire (*Fr.*, to know how to do) : common sense. [Sir Walter Scott, *Guy Mannering*, xxxv (1815)]

Savoir vivre (*Fr.*, to know how to live) : good breeding. [Sterne, *Sentimental Journey* (1768)]

Savoy, A : a variety of cabbage. Properly Fr., *chou de Savoie*, cabbage of Savoy (France).

Sawbones, A : a surgeon. [Dickens, *Pickwick Papers*, ch. 29 (1836)]

Sawdust parlance : circus language. In allusion to the sawdust strewn in the arena of a circus.

Sawney, A : a Scotsman ; also a foolish person. Variety of Sandy (*q.v.*). [Edwards, *Damon and Pithias* (1567)]

Saxon complexion, A : fair-haired, with light-blue eyes.

Scab, A : a workingman who refuses to join a trade union. First used in this sense in the U.S. in 1811. Used as early as 1590 as a general term of reproach.

Scala Coeli (*Lat.*, the ladder of heaven) : a means of reaching heaven or celestial happiness.

Scalding water, To wash one's sheep with : *see* Wash.

Scale, To turn the : to prove the deciding factor on one side or the other.

Scales to fall from one's eyes : suddenly to perceive the reality after a period of self-deception.

Scales even, To hold the : to be strictly impartial. An allusion to the scales of justice.

Scales of justice, To hold the : to decide or act with strict impartiality. [Minucius Felix, *Octavius* (150) ; Chapman, *All Fools*, V, i (1605)]

Scallawag, A : a disreputable person. Amer. slang. Orig., trade union.

Scallywag, A : *see* Scallawag.

Scamp, A : a good for nothing. Lit., one who decamps or deserts from a military camp.

Scandal-broth : tea. From the female practice of talking scandal at afternoon tea. [Scott, *Peveril of the Peak* (1822)]

Scapegoat, A : he on whom the offences of others are visited. From the goat in ancient Jewish ritual which was sent into the wilderness burdened with the sins of the people.

Scapegrace, A : a bad character. Lit., one who escapes the grace of God. [Holinshed, *History of Scotland* (1577)]

Scarab : (*Lat..*, *scarabaeus*) : a term of reproach ; properly a beetle.

Scaramouch, A : a buffoon. After Scarramuccia, an Ital. comedian who acted in London and in Paris in the 17th cent.

Scarborough warning, A : no warning at all, or one that comes too late. From the sudden capture of Scarborough Castle by Thomas Stafford in 1557. After having taken the Castle he advised the townspeople to flee.

Scarce, To make oneself : to go away in a hurry. [Ainsworth, *Rookwood*, V, 45 (1834)]

Scarecrow, A : that which frightens or is intended to frighten without doing physical harm. Lit., that which scares away crows. [*Nobody or Somebody*, l. 1791 (1592)]

Scarlet countenance, To wear (put on) a : to be brazen-faced, so that blushes pass undetected. [*Look About You*, I, xvi (1600)]

Scarlet Lady, The : the Church of Rome. In allusion to *Revelations*, xvii, 1–5.

Scarlet Lancers, The : the 16th Lancers. From the colour of their uniforms.

Scarlet Letter, The : a badge formerly borne in the Puritan states by unmarried mothers. 'Scarlet' has been from early times an equivalent of heinous in allusion to offences. [*Isaiah*, i, 18]

Scarlet Runners : Bow street runners. From the colour of their waistcoats.

Scarlet Whore, The : according to extreme Prot. controversialists, the Church of Rome. [*Revelations*, xvii]

Scarlet Woman ; Scarlet Woman (Lady) of Babylon, The : according to Prot. controversialists, the Church of Rome. [*Revelations*, xvii]

Scarlet-dyed, To be : to be brazen-faced, so that blushes pass unheeded. [*Look about You*, I, xv (1600)]

Scavenger's Daughter, The : an instrument of torture. Properly, 'Skeffington's Daughter.' From Sir William Skeffington (c. 1465-1535), governor of the Tower of London and Lord Deputy of Ireland.

Scene, To make a : to display bad temper in public.

Scenes, Behind the : in private; not in the public eye. Theatrical metaphor.

Scent, To be on the right (wrong) : to be following the right (wrong) course of deduction. Metaphor drawn from the kennels.

Scepticism, The Father of Modern : see Father.

Schiedam : Hollands gin. From Schiedam in Holland, where it is manufactured.

Schism, The : the division of authority in the R.C. Church between two, and during the last six years of the period, three rival popes, from 1378 to 1415.

Schism, The Great : the division of the Catholic Church into two branches, the eastern and the western, in 1054.

Schomburgk Line, The : the boundary between British Guiana and Venezuela fixed by Sir Robert Schomburgk in 1841-4.

Schoolboy, Macaulay's : the imaginary schoolboy who, in the course of Macaulay's writings, is frequently cited as an example of his opponent's ignorance. The phrase 'Every schoolboy knows' is, however, older than Macaulay. [Burton, *Anatomy of Melancholy* (1621)]

Schoolmaster is abroad, The : knowledge is universal. The original meaning of the phrase was, however, the opposite, *viz.*, that the schoolmaster had packed up and left the country. The phrase was popularized by Lord Brougham in the House of Commons on the 29th January, 1828.

Schoolmaster's language : pedantic language. [Sir Thos. Overbury, *Characters : What a Character Is* (1616)]

Science, The dismal : political economy. So-called by Thomas Carlyle.

Science, The gay : poetry. Properly, the poetry of the Troubadours.

Science, The noble : boxing.

Scientific frontier, A : an international frontier based on strategic grounds.

Scio's blind old bard : Homer. After Scio or Chios, which claims to have been his birthplace.

Scissors and paste : compilation. From the tools needed in the compilation of a book.

Scores, To wipe out old : to take revenge on .. [Peter Pindar, *Ode Upon Ode* (1785)]

Scot free : without payment or punishment. Lit., free of scot or tax.

Scot and Lot, To pay : to pay both general and personal taxation.

Scots Greys, The : a regt. of Scot. dragoons formerly wearing grey uniforms, now mounted on grey horses.

Scotch : *see also* Scottish.

Scotch answer, A : *see* More Scotico.

Scotch breakfast, A : a heavy breakfast.

Scotch fiddle, The : *see* Fiddle.

Scotch Hobbema, The : Peter Nasmyth (1787-1831). From the resemblance of his style to that of the Flemish painter, Meyndert Hobbema (c. 1638-1709).

Scotch marriage, A : a marriage in accordance with Scots law; also a runaway marriage, From the number formerly effected easily in Scotland by refugees from across the Border.

Scotch prize, A : capture made in error. A nautical metaphor.

Scotland, The Curse of : *see* Curse.

Scotland Yard : the headquarters of the London Police Force. From the name of the street in which its offices were formerly situated. Old Scotland Yard was the site of a palace of the Scot. kings.

Scotsman's head, To get a joke into a : from the proverbial impenetrability of the Scotch to jokes.

Scott of Belgium, The Sir Walter : Hendrik Conscience (1812-83).

Scott of Italy, The Sir Walter : Ariosto (1474-1533). So-called by Byron.

Scott, The Southern : Ariosto (1474-1533). So-called by Lord Byron.

Scottish : *see* also Scotch.

Scottish Anacreon, The : Alexander Scot (c. 1530-70). So-called by Pinkerton. Anacreon, Grk. lyric poet, lived from c. 560-475 B.C.

Scottish Boanerges, The : (1) Robert Haldane (1764-1842); (2) James Alexander Haldane (1768-1851). The Apostles, James and John, were called Boanerges or Sons of Thunder, by Jesus.

Scottish Hogarth, The : David Allan (1744-96). Wm. Hogarth, English painter and engraver, lived from 1697 to 1764.

Scottish Homer, The : William Wilkie (1721-72), author of *The Epigoniad*, written in heroic couplets based on those of the 4th Book of the *Iliad*.

Scottish Iliad, The : *see* Iliad.

Scottish mist, A : a steady soaking rain. Properly a thick damp mist characteristic of the Scottish Highlands.

Scottish novels, The : the Waverley novels.

Scottish Solomon, The : James I of England and VI of Scotland.

Scottish Teniers, The : Sir David Wilkie (1785-1841). David Teniers, Flem. artist, lived from 1610-90.

Scottish Theocritos, The : Allan Ramsay (1685-1758). Theocritos, the creator of pastoral poetry, lived in the 3rd cent. B.C.

Scourge of God, The : (1) Attila, King of the Huns (d. 453), who overran the Rom. Empire; (2) Genseric, King of the Vandals (d. 477); (3) Timur Tamerlane, the Tartar chief. (1336-1405).

Scourge of Princes, The : Pietro Aretino (1492-1556), Ital. satirist.

Scourge of Scotland, The : Edward I of England.

Scrap of paper, A : an international treaty observed so long as it suits the interests of either party to do so and then ignored. A phrase used by Herr von Bethman-Hollweg, Germ. Chancellor, in conversation with the Brit. ambassador on the 4th of August, 1914. [*The Press* (Dec. 22, 1855): ' A treaty is with them but a bit of paper.']

Scrape acquaintances, To : to claim acquaintanceship on a slight basis. [Josh. Cooke, *How a Man May Choose a Good Wife from a Bad*, III, ii (1602)]

Scrape, To get into a : to get into trouble or a difficulty. ' Scrape ' is said to denote the path cut by deer in the forests when they were plentiful in England.

Scratch, A : a competitor in a race who is given no advantage in starting. *See* next entry.

Scratch, To come up to the : to keep an implied engagement; to carry out an implied undertaking. The scratch was a line scratched on the ground which combatants in a prize fight or a race toed before the contest began. A sporting metaphor.

Scratch crew (eleven), A : a crew of a boat (cricket eleven) not carefully selected but chosen from among those most readily available.

Scratch a horse, To : to withdraw a horse which has already been announced as intended to be run in a race. To scratch its name out of the list.

Screw, A : pay. Said to have been derived from the practice of placing a man's weekly wages in a screwed-up piece of paper.

Screw loose, To have a : to be mentally unbalanced to a slight extent. Metaphor drawn from joinery.

Screw, An old : a miser.

Screw, To put on the : to bring pressure to bear, generally for payment.

Screwed on the right way, Head : possessing much shrewdness and commonsense.

Scribbler, A : a minor author ; one who writes for low pay.

Scrutin d'Arrondissement : a system of election whereby each constituency returns one member only.

Scrutin de Liste : a system of election whereby one large constituency returns several members.

Sculpture, The Father of French : (1) Jean Goujon (1510–72) ; (2) Germain Pilon (c. 1515–90).

'Scutcheon, A blot on the : *see* Blot.

Scylla and Charybdis, Between : a difficult course between two dangers. From the two whirlpools opposite one another on the coasts of Sicily and Italy, whose danger gave rise to the Lat. proverb, *Incidit in Scyllam qui vult vitare Charybdim*, Who wishes to avoid Charybdis falls into Scylla. [Ascham, *The Schoolmaster*, Bk. I (1570)]

Scythe-bearers, The : the Polish peasant revolutionaries in 1794, 1831, 1846 and 1848.

Sea, To be at : to be in a state of perplexity.

Sea, To build a bridge over the : *see* Bridge.

Sea, To seek water in the : *see* Seek.

Sea, To write on the surface of the : *see* Write.

Seas, The Four : those which surround Great Britain. [1325]

Seas, Within the Four : in Great Britain. *See* Seas, The Four.

Sea-blue bird of March, The : the wheatear.

Sea-born City, The : Venice.

Sea-dog, A : a seaman. Orig. an Eng. privateer in the early days of Elizabeth licensed by the Huguenots to prey on Fr. commerce.

Sea-girt Isle, The : Great Britain. In allusion to Shakespeare, *King Richard, II*, II, i (? 1593).

Sea-green Incorruptible, The : Robespierre. So-called by Carlyle in *The French Revolution* (1837).

Sea-legs, To get one's : to be able to keep one's balance at sea in stormy weather.

Sealed book, A : something extremely obscure or difficult to understand. Properly the standard copies of the Book of Common Prayer, annexed to the Act of Uniformity of 1662.

Seamy side, The : the unpleasant side (of life). Metaphor derived from carpets whose underside shows the seams.

Season, Big gooseberry : *see* Big.

Seat, To take a back : *see* Back seat.

Secession, Ordinance of : the declaration of South Carolina in 1860 dissolving the union with the northern states.

Second best, To come off : to be defeated in a contest. [Peter Pindar, *Farewell Odes*, Ode II (1786)]

Second Chamber, The : the less important of the two houses of a legislature.

Second Charlemagne : Charles V (1500–1558), Emp. of Germany.

Second childhood : *see* Childhood.

Second fiddle : *see* Fiddle.

Second Hogarth, The : Henry William Bunbury (1750–1811), Eng. caricaturist. Wm. Hogarth, Eng. painter and engraver, lived from 1697–1764.

Second nature : habit to which one has become so accustomed as to find it almost natural.

Second self, One's : one who is in perfect agreement with oneself.

Second sight : the power of seeing that which is invisible to ordinary people.

Second Solomon, The : *see* English Solomon.

Second thoughts : maturer consideration. [Thos. May, *The Heir*, II, i (1633)]

Second Washington, The : Henry Clay (1777–1852), Amer. statesman. After George Washington (1732–99), the founder of American independence.

Secret, The Grand : the state after death. Phrase attributed to Rabelais.

Secret as the night, As : [J. Cook, *How a Man May Choose a Good Wife from a Bad*, III, iii (1602)]

Secret, An open : *see* Open.

Secret de Polichinelle (*Fr.*) **:** an open secret ; one known to most people interested. From Punchinello who in

Ital. comedies confides a secret to a number of people each of whom is surprised to learn that it is also known to the others.

Secret Service, The : that branch of the government's service the nature and details of which are not disclosed.

Secretaries of Heaven : the Apostles.

Secretary of Nature, The : (1) Francis Bacon, Lord Verulam (1561–1626), so-called by Isaac Walton ; (2) Plato ; (3) Aristotle ; (4) Socrates, so-called by James Howell.

Sedan, A : an overwhelming defeat. After the defeat of the French by the Germans at Sedan in 1870.

Sedan, The Man of : *see* Man of Sedan.

Sedan (-chair), A : a portable chair. From Sedan, in France, where they were first made.

See through, To : to penetrate a disguise or a deceit. [*Love God*, 95 (1400)]

See which way the cat jumps, To : *see* Cat jumps.

Seek figs where only brambles grow, To : to act foolishly and to no purpose. From an ancient Grk. proverb.

Seek others and lose oneself, To : to play the fool. [Florio, *Worlde of Wordes* (1598)]

Seek water in the sea, To : to act foolishly. From an ancient Grk. proverb.

Seek wool on an ass, To : to act foolishly and to no purpose. From an ancient Grk. proverb.

Seian (Sejan) Horse, The : a possession which carries misfortune with it. After a very valuable horse which belonged to Eneiuz Seius in the 1st cent. B.C. and brought him and its other possessors dire misfortune.

Self-denying Ordinance, The : the resolution of parliament of 1646 which disqualified its members from holding commands in the Army.

Self-made man, A : a man who has raised himself to affluence by his own exertions unaided.

Sell, A : a means of deception ; a trick ; a hoax. From to sell in the sense of to trick, to deceive.

Sell a person, To : to betray a person ; to deceive a person. [Plautus, *Bacchides*, IV, vi, ll. 16-8]

Sell one's birthright for a mess of pottage, To : *see* Mess.

Sell like hot cakes, To : to sell quickly and without effort on the part of the salesman.

Sell an ox to catch a hare, To : to act foolishly. From an ancient Grk. proverb.

Sell the pass, To : to betray by turning king's evidence. From the Irish tradition that soldiers sent by Crotha to hold a pass against Trathal, sold themselves to the enemy.

Semiramis of the North, The : (1) Margaret, Queen of Denmark, Sweden and Norway (1353–1412) ; (2) Catharine II, Empress of Russia (1729–96), according to Voltaire. The original Semiramis was a great oriental ruler among whose exploits was the foundation of Babylon.

Seneca, The Christian : Joseph Hall (1574–1656), Bp. of Exeter and of Norwich. Lucius Annæus Seneca, Rom. statesman and philosopher, lived from 3 B.C. to 65 A.D.

Senior Optime, A : (Camb. Univ.) one who gains a second-class in the Honours degree in mathematics.

Senior Service, The : the Navy, which was organized on a permanent footing earlier than the army.

Senior Wrangler, A : *see* Wrangler.

Senussi, The : a N. African Mohammedan fraternity of a religious-political character. Founded by Mohammed-es-Senussi about 1830.

Separatists : advocates of the withdrawal or separation of Ireland from the United Kingdom.

Sephardi, A : a Jew of Span. or Port. descent or who employs the Span. or Sephardi ritual. From the name of a country mentioned in *Obadiah*, xx, and identified with Spain.

Sepoy, A (*Pers.*, *sipahi*, soldier) : an Indian soldier employed in European, esp. Brit., service.

September Laws, The : Fr. press laws adopted in September, 1835.

September massacres, The : the massacres of about 8,000 Fr. royalist prisoners after pretended trial in September, 1792.

Septembriseurs, The : those who took part in the September Massacres (*q.v.*).

Septuagint, The (*Lat.*, *septuaginta*, seventy) : the Grk. translation of the Bible, made in Egypt between 290 and 270 B.C., by seventy scholars. Hence the name.

Sepulchre, A whited (painted) : *see* Whitened sepulchre.

Seraphic Doctor, The : St. Bonaventura (1221–74).

Seraphic Saint, The : St. Francis of Assisi.

Serbonian bog, A : an inextricable difficulty. According to the ancient geographers the Serbonian Bog was a lake lying between Egypt and Palestine. [Milton, *Paradise Lost*, Bk. II, 592 (1667)]

Sere month, The : August.

Sere (Sear) and yellow leaf, The : old age. [Shakespeare, *Macbeth*, V, iii (1606)]

Sérieux, Au Grand (*Fr.*) : in sober earnest.

Serpent in one's bosom, To cherish a : to benefit one who afterwards proves ungrateful. The Greeks had a fable of a husbandman who found a serpent's egg which he placed in his bosom. There it was hatched by the warmth and the young serpent immediately stung him who had brought it to life. [Sir Thos. Wyatt, *Complaint Upon Love, to Reason* (1557)]

Serpent, As subtle as a : in allusion to the serpent of *Genesis*, iii, 1.

Serpent to hiss, To teach a : *see* Teach.

Serpent by the tail, To hold the : *see* Hold.

Serpent, The trail of the : evidence of sin. [Thos. Moore, *Paradise and the Peri* (1817)]

Serpent, The wisdom of the : in allusion to the serpent in the Garden of Eden, and the general belief in early times in the wisdom of the serpent. [*Matthew*, x, 16]

Serpentine : tortuous or winding ; like a serpent in motion.

Serpentine verses : verses whose lines end with the same words as those with which they commence.

Serpent's head, To love a : to be very cunning and cruel.

Serve the turn, To : to be effective for the immediate purpose. [*Knack to Know a Knave*, l. 1615 (1594)]

Serve two masters, To : [*Matthew*, vi, 24 ; *Luke*, xvi, 13]

Services, The : the Army, Navy and Air Service.

Servus Servorum Dei (*Lat.*, a servant of the servants of the Lord) : a title of the Pope.

Sesame, A ; An open sesame : a password that gives admission which would otherwise be refused. From the password in the tale of *Ali Baba and the Forty Thieves* in the *Arabian Nights*.

Settle a person's hash, To : *see* Hash.

Set-to, A : a fight. In a prize fight the combatants are set by their seconds to the scratch.

Seven ages of man, The :
' At first the infant,
Mewling and puking in the nurse's arms.
Then the whining school-boy, with his satchel,
And shining morning face, creeping like snail
Unwillingly to school. And then the lover,
Sighing like furnace, with a woful ballad
Made to his mistress' eyebrow. Then a soldier,
Full of strange oaths, and bearded like the pard.
Jealous in honour, sudden and quick in quarrel,
Seeking the bubble reputation
Even in the cannon's mouth. And then the justice,
In fair round belly with good capon lin'd,
With eyes severe, and beard of formal cut,
Full of wise saws and modern instances ;
And so he plays his part. The sixth age shifts
Into the lean and slipper'd pantaloon,
With spectacles on nose, and pouch on side ;
His youthful hose, well sav'd, a world too wide
For his shrunk shank ; and his big manly voice,
Turning again toward childish treble, pipes
And whistles in his sound. Last scene of all,
That ends this strange eventful history,
Is second childishness, and mere oblivion—
Sans teeth, sans eyes, sans taste, sans everything.'
[Shakespeare, *As You Like It*, II, vii (1600)]

Seven Arts, The : grammar, logic, rhetoric, arithmetic, geometry, music and astronomy ; the principal branches of learning in the Middle Ages.

Seven Bibles, The : the Bible of the Christians ; the Eddas of the Scandinavians ; the Five Kings of the Chinese ; the Koran of the Mohammedans ; the Tri Pitikes of the Buddhists ; the Three Vedas of the Hindus ; the Zendavesta of the Persians.

Seven Bishops, The : Archbishop Sancroft, Bishops Ken, Lake, Lloyd, Trelawney, Turner, and White, who protested in 1688 against the Declaration of Indulgence.

Seven Bodies in Alchemy, The : the Sun (gold), the Moon (silver), Mars (iron), Mercury (quicksilver), Saturn (lead), Jupiter (tin), Venus (copper).

Seven Champions of Christendom, The : St. Denis of France, St. Anthony of Italy, St. James of Spain, St. George of England, St. Andrew of Scotland, St. Patrick of Ireland and St. David of Wales ; according to Richard Johnson (1573–1659).

Seven Churches of Asia, The : Ephesus, Smyrna, Pergamos, Thyatira, Sardis, Philadelphia, Laodicea.

Seven Days' Battle, The : the battle of James River between the Federals and the Confederates in the Amer. Civil War, lasting from June 25 to July 1, 1862.

Seven Days' Campaign, The : the series of battles in Bohemia concluding in the Battle of Sadowa, July 3, 1866, in the Austro-Prussian War.

Seven deadly Sins, The : pride, idleness, envy, murder, covetousness, lust and gluttony ; according to the Rom. Catholic Church.

Seven hilled City, The : Rome, built on the Palatine, Capitoline, Quirinal, Aventine, Coelian, Esquiline and Viminal hills.

Seven Lamps of the Church, The : the Seven Bishops (*q.v.*).

Seven Sages (Wise Men) of Greece, The : Anacharsis, Bias, Chilo, Cleobulus, Pittacus, Solon and Thales (fl. c. 600 B.C.).

Seven Sciences, The : the seven arts (*q.v.*).

Seven Seas, The : the Arctic, Antarctic, North Pacific, South Pacific, North Atlantic, South Atlantic and Indian Oceans.

Seven Senses, The : animation, feeling, speech, taste, sight, hearing, smell. According to *Ecclesiasticus*, xvii, 5, seeing, hearing, tasting, feeling, understanding, speech.

Seven Sleepers of Ephesus, The : seven Christian youths who are supposed to have hidden themselves and fallen asleep during the persecution by Decius (249–251) and to have slept for two or three centuries.

Seven Spirits of God, The : wisdom, understanding, counsel, power, knowledge, righteousness, divine awfulness.

Seven Virtues, The : faith, hope, charity, prudence, justice, fortitude, temperance.

Seven Weeks' War, The : the Austro-Prussian War of June and July, 1866.

Seven Wise Masters, The : an old collection of oriental tales, called *Sandabar's Parables*.

Seven Wise Men of Greece, The : *see* Seven Sages, The.

Seven Wonders of the World, The : (in antiquity) the Pyramid of Philetion, the Pharos at Alexandria, the Walls of Babylon, Phidias' Statue of the Olympian Zeus at Athens, the Temple of Diana at Ephesus, the Tomb of King Mausolus at Helicarnassus and the Colossus at Rhodes. (In the Middle Ages) the Colosseum of Rome, the Catacombs of Alexandria, the Great Wall of China, Stonehenge, the Leaning Tower of Pisa, the Porcelain Tower of Nankin, the Mosque of St. Sophia at Constantinople.

Seven Years' War, The : the War of 1756 to 1763 between Prussia, under Frederick the Great, supported by England, and France, Russia, Austria, Sweden and Saxony.

Seven-leagued boots, To put on : to cover ground very rapidly. From the boots of the fairy-tale which enabled the wearer to cover seven leagues at a step.

Seventh Heaven, The : *see* Heaven.

Severn Capon, A : *see* Capon.

Seville, To learn manners in : a pun on 'Seville' and 'civil.' [*Appius and Virginia*, ll. 905–6 (1563)]

Sex, The fair : women.

Sex, The gentle : women. [Phillip Stubbes, *Anatomie of Abuses*, VII (1583)]

Sex, The Softer : women. [J. Beaumont, *Psyche*, XIV, i (1648)]

Sex, The weaker : women. [Purchas, *Pilgrimage* (1613)]

Shabby-genteel : shabby while obviously attempting to retain gentility. [*Connoisseur*, No. 25, 146 (1754)]

Shadow, To : to follow about like a shadow.

Shadow, To be afraid of one's own : to be unreasonably nervous.

Shadow figure, A : a profile portrait filled in in black ; a silhouette.

Shadow, To quarrel with one's own : to be so irritable as to be ready to be offended at the merest trifle.

Shadow for the Substance, To mistake the : to lose the good while vainly seeking the better. From the fable of the dog that dropped his bone into the river while vainly endeavouring to secure the enlarged reflection of it.

Shady character, A : (Orig. Univ. slang) a person justifiably the object of suspicion.

Shady side of .. On the : older than (an age).

Shaft or a bolt of it, To make either a : to apply it to one purpose or another. The bolt and the shaft were different varieties of arrow.

Shake-down, A : a bed. In allusion to the period in which men slept on a litter of straw.

Shakes, In a couple (brace) of : very quickly, in as short a time as one can shake a dice-cup twice.

Shakes, No great : no particular value.

Shakespeare of Divines, The : Jeremy Taylor (1613–67).

Shakespeare of Eloquence, The : Honoré Gabriel Riquetti, Comte de Mirabeau (1749–91). So-called by Antoine Barnave.

Shakespeare of Germany, The : August Friedrich Ferdinand von Kotzebue (1761–1819).

Shakespeare of Prose Fiction, The : Samuel Richardson (1689–1761). So-called by Isaac d'Israeli.

Shakespeare, The Spanish : Calderon (1600–81).

Shallow, A Justice : a solemn, self-important, unintelligent country magistrate. After a character in Shakespeare, 2 *King Henry IV* (1597–8) and *Merry Wives of Windsor* (1598–9).

Shalls, To be fed with : to be kept quiet by means of promises. [Churchyard, *The Challenge* (1593)]

Shandean exactness : in allusion to *Tristram Shandy* (1759–67) by Laurence Sterne. Term used by Sir Walter Scott.

Shandean vein, In a : in the manner of Tristram Shandy, the hero of a novel of that name by Laurence Sterne.

Shanghai, To : (1) to drug a person and then to ship him as a sailor ; (2) to hoax. From Shanghai, the *Daily Mail* correspondent in which city sent a spurious account of the massacre of the inhabitants of the European legations in Pekin during the Boxer troubles, which account was for a time accepted as authentic.

Shanks's mare (pony), To ride : to walk. From ' shank,' a leg.

Shannon, Dipped in the : innocent of bashfulness. According to an Irish proverb.

Shark, A : a swindler ; one who makes undue profit. [16th cent.]

Sharp practice : taking unfair advantage of others ; practice on the verge of dishonesty.

Sharp as a razor, As : (1) clever ; (2) keen. [Chaucer, *Legende of Good Women*, IX, 93 (14th cent.) ; Horman, *Vulgaria*, 277 (1519)]

Sharper, A : a swindler ; a rogue. [Luttrell (1681)] *See* Sharp practice.

Shave an ass, To : to act foolishly. From an ancient Grk. proverb.

Shave, A close : a narrow escape.

Shears of Destiny, The : in allusion to the shears which Atropos, one of the three Parcæ or Fates, used to cut the thread of life.

Sheeney, A : (slang) a Jew. Apparently from *misah meschina*, a Jewish expression which, being familiar in certain Eng. circles, suffered corruption and was applied to designate Jews themselves.

Sheep, A black : *see* Black sheep.

Sheep from the goats, To separate the : to separate the good from the bad. [*Matthew*, xxv, 32]

Sheep, A lost : a person who has got out of his natural environment. [*Jeremiah*, i, 6 ; Geo. Whetstone, *Remembrance of George Gascoigne*, st. 7 (1577)]

Sheep, To return to our : to return to the matter in hand. From the Fr. phrase ' Revenons à nos moutons' (*q.v.*).

Sheep with scalding water, To wash one's : *see* Wash.

Sheep among wolves, A : a victim among rogues. [Rob. Wilson, *Three Ladies of London*, II, 1485–6 (1584)]

Sheep's eyes at .. To cast (make) : to ogle. Formerly, to look modestly. [Skelton, *Workes* (1500)]

Sheepish : foolish looking, like a sheep.

Sheer Thursday : the Thursday before Easter, when it was the practice to shear or shave the beard.

Sheet anchor, One's : one's principal support. A nautical metaphor.

Sheet, A clean : *see* Clean sheet.

Sheet, To wear the white : to do penance ; to acknowledge one's guilt. From the costume worn by a penitent in the Rom. Catholic Church.

Sheets in the wind, To be three : to be very drunk. A nautical metaphor.

Sheffield, The Bard of : James Montgomery (1771–1854).

Shekels : money. The shekel was a weight and silver coin of the Hebrews.

Shelf, To be laid (put) on the : to be retired or unemployed ; (of a spinster) to become an old maid.

Shell out, To : to disburse. From the sense of to shell, to remove from the shell. [Maria Edgeworth, *Moral Tales* (1801)]

Shell, To come out of one's : to enter into the general conversation or activities. Metaphor derived from the poultry-yard.

Shepherd of Banbury, The : John Claridge, who assumed the name for his weather-forecasting rules, published in 1744.

Shepherd Kings, The : the Hyksos, or alien kings who ruled in Egypt from 2100 to 1650 B.C.

Shepherd of the Ocean, The : Sir Walter Raleigh. Name given to him by Edmund Spenser.

Shepherd of Salisbury Plain, The : a popular moral tale by Hannah More, based apparently on David Saunders.

Sheppard, A Jack : a highwayman. After a notorious highwayman, b. in 1702, hanged in 1724.

Sheraton : an Eng. style of furniture. After Thomas Sheraton (c. 1751–1806), the designer.

Shere Thursday : *see* Sheer Thursday.

Sherlock Holmes, A : an esp. clever amateur detective. After the hero in Conan Doyle's *Adventures of Sherlock Holmes* (1892) and other stories.

She-wolf of France, The : Isabella of France (1292–1358), wife of Edward II of England.

Shiah : one of the two great divisions of Mohammedanism ; that which bases its teachings on the Koran without the aid of tradition.

Shibboleth, A : a means of distinguishing one party from another. From the Hebrew word by the pronunciation of which the Ephraimites were identified. [*Judges*, xii]

Shield, The other side of the : the other side of the question. From the story of two knights who quarrelled over the metal composing a shield which was silver within and gold without, each knight seeing one side only. [Beaumont, *Moralities*]

Shiite : a member of the Shiah (*q.v.*) sect.

Shillalah (Shillelagh), A : a cudgel, esp. in Ireland. After a wood in Ireland, famous for its oaks.

Shillibeer, A : an omnibus. After George Shillibeer (1797–1866), who introduced that class of vehicle into the London streets.

Shilling, To cut off with a : to disinherit and in order to show that the action is intentional to bequeath an insignificant legacy to the natural heir. A vulgar error was long current that a will in which no mention of the natural heir is made is invalid. This was a fact in Rom. law.

Shilling, The King's (Queen's) : the coin formerly handed to a recruit on enlisting in the British army.

Shilling shocker, (dreadful), A : a sensational novel of an ephemeral character, published at a shilling. Introduced into the language c. 1885.

Shilly-shally : irresolution. Corrupt duplication of ' Shall I, shall I ? '

Shindy, A : a noisy quarrel. Gypsy, *chinda.*

Shining hour, To improve the : to make the best use of one's time. [Isaac Watts, *Divine and Moral Songs*, XX (1720)]

Shining light, A : an example of excellence. [*John*, v. 35]

Ship of the desert, The : the camel. So-called by G. Sandys. [*Paraphrase from Job* (1610)]

Ship comes home, When my : when I come into a fortune. An allusion to the days when argosies brought great wealth across the seas.

Ship on the sands, To run one's : to argue oneself into a wrong position.

Ship for a ha'porth of tar, To spoil the : to practice niggardliness ; to be disinclined to complete the expenditure on an object. Properly, to spoil the sheep, etc.

Ship of State, The : the state ; the national fortunes. Term originated by Machiavelli in *The Prince.*

Ships that pass in the night : people who pass into one's circle of acquaintance, stay there a brief while and then pass out again. The phrase was originated by Longfellow in *Elizabeth*, but popularized by Miss Beatrice Harraden as the title of one of her novels (1893).

Shipton, Mother : a half-mythical personage who lived (1488–c.1559). Her prophecies had much vogue and are still quoted.

Shirt to one's back, Not a : penniless.

Shirt of Nessus, The : given to Hercules and, when worn by him, poisoned his flesh so that he died in agony.

Shirt-sleeves diplomacy : diplomacy which takes the press, and through it the public, into its confidence, as practiced in the U.S. where the President used to grant weekly interviews to representatives of the press and give them much information on the course of foreign affairs.

Shoddy : material worthless or of little value. Properly woollen cloth remade out of woollen rags and refuse.

Shoe after .. To cast (fling) an old : to wish good luck to .. From the practice of throwing an old shoe at a bridal couple in order to bring them luck. [Heywood, *Proverbs* (1546)]

Shoe the gosling, To : to engage in a profitless task. [Heywood, *Proverbes* (1546)]

Shoe the grey goose, To : to undertake a difficult and thankless task.

Shoe the horse, To : to cheat an employer out of small amounts. Apparently from the practice of grooms of charging their masters for shoeing horses and pocketing the proceeds.

Shoe the mockish (wild) mare, To : to undertake a difficult and dangerous task.

Shoe pinches, To know where the : to suffer trouble not patent to the stranger. Lucius Aemilius Paulus (c. 229–160 B.C.), Rom. general, when asked why he had divorced his wife, held out his shoe and remarked, ' None of you know where it pinches but he that wears it.' [Chaucer, *The Marchand's Tale* (14th cent.)]

Shoe on the right foot, To put the : to attribute the blame to the proper person.

Shoes, To get too big for one's : to become conceited.

Shoes, To die in one's : to die a violent death, esp. to be hanged. [Urquhart, *Rabelais*, IV, 45 (1653)]

Shoes, Another pair of : another matter altogether.

Shoes, To step into another's : to succeed another person in office.

Shoes, To wait for dead men's : to await the death of a person in order to succeed him in office or possessions.

Shoot one's bolt, To : *see* Shot one's bolt.

Shoot folly as it flies, To : *see* Folly.

Shoot the moon, To : to evacuate one's house surreptitiously without paying one's rent.

Shoot wide of the mark, To : to be altogether in error. An archery metaphor.

Shop, To talk : to talk about one's business in company after business hours.

Shop, The wrong : the wrong person or destination.

Shopkeepers, A nation of : the English. Remark attributed to Napoleon, but proper to Barère de Vieuzac in a speech in the Convention on the 16th of June, 1794. In 1805 the Emp. Francis II in conversation with Napoleon called the English a nation of merchants. Samuel Adams is said to have used the same phrase in allusion to England in a speech alleged to have been delivered by him at Philadelphia on the 1st of August, 1776. It was used in a general sense by J. Tucker, Dean of Gloucester, in 1766, and by Adam Smith [*Wealth of Nations*, Vol. II, Bk. IV, ch. 7, pt. 3 (1775)] and also by Louis XIV in allusion to the United Provinces.

Shoplifting : stealing from a shop under the guise of a customer. [*William III*, Act II, ch. 12 (1698)]

Shore Thursday : *see* Sheer Thursday.

Short cut, A : a quick route, out of the ordinary way. [Lyly, *Euphues : Anatomy of Wit* (1579)]

Short work of .. To make : to deal with or complete rapidly. [Peter Pindar, *Frogmore Fête* (1795)]

Shot, A bad (good) : a bad (good) guess. A shooting metaphor.

Shot one's bolt, To have : to have made one's last effort. An archery metaphor.

Shot, Like a : promptly.

Shot in one's locker, Not to have a : to be penniless. A nautical metaphor.

Shot, To pay the : to pay the reckoning. [Heywood, *Proverbes* (1546)]

Shotten herring, A : a person without spirit, like a herring that has shot out its spawn.

Shoulder, Over the : to be understood in the opposite sense. [Nashe, *Saffron Walden* (1596)]

Shoulder, To show the cold : to receive with coldness and discouragement.

Shoulder, Straight from the : direct or downright. A boxing metaphor.

Shoulder to the wheel, To set one's : to set to work energetically. A metaphor drawn from the calling of a carter.

Shoulders, Narrow in the : impatient of ridicule.

Shoulders, An old head on young : abnormally wise or experienced for one's age.

Shoulders, To take upon one's own : to accept responsibility for .. In allusion to the carrying of the key on the shoulder of stewards. [*Isaiah*, ix, 6]

Shoulders with .. To rub : to associate with ..

Shoulder-knot, A gentleman of the : a footman. In allusion to the shoulder-knots worn by them.

Show one's hand, To : *see* Hand.

Show, To run the : to manage the business.

Shrapnel : an artillery shell which on bursting scatters bullets. From Henry Shrapnel (1761–1842), Brit. general.

Shrieking Sisterhood, The : a nickname given to the advocates of Women's Rights.

Shrift, To give short : to allow little leisure or breathing time. Orig. to allow a criminal a short period for confession before execution.

Shrovetide : the day before Ash Wednesday, on which it was customary for people to confess their sins and be shriven.

Shunamite woman, Like the : extremely hospitable. From the Shunamite woman mentioned in II *Kings*, iv.

Shuttlecock, A : a person or object bandied to and fro by two external powers over which he has no influence. From the piece of cork used in the game of battledore and shuttlecock.

Shy, To fight : *see* Fight.

Shylock, A : a heartless usurer. After the principal character in Shakespeare, *Merchant of Venice* (1596).

Sibyl, A : a fortune-teller. From the Sibyllae or prophetic women who flourished in the ancient world. These were the Sibyls of Persia, of Libya, of Delphi, of Cumae in Italy, of Erythræa, of Samos, of Cumae in Aeolia, of Marpessa, of Ancyrae and of Tiburtis.

Sibylline Books, The price of the : the following is the legend of the sale of the Sibylline Books. The Sibyl of Cumae offered nine books for sale to Tarquinius Superbus. He refused to buy them and she thereupon destroyed three of them and offered him the remaining six at the original price. He again refused and she destroyed a second three, offering the three survivors at the original price. These Tarquinius purchased. They were preserved as sacred until their accidental destruction with the Temple of Jupiter in 83 B.C.

Sic transit gloria mundi (*Lat.*, thus passeth away the glory of the world) : [Peter Pindar, *Instructions to a Celebrated Laureat* (1786)]

Sic vos non vobis (*Lat.*, thus you (labour) but not for yourselves).

Sicilian dishes : luxurious food. In ancient Rome the most sought-after cooks came from Sicily.

Sicilian Muses, The : the pastoral poets, because Theocritus, who was Virgil's model for his *Eclogues*, was a Sicilian poet.

Sicilian Vespers, The : a rising in Sicily in March, 1282, which arose from a French soldier, who had insulted a Sicilian bride on her way to Church, being promptly stabbed by a Sicilian, and which resulted in the extermination of the Frenchmen in the island. The massacre commenced at Vespers on Easter Monday.

Sick as a horse, As : suffering from nausea without being able to vomit, like a horse. [Burton, *Anatomy of Melancholy*, III, 336 (1621)]

Sick Man of Europe (the East), The : the Turkish Empire, which for long apparently on the verge of collapse, yet managed to continue. The epithet was first applied by the Czar Nicholas in 1853. A parallel is the designation of the same empire as ' Ce corps malade ' by Charles Louis de Montesquieu in his *Lettres Persanes* (1721), and by Sir Thomas Roe, ambassador of James II to Constantinople, ' the body of a sick old man, who tried to appear healthy although his end was near.' In 1579 Don John, the Governor-General of the Netherlands, writing to Philip II, described the Prince of Orange as ' the sick man.'

Side : pretence ; swagger. In use as an adjective in 1508 in the sense of haughty, proud.

Side, To put on : to swagger ; to adopt a boastful attitude.

Sidetrack, To : to push aside. An Amer. railway metaphor.

Sidonian tincture, The : purple dye. After Sidon in Syria, whence it was obtained.

Sieve, To draw water with a : *see* Draw.

Sikes, A Bill : a burglar. After the name of a character in Dickens, *Oliver Twist* (1838).

Silence gives consent : a favourite phrase of Pope Boniface VIII who derived it from the Canon Law, *Decretals*, Bk. V, xii, 43. [Plato, *Cratylus*]

Silence, The Great : death.

Silent as a mouse, As : [Dryden, *Amphitrion*, VII, 49 (1690)]

Silent as Pythagoras, As : *see* Pythagoras.

Silenus, A : an old drunkard. After one of the subordinate deities attendant on Bacchus.

Silhouette, A : a profile portrait in black and cut out. After Etienne de Silhouette (1709–67), Fr. statesman and political writer, noteworthy for his extremely economical methods.

Silk Gown, A : a King's Counsel. After the material of his official robe.

Silk purse out of a sow's ear, To make a : to attempt the impossible. From the proverb, ' You cannot make a silk purse of a sow's ear.' [Peter Pindar, *Lord B. and His Motions* (c. 1800)]

Silk Street : the ancient trade highway from Europe to the East.

Silk, To take : of a barrister, to become a King's Counsel. *See* Silk Gown.

Silly Billy : William IV of England.

Silly season, The : the period after Parliament has risen, when news being scarce, the newspapers used to encourage correspondence on non-topical subjects.

Silurist, The : Henry Vaughan (1622–1695), Welsh physician and poet. On account of his Welsh birth, the Silures being the ancient name for the inhabitants of South Wales.

Silver age of a literature, The : the period that follows the Golden Age (*q.v.*), from which it is a degeneration.

Silver Fork School, The : a school of Eng. novelists—Theodore Hook, Mrs. Trollope, Lady Blessington and others —who laid much emphasis on etiquette.

Silver Grays : Conservative Whigs, many of whom were old and grey-haired, who seceded from the New York Convention of 1848.

Silver Latin : the literary period which followed immediately after the Golden or Augustan period of Lat. literature.

Silver pheasant, A : a beautiful young woman of gentle birth.

Silver spoon in one's mouth, To be born with a : to be born of wealthy parents. In allusion to the silver apostle spoon given to the children of the rich at baptism.

Silver State, The : Nevada.

Silver Streak, The : the English Channel.

Silver, To think one's farthing (halfpenny) good : to be unduly proud of one's property or achievements. [Heywood, *Proverbes* (1546)]

Silver trumpet, A : an eloquent orator.

Silver wedding, A : the twenty-fifth anniversary of a wedding, when in Germany the wife was presented with a silver wreath.

Silverstick : the title of an officer of the Royal Household.

Simnel Sunday : mid Lent, on which day, in some places, simnel cakes are sent as presents. *See* Mothering Sunday.

Simon Pure, The real : a genuine person ; one who is indeed the person he claims to be. After a character in Mrs. Susanna Cantlivre, *A Bold Stroke for a Wife* (1718).

Simony : the offence of dealing in ecclesiastical preferment. After Simon Magus, who endeavoured to purchase the power of conferring the Holy Spirit. [*Acts*, viii]

Simple life, The : plain, non-luxurious living. After the title of a book by Charles Wagner.

Simple Simon, A : a simple, unaffected person. After the hero of a nursery rhyme so entitled.

Sin cast the first stone, Let him who is without : who can in his heart admit that he's clean of all sin ? From the saying of Jesus, recorded in *John*, viii, 7.

Sin of the new world, The first : drunkenness, the first recorded sin after the Flood and the landing of Noah and his family.

Sins are sure to find one out, One's : a sin cannot be concealed for ever. [Homer, *Odyssey*, IX, 477]

Sins be as scarlet, Though your : in allusion to the scarlet fillet which was bound round the head of the scapegoat which was sent into the wilderness by the high priest of the Jews on the occasion of the High Festival. [*Isaiah*, i, 18]

Sins, The seven deadly : *see* Seven.

Sine qua non, A (*Lat., sine qua non potest esse*, without which it cannot be) : something indispensable. [J. Castle, *Court and Times of James I*, Vol. I (1615)]

Sinecure, A (*Lat., sine cura*, without care) : an office that carries with it no duties or responsibilities.

Sinews of war, The : money. Phrase first used by Cicero in his fifth *Philippic*, ch. II.

Sing another song (tune) (note), To : to tell a different story. [*Everyman*, ll. 410–3 (1520)]

Sing small, To : to cease from boasting.

Single blessedness : bachelorhood. [Shakespeare, *Midsummer Night's Dream* (1595)]

Single speech Hamilton : William Gerard Hamilton, Eng. politician (1729–96). From the brilliant but solitary speech he delivered in the House of Commons in the debate on the Address in 1755.

Sinister (*Lat.*, *sinister*, left) : threatening ; of ill omen. By the Rom. augurs the left side was considered ill-omened.

Sink or swim : fail or succeed. In allusion to the ordeal undergone by suspected witches. [*Ralph Roister Doister*, I, iii, l. 75 (1550)]

Sinkhole of the East, The : Port Said. On account of its reputation for vice.

Sinn Fein (*Erse*, ourselves alone) : the Irish political organization formed to secure the complete independence of Ireland.

Sinon, A : one who deceives in order to betray. After the name of the Grk. who induced the Trojans to admit the wooden horse into their city.

Sir Boyle Roche's bird : Sir Boyle Roche (1743–1807), Irish member of parliament, famous for his bulls, on one occasion defended a man by saying, ' Did he think he could be, like a bird, in two places at the same time ? ' The same bull was perpetrated at the end of the 17th cent. by Thos. Jevon (1652–88) in *The Devil of a Wife* (1686).

Sir Hubert : *see* Praise from Sir Hubert.

Sir Oracle : a dogmatic individual. From the dogmatism of the ancient oracles. [Shakespeare, *The Merchant of Venice*, I, i (1596)]

Siren, A : an instrument designed to utter warnings by means of a piercing sound ; an enticing woman. From the mythical monsters, half women, who, inhabiting an island in the Mediterranean, used to lure seafarers to their doom by their singing.

Siren song, A : a song that allures or betrays ; such as that sung by the mythical sirens who thereby lured mariners to disaster.

Sirocco to one's flowers, To let in the : to bring misery on oneself by one's own fault or carelessness. From a Rom. proverb. [Virgil, *Eclogue*, I, ll. 58–9]

Sister Ann : *see* Ann.

Sister Arts : related arts, such as painting and sculpture, poetry and music.

Sister Isle, The : Ireland, in her relationship to Great Britain.

Sister Kingdom, The : Ireland, in her relationship to Great Britain.

Sister Kingdoms, The : England and Scotland.

Sisters of the Bank : *see* Bankside.

Sisters Nine, The : *see* Nine.

Sisters, The Three : the Fates.

Sisters, The Weird : the Fates.

Sistine : of or relating to one of the popes named Sixtus.

Sisyphus : a Grk. mythological personage who was condemned unceasingly to roll a large stone to the top of a hill, on reaching which it immediately fell to the bottom.

Sisyphus' stone : *see* Sisyphus.

Sit under .. To : to receive the religious ministrations of ..

Sit up, To make a person : to astonish ; to have a powerful moral effect on a person.

Sit upon, To : to suppress ; to snub.

Sit on the rail (fence), To : to remain neutral ; not to commit oneself to either party in a discussion or dispute.

Six feet of English ground : a grave (on Eng. soil). [Sir T. Browne, *Hydrotaphia*, ch. 5 (1658)]

Six Months' War, The : the Franco-German war, July, 1870–Jan., 1871.

Six of one and half a dozen of the other : nothing to choose between one and the other.

Sixes and sevens, At : in a state of neglect. Possibly from the game of backgammon ; or from the Arabic numerals, of which one to five are regular, but six and seven extend above and below the line respectively. [*The Towneley Mysteries*, 143 (14th cent.) ; *The Impeachment of Wolsey*, 205 (1528)]

Six-shooter, A : a revolver with six chambers.

Six-stringed whip, The : the statute of the six Articles (1539).

Sizar, A (Camb. and T.C.D.) an undergraduate enjoying a bursary. Formerly a poor scholar at a university whose assize of food (bread, butter and milk) was given to him.

Skedaddle, To : to run away hastily. Orig. Amer. military slang, introduced at the time of the Amer. Civil War.

Skeffington's Daughter : *see* Scavenger's Daughter.

Skeleton in the closet (cupboard), A : a concealed anxiety or cause of shame. [*Italian Tales of Love, Gallantry and Divorce* (1824)]

Skeleton at the feast, The : a reminder of pain and sorrow in the midst of pleasure.

Skevington's irons : the Scavenger's Daughter (*q.v.*).

Skibbereen and Connemara : types of poverty and distress. In allusion to the proverbial poverty of these Irish districts.

Skibbereen Eagle, The : *The Skibbereen Eagle* newspaper on one occasion informed Lord Palmerston that it had ' its eye both upon him and on the Emperor of Russia.' From that time *The Skibbereen Eagle* became the type of self-important insignificance.

Skies, To drop from the : to appear suddenly on the scene, without warning.

Skies, To praise to the : to praise very highly, as if to the skies. [Smollett, *Peregrine Pickle*, ch. 51 (1751)]

Skilligalee, Not worth a : of practically no value. A skilligalee is a coin of the lowest value.

Skilly : thin gruel or porridge. Contraction of skilligalee (*q.v.*).

Skin, To be in another person's : to be in another person's situation.

Skin, To be in a whole : to be uninjured. [Bunyan, *Pilgrim's Progress*, Pt. II (1684)] For ' skin whole ' *see* Shakespeare, *Merry Wives of Windsor*, III, i, ll. 111–2 (1600).

Skin before catching the bear, To sell the : to anticipate with undue optimism.

Skin, To cast one's : to change one's habits of thought.

Skin, To cultivate one's : to be luxurious.

Skin of .. To get into the very : of an actor, to play the part of .. exactly. Phrase used by the Fr. actor, Eugene Bignon (b. 1812), in allusion to his representation of Danton in François Ponsard, *Charlotte Corday*.

Skin, To save one's : to avoid harm or loss. [Pseudo-Marlowe, *Lust's Dominion*, IV, ii (1637)]

Skin of one's teeth, By the : very narrowly (of an escape). *Job*, xix, 20: ' I am escaped with the skin of my teeth.'

Skinflint, A : a miser ; one who would skin a flint if he could.

Skirts, To sit upon one's : to meditate revenge against ; to persecute. [Howell, *Familiar Letters* (1650)]

Skull and crossbones, The : the symbol of piracy.

Sky, To : to hang a picture in an exhibition close under the ceiling, where viewing is difficult.

Sky pilot, A : a parson. Nautical slang.

Skylarking : rough amusement. Orig. nautical, when it comprised climbing as high as possible into the rigging.

Skyscraper, A : a very lofty building that appears to reach almost to the sky.

Slap in the face, A : a sudden, sharp rebuff.

Slapdash : hastily and without consideration. With a slap and a dash.

Slate, To : to criticize ruthlessly. Formerly a school term alluding to the names of offenders which were entered on a slate.

Slate, With a clean : with a fresh start, expunging all past unfavourable records.

Slate Club, A : a local thrift society drawing its membership from among the working classes. The original ones met in school-rooms and had their accounts entered on slates.

Slate, To wipe off the : to place out of consideration. [Chaucer, *Merciles Beaute*, III, ll. 8–9 (14th cent.)]

Slating, A : a severe review of a book, etc. ; a reproof. *See* Slate, To.

Slave, A : one who is entirely subjected to another. From the Slavs, who in former days supplied a large proportion of the slaves of Rome.

Slave power : power based on the institution of slavery.

Slave States, The : Virginia, the two Carolinas, Georgia, Florida, Alabama Mississippi, Louisiana, Texas, Arkansas, Tennessee, Missouri, Kentucky, Maryland and Delaware ; the last of the United States in which slavery was legal.

Slaveocracy : a dominant class resting on a system of slavery. [*New York Express*, Sept. 4, 1848]

Slavophil, A : a member of a party of Russian intellectuals about the middle of the 19th cent. who led the reaction against occidentalization in Russia.

Slavophobe, A : one who is possessed by an unreasoning hatred of Slavs or Russia.

Sledge-hammer argument, A : a decisive and deciding argument, which settles a case like a sledge-hammer.

Sleep like a top, To (*Fr., taupe*, a mole) : to sleep soundly.

Sleep upon .. To : to consider (a proposal) at leisure, *e.g.*, after a night's rest. [Arth. Murphy, *Three Weeks after Marriage*, II (1776)]

Sleep a wink, Not to : to be sleepless. [Maria Edgeworth, *Castle Rackrent* (1799)]

Sleeping dogs lie, Let : do not arouse a source of possible trouble unnecessarily. From an ancient Grk. proverb. [Jno. Heywood, *Proverbes* (1546)]

Sleeping partner, A : a partner in a business who takes no part in its management.

Sleeping sickness, The : a fatal disease prevalent in certain parts of Africa.

Sleeve of .. To creep up the : see Creep.

Sleeve, To hang on a person's : to surrender one's judgment to another, as a child which still hangs to his mother's sleeve. [Sir Thos. Wyatt, *Of the Courtier's Life* (1557)]

Sleeve, To have up one's : to have in reserve. [F. de Lisle, *Legendarie*, VII (1577)]

Sleeve, To laugh in one's : to get the better of a person and therefore to laugh at him in secret. [Heywood, *Proverbes* (1546)]

Sleeve, To wear one's heart on one's : to practice no concealment about one's own feelings. [Shakespeare, *Othello*, I, i (1604)]

Sleeveless errand, A : a fruitless errand. [Chaucer, *The Testament of Love* (14th cent.)]

Slick : clever, quick. [*Doctor Faustus* (1588)]

Slick-tongued : smooth-tongued ; plausible. [Marlowe and Chapman, *Hero and Leander* (1598)]

Sliding scale : a system of graduated import duties on corn which depended on the price fetched by wheat grown in England.

Slim (*S. Afr. Dutch*) : sly ; cunning.

Slip to .. To give the : to escape from, unperceived. [Wm. Haughton, *Englishmen for My Money*, IV, ii (1597)]

Slip of the tongue, A : Lapsus linguæ (*q.v.*). [Benja. Franklin, *Poor Richard's Almanac* for 1734, January]

Slippers, To walk in golden (silver) : to be in the height of prosperity. [Bunyan, *Pilgrim's Progress*, Pt. I (1678)]

Slippery as an eel, As : quite unreliable, not to be trusted. [Heywood, *Proverbes* (1546) ; Earl of Surrey, *The Frailtie of Beautie*, l. 7 (1557)]

Slipshod : careless. Properly, wearing loose, ill-fitting slippers or shoes. [Shakespeare, *King Lear*, I, v (1605-6)]

Slop clothing : cheap, ready-made clothing. Orig. such as was supplied to seamen. [Lodowick Barrey, *Ram-Alley* (1611)]

Slops : ready-made clothing. [Lodowick Barrey, *Ram-Alley*, IV, i, ll. 284-5 (1611)]

Slope, To : to decamp ; to slip away. From the more general sense of to proceed in an oblique direction.

Slough of Despond, The : a state of depression. From the name of a bog described in Bunyan, *Pilgrim's Progress* (1678)]

Slow coach, A : a person who dawdles or moves or acts slowly.

Slug-abed, A : one who rises late in the morning. [Shakespeare, *Romeo and Juliet*, IV, v, 2 (1591-3)]

Sluice of life up, To draw the : to die. [*Jacke Drum's Entertainment*, III, ll. 287-9 (1616)]

Slum, A : one of the low, poverty-stricken, insalubrious districts of a city.

Slumland : a poverty-stricken district of a town. See Slum.

Sly-boots, A : a person who pretends to be stupid but is by no means really so.

Small ale (beer) : see Beer, Small.

Small hours (of the morning), The : those between midnight and an early dawn.

Small talk : gossip ; conversation of little consequence. [Lord Chesterfield, *Letters* (1751)]

Small wares : textile manufactures of a subordinate character (tape, cottons, etc.). [Bacon, *Essayes : Of Cunning* (1625)]

Smart Set, The : fashionable society, tending towards vulgarity and ostentation. The original Smart Set was the most exclusive circle in Boston (U.S.A.) society.

Smart Society : the fashionable and slightly fast class of society. 'Smart' in this sense was in use as early as the beginning of the 18th cent., but it passed into desuetude, to be revived about 1885.

Smell of the apron, To : of an action or remark, to show traces of the influences to which the actor or speaker has been subject. Aristodemus, supposed to be a cook's son, advised Antigonus to be more moderate in his expenditure. 'Thy words,' replied Antigonus, 'Aristodemus, smell of the apron.' [Plutarch, *Antigonus*, I]

Smell of the lamp, To : to show traces of the process of preparation. Pytheas, Grk. orator (fl. 325-322 B.C.), used the phrase of the orations of Demosthenes, who prepared them in an underground cave by artificial light. [Plutarch, *Life of Demosthenes*]

Smell powder, To : to have actual experience of battle.

Smell a rat, To : to suspect something wrong. From the instinct of a dog or cat. [Ben Jonson, *Tale of a Tub*, IV, 3 (1633)]

Smith of Nottingham : a conceited person. From the couplet :
'The little smith of Nottingham
Who doth the work that no man can.'
[Ray, *Collection of Proverbs* (1670)]

Smithereens : tiny fragments.

Smithfield bargain, To make a : to trick the purchaser ; to make a marriage in which money is the chief interest. From Smithfield Market, London.

Smoke, To end in : to have no result of any value. From the fire that smokes but does not burn. [E. Grimstone, *Siege of Ostend*, 184 (1604) ; *Temple* (1683)]

Smoke the pipe of peace, To : *see* Pipe of peace.

Smoke, To sell : to give only words in return for money. [Martial, *Epigrams*, Bk. IV, v ; Sir Jno. Davies, *Yet Other Twelve Wonders of the World*, ll. 1–2 (1611)]

Smoker's heart : disease of the heart due to excessive tobacco smoking.

Smoky City, The : Pittsburgh, U.S.A.

Smollett of the stage, The : George Farquhar (1678–1707). After Tobias Smollett, Eng. novelist, who lived from 1721 to 1771.

Smooth as oil, As : [*Proverbs*, v, 3]

Smooth-tongued : plausible. [Marlowe, *Edward II*, IV, v (1594)]

Snacks, To go : to share profits. [Jas. Puckle, *The Club* (1711)]

Snake in the grass, A : a secret enemy. [Virgil, *Eclogue*, III, l. 93 ; Bradford, *Sermons, etc.* (1555)]

Snakes in one's boots, To have : to suffer from delirium tremens, one of the delusions connected with which disease is the belief in being pursued by snakes.

Snakes in Iceland (Ireland), As rare as : it is said that snakes are to be found in neither Iceland nor Ireland.

Snark, To hunt the : to hunt an imaginary animal. From *The Hunting of the Snark* by 'Lewis Carroll' (1876).

Snatch a club from Hercules, To : *see* Hercules.

Sneerwell, A Lady : a scandalmonger. From a character in Sheridan, *School for Scandal* (1777).

Sneezed at, Not to be : not valueless.

Snip, A : a tailor. [Randolph, *Muses' Looking-Glasse* (1643)]

Snob, A : one who vulgarly pretends to a higher social status than that which is proper to him ; said to have been derived from nob.

Snobocracy : snobs as a class.

Snore like a tinker, To : to snore loudly or sleep deeply. In allusion to the supposed fatigue of a travelling tinker at the end of his day's journey. [Geo. Coleman, jun., *Sylvester Daggerwood*, i (1795)]

Snow in a furnace, To roast : *see* Roast.

Snow King, The : Gustavus Adolphus of Sweden (1594–1632). The name given to him by the Viennese, because as he proceeded south his successes diminished or melted away.

Snow Queen, The : Christina of Sweden (1626–89).

Snuff, Up to : wideawake, to be deceived with great difficulty.

Soaped-pig fashion, In : of writing or speaking, vaguely, so that an opportunity is always left for an alternative explanation. In allusion to the practice at country fairs of soaping a pig's tail and then setting it free to be caught by the crowd.

Soapy Sam : Samuel Wilberforce (1805–73), Bishop of Oxford and of Winchester.

Socinians : the forerunners of the modern Unitarians, founded by Laelius Socinus (1525–62) and Faustus Socinus (1539–1604).

Socrates, The English : Dr. Samuel Johnson. So-called by Boswell. After Socrates, the famous Athenian philosopher, who lived from about 470 to 399 B.C.

Socrates, The Jewish : Moses Mendelssohn (1729–86).

Socrates, The Mad : Diogenes (c. 412–323 B.C.), Grk. cynic philosopher.

Socrates, The Roman : Sapiens Laelius (186-post 122 B.C.).

Socratic : of teaching based on a series of questions. After Socrates (c. 470–399 B.C.), Athenian philosopher.

Socratic irony : a method of dialectics by which, through pretended ignorance, the ignorance of one's opponent is disclosed. *See* Socratic.

Soft job, A : an easy occupation.

Soft sawder : flattery.

Soft soap : flattery.

Softly, To walk : to be low-spirited. Walking softly was in ancient Greece a display of mourning. [I *Kings*, xxi, 27]

Y

Softy, A : a foolish person.

Soi-disant (*Fr.*) : self-styled. [Lord Chesterfield, *Letters*, Vol. II, No. 71 (1752)]

Sold, To be : to be betrayed.

Soldier of fortune, A : one who lives by his wits ; in medieval times, who hired himself out to any party that wished to employ him. [*The Last Will and Testament of Charyng Crosse* (1646)]

Soldier over .. To come the old : to impose on.

Soldier's Battle, The : (1) Malplaquet (1709) ; (2) Inkerman (1854). On account of the extent to which the Brit. rank and file were thrown on their own responsibility on account of the splitting up of units and separation from officers by the fog.

Soldier's heart : a complaint of the chest induced by excessive military drill.

Solecism, A : a misapplication of words. From Soli, in Cilicia, where an Athenian colony settled and allowed its native language to degenerate. [Bacon, *Essays : Of Empire* (1625)]

Solemn League and Covenant, The : the agreement between the Eng. parliament and the Scots in March, 1643, whereby it was determined to extirpate popery, prelacy, etc., and incidentally to join forces in opposition to Charles I. The signatories were known as Covenanters.

Solid South, The : the Southern States of the Union which were solid in their support of the Democratic Party from the Civil War until 1896.

Solitary Monk, The : Martin Luther (1483–1546), the founder of Protestantism. So-called by Robert Montgomery in *Luther* (1842).

Solomon, A : a wise man. After Solomon, King of Israel.

Solomon of England, The : *see* English Solomon.

Solomon of France, The : (1) Louis IX (1215–70) ; (2) Charles V (1337–80).

Solomon, The Second : (1) Henry VII of England ; (2) James I of England.

Solomon, As wise as : in allusion to King Solomon. [*Chester Plays* (1327)]

Solon, A : a man of great wisdom. After Solon, the Athenian legislator and one of the seven sages of Greece.

Solon of French Prose, The : Balzac (1596–1655).

Solon of Parnassus, The : Jean Jacques Boileau (1649–1735). So-called by Voltaire.

Solon's happiness : death. From Solon's remark, ' Call no one happy until his death.'

Solvitur ambulando (*Lat.*, it is solved by walking) : the difficulty will settle itself.

Soma, To drink the : to become immortal. From the belief expressed in the Vedic hymns that the juice of the soma or moonplant confers immortality.

Son, The : Jesus Christ, Son of God.

Son of a sea cook, A : an address of contempt.

Son of Belial, A : a wicked man. [*Judges*, xix, 22]

Son of dripping, A : a male cook. [Peter Pindar, *The Lousiad*, canto ii (1786)]

Son of earth, A : a person of mean birth.

Son of Jupiter Ammon, The : Alexander the Great, the greatest monarch of ancient times. Traditionally descended from Jupiter and saluted as a god at the temple of Ammon.

Son of the Last Man, The : Charles II of England. So-called by the Puritans to indicate that his father, Charles I, was the last king of England.

Son of lather, A : a barber. [Peter Pindar, *Lyric Odes to the Royal Academicians* for 1785, Ode I]

Son of Mars, A : a soldier. [*Bartholomew Faire*, p. 2 (1641)]

Son of Mercury, A : a wit.

Son of the morning, A : a traveller. In allusion to the practice in the East of travellers rising early in order to avoid the fatigue of travelling in the heat of the day.

Son of the Nine, A : a poet. In allusion to the nine Muses. [Peter Pindar, *Instructions to a Celebrated Laureat* (1786)]

Son of parchment, A : a lawyer.

Son of Neptune, A : *see* Neptune.

Son of Perdition, The : Judas Iscariot. [*John*, xvii, 12]

Son of the rock, A : an echo.

Son of Saint Crispin, A : *see* Saint Crispin.

Sons of morning, The : the angels. [Milton, *On the Morning of Christ's Nativity : the Hymn* (1629)]

Sons of Phidias : sculptors. In allusion to Phidias (c. 500–434 B.C.), the greatest sculptor of ancient Greece.

Song, The Father of Modern French : Charles François Panard (1689–1765).

Sop to Cerberus, A : a gift to quieten one who disturbs one's peace. From the practice among the ancients of placing a cake in the hands of the dead as a gift to Cerberus, the three-headed dog of Pluto which guarded the entrance to the lower regions.

Sop in the pan, A : a bribe.

Sorbonne, The : the University of Paris. After Robert de Sorbon, Canon of Cambrai, who founded a learned institution in Paris in 1252.

Sort of war, A : the later stages of the Boer War of 1899 *et seq.*, as described by the Earl of Halsbury at Sheffield (Oct. 3, 1901). 'It may be, and may be perfectly true, that there is going on now a sort of warfare. But is it war ? '

Sortes Biblicae : fortune-telling by opening the Bible at random.

Sortes Virgilianae (*Lat.*, Virgilian lots) : fortune-telling by opening Virgil's *Æneid* at random. [Sir P. Sidney, *Defence of Poesie*, Pt. I, § 4 (1595)]

Sorts, Out of : in indifferent health. From the Fr., *être dérangé*, to be disarranged. If cards are disarranged they are out of sorts. [Peter Pindar, *Pindariana : Apology for Inconstancy* (1794)]

Sosia, A : a double. After a character in Plautus's comedy, *Amphitryon*.

Sotadics ; Sotadic Verse : verses or lines that read the same backwards and forwards. After Sotades of Maroneia (d. c. 285 B.C.), the inventor.

Sotto voce (*Ital.*, under the voice) : in a low voice.

Sough, To keep a calm (*Scot.*) : to keep quiet. Sough, a breath.

Soul of .. To be the : to be the inspiration of ..

Soul one's own, Not to be able to call one's : to be entirely under the control of another person.

Soul, The palace of the : the head. [Waller, *On Tea* (c. 1645)]

Soul Mass Day : All Souls' Day.

Soul-cakes : cakes given to the poor on All Souls' Day in Staffordshire and Cheshire.

Sound a person, To : to examine indirectly. From 'to sound,' in the sense of to measure the depth of water.

Sound as a bell, As : quite sound. When a bell is cracked it is useless. [Chapman, *All Fools*, III, i (1605)]

Sound as a roach, As : in perfect health. After St. Roche, the guardian against pestilence. [Moufet and Bennet, *Health's Improvement* (1655)]

Sound as a rock, As : sound as a roach (*q.v.*).

Sound the trumpet before victory, To : to act foolishly. From an ancient Grk. proverb.

Soup, To be in the : to be in a difficulty ; to be defeated. The phrase came into general use in the United States during the election of 1888. It was, however, in use in Germany much earlier.

Souper, A (*Anglo-Irish*) : a missionary who makes converts with the assistance of free soup ; one converted to Protestantism in this manner.

Sour grapes : *see* Grapes.

South Sea Bubble, The : the financial scheme which, after a period of wild speculation, collapsed in 1720 and involved a large number of people in ruin.

Sow discord, To : to cause dissension. [*Proverbs*, vi, 19]

Sow dragon's teeth, To : to lay up trouble. *See* Dragon's teeth.

Sow by the ear, To have the right : to hit upon the right conclusion. A sow is a large tub with two handles, used for pickling. The phrase is attributed to Henry VIII of England in allusion to Cardinal Wolsey, who made a pleasing suggestion regarding the pro-projected royal divorce. For the opposite, ' to take the wrong sow by the ear,' *see* Heywood, *Proverbes* (1546). The latter metaphor was also used by Cervantes in *Don Quixote*, Pt. I, Bk. III, ch. iv.

Sow playing on a trump, To look like a : to look dissatisfied and angry. [Scott, *Rob Roy*, ch. 25 (1818)]

Sow what another reaps, To : to work for another's profit. [*John*, iv, 36]

Sow on the sand, To : to act foolishly and to no purpose. [Diogenes, *Vindol*, III, 71 ; Rob. Southwell, *St. Peter's Complaint : Love's Servile Lot*, ll. 73–4 (1595)]

Sow to the tail of the grice, To lay the head of the : to make the cheapness of one thing cover the cost of another ; to take the good with the bad. [Scott, *Rob Roy*, ch. 24 (1818)]

Sow tares amongst the wheat by night, To : to cause evil by deceit. [*Matthew*, xiii, 25]

Sow in tears and reap in joy, To : sorrow to be succeeded by gladness. [*Psalms*, cxxvi, 5–6]

Sow wild oats, To : to give free rein to the calls of youth. The word ' oats ' has two allusions : (1) to the spirit given by a diet of oats to horses ;

(2) to the parable of the sower. [*Bacon, Workes*, 240 (1570)]

Sow the wind, To : to do evil or cause trouble and to be repaid a thousand-fold. [*Hosea*, viii, 7]

Spade a spade, To call a : to speak bluntly and frankly without verbal embroidery. Philip II of Macedon (382–336 B.C.) described his subjects as people who call a spade a spade. [Gosson, *Ephemerides of Phials* (1579)]

Spadish language : plain, blunt language. From ' to call a spade a spade.' *See* previous entry.

Spain, Castles in : *see* Castles.

Spanish Ennius, The : Juan de Mena (1411–56). After Quintus Ennius, Lat. poet (239–170 B.C.).

Spanish Fury, The : the sack of Antwerp by the Span. troops in 1576.

Spanish Main, The : generally the Caribbean Sea, but more properly the lands surrounding that sea which were, until early in the 19th cent., in Spanish possession.

Spanish Molière, The : Leandro Fernandez de Moratin (1760–1828). After Molière (1622–73). Fr. dramatist.

Spanish money : fair words only. From the reputation of the Span. government of neglecting to pay its debts.

Spanish Phoenix, The : Lope de Vega-Carpio (1562–1635), poet and dramatist. So-called by G. H. Lewes.

Spanish pike, The : the needle. Needles are said to have been introduced into England from Spain.

Spanish Shakespeare, The : *see* Shakespeare.

Spanish, To walk : to compel a person to walk, by holding him by the collar and the seat of his trousers.

Spartacist, A : an extreme communist. After Spartacus, leader of the insurgent slaves in their war against Rome (73–71 B.C.).

Spartan, A : (1) a person of tried hardihood ; (2) undaunted. After Sparta, in Greece, whose inhabitants were famous in history for their hardihood and dauntlessness.

Spartan dog, A : a bloodhound.

Spasmodic School, The : a group of 19th cent. Eng. writers—Gerald Massey, Sydney Dobell, Philip James Bailey, Alexander Smith, George Gilfillan and others, grouped together on account of their artificial literary style.

Spatchcock, To : to interpolate a remark or passage. Properly, to split a fowl

open and to grill it, as a quick method of cooking.

Speak of things more ancient than chaos, To : to act to no purpose. From an ancient Grk. proverb.

Speak volumes, To : *see* Volumes.

Speak the word, To : to give a command. [J. T., *Grim, the Colier of Croydon*, IV, i (1662)]

Speaker, The : the chairman of a parliament.

Speaker's eye, To catch the : to be called on by the Speaker to address the House of Commons.

Speaking terms, Not to be on : to know one another but not to be friendly enough to speak to one another.

Spear to kill a fly, To take a : *see* Take.

Spear, To pass under the : to sell by auction.

Spear, To run against the point of a : *see* Run.

Spear, To sell under (at) the : to sell by auction.

Spear half : the male side of a family. The opposite of spindle half (*q.v.*).

Spell-binder, A : an orator who binds his hearers as if by a spell. Orig. an American political term introduced about 1888.

Spenlow and Jorkins : a partnership in which one party always uses the other as an excuse for any unjust or unpleasant action. After a firm in Dickens, *David Copperfield* (1849).

Spenser of English Prose, The : Jeremy Taylor (1613–67). After Edmund Spenser (c. 1552–99), the great romantic poet of Elizabethan England.

Spenser to Fleeknoe, From : from the sublime to the ridiculous. [Dryden, *Comment on Spenser*]

Sphere of Influence, A : a region inhabited by a population in a backward state of civilization or otherwise incapable of repelling foreign aggression, which is agreed to be within the province of one of the powers, without that power being required to take any responsibility for its administration.

Sphinx, A : an inscrutable person. After an Egyptian monument, half human, half lion.

Spick and span : absolutely new. Several derivations have been suggested for this phrase. (1) From Lat., *spica*, an ear of corn, and the spawn of a fresh fish ; (2) from Ital., *spiccata de la spanna*, snatched from the hand, *i.e.*, freshly made ; (3) a spinning metaphor, newly spun from the spike or brooch ; (4) from spike, a sixteenth part of a yard, and span, a quarter of a yard, implying therefore, of a suit of clothes, fresh from the tailor ; (5) from the spannans (stretchers) and the spikes (hooks) on which cloth was hung. [Chaucer, *Troilus*, III, 1665–6 (1386) ; Middleton, *The Familie of Love*, IV, 3 (1608)]

Spies but in battalions, Not single : of several incidents, *e.g.*, misfortunes, following in quick succession. [Shakespeare, *Hamlet*, IV, v (1602–3)]

Spigot and spill at the bung, To spare at the : to be miserly in small matters and extravagant in great.

Spilt milk, To cry over : *see* Cry.

Spindle City, The : Lowell, Mass. In allusion to its cotton spinning industry.

Spindle half, The : the female side of the family. After the spindle employed in spinning, the former general occupation of women in England.

Spindle-side, On the : on the female side. *See* Spindle half.

Spinning Jenny, A : a machine for spinning. Jenny is a diminutive of engine.

Spirit away, To : to kidnap ; to carry away surreptitiously. Seventeenth century kidnappers, who sold their victims to the West Indian planters, used to be known as 'spirits.'

Spitfire, A : a person whose anger is easily aroused.

Spit vinegar, To : to utter spiteful remarks. [Lyly, *Sappho and Phao*, IV, iv (1591)]

Spite and spurn, To : to be enraged. [Ingeland, *Disobedient Child*, l. 573 (1560)]

Splay-mouth, A : a Presbyterian. Properly a crooked mouth.

Splendid Isolation : Lord Salisbury's Foreign Policy, that of independence of all foreign alliances. So-described by George Joachim, Viscount Goschen (1831–1907).

Splendide mendax (*Lat.*) : magnificently deceiving. [Horace, *Odes*, III, xi, 55]

Split upon .. To : to betray a confidence.

Split the difference, To : to compromise ; to meet halfway. [Benj. Franklin, *Poor Richard's Almanac* for 1750]

Split straws (hairs), To : to argue or dispute over infinitesimal differences. [Congreve, *Old Bachelor*, II, ii (1693)]

Spoil for a fight, To : to be eager for a contest.

Spoilsport, A : one who interferes gratuitously to upset the plans of others. [Haughton, *Woman Will Have Her Will* (1597)]

Spoils System, The : the Amer. system of making office in the Civil Service the reward for political services, involving as a consequence widespread dismissal of officials whenever a change of party in office occurred. The system was introduced by President Andrew Jackson (1767–1845) on the ground that, as epigrammatically expressed by William Learned Marcy (1786–1857) in the U.S. Senate in Jan., 1832, 'to the victors belong the spoils of the enemy.'

Spoke in the wheel of .. To put a : to interfere in another person's affairs. [Lyly, *Euphues* (1581) ; Beaumont and Fletcher, *The Mad Lover* (1647)] Orig. this phrase had the opposite meaning, *viz.*, to increase a person's force by adding to the number of the spokes in his wheel.

Spolia opima (*Lat.*) : the richest spoils of victory. [*Livy*, I, 10 ; Virgil, *Æneid*, vi, 856]

Sponge on .. To : to live at the expense of others as a parasite, *i.e.*, to suck in like a sponge without repayment of any kind. [Miége, *French Dictionary* (1677)]

Sponge, To throw up the : to abandon the contest. A prizefighting term.

Sponging house, A : a place of internment for debtors. From 'to sponge' in the sense, 'to squeeze.'

Spoon in one's mouth, To be born with a silver : *see* Silver spoon.

Spoon or spoil a horn, To make a : to make a determined effort which may result in success or failure. In allusion to the practice in Scotland, until late in the 19th cent., of making spoons out of the horns of cattle.

Spoon in the wall, To stick one's : to die. In allusion to the early practice of hanging one's spoon and other articles of daily use in an available place on the wall of one's home.

Spoon, To gain the wooden : *see* Wooden spoon.

Spoonerism, A : an accidental exchange of two sounds in speech. After the Rev. William Archibald Spooner (b. 1844), Warden of New College, Oxford.

Spoon-feed, To : to feed with a spoon, *i.e.*, to nurse as a child.

Sport, To be : to be good fun. [R. B., *Appius and Virginia*, 605 (1563)]

Sport of kings, The : (1) horseracing ; (2) hunting. According to Somervile. [*The Chace*, I, 13 (1735)]

Spotted dog (duff) : plain plum pudding. Spotted dough (dog).

Sprat to catch a whale (herring) (mackerel), To throw a : to risk a small loss in the hope of securing a great gain.

Spread a plaster, To take a hammer to : *see* Take.

Spread-eagle, To : *see* Spreadeagleism.

Spreadeagle oratory : exaggerated, bombastic, extravagant oratory.

Spreadeagleism : extravagant boasting and praise of the United States, their institutions, etc. After the eagle as the Amer. national symbol.

Spring from the years, To take the : *see* Take.

Sprinkle incense on a dunghill, To : to act foolishly and to no purpose. From an ancient Grk. proverb.

Spruce : neatly attired. From Prussia. To be spruce meant originally to dress in Prussian fashion.

Spur of the moment, On the : spontaneously ; without hesitation.

Spurs, To dish up the : to hint to guests that it is time to depart. The custom arose in the Eng.-Scot. borderlands, when provisions ran out, for a pair of spurs to be sent to table as a hint that a raid for provisions was desirable.

Spurs, To win one's : to earn admission into a certain rank or class. Properly, to gain by one's deeds the spurs of knighthood. [*Paston Letters*, No. 732 (1473)]

Spy Wednesday : the Wednesday before Good Friday on which Judas is reputed to have decided to act as a spy.

Squad, The awkward : a squadron of raw recruits, not yet trained.

Squalls, To look out for : to prepare for trouble. A nautical metaphor.

Square a person, To : to satisfy ; to make satisfactory arrangements with. Esp. by means of a bribe.

Square an account, To : to balance an account.

Square, To act on the : to act straightforwardly. [Chapman, *Iliad*, XIII, 138 (1611)]

Square, Out of : out of order. [*Damon and Pithias*, 1045–6 (1567)]

Square with .. To : to make agree with ..

Square the circle, To : to effect the apparently impossible. It is mathematically impossible to construct a square occupying exactly the same amount of space as a circle.

Square dealing : straightforward, honourable dealing. [Overbury, *Characters : A Puritan* (1616)]

Square peg in a round hole, A : *see* Round peg in a square hole.

Square-toes, Old : a precisian. [Peter Pindar, *Pathetic Odes : The Duke of Richmond's Dog* (1794)]

Squarson, A : the combination in one person of squire and parson. Term invented by Henry Mereweather before a committee of the House of Commons in 1861 and popularized by Samuel Wilberforce, Bp. of Oxford and of Winchester.

Squatter sovereignty : the doctrine of popular sovereignty in the United States as formulated by Lewis Cass in 1847. So-called by John Caldwell Calhoun (1782–1850).

Squattocracy, The : the class of squatters or large landowners in Australia.

Squeers, A : a cruel schoolmaster. After a character in Dickens, *Nicholas Nickleby* (1838).

Squeeze a person, To : to bring pressure to bear on a person, esp. with a view to extorting money. [Swift, *The Beast's Confession* (1732)]

Squib, A : a political pleasantry.

Squirarchy, The : the class of squires or resident landowners.

Squire of the Body, A : an Apple squire (*q.v.*).

Squire of dames, A : a man who pays much attention to women. A squire of dames was introduced by Spenser in the *Faerie Queen*, Bk. III, c. vii (1590–6).

Squireen, A : a small landowner in Ireland who farms his own land.

Stab in the back, A : a cowardly betrayal.

Stable door after the steed is stolen, To lock the : to take precautions after the harm has been effected. [*Les Proverbes del Vilain* (1300) ; Heywood, *Proverbes* (1546)]

Staff in a place, To put one's : to take up one's residence in a place. In allusion to the tent-staff of the nomads.

Staff in one's own hand, To keep the : to retain possession. In allusion to the staff or sceptre as the symbol of power and authority.

Staff of life, The : bread. ' Staff ' being used in the sense of ' support.'

Staff, To part with one's : to give up office or possession. In allusion to the staff of office.

Stafford Court, To have a treat in : to be well beaten. A play on ' staff,' a cudgel.

Stafford law : the law of the cudgel. A play on the word ' staff.'

Stage fright : nervousness in public. Properly, the shyness or nervousness of an actor on his first appearance on the stage.

Stager, An old : a veteran ; one who has had prolonged experience. Med. Lat., *Stagiarius*, an aged monk past activity.

Stagyrite, A ; Stagirite, A : a disciple of Aristotle (384–322 B.C.). After his birthplace, Stageira, in Macedonia.

Stalemate, A : a deadlock in which neither party has the advantage. A chess-playing term.

Stalking-horse, A : anything used for the purpose of concealing one's purpose. Properly a real or imitation horse used as a cover when shooting wild-fowl.

Stamp Act, The : an act of the British parliament (1765) imposing stamp duties on the Amer. colonies, which led direct to the secession of those colonies and the establishment of the United States of America.

Stamp Duty, A : an inland revenue tax paid by means of a stamp.

Stand on ceremony, To : to be punctilious in regard to matters of etiquette.

Stand and deliver, To : to surrender. Properly, to stand still and deliver over one's property to a highway-man.

Stand or fall, To : to succeed or fail. [Burton, *Anatomy of Melancholy*, Pt. I, Sect. ii, Mem. 1 (1621)]

Stand on one's own feet, To : *see* Feet.

Stand in good stead, To : to be of great assistance or service to .. [Rich. Edwards, *Damon and Pithias*, 1407 (1567)]

Stand to one's guns, To : to adhere to one's expressed opinion. A military metaphor.

Stand in the light of .. To : to impede the advantage of .. [Earle, *Micro-cosmography : A Suspitious Man* (1628)]

Stand in one's own light, To : to neutralize one's own opportunities. [Seneca, *Epistulae*, XCIV, 28 ; Heywood, *Proverbes* (1546)]

Stand to reason, To : to be obvious.

Stang, To ride the : to be ruled by one's wife or other female relative. After the stang or pole on which a man who ill-treated his wife used to be placed.

Star, A : (1) a prominent actor or vocalist ; (2) one who ' shines ' in society or literature or art, etc. [Ascham, *The Schoolmaster*, Bk. II (1570)]

Star to be in the ascendant, One's : to be fortunate in one's affairs. An astrological metaphor.

Star Chamber, A : a secret, irresponsible tribunal. After the Star Chamber (so-called from the decoration of the ceiling of the room in which the Court met), a court established in 1487 which ultimately became an instrument of oppression and of the suppression of liberty. It was abolished in 1641.

Star, One's evil (lucky) : one's evil (fortunate) influence. Term derived from astrology. [Lyly, *Endimion*, IV, iii (1591)]

Star of the North, The : Gustavus Adolphus of Sweden (1594–1632). So-called by the Protestants of Germany.

Stars and Bars, The : the flag of the Confederate States of America.

Stars from the sky, To snatch the : to attempt the impossible.

Stars and Stripes, The : the flag of the U.S., which consists of 13 stripes, one for each of the original states of the Union, and a number of stars, one for each of the present states.

Star-crossed : unfortunate. An astrological metaphor.

Starred, Ill : unlucky ; properly, born under an unfavourable star. An astrological metaphor.

Star-spangled Banner, The : the national flag of the United States which contains a star for every one of the states of the Union. After the title of an Amer. national song by Francis Scott Key (1780–1843).

Starving it, To take a town by : *see* Take.

State, The three ages of a : ' In the youth of a state arms do flourish ; in the middle age of the state, learning ; and then both of them together for a time ; in the declining age of a state, mechanical arts and merchandize.'

[Bacon, *Essayes: Of Vicissitudes of Things* (1625)]

Status quo, The ; In statu quo (*Lat.*, state in which) : the existing state of affairs. [Burton, *Anatomy of Melancholy*, To the Reader (1621)]

Steady Habits, The Land of : the State of Connecticut. In allusion to the staid deportment and high morality of its people.

Steady as the Polar Star, As : consistent. [Mercurius Rusticus, *Bibliophobia*, p. 94 (1832)]

Steal a march on .. To : to overtake or take advantage of secretly. A military metaphor.

Steal one's thunder, To : to appropriate another person's principal arguments. John Dennis (1657–1734) invented artificial thunder for a play of his which proved unsuccessful. Shortly afterwards, at a representation of *Macbeth* at Drury Lane Theatre, he found that his invention was being utilized and exclaimed, ' They will not let my play run, yet they steal my thunder.'

Steals my purse steals trash, Who : the greatest treasure is not material and is therefore secure from the thief. [Shakespeare, *Othello*, III, iii (1604)]

Stealthy School of Criticism, The : pseudonymous criticism. Phrase invented by Dante Gabriel Rossetti in a letter to the *Athenaeum*, Dec. 16, 1871, in allusion to Robert Buchanan, the author, under a nom-de-plume, of ' The Fleshly School of Poetry,' in the *Contemporary Review* of October, 1871.

Steel the heart, To : to harden the heart.

Steelboys, The : an Irish agrarian secret society, active in Down and Antrim about 1770.

Steelyard, The : the headquarters of a guild of Germ. merchants which was active in London from the 13th to the 16th cents.

Steer clear of .. To : to avoid. [Fielding, *Voyage to Lisbon*, July 26th, 1755]

Stellenbosch, To : to transfer to a less important military post. After Stellenbosch, Cape Colony, to which town officers who failed in the Kaffir wars were transferred, as a supercession without a formal disgrace.

Stentorian : (of voices) very loud. After Stentor, a Grk. herald at Troy, mentioned by Homer.

Steps of .. To tread in the : to follow the example of .. [Bunyan, *Pilgrim's Progress*, Pt. II (1684)]

Stephen's bread, St. : stones. In allusion to the stoning of St. Stephen.

Stephen's bread, To be fed with : to be stoned. *See* Stephen's bread, St.

Stern chase, A : *see* Chase.

Stew in one's own juice, To : to be refused assistance to escape from a difficult position and to be left to get out of it as best one can. [Chaucer, *Wife of Bath's Tale*, Prologue (14th cent.)]

Stick to one's guns, To : to maintain one's position ; to stand fast before an attack.

Stick, To get hold of the wrong end of the : (1) to have the disadvantage in a controversy or contest ; (2) to get hold of the wrong story or facts. [Heywood, *Proverbes* (1546)]

Stick to one's last, To : not to interfere in matters with which one is unfamiliar. Apelles (fl. 332 B.C.), the Grk. painter, was accustomed to exhibit his pictures to the public while he in concealment listened to their criticisms. A bootmaker criticised the shoes in a picture, whereupon Apelles altered them to meet the criticism. The following day the bootmaker, returning, began to criticize the anatomy of one of the figures, whereupon the painter, from his place of concealment, ejaculated, ' Cobbler, stick to your last.' A similar story is told of Phidias (c. 490–432 B.C.), the Grk. sculptor.

Stick-in-the-mud, A : a slow person ; one who is left behind in the race of life.

Stick at nothing, To : to reject no measure calculated to assist towards one's object. [Thos. Preston, *King Cambyses*, 361–2 (1561) ; *Joe Miller's Jests*, No. 44 (1739)]

Sticks, To beat to : to out-do ; surpass.

Sticks, In quick : quickly.

Stickit minister, A (*Scot.*) : a disqualified parson, esp. one who has failed in his first attempt to preach and never made another.

Stiff as a poker, As : rigid.

Stiggins, A : an intemperate, hypocritical parson. From a character in Dickens, *Pickwick Papers* (1836).

Still as a rock, As : motionless. [Vanbrugh, *The Provoked Wife*, IV, i (1697)]

Still as a stone, As : without motion. [*Exodus*, xv, 16 ; Chaucer, *Legende of Good Women*, 308–10 (14th cent.)]

Still-room maid, A : a female domestic servant. Orig. from the room in the house in which the still for the distillation of perfumes and cordials was kept.

Sting in the tail, The : the difficulty or unpleasantness in the conclusion. An allusion to the scorpion which carries its sting in its tail. [Defoe, *Tour in the Eastern Counties*, Letter I (1724)]

Stink in the nostrils, To : to be abhorrent.

Stinking fish, To cry : to depreciate one's own interests.

Stir one's stumps, To : to move ; to walk. 'Stumps' in the sense of 'legs.'

Stirrup-cup, A : a parting drink given when the guest is already in the saddle.

Stitch in time, A : a timely remedy. From the proverb, ' A stitch in time saves nine.'

Stiver, A : an insignificant amount of money. Properly, a Dutch coin worth about a halfpenny.

Stock in, To take no : to have nothing to do with.

Stock, lock and barrel : the whole, in its entirety. After the different parts of a rifle.

Stocks, To be on the : to be in preparation. A ship-building metaphor.

Stocks and stones : an idol (made out of wood or stone). [*Deuteronomy*, xxviii, 36]

Stocking, A long : a store of money. Properly a stocking used as a receptacle for money savings.

Stoic, A : one who suppresses all expressions of pain and pleasure and cultivates the virtue of patient endurance. After the *stoa* or porch in which Zeno (fl. 300 B.C.), the founder of a Grk. school of philosophy whose doctrines were characterized by extreme austerity, taught.

Stole, Groom of the : a household official in the Eng. court.

Stolypin's necktie : the hangman's rope. After Piotr Arkadievitch Stolypin (1863–1911), oppressive Russ. statesman. The phrase was coined in 1907 by Rodicheff, a member of the Duma.

Stone Age, The : a remote period. Properly, that early period in human development in which stone was almost exclusively used for the manufacture of weapons and other implements.

Stone, Blood from a : *see* Blood.

Stone broke : absolutely without means.

Stone, To cast the first : to make a charge against .. ; with reference to *John*, viii, 7.

Stone, To kill two birds with one : to accomplish two purposes by one effort. [Hobbes, *Letter Upon Liberty and Necessity*, 117 (1654)]

Stone rolling, To set a : to commence an undertaking whose results cannot be foreseen. [Shakespeare, *Henry VIII*, V, iii (1612–3)]

Stone unturned, To leave no : to avoid no possible effort. ' Turn every stone ' was the advice given by the Delphic Oracle to Polycrates (d. 515 B.C.), Tyrant of Samos. ' To leave no stone unturned,' *see* Euripides, *Heraclidae*.

Stones instead of bread : harshness where sympathy is expected. [*Matthew*, vii 9]

Stones at .. To cast : to make charges against .. [Fulke, *Heskins' Parliament* (1579)]

Stones in one's mouth, To have : to stammer. In allusion to Demosthenes (382–22 B.C.), Athenian orator and statesman, who is said to have cured himself of stuttering by reciting with pebbles in his mouth.

Stone's throw, Within a : within a moderate distance. Properly, that to which the average man could cast a stone. [A. Hall, *Iliad*, III, 45 (1581)]

Stonemason of Cromarty, The : Hugh Miller (1802–1856), geologist and man of letters.

Stonewall Jackson : Thomas Jonathan Jackson (1824–63), Amer. Confederate general. The name is derived from a remark by Gen. Bernard E. Bee, made at the Battle of Bull Run, ' See, there is Jackson standing like a stone wall.'

Stonewalling tactics : a purely defensive policy, allowing the enemy to throw himself, as it were, against a stone wall.

Stony hearted : impervious to mercy. [Underdowne, *Heliodorus*, VII, 93 (1569)]

Stools, Between two : indecisive ; between two alternatives and therefore likely to secure neither. [Heywood, *Proverbes*, ' While betweene two stooles my taile go to the grounde.' (1546)] The proverb is, however, Fr. in origin, being found in *Les Proverbes del Vilain* (1300).

Stop gap Administration, The : that of Lord Salisbury in 1885 which held office for a few months pending a general election. Phrase coined by Joseph Chamberlain.

Stop gaps with rushes, To : to make a useless effort. [Heywood, *Proverbes* (1546)]

Stop two gaps with one bush, To : to achieve a double purpose. [Heywood, *Proverbes* (1546)]

Stork, A visit from the : birth of a child. From the explanation given in Germany to children.

Storks' Law : the Rom. law which compelled children to support their aged parents, as storks are said to do.

Storm in a teacup, A : great excitement and perhaps acrimony over a matter of little consequence. The phrase is derived from a Rom. proverb ' Excitabat enim fluctus in simpulo.' Lit., he aroused a storm in a ladle, quoted by Cicero in *De Legibus*, III, 16, 36. Paul I of Russia, at the end of the 18th cent., referred to the troubles in Geneva as a tempest in a glass of water.

Stormy petrel, A : one who delights in contention or whose intervention generally forecasts trouble. Properly, a bird that is active in stormy weather.

Stormy Petrel of Politics, The : John Scott, Earl of Eldon (1751–1838).

Stove-pipe hat, A : a tall black silk hat.

Stradivarius (Strad), A : a very valuable violin, one of those made by Antonio Stradivari of Cremona (1644–1737).

Straight as a die, As : absolutely upright and straightforward. Apparently in reference to the absolute regularity and smoothness of the die.

Straight tip, The : a definite and clear hint.

Strain at a gnat and swallow a camel, To : to cause trouble over a trifle but to let a more important matter pass unheeded. [*Matthew*, xxiii, 24]

Strasburg goose, A : a person crammed with instruction at the expense of bodily exercise. Properly, a goose fattened for the purpose of enlarging its liver.

Straw, In the : (1) in childbed, possibly in allusion to the straw laid down before the house of a sick person to soften the noise of the passing traffic, or to the straw with which beds were at one time stuffed ; [E. Ward, *Hudibras Redivivus*, IV, 18 (1705)]

(2) in extreme poverty. [Lyly, *Euphues : Anatomy of Wit* (1579)]

Straw bail : a man who made a profession of standing security for another. *See* Man of straw.

Straw to break with a person, To have a : to be about to reprove a person. In allusion to the feudal custom of breaking a straw as an indication of the cancellation of a contract of a tenancy.

Straw, To make bricks without : to attempt a task with insufficient means. In allusion to the task imposed on the Israelites in Egypt. [*Exodus*, v ; *Verney Memoirs*, II, 79 (1658)]

Straw (two, three straws), Not to care a : not to trouble about .. [Chaucer, *Dethe Blaunche*, 718 (c. 1369)]

Straw, To clutch at any : to have recourse to any expedient, no matter how futile it may appear. From the proverb, ' A drowning man clutches at a straw.'

Straw to one's dog and bones to one's ass, To give : *see* Give.

Straw in one's ear, To wear a : to be on the look-out for a second husband. In allusion to the former Fr. fashion of placing a straw between the ears of a horse offered for sale.

Straw, The last : the last of a series of events or burdens that leads to a catastrophe. From the proverb, ' It is the last straw which breaks the camel's back.'

Straw, A man of : *see* Man of straw.

Straw, To strike with a : *see* Strike.

Straw, To stumble at a : *see* Stumble.

Straw, Not worth a : of no appreciable value. [Chaucer, *Tale of Melibeus* (14th cent.)]

Straws, To draw (gather, pick) : to be sleepy. [Mrs. D'Anvers, *Academia*, 36 (1691)]

Straws, To pick : *see* Pick straws.

Straws, To pluck at : *see* Pluck at straws.

Straws against the wind, To throw : to struggle hopelessly against that which cannot be overcome.

Strawberry Leaves : the token of ducal rank. After the strawberry leaves that form part of the decoration of the coronet of a duke.

Strawberry mark, A : a birth mark. From its supposed resemblance to a strawberry.

Strawberry Preacher, A : a non-resident parson who attended to his duties only at long intervals, once a year. So-called by Bp. Latimer.

Stream, To go (sail, swim) with the : to act in accord with the prevailing influence.

Stream, To strive against the : to oppose prevailing influences. [Heywood, *Proverbes* (1546) ; Seneca, *Epistulae*, CXXII, 19]

Stream, To swim against the : *see* Swim.

Street, The : (1) Wall Street, New York, and district ; (2) the financial quarter ; (3) the money market.

Street, In Easy : in comfortable circumstances.

Street of Ink, The : Fleet Street, London, the headquarters of most of the principal London newspapers. *See* H. Simoni's book with that title.

Street, In Queer : *see* Queer Street.

Street with .. Not in the same : to be quite inferior to ..

Street and Walker, Messrs. : unemployed, who walk about the streets.

Streets, The : a life of prostitution. [Shebbeare, *Matrimony*, II, 227 (1754)]

Street-walker, A : a prostitute, who walks the streets. [Mynshul, *Essays on a Prison* (1618)]

Strength, On the : of soldiers' wives, whose marriage is recognized by the military authorities.

Stretch a point, To : to make a concession ; to exceed a limit. [Rich. Edwards, *Damon and Pithias*, 1405 (1567)]

Stricken field, The : the field on which a battle has been fought.

Strict Q.T., On the : in confidence ; quietly ; secretly. Q.T. = quiet.

Stride, To take in one's : to deal with incidentally without interruption to one's main pursuit.

Strike hands, To : to ratify a bargain. From the practice of shaking hands on concluding a bargain.

Strike up the heels of .. To : to overthrow. [Marston, *Antony and Mel.* (1599)]

Strike while the iron is hot, To : to act while the occasion is favourable.

Strike oil, To : to be successful. A metaphor derived from the oilfields.

Strike with a straw, To : to act foolishly and to no purpose. From an ancient Grk. proverb.

Strike thirteen, To : *see* Thirteen.

Strike one's truth, To : to pledge oneself by striking or clasping hands.

String, To draw by one : to be in agreement. [W. Forrest, *Grysilde Seconde* (1558)]

String, To hang together on a : to act together. [*Hist. Jetzer* (1679)]

String, To harp on the one : to keep or return to the one subject. [*Two Lancashire Lovers*, 14 (1640)]

String, To have on a (lead in a) : to have under complete control. [Melbancke, *Philotimus*, I, i (1583) ; Lyly, *Euphues and His England* (1580)]

Strings to one's bow, To have two : to have alternative courses or resources. [Wolsey, *State Papers, Henry VIII*, IV, 103 (1524)]

Strings, To pull the : to control while remaining out of sight.

Stroke a person the right way, To : to soothe, coax or flatter a person.

Strong as death, As : [*Song of Solomon*, viii, 6]

Strong hand, By the : *see* Hand.

Struldbrug : incapable of dying but living in a state of decrepitude and misery. After a race of immortals described by Swift in *Gulliver's Travels*.

Stuff Gown, A : a barrister of the outer bar, in distinction from a silk gown or King's Counsel.

Stumble at a straw, To : to stumble without excuse.

Stumble over a straw and leap over a block, To : to hesitate at a trifle, but face a greater difficulty unconcerned. [Heywood, *Proverbes* (1546)]

Stumble at (on) the threshold, To : to fail at the beginning of an undertaking. [Langland, *Piers Plowman*, V, 357 (1377)]

Stump, On the : public speaking to the mob, rather than to intelligent audiences. *See* Stump orator.

Stump the country, To : to make political speeches in all parts of the country. *See* Stump orator.

Stump orator, A : a political advocate, who speaks down to the level of the mob. In America, where the term and practice originated, they used to speak from the stumps of trees or any other chance elevation.

Stumps, To stir one's : *see* Stir.

Stunt, A : anything that attracts attention or creates a sensation. In the first instance an undersized, stunted acrobat.

Stupid Boy, The : Thomas Aquinas (1224–74), scholastic philosopher.

Sturm und Drang (*Germ.*, storm and stress.)

Sturm und Drang Zeit, The (*Germ.*, period of storm and stress): the end of the 18th cent., when the Fr. Revolution had aroused in the minds of thinking men a certain fermentation. After a title of a play by Friedrich Maximilian von Klinger.

Stygian: infernal; relating to the lower regions. After Styx, the mythical river which forms the boundary of Hell.

Styles, Tom (John-a): *see* John-a-Styles.

Styx: *see* Stygian.

Suaviter in modo, fortiter in re (*Lat.*, pleasantly in manner, determinedly in fact): with resolution in combination with politeness. [Trapp, *Commentary on the O.T.* (1654)]

Sub judice (*Lat.*, under the judge): under judicial consideration. [J. Chamberlain, *Court and Times of James I*, Vol. I (1613)]

Sub rosa: *see* Rosa.

Sublime Porte, The: *see* Porte.

Submerged Tenth, The: the poorest class (estimated at ten per cent. of the population) always below the poverty line. Phrase coined by William Booth of the Salvation Army in 1890.

Subtle as a fox, As: very cunning. [Ascham, *The Schoolmaster*, Bk. I (1570)]

Subtle as a serpent, As: *see* Serpent.

Subtle Doctor, The: Duns Scotus (1265–1308), schoolman. On account of his metaphysical acuteness.

Succès d'estime, A (*Fr.*): a success of honourable approval if not of profit.

Succès de scandale: a success, usually literary, due to impropriety and not to intrinsic merits.

Suck a person's brains, To: to take advantage of another person's knowledge.

Sucker State, The: Illinois. So-termed in derision by the other western states of the Union. The 'Suckers' were the early settlers in the lead diggings of Wisconsin, who used regularly to return to their homes in Illinois for the winter.

Suds, Mrs.: a laundress. In reference to soapsuds.

Suffolk Punch, A: a man of Suffolk. A punch is a species of horse.

Sugar loaf hat, A: a high-crowned hat conical like a sugar loaf.

Sugared words (speech): pleasant but insincere speech. [*The Louer Accusing hys Loue* ll. 19–22 (1557)]

Sui generis (*Lat.*): of its own character.

Suit one's book, To: to serve one's purpose; to fall in with one's arrangements. A betting metaphor.

Suit of dittos, A: a suit of clothes, all made of the same cloth.

Suit, To follow: to follow an example already set. A cardplaying metaphor.

Summa summarum (*Lat.* the sum of sums): the grand total. [Plautus *Truculentus* 22–7; Jno. Jewel, *A Defence of the Apologie of the Church of England* I, ix, 65 (1567)]

Summer of All Saints, A: a return of summer weather about All Saints' Day, Nov. 1.

Summer King, The: Amadeus of Spain (1845–90), who reigned from Nov., 1870 to Feb. 1873, when he abdicated.

Summum bonum (*Lat.*): the highest good. [Burton, *Anatomy of Melancholy*, To the Reader (1621)]

Sumptuary Laws: laws directed against luxury and extravagance.

Sun never sets, On which the: (of an empire) world-wide. Orig. applied to the Span. dominions, now to the British.

Sun, A place in the: *see* Place in the sun.

Sun, To leave the setting to court the rising: to transfer one's support from the present to the future leader. Said by the Emperor Tiberius of the attitude of the Rom. people towards his prospective successor, Caligula.

Sun, To worship the rising: to give one's support or adhesion to the successful.

Sunbeams out of cucumbers, To extract: to engage in a foolish and profitless business. [Swift, *Gulliver's Travels: Voyage to Laputa*, ch. 5 (1726)]

Sunday go-to-meeting clothes: Sunday clothes; best clothes. Properly clothes suitable for attendance at divine worship.

Sunday Saint, A: one who observes the ordinances of his religion on Sundays, but ignores them on other days of the week.

Sundays come together, When: never. [Ray, *Proverbs* (1670)]

Sundays, A month of: a very long period.

Sundowner, A: an idler; a ne'er-do-well. One who makes it a custom of applying for work in the evening (at sundown) when the working day is ended and thus makes himself practically assured of a meal and accommodation for nothing.

Sunnite, A : a member of one of the two great divisions of Mohammedanism, that which accepts the Sunna, a collection of laws and precepts, as a supplement to the Koran.

Sunset of one's days, The : the concluding period of one's life. [Chapman, *Monsieur d'Olive*, IV, i (1606)]

Sunset Land : the state of Arizona. In allusion to its magnificent sunsets.

Sup, A bit and : *see* Bit.

Superba, La (*Ital.*, the superb) : Genoa. On account of its beautiful situation.

Superman, A : an ideal superior man conceived by F. W. Nietzsche (1844–1900), Germ. philosopher, as being evolved from the normal human type.

Superfine Review, The : the *Saturday Review*. So-called by Thackeray in *The Roundabout Papers* (1861–2).

Supped all one's porridge, To have : to be dead.

Suppressio veri, suggestio falsi (*Lat.*) : the suppression of the true (is) a suggestion of the false. [Lord Chesterfield, *World*, No. 105 (1755)]

Surat, A : (1) an Anglo-Malay term for a compact between two persons of a gambling character ; (2) anything of an inferior description. After Surat cotton, of worse quality than that from North America.

Sure card, A : a certainty. [*Thersites* in Dodsley's *Old Plays*, I, 363 (1537)]

Sure as death, As : as certain as anything can be. [Spenser, *Faerie Queen*, I, xi, 12 (1590)]

Sure as Demoivre, As : absolutely reliable. After Abraham de Moivre, F.R.S. (1667–1754), author of *The Doctrine of Chances*, of whom Pope said, ' Sure as Demoivre, without rule or line.'

Sure as four and four make eight, As : certain. [Wm. Combe, *Tour of Dr. Syntax*, Canto XXV (1812)]

Sure as a gun, As : absolutely certain. In allusion to the superior reliability of guns as compared with bows and arrows, or to the regular firing of guns at stated times. [1655]

Surface, A Charles : a light-hearted, generous, pleasure-loving, extravagant young man. After a character in Sheridan, *School for Scandal* (1777).

Surface, A Joseph : a young hypocrite (*ibidem*).

Surgery, The Father of French : Ambrose Paré (1517–90).

Sursum corda (*Lat.*, hearts upwards) : lift up your hearts. From the Communion Service of the Eng. church.

Survival of the fittest, The : phrase invented by Herbert Spencer (1820–1903), in elucidation of Darwin's theory of natural selection.

Sus Minervam (*Lat.*, a sow (teaching) Minerva (the goddess of wisdom) : an ignorant person attempting to instruct the learned. [Cicero, *Academica*, I, v, 18 ; Burton, *Anatomy of Melancholy*, To the Reader (1621)]

Suum cuique (*Lat.*, to each his own) : [Cicero, *De Finibus*, V, xxiii, 67 ; Shakespeare, *Titus Andronicus*, I, ii (1591)] The phrase was adopted by Frederick I in 1701 as the motto of the kingdom of Prussia.

Swaddler, A : a Protestant. So-called by Rom. Catholics. Said to have been taken from the text of a sermon preached by John Cennick (1718–55), at which a Rom. Catholic happened to be present. Also a Rom. Catholic who turns Protestant temporarily in order to obtain doles of clothing, blankets, etc.

Swaddling-clothes, Not to be out of : to behave childishly. [Lyly, *Gallattea*, III, i (1592)]

Swallow gudgeons ere they are caught, To : *see* Gudgeon. [Butler, *Hudibras*, Pt. II, canto iii, 923 (1663)]

Swallow-tails : a dress coat. After the fancied resemblance to the tail of a swallow.

Swan of Avon, The : Shakespeare, who lived at Stratford-on-Avon. So-called by Ben Jonson. According to the Pythagorean system poets at death were metamorphosed into swans.

Swan, A black : a great rarity. [Juvenal *Satires*, VI, xvi, 4 (1st cent.) ; Gosson, *Schoole of Abuse* (1579)]

Swan of Cambray, The : François de Salignac de la Mothe Fénelon (1651–1715), man of letters and Archbp. of Cambrai.

Swan of Lichfield, The : Anna Seward (1747–1809), Eng. poetess and writer;

Swan of Mantua, The : Virgil (70–29 B.C.), who was born at Mantua.

Swan of Meander, The : Homer, who lived on the banks of the Meander.

Swan of Padua, The : Francesco Algarotti (1712–64), Ital. man of letters.

Swan of the Thames, The : John Taylor (1580–1654), the water poet.

Swans, All one's geese are : one exaggerates the virtues of one's own property or productions.

Swans, A goose among : an ill-favoured person in the midst of beautiful ones.

Swansong, A : the last work of a poet or musician, or other farewell performance. In allusion to the song popularly believed to be sung by the swan when dying. [Martial, *Epigrams*, XIII, 77; Shakespeare, *Merchant of Venice*, III, ii, 44–5 (1595)]

Swap horses when crossing a stream, To : to change one's instruments while in the midst of a difficult task. Abraham Lincoln (1809–65), on being re-nominated for the office of Pres. of the U.S., said ' I am reminded of the story of an old Dutch farmer who remarked that it was not best to swap horses when crossing a stream.' (June 9, 1864).

Swashbuckler, A : a bully. Properly, one who swashes or makes a noise on a buckler. [Pilkington, *Works* (1560)]

Sway and say, To have great : to possess great influence. [Scott, *Rob Roy* (1818)]

Swear black is white, To : to commit perjury without hesitation.

Swear like a lord, To : [Elyot, *Governour* (1531)]

Swear like a trooper in Flanders, To : in allusion to the habits acquired by the Eng. troops in Flanders in the 16th cent. [Richardson, *Pamela* (1741)]

Sweat of one's brow, To live by the : to earn one's living by hard work. [*Genesis* iii. 19; Gosson, *Schoole of Abuse* (1579)]

Sweat coin, To : to remove a portion of the metal of a coin without affecting its appearance or its value as currency.

Swedenborgian, A : a follower of Emanuel Swedenborg, Swed. philosopher and theosophist and founder of the New Church.

Swedish Nightingale, The : Jenny Lind (1820–87), vocalist.

Sweep the board, To : to carry everything before one ; to secure a thorough success. Orig. a gaming phrase. [Singer, *History of Cards*, 346 (1680)]

Sweep the deck, To : to win all the stakes. From deck = a pack of cards.

Sweep, To make a clean : to remove entirely ; to make a complete change.

Sweet on .. To be : to be in love with .. [Echard, *Plautus* (1694)]

Sweet as hartshorn, As : spirit of hartshorn was employed in the 18th cent. as a protection against fainting. [Fielding, *The Miser*, II, iii (1733)]

Sweet as honey, As : [Fisher (1508)]

Sweet Singer of Israel, A : King David, reputed author of the Psalms. [II *Samuel*, xxiii, i]

Sweet tooth, To have a : *see* Tooth.

Sweet with the sour, To take the : to take philosophically the good and the evil in life.

Sweet will, At one's own : in accordance with one's own wishes. [Wordsworth, *Sonnet to Westminster Bridge*, 12 (1802)]

Sweetness and light : ' a harmonious perfection, a perfection in which the characters of beauty and intelligence are both present, which unites the two noblest of things .. sweetness and light.' [Matthew Arnold, *Culture and Anarchy* (1869)] Arnold acquired the phrase, with acknowledgments, from Swift [*Battle of the Books* (1704)] but it had been used centuries earlier by Philo Judæus.

Swell mob, The : the class of well-dressed criminals. After ' swell,' a well-dressed man. So-called generally by one lower in social rank.

Swell mobsman, A : a well-dressed pickpocket.

Swelled head : excessive self-conceit.

Swift as a pudding can creep, As : very slowly. [Rob. Arnim, *A Nest of Ninnies* (1608)]

Swift as the wind, As : [Spenser, *Faerie Queen*, V, vi, 7 (1590)]

Swim, In the : of a member of a coterie or clique, the members of which support one another to their mutual advantage. Said to be derived from the habit of river fish of swimming in shoals.

Swim without cork, To : to proceed on one's career unaided.

Swim against the stream, To : to oppose prevailing influences. [Juvenal, *Satires*, IV, 89–91 ; Lyly, *Endimion*, III, v (1584)]

Swim with the stream, To : *see* Stream.

Swim, To teach iron to : *see* Teach.

Swim between two waters, To : to pursue a middle course. From a Fr. proverb.

Swiss Admiral, A : a pretender to naval rank. Switzerland has no navy.

Switzerland of America, The : West Virginia.

Swollen head, To suffer from : to be conceited.

Sword and Cloak plays : comedies in which the characters wear swords and cloaks, as compared with plays of an earlier or later costume period.

Sword of Damocles : *see* Damocles.

Sword, A Delphic : *see* Delphic.

Sword of God, The : Khaled (582–642 c.), Saracen conqueror. So-called on account of his prowess at the Battle of Muta.

Sword, To put to the : to kill.

Sword of Rome, The : Marcellus (c. 270–208 B.C.), Rom. general.

Sword and throw away the scabbard, To draw the : to determine to carry through, at no matter what cost, the task that one has undertaken.

Sword, A two-edged : *see* Two-edged.

Sworn brothers : friends sworn to share one another's fortune. Orig. brothers-in-arms.

Sybarite, A : a slave to luxury and pleasure. After Sybaris in S. Italy, whose inhabitants were noted for addiction to luxury and pleasure.

Symphony, The Father of : Francis Joseph Haydn (1732–1809).

Synoptic Gospels, The : Matthew, Mark and Luke, which present a *sunopsis* (Grk.) or general conspectus.

Syphilis : venereal disease. After Syphilis, a shepherd, in a Lat. poem, *Syphilus sive Morbus Gallicus* (1530) by Girolamo Fracastoro.

Syren, A : *see* Siren.

Syren of Antiquity, The : Xenophon (c. 420–357 B.C.), Grk. historian and narrator of the exploits of the 10,000 Greeks who retreated to the Black Sea. So-called by the Duke of Urbino.

Syrens of the ditch : frogs. So-called by Tasso.

Syren's song, A : *see* Siren's song.

T, To a : exactly. Apparently a contraction of ' To a tittle,' the smallest possible amount or fraction. [Farquhar, *Love and a Bottle* (1698)]

T, Marked with a : branded as a criminal. In allusion to the medieval practice of branding the thumbs of criminals admitted to benefit of clergy with a T (thief).

T.D. pipe, A : a cheap clay pipe. After Timothy Dexter (b. 1793), a wealthy Amer. eccentric, who bequeathed a large sum of money for the manufacture of such pipes.

T's and dot the i's, To cross the : to be meticulously exact ; to emphasize the details.

T.G., A : a temporary gentleman. A colloquial term used in the army for temporary officers in the British Armies raised during the European War of 1914–18.

Tab, An old : an old maid. From the tabby or cat generally made a companion of by an old maid.

Tabarder, A : a foundation scholar at Queen's Coll., Oxford. After the tabard or tunic worn by them.

Tabarin, To be a : to act like a clown. After Tabarin, the witty assistant of Mondor, a vendor of quack medicines in the reign of Charles IX of France.

Tabby, A : a cat. In allusion to the brindled colour frequently met with in cats similar to that of tabby silk ; also a kind of silk. From Utabi, a district of Baghdad, where it was made.

Tabernacle, A : (1) the figurative clothing of the principles of a political party ; properly the movable temple or place of worship of the Israelites in the wilderness ; (2) nonconformity, so-called by members of the Church of England. After the Tabernacle in Moorfields, the original meeting place of the Wesleyan Methodists.

Table d'Hote, A (*Fr.*, table of the host) : a meal provided at a restaurant according to the selection of the proprietor.

Table, To lay on the : to postpone indefinitely. A parliamentary metaphor.

Table in a roar, To set the : to cause the company at table to laugh heartily. [Garrick's epitaph on James Quin in Bath Abbey Church (1766)]

Tables on .. To turn the : to make a counter attack on .. or bring a counter charge against .. [T. Shipman, *Henry III of France* (1678)]

Table-money : money appropriated for the expenses of the table.

Table-talk : the social conversation of distinguished men preserved in literary form. Orig. conversation at meals.

Taboo, To be : to be forbidden, consecrated to a special (religious) use. Tongan.

Tabula rasa, A (*Lat.*, an erased tablet) : a clean slate. [Wotton, *Letters*, Vol. II (1607)]

Tack, On the wrong : in the wrong direction. A naval metaphor.

Tadpoles and Tapers, The : professional politicians. After two characters in B. Disraeli, *Coningsby* (1844).

Taffeta phrases : bombastic, flowery language. From taffeta, a silk fabric. After Utabi, a district of Baghdad, where it used to be made. [Shakespeare, *Love's Labour Lost*, V, ii, 406 (1588)]

Taffy, A : a Welshman. Corruption of David, the patron saint of Wales and a name frequently met with among Welshmen. [Harrison, *Description of England* (1577)]

Tag, Rag and Bobtail, The : the common people. Tag, rag and bobtail orig. indicated different breeds of dogs. [Spenser, *State of Ireland* (1633)]

Tail between one's legs, With one's : dejected and suppressed. As a dog in such a condition.

Tail, To hold the serpent by the : *see* Hold.

Tail, To turn : to run away. A falconry metaphor. [*Interlude of Youth*, l. 393 (1554)]

Tail twisting : *see* Lion's tail, To twist the.

Tailor's hell, A : the place in which a tailor deposits the pieces of cloth, etc., which he treats as perquisites.

Tailor's sword (dagger), A : a needle. [Peter Pindar, *Great Cry and Little Wool* (1794)]

Tailors of Tooley Street, The three : the apocryphal tailors who are said to have presented a petition to parliament, commencing, ' We, the people of England.' They were quoted by George Canning.

Take down a person, To : to humiliate ; to rebuke. [*Child-marriages* (1562)]

Take in a person, To : to trick. [Hy. Mackenzie, *The Man of Feeling*, ch. 25 (1771)]

Take off a person, To : to caricature. [Lyly, *Endimion*, II, ii (1591) ; Lord Chesterfield, *Letters* (1750)]

Take the bull by the horns, To : to face a difficulty resolutely. From an ancient Grk. proverb.

Take a hair to draw a waggon, To : to act foolishly and to no purpose. From an ancient Grk. proverb.

Take a hammer to spread a plaster, To : to act foolishly. From an ancient Grk. proverb.

Take one's life in one's hand, To : deliberately to run considerable risks.

Take lying down, To : to suffer passively ; like a party to a fight who when knocked down refuses to rise in order to continue the fight. The phrase was derived from a passage in *The Conversion of Colonel Quagg* by G. A. Sala which appeared orig. in *Household Words*, and was reprinted in a volume of *Papers Humorous and Pathetic* in 1872.

Take oil to extinguish the fire, To : to act foolishly. From an ancient Grk. proverb. [Lyly, *Euphues : Anatomy of Wit* (1579)]

Take a post to kill a bee, To : to act foolishly. From an ancient Grk. proverb.

Take the ribbons, To : *see* Ribbons.

Take a spear to kill a fly, To : to act foolishly. From an ancient Grk. proverb.

Take the spring from the year, To : to act foolishly and to no purpose. From an ancient Grk. proverb.

Take a town by starving it, To : to take advantage of a man's wants. From a Span. proverb supposed to be derived from a stratagem employed by Louis XIV to recruit his army.

Take by storm, To : generally of a speaker, actor, etc., to carry away an audience by the excellence or apparent excellence of his performance. A military metaphor.

Take a person at his word, To : to rely on what a person says.

Taking, To be in a : to be in trouble, in distress. [Chapman, *Blinde Beggar of Alexandria* (1598)]

Tale of the man in the moon, A : a wildly improbable story. [Lilly, *Endimion, the Man in the Moone*, Prologue (1591)]

Tale of a roasted horse, A : an invented story. [*Marriage of Wit and Science*, IV, i (1570)]

Tale of a Tub, A : *see* Tub.

Tales out of school, To tell : to romance ; to betray confidences (in a minor degree). [Tyndale (16th cent.) ; Heywood, *Proverbes* (1546)]

Talents, All the : *see* All the Talents.

Talk big, To : to boast. [*Tibullus*, II, vi, 9–12 ; Lyly, *Campaspe*, V, iii (1584) ; Earle, *Microcosmography*, IV (1633)]

Talk through one's hat, To : to speak irresponsibly, seeking to force one's argument without any facts behind one.

Talk shop, To : to talk about one's business or profession in social gatherings.

Talk turkey to .. To : to say pleasant things to ..

Talking Mill (Shop), The : (contemptuously) the House of Commons.

Tall talk : boastful language.

Tamberlain, As cruel as : in allusion to Timur Tamerlane (1336–1405), Tartar conqueror, as depicted in Marlowe, *Tamburlaine the Greate* (1587)]

Tammany ; Tammany Hall : a strong political organization in New York City which forms a part of the Democratic Party, notorious for its corruption and its power. It grew out of the Tammany Society, a charitable and political organization founded in 1805, which derived its name from Tamanend, that of a chief of the Delaware nation of the 17th cent.

Tammany Ring : a group of New York officials belonging to the Democratic Party who were punished for corruption in 1871. *See* Tammany.

Tamson, John : *see* John Thomson's man.

Tansy, Like a : in proper manner. The tansy is (1) a medicinal plant ; (2) a sort of custard.

Tantalize, To : to teaze or torment. After Tantalus, a mythical king of Lydia, who was condemned to perpetual thirst while almost within reach of water to which he could never attain.

Tantalus, A : a set of spirit decanters, visible but locked in a case. *See* Tantalize.

Tapers and Tadpoles : *see* Tadpoles.

Tapis, On the : under, or about to be under, discussion. Lit., on the (Fr.) tapestry or green baize (of the council table).

Tapley, A Mark : an incurable optimist, cheerful in all circumstances. After a character in Dickens, *Martin Chuzzlewit* (1843).

Tar ; Tar, Jack : a sailor. From tarpaulins frequently in use on board ship. [Wycherley, *Plain Dealer*, II, i (1676)]

Tar-brush, A knight of the : a sailor. In allusion to the use of tar aboard ship.

Tarheel, A : an inhabitant of South Carolina. From tar, one of the principal products of the state.

Tarred with the same brush, To be : to be equally to blame. From the

former practice of marking sheep with tar.

Tartar, To catch a : to be in the power of one's supposed prisoner. In allusion to the story of an Irish soldier who claimed to have taken a Tartar opponent prisoner, but explained that his captive would not permit himself to be taken to the camp, nor would he permit him to return himself. [Defoe, *Captain Singleton*, ch. 16 (1720)]

Tartarean ; Tartarian : infernal. After Tartarus, the infernal regions, in Grk. mythology.

Tartuffe A : a hypocrite. After the hero of Molière's play of that name.

Tartufish : hypocritical. *See* Tartuffe.

Tatters, To tear a passion to : to overdo a pretended rage. [Shakespeare, *Hamlet*, III, ii (1602–3)]

Tattoo, The Devil's : a monotonous drumming with a finger or a foot, tending to cause the blue devils.

Tattooed Man, The : James Gillespie Blaine (1830–93), Amer. statesman. After a caricature of him in *Puck* (1884), depicted as Phryne before her judges, tattooed with the names of the various scandals with which he had been connected.

Tau, Marked with a : marked with a cross. From the Grk. letter Υ.

Tavern of Europe, The : Paris. So-called by Prince Bismarck.

Tawdry : cheap and showy. After St. Audrey or St. Ethelreda, at whose fair in the Isle of Ely tawdry articles were sold.

Tawny Tribe, The : gypsies. In allusion to their complexion.

Te Deum, A : a hymn or service of praise and thanks. From the opening words of a Lat. hymn, *Te Deum laudamus*, We praise Thee, O Lord.

Teach a bull to roar, To : to act unnecessarily. From an ancient Grk. proverb.

Teach a cock to crow, To : to act unnecessarily. From an ancient Grk. proverb.

Teach a dog to bark, To : to act unnecessarily. From an ancient Grk. proverb.

Teach a fish to bite, To : to act unnecessarily. From an ancient Grk. proverb.

Teach a hen to chuck, To : to act unnecessarily. From an ancient Grk. proverb.

z

Teach iron to swim, To : to act foolishly and to no purpose. From an ancient Grk. proverb.

Teach an old woman to dance, To : to act foolishly and to no purpose. From an ancient Grk. proverb.

Teach a pig to play on a flute, To : to act foolishly and to no purpose. From an ancient Grk. proverb.

Teach a serpent to hiss, To : to act unnecessarily. From an ancient Grk. proverb.

Teacher of Germany, The : Philip Melanchthon (1497–1560).

Tea-cup, A storm in a : see Storm.

Teague, A : an Irishman. After the former popularity of the word as an Irish name.

Teanlay Night : the vigil of All Souls, or the last night in October.

Tear a cat, To : to rant, esp. on the theatrical stage. Apparently from the exploit of one who once desired to attract attention. [Shakespeare, *Midsummer Night's Dream* I, ii (1590)]

Tear Christ's body, To : to utter oaths. In allusion to the mdieval oaths in which parts of Christ's body were mentioned.

Tear a passion to rags and tatters, To : see Tatters.

Tears of Eos : morning dewdrops. So-called by the Greeks. Eos was the mother of Memnon, who was killed in the defence of Troy.

Tears, St. Lawrence's : see St. Lawrence.

Tecton Brook, As crooked as : in allusion to a brook in Northamptonshire famous for its windings.

Teens, In one's : between the ages of twelve and twenty, *i.e.,* thirteen to nineteen. [*The Spectator,* No. 311 (1712)]

Teeth of .. In the : in opposition to .. in defiance of .. [Fielding, *Voyage to Lisbon,* July 25, 1754]

Teeth, To cast in the : to reproach with.. [Lyly, *Euphues : Anatomy of Wit* (1579)]

Teeth of .. To draw the : see Draw.

Teeth outwards, From the : insincerely ; empty talk. [Rob. Wilson, *Three Ladies of London,* II, 1244–5 (1584)]

Teeth, By the skin of one's : see Skin.

Teeth, In spite of one's : in defiance of .. [Skelton, *Colyn Cloute,* 939 (c. 1500) ; Shakespeare, *Merry Wives of Windsor,* V, iv (1598–9)]

Teetotaler, A : a total abstainer from alcoholic drink The word was in-

vented about 1833 by Rich. Turner (1790–1846), a temperance advocate, who, as a means of emphasis or in consequence of a stammer, duplicated the initial letter in the phrase, ' total abstinence.' According to another derivation the Hector, New York, Temperance Society, introduced in January, 1827, a second form of pledge in addition to that hitherto in force. The old pledge was then known as O.P. (Old Pledge) and the new as T. (Total). The many explanations required of the latter symbol led ultimately to the incorporation into the language of T-Total, or Teetotal.

Teian Muse, The : Anacreon (550–465 B.C.), who was born in Teos, Asia Minor.

Temper the wind to the shorn lamb, To : to afford some assistance or protection to the weak. [Laurence Sterne, *Sentimental Journey* (1768)]

Tempest in a teapot, A : see Storm in a teacup.

Templar ; Templar, Knight, A : a member of a military order of knighthood founded in Palestine in 1118, with its headquarters on the site of the Temple. The order was suppressed in 1312.

Templar, To drink like a : to drink copiously. ' Templar ' is a corruption of ' Temprier ' (O.F.), glass-blower. The work of glass blowing encourages drinking.

Tempora, O mores ! O (*Lat.*) : Alas for the times, alas for the morals ! [Cicero, *Catilina,* I, i, 2]

Tempora mutantur (*Lat.,* times change) : [Greene, *Groat's-worth of Wit* (1592)] The phrase has been attributed to the Emperor Lothair (c. 830).

Temporal, Lords : the members of the House of Lords apart from the bishops or spiritual peers.

Tempus fugit (*Lat.,* time flies) : [Virgil, *Georgics,* III, 284]

Ten, The Council of : the secret tribunal which exercised unrestrained power in the Rep. of Venice. It was abolished in 1797.

Ten in the Hundred, Old : a usurer ; one who demands ten per cent. [*Death of Usury* (1594)]

Ten Minutes' Bill, A : a bill introduced into parliament under the Ten Minutes' Rule, whereby only two short speeches are permitted, one in favour and the other against.

Ten Thousand, The Retreat of the : the retreat in 401 B.C. of the Grk. auxiliaries who had assisted Cyrus in his revolt against his brother, Artaxerxes. Their campaign had been successful, but resolving to return to Greece, under the leadership of Xenophon, they marched 3,645 miles across very difficult country in 215 days.

Tender passion, The : Love.

Tender years : youth. [Ovid, *Heroides : Phaedra Hippolyto*, l. 25]

Tenderfoot, A : an inexperienced person. Orig. in use in the newly settled western districts of the U.S.

Tenderloin : the part of a city in which most of the theatres and other places of entertainment are grouped. After that district of New York which is known as the Tenderloin District. The word means literally the tenderest or most juicy part of a loin of beef or other meat, and is supposed to have reference to the considerable amount of bribery accepted by the police of New York for the protection of lawbreakers in that district.

Tendon, Achilles' : the tendon which connects the heel with the calf. That in which, according to mythology, Achilles was mortally wounded.

Teniers of Comedy, The : Florent Carton Dancourt (1661–1726). After David Teniers, (1610–90), Flem. artist.

Teniers, The English : George Morland (1763–1804).

Teniers, The Scotch : Sir David Wilkie (1785–1841).

Tennis Ball of Fortune, The : Pertinax (126–193), Rom. emperor, who was successively a seller of charcoal, schoolmaster, soldier and emperor. After a reign of three months he was deposed and murdered.

Tenor's farewell, A : a farewell destined to be often repeated. In allusion to the practice of vocalists of giving more than one farewell recital or appearance.

Tenterhooks, To be on : to have one's expectation stretched. The tenterhooks were the hooks on which cloth was stretched after it had been woven. [Heywood, *Fair Maid* (1607)]

Tenth Legion, The : the submerged Tenth (*q.v.*).

Tenth Muse, The : Madame Antoinette du Ligier de la Garde Deshoulières (c. 1635–94), Fr. poetess.

Tentmaker, The Great : Omar Khayyám (d. 1123), Persian poet, philosopher and epigrammatist. Persian, *Khayyam*, tent-maker; probably the occupation of his father.

Tents, oh Israel ! To your : the signal for a revolt. [I *Kings*, xii, 16]

Terence of England, The : Richard Cumberland (1732–1811). So-called by Oliver Goldsmith. After Terence (b. 185 B.C.), Lat. dramatist.

Termagant, A : a shrew ; a quarrelsome, nagging woman. After Tervagant, the Moslem demon in the morality plays ; more remotely after Diana Trivia, a goddess of the Scythians.

Terminological inexactitude, A : a euphemism for a falsehood. Term invented by Mr. Winston Churchill in a debate in the House of Commons.

Term-trotter, A : one who attends the Law Courts for the term.

Terpsichorean : relating to dancing. After Terpsichore, the Muse of the choral song and dance.

Terra firma : the dry land ; more esp. the Ital. mainland formerly subject to Venice, and the coast of America, between Paria and Costa Rica.

Terra incognita (*Lat.*, an unknown land).

Terrestial Sun, The : gold, which in alchemy corresponded to the sun.

Terrible Cornet of Horse, The : *see* Cornet of Horse.

Terror, The : *see* Reign of Terror.

Terror of the World, The : Attila (406–53), King of the Huns.

Terrorists : agitators in a time of political disturbance who by their threats and action terrify citizens and satisfy their desires at their expense. Also anarchists and other advocates of violence who seek to terrify the government into acquiescence in their demands. In the Fr. Rev. of 1848 the extreme party seized the Hotel de Ville and attempted unsuccessfully to overpower the National Assembly.

Tertium quid, A (*Lat.*, some third thing) : a third course, person, object, etc. The term is attributed to Pythagoras. [*Theatrum Chemicum* (1613)]

Tertius gaudens (*Lat.*, a third, rejoicing) : a third party who derives benefit from the disputes of two others.

Terza rima : a form of verse in which the second lines always rhyme with the first and third lines of the succeeding triplet.

Tesserarian Art, The (*Lat.*, *tessera*, a die) : gambling.

Tête à tête (*Fr.*, head to head) : a private conversation between two people. [Vanbrugh and Cibber, *The Provoked Husband*, III, i (1728)]

Tether, To come to (reach) the end of one's : to come to the end of one's resources. A grazing metaphor.

Tetragrammaton, The : J.H.V.H., the four letters that denote and also conceal the name of the Deity.

Texas, Gone to : decamped.

Thales, A : a renowned philosopher and scientist. After Thales of Miletus (640–546 B.C.), the founder of Grk. geometry, astronomy and philosophy.

Thames afire, To set the : to display great energy. 'Thames' is a corruption of 'temse,' a sieve. A sifter would have to exercise very great energy before the friction he caused set fire to the sieve. [Langland, *Piers Plowman*, VII, 335 (1363)]

Thames, To cast water in the : to undertake a useless work. [Heywood, *Proverbes*, (1546)]

Thank one's stars, To : to be grateful. An astrological metaphor.

Thanksgiving Day : in the U.S., the fourth Thursday in November, a day set apart for the expression of gratitude to God.

Thatched head, A : one who wore the hair matted, like the native Irish in earlier times. [Beaumont and Fletcher, *Coxcomb*, II (1612)]

Theban Bard (Eagle), The : Pindar (c. 522–443 B.C.), who was born near Thebes and lived there.

Thelusson Act, The : the 39th and 40th of George III, cap. 98, which forbids the accumulation of a legacy of a testator for more than twenty-one years. After a Mr. Thelusson who provided for the accumulation of his estate after his death until it would have amounted to nineteen million pounds.

Themis : law ; justice. After the Grk. goddess of law and justice.

Theocritus, The Scottish : Allan Ramsay (1685–1758). After Theocritus of Syracuse (fl. 280 B.C.) who was celebrated for his idylls.

Theocritus, The Sicilian : Giovanni Meli of Palermo (1740–1815).

Theon's tooth : ill-natured cricitism. After Theon, a spiteful Rom. grammarian. [Horace, *Epistles*, I, xviii, 82]

Thermidorians : the moderate party in the Fr. Revol. who approved of the overthrow of Robespierre on the 9th of Thermidor, 1794.

Thermopylæ, A : a pass which serves as the means of entrance for an invading army. After Thermopylæ, where Leonidas and his Greeks withstood the Persian invasion in 480 B.C.

Thersites, A : an ill-tempered critic of the authorized powers. After Thersites, an officer in the Grk. army which besieged Troy.

Theseus, A : a Hercules. After Theseus, the Hercules of Ionian-Attic fable.

Theseus, The Christian : Roland, the Paladin.

Theseus and Pirithous : a pair of devoted friends. After Theseus, the great hero of Attic legend, and Pirithous, King of the Lapiths.

Thespian : (1) tragic, dramatic ; (2) an actor. After Thespis (fl. 535 B.C.), the founder of the Grk. drama.

Thespian Maids, The : the Muses. After Thespiæ, a centre of their worship.

Thespian rage, A : an assumed, pretended rage. *See* Thespian.

Thespis, A Son of : a tragic poet. *See* Thespian.

Thessalian : deceitful. In allusion to the proverbial treachery of the Thessalians.

Thestylis, A : a country maid. After a character in *The Idylls* of Theocritos.

Theta on .. To put the letter : to condemn to death. From the ancient Grk. practice of marking the ballot used in voting for a death sentence with the letter *theta*, the initial of θάνατος, death.

Thetis, In the lap of : in the sea. After Thetis, one of the Nereids or sea-nymphs. [*Verses at Time of Execution of Lord Strafford* (1650)]

Thick of .. To be in the : to be in the midst of .. ; in the most active part of an action or event. [Flavel, *Method of Grace*, X, 214 (1681)]

Thick with .. To be : to be very friendly with ..

Thick as hail, As : in rapid succession ; very thick. [Chaucer, *The Legende of Goode Women*, I, 76 (14th cent.)]

Thick as herrings, As : in allusion to the shoals of herrings familiar on the Eng. coasts. [Peter Pindar, *Subjects for Painters : The Soldier and the Virgin Mary* (1795)]

Thick as hops, As : very plentiful and compact. [Taylor, *Workes* (1630)]

Thick, To lay it on : to act or speak with excessive earnestness, energy, vehemence or exaggeration.

Thick-skinned : impervious to ordinary insults or offence. [*Histrio-mastix*, III, i, 189–90 (1610)]

Thick as thieves, As : as close together in confidence as confederates in crime. [Theodore Hook, *Parson's Daughter*, II, ii (1833)]

Thick and thin, Through : despite all obstacles ; in any circumstances. [Chaucer, *Reeve's Tale* (1386) ; *Kyng and Hermyt* (1380)]

Thick and threefold : in large numbers and in quick succession. [Hall, *Chronicle of Henry VIII*, 186 (1548)]

Thieves' Latin : the cant language used by thieves and other members of the lowest class.

Thievish as a daw, As : from the reputation for stealing which has been acquired by the race of magpies. [Ovid, *Metamorphoses*, Bk. VII, 466–7]

Thimblerigging : cheating. In allusion to the trick of swindling by means of three small cups or thimbles and a pea.

Thin Red Line, The : the Argyll and Sutherland (formerly 93rd) Highlanders. So-called by Sir W. H. Russell from the colour of their uniforms and their formation at the Battle of Balaclava. [*A Hist. of the War in the Crimea* (1863–77)]

Thin-skinned : sensitive in the extreme.

Thing or two, To know a : to be mentally alert.

Thinking cap, To put on the : to take leisure for consideration.

Third Estate, The : the Commons.

Third House, The : the lobby, the other two being the Amer. Senate and the House of Representatives.

Third Section, The : the Russ. secret political police, formed by Nicholas I in 1865.

Thirteenpence-halfpenny, A : a hangman. In allusion to the fee paid at the beginning of the 17th cent. for executions.

Thirteen States, The : the thirteen colonies that combined to form the U.S. of America, *viz.*, Connecticut, Delaware, Georgia, Maryland, Massachusetts, New Hampshire, New Jersey, New York, North Carolina, Pennsylvania, Rhode Island, South Carolina and Virginia.

Thirteen, To strike : to exceed the normal by one point.

Thirteenth juryman, The : a judge who displays bias.

Thirteen to the dozen, To talk : to talk very rapidly and not too intelligently. Related to the thirteen in a baker's dozen and in a publisher's dozen.

Thirty-nine Articles, The : the Articles of Faith of the Church of England. Orig. 42, but reduced to 39 in 1563.

Thirty-pound Knights : the knights created by James I for payment, the rumoured price being as low as £30.

Thirty Years' War, The : the war between the Catholics of Germany under the Emp. Ferdinand II and the Prot. princes, which lasted from 1618 to 1648.

Thistle, The Order of the : the principal Scot. order of knighthood, founded in 809.

Thomas, A : a footman ; a waiter.

Thomas (Tommy) Atkins ; Tommy, A : a Brit. private soldier. Two derivations are given for this term. According to the one, the name was selected, probably haphazard, as a specimen in some directions for furnishing a return of particulars relating to the individual soldiers of the Brit. Army. According to the other, the name was borne by a private soldier who distinguished himself for bravery and devotion to duty in the course of the rebellion at Lucknow in 1857. The term thus came to be used for a brave soldier, and subsequently for any soldier of the Brit. Army.

Thomasing : (1) the practice of collecting money to be spent on Christmas festivities on St. Thomas' Day (Dec. 21) ; (2) begging.

Thomasite, A : a Christadelphian. After John Thomas, the founder of the sect.

Thorn in the flesh (side), A : a perpetual source of annoyance.

Thorns, A bed of : *see* Bed.

Thorpe's wife, As busy as : *see* Throp's wife.

Thracian Art, The : riding.

Thrasonic ; Thrasonical : boastful. After a character in Terence's comedy, *Eunuchus*.

Thread and thrum : the good and the bad together. A metaphor drawn from weaving. Thrums are the weaver's wastage. [Shakespeare, *Midsummer Night's Dream* (1592)]

Threadbare friend, A : one who will render no assistance. [*Paston Letters*, No. 435 (1462)]

Three acres and a cow : the agricultural policy of the Liberal party in 1882, *viz.*, the availability of allotments for all agricultural labourers. The phrase was coined by Mr. Jesse Collings (1831-1920), or by George Smith of Coalville (1831-95).

Three Ages of Man, The : *see* Ages.

Three Ages of a State, The : *see* Ages of a State.

Three Emperors, The Battle of the : Austerlitz (Dec. 2, 1805) in which Napoleon, the Emperor and the Czar all took part.

Three Estates of the Realm, The : the peerage, the clergy, the common people.

Three Exes, The : the 30th (XXX) Regt. of Foot.

Three F's, The : the programme of the Irish Land League in 1880—Fixity of Tenure, Fair Rent, Free Sale.

Three K's, The : King, Constitution and Church.

Three Kings, The Alliance of the : the alliance of 1849 between the Kings of Prussia, Saxony and Hanover, directed towards the preservation of order in Germany.

Three Kings of Cologne, The : *see* Cologne.

Three Kings' Day : Epiphany. In memory of the visit of the Three Kings or Wise Men of the East to the Infant Jesus.

Three legs, To go on : to walk with the help of a stick. [Earl of Dorset, *A Mirrour for Magistrates* (1563)]

Three pair back, A : a garret. Presumably on the third storey at the back of the house.

Three R's, The : *see* R's.

Three sheets in the wind : inebriated. A nautical metaphor.

Three Sisters, The : *see* Sisters.

Three tailors of Tooley Street, The : *see* Tailors.

Three-cornered constituency, A : a parliamentary constituency returning three members, the electors in which had two votes only apiece.

Three-decker, A : a person or object of great importance. Properly a three-decked or line of battle ship.

Throp's wife, As busy as : of a woman who is very busy in domestic affairs but seems always in a muddle. This simile originated in the North of England.

Throw up the sponge, To : to abandon the contest. A metaphor drawn from the prize-ring.

Thrum one's cap, To : to idle one's time. Properly to cover one's cap with thrums or pieces of waste thread, etc. [Dekker and Webster, *Northward Ho*, IV, i (1607)]

Thumb, Under one's : under one's complete influence or control. [Samuel Richardson, *Grandison*, V, 56 (1753)]

Thumb at .. To bite one's : to insult. [Shakespeare, *Romeo and Juliet*, I, i (1591-3)]

Thumbs, With one's fingers all : clumsy.

Thumbs up ; thumbs down : sentence of death ; announcement of release. By these signs the Rom. emperors used to give their decisions of life and death after the gladiatorial contests.

Thump-cushion, A : a preacher given to gesticulation. Lit., one who thumps the cushion of the pulpit. [Peter Pindar, *Pindariana : Sea Courtship* (1794)]

Thunder and Lightning : Stephen II of Hungary (1100-31).

Thunder, To steal one's : *see* Steal.

Thunderbolt of Italy, The : Gaston de Foix, Duc de Nemours (1489-1512), Fr. soldier who waged a great campaign against the Spaniards in Italy.

Thunderer, The : (1) the *Times* newspaper, after a leading article which opened, ' We thundered forth the other day ' ; (2) Jupiter, in allusion to his weapon, the thunderbolt ; (3) Homer, so-called by Wordsworth.

Thursdays meet, When : never.

Thyestean banquet, A : a cannibal feast. After the classical story of Thyestes and Atreus.

Thyestean revenge : the law of reprisals. *See* Thyestean banquet.

Tibb's Eve, St. : *see* Saint Tib's Eve.

Tiberius, A : a monster of vice and cruelty. After Tiberius (B.C. 42-37 A.D.), Rom. emperor.

Tibullus, The French : Evariste Désiré Duforges (1753-1814). After Albius Tibullus (54 to 19 B.C.), Lat. elegiac poet.

Tick, On : on credit; contraction for ' on ticket.' In allusion to the former habit of making credit purchases by a system of tickets. [Sedley, *The Mulberry Garden* (1668)]

Ticket, A : a list of candidates put forward by a caucus or political party.

Ticket of leave : a warrant releasing a prisoner prematurely, subject to his good behaviour.

Tickle the ears of .. To : to amuse or please, esp. by means of light talk or flattery. [Gosson, *Schoole of Abuse* (1579)]

Ticklish times : critical times. [Bacon, *Essayes : Of Seditions and Troubles* (1625)]

Tide of public opinion, To turn the : to influence public opinion in a new direction.

Tide-waiter, A : one who votes contrary to his own opinion. [Sydney Smith, *Peter Plymley's Letters*, letter V (1808)]

Tied house, A : a public-house owned or otherwise controlled by a firm of brewers, from which alone it must obtain its beer.

Tiers Etat : the Commoners or Third Estate of the Realm in monarchical France.

Tiger of France, The : Georges Clemenceau (b. 1841), Prime Minister of France.

Tight hand on .. To keep a : to keep close control over .. [Sheridan, *The Rivals*, I, ii (1775)]

Tight place, To be in a : to be in a difficult situation.

Tile loose, To have a : to be mentally afflicted slightly.

Tilt against windmills, To : to undertake an absurd, impossible task. In allusion to an episode related of Don Quixote in Cervantes' romance of that title.

Time, To do (serve) : to undergo imprisonment.

Time by the forelock, To take : to seize the opportunity as soon as it offers. Time is traditionally depicted as an old man with a solitary lock of hair in front. [Spenser, *Amoretti*, LXX, 7–8 (1595)]

Time on one's hands, To have : to be unemployed.

Time, To kill : to idle ; to perform some useless occupation merely to avoid ennui.

Time out of mind : on numerous occasions. [Shakespeare, *Romeo and Juliet*, I, iv, 67–9 (1592)]

Time-server, A : a trimmer ; one who adapts his principles to circumstances. [G. Babington, *Frailty and Faith* (1584)]

Timeo Danaos et dona ferentes (*Lat.*, I fear the Greeks even when they are bringing gifts) : I distrust certain people even though they appear to be friendly. In allusion to the artifice of a gift horse by means of which the Greeks secured admittance into Troy. [Virgil, *Æneid*, II, 49]

Timothy ; Timothy grass : a species of grass. After Timothy Hanson, who introduced it into England from America about 1780.

Tin gods, The little : mean, petty, officious persons in office or positions of influence. [Kipling, *Departmental Ditties* (1886)]

Tinker, The Immortal : John Bunyan (1628–1688).

Tinker's budget, A : stale news. [Greene, *Liberality and Prodigality*, IV, iv (1602)]

Tinker's mufti : a combination of army uniform and civilian costume.

Tintoretto of England, The : William Dobson (1610–46). So-called by Charles I. After Tintoretto (1512–94), the great Venetian historical painter.

Tintoretto of Switzerland, The : Jean Huber (1722–90).

Tip of one's tongue, On the : on the point of being uttered. [Persius, *Satires*, I, 103–6 ; De Foe, *Moll Flanders* (1722)]

Tipperary rifle, A : a shillelagh (*q.v.*).

Tippet, To turn : to undergo an entire change. [Heywood, *Proverbes* (1546)

Tip-staff, A : a constable. In allusion to the staff tipped with horn, formerly carried by them.

Tiresias, As blind as : in allusion to Tiresias, the Theban, who accidentally saw Athena bathing and was struck by her with blindness.

Tironian sign, The : & (and), said to have been invented by Tullius Tiro.

Tirynthian Swain, The : Hercules, who resided at Tiryns in Argolis. So-called by Edmund Spenser.

Tissue ballots : ballot papers printed on paper so thin that several can be inserted in the box simultaneously. Invented in North Carolina in 1876 so as to defeat the negro majority.

Titan ; Titanic : gigantic. In allusion to the Titans, the earth-giants of mythology.

Tite Barnacle, A : a typical official whose only instinct is to cling to office. After a character in Dickens, *Little Dorrit* (1855).

Tithonus, A : (1) an old man ; (2) a grasshopper. After a personage in Grk. mythology who received the gift of immortality but not eternal youth and was in extreme old age changed to a grasshopper.

Titian of France, The : Jacques Blanchard (1600–38). After Titian (1477–1576), the great Venetian painter.

Titian of Portugal, The : Alonzo Sanchez Coello (1515–90).

Tityre Tus, A : a fashionable rowdy of the London streets at the end of the 17th cent. After a character in Virgil's First Eclogue. *Tityre tu patulae recubans sub tegmine fagi.* (Tityrus was a wanton shepherd in Virgil's *Eclogues*.

Tityrus, A : a shepherd. After a name frequently used in Grk. idylls and Virgil's First Eclogue.

Toad under a harrow, Like a : suffering persecution or oppression, like a toad dragged along by a harrow. [Scott, *Rob Roy*, ch. 27 (1818)]

Toad-eater, A ; A Toady : a sycophant ; an obsequious parasite. In allusion to the practice of conjuror's attendants of eating toads, supposed to be poisonous, in order to enable their employers to effect seemingly miraculous cures. [Knox, *Spirit of Despotism* (1555)]

Toady, A : *see* Toad-eater.

Toast, To (A) : to drink to the health of .. ; a person whose health is drunk ; the offer of a compliment by means of a drink. In allusion to the piece of toast that used formerly to be placed in the glass of wine.

Toast, On : swindled ; tricked.

Toby jug, A : a jug formed to resemble a stout old man in 18th cent. costume.

Toby-man, A : a robber. A high tobyman is a highwayman ; a low tobyman, a footpad.

Tocsin, To sound the : to sound the alarm. From the tocsin bell.

Toga virilis (*Lat.*, the toga (or robe) of manhood) : full age. [Sir Thos. Overbury, *Characters : A Flatterer* (1616)]

Toga'd Nation, The : the Romans. In allusion to the togas which they used to wear. [Virgil, *Æneid*, I, 282]

Toledo, A : a sword. After Toledo in Spain, famous for its manufacture of sword blades.

Tolosa, To have the gold of : to possess that which will bring one no good. In allusion to the sacred treasures of Tolosa or Toulouse which were seized by Caepio in 106 B.C. He was shortly afterwards slain in battle.

Tom o' Bedlam : a wandering lunatic. After Bedlam Lunatic Asylum, London.

Tom Bowling, A : a sailor. After a character in Smollett, *Roderick Random* (1748).

Tom Coney (Conney), A : a simpleton.

Tom, Dick and Harry : a number of people of no consequence. From three popular Eng. Christian names.

Tom Double, A : an equivocator.

Tom Drum's entertainment : clumsy horseplay or rough joking.

Tom Farthing, A : a natural fool.

Tom Folio : Thomas Rawlinson (1681–1725), bibliomaniac.

Tom Fool, A : a stupid fool ; a practical joker. [Killigrew, *The Parson's Wedding*, II, v (1663)]

Tom Fool's colours : red and yellow ; the colours of the professional fool.

Tom and Jerry days : the period of the Regency (1810–20). After characters in Pierce Egan, *Life in London* (1821)]

Tom of Lincoln, As loud as : in allusion to the great church bell of Lincoln, cast in 1610. [Fuller, *Worthies*, II, 267 (1662)]

Tom Long, A : a sluggard.

Tom, Long : a heavy gun carried on board a man-of-war.

Tom Lony : a simpleton.

Tom Noddy : a foolish person. From noddy, a fool or noodle.

Tom Noodle : an empty-headed creature.

Tom, Old : rum.

Tom Pepper : a liar.

Tom Tailor : a tailor.

Tom Thumb : a diminutive person ; a dwarf. Popularized from the adopted name of Charles Sherwood Stratton (1838–83), an Amer. dwarf ; but in use as early as the 16th cent. [Hazlitt, *Early Popular Poetry*, II, 167 (1866)]

Tom Tiddler's ground : no man's land[*]; esp. land lying between two countries or provinces.

Tom Tiller (Tiler), A : (1) a henpecked husband ; (2) an ordinary man.

Tom Titivil : the devil. So-called in the old Moralities. From 'titivil,' a rogue.

Tom Towly : a simpleton.

Tom Tram : a buffoon.

Tom Tug, A : a waterman, who 'tugs' at the oars.

Tom Tyler : Tom Tiller (*q.v.*).

Tommy ; Tommy Atkins, A : *see* Thomas Atkins.

Tommy Dodd : the odd man in a game. From the refrain of a music hall song (c. 1866).

Tongue in one's cheek, To speak with one's : to speak without sincerity.

Tongue, To hold one's : to keep silent. [King Alfred, *Gregory's Pastorals*, C, xxxviii, 276 (897)]

Tongue run, To let one's : to be talkative. [Vanbrugh and Cibber, *The Provoked Husband*, IV, i (1728)]

Tongue, To wag one's : to be talkative. [Wm. Combe, *Tour of Dr. Syntax*, canto IV (1820)]

Tongues, The Three : the three learned languages—Hebrew, Greek and Latin.

Tonkinois, Le : Jules Ferry (1832–93), Fr. statesman. In allusion to his responsibility for the unpopular Tonkin expedition.

Tonsure, To receive the : to become a priest or monk.

Tontine, A : a system of life-insurance of the nature of a lottery. After its inventor, Lorenzo Tonti (fl. 1653), an It. banker.

Tony Lumpkin, A : a rustic clown. After a character in Oliver Goldsmith, *She Stoops to Conquer* (1773).

Too good to be true : of unexpectedly good news. [Maria Edgeworth, *Castle Rackrent* (1799)]

Too many for .. To be : to be more than a match for .. [Wm. Penn, *Some Fruits of Solitude*, Pt. I, § 343 (1718)]

Too much of a good thing : an excess ; more than can be endured with patience. [Sydney Smith, *Works*, I, 175 (1809)]

Tooley Street tailor, A : a conceited, self-opinionated person. *See* Tailors of Tooley Street.

Tooth and nail : fiercely and vigorously. Orig. with tooth and nail, *i.e.*, biting and scratching. [*Jyl of Brentford Testament* (1550)]

Tooth, To have a sweet : to have a liking for sweetmeats, sugar, etc. [Lyly, *Euphues and His England* (1580)]

Top ropes, A display of the : a pretence of friendliness. The top-rope is that used on board ship in raising and lowering the top-mast.

Top to toe, From : completely. [Ascham, *Toxophilus*, Bk. I (1545)]

Top of the Tree, At the : at the top of one's profession, etc. [Jos. Lunn, *Lofty Projects*, i (1825)]

Tophet : Hell. After a place in the neighbourhood of Jerusalem where there was a perpetual fire for the destruction of the City's refuse.

Topiarian Art, The : the art of cutting trees and shrubs into strange shapes. Grk., *topiarios*, an ornamental gardener.

Top-sawyer, A : a person in a superior position. Properly, the sawyer who works the upper handle of a pit-saw.

Topsy, To grow like : in allusion to a young negro girl in Mrs. Harriet Beecher Stowe, *Uncle Tom's Cabin* (1851), who, not knowing her parentage or origin, expected that she grew like a plant.

Torquemada, A : a persecutor. After Tomas de Torquemada (c. 1420–98), first Inquisitor-General for Castile.

Torrens System, The : a system of conveyance of land. After Sir Robert Rich. Torrens (1814–84), Austral. statesman.

Tory, A : an extreme conservative. The Tory Party grew out of the Cavaliers and their successors, the Abhorrers, and was one of the two principal parties in the State until after the Reform Act of 1832 it became known as the Conservative Party. The name Tory was first applied about the year 1679 as a term of derision. It was derived from the designation of bands of Irish robbers.

Tory Democracy : a term invented by Lord Randolph Churchill (1849–95) to indicate the combination of conservative and democratic principles.

Toto cœlo (*Lat.*, by the whole heavens) : as the poles asunder. [Macrobius, *Satires*, III, xii, 10)]

Touch bottom, To : to reach the lowest point.

Touch and go : a very narrow escape. Metaphor drawn from coaching, when the drivers were fond of driving within hair-breadths of obstacles.

Touch, To keep in : to keep within the possibility of communication with ..

Touch, To keep : to keep faith. [Rob. Wilson, *Three Ladies of London*, II, 1065 (1584)]

Touch, To put to the : to put to the test. [*A Warning for Faire Women*, II, 1553-4 (1599)] An allusion to the touchstone.

Touched, To be : to be mentally deranged to a slight extent. [W. T.

Moncrieff, *The Spectre Bridegroom*, II, i (1821)]

Touchstone of .. The: the criterion of .. Properly, a stone used for testing the quality of an alloy. [Ascham, *The Schoolmaster*, Bk. II (1570)]

Tough yarn, To spin a: to tell an incredible story.

Toujours perdrix (*Fr.*, always partridge): something repeated *ad nauseam*. The traditional origin of the phrase rests with Henri IV of France (1553–1610). His spiritual adviser remonstrated with him on his marital infidelities. The King thereupon enquired his confessor's favourite dish, and learning that it was partridge, gave instructions for him to be supplied with it at every meal. The confessor at the earliest opportunity complained of the lack of change of fare, which he now contemplated with loathing, and the King promptly pointed the moral as it applied to himself.

Tour de force, A (*Fr.*): a masterwork; a feat of strength.

Tour, The Grand: the completion of a young gentleman's education in the early 19th cent., consisting of a journey through Western and Central Europe.

Tout ensemble, The (*Fr.*): the general effect. [Gray, *Letter to Mason*, June, 1757]

Tout le monde (*Fr.*, all the world): everybody.

Tout est perdu fors l'honneur (*Fr.*, everything is lost except honour): the message sent by Francis I of France to his mother after his defeat at Pavia (1525).

Tow on the distaff, To have: to have business to attend to. [Chaucer, *The Miller's Tale* (14th cent.)]

Towering passion, In a: in extreme anger.

Town and gown row, A: a fight between undergraduates and town roughs at Oxford or Cambridge.

Town, A man about: a man who is frequently spending his leisure in public. [Nash, *Works*, II, 283 (1593)]

Town by starving it, To take a: *see* Take.

Toyshop of the world, The: Birmingham. So-called by Edmund Burke. By toys are intended small articles of steel.

Traces, To kick over the: to break loose from restraint. A metaphor drawn from the stableyard.

Track, The beaten: the habitual course. [Francis Junius, *The Painting of the Ancients*, 242 (1638)]

Tracks, To make: to go off rapidly.

Tractarians: *see* Oxford Movement.

Trade, The: tradesmen as a body engaged in a particular trade, esp. the liquor trade.

Tragedy, The Father of: *see* Father.

Tragedy, The Father of French: *see* Father.

Trail one's coat, To: to offer defiance to all and sundry.

Train bands: properly, 'trained bands.' Eng. urban militia in existence from 1604 to 1660.

Tramp steamer, A: a cargo vessel which does not run on any regular route, but plies between any ports at which business offers.

Transpontine (*Lat. trans* across and *pons.* the bridge): melodramatic. In allusion to the melodrama played in the theatres on the Surrey side of the Thames at London.

Traveller on a person, To put the: to tell fables to .. *See* Traveller's tale.

Traveller's license: exaggeration. In allusion to the reputation acquired by travellers.

Traveller's tale, A: an exaggerated acount. In allusion to the reputation for exaggeration acquired by travellers as a class.

Treacle Town: (1) Bristol, a centre of the sugar refining industry; (2) Macclesfield, in allusion to the accidental overturning of a cask of treacle in one of the principal streets of the town and the consequent widespread eating in the streets of bread and treacle.

Tread on air, To: to be lighthearted as if buoyant.

Tread on the tail of one's coat, To: to give gratuitous offence in order to give an opportunity for a fight. A practice attributed to the Irish.

Treasury Bench, The: the seat in Parliament on which the members of the Government sit.

Treaty Ports: ports. esp. in China and other countries where foreign trade is under restrictions, which have been freed by treaty with European powers, to commerce.

Trecentisti, The: the famous men of Italy of the Trecento or 13th cent., *viz.*, Dante, Petrarch and Boccaccio, and to a less extent Giotto, Giovanni da Pisa and Andrea Orcagna.

Tree, Between the bark and the : *see* Bark and the tree.

Tree, To bark up the wrong : to make a mistake.

Tree, At the top of the : *see* Top of the tree.

Tree, Up a : *see* Up a tree.

Tree-geese : barnacles. In allusion to their supposed metamorphosis into geese.

Tregeagle, To roar like : Tregeagle is in mythology a Cornish giant. His roaring is the howling of the wind over the downs.

Trek, The Great : the wholesale migration in 1836 and 1837 of Dutch settlers in Cape Colony northwards and eastwards which led to the formation of Dutch autonomous settlements beyond the Orange River and in Natal.

Trencher friend, A : one whose friendship is dependent on hospitality.

Trencher knight, A : one who shines most at table. [Shakespeare, *Love's Labour Lost*, V, ii (1594)]

Trencher, To lick the : to behave as a parasite. [Withal, *Dictionarie* (1608)]

Trent Incident, The : the forcible arrest in 1861 on board a British steamer, by the captain of an Amer. man-of-war, of two representatives of the Southern States who were on their way to Europe. The incident led to very strained relations between Great Britain and the United States.

Tribune of the People, The : John Bright (1811–89), Eng. radical statesman and orator.

Tribunes, The Last of the : Cola di Rienzi (1313–54), Rom. revolutionist.

Tribute of the dead, To demand : to act foolishly and to no purpose. From an ancient Grk. proverb.

Trice, In a (*Span.*, *tris*, an instant) : in a very short time. [Shakespeare, *King Lear*, I, i (1605–6)]

Tricolour, The : the Fr. national flag, adopted at the Revolution, in three colours—blue, white and red.

Tricoteuse, A (*Fr.*, a woman who knits) : a woman who engages in politics. In allusion to the women who knitted while watching executions during the Fr. revolution.

Trident, To wield the : to be supreme on the sea. After the trident, depicted as the weapon of Neptune, the god of the ocean.

Tried in the balance and found wanting : tested in character. In allusion to the ancient Egyptian belief that souls were weighed after death. *See* Weighed in the balance.

Triennial Act, The : an Act of 1694 limiting the duration of a parliament to three years. Repealed in 1716.

Trilbies : bare feet. After Trilby, a character who went barefooted in George du Maurier's novel of that title (1894).

Trim, In good (bad) : in good (bad) form.

Trimmer, A : a political opportunist who transfers his adherence from one party to the other. The Marquis of Halifax (1633–95) was known as 'The Trimmer.' A nautical metaphor.

Trinity House : a guild established in the reign of Henry VIII for the regulation of British shipping.

Trink-geld (*Germ.*, drink-money) : a tip.

Triple Alliance, The : the Alliance between Germany, Austria and Italy, formed in 1883 and dissolved in 1915. Previous triple alliances were between (1) England, Sweden and Holland against France in 1668 ; (2) England, France and Holland against Sweden in 1717, and (3) Great Britain, Holland and Prussia against Russia in 1789.

Triple Tyrant, The : the Pope. In allusion to his three-tiered crown.

Tripoli, To come from : to be extremely agile and active. In allusion to the tricks of the apes imported from Tripoli, North Africa.

Tripos, The : the final honours examination for the B.A. degree at the University of Cambridge. Properly, the final honours degree in mathematics only. From the three-legged stool on which the Bachelor of Arts used to sit when he disputed with the candidates for the degree.

Tripping, To catch : to detect in error. [*The Spectator*, No. 105 (1711)]

Trismegistus, A young : a young chemist whose achievements give much promise. After Trismegistos (Grk., thrice-greatest), a title of the Egyptian Hermes, the god of the secrets of alchemy.

Triton among minnows, A : one who far outshines or outdistances his associates. After Triton, a Grk. and Rom. god that lived under the sea. [Shakespeare. *Coriolanus*, III, i (1609)]

Triumvirate of Italian Poets, The : Dante, Boccaccio and Petrarch.

Trivet, As right as a : absolutely right. In allusion to the firmness of a trivet standing on its three feet. [Hood, *Dead Robbery* (1835) ; Dickens, *Pickwick Papers* (1836)] Other derivations are from Truefits, the famous London wigmakers, and from Sir Thomas Trivet (d. 1388), Eng. admiral, who escaped when the greater portion of the fleet was wrecked.

Troilus, As true as : after Troilus, the faithful lover, in the *Iliad*, Shakespeare, etc.

Trojan, A : a person who devotes himself to his task. In this sense the word has been used at least since the Elizabethan era.

Trojan horse, A : a gift that brings evil instead of good. In allusion to the wooden horse, by means of which Troy was betrayed, left by the Greeks as a parting gift.

Trojan, A regular : a valiant fighter ; a hero. In allusion to the Trojans who withstood the Greeks for ten years, as narrated by Homer.

Trophonios, To have visited the cave of : to become sad and melancholy. After the cave of Trophonios, one of the most celebrated of the oracles of Greece, from which enquirers invariably returned in a state of terror.

Trouble the waters, To : to disturb the peace ; to stir up trouble. [Rob. Tailor, *The Hog Hath Lost His Pearl*, IV, i (1614) ; Bacon, *Henry VII* (1622)]

Troubled waters, To fish in : *see* Fish.

Trouillogan's advice : advice to which can be given two opposite interpretations. In allusion to the advice given by Trouillogan to Pantragruel in Rabelais, *Gargantua and Pantagruel*.

Troy, New-reared : London. After the early British name, Troy-novant.

Truck Acts, The : the Acts of Parliament of 1831 and 1887 forbidding the payment of wages in kind.

True blue : *see* Blue.

True colours : *see* Colours.

True as fate, As : absolutely reliable. [Thomas Dekker, *The Honest Whore*, Pt. I, iv, 4 (1604)]

True as the needle to the pole, As : in allusion to the magnetic pole and the needle of the compass. [*The Spectator*, No. 596 (1714)]

True as the pole-star to the north, As : absolutely reliable.

True ring, To have the : *see* Ring.

True as steel, As : absolutely trustworthy. [Chaucer, *Troilus and Creseide*, Bk. V (14th cent.) ; *Towneley Plays*, XIII ; *Shepherds Play*, II (1450) ; *Interlude of Youth*, l. 471 (1554)]

True as touch, As : thoroughly reliable. In allusion to the testing of gold by the touchstone. [*Love Me Little, Love Me Long* (1570) ; Spenser, *Faerie Queen*, I, iii, 2 (1590)]

True as a turtle-dove, As : in allusion to the proverbial conjugal affection and faithfulness of doves. [Spenser, *Faerie Queen*, III, xi, 2 (1590)]

Trump card, To play one's : to take a step calculated to settle finally a matter in one's own favour. A cardplaying metaphor.

Trumps, To be put to one's : to be driven to the last push. Cardplaying metaphor. [Lyly, *Endimion*, III, iv (1584)]

Trumps, To turn up : to be successful, half unexpectedly. A cardplaying metaphor. [Sir Thos. Overbury, *Newes from Court* (1616)]

Trumpet one's own deeds, To : to advertise one's own virtues. After the practice of the Pharisaic sect of the Almsgivers of having a trumpet sounded before them in the streets in in order to summon the poor.

Trumpet, To sound (blow) one's own : to sing one's own praises. After the practice of heralds of announcing by means of flourishes of trumpets. [Anth. Brewer, *Lingua*, IV, i (1607)]

Trumpet before victory, To sound the : *see* Sound.

Trumpeter is dead, Your : a suggestion that one is boasting, that since no one else is available one must oneself advertise one's virtues.

Trumpington, To be born in : to be a fool. [*Interlude of Youth*, 498–9 (1554)]

Tu quoque, A (*Lat.*, you also) : a countercharge, similar in character to the original charge. The phrase formed the title and also a frequent refrain in a comedy by John Cooke (1614).

Tu quoque argument, A : *see* Tu quoque.

Tub, A tale of a : an incredible story. Popularised from the name of a satire by Jonathan Swift (1704). [Bale, *Com. Concerning Three Laws* (1538)]

Tub to the whale, To throw a : to create a diversion. A whaling metaphor. [Susan Ferrier, *Inheritance*, ch. 52 (1824)]

Tuck, Friar : a vagabond monk who appears in Eng. medieval folklore.

Tuckshop, A : a shop where confectionery, etc., is sold to school-boys.

Tuft-hunter, A : a toady. From the Oxford term, tuft, denoting a nobleman-undergraduate. In allusion to the gold tufts or tassels they used to wear.

Tug of war, A : a decisive contest for supremacy.

Tulcan Bishops : Scottish bishops appointed by James I on the understanding that they would surrender to him a portion of their revenues. From tulcan, a stuffed calfskin used to encourage a cow to yield her milk.

Tune, To change one's : to change one's attitude to a matter under consideration. [Dekker and Webster, *Northward Ho*, II, i (1607)]

Tune the old cow died of, The : advice instead of relief. After a passage in an early ballad, *Jack Whaley had a Cow*.

Turf, The : the sport of horse-racing.

Turf, The Blue Ribbon of the : see Blue.

Turk, Not to have rounded Cape : still to regard women from the oriental point of view.

Turk, To turn : to change for the worse. Formerly to become a renegade. [Dekker, *The Seuen Deadly Sinnes : Politick Bankruptisme* (1606)]

Turk, A Young : a member of the Turkish Reform Party which effected the Revolution of 1909.

Turn one's coat, To : see Coat.

Turn, A good : a favour. [Heywood, *Proverbes* (1546) ; *Paston Letters*, No. 490 (1464)]

Turn in one's grave, To cause to : to reverse the policy of one who is dead or to take such other action as would, if he had been still alive, have caused him much annoyance.

Turn a person's head, To : to infatuate.

Turn over a new leaf, To : see Leaf.

Turn, To serve a person's : to be useful on an occasion and then probably be discarded. [*Damon and Pithias*, l. 28 (1567)]

Turn the tables on .. To : see Tables.

Turn of the tide, The : a change in one's fortunes.

Turnbull Street rogue, A : in allusion to the frequenters of Turnmill (Turnbull) Street, Clerkenwell, London.

Turncoat, A : a renegade ; one who changes his party. Said to have been first applied to an early duke of Savoy whose dominions marched with those of both France and Spain. His policy was always to be friendly with the stronger of these two rival powers. The balance between these two was, however, continually changing and the Duke had, therefore, a coat made blue (the Span. colour) on one side and white (Fr.) on the other, which he wore either side outwards as the necessity arose. [Burton, *Anatomy of Melancholy :* To the Reader (1621)]

Turpentine State, The : North Carolina. On account of its large production of turpentine.

Turpin, A Dick : a highwayman. After a notorious highwayman who was executed in 1739.

Turtle, To turn : to capsize ; to turn over.

Tweed comes to Melrose, As the : in a roundabout manner. In allusion to the twisting of the River Tweed before it reaches Melrose.

Tweedledum and Tweedledee : two parties or causes the difference between which is very slight. [John Byrom, *On the Feuds between Handel and Bononcini* (1730)]

Twelfth, The : the 12th of August, the day on which grouse shooting commences in England.

Twelfth Night : the Festival of Epiphany; the eve of the twelfth day after Christmas, and the conclusion of the medieval Christmas festivities.

Twelve Tables, The : the codification of the Rom. Laws of 451 and 450 B.C.

Twice-told tale, A : a story that is already familiar.

Twickenham Bard, The : Alexander Pope (1688–1744), who lived at Twickenham.

Twin relics of barbarism : slavery and polygamy. So-called by Charles Sumner (1811–74) in a speech before the United States Senate.

Twins, The Sacred : Romulus and Remus, the reputed founders of Rome.

Twinkling of an eye, In the : in the passing of an infinitesimal period of time. [Jno. Heywood, *The Four P.P.*, ll. 723–5 (1540)]

Twist round one's finger, To : to influence and control with extreme ease.

Twist the lion's tail, To : see Lion's tail.

Two masters, To serve : to endeavour to satisfy two opposing demands simultaneously. [*Matthew*, vi, 24]

Two minds, To be of : to be undecided in opinion.

Two strings to one's bow, To have : *see* Strings.

Two and two together, To put : to deduce from the evidence.

Two-edged sword, A : an argument or instrument capable of harming as well as of benefitting the user. [*Proverbs,* v, 4]

Two-legged mare, The : the gallows.

Twopenny damn, Not worth a : of practically no value. In allusion to an Indian coin, a dam, which much depreciated in value.

Tyburn Cross, To preach at : to be hanged. In allusion to the gallows, formerly erected at Tyburn, near London. [Geo. Gascoigne, *The Steel Glass* (1576)]

Tyburn face, A : a criminal appearance. After Tyburn, near London, the former place of execution.

Tyburn jig, To dance the : *see* Dance.

Tyburn tippet, A : a halter. After Tyburn, the place of execution near London.

Tyburn tree : the gallows.

Tyrtæus, The Spanish : Manuel José Quintana (1772–1857). After Tyrtæus (7th cent. B.C.) who wrote war songs for the Spartans.

U.P, It's all : the game is lost. It's all up. [Dickens, *Oliver Twist,* ch. 24 (1837)]

Ugly affair, An : an unpleasant business.

Ugly customer, An : a person intercourse with whom is to be avoided ; one liable to have recourse to physical force or other crime.

Ugly as the devil, As : extremely ugly. [Fielding, *Tom Thumb,* II, 7 (1730)]

Ulster, The Red Hand of : a portion of the arms of Ulster ; said to have been derived from the exploit of O'Neile who, vowing on the occasion of the invasion that he would be the first to land, found his boat outstripped and, in order to fulfil his vow, cut off his hand and threw it ashore.

Ultima Ratio Regum (*Lat.,* the last argument of kings.) : a motto which Louis XIV of France had inscribed on his cannon.

Ultima Thule (*Lat.,* furthest Thule) : the most remote district of the world. Thule was the most northerly land known to the Romans. [Pliny, 4, 16, 30, § 104]

Ultimum vale (*Lat.,* the last farewell) : a finishing stroke.

Ultimus Romanorum (*Lat.,* the last of the Romans) : (1) Horace Walpole (1717–97), Earl of Orford, politician and man of letters ; (2) Samuel Johnson (1709–84), so-called by Thos. Carlyle. [*Heroes,* V (1841)]

Ultra vires (*Lat.,* beyond the power) : in excess of one's legitimate rights.

Ultramontane, An : a member of a Continental, esp. Germ., political party which supports the temporal claims of the Pope. Lat., *ultra,* beyond, *montes,* the mountains, *i.e.,* the Alps, *i.e.,* from Italy or Rome.

Ulysses' bow : the bow which Ulysses alone could bend and with which he shot the suitors who had been pestering his wife Penelope during his absence at and subsequent to the Siege of Troy.

Ulysses of the Highlands, The : Sir Evan Cameron, Lord of Lochiel (d. 1719). After the hero of Homer's *Iliad.*

Umbrage, To take : to take offence. Lat., *umbra,* a shade, *i.e.,* a gloomy view. [Jas. Puckle, *The Club : Buffoon* (1711)]

Umbrella, Under a person's : under a person's influence or control. In allusion to the umbrella of state carried over certain African potentates.

Uncial letters : letters an inch high, in use from the 5th to the 9th cents. Lat., *uncia,* an inch.

Unclasp the purple leaves of war, To : to proclaim war. [Thos. Kyd, *Jeronimo,* Pt. I, ll. 435–6 (1591)]

Uncle, An : a pawnbroker. Lat., *uncus,* a hook, on which pledges used to be hung. [Dekker, *Northward Ho,* I, ii (1607)]

Uncle over, To come the : to exceed one's privilege of reproving or punishing. Among the Romans an uncle, when left the guardian of his nephews, proverbially showed himself exceedingly strict and severe.

Uncle Sam : a popular name for the United States Government. The initial letters of both are identical. It has also been attributed to the popular name of Samuel Wilson (1770–1854), a government inspector whose duty it was to pass supplies during the war of 1812, and who was accustomed to mark those he had passed ' U.S.' (Uncle Sam.).

Uncle Sam's heel : Florida. In allusion both to its shape and to its geographical position in the U.S.

Uncle Sam's icebox : Alaska, in U.S. territory.

Unco guid (*Scot.*) : extremely good ; religious.

Uncrowned King, The : Charles Stewart Parnell (1846–91), the leader of the Irish Nationalist Party. So-called by Wm. Edw. Forster in a speech in the House of Commons (Feb. 22, 1883).

Under which King Bezonian ? : make your choice of two alternatives. *See* Bezonian.

Under-dog, To be : to be the weaker of two parties. From *The Under Dog in the Fight*, a song by David Barker (1876)]

Underground Railway, The : an organisation for the secret conveyance of fugitive slaves into Canada from the U.S. before the abolition of slavery.

Underground Russia : Nihilistic Russia.

Undiscovered country from whose bourn no traveller returns, The : death. [Shakespeare, *Hamlet*, II, ii (1602–3)]

Unearned increment: increase in the value of property due to no action on the part of the owner, but to public improvements in the neighbourhood or other extraneous cause.

Unguem, Ad (*Lat.*, to the nail) : exactly.

Unigenitus, The : the papal bull of 1713 directed against Jansenism, the first word of which is *unigenitus*.

Union Jack, The : the national flag of the United Kingdom. Properly, a small form of it used as a Jack. The union is that of the crosses of St. George, St. Andrew and St. Patrick.

Unionist, A : a member of the Brit. political party formed in 1886 of a union of Conservatives and secessionist Liberals, to oppose the grant of Home Rule to Ireland.

United Brotherhood, The : *see* Clan-na-Gael.

United Irishmen, The : an Irish political body consisting of Irish Catholics and Protestants united in opposition to the Brit. Government, formed in 1789.

United Provinces, The : the seven provinces of Holland, Zeeland, Utrecht, Friesland, Groningen, Gelderland and Oberyssel, which were combined in 1579 to form the Netherlands.

Universal Doctor, The : (1) Thomas Aquinas (c. 1226–74), Ital. scholastic

philosopher ; (2) Alain de Lille (c. 1128–1203), philosopher and poet.

Unknown, The Great : Sir Walter Scott (1771–1832), as the anonymous author of the Waverley novels. So-called by James Ballantyne, the printer.

Unlearned Parliament, The : *see* Parliament of Dunces.

Unlicked Cub, An : *see* Cub.

Unmerciful Parliament, The : *see* Parliament.

Unparliamentary language : language not permissible in parliamentary debate or interjection.

Unser Fritz : *see* Fritz.

Unspeakable Turk, The : an epithet first applied to the Turkish Government by Thos. Carlyle, in a letter read at a meeting in the St. James's Hall, London, in 1876.

Unstable as water, As : [*Genesis*, xlix, 4]

Unwashed, The Great : the common people. So-called first by Edmund Burke.

Unwritten Law, The : punishment, generally the murder, of an offender by one who has suffered from his offence, generally in a case of seduction.

Up and doing, To be : to be active. [Bunyan, *Pilgrim's Progress*, Pt. 2 (1684)]

Up to snuff : wideawake ; not easily deceived.

Up the spout : in pawn ; in a hopeless condition.

Up train, An : a train proceeding towards the railway headquarters. *See* Go up, To.

Up a tree : in a difficulty ; like an opossum up a gum tree with the hunter waiting below.

Up with .. To be all : the last chance to have been lost by ..

Ups and downs : alternating prosperity and adversity.

Upas tree, A : anything baneful. Properly a poison tree, native to Macassar.

Upper Circles, The : the higher ranks of society.

Upper hand, To gain the : to gain control over .. [Thos. Preston, *King Cambyses*, ll. 191–2 (1561)]

Upper House, The : the House of Lords. As distinguished from the Lower House or House of Commons.

Upper Ten (Thousand), The : the wealthiest and most influential class in the country ; nominally estimated at 10,000 souls. So designated by

Nathaniel Parker Willis (1806–67), Amer. poet and writer.

Uppertendom : the aristocracy. *See* Upper Ten.

Upset the apple-cart, To : *see* Apple-cart.

Upset price, An : the minimum price fixed for an auction sale.

Urbi et Orbi (*Lat.*, to the city and the world) : (1) of an announcement intended to be as public as possible ; (2) the formula relating to the papal blessing uttered from the balcony of the Church of St. John Lateran.

Uriah Heep, An : a hypocritical schemer. After a character in Dickens, *David Copperfield* (1849).

Useless Parliament, The : *see* Parliament, Useless.

Utas of a feast, The : any day not more than eight days after a feast. Fr., *huit*, eight. [*Paston Letters*, No. 482 (1464)]

Uti possidetis (*Lat.*, as you possess) : a diplomatic term, used in treaties to signify the retention of territory then in the possession of the parties.

Utopia, An (*Grk.*, nowhere) : an ideal land of perfection. After the title of a work (1516) by Sir Thomas More (1478–1535).

Utopian : ideal and impracticable. *See* Utopia.

Vade mecum, A (*Lat.*, go with me) : a handy guide-book or other work of reference. [*A Manual or a Justice of the Peace, His Vade Mecum* (1642)]

Væ victis ! (*Lat.*, woe to the conquered) : a remark of Brennus, the Gaulish conqueror of Rome (fl. 390 B.C.). He consented to evacuate the city on payment of a thousand talents. The Rom. representatives complained that his weights were false whereupon he threw his sword into the scale, exclaiming, 'Væ victis !'

Valentine's Day, St. : *see* Saint Valentine's Day.

Valhalla, A : a pantheon ; a place where a nation's most illustrious dead are buried. In Scand. mythology, the place where Odin entertained the spirits of the illustrious dead.

Valkyrie, A : a nymph of Valhalla, who, attending the army in battle, selected the heroes intended for death and conducted them to Valhalla. (Scand. mythology).

Valley of the Shadow of Death, The : a very serious illness or other state in which the risk of death is considerable. From a locality described in Bunyan's *Pilgrim's Progress* (1678). [*Psalm*, xxiii, 4]

Vandal, A : one who has no consideration for the claims of art or literature. After the Vandals, a rude, barbaric northern race who overran the Rom. empire in the 5th cent. and ruthlessly destroyed, heedless of the claims of art.

Vandalism, A : an action, worthy of a vandal (*q.v.*).

Vanderbilt, A : a very wealthy man. In allusion to the proverbial wealth of the Vanderbilt family of the U.S.

Vandyck, The English : William Dobson (1610–47). After Sir Anthony van Dyck (1599–1641), a great Flemish-English portrait painter.

Vandyck of France, The : Hyacinth Rigaud y Ros (1659–1743).

Vandyck of Sculpture, The : Antoine Coysevox (1640–1720).

Vanity Fair : the world and its worldliness. After a fair described in Bunyan, *Pilgrim's Progress* (1678).

Vantage loaf, The : the thirteenth loaf of a baker's dozen.

Variorum ; Variorum Edition : an edition of a classical work that contains the notes and comments of more than one editor. Lat., *editio cum notis variorum*, an edition with the notes of different (authorities).

Vatican, The : the papal authority. After the palace of the popes which stands on the Vatican hill at Rome.

Vaticanism : the doctrine of absolute papal supremacy. After the Vatican Council of 1869–70 which proclaimed that doctrine.

Vauban, A : a distinguished military engineer. After Sébastien le Prestre de Vauban (1633–1707).

Vaudeville : light opera or musical comedy. Orig. songs of a light and lively character. After Vau-de-Vire in Normandy where Olivier Basselin (c. 1400–50), composed such songs.

Vaudeville, The Father of : Olivier Basselin (c. 1400–50), of Vau-de-Vire Normandy.

Vaugirard, The Deputies of : a one-man company. In allusion to an incident of the reign of Charles VIII of France when a solitary individual was announced, to increase his importance, as 'The Deputies of Vaugirard.'

Vehmgericht, A : one of several secret tribunals which flourished in South Germany in the 14th and 15th cents.

Velvet, To be on : so to arrange one's bets as to render loss impossible.

Venereal disease : after Venus, the goddess of love.

Venetian Addison, The : Gaspare Gozzi (1713–86). On account of the modelling of his writings on the essays in *The Spectator*, of which Joseph Addison (1672–1719) was the author.

Veni, vidi, vici (*Lat.*, I came, I saw, I conquered) : report of Julius Cæsar after his victory at Zela over Pharnaces, King of Pontus (47 B.C.).

Venice of the East, The : Bangkok.

Venice of the North, The : (1) Stockholm ; (2) Amsterdam.

Venice of the West, The : Glasgow.

Ventre à terre (*Fr.*, belly to the ground) : at full gallop.

Venus, A : a beautiful woman. After the goddess of beauty and love.

Venus' lap : the sea. In allusion to the Grk. goddess, Aphrodite (with whom the Rom. goddess, Venus, was identified) who, according to legend, rose out of the sea.

Verb. sap. ; Verbum sap. (*Lat.*, *verbum sapienti sat est*, a word to the wise is sufficient) : the expression of a hint.

Verba, Ipsissima : *see* Ipsissma.

Verbatim et literatim (*Lat.*, word for word and letter for letter) : exactly.

Verdant Green, A : a simpleton ; an easily deceived young man. After a character in Cuthbert Bede's novel of that name (1853).

Vere de Vere, Caste of : the stamp of aristocracy. [Tennyson, *Lady Clara Vere de Vere* (1842)]

Veronese Vespers : a rising in 1797 of the Veronese against the Fr. army of occupation in which a number of Fr. wounded were massacred.

Vers de Société (*Fr.*, Society verses) : social or familiar poetry. First introduced into English at the beginning of the 19th cent.

Versailles, The German : Cassel. On account of its gardens, fountains, etc.

Versi Berneschi : humorous verses. After Franceso Berni (1490–1536), the Ital. poet.

Vesta, A : a wax lucifer match. After the sacred fire which was kept alight by the Vestal virgins.

Vestal : chaste. In allusion to the Vestal virgins who served in the temple of the Rom. virgin goddess of the hearth, Vesta.

Vestal Virgin, A : *see* Vestal.

Veto, Monsieur et Madame : *see* Monsieur Veto *and* Madame Veto.

Vexed Question, A : a much debated question. [Heylin, *Ecclesia Vindicata*, 215 (1657)]

Vi et armis (*Lat.*) : by force and arms.

Via Dolorosa, A (*Lat.*, grievous way) : a painful course. After the name given by the Christians to the road from the Mount of Olives to the place of the Crucifixion.

Vicar of Bray, A : a turncoat. Symon Symonds is said to have been twice a Rom. Catholic and twice a Protestant in the successive reigns of Henry VIII, Edward VI, Mary and Elizabeth. When charged with being a turncoat he replied that he stuck to his principles, to die Vicar of Bray.

Vicar of Christ, The : a title of the Pope. Lit., one who acts for Christ.

Vice versa (*Lat.*, in a turned position) : in the opposite manner. [A. Copley, *Answer to a Letter of a Jesuited Gentleman* (1601)]

Vicious circle, A : a difficulty, the solution of which creates a second difficulty to meet which the original difficulty has to be increased.

Victorians, The Great : the famous men of letters, statesmen, scientists, etc., of the Victorian era.

Vieux Renard (*Fr.*, old fox) : Nicholas Jean Soult (1769–1851), Marshal of France. The name given to him by his soldiers.

Vigilance Committee, A : a self-appointed committee, nominally intended to uphold the law and preserve order, but given in practice to the exercise of Lynch Law (*q.v.*) and other atrocities. Originated in California at the time of the Gold rush.

Villadom : (1) the Middle class ; (2) the suburbs and their inhabitants. From the villas of which so much of the suburbs is composed.

Villages, To come home by the : to be drunk. A provincial expression. If, on the other hand, one comes home by the fields one has no opportunity for drinking.

Ville Lumière, La (*Fr.*, the light-city ; the city of lights) : Paris.

Vincent's law : cheating at cards.

Vine and fig-tree, Under his : in a comfortable home. [I *Kings*, iv, 25]

AA

Vino veritas, In (*Lat.*, in wine there is truth) : the suggestion that a man when drunk will tell the truth. [Pliny, *Natural History*, XIV, 141 ; Mrs. Piozzi, *Anecdotes of Samuel Johnson* (1786)]

Violet, Corporal : see Corporal.

Virgil, The Christian : (1) Marco Girolamo Vida (1490–1566), Ital. prelate, scholar and Lat. poet ; (2) Giacomo Sannazaro (1458–1530). After Virgil (70–19 B.C.), the great Rom. poet.

Virgil, The English : Alfred, Lord Tennyson (1809–92).

Virgil and Horace of the Christians, The : Aurelius Clemens Prudentius (c. 348–c. 410), Span. Lat. poet. So-called by Bentley.

Virgil of Dramatic Poets, The : Ben Jonson (1574–1637). So-called by Dryden.

Virgil of the French Drama, The : Jean Racine (1639–99). So-called by Sir Walter Scott.

Virgil of Prose, The : Robert Louis Stevenson (1850–94).

Virgin City ; Virgin Fortress, A : one that has never been captured by an enemy.

Virgin Mary's Bodyguard : the Scottish Guard of France (1448–1830), as whose Colonel, Louis XI gave them the Virgin Mary.

Virgin Queen, The : Elizabeth (1558–1603), Queen of England.

Virginia fence, As crooked as a : uneven. Fences in Virginia are said to zigzag with the soil.

Virginia fence, To make a : to walk unevenly.

Virginibus puerisque (*Lat.*, for girls and boys) : that which need not be concealed from children.

Virtue of a necessity, To make a : to do apparently of one's own free will that which one cannot avoid doing. [Jerome, *Adversus Rub.*, III, 2 ; Chaucer, *Troylus*, IV, 1586 (14th cent.)]

Virtues, The Seven : faith, hope, charity, prudence, justice, fortitude, temperance.

Vitellius, A : a glutton. After Vitellius (15–69), Rom. emperor.

Vitruvius, The English : Inigo Jones (1572–1652). After Marcus Vitruvius Pollio (fl. 15 B.C.), a great Rom. architect and engineer.

Vitus's dance, St. : see St. Vitus.

Viva voce (*Med. Lat.*, with the living voice) : orally. [W. Clarke (1581)]

Vogue la galère (*Fr.*, the galley row out) : go on whatever the result !

Voice in .. To have a : to have some influence in .. [*Rolls of Parliament*, IV, 479 (1433)]

Vole, To go the : to run great risks to win a prize. A cardplaying metaphor. [Scott, *Antiquary*, IV (1816)]

Volée, A la (*Fr.*) : at random.

Voltaire, The German : (1) Johann Wolfgang von Goethe (1749–1838) ; (2) Christoph Martin Wieland (1733–1813). After Voltaire (1694–1778), Fr. philosopher, historian and man of letters.

Voltaire, The Polish : Ignatius Krasicki (1774–1801).

Voltaire, The Russian : Alexander Sumorokow (1727–77).

Volte face, A (*Ital.*, *volta faccia*, turn face) : a reversal of policy or conduct.

Volume, The Christian : the New Testament. [Burns, *Cotter's Saturday Night*, XV (1785)]

Volume, The sacred : the Bible.

Volumes, To speak : of the eyes, to suggest most significantly. [Shelley, *Zastrozzi* IV (1810)]

Voodooism : a system of superstition prevalent among the negroes of North America and the West Indies. Probably corruption of Fr., *Vaudois*, Waldensian, a generic name for heretics.

Voortrekkers : the Boers who took part in the Great Trek of 1836–7.

Vox populi (*Lat.*, the voice of the people) : public opinion ; rumour. A contraction of the Lat. maxim, ' Vox populi, vox Dei.' [Skelton, *Works* (1550)]

Vox populi vox Dei (*Lat.*, the voice of the people is the voice of God) : a suggestion that the people united or in a majority is always right. The phrase was used as the text by Simon Mepham, Archbp. of Canterbury, of a sermon preached on the occasion of the coronation of Edward III (1327). [William of Malmesbury, *De Gestis Pontificum* (12th cent.)]

Vox et praeterea nihil (*Lat.*, a voice and nothing else) : sound or words and nothing else. [Plutarch, *Apothegmata* ; Burton, *Anatomy of Melancholy* : To the Reader (1621)]

Vulcan, A : (1) a blacksmith ; (2) a lame person. After Vulcan, the god of fire and metal-working, who was lame.

Vulgate, The : Jerome's Lat. version of the Bible. Orig. any early Lat. or

Grk. version of the Bible. Lat.,
Editio vulgata, a published edition or
one made available to the common
people.

Wages of sin, The : death. [*Romans*,
vi, 23]

Waggon Boy, The : Thomas Corwin
(1794–1865), Amer. statesman and
orator, who as a lad conveyed a
waggon-load of provisions to General
W. H. Harrison, at the time engaged
in hostilities with the Indians.

Waggon to a star, To hitch one's : to
attach oneself to a lofty ideal.
[Emerson, *Civilization* (1870)]

Waggoner, A : a book of sea-charts.
After the Baron von Waegenaar's
Speculum Nauticum.

Waldenses ; Waldensians : German
religious reformers. After their
founder, Pierre Waldo of Lyons
(d. 1179).

Walhalla : *see* Valhalla.

Walk the chalk, To : to behave properly
and soberly. Orig. Amer., to walk
along a chalked line in order to prove
one's sobriety.

Walk one's chalks, To : to decamp.

Walk the hospitals, To : to study the
practice of medicine or surgery in a
hospital.

Walk Spanish, To : *see* Spanish.

Walk-over, A : success in a contest in
which the rivalry is merely nominal ;
as in a horse-race that can be won by
walking.

Walker's bus, To go by : to walk. A pun.

Walking delegate, A : a trade union
official whose function it is to inspect
the conditions of work, etc., in
different factories.

Walking encyclopaedia, A : a person who
possesses accurate knowledge on many
subjects.

Walking gentleman, A : an actor whose
principal function is to look the part
of a gentleman or nobleman.

Walking part, A : a subordinate part in
a play that needs little beyond presence
on the scene.

Wall between, To have but a : to be
divided only by a small shade of
difference.

Wall, To drive to the : to force into a
desperate position. [Heywood, *Proverbes* (1546)]

Wall, To go to the : to be pushed aside.
[*Mucedorus*, 1045–8 (1598)]

Wall Street : the Amer. money market.
From the name of the street in New
York in which the principal financial
houses in the U.S. are situated.

Wall of .. To take the : to take
preference of .. In allusion to the
time when gutters ran down the middle
of the streets, and the nearer to the
wall, the less the chance of being
splashed. [Shakespeare, *Romeo and
Juliet*, I, i (1591–3)]

Wall to .. To give the : [*Thersites*,
150–1 (1537)] *See* previous entry.

Wall, To have the : [Lyly, *Endimion*,
V, ii (1591). *See* previous entry.

Walls, Within four : in a room.

Walls of a nation, The : (1) soldiers ;
(2) the sea. The phrase appears in
both senses in Burton, *Anatomy of
Melancholy* : To the Reader (1621).

Walls, Wooden : *see* Wooden.

Wallah, Competition : *see* Competition
Wallah.

Wallflowers : ladies at dances who fail
to secure partners and are consequently constrained to sit against the
wall.

Wallop, To : to thrash. After Sir John
Wallop (c. 1490–1551), who thoroughly
defeated the Fr. fleet in 1514.

Walpurgis Night : the witches' Sabbath ;
the night of the 30th of April immediately preceding St. Walpurgis' Day.

Waltham's calf, As wise as : utterly
foolish. In allusion to the supposed
story of the calf that ran nine miles
to be suckled by a bull. [Skelton,
Colyn Clout, 811 (1520)]

Walton, An Isaac : a person devoted to
angling. After the author of *The
Compleat Angler* (1593–1683).

Wandering Jew, The : the legendary
person who struck or insulted Christ
when on his way to execution and was
condemned by the victim ' Thou shalt
wander on the earth till I return.'

Wanion, With a (*Saxon, wanung,*
detriment) : with a vengeance. [Lati-
mer, *Sermons* (1549)]

Warhorse, An old : a veteran.

War to the knife : hostility without
cessation or moderation. ' War even
to the knife ' was the response of
Palafox, the Governor of Saragossa,
when summoned by the French to
surrender in 1808.

**War is over, To bring one's machines
after the :** *see* Bring.

War against war, The : the European War of 1914–18, justified by some as a war that would render all future wars impossible.

Wars of the Roses, The : *see* Roses.

Wardour Street English : pseudo-archaic English. After Wardour Street, London, where imitation antiquities are purchaseable.

War-paint : full dress. In allusion to the paintings with which Amer.-Indians used to adorn their faces when about to depart for war.

Warm reception, A : (1) a hostile reception ; (2) a hearty welcome.

Warming pan, A : one who holds an office temporarily until another is ready to occupy it.

Warming-pans, The : the Jacobites. So-called from the belief that the Old Pretender was not the child of James II and Marie d'Este, but had been brought to the palace in a warming pan.

Warrior Queen, The : Boadicea, Queen of the Iceni.

Wash the crow, To : to act foolishly and to no purpose. From an ancient Grk. proverb.

Wash one's dirty linen in public, To : to quarrel in public over domestic disputes ; to publish in the course of a quarrel, that of which one should be ashamed.

Wash an Ethiop white, To : *see* Wash the Ethiopian.

Wash the Ethiopian, To : to act foolishly and uselessly. From an ancient Grk. proverb.

Wash one's hands of .. To : to refuse all responsibility for or interest in .. In allusion to *Matthew*, xxvii, 24, 'When Pilate saw that he could prevail nothing. . . he took water and washed his hands before the multitude, saying, I am innocent of the blood of this just person.' [Chapman, *Blinde Beggar of Alexandria* (1578)]

Wash one's sheep with scalding water, To : to act foolishly and to no purpose. From an ancient Grk. proverb.

Washington, Bird of : *see* Bird.

Washington of Colombia, The : Simon Bolivar (1785–1831). After George Washington (1732–99), the leader of the Amer. Revolution.

Washington, The Second : *see* Second.

Wasp's nest, A : a place on entering into which one obtains a hot reception.

Water capital (stock), To : to increase the number of shares in a company and its nominal capital, without increasing the wealth or real capital of the company.

Water on .. To throw cold : to criticize adversely or otherwise to dissuade against ..

Water, Court Holy : promises without performance.

Water, In deep : *see* Waters, In deep.

Water of Dirce, As cold as the : in allusion to the spring near Thebes into which, according to Grk. legend, the murdered body of Dirce, the wife of Lycus, was thrown by her step-sons.

Water off a duck's back, To run like : of an argument, etc., to leave a person quite unaffected.

Water, Of the first : *see* Diamond.

Water, To keep one's head above : to keep solvent. A swimming metaphor.

Water, Not to hold : of an argument or statement, to be unable to survive criticism. [Mabbe, *Guzman*, II, 79 (1623) ; *Look About You*, I, 20 (1600)]

Water, In hot : in trouble.

Water on one's mill, To be : to be a source of good fortune. [Weldon, *Court of King James* (1650)]

Water, To make one's mouth : to arouse a feeling of envy. [Peter Martyr (1555)]

Water of Nonacris, As cold as the : the waterfall near Nonacris in Arcadia has been suggested as the original of the River Styx, which in Grk. mythology flowed around the abode of the dead.

Water Poet, The : John Taylor (1580–1654), who was a Thames waterman.

Water in the sea, To seek : *see* Seek.

Water, To wash one's sheep with scalding: *see* Wash.

Water in a sieve, To carry : *see* Draw water.

Water with a sieve, To draw : *see* Draw.

Water in the Thames, To cast : *see* Thames.

Water, To write in : to make an ephemeral record. [Sophocles, *Fragments*, 694 (742 N) ; Shakespeare, *Henry VIII*, IV, i (1612–3)]

Waters, In deep : in difficulties. A swimming metaphor.

Waters, The Father of : *see* Father.

Waters, To fish in troubled : *see* Fish.

Water-fox, The : the carp. [Walton, *The Compleat Angler*, ch. 17 (1653)]

Waterloo, A : (1) a final and decisive victory. In allusion to the final defeat of Napoleon by Wellington at the

Battle of Waterloo in 1815; (2) a final defeat.

Water-sheep, The : the roach. [Walton, *The Compleat Angler* (1653)]

Waves, To number the : *see* Number.

Wax in the ears, To have : to be densely stupid. [Shakespeare, *Troilus and Cressida*, V, i, 5 (1609)]

Wax fat and kick, To : to prosper and become heedless of one's responsibilities. [*Deut.*, xxxii, 15]

Wax in the hands of .. To be : to be easily influenced or controlled by ..

Way in the world, To make one's : *see* Make.

Weak as water, As : [Ascham, *Toxophilus*, Pt. I, A (1545)]

Weaker sex, The : woman. [Tacitus, *Annals*, Bk. III, 34]

Weaker vessel, The : woman ; a wife. [I *Peter*, iii, 7]

Weakest goes to the wall, The : in allusion to the time when there were no pavements to the streets and gutters ran along both sides close to the walls. [Shakespeare, *Romeo and Juliet*, I, i, 17–22 (1592)]

Wealth of Ormuz and of Ind : Hormuz was a city on the Persian Gulf, famous as late as the 16th cent. for its wealth. Ind is a poetic form of India. [Milton, *Paradise Lost*, Bk. II, 2 (1657)]

Wear one's heart on one's sleeve, To : to expose one's feelings to the public. In allusion to the former practice of wearing a lady's favour on one's sleeve.

Wear, The worse for : worn out, or almost so.

Wear the yellow, To : to be jealous. [*Look About You*, I, xxviii (1600)]

Weasel asleep, To catch a : to catch a sharp person napping.

Weather eye open, To keep a : to keep a sharp look out. A sailor looks in the direction from which the wind comes in order to foresee the weather.

Weather a storm, To : to pass successfully through a crisis.

Weathercock, A : a person of changeable mind or disposition. [Chaucer, *Balade Agaynst Women Unconstaunt* (14th cent.)]

Weather-gage of a person, To get the : to obtain advantage over a person. A nautical metaphor.

Weaver's beef of Colchester : sprats. In allusion to their prevalence at Colchester.

Web of life, The : man's destiny. In allusion to the web woven by the Fates, according to mythology.

Web by the thread, To know the : to judge the whole by the part.

Wedding, The China : the twentieth anniversary of a wedding.

Wedding, The Crystal : the fifteenth anniversary of a wedding.

Wedding, The Diamond : the sixtieth anniversary of a wedding.

Wedding, The Golden : the fiftieth anniversary of a wedding.

Wedding, The Silver : the twenty-fifth anniversary of a wedding.

Wedding, The Tin : the tenth anniversary of a wedding.

Wedding, The Wooden : the fifth anniversary of a wedding.

Wedge, The thin end of the : an apparently unimportant beginning that may lead to very important consequences.

Weed, The (Divine) : tobacco. [Dekker, *The Gull's Hornbook*, ch. 4 (1609)]

Weed of Worcester, The : the elm, which is very plentiful in Worcestershire.

Weeds, A widow's : the costume worn by a widow. Ang.-Sax., *woed*, a garment.

Weeping Cross, To come home by : to repent of an undertaking. There were three places called Weeping Cross—between Oxford and Banbury, near Stafford, and near Shrewsbury—apparently from crosses erected for the devotions of penitents. [Lyly, *Euphues and His England* (1580) ; Gosson, *Schoole of Abuse* (1579)]

Weeping Philosopher, The : Heraclitus of Ephesus (c. 540–475 B.C.)

Weeping Saint, The : St. Swithin. In allusion to the tradition that if it rains on his day (July 15) it will rain for forty days thereafter.

Weigh one's words, To : to speak deliberately.

Weighed in the balance and found wanting, To be : to be tested and found to fail. [*Daniel*, v, 27] *See* Tried in the balance.

Weight, To carry : to have influence.

Weird, To dree one's (*Scot.*) : to suffer one's fate. Saxon, *wyrd*, fate.

Weird Sisters, The : *see* Sisters.

Weissnichtwo (*Germ.*, I know not where) : a non-existent place. Invented by Thomas Carlyle in *Sartor Resartus* (1833–4)

Welch ambassador, The : the cuckoo, which migrates from the west. Also because it announces the immigration into England every spring of the Welsh agricultural labourers.

Welcome as flowers in May, As : fully welcome. [J. C. Clarke, *Paroemiologia Anglo-Latina* (1638)]

Well of English Undefiled : Geoffrey Chaucer. So-called by Edmund Spenser in *The Faerie Queen* (1590–6).

Well at the river, To dig the : see Dig.

Welsh ambassador, The : the cuckoo. *See* Welch ambassador.

Welsh cousin, A : a distant relative. In allusion to the Welsh enthusiasm for the science of genealogy.

Welsh main, A : a battle royal.

Welsh mortgage, A : a mortgage in which no date of redemption is fixed.

Welsh rabbit, A : a dish consisting of melted cheese on toast.

Welsh Shakespeare, The : Edward Williams (1745–1826).

Wen, The Monstrous : London. A wen is a tumour on the surface of the body. The origin of the term is attributed to William Cobbett [*Rural Rides* (1823)]

Wertherism : romantic sentimentalism. After the hero of Goethe's *Sorrows of Werther*.

Wessex : Hampshire, Dorsetshire, Wiltshire, Somersetshire, Surrey, Gloucestershire and Buckinghamshire. Formerly the Kingdom of Wessex.

West, To go : to die. A Gaelic idiom. perhaps from *Suas* which in Gaelic means both west and upward.

Western Church, The : the Rom. Catholic Church after the schism of 729.

Western Empire, The : the Rom. Empire after the separation from the Eastern Empire in 395.

Western States, The : the states, apart from the Southern States, west of the Alleghany Mountains.

Wet blanket, A : see Blanket.

Wet finger, To do a thing with a : to do anything with ease. Apparently from the habit of wetting one's finger to turn over the page. [Heywood, *Proverbes* (1546)]

Wharncliffe Meeting, A : a meeting of railway shareholders convened for the purpose of promoting a bill in parliament. After Lord Wharncliffe (1827–99), railway chairman.

What's what, To know : to be mentally alert and well-informed. [Skelton, *Colyn Cloute*, l. 1106 (early 16th cent.)]

Wheel of Fortune, The : fortune. In early representations of the goddess Fortune, she was represented with a wheel in her hand, as an emblem of the vicissitudes of which she was the source.

Wheels within wheels : a complication. [*Ezekiel*, i, 16]

Whigs : one of the two great Eng. political parties, the predecessors of the Liberals and the successors of the Roundheads. After the Reform Act of 1832 the designation began to pass out of general use. From Whiggamor, a cattle-driver in the south-west of Scotland.

Whigs bathing and walk away with their clothes, To catch the : in politics, to appropriate the measures or policy of the other party. Phrase coined by Lord Beaconsfield (1804–81) in referring to Sir. R. Peel's government in a debate on the opening of letters in the Post Office (Feb. 28, 1845).

Whimsicals, The : the Eng. Tories who supported the House of Hanover on the death of Queen Anne.

Whip, A : the parliamentary official whose function is to secure the attendance in Parliament of members of his party. In a famous division in the House of Commons in 1768, the government in power took measures to secure the attendance of supporters as far distant as Paris and the North of Scotland. Their industry led Edmund Burke to use a hunting term, whipping in, to describe their action.

Whip-dog Day : Oct. 18th; on which a dog is once said to have snatched up the pyx and eaten it.

Whip-hand of .. To have the : to have control over .. [Vanbrugh, *Æsop*, V, i (1697)]

Whip with Six Lashes (Strings), The : the Statute of the Six Articles, passed in 1539, which made the denial of Transubstantiation a capital offence.

Whipping-boy, A : a boy kept to receive chastisement whenever a prince was at fault.

Whirlwind, To reap the : see Wind.

Whiskey Insurrection (Rebellion), The : the Pennsylvania Rising of 1794 against the attempt to suppress the illicit distillation of spirits.

Whistle down the wind, To : to defame a person.

Whistle, To wet one's : to drink. [Chaucer, *Canterbury Tales : Reeve's Tale*, 4155 (1386)]

White bird, The : conscience. According to the Moslems.

White Caps : an Indiana (Amer.) secret society of criminals.

White choker : *see* Choker.

White Clergy : Russ. parish priests, as distinct from the monastic priesthood, the Black Clergy.

White Coat, A : an Austrian soldier. After the colour of his uniform.

White Company, The : (1) a band of assassins organized by Folquet, bp. of Toulouse in the 13th cent. for the murder of heretics ; (2) a band of freebooters wearing white crosses led by Bertrand du Guesclin in 1366 ; (3) a band of adventurers, led by Sir John Hawkwood, who ravaged northern Italy in the 14th cent.

White Cross Knights : the Knights Hospitallers.

White crow, A : a great rarity. Albino crows are occasionally met with. For ' rarer than a white crow ' *see* Juvenal, *Satires*, VII, 202.

White Czar, The : the Czar of Russia. Properly the Czar of Muscovy, from his white robes.

White Day, A : a lucky day ; a day to be remembered with pleasure. In allusion to the Rom. practice of marking lucky days in the calendar with white chalk.

White Elephant, A : a gift which instead of being useful is a source of trouble or expense to the recipient. In allusion to the practice of the earlier kings of Siam of presenting those whom they wished to injure with white elephants, which on account of their sacredness were a source of great expense but could not be put to any use.

White Elephant, The Land of the : Siam. *See* White elephant.

White Ensign, The : the flag of the Brit. Navy.

White Fast, The : the Day of Atonement. In allusion to the costume worn in the synagogues.

White Feather, To show the : to display cowardice. A white feather is never found in a game cock.

White Flag, The : the military signal of surrender.

White Friars, The : the Carmelites. After their white costume.

White Harvest, A : a late harvest, when the ground is white with hoar frost.

White Horse : cowardice. After the tradition that James II fled from the Battle of the Boyne on a white horse.

White Horse, The : the 3rd Dragoon Guards.

White Horses : waves crested with foam.

White House, The : the Presidency of the U.S. After the name of the official residence of the presidents.

White Lady of Ireland, The : a banshee.

White League, The : a military organization formed in Louisiana after the conclusion of the Civil War, to secure the supremacy of the white inhabitants.

White lie, A : an untruth that causes no harm.

White as a lily, As : pure white. [*Propertius*, II, iii, 9–10 ; Chaucer, *Knight's Tale*, 1320 (14th cent.)]

White magic : innocent conjuring.

White man, To be a : to prove oneself straightforward and honest.

White man's burden, The : the supposed responsibility of the white races for the welfare of the more backward ones. After the title of a poem in Rudyard Kipling, *The Five Nations* (1903).

White man's grave, The : Sierra Leone. In allusion to its former insalubrity.

White as milk, As : pure white. [Ovid, *Heroides*, XVI, 249–50 (1300)]

White moments of life, The : periods of happiness. In allusion to the white chalk with which the Romans used to mark lucky days in their calendar.

White night, A : a sleepless night. From the Fr. phrase, *Passer une nuit blanche*.

White Paper, A : an Eng. government publication of less extent than a blue book (*q.v.*).

White Queen, The : Mary, Queen of Scots, who wore white mourning for her husband, Lord Darnley.

White Rose and the Red, The : the Eng. royal houses of York and Lancaster.

White sheet, To wear the : *see* Sheet.

White slave, A : a prostitute ; esp. one forced into the calling against her will.

White stone, Days marked with a : happy days. *See* White moments of life.

White as the sun, As : [Hy. Constable, *Damelus' Song to His Diaphenia* (1600)]

White as a swan, As : pure white. [Virgil, *Eclogues*, VII, 37–40 ; *Alison*, st. 3 (1300)]

Whiteboys : Irish Levellers (*q.v.*) formed c. 1761. On account of the white shirts they wore outside of their other garments.

Whitehall : the permanent administration of the British Empire. After the street in London in which the principal government offices are situated.

Whitened (Whited) sepulchre, A : something outwardly fair, but inwardly corrupt. [*Matthew*, xxiii, 27]

Whitewash, To : to rehabilitate ; to restore respectability to .. [Peter Pindar, *Farewell Odes*, Ode VI (1786)]

Whitsun Ale : a festival held at Whitsuntide at which much ale is drunk.

Who Who Ministry, The : Lord Derby's Ministry of 1852. - Few of the members had held office before and when their names were recounted by Lord Derby to the Duke of Wellington, it is said that the Duke, who was deaf, received each of the unfamiliar names with the question ' Who ? Who ? '

Who's Who, A : a handbook of contemporary biography. After the annual publication ' Who's Who.'

Who's who, To know : to be able to distinguish celebrities.

Whole hog, To go the : *see* Hog.

Whole skin on one's bones, To keep a : to avoid injury.

Whole-hogger : one who adopts a policy thoroughly. Applied to those who were prepared to adopt Joseph Chamberlain's Fiscal Policy as a whole, who were prepared to go the ' whole hog.'

Whore of Babylon, The : the Rom. Catholic Church. [Sir Thos. Overbury, *Characters : A Precisian* (1616)]

Why-not, A : an arbitrary proceeding, as that of a person who furnishes no reason but in response to enquiries replies only, Why not ? [Butler, *Hudibras*, II, ii, 529 (1664) ; Harington, *Nugae Antiquae*, II, 144 (1600)]

Wicked uncle, A : a relative who treats a child dependent on him with cruelty. After a character in the nursery-tale of the *Babes in the Wood.*

Wide apart as the poles, As : widely separated. [Sir. Thos Browne, *Religio Medici*, Pt. I (1643)]

Wide-awake, A : a soft felt hat, which having no nap is therefore always wideawake.

Widow of Windsor, The : Queen Victoria, who spent much of her widowhood at Windsor.

Widow's Cruse, The : the property of the poor, which although apparently insignificant yet manages to ˙ be adequate. After the miracle of the widow and the oil narrated in II *Kings*, iv.

Widow's Man, A : an imaginary sailor borne on the books whose pay, etc., is appropriated to Greenwich Hospital.

Wigs on the Green : violent disagreement. In allusion to the violent discussions in the Irish parliament at the end of the 18th cent., when it was the fashion for the members to wear wigs and the parliament met at St. Stephen's Green.

Wild cat : reckless ; unsound ; esp. in commercial or financial matters. Apparently from the device on the notes of a Michigan bank which failed for a large amount, the failure leading to failures on the part of other banks also of unsound character.

Wild Geese : Irish followers of Sarsfield, the commander of the Irish Brigade with the French Army in the 17th and 18th cents.

Wild goose chase, A : a useless pursuit. A wild goose is very difficult to catch and when caught is found not to be worth the pursuit. [Cervantes, *Don Quixote*, Pt. I, Bk. III, ch. 11 ; Shakespeare, *Romeo and Juliet*, II, iv (1591–3)]

Wild oats, To sow one's : *see* Sow.

Wildfire, Like : with great rapidity. As fire spreads. [Webster, *The Duchess of Malfi*, III, ii (1623)]

Wilhelmstrasse, The : the German Foreign Office. After the street in which it is situated.

Wilkes, As deep as : very cunning. Probably a corruption of wilks (periwinkles).

Will, Our : William Shakespeare.

Will for the deed, To take the : to accept the intention for the action.

William the Silent : William, Prince of Orange (1533–84).

William the Talkative : William II (b. 1859), Emperor of Germany.

William Tell, A : a super-patriot. After the legendary Swiss patriot of that name.

Willow, To handle the : to bat in cricket. In allusion to the wood of which cricket bats are made.

Willow, To wear the : to go into mourning, esp. for a sweetheart or bride. [*Harpelus Complaynt of*

Phillidaes Loue Bestowed on Corin, ll. 37–40 (1557)]

Willy nilly : will I, nill I ; whether I will or not. Nill = not to be willing. [Rich. Edwards, *Damon and Pithias,* l. 1509 (1567)]

Wilmot Proviso, The : an amendment to a bill introduced into the U.S. Congress in 1846, whereby slavery was prohibited in all territory to be acquired from Mexico. The amendment was introduced by David Wilmot (1814–68).

Win the horse or lose the saddle, To : to win double or quits.

Wind of .. To get : to learn of .. [Sheridan, *The Rivals,* IV, iii (1775)]

Wind, To measure the : to undertake a futile occupation. [Lyly, *Euphues : Anatomy of Wit* (1579)]

Wind with a net, To catch : *see* Catch.

Wind, To raise the : (1) to borrow or otherwise obtain money when in need ; (2) to cause excitement or a disturbance.

Wind and reap the whirlwind, To sow the : to be punished automatically manifold for one's misdeeds. [*Hosea,* viii, 7]

Wind, To sail near the : to take great risks (esp. of transgressing the law). [Sir Thos. Wyatt, *How to Use the Court* (1557)]

Wind to the shorn lamb, To temper the : *see* Temper the wind.

Wind, Something in the : something in prospect. [Ben Jonson, *Case Is Altered,* III, iii (1609)]

Wind of .. To take (gain) the : to get the upper hand of .. [Bacon, *Essays : Of Counsell* (1625)]

Wind out of the sails, To take the : to deprive a person of his justifiably expected opportunity ; suddenly to forestall a person.

Wind up, To get one's : to get excited, frightened ; to fly into a temper.

Wind and water, To hit between : to demolish an opponent at one blow. A nautical metaphor. Lit., to strike a ship on the water line, a vulnerable spot. [Burke, *Speech on American Taxation* (1774)]

Winds, To be scattered to the four : to be absolutely irrecoverable.

Windmills, To fight with (tilt against) : *see* Tilt.

Windmills in one's head, To have : to have strange fancies. [Cervantes, *Don Quixote,* I, viii]

Window Tax, A : a tax on windows enforced in England from 1695 to 1851.

Window, To put all one's goods in the front : to make a great show while leaving little of solid behind.

Wine back in the bottle, To put the : to undo what has been done.

Wine in old bottles, New : *see* New.

Wine of one ear : corruption of wine of one year ; wine of the previous year's vintage.

Wine month, The : October, the period of the wine harvest.

Wing, To take : to fly away, depart.

Wing, Under one's : under one's protection.

Wings of, To clip the : to take steps to restrain. [Cicero, *Ad Atticum,* IV, ii, 5 ; Thos. Campion, *Airs,* II (1613)]

Winged Boy, The : Cupid, the god of love, depicted as a boy with wings.

Winged feet, With : with great rapidity. [Jerome, *Epistolae,* IV, i]

Winged rooks : cheats who have been outwitted.

Wink at .. To : to pretend not to see. [*Acts,* xvii, 30 ; *Nice Wanton* (1560)]

Winks, Forty : a short sleep during the day.

Winter of one's life (age), The : old age. [Thos. Lodge, *Rosalind* (1590)]

Winter King, The : the Elector Frederick V, King of Bohemia for the winter of 1619–20.

Winter Queen, The : Elizabeth, wife of the Winter King (*q.v.*).

Wire Age, The : the present age, that of the telegraph and telephone wires.

Wirepuller, A : a political intriguer. *See* Pull the strings.

Wisdom of many and the wit of one, The : a proverb. According to Lord John (Earl) Russell (1792–1878), English statesman.

Wisdom tooth, The : the third molar tooth in each jaw which appears between the 17th and the 25th year.

Wise after the event, To be : to gain knowledge when it is no longer of much value. [Earle, *Microcosmography,* II ; *A Young Man* (1633)]

Wise as Doctor Dodipoll, As : *see* Doctor Dodipoll.

Wise as a goat, As : in allusion to the appearance of wisdom given by the goat's beard.

Wise Man (King), The : King Solomon, proverbial for his wisdom.

Wise as the Mayor of Banbury, As : foolish. In allusion to Sir William Curtis, Mayor of Banbury, who in-

insisted that Henry III reigned before Henry II.

Wise Men of the East, The : the Magi who visited the newly-born Christ.

Wise Men of Greece, The : Solon of Athens, Chilo of Sparta, Thales of Miletos, Bias of Priene, Cleobulos of Lindos, Pittacos of Mitylene, and Periander of Corinth.

Wise as one went, To return as : to pursue a fruitless errand. [Jno. Heywood, *The Four O's*, ll. 65–6 (1540)]

Wise as the women of Mungret, As : after a legend regarding certain monks of Mungret, near Limerick, who, dressed as women. astonished some visitors from Cashel with their knowledge.

Wise as a woodcock, As : stupid. In allusion to the proverbial foolishness of woodcocks. [*Hickscorner*, ll. 815–7 (1520)] *See also* Foolish as a woodcock, As.

Wisest, brightest, meanest of mankind, The : Francis Bacon, Lord Verulam (1561–1626). So-called by Pope. [*Essay on Man*, Epist. 4, l. 282 (1732–4)]

Wisest Fool in Christendom, The : King James I of England. So-called by Henry IV of France on the occasion of the English alliance with Spain.

Wits about one, To have one's : to be mentally alert. [Dekker and Webster, *Westward Ho*, III, ii (1607)]

Wits' end, At one's : unable to find any means of escape from a difficulty. [Heywood, *Proverbes* (1546)]

Wits, To live by one's : to make one's living by sharp, not always honest, practices. [*Knack to Know a Knave*, ll. 768–70 (1594)]

Witch of Wokey, As wicked as the : *see* Wokey.

Witches' Sabbath, A : a supposed midnight meeting of witches, demons, etc., under the presidency of Satan.

Witching hour of midnight, The : midnight, when witches were supposed to congregate.

Witham, To be born at little : to be charged with being silly. A pun on 'wit.'

Withers are unwrung, Our : we are unaffected unfavourably. The metaphor is derived from a galled horse, whose withers are the ridge between the shoulder-bones. [Shakespeare, *Hamlet*, III, ii (1602–3)]

Without encumbrance : having no children. A euphuism used in respect of persons applying for living-in situations, etc. [Harriet Martineau, *Three Ages* (1833)]

Witty as a haddock, As : downright foolish. [*Hickscorner* (1520)]

Wizard of Menlo Park, The : Thos. Alva Edison (b. 1847), Amer. inventor, whose laboratory is at Menlo Park, New Jersey.

Wizard of the North, The : Sir Walter Scott.

Wokey, As wicked as the witch of : Wokey Hole is a cavern in Somerset supposed to have been the haunt of a witch who was transformed into stone.

Wolf, To cry : to utter a premature or altogether unjustified cry of warning. In allusion to the fable of the shepherd boy who was continually falsely crying ' wolf ' in order to amuse himself, but whose cries were unheeded when a wolf ultimately appeared.

Wolf from the door, To keep the : to earn sufficient to cover one's minimum expenditure and thus keep dunning creditors (wolves) at a distance. [Skelton, *Colyn Cloute*, l. 1531 (1513)]

Wolf by the ears, To hold a : to be in a situation equally dangerous to retain or to abandon. Phrase used by Augustus of his situation in Rome. [Suetonius, *Tiberius*, 25 ; *The Meane Estate Is Best*, ll. 19–24 (1557)]

Wolf, The Freshwater : the pike.

Wolf among lambs, A : a rogue among the simple. From the early fable.

Wolf Land : Ireland. So-called at the end of the 17th cent. in the belief that wolves abounded there.

Wolf in sheep's clothing, A : a dangerous person who assumes the guise of harmlessness. From the fable. [Heywood, *Proverbes* (1546), ' A wolf in a lamb's skin ' ; *Matthew*, vii, 15]

Wolverine State, The : Michigan. In allusion to the large number of its wolverines in the first period of its history.

Women, The Nine Worthy : Minerva, Semiramis, Tomyris, Jael, Deborah, Judith, Britomart, Isabella of Aragon, Johanna of Naples.

Woman, An old : *see* Old woman.

Woman, To play the : (1) to weep ; [Thos. Kyd *Jeronimo*, Pt. I, l. 187 (1591)] (2) to deceive. [Dekker and Webster, *Westward Ho*, IV, ii (1607)]

Woman's year, A : a leap year. In allusion to the privilege of women to ask marriage on those occasions. [Marston, *Jack Drum's Entertainement*, I, ll. 165-7 (1616)]

Wonder, An Eighth : a work of extraordinary mechanical ingenuity ; an addition to the Seven Wonders of the World (*q.v.*).

Wonder, The Eighth : the Palace of the Escurial at Toledo.

Wonder of the World, The : (1) the Emperor Otto III ; (2) Frederick II, Emperor of Germany.

Wonders of the World, The : *See* Seven Wonders of the World.

Wonderful Doctor, The : Roger Bacon (1214-92).

Wood, To be in a : to be perplexed. [Bacon, *Essayes : Of Ambition* (1625)]

Wood, Not to cry (halloo) until one is out of the : to be certain of having escaped a danger only when one is quite clear of it.

Wood for the trees, Not to be able to see the : to lose the larger view through being absorbed in the details. [Heywood, *Proverbes* (1546)]

Woodcock, As foolish as a : Woodcocks were supposed to be physically—and therefore mentally—brainless. [Shakespeare, *Taming of the Shrew*, I, ii, 161 : ' O this woodcock, what an ass it is! ']

Wooden Horse, The : the scaffold. [Fuller, *Holy and Profane State*, IV, ii (1642)] *See also* Trojan horse.

Wooden horse (mare), To ride the : to go on board ship.

Wooden nutmegs : inhabitants of Connecticut. In allusion to the tradition that the wooden nutmeg swindle originated in that state.

Wooden spoon, A : a stupid person. In allusion to the former practice at Cambridge University of presenting a wooden spoon to the candidate who passed lowest in the Tripos.

Wooden sword, To wear the : to impede a sale by asking too high a price. In allusion to the wooden swords worn by professional fools.

Wooden Walls of England, The : the British Navy. The phrase was first used by Thomas Lord Coventry, Lord Keeper of the Great Seal (1578-1640) in a speech to the Judges on 17th June, 1635. The term ' wooden walls ' in reference to warships was used previously by the translator (probably William Phillip, fl. 1596-1619) of John Huyghen van Linschoten, *Voyage to the East Indies* (1598), and still earlier by Themistocles (c. 514-449 B.C.).

Wooden Wedding, A : *see* Wedding.

Wooden Wedge, The : the lowest in the classical tripos at Camb. Univ. After Wedgwood, the candidate who occupied that position in 1824 when the examination was instituted.

Wool on an ass, To seek : *see* Seek.

Wool and come back shorn, To go for : to suffer the same punishment as one intended to inflict. [Cervantes, *Don Quixote*, I, 7]

Wool on the back of .. To stick : to give presents to .. [Dekker and Webster, *Westward Ho*, II, ii (1607)]

Woolgathering, To be : to be absent-minded ; *i.e.*, capable of setting out to gather wool. [John Taylor, *Wandering to See the Wonders of the West*, p. 1 (1649)]

Woolsack, The : (1) the seat of the Lord Chancellor as Chairman of the House of Lords ; (2) the office of Lord Chancellor. The seat was orig. literally stuffed with wool so as to remind the occupant of the staple trade of the country.

Woolsack, To sit on the : to be Lord Chancellor of England. In allusion to the woolsack which is the seat of that dignitary in the House of Lords.

Word for .. To take a person's : to accept a person's statement. [*Life and Death of Jack Straw*, III, ll. 98-9 (1593)]

Words, To eat one's : *see* Eat.

Words about .. To have : to have an angry dispute about .. [*Rare Triumphs of Love and Fortune*, I, ll. 85-6 (1589)]

Word-painting : a description of a scene in vivid or picturesque words.

Work cut out, To have one's : to have a difficult task in front of one.

Work on the dead horse, To : *see* Horse.

Work for the Roi de Prusse, To : *see* Roi de Prusse.

World at one's feet, To have the : to be at the opening of a career in which success is to be obtained apparently for the asking.

World, the Flesh and the Devil, The : the things of this world, pleasures and temptations to evil. [Chapman, *Monsieur d'Olive*, I, i (1606) ; Marston, *Jacke Drum's Entertainement*, II, ll. 249-52 (1601)]

World grows honest, When the : never.

World, A man of the : one well acquainted with the ways of the world.

World, Out of the : not in society.

World and his wife, All the : everybody without exception. [Jonathan Swift, *Polite Conversation*, III (1709)]

Worm in one's tongue, To have a : to be bitter in speech, cantankerous.

Worms, Food for : the dead.

Worst of .. To have the : to be the loser in an argument or a contest. [*Second Maiden's Tragedy*, IV, i (1611)]

Worth a groat, Not : of practically no value. [*Paston Letters*, No. 612 (1469) ; Heywood, *Proverbes* (1546)]

Worth a haddock, Not : of little value. [Heywood, *Proverbes* (1546)]

Worthies, The Nine : three Gentiles (Hector, son of Priam ; Alexander the Great ; Julius Cæsar), three Jews (Joshua, Conqueror of Canaan ; David, King of Israel ; Judas Maccabæus), three Christians (Arthur, King of Britain ; Charlemagne ; Godfrey of Bouillon).

Worthies of London, The Nine : Sir William Walworth, fishmonger ; Sir Henry Prichard, vintner ; Sir William Sevenoake, grocer ; Sir Thomas White, merchant-tailor ; Sir John Bonham, mercer ; Sir Christopher Croker, vintner ; Sir John Hawkwood, merchant-tailor ; Sir Hugh Calvert, silk-weaver ; Sir Henry Maleverer, grocer. (According to Rich. Johnson.)

Wound, The eternal : love. [Lucretius, *De Rer. Nat.*, Bk. I, ll. 32–4 ; Pope, *Messiah*, ll. 47–8 (1712)]

Wrangler, A : one who gains a place in the first class in the mathematical tripos at Camb. Univ. From the period when the college exercises were termed 'disputations.'

Wrangler, The Senior : the first in the class of Wranglers (*q.v.*) when the relative position in the class was still indicated.

Write in the sand, To : *see* Sand.

Write on the surface of the sea, To : to act foolishly and to no purpose. From an ancient Grk. proverb.

Write in water, To : *see* Water.

Writing on the wall, The : a warning of impending danger. [*Daniel*, v]

Wrong box, In the : in jeopardy. [Abraham Fleming, *Translation of Caius on Dogs* (1575)]

Wrong shop, The : *see* Shop.

Xantippe, A : a scolding woman. After the wife of Socrates.

Yahoo, A : a low degraded man. After a monstrous race described in Swift, *Gulliver's Travels* (1726).

Yankee, A : a slang term for an inhabitant of the U.S. First used by British soldiers in the War of Independence. Possibly an Indian corruption of Anglais, term by which the Indians, through their contact with their Fr. allies, designated the English. In the U.S. the term is applied only to residents in or natives of the NewEngland states.

Yankee Doodle : an Amer. national air.

Yankee paradise, The : Paris. In allusion to the proverbial expression, 'All good Americans go to Paris when they die.'

Yarmouth capon, A : a red herring.

Year, To take the spring from the : *see* Take.

Yellow Book, A : an official publication by the Fr. Government. After the colour of the cover.

Yellow hose, To wear : to be jealous. In allusion to yellow as expressive of jealousy. [Dekker and Webster, *Northward Ho*, I, iii (1607)]

Yellow Jack : (1) yellow fever ; (2) the yellow flag hoisted by ships to indicate contagious disease on board.

Yellow Journalism : *see* Yellow Press.

Yellow Peril, The : the threat of the yellow races (Japan and China) against Europe and European civilization. Phrase coined by the Emperor William II of Germany.

Yellow Press, The : the sensational, unreliable newspaper press. After the colour of the paper on which some of such newspapers in the U.S. were printed.

Yellow, To wear the : *see* Wear.

Yeoman's service : regular hard service. With reference to the Yeomen of the Free Companies.

Yoke, To pass under the : to submit oneself to defeat. In allusion to the Rom. practice of causing a defeated enemy to pass under a yoke or arch formed of three spears.

Yoke of .. To shake off the : to revolt against .. [Bacon, *Essays : Of Seditions and Troubles* (1625)]

Yoke-fellows : partners ; esp. a married couple.

Yorick ! Alas, Poor : an exclamation of philosophical sympathy. From an exclamation used by Hamlet in Shakespeare's play of that name (1602–3).

York is to foul Sutton, As like as : quite unlike. [H. Stephanus, *World of Wonders* (1607)]

Yorkshire bite, A : a transaction in which the trickster overreaches himself.

Young Adventurer, The : Charles Edward Stuart, the Young Pretender (1720–88).

Young Buffs, The : the 31st Regt. of Foot, which received the name to distinguish it from the Buffs (3rd Regt.) whose uniforms were similar.

Young Chevalier, The : Charles Edward Stuart, the Young Pretender (1720–88).

Young England : a group of young aristocrats formed within the Conservative party by Disraeli and Lord John Manners during the period 1833 to 1846.

Young Germany : a progressive political and literary school in Germany during the first half of the 19th cent., headed by Heinrich Heine.

Young Hickory : *see* Hickory.

Young Ireland : a group of Irish extremists whose activities culminated in the Rebellion of 1848.

Young Italy : the political movement started by Mazzini about the year 1830 for the union of Italy and freedom from foreign yoke.

Young Pretender, The : Charles Edward Stuart (1720–88), grandson of James II of England and son of the Old Pretender.

Young Roscius, The : *see* Roscius, The Young.

Young Turk, A : *see* Turk.

Zabian World of Fashion, The : the world of fashion which admires people of notoriety. From stars as the equivalent in the forefront of the world's stage, and Zabians, worshippers of the planets.

Zarp, A : a South African policeman. From the initial letters of *Zuid* (South) African Republican Police.

Zechariah, The Flying Roll of : a series of predictions of evil. [*Zechariah,* v, 1–5]

Zedland : the western counties of England, where ' s ' is pronounced as ' z.'

Zenith down to Nadir, From : *see* Nadir.

Zeppelin, A : a large dirigible airship. After Count Ferdinand Zeppelin (1838–1917), Germ. inventor.

Zeuxis' grapes : a bunch of grapes said to have been painted by Zeuxis (fl. 420–390 B.C.), Grk. painter, that was so realistic as to attract the birds.

Zoilism : harsh, ill-natured criticism. From Zoilos (400–320 B.C.), a severe critic of Homer.

Printed in Great Britain by MACKAYS LTD., Chatham.